Bilingual Education for Hispanic Students in the United States

BILINGUAL EDUCATION SERIES
Gary D. Keller, Editor

Guadalupe Valdés, Anthony G. Lozano, and Rodolfo García-Moya, *editors*
Teaching Spanish to the Hispanic Bilingual: Issues, Aims, and Methods

Joshua A. Fishman and Gary D. Keller, *editors*
Bilingual Education for Hispanic Students in the United States

Bilingual Education for Hispanic Students in the United States

Editors

JOSHUA A. FISHMAN
Yeshiva University

GARY D. KELLER
Eastern Michigan University

Teachers College, Columbia University
New York and London   1982

Published by Teachers College Press, 1234 Amsterdam Avenue, New York, N.Y. 10027

Copyright © 1982 by Teachers College, Columbia University

Library of Congress Cataloging in Publication Data

Main entry under title:

Bilingual education for Hispanic students in the United States.

    Bibliography: p.
    Includes index.
    1. Spanish Americans in the United States—Addresses, essays, lectures. 2. Education, Bilingual—United States—Addresses, essays, lectures. 3. Bilingualism—United States—Addresses, essays, lectures. 4. Language acquisition—United States—Addresses, essays, lectures.
I. Fishman, Joshua A. II. Keller, Gary D.
LC2669.B54   371.91′68′073   80-27776
ISBN 0-8077-2655-9 (cloth)
ISBN 0-8077-2603-6 (paper)

"Play Catch with Me" and "David and I" from *Something to Tell* by Mabel O'Donnell; copyright © 1972 by Harper & Row, Publishers, Inc. Reprinted by permission of the publisher.

Grateful acknowledgment is made to the following for permission to reprint articles appearing in this book:
Journal of Multilingual and Multicultural Development for Joshua A. Fishman, "Bilingualism and Biculturism as Individual and as Societal Phenomena."
The Bilingual Review/La Revista Bilingüe for fourteen articles: Richard E. Baecher, "The Instruction of Hispanic American Students: Exploring Their Educational Cognitive Styles," IV, nos. 1, 2 (January–August 1977), 81–91. Andrew D. Cohen, "Bilingual Schooling and Spanish Language Maintenance: An Experimental Analysis," II, nos. 1, 2 (January–August 1975), 3–12. Alvino E. Fantini, "Emerging Styles in Child Speech: Case Study of a Bilingual Child," V, no. 3 (September–December 1978), 169–89. Richard A. Figueroa, "Individualizing Instruction in the Bilingual Classroom," V, nos. 1, 2 (January–August 1978), 48–56. Jorge M. Guitart, "Conservative Versus Radical Dialects in Spanish: Implications for Language Instruction," V, nos. 1, 2 (January–August 1978), 57–64. Gary D. Keller, "The Ultimate Goal of Bilingual Education with Respect to Language Skills," appeared originally as "Constructing Valid Goals for Bilingual and Bidialectical Education: The Role of the Applied Linguist and the Bilingual Educator," in Gary D. Keller, Richard V. Teschner, and Silva Viera, *Bilingualism in the Bicentennial and Beyond* (New York: Bilingual Press, 1976). Gary D. Keller and Karen S. Van Hooft, "A Chronology of Bilingualism and Bilingual Education in the United States," updated from pamphlet of same name (New York: Bilingual Press, 1976). John M. Lipski, "Structural Linguistics and Bilingual Interference: Problems and Proposals," III, no. 3 (September–December 1976), 229–37. Amado M. Padilla, "Bilingual Schools: Gateways to Integration or Roads to Separation," IV, nos. 1, 2 (January–August 1977), 52–68. Amado M. Padilla and Ellen Liebman "Language Acquisition in the Bilingual Child," II, nos. 1, 2 (January–August 1975), 34–55. Amado M. Padilla and Kathryn J. Lindholm, "Development of Interrogative, Negative and Possessive Forms in the Speech of Young Spanish/English Bilinguals," III, no. 2 (May–August 1976), 122–52. Elena Parra and Ronald W. Henderson, "Mexican-American Perceptions of Parent and Teacher Roles in Child Development," IV, no. 3 (September–December 1977), 210–17. Arnulfo G. Ramírez, Edgardo Arce-Torres, and Robert L. Politzer, "Language Attitudes and the Achievement of Bilingual Pupils in English Language Arts," V, no. 3 September–December (1978), 190–206. Sally D. Tilley, "A Rank Ordering and Analysis of the Goals and Objectives of Bilingual Education," appeared originally as "An Analysis of Q-Sort Ranking of Goals and Objectives in Bilingual Education," III, no. 3 (September–December 1976), 221–28.

Manufactured in the United States of America
86 85 84 83 82 81   1 2 3 4 5 6

Contents

IV | Attitudes Toward Spanish and Bilingual Education

V | Research on Bilingual Instruction and Assessment

VI | How Young Children Become Bilingual

Introduction

Friends and foes alike of bilingual education as it is provided for under Title VII of the Elementary and Secondary Education Act (and one or two other federal, state, and local programs) agree in ascribing to United States Hispanics the critical impetus for both the initiation of such education in the United States and its continuation to this day. This being the case, it is all the more puzzling that in the sizable outpouring of texts and compendia that have been prepared for the field of bilingual education, this volume is the first to focus explicitly on the Hispanic case. Given the hundreds of thousands of children of Chicano, Puerto Rican, Cuban, and other Latin American origins who have limited proficiency in the English language (and, therefore, given the hundreds of thousands who require or qualify for participation in Title VII bilingual education in accord with several crucial court decisions and federal policies), and finally given the fact that the number of such children will remain substantial for at least several more decades, a volume such as the present one is long overdue.

Were this collection intended only for Hispanic teachers or teachers-to-be, for Hispanic teacher-trainers, and for Hispanic administrators working or planning to work with Hispanic students, at least a substantial part of it would be in Spanish. We believe that it is important for bilingual education professionals to make and keep their Spanish sufficiently proficient so that they can use it in all literacy-related higher level professional pursuits. Fortunately, a growing number of publications with this goal in mind are now available, including José A Vázquez, *El español: eslabón cultural;* Eduardo Hernández-Chávez, Andrew D. Cohen, and Anthony F. Beltramo, *El lenguaje de los chicanos;* Joshua A. Fishman, *Sociología del lenguaje;* A. Bruce Gaarder, *Bilingual Schooling and the Survival of Spanish in the United States;* and many of the papers published in *The Bilingual Review/La Revista Bilingüe.* Nevertheless, their number is still far too small to enable these professionals to be substantially trained via their own mother tongue while attending American colleges and universities.

However, our goal for this volume is to reach more than the Hispanic bilingual educator desirous of better serving the myriad educational needs of Hispanic children receiving Title VII bilingual education in

American public schools. We also wish to provide material that Anglos and other non-Hispanics can use to become better oriented with respect to the Hispanic dimension of Title VII bilingual education. Together these papers will help all those who want to know the Hispanic case better but who have not been able to search out the relevant literature in order to do so. Finally, we believe that this volume will also be a highly useful one for all those who are interested in any aspect of bilingual education, whether *by* Hispanics or not, whether *for* Hispanics or not, and whether Title VII or not. A case that has been well understood holds the distinct promise of shedding light on the general topic rather than only on its own specifics. Certainly the Hispanic case within Title VII bilingual education in the United States can serve in just this way for it has benefited from more research, speculation, and concern than have any of the others.

In view of these three goals, we have tried to provide this collection with as broad a range of substantive coverage as possible within the Hispanic fold. It includes some readings that are historical and philosophical as well as others that are psycholinguistic, sociolinguistic, and educational in focus and in methodology. It includes papers on teaching, learning, and administration, on goals and on outcomes, on attitudes and on behaviors, on instruction and on evaluation, on policy and on practice, on successes and on failures. The contents, taken together, will not only help the reader to *understand* American bilingual education better, but will help him or her *to make it better as well.*

As it stands now, Title VII bilingual education is hardly a model of efficiency and effectiveness; it is hardly an approach that genuinely values the cultural diversity and pluralism of the populations that it serves; and it has hardly established any links with the huge and relatively successful world of American bilingual education outside of Title VII auspices (at times under ethnic community auspices and at times entirely under nonethnic auspices, public and private). Constantly under political pressure—from bureaucratic governmental agencies, from teachers' unions, from traditional university departments, from jingoistic writers, from a sloganeering press, from congressional spokespersons for "the good old days" when minorities "knew their place" and didn't ask for (much less receive) specially funded opportunities—Title VII bilingual education desperately needs to be better understood and better implemented. By approaching it from its Hispanic context, this volume will help nurture the reader who will be better able to defend, improve, and revise it not only for the good of Hispanic children, but for the good of all our children.

—J.A.F. and G.D.K.

I | Historical Overview

A Chronology of Bilingualism and Bilingual Education in the United States

GARY D. KELLER   KAREN S. VAN HOOFT
Eastern Michigan University   *New York University*

COLONIAL PERIOD TO 1840

During the period of colonization of what is now the United States and continuing throughout the first half-century of this nation's independent existence, non-English or bilingual schooling was frequently the rule rather than the exception. The various non-English-speaking immigrant groups who settled in the East and Midwest often established their own schools, which were usually affiliated with the religious denomination to which a particular group belonged. In the parts of the United States originally colonized by Spain, the first schools were founded by the Spanish missionaries. Those schools that were established for the education of the Indians were often bilingual. These private and/or parochial schools played a major role in education during the period under discussion.

The data that has been collected by students of early non-English education in the United States demonstrates that instruction in a language other than English was fairly common in schools throughout Pennsylvania, Maryland, Virginia, and the Carolinas during the 1700's. In some of these early schools the native tongue was used exclusively as the medium of instruction and English was taught as an academic subject. After independence, English came to assume a greater importance. While non-English schooling continued in some schools founded by immigrants, in others English was taught as the main language and the second language was offered as a school subject and used for part of the instruction. The languages most frequently taught were German, Norwegian or another Scandinavian language, Dutch, Polish, and French.

Bilingual instruction also continued to flourish in the Southwest right up to the time of the annexation of this area by the United States after

3

the Mexican War (1848). Even after annexation, sporadic cases of bilingual schooling survived in the Southwest. For example, at the time California became a state, 18% of the education in the state was Catholic-affiliated. It primarily served students of Spanish descent, and instruction was carried on in Spanish by the *padres*. After statehood these schools were state-supported for a time. Bilingual schools also continued to exist in what is now New Mexico. In Louisiana, French-English bilingual schools were commonplace during this period.

This nation's early acceptance of the special needs of non-English speaking minorities is evidenced by one of the acts of the Continental Congress (1774–1779). The Congress provided for the publication in German of a number of documents in order to make them accessible to the German-speaking minority, which was quite sizable. In addition, federal laws were printed in French for the first time in 1806, and the federal government later mandated that all laws applying to the Louisiana territory be printed in both English and French.

1840–WORLD WAR I

This period witnessed the growth of public-school education and the United States. Private and parochial non-English or bilingual schools lost some ground to the public schools, which began to experiment with their own bilingual programs in order to attract the children of immigrants. Nevertheless, private schools continued to attract students, and with the arrival of new immigrant groups from eastern and southern Europe during the latter part of the 19th century, new non-English parochial schools were founded by such groups as the Poles, Lithuanians, Slovaks, and Italians. The second half of the century also saw the arrival, chiefly on the West Coast, of immigrants from the Orient, first the Chinese and later the Japanese. The latter, particularly, established numerous bilingual schools for their children.

The early public bilingual programs had mixed success. A major problem was the lack of widespread public support for these programs. This was due to the fact that their initiation was more often than not the result of political pressure from the German-speaking population or another minority group rather than the result of a widely shared public conviction about the desirability of bilingual programs. Another problem these programs faced was the maintenance of effective, quality teaching in the face of fluctuating public support.

The situation with respect to American Indians differed somewhat from that of immigrant groups. Official federal policy generally required that English be the sole language of instruction in Indian schools.

However, in the past few decades this policy has softened somewhat, and bilingual textbooks are often used in the early grades. In spite of this official English-only policy, some Indian groups managed to maintain their native languages, at least temporarily, through bilingual schooling. In the 1800's, for example, the Cherokees had an educational system which produced students who were 90% literate in their native language in addition to having a higher English literacy level than the white populations of Texas and Arkansas. Bilingual materials were frequently used in Cherokee schools.

Specific dates of importance during this period:

1840 A law is passed in Ohio providing for the establishment of public schools where students will be taught both German and English. Instruction in other subject areas is also to be in both languages. Passage of this law is in response to the success of private and parochial German schools in previous decades. It represents an attempt to draw German children into the public school system and give them contact with English. In Cincinnati, instruction in German is introduced in the grades as an optional subject. (There is fragmentary data showing that similar programs existed in perhaps a dozen other communities during the same period, including several of the largest cities in the United States. Possibly as many as one million school children receive a part of their instruction in German as well as English during the heyday of these programs.)

1848 Treaty of Guadalupe Hidalgo with Mexico. Spanish-speaking citizens are accorded the "rights and privileges of citizenship."

1850 Passage of the initial act governing the Territory of New Mexico. It contains no provisions recognizing the fact that over one-half of the population of the Territory is of Spanish-speaking descent.

1853 The U.S. Congress passes a provision authorizing the New Mexico legislature to employ a small number of Spanish-speaking personnel to accommodate the Spanish-speaking population.

1869 A German-English bilingual program is started in Indianapolis; it lasts until 1919. During its existence there are great fluctuations in terms of quality and public support.

1870 A law is passed in Wisconsin authorizing foreign language instruction in the public schools for a maximum of one hour a day. While this law does not specify which language is to be taught, the intention is that the language be Norwegian, in order to make the public schools more attractive to Norwegian immigrants.

1871 Founding of the Instituto San Carlos in Key West, Florida. All instruction in this private school is carried on in Spanish. At the beginning of the present century, the state of Florida designates funds to this school to pay the salary of an English teacher so that all students will receive one hour of instruction a day in English. In effect, this converts the institute into a semi-public and partially bilingual school.

1884 New Mexico passes a school law which recognizes the public Spanish-language elementary schools. In addition, the U.S. Congress authorizes funds for the translation into Spanish of bills, laws, and journals of the state legislature, on condition that legislative proceedings and laws be printed in English.

1897 Hawaii is acquired by the United States. Shortly afterwards English is introduced into the legal and educational systems.

1900 Initial organic act for Hawaii directs that all legislative proceedings be conducted in English. Initially laws are published in both English and Hawaiian, but later they are published only in English.

Soon after the acquisition of Puerto Rico, the United States establishes English and Spanish as the official languages of the Island.

1901 English is established as the language of instruction in the Philippines. Originally it is intended that Spanish be dropped as an official language after 1913, but this is not accomplished.

1903 A first attempt is made in Puerto Rico to impose English as the sole medium of instruction at all school levels. There is unexpectedly strong resistance from the public.

1911 The constitution of the new state of New Mexico requires that laws passed by its legislature be printed in both Spanish and English for twenty years after ratification and that teachers be trained in Spanish to teach Spanish-speaking students.

WORLD WAR I–1950

This period is characterized by the almost complete abandonment of bilingual education in the United States and by a declining interest in the study of foreign languages. The reasons for this are several: (1) the advent of mandatory attendance laws for public schools, (2) the elimination of public funding for church-affiliated schools, and, most importantly, (3) the isolationism and nationalism which pervaded American society after World War I. These factors led to the implementation of English-only instructional policies in many states. In 1903 only fourteen states had regulations requiring that English be the sole language of instruction; by 1923 thirty-four states had such provisions. In some states the laws that were passed forbade the use of other languages for instruction in all subject areas except foreign language classes. The state of Nebraska attempted, unsuccessfully, to go even further by passing a law severely restricting the teaching of foreign languages.

The new regulations imposing English as the only language of instruction particularly affected German Americans and Japanese Americans, the two groups which had practiced bilingual education most extensively prior to World War I.

1917　Theodore Roosevelt makes a statement to the effect that the government should provide immigrants with day schools for children and night schools for adults in order that they might learn English. If after a period of time an immigrant has not learned English, he or she "should be sent back to the land from whence he came."

1919　The U.S. government requires that all teaching in public and private schools in Hawaii be in English, but also provides that Hawaiian can be taught in addition to English in the high schools. Legislation is also proposed to severely limit the operation of the private foreign language schools which teach Japanese as a cultural supplement to the public schools. There is strong public opposition to this legislation.

1923　Legislation is passed in Hawaii regulating foreign language schools. The teaching of foreign languages is limited to one hour a day, and courses, texts, and the age of pupils are prescribed by the Territorial Department of Education. All teachers are required to read, write, and speak English and to be versed in American History. The declared purpose of this legislation is to foster Americanization.

The Supreme Court, in *Meyer* v. *Nebraska* (1923), declares that the prohibition or undue inhibition of the use or teaching of a foreign language is unconstitutional. Nevertheless, the court rules that a state provision requiring English instruction in public and private schools is permitted by the Constitution.

1927   In the case of *Farrington* v. *To Kushige* the Court declares the Territorial legislation of 1923 regulating foreign language schools to be unconstitutional. Private foreign language schools are no longer to be subject to the public authorities.

1934   The Philippine Islands are granted independence by the United States, to become effective ten years later. However, the United States insists that in the interim, public school instruction continue to be conducted in English.

Also in 1934, the language issue again comes to the fore in Puerto Rico due to renewed pressure by the federal government, despite local resistance, for recognition of English as the sole medium of instruction.

1940   Nationality Act is passed, requiring spoken English for naturalization.

1943   In reaction to the events after Pearl Harbor, new legislation is passed in Hawaii attempting to regulate private foreign language schools by setting age limits before which one is prohibited from studying a foreign language.

1945   Local officials regain control of educational policy in Puerto Rico. Spanish is re-established as the language of instruction at all levels.

1950   A law is passed in Louisiana mandating English as the language of legal notices, business records, and instruction in the public schools. Juror qualification is also to be based on English. However, contracts executed in French are recognized as valid.

In the same year, amendments of the 1940 Nationality Act require English literacy (reading, writing, and speaking) as a condition for naturalization. (People over 50 years of age who have been residents of the U.S. for 20 years are exempted.)

1950–1968

After World War II the climate of public opinion slowly began to change. This led to the renewed interest in the study of foreign languages which began to manifest itself in the 1950s and to the resurgence of bilingual education in the 1960s.

As a result of their experiences abroad during World War II (contact with societies where linguistic pluralism is the norm, inability of American GIs to communicate with their allies, etc.), many Americans became aware of the deficiencies of the public schools with respect to the teaching of foreign languages. This awareness paved the way for the great strides that were made in foreign language teaching during the next two decades. The impetus for change came from several directions. (1) In the early 1950s, U.S. Commissioner of Education Earl J. McGrath actively promoted Foreign Language in the Elementary School (FLES), which gained rapidly in popularity. (2) The Foreign Language Program of the Modern Language Association took the lead in encouraging the development of foreign language programs in secondary schools and colleges. (3) Pedagogical advances, which in large part owed their inspiration to the successful Army Language Schools, profoundly affected foreign language teaching methods. The methodology for teaching English as a Second Language (ESL) was also greatly influenced by the development of the new audio-lingual approach in language teaching.

On another front, returning veterans who belonged to minority groups were newly sensitized to the injustices of American society and to their position as second-class citizens. This growing consciousness, which coincided with changes in attitude toward minorities that began to be felt in the larger society, led to the formation of organizations for the purpose of launching literacy and educational improvement campaigns. One typical result was the "Little Schools of the 400," pre-school classes set up to help Chicano children learn the 400 most common words of American English in preparation for entering the public school system. This was a first step in recognizing the needs of linguistic minorities in the United States.

1958   In response to the Russian launching of Sputnik, the federal government passes the National Defense Education act. The funds authorized under the various provisions of this act serve as a stimulus to the study of foreign languages on all levels in addition to mathematics and science. Specifically, Titles VI and IX of this act emphasize the retention and expansion of the nation's foreign language resources. In addition to legitimizing the study of foreign languages, the NDEA provides financial assistance to minority group students who wish to attend college and specialize in mathematics, science, or foreign languages, and it funds summer training institutes for foreign language teachers.

Also in 1958, the New York City Board of Education publishes a comprehensive *Puerto Rican Study*, which brings to public attention the problems faced by this group in the New York public school system.

1959   Hawaii becomes a state. The 1943 law regulating private foreign language schools is dropped.

Fidel Castro comes to power in Cuba. This event leads to a steadily accelerating emigration of Cubans from the Island to the Miami area in the early 1960s.

1961   In response to the influx of Cuban refugees, Dade County, Florida (Miami) establishes a program of Spanish for Spanish speakers (Spanish-S). In addition, the school system begins to offer elementary school classes in Spanish supplemented by intensive instruction in ESL. The plan is for students to spend about one semester in this special program, after which time they will enter the regular school programs while continuing to be offered Spanish.

1963   In Miami (Dade County), the Coral Way elementary school undertakes a completely bilingual program in grades one through three with a plan to move the program up one grade each year. The program is started with the help of Ford Foundation funds. Academic subjects (arithmetic, history, etc.) are taught in both Spanish and English once the child has attained a foundation in the second language. The cultures of both Spanish- and English-speaking groups are incorporated in the instruction that all receive. An all-English option is offered for those parents who do not want their children to participate. The program wins almost unanimous approval and the all-English option is eliminated the second year because it is not needed. The Dade County program becomes a model for programs soon to be established in other parts of the country.

Among the reasons for the Cubans' success are the following factors: (1) many of the early refugees from Cuba belonged to the educated and politically sophisticated middle and upper classes; (2) many of these arrivals are from the professional sector and can offer trained teachers and other school personnel; (3) U.S. institutions respond to the needs of the Cuban refugees, expecting the situation to be a temporary one; and (4) most of the early refugees are of predominantly European stock, so that racism is not a significant factor.

After the establishment of the first programs in Dade County, a period of intense activity follows. The years from 1963 to 1967 witness the development of models of materials and programs and the development of political activity which makes the next stage possible. Lobbying efforts are carried out by the NEA and other teachers' groups, and by minority groups, especially by Chicano organizations in the Southwest.

1964 Two bilingual programs are launched in Texas: (1) in the Nye school of the United Consolidated Independent School District in Webb County (outside Laredo), and (2) in the San Antonio Independent School District.

1965 Bilingual programs begin in Pecos, New Mexico, and in Edinburg, Texas.

The Elementary and Secondary Education Act (ESEA) is passed. Title I of this act, which deals with the education "of the disadvantaged," eventually provides funding for bilingual programs of the type stressing ESL and the rapid transition to English.

1966 More bilingual programs are started in communities in Texas, California, and Arizona.

1967 Bilingual programs initiated in New Mexico, New Jersey, and St. Croix, Virgin Islands.

Early in 1967 the U.S. Senate Subcommittee on Bilingual Education calls for hearings on the question of federal funding for bilingual education.

1968–1980

This final period begins with passage by Congress late in 1967 of the Bilingual Education Act. It is a period which also witnesses important activity not only on the legislative front but also in the form of executive measures and judicial decisions which serve to foster the development of bilingual education programs. In addition, programs are developed on the university level for the preparation of teachers, administrators, and other personnel to work in bilingual education. The universities also take part in the preparation of materials and experts in the field, and a few bilingual programs are initiated on the university level, offering courses in languages other than English and intensive ESL instruction.

1968   On January 2, President Johnson signs into law the Bilingual Education Act, officially Title VII of the ESEA of 1965, as amended in 1967 (Public Law 90-247). Congress authorizes the appropriation of $85 million for 1968–1970 to fund programs for "children from environments where the dominant language is other than English." (Title VII ESEA funds differ from Title I funds in that the former are destined for the development of programs using *two* languages as the media of instruction.) However, no funds are appropriated for either 1968 or 1969.

1970   Congress appropriates $7.5 million to fund title VII of ESEA for 1970.

       The Department of Health, Education, and Welfare notifies 1,000 school districts throughout the United States with concentrations of 5% or more non-English speakers that they will have to take "affirmative action" to remove language barriers handicapping non-English-speaking children or face a cutoff of federal funds.

1971   Congress appropriates $21,250,000 to fund Title VII of ESEA.

1972   Massachusetts passes the Transitional Bilingual Education Act. This act makes bilingual education mandatory in all school districts having 20 or more children from the same non-English-speaking background under their jurisdiction. This legislation is later copied in general lines by other states.

1973   *Aspira* v. *Board of Education of the City of New York*, 58 F.R.D. 62 (S.D.N.Y., 1973). The court decision accepts a consent decree calling for obligatory bilingual education for all New York City children who need it. The child is not to receive instruction in any substantive course in a language which prevents his or her effective participation in the course.

       Serna v. *Portales Municipal Schools*, 351, F. Supp. 1279 (D.N.M., 1973). The court finds an Equal Protection violation in the school district's failure to adopt an education program which will guarantee equal educational opportunity to Spanish-speaking children. The plan submitted by the school district as a remedy is rejected by the court, which instead adopts a plan of its own based on expert testimony presented at the court hearing. The school district appeals. (See 1974.)

       Keyes v. *School District No. I*, 413 U.S. 189 (1973). As a result of the Supreme Court decision in this Denver school desegregation case, the district court takes testimony on proposed desegregation plans for the Denver public schools. An extensive presentation on bilingual/bicultural education is given by the Congress of Hispanic Educators as part of the testimony. The plan proposed by this group is accepted by the court, which orders its implementation on a pilot basis in several predominantly Chicano schools in 1974-75 [380 F. Supp. 673, 692 (D. Colo. 1974)]. The long range goal is implementation throughout the district. The Colorado Department of Education and the school district have appealed, charging unwarranted intrusion by the court.

1974   By this date, bills similar to the Massachusetts act have been passed in Texas, Illinois, New Mexico, New Jersey, and California. Other states have issued administrative directives that have the force of law. Most of these states also appropriate funds for bilingual education.

Lau v. *Nichols,* 414 U.S. 563 (1974). This is the Supreme Court decision according to which the educational rights of a child with deficiencies in English are violated by any school system which does not provide special programs to remedy the situation. This decision applies only to those schools which receive federal funds; nevertheless, it establishes the criterion of obligatory bilingual education on the national level. It leaves open, however, the question of what types of programs are necessary to meet the requirements of Title VI of the 1964 Civil Rights Act.

Serna v. *Portales,* 499 F. 2d 1147 (10th Cir., 1974). The Court of Appeals finds a statutory violation of the students' Title VI rights. "There was adequate evidence that appellants' proposed program was only a token plan that would not benefit appellees. Under these circumstances the trial court had a duty to fashion a program which would provide adequate relief for Spanish surnamed children. . . . Under Title VI of the Civil Rights Act of 1964 appellees have a right to bilingual education. . ." [499 F. 2d 1154]. In making this ruling the court draws on decisions issued in desegregation cases, and it rejects the contention of the appellants that the district court's decision and relief represented improper judicial interference in the internal affairs of the school district.

1974 also witnesses the passage of the Equal Educational Opportunities Act. Section 204 states that "No state shall deny equal educational opportunity to an individual on account of his or her race, color, sex, or national origin by. . . the failure by an educational agency to take appropriate action to overcome language barriers that impede equal participation by its students in the instructional program."

HEW attempts to clarify the goals of Title VII ESEA, specifically the role of the second language: "The fundamental goal of a federally supported bilingual education program is to enable children whose dominant language is other than English to develop competitive proficiency in English so that they can function successfully in the educational and occupational institutions of the larger society." Use of the home language is viewed as a means to achieving the end of giving children proficiency in the dominant language. (Memorandum, DHEW, Aug. 6, 1974)

1975   The Office of Educational Evaluation of the New York City Board of Education, in accordance with the Aspira consent decree (see 1973), develops the Language Assessment Battery (LAB) in English and Spanish, kindergarten through twelfth grade. Between 300,000-350,000 students are tested in reading, writing, listening comprehension and speaking with LAB. Between 85,000 and 100,000 children enter bilingual education programs under the consent decree provisions.

In response to *Lau* v. *Nichols* (see 1974), the U.S. Office of Education makes funds available for the creation of nine regional Bilingual General Assistance Centers—or "Lau Centers," throughout the United States. These centers provide service in the form of technical assistance to school districts and publicly supported K-12 educational agencies having at least a few students who come from environments in which the dominant language is other than English. The principal types of assistance provided by the centers are as follows: (1) Assessment of specific needs; (2) Modification of administrative structures and procedures; (3) Revision or development of curriculum materials and methods; (4) Revision or development of community relations programs; (5) Revision or development of staff training programs; (6) Technical assistance in the development of funding proposals.

1976   Office of Educational Evaluation of the New York City Board of Education revises the Language Assessment Battery (see 1975) and retests 85,000–100,000 students to assess their progress under the bilingual education program established by the Aspira consent decree.

Bilingual Education units are established in the State Education Departments of Connecticut and New Jersey.

Amendments to the Voting Rights Act are passed which require bilingual balloting and other voting assistance in areas where persons of Spanish heritage, American Indians, Asian-Americans, or Alaskan natives comprise a significant share of the voting age population. The law applies to all of Texas and Alaska as well as parts of 25 other states including California, Florida, New York, Virginia, Minnesota, Hawaii, and Louisiana.

The Chacón-Moscone Bilingual Bicultural Education Act of 1976 is passed making bilingual education mandatory in the State of California. The bill requires that each limited or non-English speaking student enrolled in the California public school system (grades K-12 inclusive) be offered, at a minimum, bilingual learning opportunities. Moreover, one of the most significant provisions of the bill is that it mandates the redirection of state, federal, and local money to meet the needs of the bilingual population under its jurisdiction.

Congress directs the Secretary of Commerce to ensure that in its data collection activities, the Bureau of the Census recognize the needs and concerns of Americans of Spanish origin or descent through the use of Spanish-language questionnaires, bilingual, census takers, and any other methods considered appropriate to their rights as American citizens (Public Law 94-311).

The National Center for Educational Statistics (NCES) is charged by Congress with the responsibility of determining the number of people in the United States who are limited in their English proficiency and thus in need of bilingual education. In 1978 the NCES completed this mission and issued official reports indicating that 28 million citizens or residents of the United States speak a mother tongue other than English or live in households where a language other than English is spoken. About 5 million of this population are children. About two-thirds of the adults and four-fifths of the children of this group of 28 million are native-born citizens of the United States. In addition, NCES determines that one out of every eight Americans has had a non-English language background of one sort or another, and that of the population described above, one-third of the adults and 60% of the school-age children have a Spanish language background. Finally, language minority persons constitute at least 10% of the population in each of 23 states.

On October 22, 1976, the U.S. District Court for the Northern District of California issues a consent decree directing the San Francisco United School District, in response to the Supreme Court *Lau* v. *Nichols* decision, to implement a Master Plan for Bilingual Bicultural Education specifically requiring bilingual education for the Chinese, Filipino, and Spanish language groups of that geographic area, with the proviso that wherever feasible, the other language groups should receive bilingual instruction.

A survey of colleges and universities in the United States conducted at the University of Texas at El Paso indicates that 134 institutions of higher education have begun to teach Spanish (e.g., reading, grammar) to native speakers of Spanish at the post-secondary level.

1977   Thirty-two centers comprising the National Network of Bilingual Education Centers receive $12 million under ESEA Title VII to provide training and to develop and disseminate materials for federally-funded bilingual education projects in local districts. Three types of centers are funded:

- 15 Training Resource Centers, whose function is to assist bilingual teachers in local districts in employing relevant techniques and evaluation procedures and in involving parents and community resources and programs.

- 14 Materials Development Centers whose primary function is to develop and/or adapt both curriculum and testing materials to be used in classrooms and teacher-training materials for use by institutions of higher learning.

- 3 Dissemination/Assessment Centers whose primary function is to evaluate, publish, and distribute products of the Materials Development Centers for classroom or training use.

National Clearinghouse for Bilingual Education (NCBE) is established as the national information center for bilingual education. The NCBE identifies and maintains current information about organizations which are involved in bilingual education, including government agencies, Title VII projects, publishers, professional organizations, and other information centers.

1978   On November 1, 1978, the education amendments of 1978, containing the Title VII amendments to the Bilingual Education Act, are signed into law. The amendments expand the definition of eligible participants to include all children of limited proficiency in English. Furthermore, children whose native language is English are permitted in bilingual education programs provided their number does not exceed 40% of the program. The amendments authorize expanded research activities in bilingual education as well as an overall appropriation of $150 million for the appropriate fiscal year.

The United States Office of Education awards $2.8 million for bilingual vocational training programs for the purpose of teacher training, materials development, and actual training of students in accordance with the procedures of vocational bilingual education. In 1979 an award of $2.5 million is made for the same purpose.

1979   The National Institute of Education (NIE) establishes the National Center for Bilingual Research in Los Alamitos, California. Established by a five-year, $5.7 million cooperative agreement with the Southwest Regional Laboratory for Educational Research and Development, the new National Center is designed to provide (1) a direct basis for improving classroom procedures and materials, (2) information for legislators and other policymakers faced with questions of equity in education for language minorities, and (3) opportunities for members of bilingual communities to participate in research seeking to benefit those communities.

A survey conducted by Dr. Gina Càntoni-Harvey and published in the December issue of the *Linguistic Reporter* indicates that by 1979 seventeen states and the District of Columbia have bilingual education certification.

The President signs into law a bill, P.L. 95-539, known variously as the "Court Interpreter's Act" or the "Bilingual Courts Act," which ensures that all individuals in federal proceedings will be provided with a certified interpreter if their primary language is not English or if they have a hearing impairment.

1980   The new cabinet-level Education Department is created in which the Office of Bilingual Education is restructured and expanded with the new title of Office of Bilingual Education and Minority Language Affairs (OBEMLA).

The Bureau of the Census of the U.S. Department of Commerce makes special efforts to obtain the best possible counts of all minorities who usually speak a language other than English. For example, census questionnaires are made available in other languages, and assistance centers are established for personalized help from bilingual, bicultural staff members.

REFERENCES

Andersson, Theodore. "Bilingual Education: The American Experience." In *Bilingual Schooling: Some Experiences in Canada and the United States,* ed. Merill Swain. Toronto: Ontario Institute for Studies in Education, 1972, pp. 55–72.

Andersson, Theodore, and Boyer, Mildred. *Bilingual Schooling in the United States.* 2d ed. Austin, Tex.: National Educational Laboratory Publishers, 1978.

Bilingual Education Current Perspectives: Law. Arlington, Va: Center for Applied Linguistics, 1977.

Cancela, Gilberto. "Florida: Bilingual Education in Dade County." In *Introduction to Bilingual Education,* ed. Luis Ortega. New York: Las Américas, 1975, pp. 47–60.

Fishman, Joshua A. *Language Loyalty in the United States.* The Hague: Mouton and Co., 1966.

Geffert, Hannah N., et al. *The Current Status of U.S. Bilingual Education Legislation.* Papers in Applied Linguistics: Bilingual Education Series No. 4. Arlington, Va: Center for Applied Linguistics, 1975.

González, Josué M. "Coming of Age in Bilingual/Bicultural Education: A Historical Perspective." *Inequality in Education,* Center for Law and Education, Harvard University, 19 (February 1975), 5–17.

Haugen, Einer I. *Bilingualism in the Americas: A Bibliography and Research Guide.* Birmingham, Ala.: University of Alabama for the American Dialect Society, 1956.

———. *The Norwegian Language in America: A Study of Bilingual Behavior.* Vol. I. Philadelphia: University of Pennsylvania Press, 1953.

Horner, Vivian M. "Bilingual Literacy." In *Toward a Literate Society,* ed. John B. Carroll and Jeanne S. Chall. New York: McGraw-Hill, 1975, pp. 190–99.

Irizarry, Ruddie A. *Bilingual Education: State and Federal Legislative Mandates.* Los Angeles: Center for the Study of Evaluation, UCLA, 1978.

Kloss, Heinz. *Excerpts from the National Minority Laws of the United States of America.* Honolulu: East-West Center, 1966.

———. *The American Bilingual Tradition.* Rowley, Mass.: Newbury House, 1977.

Leibowitz, Arnold H. "English Literacy: Legal Sanction for Discrimination." *Notre Dame Lawyer,* 45, 1 (Fall 1969), 7–67.

Mackey, William F., and Beebe, Von N. *Bilingual Schools for a Bicultural Community.* Rowley, Mass.: Newbury House, 1978.

Rice, Roger. "Recent Legal Developments in Bilingual/Bicultural Education." *Inequality in Education,* Center for Law and Education, Harvard University, 19 (February, 1975), 51–53.

Schneider, Susan G. *Revolution, Reaction or Reform: The 1974 Bilingual Education Act.* New York: Las Américas, 1976.

Teitelbaum, H., and Hiller, R. "Bilingual Education: The Legal Mandate." *Harvard Educational Review,* 47:2, (May 1977),138–70.

U.S. Department of Health, Education, and Welfare. "Task Force Findings Specifying Remedies Available for Eliminating Past Educational Practices Ruled Unlawful under *Lau* v. *Nichols.*" Washington, D.C.: U.S. Government Printing Office, 1975.

II | Defining the Goals of Bilingual Education

Bilingualism and Biculturism as Individual and as Societal Phenomena

JOSHUA A. FISHMAN
Yeshiva University

BILINGUALISM AND DIGLOSSIA

The relationship between *individual* bilingualism and *societal* diglossia is far from being a necessary or causal one, i.e., either phenomenon can occur with or without the other (Fishman, 1967). Thus we have one more example of the weak relationship obtained between various *individual* social behaviors and their corresponding *societal* counterparts. Wealthy individuals can be found in both rich and poor societies. Traditional individuals are recognizable within both modern and traditional societies. Thus diglossia differs from bilingualism in that it represents *an enduring societal arrangement,* extending at least beyond a three-generation period, such that two "languages" exist, each having its secure, phenomenologically legitimate, and widely implemented functions. This paper raises for consideration the corresponding problem of arrangements at the individual and societal levels in conjunction with the phenomenon of biculturism, particularly as these pertain to ethnic identity.

KINDS OF DIGLOSSIA: LINGUISTIC RELATIONSHIPS

Following usage that has become widely accepted ever since Ferguson's seminal article of 1959, H will be used to designate the *superposed* variety in a diglossic society, i.e., the variety that is learned *later in socialization* (and therefore is *no one's mother tongue*) under the *influence of one or another formal institution outside of the home* (and therefore is *differentially accessible* to the extent that entree to formal institutions of language/literacy learning—typically: school, church, government—is available).

Prepared under NIE Grant G-78-0133 (Project No. 8-0860).

23

However, departing from Ferguson's initial designation, several different kinds of linguistic relationships between H's and L's (the latter being the universally available and spoken [mother] tongues as well as varieties used in everyday life) will be recognized:

(a) *H as classical, L as vernacular, the two being genetically related.* Examples are classical and vernacular Arabic; classical or classicized Greek [Katarevusa] and demotiki; Latin and French among francophone scholars and clergy in earlier centuries; classical and vernacular Tamil; classical and vernacular Sinhalese; Sanscrit and Hindi; classical Mandarin and modern Pekinese.

(b) *H as classical, L as vernacular, the two being genetically unrelated.* Examples are Loshn koydesh (textual Hebrew/Aramaic) and Yiddish (Fishman, 1976) or any one of the several dozen other non-Semitic Jewish L's, as long as the latter operate primarily in vernacular functions rather than in traditional literacy-related ones (Weinreich, 1979).

(c) *H as written/formal-spoken and L as vernacular, the two being genetically unrelated.* Examples are Spanish and Guraní in Paraguay (Rubin, 1968); English (or French) and various vernaculars in post-colonial areas throughout the world (Fishman, Cooper, and Conrad, 1977).

(d) *H as written/formal-spoken and L as vernacular, the two being genetically related.* Here only significantly discrepant written/formal-spoken and informal-spoken varieties will be admitted, such that without schooling the written/formal-spoken cannot even be understood (otherwise every dialect/standard situation in the world would qualify within this rubric). Examples are High German and Swiss German; standard spoken Pekinese (Putonghua) and Cantonese; standard English and Caribbean Creole.

There are, of course, various more complex cases within each of the above major clusters. Thus there are several instances of dual H's in conjunction with a single L, one H commonly being utilized for ethnically encumbered or traditional H pursuits and the other for ethnically unencumbered or modern pursuits. For example, in conjunction with type (a) above, we find various stable Arabic speech communities that have both classical Arabic and English or French as H and a vernacular Arabic as L. The Old Order Amish also reveal a complex form of (a), involving High (Luther Bible) German and English as H and Pennsylvania German as L. On the other hand, Hasidim reveal a complex form of type (b), involving Loshn koydesh and English as H and Yiddish as L. (and in Israel, Loshn koydesh and Ivrit as H and

Yiddish as L [Fishman, 1981; Poll, 1980]). Many developing nations hope to establish a type (c) pattern involving both a Western language of wider communication and one or more favored standardized vernaculars as H's along with the same (or even more) local vernaculars as L's. Thus, in the Philippines, we find a national policy fostering English and Pilipino/Filipino as H's and, for example, Tagalog as an L. Note, however, that in all these "more complex" cases an indigenous variety/language is available at both the H and the L levels even if modern H functions are also shared with a language recently imported or imposed from without.

STABILITY VIA COMPARTMENTALIZATION OF THE SOCIETAL ALLOCATION OF FUNCTIONS

The above rapid review of a dozen or more instances of relatively stable and widespread societal bilingualism (i.e., diglossia) was intended to discount the view that only in connection with classicals can such stability be maintained. Classicals are a good example of diglossia situations, of course, but sociologically speaking, what they are an example of is not classicism per se (nor even traditional religion, with which classicals are usually linked) but of a stress on *social compartmentalization,* i.e., on the maintenance of strict boundaries between the societal functions associated with H and L respectively (Fishman, 1972). Sanctity/secularity, ascribed social stratification such as caste distinctions, indigenousness/foreignness, and traditionalism/modernism are all *possible* bases of rather rigid and stable compartmentalization in societal arrangements and, therefore, in the allocation of languages (or language varieties) to such arrangements.

There is much in modern life that militates against such compartmentalization. Among the hallmarks of modernization, as expounded by the great sociologists of the past two centuries, is the increase in open networks, in fluid role relationships, in superficial "public familiarity" between strangers or semi-strangers, in non-status-stressing interactions (even where status differences remain), and, above all, in the rationalization of the work sphere (the sphere that has, presumably, become the dominant arena of human affairs). All of these factors—plus the constantly increasing urbanization, massification, and mobility of which they are a part—tend to diminish compartmentalization, whether in the language use repertoire or in the social behavior repertoire outside of language use per se.

The presence or absence of social compartmentalization in language use in bilingual settings leads to very different *societal* arrangements with respect to bilingualism, which, after all, is an *individual* behavioral manifestation. Similarly, the presence or absence of social compartmentalization in ethnocultural behavior in bicultural settings leads to very different *societal* arrangements with respect to biculturism, which, after all, is also an *individual* behavioral manifestation. Thus, ultimately, if we are concerned with the relationship between bilingualism and biculturism, we must be concerned with the co-occurrence patterns obtaining between *societally* compartmentalized and uncompartmentalized biculturism. However, relatively little has been written so far about the possible relationships between societal ethnocultural compartmentalization and individual biculturism, certainly little in comparison to the literature on the possible relationships between societal diglossia and individual bilingualism. Let us, therefore, first reexamine the latter literature and then apply its concepts and contexts to the former topic.

TYPES OF DIGLOSSIA-BILINGUALISM RELATIONSHIPS

Both diglossia and bilingualism are continuous variables, matters of degree rather than all-or-none phenomena, even when compartmentalization obtains. Nevertheless, for purposes of initial conceptual clarity, it is simpler to treat them both as if they were dichotomous variables. Treated in this fashion there are four possible combinations between individual bilingualism and societal diglossia, as Figure 1 indicates, and we will proceed to consider them one at a time.

Bilingualism and Diglossia (cell 1)

The occurrences of bilingualism and diglossia have already been discussed above. Let us, therefore, merely summarize our observations in this connection at this time. This is a *societal arrangement* in which individual

Figure 1
The Relationships Between Bilingualism and Diglossia

Bilingualism	*Diglossia*	
	+	−
+	1. Both Diglossia and Bilingualism	2. Bilingualism without Diglossia
−	3. Diglossia without Bilingualism	4. Neither Diglossia nor Bilingualism

bilingualism is not only widespread but institutionally buttressed.*
"Membership" in the culture requires that the various languages that are
recognized as pertaining to such membership be implemented in
culturally "correct" contexts, i.e., that the H (or H's) be utilized in (the
normatively appropriate) H contexts and the L (or L's) be utilized in (the
normatively appropriate) L contexts. The separate locations in which L
and H are acquired immediately provide them with separate institutional supports. L is acquired at home, as a mother tongue, and continues to
be employed there throughout life while its use is extended also to other
familial and familiar (intimate, affect dominated, emotion and spontaneity related) interactions. H, on the other hand, is never learned at
home and is never utilized to signal such interactions. H is related to and
supported by other-than-home institutions: education, religion, government, higher/specialized work sphere, etc. The authority and the reward
systems associated with these separate institutions are sufficient for both
L and H to be required at least referentially if not—due to possible
access restrictions in the case of H—overtly for membership in the
culture, and the compartmentalization between them is sufficient for
this arrangement not to suffer from "leakage" and from the resulting
potential for language spread and shift.

The above picture is, of course, at least somewhat idealized. Diglossic
societies are marked not only by compartmentalization conventions but
by varying degrees of *access restriction*. Similarly, in addition, H-ness
(whether in lexical, phonological, or grammatical respects) does creep
into L interactions (particularly among the more educated strata of
society), viz. the case of "Middle Arabic" and "Learned Yiddish," and
conversely L-ness does creep into H interactions (particularly where
access restrictions are minimal—note, for example, the completely
Yiddish phonology of Ashkenazi Loshn koydesh). Nevertheless, the
perceived ethnocultural *legitimacy* of two languages as "our own" (i.e.,
neither of them being considered foreign, even though one or the other
might, in point of historical reality, be such), and the *normative functional
complementarity* of both languages, each in accord with its own institutionally congruent behaviors and values, remain undisturbed.

Diglossia without Bilingualism (cell 3)

Since diglossia applies to societal arrangements, *political* arrangements
may certainly be included under this rubric. Given this fact, we must
recognize political or governmental diglossia whereby two or more

---

*Obviously, we are using *bi/di* as generics and intend that our comments with respect to
them also apply to more complex cases as well, i.e., to cases of tri/ter, quadri/tetra, etc.

differently monolingual entities are brought together under one political roof. Not only were various empires of old characterized by diglossia without bilingualism (except for small commercial, military, and civil service elites) but various modern states may be so classified: Switzerland, Belgium, Canada, and, at least in terms of early Leninist idealism, the USSR. This is diglossia in accord with the territoriality principle (McRae, 1975). It requires that we set aside our earlier *intra*societal notion of widespread bilingualism and extend it to the political recognition and institutional protection thereof on an *inter*societal basis. There is full freedom of press in Switzerland; nevertheless, one cannot publish a German newspaper in Geneva or an Italian one in Bern, regardless of whether this might be desirable in terms of short-term population movements. Similarly, King Ahasuerus of old, who "reigned from India even unto Ethiopia . . . sent letters into all the King's provinces, into every province according to the writing thereof, and to every people after their language (Esther 1:1 and 22)." Thus, we note that in this great multilingual empire of old, there was not only territorial diglossia at the governmental level (as between the various written languages for governmental use) but also societal diglossia between the one written and the several spoken languages of each province.

Wherever an absent nobility controls a peasantry from afar by means of a small military, governmental, and commercial presence which mediates between the absent masters and the local indigenous populations, diglossia without bilingualism is in effect. Most forms of colonialism throughout the world (whether under capitalist or communist auspices) are therefore also instances of political/territorial diglossia without widespread demographic-indigenous bilingualism. When substantial numbers of colonizers have settled in the erstwhile colonies and access to H is not restricted insofar as indigenous populations are concerned, a transformation may ultimately take place to that of diglossia *with* bilingualism.

Bilingualism without Diglossia (cell 2)

Both diglossia *with* bilingualism and diglossia *without* bilingualism are relatively stable, long-term arrangements. However, since these are highly interpretable and judgmental dimensions (*how* stable does a sociopolitical arrangement have to be before we consider it long term?) let us once more agree to use a three-generational rule of thumb in connection with them. There are obviously innumerable bilingual situations around the world that do not last up to or beyond three generations. These are characterized not only by language spread but also by language shift. In some instances indigenous languages are swamped out by intrusive ones (B = A→B) as in the case of many Native American, aboriginal Australian, and not a few non-Russian Soviet populations as well (Silver, 1974; Kreindler, in press). In other instances, immigrant languages have disappeared as their speakers have adopted the languages of their hosts (B→A = A). What both of these otherwise quite different contexts reveal in common is an absence of social compartmentalization such that the languages of hearth and home (of indigenous peoples, on the one hand, and of immigrants, on the other) can protect themselves from the greater reward and sanction system associated with the language of new institutions to which they are exposed and in which they are involved.

As a result of the lack of successful compartmentalization, both A and B compete for realization in the same domains, situations, and role relations. Since, with the exception of fleeting metaphorical usage (humor, sarcasm, etc.), bilingual functional redundancy cannot be maintained intergenerationally and gives way to the stronger functional system, the language associated with stronger rewards and sanctions wins out. In the American and Soviet contexts three generations or less have generally been sufficient for this process to run its course where sufficiently small, impacted, and dislocated groups have been involved. Large groups, groups strong enough to maintain or to fashion a reward system under their own control (whether in the home, the community, the church, or elsewhere) may succeed in establishing and maintaining the compartmentalization needed for diglossia. Even fewer ones can opt for a completely territorial solution, implementing compartmentalization via secession or isolation. Without compartmentalization of one kind or another—at times attained by ideological/philosophical and even a degree of physical withdrawal from establishment society—the flow process from language spread to language shift is an inexorable one. Although it may at times require more than three generations for its inroads to be clearly discerned, the functionally unbalanced nature of the bilingualism that obtains (both in terms of *who* becomes bilingual and who remains monolingual, to begin with, and in terms of the power differentials/reward and sanction differentials of the remaining monolingual A and monolingual B domains) always leads displacively and replacively only in one direction.

Neither Bilingualism nor Diglossia (cell 4)

The outcome of uninterrupted (i.e., uncompartmentalized) bilingualism-without-diglossia is neither bilingualism nor diglossia. Some settings, however, are characterizable in this latter fashion without ever having gone through the former stage. Korea, Yemen, Cuba, Portugal, Norway have all experienced relatively little immigration within the past three generations and have few if any indigenous minorities. However, many settings that *have* initially had numerous immigrants or linguistic minorities or both have translinguified (or exterminated) them to a very large degree. New Zealand, insofar as its indigenous Maoris are concerned, and Ireland, insofar as Irish speakers are concerned, are examples of the "successful" implementation of policies of this kind, as are several indigenous and immigrant groups in the Soviet Union, United States, Spanish America, the Arab Moslem world, Israel, and others.

Strictly speaking, of course, no socially complex speech community is fully homogeneous linguistically. Different social experiences (in work, education, religion) lead to different socially patterned varieties of talking (and even of writing), and different regional dialects may maintain themselves in a stable fashion even after former communications and interactional barriers are gone. Nevertheless, even if we hold to a definition of bilingualism as involving consensually separate "languages," there are of course numerous *speech* networks, speech communities, and even polities that may be characterized in this fashion. Normal foreign language instruction and tourism clearly lead neither to stable bilingualism nor to diglossia.

WHAT IS THE ETHNOCULTURAL COUNTERPART TO DIGLOSSIA?

We are now ready to broaden our discussion from a treatment of sociolinguistic parameters alone (bilingualism and diglossia) to one involving ethnocultural dimensions as well. In the latter connection, however, we are faced by the lack of a terminological and conceptual distinction such as exists between bilingualism and diglossia. If we employ biculturism to designate the *individual* pattern in the ethnocultural realm, paralleling our usage of bilingualism in the sociolinguistic realm, what can we use to designate the *societal* pattern in the ethnocultural realm, paralleling our usage of diglossia in the sociolinguistic realm? Most investigators use "bicultural" in both instances with considerable confusion and circumlocution as a result. Saville-Troike (1978) has suggested the term *dinomia* (two sets of norms, i.e., two cultures) for societally widespread biculturism. This is certainly a worthwhile suggestion, but in a sense it is a bit too broad for our purposes. Culture is a much broader designation than ethnicity, particularly in connection with modern complex societies. It deals with norms pertaining to all of human behavior, belief, and valuation. Ethnicity is a narrower concept, particularly in modern times. It focuses on "peopleness relatedness," that is, on those cultural behaviors, values, and beliefs that are related to "peopleness authenticity," i.e., to membership in a particular people and its defining tradition (Fishman, 1977a). At earlier stages of social development all of culture is ethnically defined and defining. How one dresses, what one eats, the kind of work one does, how one's house or furniture is built—these are distinctively peopleness-related behaviors. At later stages of social development many of the above behaviors (and many values and beliefs as well) have become ethnically neutralized because of their widespread ("international") currency. Even though cultures continue to coincide with broad ethnic designations, ethnicity recedes into a smaller corner, indeed, at times, into a residual corner of culture, so that only a much smaller set of behaviors, values, and beliefs are considered (by "insiders" or "outsiders," be they scholars or not) as ethnicity related, implying, defining, because they are viewed as "authentic" and associated with discontinuity across ethnic boundaries and/or self-definitions. Language behavior (particularly mother tongue use) is frequently considered to be ethnicity related, implying, defining.

If what is of concern to us is the co-occurrence between bilingualism/diglossia and the enactments of single versus multiple norms and identities in the realm of ethnocultural behavior, beliefs, and values, then we may find it useful to utilize bicultural for the *individual* manifestations in this realm, but what are we to use for the *societal* counterpart thereto? It is in this connection that I would like tentatively to suggest the term *di-ethnia*. Like bilingualism, biculturism is an individual asset or debit that corresponds to no particular societal institutions or concerns. Without such it is not intergenerationally maintained. However, like diglossia, di-ethnia is a sociocultural pattern that is maintained by means of specific institutional arrangements. The arrangements, as we will see, require (as they do in the case of diglossia) repertoire compartmentalization. However, ethnic compartmentalization and linguistic compartmentalization are only weakly related to each other in any causal sense. Thus, not only can we find bilingualism with and without diglossia (cells 1 and 2), as well as diglossia with and without bilingualism (cells 1 and 3), but we can also find:

(a) multiculturism with and without di-ethnia, as well as
(b) di-ethnia with and without either bilingualism or diglossia.

As we will note, multiculturism and di-ethnia do not form a fourfold table (a counterbalanced 2×2 table) as do bilingualism and diglossia. The reason for this is that di-ethnia is a rarer phenomenon than diglossia and a far, far rarer one than biculturism as well.

Biculturism-Di-ethnia in Various Bilingualism-Diglossia Contexts

When bilingualism and diglossia obtain (cell 1 above) di-ethnia may yet be absent. Thus, Paraguayans do not view Spanish and Guaraní as pertaining to two different ethnocultural memberships. The two languages are in complementary distribution, of course, insofar as their macrosocietal functions are concerned; however, they are both accepted as indicative of the same ethnocultural membership: Paraguayans. Both languages are required for full membership in the Paraguayan people and for the implementation of complete Paraguayanness. The same is true with respect to Geez and Amharic among Ethiopian Copts. Only one peopleness is involved, albeit different functions are fulfilled by each language and the two together constitute the whole, as they do for speakers of a vernacular Arabic who read/write Koranic classical Arabic. Certainly, neither di-ethnia (societal biculturism) nor individual biculturism are involved in cases such as these.

When diglossia is absent but bilingualism is present (cell 2), multiculturism may well be present but not di-ethnia. This is the context of transitional bilingualism and transitional biculturism on the one hand, and of ordinary cross-cultural contacts on the other hand. Neither passes the three-generation test and the bilingualism they prompt is either ultimately lost, integrated, or transitioned into translinguification, just as the biculturism they prompt is ultimately either lost, integrated or transitioned into transethnification. Note, however, that language shift and ethnocultural shift need not proceed apace; indeed, language shift for American immigrants has commonly proceeded more rapidly than has their reethnification (Fishman et al., 1966 [1978]). Nevertheless, ethnicity maintenance (particularly at any creative level or in any central domain) requires strong institutional support, as does language maintenance, rendering the other culture inoperative (consensually unacceptable) in certain functions—or even rejecting the functions per se—if two ethnocultural systems are to operate side by side on a stable and widespread basis. Two sets of cultural behaviors and identities must be in complementary distribution and strongly compartmentalized, as must be their language usage counterparts, if they are to constitute something more than transitional arrangements. It is just such complementarity and compartmentalization that this cell (2) lacks, and as a result, acculturation (and, in cell 4, assimilation) finally result.

Cell 3 also is inhospitable to di-ethnia. Since the diglossia encountered there is that based upon the territoriality principle it is, once again, only a small class of middlemen (civil servants, commercial representatives, professional translators) who have any need for being bilingual, and even most of them have no need for either biculturism or di-ethnia.

STABLE SOCIETAL BICULTURISM: SOME U.S. EXAMPLES

We have made the rounds of our 2×2 table and have not encountered di-ethnia in any of its four cells. Actually, stable, societal biculturism *does* exist in *part* of cell 1, but the purpose of our initial "go-round" has been attained if it has clarified the *rarity* of the phenomenon we are pursuing. Most of modern life is inhospitable—whether ideologically or pragmatically—to compartmentalization between a people's behaviors and values. Fluidity across role and network boundaries and, indeed, the weakening and overcoming of boundaries, are both a goal and result of most modern behavior and its emphasis on efficiency and reciprocity/solidarity in social behavior. Little wonder then that our examples of di-ethnia will derive primarily from nonmodern contexts.

The Old Order Amish and the Hasidim represent two patterns of di-ethnia on American shores. Both groups maintain a pattern of bilingualism and diglossia (cell 1) for their own internal needs involving Luther German and Pennsylvania Dutch on the one hand, and Loshn koydesh and Yiddish on the other. In addition, both groups control their own schools wherein their children are taught to become proficient in English (speaking, reading, writing) so that they *can* engage in "the other culture" within carefully prescribed limits of kind and degree. The "other culture" is viewed as necessary and the "own culture" is, therefore, in necessary complementary distribution with it. In both cases actualization of the "other culture" is restricted to economic pursuits and relationships, and even in this domain limits are carefully observed. Among the Pennsylvania Dutch, electricity may be used for pasteurization (this being required by state law) but not for refrigeration of their own food or to power modern farm machinery (Hostetler, 1968, 1974). The "outside world" must be engaged to some unavoidable degree, and for such purposes the outside language must be learned, but this degree must be a limited one and, ultimately, even this is rationalized as necessary for the maintenance and well-being of the "inside world."

It is probably not accidental that the rural Old Order Amish and the urban Hasidim both accept another culture only in the econo-technical domain, this being the most universalized and therefore the least ethnically encumbered domain of modern society. Nevertheless, the primary point of generalizable interest in connection with them is not so much the specific area in which their stable societal biculturism is expressed as the fact that it is stabilized by:

(a) *Not* integrating the two cultures involved but *keeping them separate,* in a state of tension vis-à-vis each other; that is, compartmentalization is recognized as necessary so that the outside world will not intrude upon (*spread* into: Cooper, 1981; displace/replace: Fishman, 1977b) the "inner world."

(b) Not accepting or implementing "the other culture" in its entirety, but rather implementing it selectively and in a particular domain so as to keep it in complementary distribution with their "own" H-governed and L-governed domains. English is specifically excluded from home use (where it would threaten their own L mother tongues) and from religious use (where it would threaten their own sacred H's). Thus, just as no speech community can maintain two languages on a stable basis (past three generations) if they are both used in the same social functions, and therefore stable societal bilingualism (diglossia) depends on institutionally protected functional sociolinguistic compartmentalization, so no ethnocultural collectivity can maintain two cultures on a stable basis past three generations if they are both implemented in the same social functions (family, friendship, work, education, religion, etc.), and therefore stable societal multiculturism (di-ethnia) depends on institutionally protected ethnocultural compartmentalization (Fishman, 1980).

DOES DI-ETHNIA EXIST ELSEWHERE AS WELL?

Di-ethnia is a relatively rare phenomenon, much rarer than its individual counterpart, biculturism. It is found beyond the three-generation cutoff in the Moslem world, where traditional behaviors, dress, diet, and values dominate most of life but where modern econo-technical roles require different dress, diet, and languages and do so not only for *inter*group interactions but for *intra*group interactions within this arena as well. Similar compartmentalization is encountered beyond the three-generation cutoff among various segments of Japanese, Chinese (Hong Kong, Singapore), Native American, and non-Russophone Soviets.

Di-ethnia of a more marginal or peripheral kind is sometimes also found among stable populations living at long-established political borders and sharing market days and other limited collective experiences (sports contests, for example). Finally, and even more exceptionally, di-ethnia is still encountered at times even after language shift has eroded bilingualism and diglossia to the vanishing point. Thus, even with the transethnification of blacks and aborigines, a deep-seated and often conflicted di-ethnia at times reveals itself.

THE BICULTURAL "THRUST" OF BILINGUAL/BICULTURAL EDUCATION

The term "bicultural" is often introduced quite innocently in connection with Title VII bilingual education in the United States. Neither the institutional stability nor the functional compartmentalization of this phenomenon, if it is to be pursued seriously and societally, is recognized. Indeed, unknowingly, the arrangements entered into usually foster biculturism in the most dislocative sense, i.e., they are transitional and transethnifying. They are commonly condescending, trivializing and peripheralizing in connection with the marked culture ("thingification," I have called it elsewhere) and Anglo-Americanizing even when they least suspect. The basic compartmentalization of societal functions and the vital institutional protection of *marked* sociolinguistic and ethnocultural behaviors, beliefs, and values upon which stable societal biculturism (di-ethnia) crucially depends are not only unrecognized but would probably be anathema if they were recognized. In this connection, in distinction to the destructive Title VII empty-headedness is the conscious and conscientious societal multiculturism often pursued by ethnic community-sponsored "parochial" schools in the United States. Unfortunately, while the former (Title VII) programs are numerous and tragically destructive, the latter (ethnic community "parochial") programs are too few and, tragically, too weak to attain their goals. America is the poorer in each case, but for quite opposite reasons.

REFERENCES

Cooper, Robert L. "Toward a General Theory of Language Spread." In *Language Spread: Studies in Diffusion and Social Change*, ed. R. L. Cooper, Arlington, Va.: Center for Applied Linguistics, 1981.

Ferguson, Charles A. "Diglossia," *Word*, 15, (1959), 325–40.

Fishman, Joshua A. "Bilingualism with and Without Diglossia; Diglossia with and Without Bilingualism." *Journal of Social Issues*, 23, no. 2, (1967), 29–38.

————. *The Sociology of Language: An Interdisciplinary Social Science Approach to the Study of Language in Society.* Rowley, Mass.: Newbury House, 1972.

————. "Yiddish and Loshn Koydesh in Traditional Ashkenaz: The Problem of Societal Allocation of Macrofunctions." In *Language in Sociology*, ed. A. Verdoodt and R. Kjolseth. Louvain, Belgium: Peeters, 1976, pp. 39–42.

————. "Language, Ethnicity and Racism." *Georgetown University Roundtable on Languages and Linguistics*, 1977a, pp. 297–309.

————. "The Spread of English as a New Perspective for the Study of Language Maintenance and Language Shift." In *The Spread of English*, ed. J.A. Fishman, R.L. Cooper, A. Conrad, et al. Rowley, Mass.: Newbury House, 1977b, pp. 108–36.

————. "Attracting a Following to High Culture Functions for a Language of Everyday Life." In *Language Spread: Studies in Diffusion and Social Change*, ed. R. L. Cooper. Arlington, Va.: Center for Applied Linguistics, 1981.

————. "Language Maintenance and Ethnicity." *Harvard Encyclopedia of American Ethnic Groups*, Cambridge, Mass.: Harvard University Press, 1980, pp. 629–38.

Fishman, Joshua A., et al. *Language Loyalty in the United States.* The Hague: Mouton, 1966. (Reprinted: New York: Arno Press, 1978.)

Fishman, Joshua A., Robert L. Cooper, Andrew Conrad, et al. *The Spread of English.* Rowley, Mass.: Newbury House, 1977.

Hostetler, John. *Amish Society.* Rev. ed. Baltimore: Johns Hopkins, 1968.

————. *Hutterite Society.* Baltimore: Johns Hopkins, 1974.

Kreindler, Isabelle. "The Changing Status of Russian in the Soviet Union. "*International Journal of the Sociology of Language*, 33 (1982), in press.

McRae, Kenneth. "The Principle of Territoriality and the Principle of Personality in Multilingual States." *International Journal of the Sociology of Language*, 4 (1975), 33–54.

Poll, Solomon. "Loshn Koydesh, Yiddish and Ivrit among Ultra-Orthodox Jews in Israel." *International Journal of the Sociology of Language*, 1980, 24, 109–126.

Rubin, Joan. *National Bilingualism in Paraguay.* The Hague: Mouton, 1968.

Saville-Troike, Muriel. *A Guide to Culture in the Classroom.* Rosslyn, Va.: National Clearinghouse for Bilingual Education, 1978.

Silver, Brian. "The Impact of Urbanization and Geographical Dispersion on the Linguistic Russification of Soviet Nationalities." *Demography*, 11 (1974), 89–103.

Weinreich, Max. *History of the Yiddish Language.* Trans. from the Yiddish original (Geshikhte fun der yidisher shprakh. 4 vols. New York: Yivo, 1973.) by S. Noble and J.A. Fishman. Chicago: University of Chicago Press, 1979.

A Rank Ordering and Analysis of the Goals and Objectives of Bilingual Education

SALLY D. TILLEY
University of New Orleans

The goals and objectives of teaching foreign languages to English speakers, of bilingual education, and of teaching English to speakers of other languages, have often been divergent and contradictory. Bilingual education in particular has had various interpretations, causing many professional educators and lay people to disagree as to what the real purpose of bilingual education is as opposed to other language programs. Von Maltitz states: "There is still resistance to the concept of bilingual education in certain areas, and a widespread lack of knowledge and understanding of what it means, though persons deeply committed to the idea and immersed in the activities involved in operating bilingual projects tend to forget this or choose to ignore it. . . . A good deal of education of the general public still needs to be done" (von Maltitz, 1975, p. 189).

There is further confusion and controversy between those who advocate transfer-oriented (transitional) programs, which stress the goal of assimilation to mainstream society, and those who advocate maintenance-oriented programs, which stress the goal of preservation of ethnic language and culture (Baratz et al., 1973). Federal government guidelines have also led to various interpretations, as illustrated by current policies stated in the Elementary and Secondary Education Act Title VII legislation (P.L. 90-247, 1968; P.L. 92-318, 1972). The guidelines of the United States Office of Education stress both assimilationist goals,

My sincere appreciation to my major advisors, Dra. Beatriz Varela and Dr. Richard Elliott, for their suggestions and help in this study; to Dr. John Newfield for his invaluable help with the computer program; and especially to the directors of the bilingual programs who so graciously gave of their time to participate in this study.

through the teaching of English, and preservationist goals, through the teaching of native language and culture—not necessarily exclusive trends, but open to misinterpretation.

SIGNIFICANCE OF THE PROBLEM

In actuality, English as a Second Language (ESL) and Teaching English to Speakers of Other Languages (TESOL) are transfer-oriented programs, whereas bilingual education programs tend to be maintenance-oriented with assimilationist features. These program names, however, are often used synonymously or interchangeably. Von Maltitz (1975) notes that the former—that is, transfer-oriented programs—are aimed at helping students, usually new arrivals in a school system, over the difficult language hurdle, making it possible for them to keep up in their academic work while they are learning enough English to function successfully in regular English classes. On the other hand, bilingual education encourages pupils from various ethnic groups to perfect and maintain their knowledge of the mother tongue while also mastering English—in other words, it aims to develop truly and competently literate bilinguals. Dr. John Molina, Director of the Division of Bilingual Education of the United States Office of Education, expressed the view that there was a need for a more clearly defined philosophy of bilingual education and for promulgating the idea that it can be valuable for all children (cited by von Maltitz, 1975). It was in line with Dr. Molina's concern that this study was undertaken.

PURPOSE OF THE STUDY

The purpose of this study was to investigate priority rankings of goals and objectives of bilingual education by directors of bilingual education programs. The study also proposed to answer the following questions:

1. Do directors indicate by their ranking of goals and objectives a trend toward transfer- or maintenance-oriented bilingual programs?
2. Do directors rank goals and objectives in a way that differentiates ESL or TESOL programs from bilingual education programs?
3. Do directors rank goals and objectives in such a way as to indicate the relationship of bilingual home and community to bilingual education in the school?
4. Do directors rank goals and objectives in a manner that would indicate that bilingual programs promote mostly compensatory needs for the disadvantaged?

DEFINITION OF TERMS

For the purpose of clarity, the following definitions of terms will be used:

Q-Sort: a sophisticated form of rank-ordering objects and then assigning numerals to subsets of the objects for statistical purposes (Kerlinger, 1966, p.581).

Goals: the more general and remote ends of schooling (Goodlad, 1966).

Objectives: generally stated in behavioral terms, they stem from the goals. They are usually differentiated from goals in that they are more discrete and precise and have a behavioral component. For the purpose of this study, "goals" and "objectives" carry the above operational definitions. As noted by Bloom (1956), educational objectives as well as goals may illustrate general policy and directions for curriculum development.

ESEA: Elementary and Secondary Education Act, Public Law 89-10, a federal act passed by Congress in 1965. It provides funds and guidance to local school districts to improve educational opportunities for pupils from low socio-economic backgrounds. Title VII of ESEA, known as the "Bilingual Education Act," Public Law 90-247, was added in 1967 and signed into law in January, 1968.

ESL: Abbreviation for English as a Second Language, aimed at teaching English to students of non-English-speaking backgrounds.

TESOL: Acronym for Teaching English to Speakers of Other Languages, an organization established in 1966 by the National Council of Teachers of English for the development of programs to teach English to non-English-speaking people.

METHOD

The population of this study consisted of the directors of the 220 bilingual project centers in the United States, as given in the *Guide to Title VII, ESEA Bilingual-Bicultural Projects, 1973-74* (Dissemination Center for Bilingual Education, Austin, Texas). Out of an initial 60 directors chosen using a table of random digits, 24 responded to the investigator's letters asking for examinees. Because 10 of the 24 respondents chose not to participate, the same was further reduced to the 14 directors who took part in the study. The participants represented a cross-section of the United States: they were from the Northeast, North Central region, South, Southwest and West. Languages spoken by the students in the programs are presented in Table 1, with the predominant language being Spanish. Grade levels of the students ranged from kindergarten

Table 1
Percentage of Students Speaking Each Language Represented by the Sample

Language	Percentage
Spanish	
Mexican	44
Puerto Rican	6
Other	4
Total	54
French	
Canadian	4
Acadian and Creole	16
Total	20
English	20
Chinese	5
Other	1

through the twelfth grade. Unfortunately, no American Indians were represented because the five centers with Indian student populations selected in the sample chose not to participate.

In order to determine goals and objectives that were pertinent to bilingual education, a survey of the literature was made, starting with preliminary index sources: *Dissertation Abstracts, Education Index, Research in Education,* and selected books. With the exception of the books, all indexes encompassed the period from January, 1974, through December, 1974. Descriptors used in the search were "bilingualism," "bilingual education," and "objectives." The criteria for the selection of goals and objectives were that they should be both readily apparent and deemed significant in the field of bilingual education.

A tentative selection of the goals and objectives for the Q-Sort was made by three linguists who received the first screening from the library search. With the above stated criteria as a guide, they worked independently of each other in making their choices. Final selection resulted in 57 goals and objectives in the instrument, among which were represented four general categories that were in keeping with the federal guidelines: namely, actual bilingual instruction, preparation and acquisition of materials, staff development, and community participation. The directors who participated in the study were allowed to make any additional comments they wished on a card that was enclosed with the instrument. The instrument was considered sufficient for the purpose of the study in that the 57 brief descriptions of goals and objectives were representative of the range of possible goals and the open-ended card added the needed flexibility statement to cover possible error.

Each goal or objective was then printed on an IBM card, and the respondents were required to sort the 57 cards (the instrument) into eleven piles, with the number of cards per pile as shown on the scale (Table 2). The scale represents a continuum in which category "0" is the least desirable item. The center pile was to be a neutral pile consisting of those objectives which seemed to be ambiguous or to have little relevance to immediate decision.

The Q-Sort technique was examined with regard to its many difficulties. It is a somewhat novel instrument in ranking items, and it is for this reason that it was chosen. Other questionnaires using the form of a Likert Scale might have been as useful; however, the purpose of the study was to identify a list of bilingual objectives ranked in priority order and not to generalize aspects of bilingual education to a hypothetical population. Thus, the Q-Sort was deemed appropriate. It is assumed that the subjects working with the instrument understood the nature of forced- choice situations and interpreted certain objectives alike. It is also possible that the low return by the directors was due to the sorting and scoring of the instrument. As a survey instrument, the Q-Sort has the drawback that it cannot be answered quickly and requires much involvement by those participating. The instructions, however, did ensure anonymity of all respondents in accordance with stated university and government policy.

After sorting the cards, the subjects placed the category number, corresponding to the column on the scale, on the back of each card. These were the numbers used for tabulating the median rank of each objective, which was done by computer at the University of New Orleans. The 57 items were then ranked according to their median rank score. Table 3 presents the rank order of the 57 goals and objectives. For the purpose of analysis, a comparison was made between the upper 25 percent (scored 10.0 through 6.5) and the lower 25 percent—starting with objective number 44—(scored 4.0 through 0.0). Further analysis,

Table 2
Scale for Sorting Q-Sort Cards

	Least Desirable									*Most Desirable*	
Category Number	0	1	2	3	4	5	6	7	8	9	10
Number of Cards Per Pile	2	3	4	6	8	11	8	6	4	3	2

Table 3

Median Rank of Bilingual Goals and Objectives

Objective Number	Objective	Median Rank Score
24	To develop and maintain child's self-esteem in both cultures	10.0
23	To establish cooperation between school and home of bilingual child	8.0
53	To prevent students' retardation in school performance	8.0
34	To develop measurements for evaluation of bilingual programs	7.5
43	To instruct children in their cultural heritage	7.5
52	To counteract high dropout rates resulting from language handicaps	7.5
1	To teach all subject matter in 2 languages	7.0
38	To return to schools those individuals unable to attend because of language handicaps	7.0
40	To increase number of non-English dominant children receiving high school diplomas	7.0
41	To develop a bilingual staff for a self-supporting district program	7.0
45	To provide in-service training for all levels of bilingual personnel	7.0
55	To help students overcome educational handicap from minority group isolation	7.0
4	To teach all skills in 2 languages: reading, writing, listening, speaking	6.5
10	To teach native language skills so child will perform at or above grade level	6.5
11	To teach English skills so child will perform at or above grade level	6.5
9	To offer English classes to parents of bilingual children	6.0
19	To upgrade English ability for better vocational and career opportunities	6.0
57	To teach the language and culture of child's native country or community	6.0
3	To maintain instruction in 2 languages in grades K-12	5.5
47	To develop teaching personnel from bilingual non-Anglo groups	5.5
51	To develop instructional materials from a locally based source	5.5
54	To eliminate minority group segregation among students and faculty	5.5
16	To make bilingual child aware of the process of acculturation	5.0
21	To develop functional bilinguals among native English-speaking population	5.0
29	To promote understanding between privileged and deprived groups	5.0
31	To gain an economic advantage for minority groups	5.0
36	To encourage bilingual child to participate in extracurricular activities	5.0
37	To provide bilingual counselors and job placement personnel in schools	5.0
39	To develop in-service field experience for teacher certification	5.0
42	To develop demonstration programs for replication in other areas	5.0
48	To develop teaching personnel from bilingual Anglo groups	5.0
15	To make majority culture aware of the process of acculturation	4.5
17	To make minority parents aware of the process of acculturation	4.5
25	To give 2 cultures present in a society a more equal prominence	4.5

2	To teach only selected subject matter in 2 languages	4.0
5	To teach only selected skills in 2 languages	4.0
14	To teach 2 languages for future employment in bilingual positions	4.0
18	To develop bilingualism in the United States to ensure national survival	4.0
27	To introduce English-speaking monolinguals to foreign cultures via language	4.0
32	To absorb individuals or groups into mainstream society	4.0
44	To act in compensatory fashion for pre-school children	4.0
46	To act as clearinghouse for materials imported from abroad	4.0
49	To develop teaching personnel from monolingual non-Anglo groups	4.0
50	To develop teaching personnel from monolingual Anglo groups	4.0
12	To teach elementary English-speaking children another language and culture	3.5
13	To teach secondary English-speaking children another language and culture	3.5
33	To enable Americans to communicate with other nations	3.5
22	To break the monolingual pattern of a majority society	3.0
8	To urge the learning of language for its own sake	2.5
28	To reconcile different political or socially separate communities	2.5
30	To preserve ethnic or religious ties	2.5
6	To teach English skills only	2.0
35	To develop measurements for evaluation of bilingual child's performance	2.0
7	To teach child's native language skills only	2.0
20	To maintain status quo of the non-English-speaking child in his own culture	1.5
26	To embellish or strengthen the education of social elites	0.5
56	To teach the language and culture of Spain and France	0.0

such as factor analysis, was not attempted because of the small sample return and the limited background information about the directors and the centers.

RESULTS

In analyzing the data, the questions raised earlier will be restated and the findings will be presented.

1. Do directors indicate by their ranking of goals and objectives a trend toward transfer- or maintenance-oriented bilingual programs?

An analysis of the upper and the lower 25 percent of the items indicates that the rankings show neither a purely transfer-oriented (assimilationist) program nor a purely maintenance-oriented program. Objective 1 (to teach all subject matter in 2 languages) had a high median rank score of 7.0, which indicates a merging of the two philosophies. Adding support to this conclusion are objective 10 (to teach native language skills so child will perform at or above grade level), scored 6.5, and objective 11 (to teach English skills so child will perform at or above grade level), also scored 6.5. Objective 43 (to instruct children in their cultural heritage) was scored a high 7.5, but objective 30 (to preserve ethnic or religious ties) was scored a low 2.5, as was objective 20 (to maintain status quo of the non-English-speaking child in his own culture), scored 1.5. Objective 7 (to teach child's native language skills only), which was scored 2.0, coupled with objective 6 (to teach English skills only), which was also scored 2.0, shows that emphasis is placed neither on assimilationist nor on maintenance-type programs.

2. Do directors rank goals and objectives in a way that differentiates ESL or TESOL programs from bilingual education programs?

The directors did differentiate between ESL and bilingual education programs, as shown by objective 1 (to teach all subject matter in 2 languages), which was scored a high 7.0, and objective 6 (to teach English skills only), which was scored a low 2.0. The relatively high score of objective 4 (to teach all skills in two languages: reading, writing, listening, speaking) further substantiates the conclusion that the two programs are distinct. These rankings concur with the definitions of ESEA, Title VII guidelines:

> Bilingual education involves the use of two languages, one of which is English, as the media of instruction in a comprehensive school program. There is evidence that use of the child's mother tongue as a medium of instruction concurrent with an effort to strengthen his command of English acts to prevent retardation in academic skill and performance. (Public Law 93-380, 1974)

Von Maltitz (1975, p. 191) summarizes: "As has been made clear in many statements, ESL alone is not bilingual education, but it must be a major component of any bilingual program."

3. Do directors rank goals and objectives in such a way as to indicate the relationship of bilingual home and community to bilingual education in the school?

Goal 23 (to establish cooperation between school and home of bilingual children), which was ranked second highest of the 57 items, concurs with Ulibarri's statement:

> To the extent that a program divorces itself from the lives of the people, it and the school serve only as a superficial shell, totally irrelevant to the people...their language and their manner of living must be taken into consideration. To the extent that this is achieved in developing goals and objectives, the program has a chance of reaching those for whom it is intended. (Ulibarri, 1970, p.1)

4. Do directors rank goals and objectives in a manner which would indicate that bilingual programs promote mostly compensatory needs for the disadvantaged?

This question was not answered in the top or bottom 25 percent of the items. However, objective 44 (to act in compensatory fashion for pre-school children) had a median rank score of 4.0. Von Maltitz (1975) states that many speakers at the International Bilingual-Bicultural Conference in 1974 expressed disapproval of the continuing character-ization of bilingual education only as a compensatory measure for disadvantaged pupils. However, disapproval is not strongly supported by the findings of this study.

DISCUSSION

Goal 24 (to develop and maintain a child's self-esteem in both cultures) was ranked the most desirable, with the top median rank score of 10. This concurs with the federal guidelines, which state that the programs are intended "to develop the child's self-esteem and a legitimate pride in both cultures" (Public Law 93-380, 1974). Because of the stress on middle-class, Anglo values in the schools, non-English-speaking children have come to feel inferior to Anglo children and are ashamed of their native language and culture. For this reason, Ulibarri notes, "one finds statements on objectives dealing with reinforcement and development of the self-image of the bilingual-bicultural child. This seems to be one of the strongest reasons for the creation of bilingual-bicultural educational programs" (Ulibarri, 1970,p.10).

The process whereby one can achieve goal 24 is reflected in the top 25 percent of the objectives, which emphasize the importance of studying both English and the native language and culture. It is possible that the choice of many of these objectives was influenced by the directors' knowledge of the federal guidelines, which state or imply many of the high-ranked goals and objectives in this study.

At the other end of the continuum are the two least desirable objectives: 56 (to teach the language and culture of Spain and France) and 26 (to embellish or strengthen the education of social elites). These objectives support a philosophy of exclusivity that is not representative of American democratic ideals. The low rank of objective 56 also raised the following question: if this is the least desirable objective for bilingual education, why have some programs felt the need to import teachers from these countries to teach bilingual children of the same heritage living in the United States? Feedback from the Q-Sort produced the explanation that there are not enough bilingual teachers from North America to staff these newly formed programs. This fact is upheld in the legislative history, which states: "The Office of Education, in a study of 76 of its bilingual programs, found extensive incidence of inadequately prepared teachers. . . . In addition, there is a serious scarcity of trained bilingual teachers." (P.L. 93-380, 1974, p. 4150).

Objective 56 can also refer to foreign language instruction to English-speaking students, as can objective 13 (to teach secondary English-speaking children another language and culture). Objective 12 (to teach elementary English-speaking children another language and culture) would apply to Foreign Language in the Elementary School (FLES). One possible reason for the low rank scores of objectives 12 and 13 is that the Education Amendments Act signed by President Ford in 1974 (amending earlier legislation) ensures federal funding through 1978 but contains a new policy that states "In no event shall the program be designed for the purpose of teaching a foreign language to English-speaking children" (cited by von Maltitz, 1975, p. 5). This will certainly have repercussions for the Anglo children included in bilingual programs. Interestingly, 20 percent of the children represented in this study were Anglos.

SUMMARY

Within the limitations of this study, one can conclude from the rank ordering of goals and objectives by bilingual program directors that both adapting to mainstream society through the teaching of English and the preservation of ethnic ties through the teaching of native language and culture are important goals of bilingual education. There is a distinct difference, however, between goals for English as a Second Language (ESL), which emphasize assimilation only, and goals for bilingual education; consequently, the two program names should not be used arbitrarily or interchangeably. High on the list of goals of bilingual education is the desire for interrelationships between the bilingual community and the school, with major emphasis on the development of the bilingual child's positive self-concept and prevention of his academic retardation. Conversely, the bilingual program directors were not concerned with such goals as elitism, language for its own sake, or other goals which tend toward exclusivity.

REFERENCES

Baratz, Joan C., et. al. *Development of Bilingual-Bicultural Education Models.* Washington, D.C.: Education Study Center, 1973. (Eric Document Reproduction Service No. ED 083 923).

Bloom, B.S. *Taxonomy of Educational Objectives.* New York: David McKay Company, 1956.

Congressional Findings, Public Law 90–247, Title VII ESEA, January 2, 1968.

Congressional Findings, Public Law 90–318, Title VII ESEA, June 23, 1972.

Goodlad, J.I. *The Changing School Curriculum.* New York: Fund for the Advancement of Education, 1966.

Kerlinger, F.N. *Foundations of Behavioral Research.* New York: Holt, Rinehart and Winston, 1966.

Ulibarri, H. *Bilingual Education: A Handbook for Educators.* New Mexico: 1970. (ERIC Document Reproduction Service No. ED 039 078).

U.S. Code—Congressional and Administrative News, Legislative History, Public Law 93–380, Vol. 3, 1974.

von Maltitz, F.W. *Living and Learning in Two Languages.* New York: McGraw-Hill, 1975.

Bilingual Schools: Gateways to Integration or Roads to Separation

AMADO M. PADILLA
University of California, Los Angeles

Public education has long been viewed as the great social equalizer in American society. Many have pointed to public education as one of this country's greatest achievements. Because of the widespread acceptance of this belief, educational philosophy and practice has rarely been challenged, and then when it has by only a few dissidents. In recent years these dissidents have begun to raise their voices louder than ever. Although there is not unity among the critics of public education, one thing is clear: public education has not succeeded with all children. Some critics even claim that it has failed *most* children. Public education, moreover, is not the great social equalizer it is thought to be. For every child who has succeeded there are many more who have failed. The list includes, among others: immigrants, the poor, minority groups, women, the gifted, the independent, and the hyperactive. The causes of failure are many but most have to do with what we will call "extracurricular rules" to learning. These rules have little to do with that set of principles laid down by psychologists and educators about the most efficient ways to learn in the classroom. Rather, these "extracurricular rules" have to do more with the correct language to speak in the classroom, grooming, the suppression of inquisitiveness, the ability to sit reasonably still for long periods of time, etc. There is a degree of racism, sexism, ageism, and anti-intellectualism in all of this. The focus of this paper will be on the education of children and adults who because of linguistic and/or cultural reasons are unable to cope with the "extracurricular rules."

Bilingual education has been proposed as a solution to the failure of educational philosophy (i.e., equality through education) to match

Prepared for the National Institute of Education, Developmental Conference on Policy Problems in Educational Options. Chicago, Illinois, 1976.

reality (i.e., educational opportunity is not equally distributed to all segments of United States society). Only a short space will be given here to the rather long history of bilingual education. Attention will be devoted more to the variability in goals and outcomes that exists among bilingual educational programs. We will show how some of these programs do not in reality present an educational alternative to the linguistic and/or culturally different learner and how other programs are so threatening that they cannot be tolerated by the American educational system. In the analysis, we will seek to establish a balance between types of bilingual educational programs and how these programs coincide with mainstream educational policy. Finally, guidelines for making Bilingual Education a true educational alternative will be offered.

BILINGUAL EDUCATION: A HISTORICAL PERSPECTIVE

Contrary to the belief of many educators, bilingual education is not a recent educational phenomenon. Nor has bilingual education been confined to Spanish-English programs in the Southwest. The maintenance of ethnicity and a native language other than English has a long and extremely fascinating history (Fishman, et al., 1966). There have been six historical factors which have contributed to language maintenance in the United States (Kloss, 1966). These factors are:

1. Religio-societal insulation;
2. Time of immigration; earlier than or simultaneously with the first Anglo-Americans;
3. Existence of language islands;
4. Affiliation with denominations fostering parochial schools;
5. Pre-immigration experience with language maintenance efforts;
6. Use of a language other than English as the official language during the pre-Anglo-American period.

In attempting to use these factors to understand the history of bilingual education in this country, we must distinguish between consciously planned language maintenance experiences and unplanned, effortless pre-immigration language maintenance experiences. Employing this dichotomy and again relying heavily on Kloss's study of bilingual schooling (see Andersson and Boyer, 1970), the history of bilingual schooling divides itself into two main parts: pre-World War I and post-1963. The pre-World War I part can be differentiated into two segments and two phases. Table 1 summarizes the pre-World War I

Table 1
A Summary of the Pre-World War I Period in Bilingual Schooling[1]

First Segment: Public Elementary Schools
Phase I 1839–1880
German was the only non-English tongue admitted as a medium of teaching except for French in Louisiana and, from 1848, Spanish in New Mexico. The heyday of the public bilingual school was before the Civil War.
Phase II 1880–1917
There were German-English bilingual schools in Cincinnati, Indianapolis, Baltimore, New Ulm, Minnesota, and in an unknown number of rural places. In other schools German was taught as a subject, but not used as a medium of instruction. Norwegian, Czech, Italian, Polish, and Dutch were also occasionally taught but not used as teaching mediums.

Second Segment: Non-Public (Chiefly Parochial Elementary Schools)
Phase I Before 1880
German schools flourished throughout the country. Also this period saw the beginning of many French schools in New England and many Scandinavian and some Dutch schools in the Midwest. Many of these schools were not actually bilingual in their curricula; they were non-English schools where English was taught as a subject.
Phase II After 1880
This period saw the multiplication of French and Scandinavian schools as well as the founding of numerous parochial schools especially for Catholic newcomers from Eastern and Southern Europe: e.g., Poles, Lithuanians, Slovaks.

---

[1]As presented by Kloss (1942 and 1963) and adapted by Andersson and Boyer (1970).

period in bilingual schooling. The crucial thing to note in studying Table 1 is the diversity of languages employed in pre-World War I schools. Today, many of these languages are not usually associated with bilingual education.

The second period of bilingual schooling began in 1963 with the pouring into Miami of thousands of Cuban refugees. In an effort to meet the educational needs of the Cuban refugee children, school officials of the Coral Way School in Miami organized a completely bilingual program. The program began in grades one, two, and three. Plans were made to move up one grade each year. Approximately half of the instruction was given in Spanish by a Cuban teacher; the other half in English by an American teacher. Soon thereafter, bilingual programs spread to other schools in Miami and were extended through the twelfth grade (Gaarder and Richardson, 1968; Bell, 1969).

Shortly after the creation of the first bilingual public elementary school programs in Miami, a number of bilingual programs began to appear elsewhere. The first of these programs appeared in Texas, New Mexico, California, and have subsequently spread to many other states

(Andersson and Boyer, 1970). Coupled with the sudden appearance of a new and more recent period in bilingual schooling was federal legislation which established a national policy regarding bilingual education. This new policy was contained in the Bilingual Education Act, Title VII of the Elementary and Secondary Education Act of 1965. The best way to grasp the full implication of the Bilingual Education Act is to read the opening statement of the Act. The appropriate section reads as follows:

TITLE VII—BILINGUAL EDUCATION PROGRAMS

Sec. 701. This title may be cited as the "Bilingual Education Act."

Policy

Sec. 702. (a) Recognizing—

(1) that there are large numbers of children of limited.English-speaking ability;

(2) that many of such children have a cultural heritage which differs from that of English-speaking persons;

(3) that a primary means by which a child learns is through the use of such child's language and cultural heritage;

(4) that, therefore, large numbers of children of limited English-speaking ability have educational needs which can be met by the use of bilingual educational methods and techniques; and

(5) that, in addition, children of limited English-speaking ability benefit through the fullest utilization of multiple language and cultural resources;

the Congress declares it to be the policy of the United States, in order to establish equal educational opportunity for all children (A) to encourage the establishment and operation, where appropriate, of educational programs using bilingual educational practices, techniques, and methods, and (B) for that purpose, to provide financial assistance to local educational agencies, and to State educational agencies to develop and carry out such programs in elementary and secondary schools, including activities at the preschool level, which are designed to meet the educational needs of such children; and to demonstrate effective ways of providing, for children of limited English-speaking ability, instruction designed to enable them, while using their native language, to achieve competence in the English language.

The careful reader of the legislation will observe that the Bilingual Education Act:

- Recognizes that there is a large number of children of limited English-speaking ability;
- Is not limited to any linguistic/cultural group;
- Makes reference to the importance of a child's differing cultural heritage in the educational process;
- Provides for bilingual education beginning at the preschool level;
- Sets no upper limit to bilingual education;

- Emphasizes the use of the native language to achieve competence in English;
- Adheres to a policy of equal educational opportunity for all limited English-speaking ability children through the creation of biingual education programs.

With what has been presented thus far as background, let us turn our attention to the reasons for the resurgence of bilingual schooling in the United States and to the legislation which provides for such an educational experience. Bear in mind though that we have only uncovered the tip of the iceberg in our historical sketch of bilingual schooling and that we have not summarized the very long litany of opposition to this type of educational program.

A RATIONALE FOR BILINGUAL SCHOOLING

There are numerous reasons we can use to argue for bilingual education. These rest entirely on what is best for the individual child, the philosophy of education we hold, or the politics surrounding a policy of cultural pluralism. Andersson and Boyer (1970) presentan excellent discussion of a rationale for bilingual education. A summary of their discussion is presented in Table 2. The argument that Andersson and Boyer evolve is that an educational alternative is essential since mainstream American education has *not* met the needs of children whose language of the home is something other than English. In addition, they argue cogently that whatever alternative is provided, it should be organized in a way that reinforces the individual as well as the cultural identity of the learner.

Perhaps the most instructive way to understand the full significance of how American schools have failed the linguistic and culturally different student is to examine the present status of minority groups who report using a language other than English in the home. According to the 1970 census, 33.2 million Americans, or roughly 16 percent of the population, speak a language other than English as a native tongue. Spanish, German, and Italian speakers are the most numerous, in that order. Spanish is the only one of the three which has experienced substantial growth in the number of speakers since 1940, largely owing to increased immigration from Mexico and Puerto Rico. By 1973, Spanish-origin persons numbered 9,072,602 nationwide and constituted the second largest minority group in the United States.

Immigration of other groups also continues to increase the size of the country's language minority communities. Asian groups, for example,

Table 2
Ten Reasons That Justify the Importance of Bilingual Schooling[1]

1. American schooling has not met the needs of children coming from homes where non-English languages are spoken; a radical improvement is therefore urgently needed.
2. Such improvement must first of all maintain and strengthen the sense of identity of children entering the school from such homes.
3. The self-image and sense of dignity of families that speak other languages must also be preserved and strengthened.
4. The child's mother tongue is not only an essential part of his sense of identity; it is also his best instrument for learning, especially in the early stages.
5. Preliminary evidence indicates that initial learning through a child's non-English home language does not hinder learning in English or other school subjects.
6. Differences among first, second, and foreign languages need to be understood if learning through them is to be sequenced effectively.
7. The best order of the learning of basic skills in a language—whether first or second—needs to be understood and respected if best results are to be obtained; this order is normally, especially for children: listening comprehension, speaking, reading, and writing.
8. Young children have an impressive learning capacity; especially in the case of language learning, the young child learns more easily and better than adolescents or adults the sound system, the basic structure, and vocabulary of a language.
9. Closely related to bilingualism is biculturalism, which should be an integral part of bilingual instruction.
10. Bilingual education holds the promise of helping to harmonize various ethnic elements in a community into a mutually respectful and creative pluralistic society.

[1]Taken from Andersson and Boyer (1970).

have experienced rapid increases in size since restrictive legislation barring or limiting their entry was repealed. Since 1965, when all immigration quotas were liberalized, 654,736, or more than one-third of all Asian immigrants since 1820, have entered the United States. In 1973 alone, more Asians immigrated than any other group (1973 Annual Report of Immigration). Moreover, we have also recently witnessed the immigration of a very large number of Vietnamese refugees into the United States.

On another level the 1970 census estimates that 31 percent of the 760,572 Native Americans counted speak a Native American language as their first language. Unlike some other groups, the survival of Native American languages is primarily the result of their continued use by existing groups (e.g., Navajos) and their geographic isolation.

In sum, although precise data are not available on the numbers of limited- or non-English-speaking children currently in school, the U.S. Office of Education estimates that at least 5 million children need bilingual schooling. The Census Bureau reports that 4.5 million Spanish-speaking children under 20 years of age speak Spanish at home. An estimated 259,830 Asian American children (excluding Vietnamese children) speak little or no English, and some 56,493 Native American children speak a Native American language as a first language.

More important than just knowing the number of school-age children who come from non-English-speaking home environments is the question of how these same children are succeeding in school. Educators have known for many years that ethnic minority children whose primary language is not English have difficulty succeeding in English monolingual schools. (For an historical analysis of this as far as the Spanish-speaking child is concerned, see Carter, 1970, and Padilla and Ruiz, 1973). Census Bureau figures alone indicate that, compared with the median number of 12.0 school years completed for whites, the median is 8.1 for Mexican Americans, 8.6 for Puerto Ricans, 9.8 for Native Americans, and 12.4 for Asian Americans. The Civil Rights Commission Mexican American Education Study shows that 40 percent of Mexican Americans who enter first grade never complete high school (U.S. Commission on Civil Rights, *The Unfinished Education,*1971). As of 1972, the dropout rate for Puerto Ricans in New York City from tenth grade to graduation was 57 percent (U.S. Commission on Civil Rights, Staff Report, 1972). In New England, 25 percent of the Spanish-speaking student population had been retained in grade for at least 3 years; 50 percent, for at least 2 years. Only 12 percent were found to be in the correct grade for their age group (New England Regional Council, 1970). The dropout rate for Native Americans in the Southwest between grades 9 and 12 is 30.6 percent (U.S. Commission on Civil Rights, *Southwest Indian Report,* 1973). For Navajos, the largest Native American tribe, the median educational level achieved is the fifth grade.

Academic achievement scores recorded for these children lag significantly behind those for majority group children. Coleman, et al. (1966), who has looked at this particular aspect of schooling in the United States more closely than any investigator, concludes that by the twelfth grade the Mexican American student is 4.1 years behind the national norm in math achievement, 3.5 in verbal ability, and 3.3. in reading. The Puerto Rican student is 4.8 years behind the national norm in math, 3.6 in verbal ability, and 3.2 in reading. On tests of general information— including humanities, social sciences, and natural sciences—the median twelfth grade score is 43.3 for Mexican Americans, 41.7 for Puerto Ricans, 44.7 for Native Americans, and 49.0 for Asian Americans, as compared to a median score of 52.2 for whites.

It is clear from the data presented above that ethnic minority children whose primary language is something other than English have education needs that are sadly going unmet in today's schools. With these data in hand let us proceed to a discussion of the philosophy surrounding bilingual education.

BILINGUAL EDUCATION: PHILOSOPHICAL PERSPECTIVES

There is no single or unitary philosophical position on bilingual education. However, to bring some coherence to this educational approach we will discuss three divergent philosophies which have guided advocates of bilingual education. Each of these philosophical positions will be dealt with separately.

Philosophy of Cultural Assimilation. Proponents of this philosophy advocate bilingual schooling to bridge the gap between the child's home and the school. The child's native language is actually treated as a supplementary instructional tool to be used until the child has adapted to school and has acquired the necessary skills in English to participate in an English-only program. Bilingual programs built solely on this philosophy are called transitional programs since they emphasize a shift from the native language and culture to the majority language and culture. A program of this type can be categorized as a "one-way" educational experience open only to ethnic students. This philosophical position holds that non-ethnics need not participate since they are already assimilated.

A program of the type described under this philosophy usually begins with either the child's native language as a single language of instruction, or with the native language and English as dual mediums of instruction. However, as rapidly as is pragmatically deemed possible, the time and treatment of English is increased so that within a relatively short period of time the native language is used only for limited, non-essential subjects. If reading or writing skills are taught in the native language, only the minimum skills considered necessary for establishing the base skills for their transfer to English are offered to the child. Basically the educational trend in all programs of this type is towards rapid and near complete transfer to English, so that by about the third grade English alone is the language of instruction. In an analysis of the assimilation model, Kjolseth (1973) sums up this position quite nicely as follows:

> The school's policy is essentially a "burnt bridges" approach: the ethnic language is seen only as a bridge to the non-ethnic language—one to be crossed as rapidly as possible and then destroyed, at least as a legitimate medium of general instruction, although some voluntary classes in it as a foreign language may be maintained. (p. 13)

Another aspect of programs of this type is that, apart from some possible early consideration of ethnic-related culture curriculum, the content of the curriculum emphasizes majority-group, middle-class interests and values. Ethnolinguistic matters are conspicuous by their absence. Even when ethnocultural curriculum is introduced it is often done so superficially. For example, the introduction of a piñata into a single classroom activity is not enough to boast of having an ethnoculturally relevant curriculum. Although this example may be extreme, it is appropriate for the point being made here.

In sum, the linguistic and cultural content of the assimilation philosophy is metaphorically a "vertically" articulated one implying power and prestige. It emphasizes the superiority or inferiority of different varieties of language and culture and encourages restricting use to correct forms of school-approved varieties in all domains of usage. Often this educational approach is successful in alienating the student from the language and culture of his/her home and community. When this occurs the educational program has been successful—the student is on the way toward acculturation! Finally, pre-existent stereotypes about ethnolinguistic carriers held by majority, and in some cases minority-group members, are unaltered or reinforced by educational programs which describe the assimilation efforts as bringing "cultural enrichment" and a literate standard language to the "culturally deprived" and illiterate.

Philosophy of Cultural Pluralism.   Supporters of this philosophy argue that the school should recognize the legitimate right of other languages and cultures in the classroom. The essential and critical argument is that the schooling experience is enriched for all children if education is conducted bilingually *and* biculturally. Ideally, a bilingual program organized around a philosophy of cultural pluralism offers a schooling experience that is "two-way." That is, students of both the minority and majority group learn essential skills in both languages. Classes are ethnically mixed (majority student involvement usually occurring on a voluntary basis) from the beginning if initially segregated; they become mixed by the third or fourth grade.

The medium of instruction is dual—the child's native language and English—and both languages are presented by the same teacher. Each language receives equal time and equal treatment, initially through the presentation of a lesson in the student's strongest, or native, language, followed by presentation of the same materials in the second language. Later, when students have a better command of the second language, the class may alternate from one to the other without doubling or repeating the same materials in the second language. Overall, there is the conscious attempt to keep both languages in balance without relegating either to unimportant purposes.

The content of the bilingual curriculum stimulates ethnic community language planning efforts and includes considerable attention to the local and regional cultures of both the ethnolinguistic minority group and the majority group in such a way as to provide a natural context for alternate use of both languages. Moreover, bilingual schooling under this philosophy is programmed to last a minimum of nine years. Continuity in bilingual-bicultural schooling is deemed essential for cultural pluralism to blossom to maturity in students from both the minority and majority group. To ensure this continuity in schooling, parents and other community leaders are encouraged to take an active role in the program's administration. The bilingual program ideally becomes a social issue around which the community becomes politically mobilized. If the teachers and school administrators are committed to a philosophy of cultural pluralism then the school and the community jointly and in concert control the program's operation. If the school is not committed to this educational philosophy then the community can only hope to exert enough pressure on local school officials to initiate such a program. As yet there are only a few programs in existence which can truly be labelled as culturally pluralistic in orientation.

We can summarize this second major philosophical position in the following way: the administrative staff of the school maintains a policy of egalitarian distribution of power with the community and actively seeks community input from all sectors of the community. The linguistic and cultural content of the pluralistic program is "horizontally" articulated, emphasizing the complementarity of different varieties of situationally appropriate culture and language. The school environment encourages the student to become a proficient speaker of two languages and to feel comfortable in switching between them. Language skills and cultural perspectives are added without progressively destroying the student's home language and culture. Furthermore, these developments take place in *both* groups. The success or failure of this educational model depends on the commitment to cultural pluralism held by local school officials and by the community they serve.

Philosophy of Cultural Separation. In a very real sense this is the easiest position to describe, but at the same time it is the most difficult to represent accurately because of the political diversity of its advocates. The essential argument is that traditional schooling has so badly failed in meeting the educational needs of the non-English-speaking child that there is no recourse but to offer a totally separate educational alternative to these students. The charge of failure pertains to more than just academic needs. It implies that the school has failed the child: culturally, linguistically, and socially. Advocates of this educational philosophy contend that the educational failure has gone on long enough. The proposed solution is obvious. The ethnic minority community must be charged with the education of its own children. How this is implemented is as follows: first, there is the explicit philosophy that education should be in the hands of culturally similar teachers (i.e., members of the same ethnic group). Second, there is the belief that the curriculum should be as highly relevant to the culture of the student as possible. To ensure this, the medium of instruction should be weighted heavily on the side of the home language, rather than English. Finally, there is the belief that the students must be instilled with and/or reinforced for having pride in their cultural membership. This orientation is more than just cultural maintenance. It is a philosophy that espouses a position that is the antithesis of assimilation. Separatists would prefer to exclude "American" cultural values and traditions from the curriculum to the extent possible.

Advocates of this philosophy can be subdivided into one of two possible camps. The first is a somewhat hypothetical extreme manifested by hostility toward the majority culture and subsequent relegation of that language and culture to a subordinate or nonexistent position. It is the opposite of extreme assimilationism, yet is like it in its exclusionary focus. The second camp has a similar outlook, although it is less radical. It allows room for English and majority-group culture and language, but still subordinates them to the native language and culture—unlike cultural pluralism, which gives both languages and cultures equal status.

Politically, a separatist philosophy carries little threat as long as schooling continues to be maintained by the majority group and supported by public monies. In the following section we will outline a typology of bilingual programs and in doing so will illustrate the very limited range of influence separatist programs have. The limited power exercised by the separatists in their quest to establish alternate educational programs for their children is due to many of the same causes that ensure hardship, if not failure, for advocates of alternative educational programs generally. The financial strain is enormous especially for minority group communities. Related to this is the shortage of teachers from the minority group committed to an educational alternative of separation which in effect means job insecurity, political pressure from the majority group, and lack of educational materials for students.

In an effort to place the three philosophies in their proper perspective, we will, by means of several typologies, attempt to highlight how the advocates of each of these philosophies have carried out their programs in the classroom. Before we begin, however, it is essential to be clear on the fact that what will be presented here is not an exhaustive analysis of bilingual programs. Our purpose is only to isolate the most critical aspects of these programs so that their similarities and differences can be scrutinized.

BILINGUAL EDUCATION PROGRAMS: TYPOLOGIES

Since the Mexican-American population constitutes the largest identifiable bilingual group, our analysis will be focussed on the Mexican-American school-age child. However, the analysis we will present is generalizable to all bilingual communities. Models of the educational philosophies discussed above are shown in Figures 1–3. The three models are readily contrastable by means of these figures.

The Assimilation and Separatist Models are obviously the most dissimilar. The Pluralistic Model lies midway between the two. The three

Figure 1
Typology of the Assimilation Model

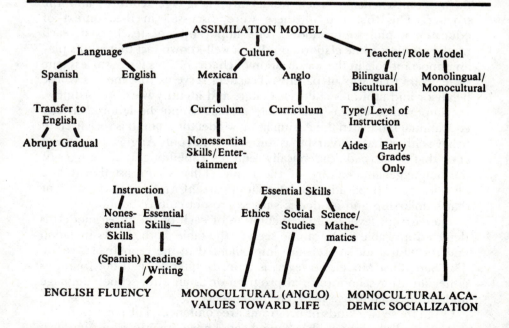

Note the recognition of the minority language and culture, but the nonuse of these in the essential skill training of the student.

Figure 2
Typology of the Pluralistic Model

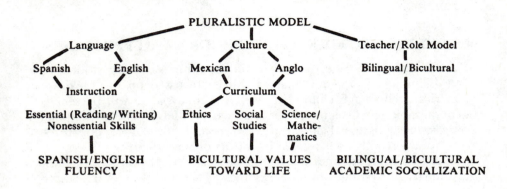

Note the dual recognition of minority and majority group language and culture and their dual use in the educational process.

major components of each model are: language, culture, and the teacher. The first two of these were discussed in the context of educational philosophy above. The importance of teachers in each model requires some elaboration. It is a well-known fact that adults play an important role in the socialization of children. This fact is no less true of teachers than it is of parents. Teachers serve as role models whose behavior and attitudes children imitate and identify with. Accordingly, the importance of teachers as role models cannot be ignored in any educational model. In the Assimilation Model the student is socialized to believe either that scholarship is something that only Anglos can succeed at or that to succeed academically requires a shedding of all vestiges of the language and culture of the home. This is contrasted with the Pluralistic and Separatist Models that impart information to the student that scholarship and academic success are not culture-bound.

The current level of implementation of each of the three models is depicted in Table 3. As can be seen in the table, both the Assimilation and the Pluralistic Models are implemented in the regular classroom. The Separatist Model, however, is more frequently than not found as either an after-school tutorial program or as an after-school language and culture-maintance program.

Often these two kinds of programs are combined. The concept of the *"escuelita"* (little school) has long been known in Mexican-American communities throughout the Southwest. The *escuelita* usually is organ-

Figure 3
Typology of the Separatist Model

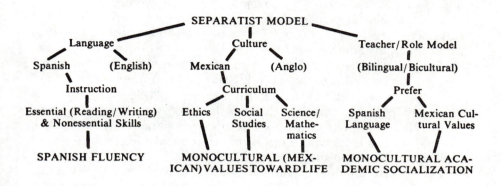

Note the recognition of majority group language and culture, but their exclusion in the educational process. Also note that teachers are bilingual/bicultural, but prefer to be role models who speak Spanish and emulate Mexican values.

ized and run by a small number of adults who contribute their time to try to provide an educational experience that the Mexican-American child is not receiving in the traditional assimilation-oriented classroom. The community is usually called on to support the *escuelita* by means of various sorts of fund-raising events. The *escuelita* in its language and culture-maintenance function closely resembles similar after-school programs organized by other ethnic minority communities (e.g., Jewish and Japanese). The tutorial function of the *escuelita* is indicative of the

Table 3
Current Level of Implementation of the Three Educational Models

Current Level of Implementation	Models		
	Assimilation	Pluralistic	Separatist
Regular Classroom	X	X	
After-School Tutorial			X
After-School/Language-Culture Maintenance			X
Elementary	X	X	X
Secondary	X	?	
Higher Education	X		
Minority Community Involvement	?	X	X

long felt belief that the assimilation-oriented school is at fault in the low educational achievement of Mexican-American children. In recent years, Chicano university students have been especially active in providing after-school alternative programs for Chicano youngsters.

It is essential to point out that regular classroom Separatist Model programs largely do not exist. There are a few that can be pointed to throughout the Southwest, but because of financial burdens no systematic network of separatist programs has yet appeared on the educational scene. Moreover, due to the severely limited socio-economic situation of the Chicano population it is doubtful whether any large move toward a separatist program will ever develop. In those very few cases where federal monies were initially used to support separatist-type programs, the money has been withdrawn owing to the exclusionary enrollment policies of the schools (Appleton, 1973).

Turning our attention again to Table 3 we can see that the Separatist Model is confined to the elementary level. There are some attempts to provide after-school experiences to Chicano secondary school students. These programs are usually less successful and/or are combined with other programs (e.g., recreationally oriented projects) which blur the educational aspect. Similarly, the Pluralistic Model is largely confined to the elementary level. Although the Bilingual Education Act does not specify an upper level to bilingual-bicultural education, the Pluralistic Model is yet to be implemented on a large-scale measure at the second-ary level. It is true that textbooks which more accurately portray ethnic minority groups in the humanities and social studies are being employed with ever-increasing frequency in secondary schools. Yet this improvement in textbooks and related educational materials does not constitute pluralistically oriented education.

At the level of higher education there is little question but that a single educational model is operating. The role of ethnic studies in colleges and universities continues to be minor. Ethnic studies have had little impact nationally in "pluralizing" higher education in the United States. In those situations where ethnic studies are moderately successful (as measured by administrative support), the curriculum is tied to bilingual-bicultural teacher credentialing programs. This may in the long run prove to be the greatest single contribution of ethnic studies programs.

There have been some attempts in recent years to establish centers of higher education for Chicanos. The most notable attempt to use federal funds from the Department of Labor to establish a center of higher education was Deganawidah-Quetzalcoatl (D-Q) University, which was founded on an abandoned military base outside of Davis, California. D-Q University was created by the joint efforts of Chicanos and Native Americans. The University was founded on the premise that an alternative higher education program had to be started for Chicanos and Native Americans which was closer to the experiential reality of its students. Several other higher education alternative programs can be found throughout the United States. Unlike D-Q University, however, these programs are associated with Antioch College. Just one example is Juárez-Lincoln University in Austin, Texas. Juárez-Lincoln traces its origins to the ideas of a group of M.A.Y.O. (Mexican American Youth Organization) members and other community people meeting in December of 1969 in Mission, Texas, in the Rio Grande Valley. An urgent need was expressed there for an alternative educational institution that would address the needs of Chicanos in Texas. Juárez-Lincoln, with an affiliation with Antioch College, moved from Mission to Fort Worth, Texas, in 1970. There, with 30 students, an educational design evolved using the university-without-walls model; no classrooms, but a combination of work and study—a performance-based education for Chicanos and other people concerned with the Chicano's situation. In 1972, Juárez-Lincoln moved again, this time to Austin, Texas, and all the while continued to gain students. In June of 1975, Juárez-Lincoln bought its own campus in Austin and legally became a university with a graduate school of education. Juárez-Lincoln University is one of the very few success stories in the quest to establish separatist educational alternatives. Yet it is too early to determine whether the limited success of Juárez-Lincoln will endure in the years ahead.

The final element in need of some discussion here is the question of community involvement. As shown in Table 3, minority community involvement in assimilation-oriented schooling is questionable. Traditionally, the assimilation-oriented school made little attempt to encourage parental and community involvement in its programs. Moreover, the minority-group deferred the responsibility of education to the schools. The obvious reasons for the lack of parental involvement in the schools had to do with the parent's lack of familiarity with the language of the school (i.e., English) and with lack of knowledge of the community participatory function in education. It is important to recognize thatschool officials who operated within the Assimilation Model made little attempt to instruct the community in its right to participate in the educational process via school boards or advisory councils.

Community involvement is essential in the two other educational models. In the Pluralistic Model, just as the method of instruction and curriculum are dual, community involvement from all sectors is encouraged. A truly pluralistic school requires total community involvement and support. Total involvement is still more the ideal than what is actually taking place in the schools. Nonetheless, it is encouraging to see the efforts being made by minority communities to begin their rightful participatory function on concerned community groups, school advisory committees, and school boards. Although there continues to be a great deal of resistance to community involvement, federal legislation mandates it for schools receiving federal monies and slowly both the community and school are adjusting to each other. The eventual beneficiary of this involvement can only be students, minority and majority alike, who will benefit from an improved educational experience which is more aligned with the cultural/linguistic diversity that exists in United States society.

As indicated earlier, separatist-type schools cannot exist without some form of community involvement and support. This support comes in many forms—from allowing children to participate to donating items (e.g., food or the use of a hall) that can be used for raising funds. Although the goals of the community do not always match the goals of the separatist-type school staff, it is important to recognize that the maintenance of language and culture are deemed essential by both. Also true is the fact that community involvement is usually less structured than it is in the other two educational models. In some cases there may be an advisory committee or *mesa directiva* whose function is to provide various forms of counsel and to serve as a support system to ensure the continuation of the program. What is important here is that regardless of the level of formality of community involvement, there is support for such programs. As noted earlier, the *"escuelita"* has existed in Chicano communities much longer than most majority-group educators would care to admit. The reasons for this are simple: linguistic and cultural maintenance are deemed essential by the community and the educational system's failure to meet the needs of the Mexican American student have long been recognized.

GUIDELINES FOR BILINGUAL SCHOOLING

We began this essay by commenting on the dissatisfaction of many with public education. We noted how "extracurricular rules" to learning were often used to exclude many students from the educational process. These "extracurricular rules" have proven especially effective in barring students who differ ethnically and linguistically from full participation in society. This problem is of long-standing historical importance and has affected large numbers of ethnolinguistic groups for over 100 years. In more recent years, this problem has come to be identified most closely with the Spanish-speaking (i.e., Mexican American, Puerto Rican, and other Spanish-origin groups), Native American, and Asian American populations. The Bilingual Education Act was proposed as one solution to the inequality in educational opportunity. Three philosophical positions and their concomitant educational models have been embroiled in the controversy of how ethnolinguistically different children should be instructed; there is as yet no agreed-upon model.

The essential argument centers on whether the American educational system should continue to carry out a policy directed at emphasizing the majority-group language and culture, or whether there should be recognition of the cultural and linguistic diversity that exists in this country. Cultural pluralists (e.g., Ramírez and Castañeda, 1974) have begun to call for a more diversified curriculum that includes the recognition and respect of other cultural groups in schooling. The philosophy of cultural pluralism asserts that an individual can remain identified with the life style and values of the home and community while at the same time learning about the life style and value system of other cultural groups. The philosophy is based on the reality that we live in a culturally pluralistic world where the United States is not an isolated island, but rather a leader in the community of world governments. To deny cultural pluralism in education is to deny cultural democracy, a denial that has existed in the public education system in this country for too long.

Bilingual schooling, then, should have two functions. The first is to provide the student from a different language and culture with the tools necessary to gain entry into mainstream society without having to give up the language and values of the home. This is integration with respect and without shame of one's home, parents, or culture. The second function is to provide majority-group students with an educational experience of another language and culture that goes beyond what can merely be presented in a textbook. This is education that is experientially based and which results in greater understanding of the world on the part of majority-group students.

How can bilingual/bicultural education be made into a meaningful educational alternative for all students? Some guidelines are:

- A clear statement on educational policy that unequivocally establishes cultural pluralism as the mode of instruction is essential.
- A public relations program directed at parents, teachers, and school officials to increase their understanding of and receptivity to this educational approach is mandatory.
- An expanded program for the development of bilingual/bicultural teaching staff committed to cultural pluralism in education is necessary.
- The development of curriculum and materials necessary to conduct a true bilingual/bicultural program is essential.
- An evaluation process for assessing bilingual/bicultural schooling must be developed.

Statement of Policy.   The Bilingual Education Act, as pointed out earlier, goes a long way in providing the kind of statement of policy necessary. It does fall short, however, in not acknowledging more convincingly that in a pluralistic society such as the United States the most effective form of intercultural socialization comes through pluralistic education. If it is to be truly effective, the policy statement must emphasize that cultural hospitality is a humanistic goal of American education, not a narrow, special, or peculiar interest of Mexican-Americans, Asian Americans, Native Americans, or anyone else. Ultimately, the policy statement must be accepted and endorsed by the widest possible audience. This must occur first on a local basis before it will ever succeed nationally. The impetus for this kind of policy can only come from parents, informed school officials, and responsive governmental policy makers.

Public Relations Campaign.   We showed earlier that bilingual schooling is not a new concept. It is true, however, that the majority of people who subscribe to an assimilation philosophy find the concept threatening. For many people, the concept of bilingual schooling arouses images of revolution and ethnic separation, rather than of a positive educational experience. The beneficial aspects of bilingual schooling must be communicated to concerned parents and school officials. For example, several hundred years ago the famous German author Goethe observed that "someone who does not know a second language does but poorly know his first." In other words, the acquisition of a second language not only introduces another store of knowledge, it also serves to raise the level of understanding of the first language. Somehow means must be found to instruct parents, minority and majority alike, of the positive consequences of knowing more than a single language. Similarly, knowledge of another culture opens vistas not possible otherwise. Once these facts can be communicated on a wide basis and understood, cultural pluralism will be readily accepted.

Staff Development.   Teachers' values, beliefs, attitudes, and expectations influence the student's chances for success or failure. As was pointed out earlier, teachers also serve as role models and influence the development of the student's orientation to language, culture, and academic achievement. In bilingual/bicultural education programs, particular attention must be given to teacher selection, since a number of diverse skills are needed in a curriculum which involves two languages and two cultures.

Consideration of teachers for bilingual/bicultural programs would cover their motives for teaching, linguistic and cultural backgrounds, competency in teaching in two languages, and knowledge of specific subject matter. Because of the scarcity of trained and certified bilingual/ bicultural teachers, Schools of Education in colleges and universities must initiate a more concentrated effort to establish bilingual/bicultural credential programs that will attract members of ethnolinguistic minority communities. Now that positions in education are difficult to secure, there is a growing trend of majority-group students with minimal knowledge of the second language and even less knowledge of the second culture to enter a bilingual/bicultural credential program. These students are possibly well-intentioned, but the fact remains that if a true cultural pluralistic learning environment is to be created, then bilingual/ bicultural staff is essential. Training centers must establish criteria by which to evaluate bilingualism and biculturalism on the part of future teachers of bilingual programs. This is especially critical in those communities with large numbers of students from different language and cultural backgrounds. To illustrate the importance of this point, the Los Angeles Unified School District recently released a breakdown of ethnic enrollment and certified staff members (teachers). The report indicated that for the entire district 29.7 percent of the students are Spanish-surnamed while only 5.7 percent of the teachers were Spanish-surnamed. In one of the twelve areas of the school district, the Spanish-surnamed enrollment reached a high of 92.3 percent. Los Angeles is just one of many communities in need of educational realignment in the balance of its staff to its minority student enrollment.

Staff development also extends to the initiation of a system-wide staff training program developed through joint staff and community effort. The program should emphasize cultural awareness training and should be directed at School Board members, key community leaders, administrative staff, teaching personnel, counseling and guidance personnel, and parents.

Curriculum Content and Materials.   Decisions as to what curriculum areas should be emphasized in a particular program obviously depend on student needs. But we would hope that in a bilingual school emphasis will be placed on the dual-medium instruction of the core subjects, such as reading, writing, math, and science, rather than on such subjects as music or art.

Materials should incorporate the contributions made by minority communities to this country and should reflect experiences familiar to all students. Due to the scarcity of materials appropriate for use in bilingual/bicultural education, many programs have adapted materials which were either produced in the United States or imported from other countries. Programs have also developed new materials, particularly in the language familiar to ethnolinguistic minority children. In some cases programs have attempted to use materials in Chinese imported from Taiwan and Hong Kong or in Spanish imported from Spain. Many of these materials have been found to be unsuitable for the Chinese- or Spanish-speaking student in the United States, especially because some of the vocabulary is not used by Chinese or Spanish speakers in this country. Consequently, these imported materials can only be used in a supplementary manner highlighting the need for the development of appropriate materials.

In sum, bilingual/bicultural curriculum specialists are needed to develop materials that integrate other cultures into the school curriculum. These materials must convey the historical, literary, political, and scientific contributions to this country of members of different linguistic/ cultural groups. The inclusion of these materials in educational course matter is another way, in addition to the teacher, that the student from a minority background is provided with role models from his own cultural group.

Evaluation of Bilingual/Bicultural Schooling.   Systematic evaluations of bilingual/bicultural education programs are necessary not only for ensuring that individual programs are effective, but also in providing some basis for identifying the most effective methods for teaching language and culture. Currently, many programs lack even the most basic data on students served.

All bilingual/bicultural education programs share a common concern for students' language development in two languages and their achievement in subject areas. Thus, at a minimum, data in these two areas must be evaluated. Since the acceptance of other cultures and people is another objective of bilingual/bicultural schooling, attitudes of students must also be assessed.

In addition to indicating the long term success of the bilingual education program, evaluation information and feedback allows program staff to make informed judgments about matters concerning student readiness to receive content instruction in the second language, the type of additional teacher training needed, and whether adjustments are needed in the general instructional program. Moreover, such information is important in determining the causes of difficulty experienced by certain individual students.

The evaluation should also be divided into three phases: (1) preprogram assessment, or the preliminary evaluation of student needs that accompanies program planning; (2) process evaluation, or the assessment of the program implementation and interim student performance for the purpose of strengthening and adjusting the instructional program; and (3) outcome evaluation, or the assessment of the program's impact on student performance over a period of several years. As for the assessment instruments themselves, both criterion-referenced *and* norm-referenced measures should be used to evaluate student progress.

CONCLUSION

Although bilingual/bicultural schooling has been criticized for nurturing ethnic separateness in this country, it can provide one of the best alternative means for diminishing such separation. Without full economic and social opportunity, ethnolinguistic minority groups will almost certainly remain isolated, outside the American mainstream in spite of Civil Rights legislation. If bilingual/bicultural schooling fulfills its promise to provide equal educational opportunity, it can be a major step in helping to remove the barriers which currently exclude minority groups from that mainstream. This will add validation to the long-standing American dictum of "Equality through Education." Moreover, it can provide opportunities for *all* students to learn about and experience the benefits of a pluralistic society.

REFERENCES

Andersson, T., and Boyer, M. *Bilingual Schooling in the United States.* Vol. 1., Washington, D.C.: U.S. Government Printing Office, 1970.

Annual Report of Immigration and Naturalization. U.S. Immigration and Naturalization Service, Department of Justice, 1973.

Appleton, S. F. Alternative schools for minority students: The constitution, the Civil Rights Act and the Berkeley Experiment. *California Law Review*, 1973, *61*, 26–86.

Bell, P. W. Bilingual education in an American elementary school. In H.H. Stern, (ed.), *Languages and the young school child.* London: Oxford University Press, 1969, pp.112–118.

Carter, T. P. *Mexican Americans in School: A history of educational neglect.* New York: College Entrance Examination Board, 1970.

Coleman, J. S., and others. *Equality of Educational Opportunity.* Office of Education, U.S. Department of Health, Education, and Welfare. Washington, D.C.: U.S. Government Printing Office, 1966.

Fishman, J. A., Nahirny, V. C., Hofman, J. E., Hayden, R. G., and others. *Language Loyalty in the United States.* The Hague: Mouton & Co., 1966.

Gaarder, A. B., and Richardson, M. W. The patterns of bilingual education in Dade County, Florida. In T. E. Bird, (ed.), *Foreign Language Learning: Research and Development: An Assessment.* Menasha, Wis.: George Banta Co., Inc., 1968, pp. 32–44.

Kjolseth, R. Bilingual education programs in the United States: For assimilation or pluralism? In P. R. Turner (ed.), *Bilingualism in the Southwest.* Tucson, Ariz.: University of Arizona Press, 1973.

Kloss, H. *Das Volksgruppenrecht in den Vereinigten Staaten von Amerika.* Essen: Essener Verlagsanstalt, 1942.

———. *Das Nationalitatenrecht der Vereinigten Staaten von Amerika.* Vienna: Braumüller, 1963.

———. German-American language maintenance efforts. In J. A. Fishman, et al., *Language loyalty in the United States.* The Hague: Mouton & Co., 1966.

New England Regional Council. *Overview of the problems encountered by New England's Spanish speaking population.* July, 1970.

Padilla, A. M., and Ruiz, R. A. *Latino mental health.* Washington, D.C.: U.S. Government Printing Office, 1973.

Ramírez, M., and Castañeda, A. *Cultural democracy, bicognitive development, and education.* New York: Academic Press, 1974.

U.S. Bureau of the Census, Department of Commerce, PC(2)—1C. *1970 Census of Population: Subject Reports—Persons of Spanish Origin,* June 1973.

———. *1970 Census of Population: Subject Reports—American Indians.*

U.S. Commission on Civil Rights. *The Unfinished Education,* Report 2, Mexican American Education Study, October 1971.

———. Staff Reports, *Public Education for Puerto Rican Children in New York City,* February 1972, as appears in Hearing Before the U.S. Commission on Civil Rights, N.Y., February 14–15, 1972, p.290.

———. *The Southwest Indian Report,* May 1973.

The Ultimate Goal
of Bilingual Education
with Respect to Language Skills

GARY D. KELLER
Eastern Michigan University

INTRODUCTION

Those of us who are applied linguists are confronted with two phenomena that are of crucial importance to us. One is a social phenomenon with profound linguistic manifestations. The other is a sweeping set of innovations in the pursuit of sociolinguistics, a radical refiguration in our professional stance as applied or sociolinguistics. The social movement and the sociolinguistic movement are closely intertwined and together they present us with opportunities, challanges, and perils never before experienced in the field of applied linguistics.

Never before in this country has the linguist had a greater opportunity to do social engineering. For example, many of us who are involved with the linguistics of bilingualism have been and will continue to be called upon to represent the linguistically and socially repressed minorities on advisory and policy-making boards of regional and even national scope. We have been called to court in places such as San Francisco and New York to give expert testimony in matters linguistic, the ramifications of which have often involved massive reallocations of educational and human resources. We have been called upon to devise language dominance and language achievement tests for bilinguals, the politico-statistical application of which has caused significant changes in the pedagogical structure and even teaching faculty of some of our major school systems. We have been acting as consultants to and textbook writers for the numerous publishers who wish to service the field of bilingual education. More generally, we have been summoned by the public, via the agencies of the press and of other mass media, to give our considered opinions as professional linguists with respect to the advantages and drawbacks of bilingual education as a whole, and of various bilingual-educational policies such as the transitional, maintenance and reciprocal models.

The social stakes in terms of funds, of the allocation of human resources, and of the general educational-philosophic impetus that this nation will take in the near and intermediate future are very high indeed, and the professional linguist occupies a crucial mediating role among the general public, the linguistic minorities, the government agencies, and the school administrators. But since the stakes are high and since opportunities carry with them weighty responsibilities, I feel that we linguists who have been so engrossed in the data of bilingualism and the application and implementation of our research to social policy must now begin to recognize our own professional status within the sociopolitical context that we are working. We must begin to generate a sociology of the sociolinguist. Moreover, once we begin to realize the sociological parameters of our own professional role, we need to devise procedures and tactics that will enhance our effectiveness. It is to the following two aspects that I will address myself: on the one hand to describing some of the relevant factors which I believe should go into an embryonic sociology of the sociolinguistic engineer, and on the other, to the plea for certain professional stances that I believe would strengthen our effectiveness in areas that are crucial to us.

THE SOCIAL MOVEMENT

The social movement that I have referred to involves, at least for certain sectors, the liquidation of the assimilationist mythos—call it the "melting pot" mythos—in favor of an identificatory policy that seeks out in the social fabric that which is unique—ethnically, racially, and most pertinently, linguistically. Especially during the last decade we have witnessed, and many of us participated in, the rise—or perhaps resurrection is the word—of the Black movement, the Native American nation, the Chicano and Boricua peoples. Even at the most basic level of group identification the semantic shifts have been momentous: among those who embrace most fully the mythos of cultural pluralism it is no longer Negro but Black or Afro-American, no longer Indian but Native American, no longer Mexican-American but Chicano or member of La Raza. The distinction between Puerto Rican and Boricua and the revitalization of *jíbaro* are less overt but fall along the same dimensions.

THE SOCIOLINGUISTIC MOVEMENT

The sociolinguistic movement that I have evoked began with Labov's work in the mid 1960s and has been expanded to the field of bilingualism and bidialectalism by linguists such as Fishman, Ferguson, Gumperz, Lambert and Wolfram.

The "socially realistic linguistics"[1] that Labov called for has led, in terms of theory, first to a realization of the dichotomy that linguists themselves had falsely constructed between structural linguistics and sociolinguistics, between *langue* and *parole;* subsequently to the breaking down, as Craddock puts it, of "the simplistic notion of the unitary ideolect or ideally homogenous speech community as the foundation of linguistic inquiry and speculation, and its replacement with the more realistic conception of multiple linguistic systems, each appropriate for given social contexts, and susceptible of linguistic description, as part of every speaker's repertoire."[2] Moreover, the theoretical breakthrough has been effectively articulated by methodological innovations with a new elegance in design, experimental parsimony, and statistical power that have permitted the sociolinguist to perform a key role as a scientific mediator within the general sociopolitical milieu.

THE EXALTATION OF THE VERNACULAR

Joshua Fishman has made some cogent observations concerning the linguistic problems of developing nations and their relation to nationalism.[3] These observations have been based on a substantial number of empirical investigations of sociolinguistic phenomena in African and Asia; nevertheless, they have relevance to the social movement being discussed here.

Fishman has shown that not all language differences that exist are noted. Language differences at the phonological, morphological or syntactic levels that can be clearly distinguished by linguists may be consciously or unconsciously ignored by millions of native speakers. Moreover, those which are noted by native speakers may or may not be the basis for an ideologized position of divisiveness. The basic point is that divisiveness is an ideologized position and it can magnify minor differences, or even manufacture differences in languages. Similarly, unification is also an ideologized position which can minimize or even ignore seemingly major differences, whether these be in the realm of language, religion, culture, race or other bases of interpersonal differentiation. Fishman sociolinguistically distinguishes between two forms of developing nations: those for whom the quest for nationism is paramount and those for whom the concern with nationalism is paramount. For those entities where nationalism is the major concern,

> that is, where populations are actively pursuing the sociocultural unification that befits those whose common nationality is manifest, the choice of a national language is not in question since it is already a prominently ideologized symbol. The major language problems of nationalism are language maintenance, reinforcement, and enrichment (including both codification

and elaboration) in order to foster the nationalistic (the vertically or ethnically single) unity, priority, or superiority of the sociocultural aggregate.[4]

Conversely,

> among those for whom *nationism* is stochastically paramount *other* kinds of language problems come to the fore. The geographic boundaries are far in advance of sociocultural unity. Thus problems of horizontal integration, such as quick language choice and widespread literary language use, become crucial to the nation's functional existence per se.[5]

The social movements of Blacks, Chicanos, Native Americans and Boricuas are analogous to the nationalistic goals of Asian and African peoples. In certain extreme left sectors, United States minority movements take a form not unlike Fishman's concept of nationism except that, of course, the quest is not only linguistic but entails a geographic entity of one's own: witness the proposal on the part of some Blacks to convert Mississippi into a Black nation or the aspiration of some Chicanos to regain hegemony over Aztlán. More pertinent for us linguists is the quest on the part of Blacks, Chicanos and Boricuas to culturally validate their tongues, their vernaculars; to convert them into the expressive instruments of their social identities and to have them generally accepted as such. This exaltation of the vernacular on the part of those Chicanos, Boricuas and Blacks who radically embrace the notion of cultural pluralism is a powerful force and one that must be reckoned with by sociolinguists and bilingual educators—often on grounds that are political, cultural, existential—since they represent a quest for cultural enfranchisement.

Moreover, the notion of the vernacular may be quite different when entertained by a community spokesperson, the sociolinguist or by the general public. (Let us include most language teachers, both public school and college, in this latter group.) For example, Lozano claims that "the regional varieties of Spanish in Mexico and the [United States] Southwest which share virtually the same morphosyntactic characteristics should be considered a binational macrodialect."[6] Lozano adduces solid linguistic reasons for subsuming Southwestern United States Spanish and Mexican Spanish but in the sociopolitical arena his conclusions are nil. The Chicano is engaged in combat not only with the "Anglo establishment" but with the disapproving "Mexican establishment" of which even such a distinguished Mexican linguist as Antonio Alatorre may be taken as a representative voice. Alatorre compares the Chicanos to the *mozárabes* of medieval Spain, intimating that the former, like the latter, have served to introduce many foreignisms into Spanish. He defines the Chicano (except that he uses the term *pocho,* which is pejorative in Mexico) as a Mexican who permits himself to be seduced by the American way of life and for whom Mexican ways are always contemptible and American ways unsurpassable. As for the language, it is the product of a border society "that has created a type of dialect or creole in which elements of English and Spanish are fused."[7]

Naturally, the Chicano, when confronted with these sorts of stark expressions of prejudice on the part of Mexicans, is compelled to systematically minimize the Mexican element in the language and systematically single out that which is autochthonous.

Let us look at the same phenomenon at the micro rather than macro level. Troike points out that "there are in fact several native dialects of Spanish spoken in Texas alone—even in a single city such as San Antonio or El Paso—and most of these are simply local varieties of the much larger regional dialect of North Mexican Spanish."[8] Troike goes on to observe the classroom implications of these differences, but once again the chances of implementing the fact of different subdialects in the Southwest into a coherent classroom pedagogy are obstructed by the overriding ideological exigency that Chicano Spanish be one and the vehicle of Chicano self-identity. Thus Fishman's observation that divisiveness is an ideologized position must be recognized as a sociolinguistic fact, a fact that is more social than linguistic, but nevertheless a fundamental consideration in analyzing the development of in-group attitudes toward the vernacular. Moreover, these attitudes will have clear expression in the educational process. For example, Gaarder attests to the fact that many Chicano Studies programs actively denigrate what he calls "world standard Spanish" and insist that for their purposes the only languages needed are English and "Barrio Spanish."[9] I believe that such a policy (or attitude) is extremely short-sighted for reasons that I will explain subsequently. In sum: it seems clear that the professional linguist, while on one hand understanding and sympathizing with the sociocultural vicissitudes that press an ideologized notion of the vernacular upon the community spokespersons of the various United States minorities, must also actively pursue a non-ideologized description of the vernacular—objectively making the necessary inter- and intralinguistic comparisons. In addition, it is the linguist's responsibility to bring to the attention of the educational community such differences between the idealized version of the vernacular and its attested reality that are pedagogically important.

Often this task will be unenviable and onerous, particularly for those of us who are members of a minority community as well as linguists. It is a necessary task and part of our professional responsibility.

DENIGRATION OF THE VERNACULAR

The problems of the sociolinguist in providing an objective counter-weight against the excesses of the idealizer of the vernacular are modest in comparison to the problem of dealing with the general public's disdainful attitude toward the vernacular. The register that a person speaks publicly provides us with a quick and easy means for assigning that individual—at least provisionally, in lieu of further evidence such as earnings and place of residence—a ranking in the social hierarchy. Those who speak a vernacular in a public context immediately earn themselves the lowest rung on the social ladder. This general identification of the vernacular with low social status accounts for much of the illogical abhorrence of the vernacular per se on the part of the middle class. The abhorrence is all the more illogical since the middle class—whether it be Spanish-speaking or English-speaking or both—is perfectly adept at its lingua franca, although, of course, the difference between the middle class and the uneducated sector is the former's ability both to speak the standard register as well as the vernacular, to read and to write the standard, and to employ either register according to the determinants of the social context. Thus, the difference between the educated person and the non-educated person is that the former is bidialectical and conscious of the pragmatics of code switching so that he or she will use the appropriate register for any given social context while the latter is monodialectical and can speak only in the vernacular whether it be in the community, or at home, or, say, at a more formal occasion such as an interview with a principal or at a board of education hearing.

The feelings of the middle class toward the vernacular are revealed in a most enlightening and ironic way in the case of Richard Nixon. No small factor in the ex-president's downfall was the fact that as a result of the transcription and publication of the presidential Watergate cover-up tapes, the august Richard Milhous Nixon was caught in the public eye speaking like Tricky Dickie in no less venerable a domain than the Oval Office of the White House. Poll takers found that many people were more concerned not with the content of Nixon's machinations, but with the fact that he spoke like a lowbrow from the poolhall or the alleyway. Alas, poor Richard's Almanac—his legacy to the people—comes not in the form of the upbeat parables of *Six Crises,* but rather in a gutsy gutterformat with all the expletives deleted!

Yet my point is that Nixon too is a fellow traveler in the vernacular as we all are. The vernacular is our first register. It develops out of our baby talk and our communion with our playmates so that even before we go to school our control over the vernacular is that of the native. In my judgment, the definition of a native speaker of a given language involves the native control of a vernacular register of that language. It is only later, after we thoroughly control our lingua franca that we are formally educated, and part and parcel of this formal education involves the systematic teaching of a second, more formal standard register of the language.

The standard forms of Spanish, English or any other language, while essential for business, commercial, diplomatic and probably most educational communication, for broadcasting, journalism, public speaking and the like, are nevertheless, dull and lifeless instruments, hopelessly inadequate for expressing love, anger or any of the other emotions, for enjoying oneself with friends, for joking, for rapping with buddies, for searching out one's hangups with one's shrink, for making it, or for getting it all together. Nixon aside, once the turtle soup has been spooned out and the chateaubriand carved up, the vernacular may even be necessary for running the country's affairs from the privacy of the Oval Office in the intimacy of one's trusted stalwarts.

We linguists are confronted with massive ignorance compounded by substantial antagonism on the part of the general public, both Spanish-speaking and/or English-speaking, concerning their attitudes toward the vernacular. If we are to take our opportunities for social engineering seriously, part of our role will be to alert the public to the fact that indeed, all of us include within our language repertoire an informal and intimate variety of speech. Moreover, we need to point out repeatedly that the child who speaks so-called Black English or Chicano or Puerto Rican Spanish must be permitted to retain her or his lingua franca. The teaching of the standard register should not, and indeed cannot be accomplished at the expense of the vernacular since to effectively remove a vernacular from the repertoire of a community would entail the effacement of that group's social identity—and no community would willingly subject itself to cultural genocide.[10]

Part of the answer I believe is for the sociolinguist to embark upon as intense a consciousness-raising campaign as possible, alerting the public to the fact that indeed all of us without exception include within our language repertoire an informal and intimate variety of speech. This in itself will be no easy task, given engrained biases in our society. For example, in a feature article in *Newsweek* magazine entitled, "Why Johnny Can't Write," the policy statement issued by the National Council of Teachers of English entitled, "Student's Rights to their Own Language" was both distorted and abused.[11] I might add that mention was made of the "pervasive influence of structural linguists"—God knows who these may be—whose meddling has helped cause a crisis in writing skills in the nation's schools. With inimitable ignorance this article failed to recognize the difference between comprehension and speaking and reading and writing. Both minority citizens and linguists generally accept the reality that in order for minority children to become upwardly mobile they will have to read and write standard English. But such a policy does not entail the effacement of the various forms of vernacular English which are spoken by all of us who are native speakers. Moreover, most linguists are hardly pedagogically permissive, for although they judge that while the standard cannot be taught at the spoken level by attempting to suppress the vernacular, conversely, at the written level, the vernacular forms should not be expanded into the formal education process at the expense of the standard. This is a point to which I will return.

In addition to the general world-wide hostility of the public to any vernacular, be it Black or Appalachian English, rural Andalusian or Río de la Plata *lunfardo,* there is in the United States and Canada a special, even more intense hostility directed toward non-English vernaculars which linguistically display the evidence of daily English language contact. Specifically, I am referring to what in this country is popularly termed as "Spanglish" and what in Canada and Northern New England is referred to as "franglais" or "Franglish." "Spanglish" implies in the popular mind that United States Hispanos speak a mixed language, some hybrid—the illegitimate fruit of English-Spanish contact. In fact "Spanglish," if characterized in the way that I have described above, as the fusion or cross-breeding of two languages, in other words, as a pidgin, does not exist. We need to distinguish two separate factors that go into the confused, popular designation, "Spanglish." One factor is the phenomenon of code switching. The second is the phenomenon of a vernacular that incorporates Anglicisms at the lexical and idiomatic levels.

Code switching merits intensive future research but evidence from Gumperz and Hernández's landmark study[12] (subsequently replicated by McMenamin)[13] suggests that code switching between English and Spanish among Hispanos is patterned rather than random and relates to such factors as the establishment of ethnic identity markers, semantic domains that are more characteristic either of Anglo or Hispanic cultural values, and most important of all, transitions in the conversation such as in the direction of greater informality or personal warmth.

There is nothing in either study that would imply that United States Hispanos are not able to control the English or the Spanish codes separately. Quite to the contrary, when expressing themselves more formally, the frequency of code switching among bilinguals is much reduced. Similar evidence is available from the study of the developmental psycholinguistics of bilingualism, particularly in a study by Padilla and Liebman.[14] Just as in the case of all examples of adult bilingual speech that I have seen attested to, children express bilingual structures which invariably respect the constituent phrase boundaries of each language: from a syntactic and semantic point of view there is no redundancy. Consider the following examples from Padilla and Liebman:

Chanclas por here.	Not: *Chanclas por by here.
Está raining.	Not: *Raining está.
Dame that.	Not: *Dámelo that.
Es a baby.	Not: *Es un a baby.
Es un baby pony.	Not: *Es un a baby pony.

This careful control and respect for the syntactic particularities of each of the combined languages even by three-year-old incipient bilinguals militates strongly against the position Peñalosa hypothesizes, only as a speculation, that "the bilingual may be combining English and Spanish into a new separate code that can properly be said to act as a mother tongue."[15]

Moreover, from a theoretical point of view we need to distinguish between voluntary and involuntary code switching. Involuntary code switching may be taken as evidence of an interference effect, usually of English upon the control of Spanish. However, the point of the Gumperz-Hernández and akin studies is precisely that the code switching is not involuntary but rather the result of definite social strategies. In addition, as the logic of the conclusions of the above-mentioned studies imply, a great deal of code switching probably represents individual or community creativity, prowess with the combination of both codes. We would expect that a bilingual person would use a mixed medium either in order to express her or himself more originally or in order to make linguistic shortcuts. I suspect that little code switching is of the involuntary sort.

Having broached the question of involuntary code switching as a form of interference, I will turn now to the second factor that goes into the stereotype popularly designated as "Spanglish"—namely the Anglicisms that have been incorporated into United States Spanish. Following Haugen, these borrowings may be classified into three basic categories: (1) loanwords, (2) loanblends and (3) loanshifts which include loantranslation, calques and the semantic loan.[16]

However, the critical point is that what is being incorporated into Spanish in the United States is the most superficial and flexible element of a language, mere lexicon and idiomatic expressions. The Spanish language can accept an immense number of such borrowings and it will remain Spanish. The introduction of *estar supuesto* does not change the rules governing the use of *ser* and *estar,* nor will any other English language borrowings change the tense and mood aspects of Spanish grammar, the way object pronouns are formed and placed, the rules governing the formation of commands, the positioning of quantitative and qualitative adjectives, the use of conjunctions, or the conjugation of verbs. The regularization of certain irregular verbs and even the randomization of certain noun genders on the part of a few speakers will not alter the system of agreement of number and gender. The grammar and syntax of Spanish remains secure. It is protected above all by its own structural integrity, and by an educated class of speakers, by language academies in all of the Spanish-speaking countries (including the recently established academy in the United States), and by the mass media, which are a strong influence in standardizing language. The phonology and the lexicon of Spanish are subject to the input of regional and local requirements, and this is as it should be. Moreover, we should in no way think that United States vernacular Spanish is characterized merely by its borrowings from English; Spanish in the United States has developed diachronically apart from English language contact.[17] From a linguistic point of view we can categorically state that United States vernacular Spanish does not present any danger to the sovereign structure of Spanish, quite to the contrary, this vernacular, as do all vernaculars, tends to enrich the language in the area of lexicon and idioms. It is a well-established fact that apart from writers, poets and so on, the stimulus for creativity in language rests among the poor (and among children and adolescents). Language creativity is substantially a function of the vernacular. Moreover, in a separate paper[18] I have pointed out that United States vernacular does not vary more radically from standard Spanish than does any other vernacular. There are differences, say, between rural Castilian and United States vernacular Spanish but these are differences of quality—usually at the lexical level, not of degree of deviance from the standard.

Nevertheless, in this country United States Spanish vernacular is stigmatized to an extreme that is not experienced in connection with any other vernacular in the Hispanic world. For those of you who are interested in reading some of the depressing testimony with respect to the ill effects of such stigmatization, I refer you to A.M. Padilla's book, *Latino Mental Health* and to articles that I have written in *The Bilingual Review/La revista bilingüe* and elsewhere.[19] But we must recognize the profoundly psychopolitical motivation behind the manifest antagonism to United States vernacular Spanish. Alfonso Reyes, the Mexican thinker, once observed about his people. "Pity us who are so removed from God and so near the United States." It is especially painful for many

Spanish-speaking persons to see the English language affect Spanish because of the obvious analogues with imperialistic exploitation. Those feelings of frustration are linguistically spurious but are psychologically intense. Yet, while we can understand some of the motivation as attributable to a feeling of anger and frustration directed toward what is seen as another instance of United States domination—what we cannot accept is the result: stigmatizing both United States vernacular Spanish and its legitimate speakers.

In sum, we linguists need to campaign actively in order to make the general public aware, first, that all of us without exception control a vernacular register, second, that the vernacular is not only entirely acceptable in certain social contexts, but absolutely necessary: there is no substitute for the vernacular in intimate or informal contexts; finally, that one vernacular is not necessarily better or worse than another simply because its linguistic variations from the standard are the result of different historical circumstances.

LANGUAGE IN THE SCHOOL: THE GOAL OF BILINGUALISM, BIDIALECTALISM AND MULTIGLOSSIA

And yet, even though we are obliged to defend the validity of the vernacular, such a defense does not carry with it the supposition that we should encourage its use in the classroom as part of the process of formal education except under circumscribed conditions.

There is a problem that arises in connection with all vernaculars that must be appraised realistically. The problem is not that United States bilinguals speak a specific type of vernacular but that all peoples who only speak a vernacular are condemned to limited social mobility in any society. The classroom problem is equal for the Castilian peasant, the Argentine gaucho, the Mexican peon, the Puerto Rican *jíbaro* and the urban or farm-dwelling United States Hispano. It is the same for the Appalachian hillbilly, the child of the Mississippi delta and indeed for all English monolinguals when they enter the school system. All of us come into the first grade (or kindergarten) with competence in a vernacular; it is the responsibility of the school system to teach us a second register, a more formal variant that permits us to communicate beyond the hearth to society at large. Keeping this fact in mind, certain recommendations can be made with respect to classroom activities and with respect to the development of instructional materials.

While United States vernacular Spanish with its linguistic manifestations of English influence must be looked upon with sympathy by our educators, it also must be understood that the purpose of formal education is to teach a second, non-colloquial register both in English and in Spanish.

Peñalosa,[20] following Ferguson, Gumperz, Fishman and most especially Kloss, has posited that the speech of the Chicano community (for our purposes the United States Hispanic community) is characterized by multiglossia (or complex diglossia). Let us recall that, in contrast to bilingualism, which refers to individual linguistic behavior, diglossia may be characterized as the societal normification of bilingualism and/or bidialectalism. Peñalosa proposes that in the Chicano bilingual we recognize in-diglossia which refers, in Spanish, to the socioculturally controlled usage of standard Mexican Spanish as the prestige dialect and of the Spanish of the peasantry and lower class of Mexico as the basis of one and perhaps two separate vernaculars. With respect to English we also have an in-diglossic relationship, that which relates to norms governing the Chicano's use of colloquial English versus standard English. Thus in-diglossia refers to the Chicano's choice of register or dialect within languages, be they English or Spanish.

Moreover, out-diglossia refers to the sociocultural norms that govern the Chicano's choice of English versus Spanish per se, without regard to the registers available within each. The term multiglossia or complex diglossia is suggested to describe those societies which are characterized by both in-diglossia and out-diglossia.

Certainly some of the United States Hispanic community may be characterized according to Peñalosa's model. This sector has control over at least four separate registers: a vernacular and a standard both in Spanish and in English, and in addition to control over the four registers, has developed group norms governing the use of registers within each language as well as norms governing code switching between languages. Which sector may be characterized in this fashion? The United States bilingual Hispano who has been formally educated, usually through the university level.

However, the majority of United States Hispanos are observed to be lacking to a greater or lesser degree in the competencies presupposed by the Peñalosa model. The majority of United States Hispanos are not proficient in either one or even both of the standard registers. From the point of view of bilingualism, a common characteristic among United States Hispanic bilinguals is a lack of control over the standard register of the language in which they are less fluent; another common phenomenon is bilingualism without bidialectalism, that is, control only over the vernacular registers in both Spanish and English. From the point of view of multiglossia, some Hispanic bilinguals possibly should be characterized according to the Fishman 1967 model within the quadrant, "bilingualism without diglossia."[21] These bilinguals, in contrast to the

Gumperz-Hernández subjects, would function without the benefit of well-understood and widely accepted norms as to which language or which language variety should be used among interlocutors over varied social contexts. Fishman has characterized the historical and sociological circumstances of bilingualism without diglossia and the factors that he describes have relevance to the United States Hispanic community. Some of the basic factors underlying this phenomenon include simultaneous immigration, industrialization, and urbanization, with a consequent dislocation of values and norms; and the acquisition of the language of the means of production—the language of the "work force"—while at the same time being removed from the "power class" who might serve as the standard other-tongue models. Fishman observes that in response to this imbalance

> some react(ed) by further stressing the advantages of the newly gained language of education and industry while others react(ed) by seeking to replace the latter by an elaborated version of their own largely pre-industrial, pre-urban, pre-mobilization tongue. . . . Under circumstances such as these no well established, socially recognized and protected functional differentiation of languages obtains in many speech communities of the lower and lower middle classes.[22]

In my opinion, Peñalosa's useful model of multilingualism (that is, bilingualism and bidialectalism) and multiglossia (in-diglossia and out-diglossia) represents not the current reality of the United States Hispanic community in general but the ideal that we should be striving for as applied linguists and edcuators, with the added proviso that our bilingual students be taught to read and write the standard registers of both English and Spanish.

On one hand it is my fear of a chaotic and normless situation in the future with its potential that Fishman recognizes for pidginization, where more and more inexplicable, perhaps random code switching within and between languages operates, on the other hand it is my desire to ensure the upward mobility of American Hispanic youth and adults, the prerequisite of which is proficiency in reading and writing skills, that leads me to the position that vernacular usage not be actively encouraged within the formal education process. School is school, linguistically just as behaviorally, quite apart from peer life or neighborhood life. It is my considered judgment that the teacher, while never downgrading the vernacular in the classroom, likewise should not encourage its active expression in class. The children already *know* the vernacular—they are in school precisely to learn a more formal register—this is perhaps the basic meaning of receiving a *formal* education.

By the same token I believe that (with certain exceptions such as in transitional bidialectical education) those textbooks which attempt to teach reading and writing skills in the vernacular are based upon a misguided pedagogy and are doing a disservice to our youngsters which may be irreparable. The rationale of such textbooks is that they are somehow embarked upon a liberal and enlightened enterprise, they are telling us (students and teachers alike) "how it is"—they are reflecting the true speech of the community. However, reading and writing must reflect the standard language; if not, American Hispanic children will not be able to achieve the social mobility, the type of employment, nor even the ability to read sophisticated materials that we all ardently desire for them.

For the reasons stated above I cannot agree with González's position which for me does not ensure enough the reinforcement of standard Spanish in the area of reading and writing. González advocates correcting such "baby talk" overgeneralizations as *sabo, ero* and *pongaba* on the grounds that "our guide should be the language spoken by the adult Chicano community. "[23] For that reason he considers *pidí* and *siguí* to be acceptable in the classroom, claiming that their standard alternates, *pedí* and *seguí* should not be banned since "failure to learn (at least passively) other forms of Spanish will limit the Chicano in his exchange of ideas with other people—especially the writings of our ancestors. Or should we wait for the English translation?[24] First of all, what is to guarantee that Chicanos will be able to read the English translation once someone gets around to doing it, if beforehand standard English has not been instructed to Chicanos? Second, what constructive purpose is served by accepting written *pidí* and *siguí* (if this is what González means by classroom-acceptable)? Alternates such as these will be used by readers and writers of standard Spanish to downgrade Chicanos. I have no complaint against anyone saying "pidí" or "siguí" in the proper. community context, that is, in a context where the community accepts such usage. It is hard to see how, where, or when written *siguí* and *pidí* on the part of students would be socioculturally accepted in the classroom.

I have argued for the encouragement of the standard register, be it Spanish or English, depending on the classroom, in relation to the formal education process. On the other hand I have mentioned exceptional circumstances where the vernacular may be used. What are these exceptions? Moreover, how is the crucial concept of biculturalism to fit into a policy of this sort? In addition, what is the teacher to do when confronted with students who insist upon using the vernacular in class?

I will attempt to clarify my position in the light of such complexifying circumstances. First, what I argue for on behalf of Hispanic bilinguals in both Spanish and English is no more, but also no less than what is generally practiced for English-speaking monolinguals in the United States and for Spanish-speaking monolinguals within the Hispanic world at large. Do educators in southern Spain propose that Andalusians be taught to read and write in their own vernacular rather than in standard Spanish? The idea seems absurd. In Argentina, although *voseo* is widespread, societal norms prescribe that the teacher use *tú* with grade school students, who in turn respond with *Ud.* Moreover, training in the grammar does not reinforce *voseo* nor the verbal conjugations peculiar to it in Argentina. The net result is that the vernacular is unaffected; it flourishes outside the classroom, but the standard register is learned and reinforced as well. In the United States the situation is analogous. Training in language arts is conducted in standard English. We must not let our defense of United States vernacular Spanish sway us into believing that either the vernacular itself should be the register that we will employ in formal education or that United States Spanish is so different from standard (school) Spanish that it should enjoy the status of an independent language.

When then is the vernacular to be used in the schools? Certainly there will be a host of practical pedagogical issues that will present themselves in the implementation of the policy that I have stated above. Of course, these must be identified and resolved in an ongoing fashion, as a result of actual prolonged experience with a policy attempting to separate the relative domains of vernacular United States Spanish and standard Spanish and to reserve the latter register for the formal educational process. In this paper I will limit myself to certain obvious issues.

Clearly the vernacular may be employed in transitional bidialectical education. While textbooks should teach language arts, reading and writing in the standard register, an exception could be defended in the area of transitional education within languages. When students enter the school system with only a knowledge of the vernacular, it is incumbent to build upon their knowledge, to teach them what they don't know on the basis of what they are competent in. Children who enter the school system in kindergarten or the first grade are clear examples. (One might also want to consider a transitional bidialectical program for foreign students who have had little or no exposure to standard [school] Spanish in their native lands. However, here the problem is more difficult since such students will speak a vernacular other than United States Spanish). Moreover, the pedagogy of beginning language arts, with its use of rhyme and of matching techniques between pictures and words, together with the limited vocabulary and memory capacity of the young child, all argue for utilizing vernacular lexicon at the very elementary level. However, certainly by the third grade it would be appropriate to change over to standard lexical items instead of regional ones. Moreover, even at the very elementary level, the use of vernacular Spanish presents problems in the development of instructional materials. For example, since there are a number of lexical variants between northeastern (and southeastern) United States Spanish and its variant in the southwest (for example: *guagua* vs. *camión* for bus; *cometa* vs. *papalote* for kite, etc.), it is measurably more difficult to develop national editions if the vernacular is being used. On the other hand, national editions, valid for all Spanish-speaking children in the United States, can be developed fairly easily if regional lexicon is controlled for and the active vocabulary limits itself to words of universal currency in the Hispanic world (for example: *rodilla, aire, tierra, mamá,* etc.).[25]

With respect to biculturalism, most concepts relevant to the cultures of Chicanos, Boricuas, Cuban-Americans and so on can easily be grasped and discussed in standard (school) Spanish, provided that we incorporate into the standard register lexicon for which there is no available equivalent. Essential lexicon of ethnic self-identification such as *chicano, boricua, Aztlán, La Raza,* must enter the linguistic mainstream, that is, become part of United States Spanish in its formal manifestations. However, *troque, guagua, marqueta, boila, norsa,* etc., for which standard equivalents exist should not be actively reinforced in the process of teaching to read and write in Spanish. Moreover, at the level of vocabulary the problems are trivial. Lexicon is the most superficial and flexible stratum of language. Certainly United States Hispanic culture can be taught with standard idioms and morphosyntax. (Thus, vernacular morphosyntax such as *llamar para atrás* and *estar supuesto* should not be reinforced.)

The argument may be made that the policy that I have outlined will not permit the teaching of Chicano and United States Puerto Rican literatures which reflect the speech of the community. How will we deal with this growing body of excellent literature? We certainly would not wish to suppress it in the classroom.

A little common sense adequately resolves this pseudo-problem. The notion that the vernacular must be used in the classroom in order to teach ethnic literature is spurious. This is akin to having our monolingual English-speaking children talk (and write?) like Huck Finn in order to discuss or appreciate Mark Twain. Actually, two myths are involved here. One is that bilingual literature—say of Alurista, El Huitlacoche, Eduardo Rivera or Víctor Hernández Cruz—reflects in mirror-like fashion the speech modalities of the bilingual community. Untrue! In a separate analysis I evaluated bilingual fiction including that of Hemingway and contemporary Chicano and Boricua writers.[26] Ortega y Gasset has likened language to the municipal trolley system which people get on and off at will. The language of bilingual writers is more akin to a one-man rocket ship, a subjective submarine. While these stylists often evoke the speech patterns of the bilingual community, their essential creativity, their cross-cultural quips, comparisons, ironies and implications far surpass the resources of language used for mere practical communication.

The second myth is that we should expose our students to literature written in the vernacular because it will be "easy" for them. As I have pointed out, bilingual literature, strictly speaking, is not written in the vernacular but creates its own, artistic medium, a separate register. Nor is it easy. Of course we want to expose our students both to bilingual fiction and poetry (which uses a good deal of code switching within the sentence) and to United States Hispanic literature, be it written exclusively in Spanish or in English; but the reasons for such exposure are cultural and literary. The children *must* be exposed to such literature once they know how to read, and the going will be difficult for them, as it is for all children in any language who are being taught to appreciate literature. But the necessity of such exposure does not imply that we should use such materials to teach our children *how* to read and write. Moreover, the students will need to discuss the works of United States Hispanic writers as they would Shakespeare or Cervantes or J.D. Salinger or García Lorca: in terms of the formal lexicon of literary appreciation (theme, plot, characters, symbols, implications, etc.).

Finally, while I propose not to actively encourage the vernacular in the formal educational process, I do not mean that it should be barred from the school nor do I imply a rigid policy of discipline. To the degree that school life such as gym, cafeteria, and after-school activities approximates peer life or community life, to that degree the vernacular is in order. As for the classroom itself, Valdés observes that students will often use the vernacular when they become excited and argue a point—and they should not be slapped on the wrists for such usage. Equally important is her observation that the students eagerly absorb patterns and constructions in imitation of the teacher conducting the discussion.[27] It is for this reason that our teachers and our textbooks must reflect standard rather than vernacular usage. They are the mediating agents that will conduct our children to the opportunities of the world at large. There are no others.

CONCLUSION

In this paper I have attempted to present a number of fundamental sociolinguistic phenomena in a context permitting the linguist to grasp her or his role as a social engineer or scientist-activist. In particular, I have discussed from this social engineering perspective, the problems of exalting or denigrating the vernacular and of situating the vernacular and the standard register in their proper contexts in school, home and society at large. In addition, I have proposed a model of linguistic competencies for our linguistic minorities which I have suggested should represent the ideal goal of bilingual education. The model presupposes competence in both the vernacular and the standard registers of each language, competence in the pragmatics of code switching within and between languages, and the ability to read and write the standard register of each language.

NOTES

1. William Labov, *Sociolinguistic Patterns*, (Philadelphia: University of Pennsylvania Press, 1972), p. xiii.

2. Jerry R. Craddock, "Spanish in North America" in *Current Trends in Linguistics, Vol. 4: Ibero-American and Caribbean Linguistics*, ed. by Thomas A. Sebeok (The Hague: Mouton, 1968), p. 468.

3. Joshua A. Fishman, "Nationality-Nationalism and Nation-Nationism," in *Language Problems of Developing Nations*, ed. by Joshua A. Fishman, Charles A. Ferguson and Jyatirindra Das Gupta (New York: John Wiley and Sons, 1968).

4. *Ibid.*, p. 43.

5. *Ibid.*

6. Anthony G. Lozano, "Grammatical Notes on Chicano Spanish," *The Bilingual Review/La revista bilíngüe*, Vol. I, No. 2, May–Aug. 1974, p. 147.

7. Antonio Alatorre, "El idioma de los mexicanos," *Revista de la Universidad Nacional Autónoma de México*, Vol. 10 (1955), pp. 11–15.

8. Rudolph C. Troike, "Social Dialects and Language Learning: Implications for TESOL," *Tesol Quarterly*, Vol. II (1968), pp. 176–180.

9. A. Bruce Gaarder, "Language Maintenance or Language Shift: The Prospect for Spanish in the United States," in Theodore Andersson and W. F. Mackey, eds., *Bilingualism in Early Childhood* (Rowley, Mass.: Newbury House, 1977) pp. 409–434. For a summary see Richard V. Teschner, Garland D. Bills, and Jerry R. Craddock, *Spanish and English of United States Hispanos: A Critical, Annotated, Linguistic Bibliography* (Arlington, Va.: Center for Applied Linguistics, 1975).

10. It is possible in principle (and practice) to suppress the vernacular of a people (a brutal procedure), but the only result would be that the suppressed group would substitute the vernacular of the suppressor for their own. Only very small, isolated communities do not maintain at least two different registers: a vernacular and a standard. See Joshua A. Fishman, "Bilingualism With and Without Diglossia; Diglossia With and Without Bilingualism," *Journal of Social Issues*, Vol. XXIII, No. 2 (1967), pp. 29–38.

11. "Why Johnny Can't Write," *Newsweek*, December 8, 1975, pp. 58–63.

12. John J. Gumperz and Eduardo Hernández-Chávez, "Bilingualism, Bidialectalism, and Classroom Interaction," in *Functions of Language in the*

Classroom (New York: Teachers College Press, 1972), pp. 85–108. See also John J. Gumperz, "Verbal Strategies in Multilingual Communication," *Monograph Series on Language and Linguistics* (Georgetown University.) Vol. 23, pp. 129–143; John J. Gumperz and Eduardo Hernández-Chávez, "Cognitive Aspects of Bilingual Communication," in *Language Use and Social Change*, ed. by W. H. Witeley (New York and London: Oxford University Press, 1970), pp. 111–125.

13. Jerry McMenamin, "Rapid Code Switching Among Chicano Bilinguals," *Orbis: Bulletin International de Documentation Linguistique*, Vol. 22 (1973), pp. 474–487.

14. Amado M. Padilla and Ellen Liebman, "Language Acquisition in the Bilingual Child," *The Bilingual Review/La revista bilíngüe*, Vol. II, Numbers 1 and 2 (1975), pp. 34–55.

15. Fernando Peñalosa, "Chicano Multilingualism and Multiglossia" *Aztlán*, Vol. III (1972) pp. 215–222.

16. Einar Haugen, "The Analysis of Linguistic Borrowing." *Language*, Vol. 26 (1950) pp. 210–231.

17. See Rosaura Sánchez, "Nuestra circunstancia lingüística," *El Grito*, Vol. VI (1972).

18. Gary D. Keller, "Psychological Stress Among Speakers of United States Vernacular Spanish," in *Introduction to Bilingual Education/Introducción a la educación bilingüe*, ed. by Luis Ortega (New York: L.A. Publishing Co., 1975), pp. 71–78.

19. Amado M. Padilla and René A. Ruíz, *Latino Mental Health: A Review of the Literature* (Rockville, Md.: National Institute of Mental Health, 1973); Gary D. Keller, "The Systematic Exclusion of the Language and Culture of Boricuas, Chicanos and Other U.S. Hispanos in Elementary Spanish Grammar Textbooks Published in the United States," *The Bilingual Review/La revista bilingüe*, Vol. I, No. 3 (1974), pp. 228–235; Gary D. Keller, "Psychological Stress Among Speakers."

20. Fernando Peñalosa, "Chicano Multilingualism."

21. Joshua A. Fishman, "Bilingualism With and Without Diglossia."

22. *Ibid.*, p. 35.

23. Gustavo González, "The Analysis of Chicano Spanish and the 'Problem' of Usage: A Critique of 'Chicano Spanish Dialects and Education,' " *Aztlán*, Vol. III (1973), pp. 223–231.

24. *Ibid.*

25. I have constructed a program of this sort which controls for regional and nonstandard lexicon, idioms and syntax, for children kindergarten through third grade and introduces children to the vowel and consonant system of written Spanish as well as teaching them numerous reading and language art skills. See Gary D. Keller, *Mi escuela (Guía del maestro)* (Chicago: Science Research Associates, 1976).

26. Gary D. Keller, "Toward a Stylistic Analysis of Bilingual Texts: From Ernest Hemingway to Contemporary Boricua and Chicano Literature," in *The Analysis of Hispanic Texts: Current Trends in Methodology. First York College Colloquium*, ed. by Mary A. Beck, Lisa E. Davis, José Hernández, Gary D. Keller and

Isabel C. Tarán (New York: Bilingual Press/Editorial bilingüe, 1976), pp. 130–149.

27. Guadalupe Valdés-Fallis, "Spanish as a Native Language" (Letter to the Editor), *Hispania*, Vol. 56 (1973), pp. 1041–1043.

A Generative Analysis
of the Constituent Dimensions
# of Bilingual Education

WILLIAM G. MILÁN
Yeshiva University

Bilingual education can hardly be considered a curricular innovation if we take into account the long tradition of pedagogical pluralism that the great civilizatons of all times have maintained throughout the centuries (Lewis, 1976). In that sense, the United States, which is considered by many to be "the great civilization of our times," has failed to live up to these standards. We should wonder how and why we have been so deprived! We must admit that we have no satisfactory way of explaining why our government is willing to let our precious language resources go to waste, especially when we consider that linguistic pluralism today is broadly cultivated through instructional means in many nations (Fishman, 1976), that the history of our own nation is dotted with highly significant bilingual education accomplishments (see the chronology by Keller and Van Hooft in this volume), and that current research findings clearly show that there are over a hundred live and socially institutionalized languages in the United States today (Fishman and Milán, 1980). There is, of course a great deal of varied and successful bilingual education activity in the private sector. Fortunately, the ethnic mother-tongue, community-based private school is still alive and doing very well (Fishman and Markman, 1980). The public sector, however, presents a very different picture. Even though more than a decade has already elapsed since the enactment of the Bilingual Education Act (United States Congress, 1968), American publicly funded bilingual education remains grossly underdeveloped. We have reached the point where the academic community is under serious pressure to propose some sound research strategies that will enable policy makers and educators alike to get a better understanding of both the issues and problems surrounding the education of children of limited English proficiency and the broader possibilities of bilingual education as a way to support and promote our nation's ethnolinguistic pluralism.

At this stage, four major goals must be met by researchers who wish to contribute to our national bilingual education inquiry:

1. to identify the key theoretical and programmatic dimensions of bilingual education programs (be they public or private) and of the communities where they exist,
2. to identify those ways and means through which these dimensions are actually represented in the programs themselves,
3. to formulate relative interdimensional hypotheses for the prediction and assessment of bilingual program outcomes, and
4. to propose some research procedures through which these dimensions can be identified and studied in actual programmatic cases.

This paper does not propose to meet these four goals. Instead, it seeks only to take some preliminary steps in their direction by presenting a generative analysis of the constituent dimensions of bilingual education programs. Naturally, it addresses the four points listed above, but it should be viewed only as a possible model for their consideration, rather than as a definitive design for their attainment.

Even this relatively modest task must be undertaken with caution. The field of bilingual education is smothered with theoretical extravaganzas totally lacking in empirical validity, practical value, or both. There is surely no need to aggravate the already existing philosophical chaos. In addition, any kind of dimensional study, out of necessity, requires some terminological adjustments. It is difficult to label or even to qualify bilingual program designs without contributing to the ongoing semantic crisis. Words such as *maintenance, enrichment,* and *compensatory* are bandied about without much regard for their meaning, not to mention their relevance. Care must be taken, therefore, to propose some operational or at least structurally significant definitions for the terms we *must* use. Finally, anyone who undertakes the task of proposing a comprehensive, multidimensional inquiry into *all* of American bilingual education is handicapped by the limitations of his or her own experience. My own experience has been primarily in the area of publicly funded, educational, equity-oriented bilingual programs, and such is the reality that most of my propositions reflect. That is why, as I present the following options, I look forward to seeing what other alternatives can be offered that will supplement, complement, and (why not?) even diverge from those I propose.

THEORETICAL AND PROGRAMMATIC DIMENSIONS OF BILINGUAL PROGRAMS AND OF THE COMMUNITIES WHERE THEY EXIST

I have chosen to limit my consideration of theoretical dimensions to those that can in fact have some programmatic impact, leaving out peripheral considerations that, although theoretically possible, are not likely to have much curricular validity. I have resisted the temptation to produce a massive typological matrix. Theoretical typologies not only have been successfully developed (Paulston 1975); they have even been dramatically exhausted (Mackey 1972). In essence what I have done is draw from the actual curricular design of those programs with which I am familiar the theoretical abstractions that seem to have had some structural significance in their development. I have organized these abstractions into six critical theoretical considerations. Each theoretical consideration is made up of a cluster of theoretical dimensions, some of them community-specific, some of them school-system-specific, and some of them applying to both the community and the school system. Each theoretical consideration will yield one programmatic dimension. The programmatic dimensions will then be used as dimensional criteria for the empirical analysis of each type of bilingual program in terms of its predictable outcomes.

In order to facilitate the characterization of each type of program, each programmatic dimension has been assigned the value of a "feature" comparable to that of the phonological features used in generative phonology. It is not my intention to apply generative principles to my analysis with the same structural value that they have in linguistics. Even though generative phonologists are no more sure about the exactness of the features they use than I am about the precision of those I propose here, I do not claim correspondence. The use of generative notation is intended only to provide a structure for the organization of certain key concepts that are too abstract to be tossed around loosely. A distinctive-feature matrix will give us an "at a glance" dimensional profile of each type of curriculum: the ordered rules that will be required to fill in the completely specified matrix will serve to establish some hypotheses for dimensions relative to other dimensions with regard to different program outcomes.

Theoretical Consideration 1: Attitudes Toward Bilingualism

Attitudes toward bilingualism have always been the result of community perspectives and/or community dynamics. Even in the days when bilingualism was suspected of having serious detrimental effects on the cognitive growth of young children, many communities still chose to educate their children bilingually. Luckily, extensive research in the area of bilingualism and cognition has put the issue of the undesirability of bilingualism to rest, at least temporarily. Today, the arguments against bilingualism will not be addressed so much to whether it is desirable as to whether it is feasible, productive, or necessary. Assuming that bilingualism is desirable, is it feasible? Is it a worthy community goal? More to the point, is it a reasonable goal for a school system? It is impossible to determine the feasibility of bilingualism through *a priori* considerations. Like anything else that costs money, bilingualism must be justified in terms of productivity or necessity. It is precisely in this realm that advocates of bilingual education are at a disadvantage. It is difficult to argue the productivity of bilingualism in communities with limited bilingual experience. And surely we are completely lost when we try to argue its necessity, living as we do in a nation with a long history of monolingualism that gives the impression of having accomplished so much thanks to its linguistic unity.

In any event, the ultimate key to determining attitudes toward bilingualism will depend not so much on philosophical arguments as on sociological realities. Here is where we begin to consider some of the social factors with dimensional significance in the determination of those attitudes. First we need to look at the community itself. If we are talking here about a single-group community that has decided to support an educational program fostering an elitist type of intragroup bilingualism, we really do not need to conduct an elaborate dimensional study of attitudes toward bilingualism, since the basic premise of such a bilingual program · is that bilingualism is desirable, feasible, productive, and necessary. Dimensional considerations are truly critical when we are dealing with a community that is made up of two or more language groups. Here, at least two kinds of considerations must be taken into account: those pertaining to the societal status of the individual groups, and those pertaining to intergroup relations. For the dimensional study of group status, I propose the following criteria: origin of the group (migrant/aboriginal), size of the group (majority/minority), relative political power (ruling class/powerless), intellectual and socioeconomic achievement (high/low), ethnic or racial status (perceived as inferior or superior). Insofar as intergroup relations are usually the result of dynamic concretizations of group status, a theory of intergroup relations must take into consideration the dimensions that go into determining such status. I would therefore like to endorse Paulston's (1975) societal model for the dimensional study of intergroup relations. This model not only takes into consideration group status dimensions, it also projects them in a way that is quite representative of the typical community context of bilingual programs in the United States.

Having given full consideration to the societal dimensions that determine the status of each language group and the relations that exist among the different groups, we can then ascertain the prevailing attitudes toward bilingualism in a given community. Such attitudes will inevitably be reflected in programmatic dimensions or features. The first of such programmatic features that can be abstracted will, therefore, be whether the bilingual program in question is likely to have a *developmental* emphasis. For the purposes of our feature analysis, a developmental bilingual program is one that reflects community attitudes that endorse bilingualism as a worthy community goal to be achieved through the educational system. As the term I have chosen implies, such a program seeks to *develop* bilingualism and is geared toward promoting *permanent* rather than transitional linguistic diversity.

Theoretical Consideration 2: Attitudes Toward the Languages in Question

Moving on from attitudes toward bilingualism in general to attitudes toward the specific languages in question, we need to change our focus. The acquisition and mastery of the language of the mainstream is a given, so we will not make that our focus. What we need to know is how the community as a whole reacts to the acquisition of a marked language. When we say that a program is developmental, all we have said is that it reflects the fact that the community where it exists endorses bilingualism as a worthy community goal to be achieved through the educational system; we have not specified which segment of the population should be bilingual, nor in which languages. Nor have we specified whether the development of bilingualism by a given segment of the population requires just the reinforcement of a marked language already learned in the home, or a systematic and deliberate acquisition of a language other than that of the mainstream. The issue here becomes one of the community's willingness to support the acquisition of a marked language whether it be by a marked or an unmarked population. Two types of dimensions need to be considered: socioattitudinal dimensions, and what we can call purely linguistic or structural dimensions. The socioattitudinal dimensions would include the following: the role of the marked language in promoting social unification or diversity; the possible stigmatization of a language because of its association with a given culture, race, or ethnicity; the assumed aesthetic attributes of the marked language, including the bulk of literature or knowledge accessible through it; its possible societal (diglossic) functions for both the marked and the unmarked groups; access to new social roles; and the relative proficiency that members of the unmarked group may have in the marked language. The structural dimensions will also end up being reflected in an attitudinal framework. Here we must consider, at least, the structural separation between the marked and the unmarked language, as well as the school-worthiness of the marked language in terms of standardization, availability of teaching materials, etc.

Having given full consideration to the socioattitudinal and structural dimensions determining the community's attitudes toward the marked language, we are now ready to abstract a second programmatic dimension or feature. In the area of attitudes toward the language in question, the one factor that will most clearly identify the position of the community will be whether the bilingual program in question is likely to have an *acquisitional* thrust in which a marked language is the target language. Acquisitional programs are characterized by a curricular focus that emphasizes the acquisition and mastery of a language other than that of the mainstream.

Theoretical Consideration 3: School System's Position toward Dominance in a Marked Language

Of all our theoretical considerations, this is the one that is most likely to have a decisive programmatic impact. In the American system of education, whether public or private, the philosophy of the school system is supposed to reflect the values of the community that supports it, and the school system's curricular design is supposed to be an enactment of the community's views. Therefore, it becomes necessary to find within the social dimensions of the community at large some theoretical basis for the school system's position toward dominance in a marked language. To do this we can fall back on the dimensions mentioned in theoretical considerations 1 and 2 and highlight two salient factors likely to be manifested here. First, what are the community's perceptions with regard to the identifying effect of the marked language? Is dominance in a marked language seen as a threat to social unity? Second, what are the overall community views on diversity? In other words, does difference imply inferiority? Of course other dimensions, which are not necessarily community-based, go into the determination of the school system's position toward dominance in a marked language. These other dimensions are tied to the logistics of education, particularly in the public sector. When a school system recognizes a language-related learning problem, it often chooses to treat it as a deficiency, not so much because of inbred prejudices, but for the sake of administrative expediency. It is a lot easier to argue in favor of remediation, and it is less controversial to divert financial and human resources toward something that is labeled as deficient, than to attempt to present a case in favor of alternative means of education for a particular segment of the population. Unfortunately, whether the school system's condemnation of dominance in a marked language has its roots in purely social dimensions or in the realities of mass education, the programmatic design that such condemnation brings about is equally detrimental, and the program outcomes are likely to be equally poor.

Having assessed the school system's position toward dominance in a marked language through a consideration of both social and educational factors, we are now ready to introduce our third programmatic feature. When a school system takes a position that dominance in a marked language is a deficiency that needs to be corrected, we are likely to see a bilingual program that will be *remedial* in emphasis. What is so devastating about such programs is that they generate the kind of curriculum that is based on a theory of *learning*. The student is provided with some services to remedy a perceived deficiency, but when it comes to pupil success, the burden of proof is on the student, not on the system. In addition, the content of the program is geared primarily, if not exclusively, to the acquisition of the unmarked language. The preservation of the marked language is not encouraged, this being considered a retarding factor that needs to be outrooted. Traditionally, this condescending type of remediation is initiated by the school system and takes into consideration neither community expectations nor the policies of the state in this area.

The types of programs described here are not to be confused with the nonremedial types of programs that present alternative means of education for the student who is dominant in a marked language. These alternative programs are based not on a theory of learning but on a theory of instruction, in which the school system assumes responsibility for addressing the different educational needs of its diverse student population. In this context, dominance in a marked language is not viewed as a deficiency that requires remediation, but as a difference that must be dealt with for the sake of educational equity.

Theoretical Consideration 4: Determination of the Bilingual Education Clientele

The issue that is addressed here is *who* shall be the consumer of bilingual education? For a single-language-group community that wishes to engage in an elitist intragroup bilingual program this is not an issue, since the clientele for bilingual education is determined by design. It becomes an issue requiring dimensional considerations when we are dealing with a community with two or more language groups, all of them potential consumers. The theoretical basis for the determination of this issue lies in the same societal dimensions mentioned in theoretical consideration 1. These dimensions, however, should be refocused and three basic dimensional components should be highlighted: *who* needs to be bilingual, in *which* languages, and *why?* Since we are talking here about actual marketable services, we cannot discuss the issue in terms of its social dimensions only. Once again we need to address the issue of administrative feasibility, particularly in the area of cost. So even when the community's attitudes toward bilingualism in general, and toward the specific languages and language groups in particular, may be very positive, access to bilingual education is going to be limited by the availability of resources. As far as American bilingual education is concerned, whenever two or more groups are involved we need only to distinguish those programs in which only a given segment of the population is designated as the consumer of bilingual education. In the realm of public education these are usually the programs in which the marked group is designated as the consumer for the sake of achieving a bilingual capacity that will enable its members to enter the mainstream. In the private sector this usually involves also one specific segment of the population or single-group community that chooses bilingual education as a better alternative. For the purposes of our feature analysis we shall designate as *unilateral* those programs that offer bilingual education to a segment of the population or to a single-language-group community exclusively. *Nonunilateral* programs will be those in which bilingual education is available to all segments of the population wherever there is more than one language group.

Theoretical Consideration 5: Amount of Community Participation in the Formulation of the Bilingual Curriculum

The social dimensions to be considered when we talk about the amount of community input in the formulation of educational policy are basically the same as those mentioned in theoretical consideration 1. They need, however, to be refocused, and a sharper perspective on the dimensions needs to be abstracted. For this specific dimensional cluster we need to consider primarily the status of each of the language groups vis-a-vis the state in general and the school system in particular, in terms of political power. Since the amount of community input will depend largely on the community's ability to make itself heard, in the private sector the amount of community participation is not a major issue. In the private programs direct support of the system entitles the consumer to participation in the formulation of educational policy. In the public arena, however, we end up falling back on group status and on intergroup relations. Ordinarily, public education is controlled by a single segment of the population, usually the segment that speaks the unmarked language. The amount of input that each segment of the population will have in curricular planning will be determined by the way in which each group relates to the school system. The unmarked group, which in fact constitutes the school officers' own ethnolinguistic constituency, will have no problem making its wishes known. Participation of the marked groups will be determined mostly by the extent to which these are aware of their rights, interested in education, and willing to assume the responsibilities that come along with participation. Of critical importance here also will be the manner in which the marked group relates politically to the state in general, and whether it is considered, at least by some, as a source of political power.

Finally, we cannot neglect to consider the ultimate determiner of community participation, and that of course is money. Very often, the same segments of the population in control of public education are the ones most visibly supporting it. For example, in those communities where education is financed through real estate taxes the ultimate source of fiscal power is that segment of the population designated as property owners. Ordinarily, property owners belong to the unmarked group, and although they may agree philosophically that bilingual education is a desirable and worthy community goal, they unquestionably will want to know how much it is going to cost them. For the purposes of our study of programmatic dimensions we shall designate as our fifth feature the extent to which a bilingual curriculum is *community-based*. By community-based we mean that a segment or segments of the community engage in active dialogue with the school system, be this directly or through a higher agency of the state, for the sake of programmatic formulation.

Theoretical Consideration 6: Manner in Which Community Input Is Delivered

It is not enough to note that a segment or segments of the community assume an active role in the formulation of educational policy. As is the case with most bureaucracies, the impact that external influences may have on the school system will not depend exclusively on the substance of the input; it will be equally dependent on the manner in which such input is delivered. The most critical dimensions to be considered for the determination of the manner in which community input is delivered are the accessibility of the school system to the community, and the means available to the community to express its views and concerns. We will further refine our fifth programmatic feature by determining whether the input of the community can be said to be *direct* or not. Direct community input is delivered through community-specific dialogue in which the segments of the population in question and the school system engage in any type of negotiation, be it adversary or conciliatory, that results in curricular planning.

Summary of Programmatic Feature Definitions

Developmental vs. nondevelopmental.   This feature determines whether a bilingual program is designed to accomplish permanent bilingualism in a society that considers linguistic diversity a worthy community goal.

Acquisitional vs. nonacquisitional. This feature determines whether a bilingual program favors the acquisition of a marked language. (Programs that are geared toward reinforcing a marked language already acquired in the home are considered nonacquisitional.)

Remedial vs. nonremedial.   This feature determines whether a bilingual program has been initiated by the school system as a means to eradicate dominance in a marked language. This feature also determines whether the bilingual curriculum is based on a theory of learning or on a theory of instruction, whether the burden of achievement is placed on the student or on the system.

Unilateral vs. nonunilateral.   This feature determines whether a bilingual program is designed to serve the educational needs of a limited segment or segments of the community or is intended to provide bilingual education for everybody.

Community-based vs. non-community-based.   This feature determines whether a bilingual program is born out of a dialogue between the school system and the community it serves. (Because in our system of educational policy-making the ultimate responsibility for the education of the citizenry rests on the state government, a bilingual program will be considered to be community-based if it results from state legislation based on a community lobby.)

Direct vs. nondirect.   This feature determines whether citizen participation in the formulation of educational policy is community-specific or not. (The term *community-specific* refers to community-system dialogue at the local level. It excludes the intervention of a state-level authority.)

PROGRAMMATIC FEATURES AND PROGRAMS

Study of the programmatic features discussed in this part of the paper does not, of course, have much practical value unless those features are discussed in terms of actual types of programs. In the second part of this paper, in which I will be discussing the likelihood of finding representations of the dimensions discussed so far, I will begin by presenting distinctive-feature descriptions of the seven major types of bilingual programs. To facilitate this process, I am presenting here two tables. In Figure 1 a branch-tree diagram serves to cluster and score the *distinctive* programmatic dimensions or features of each type of bilingual curriculum. A feature is scored with a plus sign (+) whenever its programmatic manifestation is inherent in a particular type of curriculum. In the terminal string we come up with the seven major types of bilingual programs as determined by the different combinations of programmatic features. At this point, I must, out of necessity, use some labels to identify what I see as being different types of bilingual programs. Some of these terms will sound familiar. I caution the reader *not* to assume any meaning for any of these terms other than the ones I propose here. I have chosen the labels based on the frequency with which certain dimensions or features are represented in certain contexts. The terms, therefore, refer to curricular contexts rather than to conceptual issues. This distinction is crucial!

In Table 1 we have a distinctive-feature matrix that provides an "at a glance" *essential* programmatic feature profile for each of the seven types of bilingual curricula.

Figure 1

Branch-Tree Diagram of the Clustering and Scoring of Programmatic Features Used to Produce a Terminal String of Major Types of Bilingual Curricula

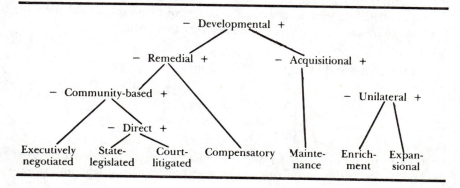

Table 1
Distinctive-Feature Matrix

	Executively Negotiated	State-Legislated	Court-Litigated	Compensatory	Maintenance	Enrichment	Expansional
Developmental	−	−	−	−	+	+	+
Acquisitional					−	+	+
Remedial	−	−	−	+			
Unilateral						−	+
Community-based	−	+	+				
Direct		−	+				

DIMENSIONAL REPRESENTATIONS

In order to establish the likelihood of finding representations of the theoretical and programmatic dimensions discussed so far in both public and private bilingual programs, we need first to describe each major type of bilingual curriculum in terms of its distinctive features. Then it will be easy to establish dimensional representations. Each type of curriculum can be described in terms of its *essential* programmatic dimensions (or features) and the way in which these relate to their supporting theoretical dimensions. In this second part of the paper, each type of program identified in Table 1 will be profiled, described, and briefly analyzed; whenever possible a concrete example will be given from either the public or the private sector. One can indeed find representations of theoretical and programmatic dimensions other than the ones given in each of the program profiles; however, such representations, if overt, will be subordinated to or contained within the representations of those dimensions, theoretical or programmatic, that are distinctively essential to the specific type of program. The discussion of the following profiles will illustrate this proposition.

Enrichment Bilingual Education

$$\begin{bmatrix} + & \text{developmental} \\ + & \text{acquisitional} \\ - & \text{unilateral} \end{bmatrix}$$

Many bilingual educators will consider a program that encourages maintenance and/or acquisition of more than one language an enrichment program. However, I choose to define true enrichment-oriented bilingual education by much stricter standards. I can see no true enrichment in a bilingual curriculum without the presence and dynamic interaction of two distinct language groups, both of which enjoy comparable social status and have high regard for each other. True linguistic and cultural enrichment, therefore, is not really contained within the school context alone, but depends primarily on the kind of community-based reinforcement that can be found only in a nonschool context. In effect, the true enrichment program is nothing but an extension and formalization of a well-established and prevalent social pluralism.

An enrichment program must have three distinctive programmatic features or dimensions. It must be developmental; it must be acquisitional; and it must not be unilateral. These features are drawn from theoretical considerations 1, 2, and 4. The theoretical dimensions clustered under theoretical consideration 1—those pertaining to group status and intergroup relations—will be reflected in an extremely positive representation of both languages and of both cultures in the bilingual curriculum. In the same manner as the groups in question enjoy comparable societal status, the languages in question will enjoy comparable curricular distribution. In the same manner as the two groups enjoy positive relations, the two cultures will enjoy comparable programmatic reinforcement. The school system, therefore, will assume a commitment to foster, promote, and preserve bilingualism as a community-based effort.

Moving on to theoretical consideration 2, which addresses attitudes toward the languages themselves, we can already anticipate a favorable socioattitudinal perspective toward the marked language, based on the favorable social status enjoyed by the group that speaks it. Structural dimensions such as the grammatical complexity and schoolworthiness of the marked language are also subordinated to a great extent to the status enjoyed by the marked group. The grammatical complexity of the marked language will not be seen as a major obstacle from a community standpoint. If anything, such complexity is likely to receive very special attention in the design of the curriculum. The school system will invest its resources generously in making the marked language schoolworthy and in facilitating its acquisition by the unmarked group. Structural dimensions, therefore, are not likely to be absolute predictors of the role that the marked language will have in the actual curricular design. They do stand the chance, however, of being a good test of the socioattitudinal dimensions. As far as their possible representation in the actual program design is concerned, we are likely to find that the program components intended to promote the acquisition of the marked language will be better distributed, better structured, and better supported than those designed to facilitate the acquisition of the unmarked language. Thus the acquisition of the marked language by the unmarked group is in fact considered one of the major priorities of the school system, and there is a strong possibility of some Hawthorne effect in the eventual outcome.

The final essential programmatic feature of this type of program is drawn from theoretical consideration 4 and is precisely the one that makes it different from all other curricula. Enrichment programs are based on the premise that bilingualism is good for all the segments of the population. Therefore, the acquisition of a language other than the mother tongue is a curricular goal for all segments of the community. In making bilingual education available to everybody, the community evidences its true commitment to bilingualism and its true positive attitudes toward its languages and language groups.

We cannot forget, however, the administrative dimensions of bilingual education, particularly in the public sector where all the positive attitudes in the world are likely to have no curricular impact whatsoever unless they can be translated into dollars and cents. These system-specific dimensions are decisive predictors. Given the current policies of the state, it is unlikely that an enrichment program such as the one described above will have a chance to be financed out of either federal or state budgets. Accordingly, the chances for the implementation of such a curriculum are limited by the system's ability to generate its own funds either from its immediate clientele or from private sources. Fortunately, school financing bears a close relationship to community goals; if the community chooses to endorse bilingual education for everybody, we can at least count on a genuine effort to raise the money necessary for its implementation.

Given this profile of true enrichment-oriented bilingual education, we are not going to find many examples of it in American schooling. At least the northeastern part of the country does not to my knowledge have an enrichment bilingual program that would satisfy the requirements I have outlined here. My guess is that the closest we are likely to come to such a model will be found in Dade County, Florida, or in the Miami vicinity, for only in this part of the country can we find a marked language group that has achieved the social status necessary to promote the kind of attitudes toward bilingualism and toward the marked language and culture that are prerequisite to the formulation of an enrichment-oriented curriculum.

Maintenance Bilingual Education

$$\begin{bmatrix} + \text{ developmental} \\ - \text{ acquisitional} \end{bmatrix}$$

As the term implies, a maintenance-oriented bilingual program is intended to maintain a language initially acquired in a nonschool context, presumably the home. That is why maintenance programs fit the label of "nonacquisitional." The maintenance curriculum presupposes two things: that the language in question does not have to be taught anew, and that it will have ample reinforcement outside of the school environment. Maintenance bilingual education is also "developmental" in nature. It finds its rationale in a community perspective that endorses bilingualism as a desirable and worthy goal and that seeks to support a school system that will help to promote bilingualism as a permanent social characteristic. Such are the essential programmatic features or dimensions of maintenance bilingual education. Representations of these dimensional traits, which are drawn from theoretical considerations 1 and 2, will be seen in all maintenance curricula, manifested through very strong conceptual and programmatic endorsement of the marked language and culture (which is in fact the locus of the maintenance) and through an instructional design that takes for granted community-based acquisition of the marked language and community reinforcement of its usage. The maintenance curriculum is designed, therefore, to strengthen an already existing social phenomenon, not to create a new one. While all maintenance programs are likely to exhibit these essential characteristics, the curricular configuration of those characteristics will vary considerably from the public to the private sector and, to a great extent, even within the private sector.

Most maintenance bilingual programs in this country are in the private sector. Consequently, they involve a single language group that seeks to preserve its native tongue while still becoming proficient in the language of the mainstream. In the Northeast we have two ethnic groups with long educational traditions that can be credited as having the most experience with maintenance curricula. These are the Jews and the Chinese. These two communities have sought through the years to preserve their native languages by supporting their own schools in which the marked language is taught in addition to the language of the mainstream. Very often, the maintenance component of their education is actually a supplemental component, added on to a regular unmarked language curriculum selected from either the private sector or the public school system. Other community institutions have also supported maintenance bilingual education, particularly for ethnolinguistic groups of very limited financial resources. Such is the case of the bilingual schools sponsored by the Catholic Church for the Portuguese in Massachusetts and for the French-speaking populations in upper New England. Single-group-sponsored maintenance-oriented bilingual education in the private sector does not require an elaborate dimensional analysis. It presumes that the community that supports it is committed to bilingualism as a permanent social goal and seeks to maintain (rather than to acquire) the marked language. But when we deal with maintenance bilingual education in the public arena, we have to account for the role played by the unmarked group. This will require a more careful dimensional study, and in all probability the representations of the essential programmatic dimensions will differ from those found in the maintenance programs of the private sector.

Publicly supported maintenance bilingual programs are for the most part experimental or pilot programs. Most of them lack a solid financial commitment due to the fact that federal and state budgets are unlikely sources for their support and local funds are usually very limited and constrained.

Turning now to the theoretical considerations (1 and 2) that yield the essential programmatic dimensions that make maintenance programs developmental but nonacquisitional, we need to consider more carefully the interaction of the different groups involved. In order for maintenance programs to be developmental, i.e., in order for them to seek the preservation of bilingualism, the unmarked group must be at least passively supportive of bilingualism as a community goal. This means that while the unmarked group may not seek to participate in bilingual education nor wish to benefit from the advantages of bilingualism, its attitudes toward bilingualism must be sufficiently positive for it to be willing to tolerate the spending of public funds so that the marked group can enjoy these rare commodities. This will require a set of dimensional considerations that will place the marked group in a fairly favorable position within the community as a whole. My personal experience with most maintenance programs that I know of in the public sector is that they are usually dressed-up showcases wherein the unmarked group (usually the one in control of the school system) displays its goodwill toward the marked group for everybody to see. This is not necessarily bad, but it does fall short of the true commitment to pluralism that maintenance programs usually pretend to imply. We can at least be glad that the unmarked group recognizes, endorses, and is willing to support the right of the marked group to preserve its language and that it helps provide a curriculum that will promote bilingualism for the minority. But when these theoretical and programmatic dimensions are translated into actual curricular design, we usually end up with an alarming ethnolinguistic segregation.

In order to establish maintenance programs, a school district needs to have large numbers of students who speak the marked language and it must offer them a substantial range of instructional services for their exclusive use, services which are not within the reach of the student who is a member of the unmarked group. Consequently, maintenance bilingual programs in the public sector usually end up as ghettoized, ethnically identifiable, educational nuclei (sort of a system within a system) that very seldom offer the same quality education that is available to the rest of the district's population.

This curricular structure, ironically enough, is quite representative of the dimensional realities of the community as a whole. The marked group enjoys the social acceptance of the unmarked ruling class. It is entitled to its identity, its culture, its language, and a chance to receive a special kind of education. The unmarked group not only is willing to facilitate it, but is even willing to help pay for it. However, this in no way commits the unmarked group to granting equal status to the minority or to assuming responsibility for its integration into the rest of society.

The fact is that all maintenance bilingual education requires ethno-linguistic segregation. This is not an alarming issue when we are talking about single-group-sponsored maintenance programs in the private sector. After all, all private education is *de jure* segregated in one way or another, and participation in such a segregated system is voluntary and quite deliberate. Furthermore, the fact that the unmarked ruling class endorses maintenance bilingual education in the private sector for those marked groups that so desire it is also a tacit approval of their segregation and representative of broader dimensional realities not much different from those described above for the public sector. What is truly alarming about maintenance bilingual education in the public school system is that it is often used as an instrument of segregation in disguise, and that it much too often sets as its primary goal the preservation of the mother tongue at the expense of a good quality education that will enable the members of the marked group to compete in an unmarked job market. The end result could easily be the restoration of the tracking system, a new programmatic configuration for one of the greatest evils of the past.

Expansional Bilingual Education

$$\begin{bmatrix} + \text{ developmental} \\ + \text{ acquisitional} \\ + \text{ unilateral} \end{bmatrix}$$

Expansional bilingual programs are very rare. They occur mostly in the private sector and are primarily intended to promote a kind of intragroup elitist bilingualism that very seldom has any real practical social significance. Ordinarily, they involve a monolingual group or a once bilingual group that has become functionally monolingual. Their distinctive programmatic features—that they are developmental, acquisitional, and unilateral—are drawn from theoretical considerations 1, 2, and 4.

The developmental dimension of expansional programs lies in the positive community attitudes toward bilingualism that motivate the community to seek bilingualism through the educational system. Because most expansional programs are the work of unmarked groups acting on their own, they really have no major dimensional implications with regard to group status or intergroup relations.

They can readily be labeled as acquisitional, since the groups that support expansional programs are traditionally speakers of the mainstream language who seek to acquire a marked language. The theoretical dimensions determining the acquisitional nature of these programs are rather significant, particularly when they involve the participation of well-to-do members of the ruling class who voluntarily seek to acquire a marked language that is not part of their daily lives and is not spoken by any of the ethnolinguistic groups with which they have social contact. It is precisely this acquisitional feature that distinguishes expansional programs from maintenance curricula. Also, expansional programs do not usually seek to establish bilingualism on a full social scale, since the dimensional realities of the communities that support them are such that chances for community reinforcement of the marked language are limited to a very small social elite. Expansional programs exhibit positive attitudes toward the acquisition of the marked language, more so than any other type of program. As a matter of fact, it could be said that the acquisition of the marked language is their primary curricular goal. By inference, it is also possible to assume that the unmarked group has very positive feelings toward the culture usually associated with the marked language, and with the people who speak it, even though they may have no contact with them.

Expansional programs are also unilateral, since they entail only a one-way participation in bilingual schooling by speakers of the unmarked language.

The typical consumer of expansional bilingual education is the upper Fifth Avenue resident who would rather keep his or her children at home than send them to a neighborhood public school where they might be able to participate in a bilingual program with the local Spanish-speaking children, but who will spend a fortune to send the children to a private school where they can learn French and participate in the greatness of the French people without ever seeing a French person.

Still, within the private sector, and to some extent in a publicly funded system of education, I can see some possible use of an expansional type of curriculum, which could have very beneficial and rather interesting dimensional implications. I am talking here about something that I would call "language restoration." This would involve groups that have had a history of bilingualism but that, unfortunately, through social evolution and deprivation, have lost or nearly lost their marked languages and are now primarily dominant or monolingual in the language of the mainstream. Because the marked languages in question have lost social vitality and are no longer learned as the first language in the home environment, these groups could not readily avail themselves of a maintenance curriculum. For these groups, the once dominant marked language must be taught from scratch as if it were a second language, and its possible social reinforcement would be minimal, confined perhaps to some traditional religious institutions. German, Yiddish, Hebrew, and the Native American languages are among the national linguistic resources that could be cultivated through expansional bilingual education programs and other non-school-based language restoration efforts.

Compensatory Bilingual Education

$$\begin{bmatrix} -\text{ developmental} \\ +\text{ remedial} \end{bmatrix}$$

Dimensionally speaking, compensatory bilingual education epitomizes either the ultimate in condescending and patronizing attitudes on the part of the unmarked group toward the marked group, or the ultimate in fiscal and administrative hardship on the part of a school system that tries to correct what it perceives as a language deficiency in the most expeditious way, given its limited resources. Very often it represents a combination of both. But regardless of the configuration of its dimensional framework, the programmatic reality is the same. Compensatory bilingual education is essentially a tool to eradicate the marked language as soon as possible.

Compensatory bilingual education has two distinctive programmatic features drawn from theoretical considerations 1 and 3. It goes without saying that compensatory programs are *de facto* nondevelopmental. In this respect, they stand at the opposite end of the spectrum from the enrichment programs. Community attitudes toward bilingualism, particularly the attitudes of the unmarked group, score at the extreme negative. Neither the status of the marked group nor its relationship to the ruling class can be said to be favorable.

Characteristically, compensatory programs have a remedial posture. The theoretical consideration behind this posture brings together social and administrative dimensions that account for the school district's perception of dominance in a marked language as a deficiency that needs to be corrected. In the realm of social dimensions we can assume that the groups in question are extremely disparate in status and that intergroup relations can best be termed as a display of a very small measure of tolerance. Bilingualism is not considered a desirable or worthy community goal, and the marked language is considered a threat to social unity and an obstacle to learning. Accordingly, bilingual education is approached with a certain degree of hostility, and a minimum of human and financial resources are invested in it.

However, we should not be so harsh on a school system as to assume that a remedial posture automatically means discrimination or a negative position toward diversity, *de facto* categorizing difference as inferiority. It is possible that the school system's position may not be determined entirely by the external social context but may also be largely dependent on internal administrative factors. Given the fiscal constraints of public education, it is virtually impossible to argue in favor of alternative means of education for a given segment of the population without strong external political and even legal pressure. Since compensatory programs are by their very nature system-initiated, they must find their rationale within traditional instructional practices. The concept of bilingual education as a means to achieve educational equity not only is a recent innovation, but also has its origin outside of the educational community. Therefore, in order for the system to justify spontaneous services for the marked segment of the student population, these must give the appearance of conforming to existing educational procedures. The dialogue usually takes place between the administrative officials of the school system (the superintendent, curriculum designer, principals, etc.) and the policy makers of the school system (the Board of Education). The administrators must justify these services to the policy makers. From an administrative perspective, it is a lot easier to present a case in favor of *remediation* than in favor of *alternative equity-oriented education*.

But whether we trace the district's remedial posture to its administrative realities, to its broader social dimensions, or to a combination of the two, the programmatic representation of any and all possible combinations of these factors will still yield a program that will inevitably result in the demise of the marked language.

The main curricular feature of a compensatory program is that it is based on a theory of learning rather than on a theory of instruction. The school system, confronted with another "learning disability," addresses its expertise to its correction. However, the implementation of special services is justified by the student's suspected *deficiency;* accordingly, the burden of success is on the student. If the student succeeds, he is mainstreamed; if he fails, he is termed "ineducable." At no time does the system acknowledge diversity as an inherent characteristic of its student clientele and at no time does it assume a responsibility for providing alternative means of education that will ensure the best possible educational opportunity for each segment of that clientele.

Compensatory programs are known for making very limited use of the marked language. Ordinarily, use of the marked language is restricted to the teaching of literacy skills in the lower grades, and only when absolutely necessary. The most important component of compensatory programs is usually the ESL component, which is intended to facilitate the acquisition of the unmarked language as soon as possible. Even ESL services are usually provided within the already existing school-day structure, so as to avoid resembling a curricular overlay. Most of the time, the ESL services are offered concurrently with the rest of the classes, and so the children who are to receive them must be "pulled out" of regular classes in order to gain access to them. Compensatory programs are usually found sorely lacking in bilingual personnel capable of speaking the marked language, and they usually rely on soft money for financing.

What comes out loud and clear through the curricular design is the school system's position that the marked language is a learning disability and that immediate acquisition of the language of the mainstream is the real priority. What is not always sufficiently clear is whether such a posture is the result of social dimensions, administrative realities, or a combination of the two. An in-depth analysis of the dimensions relevant to compensatory programs is needed, since their program design is usually so amorphous and so far from being comprehensive that representations of their dimensions can be expected only to be global and undefined rather than specific.

Equity-Oriented Bilingual Education

The concept of bilingual education for educational equity is fairly new; it still has not caught on within the ranks of the profession. To many educators, equity-oriented programs do not differ much from already existing curricula, and since their institution is so recent, we are unable as of yet to assess their outcomes. In order to facilitate the description of those dimensional characteristics that set equity-oriented programs apart from other types of bilingual education, and in order to avoid repetition of the basic conceptual and programmatic framework that all equity-oriented programs share, I would like at this point to discuss the overall concept of educational equity through bilingual education and to go over the fundamental dimensional characteristics that all equity programs have in common.

I distinguish three types of educational equity programs: (1) executively negotiated programs, (2) state-legislated programs, and (3) court-litigated programs. I will elaborate later on the specific dimensional characteristics of each. In the meantime, here are their essential programmatic features, drawn from theoretical considerations 1 and 3.

1. They are all nondevelopmental (theoretical consideration 1). The status and the interrelationships of the groups that comprise their constituent communities are such that bilingualism is not proclaimed as a worthy community goal to be achieved through the educational system.
2. They are nonremedial (theoretical consideration 3). As a matter of fact, equity-oriented programs ordinarily come about as a reaction against compensatory remedial bilingual programs that have been proven to be ineffective.

Within an educational equity framework, neither the school system nor its constituent community has to endorse bilingualism as a worthy community goal, but the school system is not allowed to assume a position in which dominance in a marked language may be regarded as a learning disability. Instead, the educational equity thrust is initiated outside of the educational community, generating through legal means a series of curricular patterns in which dominance in a marked language is to be regarded as just another aspect of the diversity of the student population. The special services that the children of the marked group may require are to be designed not as instruments for remediation, but as educational alternatives that will ensure equal educational opportunity. Educational equity seeks to abolish the deficiency model and to replace it with a model that stresses diversity and alternativeness. Finally, equity-oriented bilingual education seeks to shift the burden of pupil success from the student to the school system, by basing the bilingual curriculum on a theory of instruction instead of on a theory of learning.

Equity-oriented bilingual programs can occur only in the public sector. Not only are they initiated outside of the educational system, but they are also implemented through the power of a government agency that exercises legal pressure on the system. It is precisely because of this character of external enforcement that equity-oriented bilingual education can be truly innovative. It addresses a much higher principle than that usually addressed by a school system internally, and this affords it the luxury of structuring curricula using novel approaches that are not necessarily found in traditional education.

In terms of the social dimensions that we are likely to find represented in equity-oriented programs, we can focus briefly on those that determine the lack of community endorsement for bilingualism as a worthy community goal. The fact that legal or quasi-legal action is needed to establish an educational equity bilingual program, and the fact that legal pressure and oversight are required to implement it, are the best possible dimensional representations of the sociopolitical status of the groups in question and of the kind of intergroup relations that prevail in the community.

As far as the school system's attitudes toward dominance in a marked language are concerned, we know very well that if these were originally negative and condescending due to intragroup conflicts and prejudice, they are not likely to change just because an external legal force has stepped in. However, in the educational realm, administrative expediency is no longer a dimensional issue, since the equity framework does away with the deficiency approach and lays down the foundation for better educational alternatives. Furthermore, the agencies that enforce equity-oriented bilingual programs do not accept administrative problems nor fiscal crisis as justifications for their faulty design or implementation. And even if the social dimensions that go into determining the system's position toward dominance in a marked language still score at the extreme negative, these are prevented from surfacing and overtly interfering with the programmatic design.

Executively Negotiated Bilingual Education

$$
\begin{bmatrix}
- \text{ developmental} \\
- \text{ remedial} \\
- \text{ community-based}
\end{bmatrix}
$$

When we think of executively negotiated bilingual education, we automatically think of a new breed of bilingual program that is coming about as a result of the Office for Civil Rights' efforts to help implement the *Lau* v. *Nichols* decision (1974). This simplistic analysis of executively negotiated bilingual education has been the cause of multiple misunderstandings and of much unfair treatment of the Office for Civil Rights (OCR) by the members of the educational community who find their own ideals at odds with the Office's posture on bilingual education, and who insist on judging *Lau*-oriented curricula standards of conventional bilingual programs.

The theoretical considerations that need to be discussed in terms of essential programmatic features for these programs are numbers 1, 3, and 5. The first two have been discussed in the preceding section. It is the third consideration that makes these programs characteristically different. It is indeed ironic that a movement such as *Lau*'s, which has a long tradition of community involvement, should result in a style of programming that usually does not take into consideration the community's expectations. To clarify this point, we need a little bit of background history.

First of all, executively negotiated bilingual education is an alternative, not a prescription. Second, it did not begin as a community movement, nor was it ever intended to be one. It began with an executive directive issued by OCR on May 25, 1970. Finally, at no time has the position of OCR been, nor can it ever be, educational *quality*. OCR can address education only in terms of *equity*, in the same manner as it addresses employment issues, housing disputes, voting rights, sex discrimination, etc. To put it bluntly, as far as OCR is concerned, the education of the marked group does not have to be good, it just has to be equal to that of the unmarked group in terms of relative outcomes. Such an education can be *equally* poor, *equally* worthless, *equally* ineffective. The May 25th Memorandum only directed districts to take affirmative steps to ensure an *equal educational opportunity* for the children of the marked group. All that the Supreme Court's decision in *Lau*. v. *Nichols* did was to uphold the directive contained in the May 25th Memorandum. The so-called "Lau Guidelines," which have been the object of so much publicity, controversy, and misunderstanding, were never intended to have the force of law. It is precisely in these Guidelines that the term *bilingual education* is used to address the educational needs of the marked group. The Guidelines were drafted in consultation with a multi-ethnic task force composed of educators representing several marked groups in the country. The members of the task force did *not* write a document; they just offered their suggestions. The position of OCR is that bilingual education is *not* the ultimate panacea for solving past educational inequities, but that since so many experts are willing to endorse it, OCR is willing to accept it. However, this in no way precludes a school district's offering its own solutions to make up for past educational inequities if it can convince OCR that its methods are likely to succeed. And regardless of whether the school system chooses to follow the Guidelines or to propose its own alternative, it must still bear the burden of proof. In other words a *Lau* compliance plan can follow the Guidelines to the letter and still fail, or it could ignore them completely and still succeed. In either case, the role of OCR is only to judge the plan's *outcome*.

Now that we know where we stand in the area of *Lau* compliance planning, we can address the issue of community participation. I am sure that neither OCR nor the Supreme Court ever intended to exclude the community, particularly the members of the marked group, from active participation in program design, especially if such a program was to involve a bilingual curriculum. However, if we look closely at the process through which these programs come about, we will understand how it is that the community has been neutralized. When OCR finds a school system out of compliance with *Lau*, it demands that the district submit for consideration a plan outlining the steps it is going to take to make up for past inequities. Failure to submit such a plan will result in legal action that can lead to defunding. Since a *Lau* district usually has a long history of inequities and neglect, we can assume that the marked group in question is politically powerless. OCR therefore assumes the responsibility of looking after what it considers the best interest of the minority group. Within the civil rights context, "best interest" is defined in terms of group equity, not necessarily in terms of group preference. The school district perceives both the legal thrust and the curricular innovation that results from OCR's intervention as coming from *outside* of the system and its constituent community. Therefore, the program of instruction that is adopted in order to comply with the spirit of *Lau*, be it bilingual or otherwise, need not conform to community expectations but to OCR standards. If the school district chooses to go the bilingual route, the curriculum of the bilingual program is negotiated with OCR officials, and the only legally permissible standards that OCR can apply are those of *minimum* chances of program success. In the final analysis, the design of the bilingual program is reduced to a contractual agreement between the school district and OCR. The community does not have to be pleased, OCR does. The community may have very high expectations for the intended bilingual curriculum, but if these cannot be contained within the realm of *minimal* acceptable standards likely to promise *minimum* chances of program success *in terms of educational equity*, these expectations are not even at issue. For example, at no time may the preservation of the mother tongue for the marked group be considered as having any relevance to program design, unless it can be demonstrated *conclusively* that the marked population will not have even the barest minimum chance of educational achievement without such a programmatic feature. Programmatic representations of this dimensional absence of community support are found in the way in which *Lau* compliance plans usually turn to the Lau Guidelines in search of the barest minimum standards acceptable. There is usually no dialogue with the community, just a negotiation with OCR. As a regional Lau Center Director, I observed that most of the school-community relations programs that my colleagues and I so enthusiastically advocated ended up fulfilling a symbolic public relations function rather than generating a substantial community-based organism to help in the making of educational policy.

The one redeeming feature that OCR-negotiated *Lau* compliance bilingual programs have that makes this absence of community participation forgivable is their very strict system of "product and process evaluation." When OCR assumes a position of advocacy for the community, it goes all the way. Not satisfied with the mere design of an equity-oriented bilingual program, OCR will monitor the implementation of such a program and will hold the school system accountable for its success. While the community may not be getting what it wanted, at least it can rest assured that it will get what it was promised.

State-Legislated Bilingual Education

$$\begin{bmatrix} - \text{ developmental} \\ - \text{ remedial} \\ + \text{ community-based} \\ - \text{ direct} \end{bmatrix}$$

State-legislated bilingual education is an innovation of the 1970's. To those of us who approach all education from a public perspective, the idea of the state government actually taking charge of the education of the non-English-speaking children represents a dream come true. After all, education of the citizenry is the responsibility of the state, and the members of the marked group are tax-paying citizens. If it really worked, state-legislated bilingual education would be the solution to all our problems.

The distinctive programmatic features of state-legislated programs—that they are nondevelopmental, nonremedial, community-based, and nondirect—are drawn from theoretical considerations 1, 3, 5, and 6. Of all the types of educational equity programs, it is the state-legislated ones that most effectively illustrate the social dimensions clustered under theoretical consideration 1. This is so because program parameters are established at a very high level of policy-making, where the statewide community's attitudes toward bilingualism, as determined by the status and interrelationship of that community's component groups, are visible on a very large scale. The unmarked group is the ruling class in control of the government and the educational system. The marked segment of the community seeks an opportunity for an equal education by lobbying in favor of better educational alternatives. The state, at all cost, will refrain from legislating bilingualism or marked-language preservation. The legislation, however, will contain a standard educational equity curriculum to be implemented statewide.

State laws affecting bilingual education often use the term "compensatory" without this having any *remedial* implication (as *remedial* is defined in theoretical consideration 3). All equity-oriented movements try to respond to the ineffectiveness of deficiency-based remediation. In order to convince a state legislature to establish equity-oriented bilingual education as "the policy of the state," it is necessary to produce not just one but many cases that will illustrate the failure of system-initiated efforts based on deficiency models. Therefore, when state legislatures use the term "compensatory," they do so from a legal standpoint, not from a pedagogical one.

Theoretical consideration 5 is very important when we talk about state-legislated programs. Unlike OCR-negotiated programs, state-legislated curricula *do* have some community participation. Community participation starts with a strong lobby that eventually generates a legislative task force to work on a bill. Later on, expert witnesses, many of them drawn from the state's community at large, offer the testimony that serves as the basis for the drafting of the legislation itself. There is also community participation in the design of the statewide curriculum that is going to be contained within the legislation. Finally, the legislation itself may propose some guidelines determining the role of the community in the implementation of the programs.

But what actually happens to community participation at the local level? Once the community has delivered its input at the state level and the statewide curriculum has been determined, how much impact does the community actually have when it comes to applying statewide solutions to community-specific educational needs? Here is where we consider theoretical consideration 6, whether community participation is direct or not. In a state-legislated bilingual program, the input of the community is delivered to the state authorities at the time the legislation is drafted. Once the law is enacted and a bureaucracy for its implementation created, the role of the community is considerably reduced. The curriculum contained in the state legislation is supposed to serve as the blueprint for *all* the bilingual programs of the state. Limited staff and financial resources make it impossible for the state to give careful attention to the implementation of each program in each individual school district. Some states with legislated bilingual education (for example, Commonwealth of Massachusetts, 1971) have made provisions for the establishment of Parent Advisory Councils (PAC's) to assist the school districts in implementation. But the role of these PAC's is neither executive nor legislative; it is merely advisory; when it comes to program implementation, the school district is *not* accountable to the PAC nor to the community it represents, but to the State Bureau of Transitional

Bilingual Education. In other words, there is still no mechanism through which the community can deliver substantial input in the actual formulation of educational policy at the local level. Like anything else that is entrusted to the elected lawmakers, the education of the marked students is taken out of the hands of the local groups and placed in the hands of state bureaucracies that will accept community participation only *indirectly*.

It is possible to find clear representations of the theoretical and programmatic dimensions that distinguish state-legislated bilingual education from other types of bilingual education within the programs themselves. The most significant of these representations is precisely the role of the state in supporting a bilingual curriculum. This represents the effect that the political pressure exercised by the marked group has had on the overall formulation of state policy and is also quite representative of the extent to which the ruling unmarked group is willing to be pressured by the minority constituency. In plain political language, the extent to which the state has singled out and endorsed bilingual education as the better alternative to educate the marked segment of the population is decidedly the most revealing illustration of the marked group's interest in education and knowledge of its rights and of the unmarked group's willingness to respond to the marked group's specific needs. Through its role in the actual drafting of the legislation, the community makes its presence felt and its wishes known. But these programs also illustrate quite representatively those social dimensions that make community participation indirect, and therefore less effective. The curricular design of these programs has been shaped at a very high level of abstraction, the state legislature. Consequently, local realities are not always taken into consideration, much less represented. The fact that so often the blueprint put together in the legislature does not seem to work out when applied to a local educational agency, and the fact that the local community still has no available means to really effect change in the formulation of educational policy at the local level, are unquestionable evidence of the community's lack of accessibility to the school system and of its inability to deliver its input *directly*.

Court-Litigated Bilingual Education

$$
\begin{bmatrix}
- \text{ developmental} \\
- \text{ remedial} \\
+ \text{ community-based} \\
+ \text{ direct}
\end{bmatrix}
$$

Court-litigated bilingual education epitomizes the ultimate in negative relations between the marked groups and the unmarked majority. Whether we are talking about the Chicanos in *Serna* v. *Portales* (1974) or about the Puerto Ricans in *Aspira* v. *New York* (1974), the story of court-litigated bilingual education is always the story of oppressed minority groups with long histories of neglect, mistreatment, social deprivation, and underachievement taking an adversary position against a system that has done them wrong and against the unmarked group that controls that system. While in a state-legislated bilingual education program the dimensional characteristics of the status and the interrelationships of the groups in question are displayed on such a large scale that they cannot be missed, in court-litigated bilingual education those dimensions are represented in the most drastic, pointed, and inflammatory fashion. The court's own language sets the tone for the development of the bilingual program. The marked group is designated as the "plaintiff"; the ruling class who are members of the unmarked group are designated as "defendants." And the program that results from the litigation is designated as the "plaintiff's relief."

The distinctive programmatic features of court-litigated programs—that they are nondevelopmental, nonremedial, community-based, and direct—are drawn from theoretical considerations 1, 3, 5, and 6. As far as theoretical consideration 1 goes, the social dimensions that would endorse the pursuit of bilingualism as a worthy community goal are absent. Occasionally, a sentence or two blessing the continued development of the marked group's mother tongue manages to sneak into the text of the program that is finally approved by the court. But such quiet endorsements of bilingualism and/or maintenance are never more than traces of altruism or expressions of goodwill that never see the light of curricular implementation. The reason for that is obvious: if a marked group attempted to convince a court that the only way that their children could receive an equal education enabling them to compete in an English-speaking society was through maintenance of their native marked tongue, it would not be able to bear the burden of proof.

When it comes to theoretical consideration 3, court-litigated bilingual education also offers a picture of extremes. In order to obtain bilingual education through the judicial route, the marked group must present conclusive evidence that the school district's previous efforts to open the educational process to the children of the marked group have resulted in failure. Like any litigation, educational litigation requires massive aggregates of evidence. In the case of students of limited English-speaking ability, only a considerable amount of data showing a gross disproportion in student underachievement as compared to other groups are considered acceptable. These data are very difficult to obtain, since they must be extracted from the school system itself. What must be proved in court is that the defendant school system has failed to educate a segment of the population through either traditional educational practices or those special services that the system has thus far provided under the rubric of "currently acceptable corrective procedures." Furthermore, the plaintiffs must make a projection stating that under the present circumstances there is no likelihood that the situation will change. The final product of the litigation will be a *new* curriculum, based on a theory of instruction, student diversity, and educational alternativeness. Under the new curriculum, the school system must withdraw its position of intolerance toward the marked language and discard the deficiency model that has been proved inadequate. Whether or not the system is happy with this philosophy, neither the social nor the administrative realities that could have possible dimensional implications can enter into the program design or implementation.

As far as theoretical consideration 5 is concerned, court-litigated bilingual education is the prototype of community-based curricular innovation. In our judicial system, the burden of proof is on the plaintiff. Therefore, the marked group must state the problem, assess the situation, produce the evidence, and propose the solution. All of these community functions are dimensional representations of the marked group's interest in education and awareness of its rights. These representations are seen not only in the litigation process itself, but in the ultimate curricular design. The program that comes out of the litigation must reflect community expectations within the framework of educational equity. The curricular negotiations take place not between the district and the state but between the school district and the community. The function of the court is to sanction the negotiation from a legal perspective and to oversee the implementation of what has been negotiated.

Finally, we must consider theoretical consideration 6. As far as this is concerned we find that such dimensions as the accessibility of the school district to the community and the means available to the community to deliver its input are best represented by the role of the courts. The design and implementation of a court-litigated program is an ongoing process in which the court is an active participant. The court's continued support of the plaintiff marked group ensures the latter's ability to evaluate and pass judgment on the performance of the defendant school system and ensures its constant participation in the solution of community-specific educational issues affecting the marked student population.

DEVELOPING RELATIVE INTERDIMENSIONAL HYPOTHESES FOR PREDICTING AND ASSESSING PROGRAM OUTCOMES

Before I can start to formulate specific hypotheses interrelating two or more dimensions for the determination and evaluation of program outcomes, I must first issue a series of ordered rules to complete the programmatic feature matrix contained in Table 2. This will serve two purposes. First, it will complete the dimensional profile of each type of program. Second, it will begin to establish the kind of interdimensional relationships upon which such hypotheses can be based. This process will also serve to illustrate the close relationships that exist among specific programmatic dimensions or features. The reason for that is obvious. Most programmatic dimensions draw their supporting theoretical considerations from the same pool of theoretical dimensions. As a matter of fact, what makes these programmatic features characteristically different is only the different way in which these theoretical dimensions are clustered and refocused for each one of them. So it is reasonable to expect that there will be parallel relationships, or even cause and effect relationships, among the structurally significant dimensional sets.

The following rules *must* be applied in this order:

Rule 1

[− developmental] → [− acquisitional]

All programs that are nondevelopmental are *de facto* nonacquisitional.

Rule 2

$$[+ \text{developmental}] \rightarrow \begin{bmatrix} - \text{ remedial} \\ + \text{ community-based} \\ + \text{ direct} \end{bmatrix}$$

All programs that are developmental are *de facto* nonremedial, community-based, and direct.

Rule 3

[− acquisitional] → [+ unilateral]

All programs that are nonacquisitional are *de facto* unilateral.

Rule 4

[+ remedial] → [− community-based]
All programs that are remedial are *de facto* non-community-based.

Rule 5

[− community-based] → [− direct]
All programs that are non-community-based are *de facto* nondirect.

After all these rules have been applied we will have a completely specified matrix showing not just the distinctive features of each type of program but their complete dimensional profile (see Table 2).

Numerous interdimensional relationships among programmatic features are already contained in the original program profiles described in the second part of this paper. In the case of every program, some consideration is given to these program outcomes within the context of those interdimensional relations that are inherent in each type of program. I see no need to restate those relationships here, particularly when the fact that they are programmatically *inherent* and *distinctively* clustered makes them more axiomatic than hypothetical. In this third part of the paper I would like to articulate those hypotheses that can be established within the context of a *complete* program profile.

First Cut of Hypotheses: From the Inherent to the Predictable

It is possible to establish hypotheses at different levels of abstraction, moving from the interrelationship of concrete programmatic features out toward the overlappings and oppositions of more theoretical and

Table 2
Completely Specified Matrix

	Executively Negotiated	State Legislated	Court Litigated	Compensatory	Maintenance	Enrichment	Expansional
Developmental	−	−	−	−	+	+	+
Acquisitional	−	−	−	−	−	+	+
Remedial	−	−	−	+	−	−	−
Unilateral	+	+	+	+	+	−	+
Community-based	−	+	+	−	+	+	+
Direct	−	−	+	−	+	+	+

general factors. In the first cut of hypotheses, I would like to discuss my ordered rules briefly, since they are in fact structural hypotheses that are used to predict the programmatic features needed to complete each curricular profile.

Hypothesis 1. All programs that are nondevelopmental are also nonacquisitional.

A curriculum that is based on a premise that does not endorse bilingualism as a worthy community goal is not likely to encourage or facilitate the learning of the marked language. Four types of programs fit within this hypothesis: executively negotiated, state-legislated, court-litigated, and compensatory. We can say with certainty that, in fact, none of them is going to produce a bilingual student. If anything, they are likely to contribute to the monolingualization of those who have been bilingual before they entered them. In terms of curricular design, both the remedial programs such as compensatory bilingual education, and the three types of equity-oriented programs mentioned above are unlikely to contain much more than the bare essentials for mainstreaming. Transitional Bilingual Education is the preferred curricular model for equity programs, while compensatory programs rely heavily on ESL and HILT. These curricula are not likely to contribute much to the development of bilingualism, since they primarily seek to develop English language competency in the students. The marked language may be used as a means of instruction temporarily, but its use is no longer reinforced, nor is competence in it developed once the student is past the assimilation point.

Hypothesis 2. All developmental programs are nonremedial and community-based, and in all of them community input is delivered directly.

Three types of program fit within this hypothesis: maintenance, enrichment, and expansional. All three of them are based on a curricular principle that endorses bilingualism as a community-worthy goal to be accomplished through the school system. It goes without saying that attitudes toward the marked languge in these dimensional contexts are very positive. Surely, of the three, only the enrichment and expansional programs are geared for acquisition of the marked language. However, though the curricular configuration of the maintenance program may not be addressed to marked language acquisition, this does not mean that the attitudes toward it are negative. A maintenance bilingual program is not designed for the acquisition of the marked language, but for its reinforcement and formalization. Therefore, we can confidently state, axiomatically more than hypothetically, that these types of developmental programs will not be remedial in their approach.

Developmental programs that seek to enact bilingualism as a community value are usually the kinds of programs with the most substantial community input, and for which such community input is likely to be most direct. There is, therefore, a necessary connection between the kinds of social attitudes that seek to promote bilingualism through schooling and the kinds of social attitudes that advocate and promote intense and direct community participation in the formulation of educational policy. Given this curricular and dimensional profile, in which we have both community support of bilingualism and community participation in curricular design, we can hold reasonably high expectations for the development of true bilingual students.

Of the three models mentioned above, I would have highest expectations of the enrichment program, which is designed not for one single group but for all the component groups of the community. Because enrichment programs are not unilateral, they offer the best chances of accomplishing community goals in the development of bilingualism. Furthermore, their curricular design reflects the kind of intergroup dynamics that is likely to reinforce most positively the development of bilingualism in a nonschool context.

In spite of the fact that maintenance programs are unilateral, the fact that they are designed to build upon an already existing base and to draw reinforcement from an already existing source gives them the next best chance of success. Since these are programs that are created to accommodate the marked group *exclusively,* the group's strong participation in program design, as well as its provision of external support to the program, is very likely.

Expansional programs, at least in the private sector, are my last choice in terms of probabilities of success because, although they are acquisitional by design, they are essentially unilateral on account of their social reality, usually lacking a social experience that will reinforce the marked language.

Hypothesis 3. Those programs that are nonacquisitional are always unilateral.

A program that does not promote the *acquisition* of a marked language has as its *only* clientele the members of the marked group. In the public sector, all programs that are unilateral and that are targeted exclusively for the marked group are going to result in some segregation. The amount of segregation depends, ironically enough, on the amount of effort invested in the preservation of the marked language. Five types of programs fit within this hypothesis: compensatory, executively negotiated, state-legislated, court-litigated, and maintenance-oriented. The first four types of programs are not intended for the development of bilingualism, since they are after all nondevelopmental. They are supposedly geared for mainstreaming. The compensatory program seeks mainstreaming at the expense of the student. The three equity-oriented programs seek mainstreaming at the expense of the system. Maintenance programs (which are developmental) seek to develop a bilingual student. The likelihood that the maintenance program may succeed in this goal has already been discussed in Hypothesis 2.

I would like to explore the chances of this third hypothesis for pupil success in terms of access to learning resources and possibilities for cognitive growth. The five programs that can be classified as being nonacquisitional and unilateral present a continuum of possible outcomes. If the outcome that we seek is bilingualism, the maintenance program has the best chances, the compensatory program has the least possibilities, and the three equity programs stand somewhere in between. However, such a criterion is not a fair measure since four out of the five programs in question are overtly in favor of mainstreaming. The one fair criterion that we should be using to compare these programs in terms of their possible outcomes is their chance of pupil success. Here is where we must consider cognitive growth as a goal, and access to learning resources as a predictor.

The compensatory program is not a likely medium for achieving cognitive growth, not because it segregates the marked group but because it treats it unfairly. The issue here is not a denial of access to learning resources available to other students, but a remedial posture that fails to meet the student's needs. The three equity-oriented models should have the best chances of academic success since, after all, that is where all their efforts are concentrated. In this context, however, we would have to accept that there can be academic success at the expense of bilingualism.

The maintenance program presents an interesting dilemma. Like the other programs, it is nonacquisitional and unilateral but, unlike them, it is developmental. Being developmental, it concentrates its efforts on the preservation of the marked language and the development of bilingualism in general. Given its unilateral nature, there is just no way that this can be accomplished without segregation. In the public sector, this becomes a real danger. Segregation is likely to result in the curtailment of access to many important learning resources. It would be unrealistic to expect that a school district can duplicate all its learning resources for the marked language group, and even if districtwide resources were available to the marked population, how would they make use of them when they are locked into a cellular curriculum? Also, to what extent are these children hurt *pedagogically* on account of that segregation, just by the fact that they miss some good opportunities of intergroup socialization? It is not my intention to discredit maintenance programs. I simply do not want to see us lose sight of the fact that, as desirable as bilingualism might be, we are still in the business of student achievement. I want everybody to stop and think for a second what the price of maintenance could be. We cannot ignore the fact that a maintenance track stands a good chance of cutting the marked students off from some educational resources. How important are these resources for cognitive growth? Are we selling the children short? Is it worth the trade-off? More to the point, what can we do to make sure that there is no trade-off?

Hypothesis 4.   Remedial programs are non-community-based.

Only compensatory programs fit this hypothesis, and it is not surprising at all that they exemplify the ultimate in lack of community participation. When a school district perceives dominance in a marked language as a learning disability, it is most unlikely that it may want to discuss this issue with the marked population. It is even less likely that it may want to seek the marked population's input to determine what "corrective" measures it should apply. It is no surprise, therefore, that compensatory programs consistently have the least chances of success. It is precisely this kind of faulty perception of the problem, this kind of ill-advised approach to it, and the way in which the district proceeds behind the community's back, that sabotage the program's outcomes in advance. Even when program goals are set at the lowest, pupil achievement is not likely because of the way in which the program deals with diversity as a disability rather than as a characteristic.

Hypothesis 5.   Non-community-based programs are also nondirect.

There can be no direct community participation if there is no community participation at all. Two programs fit this hypothesis: those that are executively negotiated and those that are compensatory. It is interesting to note that, in addition to sharing these two features, these programs share all other features except for the one dealing with the district's position toward dominance in a marked language. Therein lies the key to predictable outcomes. The fact that there is no community participation in either one is regrettable. But while the compensatory program prejudices its outcomes by taking a remedial approach, the executively negotiated program has a better chance of improving cognitive growth by approaching diversity with alternative means of education.

Second Cut of Hypotheses: Primary Curricular Goals and Programs

In this section of the paper I would like to lay down some of the primary curricular goals that are often articulated in connection with bilingual programs aimed at specific clienteles. Under each curricular goal, I will list the necessary interdimensional relations (at the programmatic level) that I see as being essential for the accomplishment of that goal for the particular community in question. This will serve to identify which of the programs already profiled can best be applied for the fulfillment of the goal in question. For the purposes of this analysis, we may think of each primary curricular goal as the *product;* we should then view the interdimensional relations contained in the suggested programmatic configuration as the *process.*

Primary Curricular Goal 1. Bilingual education will be used to ensure that *all* children are fully bilingual by the time they complete their schooling.
HYPOTHESES:
1. The bilingual program must be nonunilateral.
2. A nonunilateral program is out of necessity developmental and acquisitional.
3. In a nonunilateral program, direct community participation is needed, and the groups (marked or unmarked) must be represented. Also, considerable community reinforcement of the two languages in a nonschool context is expected.
CONCLUSION: An enrichment program is the one most likely to accomplish this curricular goal.

Primary Curricular Goal 2. Bilingual education will be used to ensure that *speakers of a marked language* are able to preserve their mother tongue.
HYPOTHESES:
1. The bilingual program must be developmental, but need not be acquisitional.
2. The bilingual program must rely heavily on direct community participation and language reinforcement on the part of the *marked group.*
3. A program that seeks to develop bilingualism but does not have a marked language acquisition component will inevitably have to be unilateral, and its clientele will be the *marked group* exclusively.
CONCLUSION: A maintenance program will be sufficient to accomplish this curricular goal.

Primary Curricular Goal 3. Bilingual education will be used so that the *speakers of the unmarked language* can learn another language.
HYPOTHESES:
1. The program must be essentially acquisitional.

2. The fact that it is acquisitional presupposes that it is developmental.
3. Although it must be acquisitional, it will suffice if it is unilateral.
4. Direct community participation is needed to ensure that the community's expectations are being met.

CONCLUSION: An expansional program will be sufficient to accomplish this curricular goal.

Primary Curricular Goal 4.   Bilingual education will be used to restore the once widely spoken mother tongue of an *ethnically marked group* that has now become monolingual in the language of the mainstream.
HYPOTHESES:
1. The program must be essentially acquisitional.
2. The fact that it is acquisitional presupposes that it is developmental.
3. Because it is intended to serve the needs of a specific group, there is no reason why it should not be unilateral.
4. Direct community participation is needed to ensure that community expectations are being met. The burden of quality control rests primarily with the marked group.

CONCLUSION: A program with the basic programmatic features of an expansional program should be a good starting point for the fulfillment of this curricular goal.

Primary Curricular Goal 5.   Bilingual education will be used as a means to ensure equal educational opportunity *for the members of the marked group only.* (Equal educational opportunity is defined as eventual mainstreaming on a competitive basis without any loss in cognitive growth.)
HYPOTHESES:
1. Since neither bilingualism in general nor the marked language in particular needs to be reinforced, the program need not be developmental or acquisitional.
2. In order to serve the specific needs of the *marked group* by dealing with its linguistic identity as a diversity issue rather than as a deficiency, the program needs to be unilateral and nonremedial.
3. The community as a whole, particularly the marked segment of the community, should participate directly in the formulation of the curriculum and should retain some means for making sure that its expectations are being met.

CONCLUSION: At the moment, a court-litigated program is the only one that has a chance of delivering all of these programmatic configurations; it therefore is the one most likely to fulfill the curricular goal in question.

Third Cut of Hypotheses: Theoretical Interrelations and Program Outcomes

In this section of the paper I would like to formulate some hypotheses interrelating the dimensions that are mostly theoretical. There is no need to establish relationships between the theoretical dimensions and the programmatic dimensions, since such relationships have already been established through the six theoretical considerations discussed in the first part of this paper.

Hypothesis 1.   Group status is a determiner of intergroup relations.

This hypothesis has critical implications for bilingual programs that propose to encourage bilingualism as a worthy community goal. Such programs require community reinforcement of the school curriculum. A multigroup community where intergroup relations are not positive and where the status of each group is not favorable is an unlikely ally for developmental bilingual education. This hypothesis also has critical implications for equity-oriented programs. Because these programs require the protection of the law, only a community situation where the marked group's status can justify legal intervention will ensure the participation and oversight of external forces. Equity-oriented programs will last only as long as the group status and intergroup relations that brought them about prevail. In other words, there is no justification for an equity-oriented bilingual program unless there is a social inequity to be corrected. And in the final analysis, once the program has accomplished its intended goals of leveling off educational opportunity, improving the status of the marked group, and improving the community's intergroup relations as a whole, it is unnecessary.

Hypothesis 2.   All educational policy generated by the system itself without any outside interference will reflect to a great extent community objectives, intergroup relations, and the status of the groups themselves.

This hypothesis has significant implications for compensatory programs. The lack of external forces that can affect internal policy leaves the curriculum at the mercy of community-specific and system-specific circumstances. This hypothesis addresses primarily the realities of the community that proposes the program. A community that is controlled by an unmarked group that views the differences of the marked group as deficiencies is not likely to be a good contributor to any kind of academic success, particularly when these views are manifested in educational policy. Compensatory programs based on such community attitudes are preprogrammed for failure.

Hypothesis 3.   Both the amount and the manner of participation that any given segment of the community may have in the formulation of educational policy will be determined by the social status of the said segment and by the possibility of intervention by external forces.

In developmental programs, community participation is inherent. The status of the group or groups that serve as program clientele is high enough to give that group a role in educational policy-making. The group's active participation will be a determiner of program success.

Equity-oriented programs present different configurations of community participation. Since these programs rely on external forces, the participation of both the marked and the unmarked groups will be largely determined (or negotiated) by the intervening agency. Program outcomes in this context will depend considerably on the roles assigned to each segment of the community and on the role reserved to the external forces. The achievement of goals and quality controls is essentially determined by the amount of participation that is given to the marked group, or by the extent to which the intervening agency is willing to assume responsibility for the interests of the marked group. The best example of the first case is the court-litigated program where the court backs up the minority. The best example of the second case is the executively negotiated program in which OCR assumes responsibility for minority interests. Both of these programs have good chances of success. However, state-legislated programs in which the external forces neither put quality control in the hands of the community nor assume that responsibility for every specific local educational agency are not as likely to succeed.

Hypothesis 4. The intervention of external forces (OCR, the state, the courts) in favor of the marked group is likely to occur only in the public sector.

This hypothesis holds for two major reasons. First, the kind of external forces mentioned above are not likely to have jurisdiction over most private education. Second, the intervention of an external force should *not* be necessary in a system that receives its financial support *directly* from its clientele.

Hypothesis 5. System-specific administrative and fiscal constraints will be a major determiner of program design (more so than community objectives).

This hypothesis is particularly relevant to compensatory programs, but it is likely to hold true for all types of programs. Regardless of the good intentions of the community, the hard realities of the system's limitations in terms of structure and resources will be major predictors of program configuration and, to a large extent (almost consequently), of program success.

Hypothesis 6. Intervention of external forces can redefine the system-specific programmatic structure.

External forces with legal strength can negotiate or mandate curricular innovations regardless of community attitudes. They cannot change attitudes, but they can modify administrative structures and processes, restructure programs, redefine curricular goals, and bring about a new distribution of resources. Since external interventions can occur only when system-specific realities and results are *really* bad, the changes brought about by the intervention of external forces can only improve program outcomes.

Hypothesis 7. The size of the student clientele for bilingual education will be a primary determiner of curricular design (more so than will community objectives).

This hypothesis will hold true for all programs. If the clientele is too small, certain curricular models are simply not administratively feasible. If the clientele is too large, certain curricular models are simply too costly.

Developmental programs that are privately supported have better chances of success because they generate both their own curriculum and their own funding. Equity-oriented programs, on the other hand, are very much at the mercy of numbers. Laws such as the Massachusetts Transitional Bilingual Education Act (1971) have arbitrary cutoff points of twenty students for the establishment of programs. Court cases such as *Serna* v. *Portales* (1974) and even *Lau* v. *Nichols* (1974) have been decided largely on the basis of numbers. Even the Lau Guidelines (OCR 1975) have an arbitrary cutoff point for plan submission.

In terms of program outcomes, this hypothesis is rather significant. Children who may require specific services may never get them simply because there are not *enough of them* to justify what they need. On the other hand, a large group of children who could best benefit from a given type of curriculum will have to settle for a less beneficial program that will be less expensive.

IN SEARCH OF THE DIMENSIONS

It is my belief that all bilingual curricula can be profiled in terms of their significant programmatic features. Such profiles can first be composed from surface curricular configurations and later validated through a more complex analysis. The process as I envision it would have four steps.

Step 1. Surface Profile

Looking into the curricular design, first-cut determinations could be made as to the status of each of the programmatic features presented earlier in this paper. In all probability, an initial profile of this type would conform to the program analysis presented here. For example, the profile for most enrichment programs is likely to look very much like the one presented in Table 2. The same is likely to hold true for the other programs as well. This is the point at which we should go full-scale generative, do away with all the labels, and deal with each program profile in terms of feature clusters *exclusively*. For example, what *appears* to be an enrichment program as defined by its initial feature profile will not be called an enrichment program but simply a program that is:

$$
\begin{bmatrix}
+ \text{ developmental} \\
+ \text{ acquisitional} \\
- \text{ remedial} \\
- \text{ unilateral} \\
+ \text{ community-based} \\
+ \text{ direct}
\end{bmatrix}
$$

Step 2. Validation: The Relevant Data

The following aggregates of information are needed:

1. Complete demographic census describing all the social characteristics of the population in question, with emphasis on group differentiation.
2. Complete intergroup relations profile based on Paulston's model (1975).
3. Representative polling of all the segments of the population (marked and unmarked), such poll designed to identify community-specific and group-specific attitudes toward and behaviors pertaining to bilingualism, diversity, ethnicity, and education.
4. Comprehensive profile of the system that is operating the program, with emphasis on administrative and fiscal structure.
5. Comprehensive definition and assessment of the roles assumed in the formulation of educational policy by different segments of the population, the educational establishment, and the external forces (if any).

Step 3. Validation: The Instrument

An instrument should be developed with items that will address the theoretical dimensions clustered under the six theoretical considerations discussed in the first part of this paper, with special emphasis on the dimensions restated in the third cut of the hypotheses in the third part of this paper.

Step 4. The Process and the Final Product

The five aggregates of information listed under Step 2 will then be used to respond to the instrument developed in Step 3 and to define each item. If the interdimensional relationships that I propose are valid, a rotational solution of the intercorrelation of the items will yield six factors that will correspond to the six programmatic features discussed in this paper, with the relevant items loading on the relevant factors. Each programmatic feature of the program in question will then be reassessed, and if any one of them needs to be altered ($+ > -$ or $+ > -$), the relevant rule will be inserted and the change effected generatively. For example, if after reassessing each one of the features of the program described in step 1 above we find that the program is not [+ direct] but [− direct], it should simply be stated as a rule to the effect that in this particular program

$$[+ \text{ direct }] \rightarrow [- \text{ direct }].$$

Our revised program profile will therefore look like this:

$$
\begin{bmatrix}
+ \text{ developmental} \\
+ \text{ acquisitional} \\
- \text{ remedial} \\
- \text{ unilateral} \\
+ \text{ community based} \\
+ \text{ direct}
\end{bmatrix}
$$

An explanation accounting for the incongruency between [+ developmental] and [− direct] is in order, since obviously this program presents a different dimensional interrelationship than what we would expect ordinarily. In Rule 2 presented in the third part of this paper it was determined that all developmental programs would have direct community participation. If this particular developmental program does not, we are likely to find among its dimensions several incongruencies of the kind that could jeopardize its outcomes.

If, after reassessment, none of the features of a program needs to be altered, they will simply remain as they are, with the results of the instrument and the factor analysis used to validate them on hand for support and clarification.

CONCLUSION

I see the future of the study of the dimensions of bilingual programs as depending on three major factors:

1. Our ability to correlate our concepts with programmatic realities; or, better still, our ability to abstract our concepts *from* these realities, rather than impose our concepts *upon* them.
2. Our ability to study the communities where bilingual programs exist as extensively and as thoroughly as we study the programs themselves, and our ability to contextualize our program inquiry within that total social milieu.
3. Our ability to free ourselves from meaningless labels and obscure definitions and to address only the relevant issues directly, comprehensively, and economically.

The generative approach that I have proposed here is a daring attempt to meet these three objectives.

REFERENCES

Commonwealth of Massachusetts. *Massachusetts Transitional Bilingual Education Act.* C.71A, Boston, 1971.

Fishman, Joshua A. *Bilingual Education: An International Sociological Perspective.* Rowley, Mass: Newbury House, 1976.

Fishman, Joshua A., and Markman, Barbara. *The Ethnic Mother-Tongue School in America: Assumptions, Findings, Directory.* Research Report, N.I.E. Grant G-78-0133. New York, 1980.

Fishman, Joshua A., and Milan, William G. "Spanish Language Resources of the United States: Some Preliminary Findings." In *Conference on the Spanish Language in the United States: Beyond the Southwest Setting.* Chicago, University of Illinois, October, 1980.

Lewis, E. Glyn. "Bilingualism and Bilingual Education: The Ancient World to the Renaissance." In *Bilingual Education: An International Sociological Perspective,* ed. Joshua A. Fishman. Rowley, Mass.: Newbury House, 1976, pp. 150–200.

Mackey, William F. "A Typology of Bilingual Education." In *Advances in the Sociology of Language II,* ed. J. A. Fishman. Mouton: The Hague, 1972.

Office of Civil Rights. "May 25th Memorandum." In *A Better Chance to Learn: Bilingual-Bicultural Education*. Clearinghouse Publication 51, United States Commission on Civil Rights, Washington, 1975a.

Office for Civil Rights. "Task Force Findings Specifying Remedies Available for Eliminating Past Educational Practices Ruled Unlawful Under *Lau v. Nichols*." Washington, 1975b.

Paulston, Christina Bratt. "Ethnic Relations and Bilingual Education: Accounting for Contradictory Data." In *Proceedings of the First Inter-American Conference on Bilingual Education*, ed. R. C. Troike and N. Modiano. Arlington, Va.: Center for Applied Linguistics, 1975.

United States Congress. *The Bilingual Education Act*. Title VII of the Elementary and Secondary Education Act, Washington, D.C., 1968.

United States Court of Appeals, Tenth Circuit. *Serna* v. *Portales*, 499 F2nd 1147. Dallas, 1974.

United States District Court, New York Southern District. *Aspira* v. *New York*. 72 Civ. 4002, New York, 1974.

United States Supreme Court. *Lau* v. *Nichols*, 414 U.S. 563, Washington, 1974.

III | United States Spanish: Issues in Language Diversity and Language Standardization

Expanded Subcategorization of Spanish-English Bilingual Spelling Strategies

JOHN J. STACZEK
Florida International University

A preliminary study (Staczek and Aid, 1981) of the Spanish language spelling habits of Spanish-English bilingual students (kindergarten through university) revealed that spelling strategies of these bilinguals could be categorized as Spanish-based, English-based, or simply random. Subcategories, with appropriate linguistic descriptions and justifications, were listed. Subsequent research[2] on the basis of a locally designed instrument consisting of word, phrase, and sentence dictations, written story retelling, and free composition has led to some further subcategorization of the orthographic errors and strategies. The new data, categorized and described below, confirm the strategies described in 1977 and provide additional information on all categories, including the random errors. The basis for random errors seems to be perceptual problems such as the orientation of graphemic <p q b d>, aural misperceptions, and incomplete mastery of the orthographic conventions of either Spanish or English.

1

The instrument (Appendix) designed for data elicitation consisted of a series of four 20-word dictation lists for a total of 80 words, two 25-word combination single-word and phrase-level dictations, a 6-sentence dicta-

I would like to express my appreciation to the School of Education, Florida International University, for the Faculty Development Award in the Spring Quarter of 1978 for the design and preparation of the instrument and for the collection and collation of data, and to the Dade County Public Schools and Christopher Columbus High School for allowing me to use their students as subjects in the research project. Moreover, I would like to express my thanks to the 384 bilingual subjects in Miami and to the 120 monolingual subjects in Bogotá, Colombia.

139

tion list, and two short narrative listening comprehension paragraphs for subsequent written retelling. Free composition was also used to elicit data from the monolingual control group. The tests were administered over a three-day period in an effort to eliminate practice effect and boredom and to detract as little as possible from the daily classroom activities of the Spanish-S or Spanish for Native Speaker classes. The items selected for the instrument are of high frequency, including several Spanish-English cognates. Many of the items have been taken from the preliminary informal collection reported on by Staczek and Aid.

Test group subjects included 384 students enrolled in six junior and senior high schools in the Miami area. Personal data from the students indicate a 2- to 14-year range of formal Spanish and/or English language study. The participants are predominantly Cuban or Cuban-American, with about 20 percent coming from other countries of the Hispanic Caribbean, Central America, and South America. Control group subjects, monolingual Spanish speakers, are 120 eighth-, ninth-, tenth-, and eleventh-grade Colombian students from Bogotá.

The spelling strategies revealed in the preliminary study were apparently developed as an independent accommodation to two different spelling systems available to the bilingual. The new data suggest a similar accommodation. It is my intent here to describe the findings from a purely linguistic point of view and not to judge them. There is no doubt that the derived spelling strategies are an attempt on the part of the bilingual to cope with learning to write the acquired language, Spanish, while at the same time learning to read and write the learned language, English.

2

Prior to the present study, the underlying sources of deviance from standard Spanish orthography were described as: (1) intralanguage problems or Spanish-based problems that arise because of inconsistencies or irregularities in the orthographic patterns of Spanish, (2) interlanguage problems or English-based problems that arise because of interference based on similarity of morphemes and graphemes, and (3) random errors for which no attempts at categorization were deemed possible.

In the Spanish orthographic system it is expected that the monolingual will have difficulty spelling words (1) in which more than a single grapheme may be used for a single phoneme segment, (2) in which two graphemes are in complementary distribution yet have the same phonemic value, (3) where dialectal variation leads the writer to spell phonetically on the basis of aural perception, and (4) where certain historical processes are independently and unwittingly resurrected.

Rather than approach the new data in terms of the classification of the preliminary data, I find it more profitable to describe the data in terms of a standard and all its intralanguage variants in order to emphasize the degree of deviance and the multiplicity of forms. Although I point out frequencies of occurrence, I make no attempt at a statistical interpretation. The data here are simply described.

Intralanguage phenomena.

a.	HAY	ay	10
		ai	2
		ai	3
		ahi	3
		hay	3
		hoi	1
		hai	1
b.	MUY	mui	10
		mui	2
		moi	1
c.	MIS	miz	1
		mis	6
		mi	1
d.	IBAN	hiban	39
		hivan	8
		ivan	33
		iba	1
e.	CEBOLLA	sebolla	37
		cevolla	3
		sevolla	9
		sevoya	3
		sevoilla	1
		seboya	18
f.	VISITAN	bisita	1
		bisitan	4
g.	RECIBAN	recivan	19
		resiban	44
		resiba	1
		resivan	13
h.	SIGUE	sige	40
		sigen	1
		cigue	3

i. ESTRICTO	extricto	6
	estrixto	1
j. RELACIÓN	relazion	1
	relasion	9
k. HICIMOS	isimos	13
	hizimo	3
	icimos	3
	hisimos	13
	hizimos	4
l. AGENTE	ahente	2
	hajente	5
	hagente	3
	ajente	7
	adjente	2
m. JARRO	jaro	14
	haro	5
	harro	5
	garro	2
	jarro	2
n. ACERCA	hacelca	3
	hacerca	11
	aserca	8
	aselca	2

The above data are consistent with the data collected from the monolingual Spanish control group. In gross terms, there seems to be nothing new under the sun that is not Spanish-based. There does appear, however, to be a growing, though perhaps still minor, tendency toward the voicing of voiceless consonants in Spanish, as shown in the following examples:

a. MELANCOLÍA	melegonia	2
	melangolia	5
	melagoria	1
	malangolia	5
b. ACERCA	acerga	2
c. CASTIGAR	gastigar	1
d. PULGA	bulga	2

Other types of errors include the difficulty with consonant clusters; metathesis; intrusion of extra consonants or vowels; loss of consonant, vowel or syllable; confusion in syllabication, and the like. These types of errors are seen below:

a. RELACIÓN	relason	2
b. CALIFICACIONES	calicafion	2
	caficaciones	1
c. ME SIENTO	me semto	2
	me siemto	1
d. RECIBAN	recinban	2
e. BIBLIOTECA	bivoteca	1
	didiloteca	1
f. ENTONCES	entocis	1
	entoses	1
g. ESTRELLA	esella	1
	esterlla	1
h. MALTRATAN	martratan	1
	paltratan	1
	antrata	1
	malestranscan	1

Many of the above examples, though infrequent, show some degree of consistency across words and from writer to writer. Though one or another may seem arbitrary and independently motivated, there are reasons to believe that across speakers there is a strategy being employed.

3

The second class of errors alluded to in the preliminary study stems from the regularities and patterns of English orthography. Those errors were classified as related to four phenomena: naming of the alphabet, spelling of the English vowels, spelling of English consonants, and the transfer of English morphemes.

The naming of the alphabet is a strategy employed by the bilingual whereby the learning of the L_2 affects the spelling in the L_1 because of the fact that greater emphasis is being given to the learning of the L_2 and the techniques to teach it, namely, spelling aloud, alphabet repetition, and the use of phonics.

In an effort to summarize earlier categorizations, I chose to list the repeated errors for the purpose of dramatizing their frequency and multiplicity of style. The strategies suggested earlier continue to be employed.

Interlanguage phenomena.

a. HAY	I	4
	hi	2

b.	MUY	my	1
		muey	1
		mue	1
c.	MIS	miss	1
		mes	1
d.	IBAN	eban	7
		evan	5
		evas	1
e.	VISITAN	visentan	1
		besetan	1
		besitan	3
		decintan	1
f.	CEBOLLA	ceboje	1
		cevoja	1
g.	RECIBAN	reseban	2
		raseban	3
h.	SIGUE	sege	1
		segian	1
		cege	1
i.	QUESO	qeso	1
		ceso	1
		cheso	2
		quesso	2
j.	CUÑADO	cunjado	1
k.	BÉISBOL	baseball	7
		basebol	2
		baesboll	1
		baesbal	1
		basboll	1
		beisbal	1
l.	MOTOCICLETA	motocyclas	1
		motorcicleta	6
		motociqleta	1
		motocikleta	1
		motocycleta	8
		motociquleta	1
		motociqueta	1
m.	DIJO	deho	2
		dejo	2
n.	INTELIGENTE	inteligente	3
		intelijante	1

| o. QUIERO | cero | 3 |
| | ciero | 2 |

As there was with the intralanguage phenomena, there is also with the above phenomena a certain predictability. Movement beyond the four categories described above for English-based errors seems to be limited.

4

In the 1977 study there were too little data to suggest any kind of categorization of the random errors, errors that appeared to have their basis in arbitrary spelling assignments as well as in totally misperceived cues and in incomplete mastery of either system. It was suggested at that time that the chaotic forms defied the above systematic description and that mastery of either system had not yet begun. Ignorance of spelling conventions produced some very strange errors but not enough to warrant classification. However, in the collection of the new data there began to appear some consistencies in the chaotic data that suggested a categorization, specifically in terms of such visual-perceptual phenomena as the orientation of <p q b d>, aural misperceptions, phonetic guesswork, and the simple lack of understanding of the conventions of a system.

The graphemes <g p q b d>, it is to be understood, are problematic for many students who are learning to write the Roman alphabet because of the mirror image likeness of the symbols. It is not my intent here to label these errors as unique but only to point out that among Spanish-English bilinguals the perception and the consequent confusion of the letters do indeed present some spelling problems. Though the errors disappear by midadolescence among monolinguals, the errors here are common. It would appear that the strategy in dealing with this problem is more or less arbitrary. They are neither Spanish- nor English-based but are simply Roman-alphabet-based. Some of the confusion, in fact, results from the phonetic cue confusion over the <b v> distinction.

Graphemic confusion of <g p q b d>.

| a. CABALLO | cadallo | 3 |
| b. VOCECITA | dosesita | 2 |

   This confusion also produces *todadia* from *todavía*.

c. BIBLIOTECA	didioteca	2
	didotica	1
d. QUESO	gueso	3
	gweso	2

e. PEQUEÑO	pegueno 2
f. QUIERO	guiero 2
	giero 3

Aural misperception of cues, including total misperception of phonetic features or surrounding environments, accounts for a number of random errors. In several cases there is a recurring redundant palatal, either oral to nasal or nasal to oral.

Aural misperceptions.

a. CUÑADO	punado 2
	guyado 1
b. MELANCOLÍA	melegonia 2
	melogonia 2
	melagoria 1
c. CEBOLLA	tevoya 3
	tevofoya 1
d. TANTO	santo 1
	canto 1
e. LECCIONES	tecchines 1
f. VOCECITA	bolsetita 1
g. GRINGO	gueringo 1
h. DESAYUNAR	decaunal 1
	desallnar 2
	diesala 1
i. BIBLIOTECA	bleboteca 2
	bibogeta 1
	bibletica 1
	biotegla 1
j. TODAVÍA	dovinga 1

Phonetic guesswork, however it is accomplished, accounts for a number of inaccuracies in spelling. The student might totally misperceive and attempt to guess but, because of poor short-term memory, recall a sound from a previous word or one at another boundary and consequently produce what might be termed a barbarism. The student may also recognize a feature of one sound yet write its corresponding grapheme in terms of another with a similar feature.

Phonetic guesswork.

a. GRINGO	trinco 2
b. AÑO	allo 3
	anllo 4
c. PRESENCIA	preciaca 1

d. AGENTE	ajuerte	1
e. PEQUEÑO	pecenllo	1
f. EXPLICADO	exbecado	1
g. DESAYUNAR	desallnar	2
h. MEJOR	mehoy	1
i. OJALÁ	uchala	1
j. CALIFICACIONES	caniricanes	1
	califactiere	1

A lack of understanding of either phonetic and graphemic system leads to errors for which there are no apparent categorizations. There are documented cases in the data where a student's misunderstanding or inability to spell correctly results from a lack of familiarity with an orthographic system, compounded by the fact that the student's aural ability is not at all matched by his or her writing or spelling ability.

Lack of understanding of the graphemic system.
a. Fuimos a los cayos a pescar.
   F mos as cajo a pezca.
   Fimos a lo callos a pecar.
   Fuymos a los callos a petar.
b. La casa blanca está en la loma.
       blanra   roja
c. Los niños juegan con los gatos y los perros.
       jugegan
       guelgan
       gedan

Before concluding, I would like to share with you the most enjoyable of the free compositions, not because it contains any errors but because its theme gives one pause while conducting research. It comes from one of the students in the Bogotá, Colombia, control group.

> Los norteamericanos son faltos de imaginacion porque debé primero mirar su idioma corregirlo y despues cuando lo tenga bien adaptado mirar los de los demás y criticarlos.
> Pero no obstante sabén hacer las cosas y por esto se aprovechan de los paises subdesarrollados como el nuestro y hasta lográn apoderace de paises como Cuba pero luego se tienen que retirar cuando se les muestra que uno también pueden.

SUMMARY

To summarize: What I have undertaken is to study the problems in the spelling habits of Spanish-English bilinguals, to analyze them, and to see what strategies are used in spelling. Doubtless, more needs to be done with these data and with more data to be collected from other bilingual areas in the United States. At the same time, similar research needs to be done in English as a second language. The goal of such research necessarily will have to be a program of teaching and remediation of the spelling rules of Spanish and English.

REFERENCE

Staczek, John J., and Aid, Frances. "Hortographia Himortal: Spelling Problems Among Bilingual Students." In *Teaching Spanish to the Hispanic Bilingual: Issues, Aims, and Methods*, ed. Guadalupe Valdés, Anthony G. Lozano, and Rodolfo García-Moya. New York: Teachers College Press, 1981.

APPENDIX: ORTHOGRAPHIC RESEARCH

Palabras para el dictado

1. hay	1. cuñado
2. muy	2. melancolía
3. estoy	3. que
4. hoy	4. cuando
5. mis	5. biblioteca
6. iban	6. porque
7. visitan	7. cebolla
8. reciban	8. desayunar
9. sigue	9. reír
10. cebolla	10. pasear
11. expresar	11. hermano
12. estricto	12. algunas
13. relación	13. hacer
14. hicimos	14. entonces
15. calificaciones	15. plástico
16. me siento	16. estrella
17. días	17. maltratan
18. agente	18. acerca
19. jarro	19. haber
20. queso	20. poesía
1. mucho	1. dijo
2. creo	2. mejor
3. gatos	3. caballo
4. castigar	4. cebolla

5. pequeño
6. todavía
7. poner
8. pulga
9. trato
10. gringo
11. pluma
12. tratar
13. dolor
14. feliz
15. atención
16. presencia
17. responder
18. podrán
19. tanto
20. siempre

1. de mis notas
2. estudio mis lecciones
3. se podrán
4. ha explicado
5. debo
6. calificaciones
7. de haber estudiado
8. hicimos
9. me siento
10. contento
11. siempre
12. tanto
13. explicado
14. biblioteca
15. a las preguntas
16. acerca
17. peña
18. pirata
19. bonita
20. frío
21. había
22. queso
23. entendí
24. perdón
25. fue

5. elefante
6. teléfono
7. cuando
8. démelo
9. nada
10. después
11. pero
12. hicieron
13. amistad
14. béisbol
15. vocecita
16. motocicleta
17. reciban
18. calificaciones
19. examen
20. hoy

1. quiero
2. irás
3. queso
4. y gatos
5. año
6. amistad
7. cuando
8. vine
9. reciban
10. de mis notas
11. que
12. buque
13. trucha
14. hecho
15. encontró
16. caballo
17. pájaro
18. inteligente
19. fueron
20. catarro
21. azúcar
22. posesión
23. después
24. más tarde
25. ojala

Frases para el dictado

1. Me gusta mucho estudiar.
2. Fuimos a los cayos a pescar.
3. La casa blanca está en la loma.
4. Los niños juegan con los perros y los gatos.
5. ¿Cuándo irás a la biblioteca?
6. Estoy pensando en lo que digan mis padres cuando reciban mis notas.

Párrafos[1]

La maestra leerá en voz alta el párrafo siguiente. Luego, los muchachos se lo recontarán en forma escrita.

I.   Los primeros viajes de exploración que hizo Francisco Pizarro con su socio Diego de Almagro fuéron un verdadero fracaso. Exploraron la costa de Tierra Firme, nombre que la daban entonces al continente sudamericano, y llegaron hasta la costa del Ecuador. Sin embargo, en vez del fabuloso país que esperaban descubrir, los dos viejos capitanes y sus hombres encontraron un "infierno verde" de impenetrable vegetación tropical. Estaba lleno de animales feroces y de insectos venenosos que producían fiebre y enfermedades mortales. Los pocos grupos de indios que vivían en la costa colombiana eran pobres y no tenían una civilización avanzada.

II.   El tigre es un animal muy común en Norte América y también en Sud América. Este animal se llama en inglés *cougar*. Hay gente que lo llama *puma* en inglés y en español. También tiene otro nombre en español: *jaguar*. La palabra "tigre" es muy común en los países latinoamericános. En España esta palabra se refiere al famoso tigre de India, un animal bastante diferente al tigre de las Américas.

El tigre vive en Canadá, en Argentina, y en muchos otros países de las Américas. Este animal corre muy rápido y sube montañas fácilmente. Entra en los corrales, pero no en las casas. No es un animal doméstico. Vive en el campo y en las montañas. No vive en la ciudad. En muchas ciudades hay parque o jardines especiales que se llaman zoológicos. En los parques zoológicos hay muchos animales. Hay muchos tigres que viven en los zoológicos.

---

[1]William Bull, Enrique Lamadrid, and Laurel Briscoe, *Communicating in Spanish, Teacher's Manual* (Boston: Houghton Mifflin, 1974.)

Language Diversity in Chicano Speech Communities: Implications for Language Teaching

LUCÍA ELÍAS-OLIVARES   GUADALUPE VALDÉS
University of Illinois, at Chicago Circle   *New Mexico State University*

This paper focuses on language diversity in Chicano speech communities[1] in the United States and its relation to the teaching of Spanish to Chicano bilinguals. As a result of an increasing interest in the teaching of Spanish to Spanish-speakers in the United States, attempts have been made to improve the teaching of that language to speakers who already speak varieties which differ from standard Spanish. These efforts have been for the most part unsuccessful because the schools recognize only a single standard of "correctness," which is not always the same as that used in these communities. This paper reviews these attempts and addresses the need to establish guidelines for the evaluation of current positions and programs in the teaching of Spanish as a mother tongue to Chicano students.

Linguistic characteristics of speech communities are usually viewed as separate entities rather than the result of factors within the societal context. We believe that the following review of the sociopolitical, socioeconomic, and educational experience of Chicanos is appropriate because it has contributed to the development of the present sociolinguistic situation: a language repertoire with various codes which depart from the Mexican-Spanish linguistic tradition, an asymmetrical type of bilingualism, and a use of Spanish that is viewed as transitional and not valued in the broader society.

Presented at the 9th World Congress of Sociology, Sociolinguistics Program, Uppsala, Sweden, August 14–19, 1978.

SOCIOPOLITICAL CONTEXT

The Chicanos constitute the largest linguistic minority in the United States, with a population estimated at 10 to 12 million, 87 percent of them residing in the five Southwestern states. Unlike most ethnic groups of European extraction, which have been accepted as equal in mainstream America, the Chicanos have had a history of racial, economic, and linguistic discrimination since the days of the conquest of the Southwest, a pattern similar to that experienced by the black population.[2]

With regard to educational achievement, the findings of several studies—particularly those conducted in 1974 and 1975 by the U.S. Commission on Civil Rights (USCCR)—reflect the systematic process of discrimination and exclusion suffered by the majority of Chicanos in education. Schools have generally not succeeded in narrowing the serious gap between advantaged and disadvantaged students; on the contrary, "the longer language minority students stay in school, the further they fall behind their classmates in grade level achievement" (USCCR, 1975:19).[3] Educational institutions have always been committed to the maintenance of racial and ethnic barriers, and to the status quo in general, with the implicit collaboration of professional organizations of educators who have chosen to ignore those socioeconomic, racial, and ethnic issues which have not usually been included in standard histories of education in this country.[4] Thus, Chicanos have been low achievers in the public schools, particularly in the Southwest, where the language policies of the schools were dictated by an English-speaking landholding class whose aim was not to enhance the opportunities of the Spanish-speaking people but to have access to an illiterate, unskilled, and cheap labor force. The majority of Chicanos live today in urban areas but are still absent from all important decision-making levels.[5] The role of the school as a "melting pot" and social class equalizer has been a myth in this country as far as Chicanos are concerned. Schools have not been able to educate the poor and/or culturally different child because they are middle-class institutions whose aim is to teach the mainstream society values, a common language, work habits, and the political faith of the dominant culture. Unable or not willing to cope with the particular characteristics of Chicanos, the schools simply labeled them as "disadvantaged," "culturally deficient," and "linguistically deprived," failing to realize that they came to school with a rich potential to be fully bilingual, bicultural individuals, an asset in almost every country in the world but a liability in an assimilationist and ethnocentric society.

Even though research studies that show no negative effects of bilingualism on school learning have long been available to this country (Andersson and Boyer, 1970), all instruction in schools for the Spanish-speaking child was to take place in English. Only in the last decade, and to a large extent as a result of demands made by the Spanish-speaking communities, have the U.S. Congress and the Courts mandated that school districts with a large Spanish-speaking constituency offer bilingual education. Unfortunately, the great majority of these programs are compensatory and assimilationist (Kjolseth, 1973; Gaarder, 1978). Their goal is not to foster cultural and linguistic pluralism but simply to ease the transition of the Chicano from Spanish monolingualism or incipient bilingualism to English monolingualism. They are in reality English as a Second Language programs, "a way to hold closed the floodgates of discontent and to more efficiently transform the child to the desired world" (Hernández-Chávez, 1977, p. 51). Furthermore, the assumption that any compensatory or remedial program—including present bilingual education programs—produces higher academic levels of achievement has yet to be demonstrated (Cordasco, 1974).

The educational system and the public at large have always supported the theory that blames failure on the child's cultural and linguistic distinctiveness, avoiding in this way the need to confront the economic and political issues related to the situation. In reality, linguistic problems present in a society are often the reflection of less obvious economic conflicts between groups of people in contact, such as the case of Anglos and Chicanos, and linguistic differences serve as an excuse for maintaining economic and social inequalities. In fact, one could say that the economic and political domination experienced by Chicanos has contributed greatly to their linguistic isolation and to the present sociolinguistic reality of these communities, which is slowly emerging from the studies currently being undertaken. As Sánchez (1978, p. 186) points out, the process of urbanization which produces contact between groups has not influenced the situation either, because the two groups continue to be kept apart because of the way American society is stratified. This situation has helped to produce an asymmetrical type of bilingualism in which Spanish, one of the great world languages of wider communication, has a very low prestige as a language of the people, although, ironically, it is the most widely studied language in the high schools and colleges of this country (Gaarder, 1978). Lack of respect for the language of the inferior dominated group, as well as lack of uses for Spanish outside intimate domains, has contributed to the creation of the present trend of shift from Spanish monolingualism to functional English bilingualism or English monolingualism, as has been mentioned in several studies (Solé, 1977; Sánchez, 1978; Aguirre, 1978); such a process could be completed within two to three generations after migration. Nevertheless, there are several factors, such as the constant incorporation of newly arriving Mexican workers into the *barrios,* that reinforce Spanish language loyalty in these communities.

The sociolinguistic reality of Chicanos in this country, and particularly in the Southwest, should not be viewed simply as a static phenomenon but as a dynamic reflection of the societal framework in which these linguistic events take place, a framework often neglected in the polemics around linguistic issues, bilingualism, and bilingual education.

THE SOCIOLINGUISTIC SITUATION

Regardless of the fact that Chicanos constitute the most important linguistic minority in America, little is known at present about their language varieties, their patterns of language use and language loyalty, and their attitudes toward English and Spanish. Research on bilinguals in this country in the 1960's was heavily influenced by the works of linguists who dealt primarily with the concept of interference, the various ways in which two "pure" codes influence each other in phonology, syntax, and lexicon. The term "interference" has been an umbrella term covering different aspects of bilingualism, addressing partially the cause of the phenomena rather than describing it. This trend has influenced research on Chicano Spanish, which tends to be looked at not as a self-contained system but as a deviation from standard Spanish, with special emphasis on long lists of borrowings and loan translations from English. And although heterogeneity is the rule in bilingual communities as much as it is in monolingual settings, variation in style is ignored, as if to say that Chicanos were single-style speakers.

Another criticism that has been voiced by some scholars is that research has not involved the nonacademic community. We need to find out how the community perceives its linguistic situation, what types of linguistic issues they identify with, and so on. The issue of which variety should be used in school, for example, could certainly benefit from community participation. As Fishman has said, "languages live in communities and if they 'belong' to anyone, they belong to their speech communities" (1977, p. 321).

More recent studies on bilingualism in Chicano communities have argued that previous studies based on the interference model have tried to account for an ideal bilingual who controls his or her choice of language rigidly, alternating between the two only when there is a change in topic or in the participants in the speech event. This ideal type of bilingualism, however, is seldom found in bilingual and multilingual communities, where many speakers have not been exposed to formal instruction in the two languages, or even in one of them. Susan Ervin-Tripp has pointd out that where bilinguals have for a long time interacted mainly with other bilinguals, "the model for each of these languages is not monolingual usage of these languages but rather the languages spoken by the bilinguals themselves" (1967, p. 78). Departing from the limiting view of those who have considered speech communities as homogeneous with no room for variation or language interplay, new investigators have approached the study of bilingual speech from a more functional perspective which has been particularly influenced by ideas put forward by Hymes (1964), Gumperz (1964), and Labov (1966).

A Chicano speech community repertoire can be described as a sociolinguistic continuum in which the distance between the two extremes is bridged by intermediate varieties, some of them interlingual, with various degrees of borrowing and code switching (see Figure 1). If one looks at this continuum, one sees very clearly that instead of being internally homogeneous systems, each of the languages used for daily interaction in the community is composed of varieties which in turn show varying degrees of similarity to each other.[6]

Mixed Spanish and code switching are particularly interesting because they can also be discussed in terms of a continuum, with code switching at one end of the spectrum and integration (borrowings, loan translations) at the other.

There are no "pure" mixed-Spanish speakers just as there are no "pure" code-switching speakers. Each speaker in the community has either productive or receptive competence of a span of this continuum. Movement along this continuum is governed by factors such as social domain, geographical origin, extent of usage of the two languages at home, and pressure to acquire the formal variety, but above all by intergenerational variables.

The breakdown between formal Spanish and popular Spanish, Caló, and code switching is fairly clear. Mixed Spanish, however, is assigned separate status because some speakers, particularly those who are

Figure 1

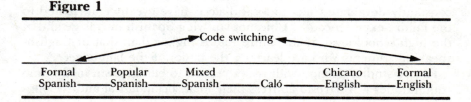

first-generation English speakers or those who have had greater exposure to formal Spanish, avoid using it and condemn its use.[7]

There have been a few authors who have addressed the possibility of
certain varieties of Chicano speech being a pidgin or a creole. However,
pidgins and creoles can be explained only by reference to other
languages, and they are often mutually unintelligible to each other and
to the standard variety. The varieties in question are mutually intelligible
since any bilingual speaker could easily understand exchanges in these
varieties if sufficient context is provided. One could acknowledge that
processes of pidginization such as reduction and simplification are
indeed present in mixed Spanish, but we are not in the presence of a
drastic restructuring of Spanish grammar, and furthermore, mixed
Spanish shares a large number of linguistic features with formal
Spanish. The morphosyntactic organization is predominantly Spanish,
and cases of syntactical influence from English are generally more
common in formal domains. There is also an important factor that will
always hinder the development of a pidgin, and that is the constant
exposure to more formal varieties of Spanish, especially because of
contact with Mexican nationals and new immigrants.

Nevertheless, negative attitudes toward these varieties are similar to
those held by laypeople with regard to pidgins and creoles, due perhaps
to a failure to distinguish between attitudes toward language varieties
and attitudes toward speakers of those varieties. Hymes has stated that
pidgins and creoles "have been explained not by historical and social
forces, but by inherent ignorance, insolence and inferiority" (1971, p. 3).
In effect, mixed Spanish, codeswitching, and Caló are varieties which
have come to be evaluated primarily in terms of the low status of their
speakers.[8] Especially within Spanish language teaching circles, as a result
of narrow and unrealistic standards of linguistic purity and prescriptive-
ness, these interlingual varieties are perceived as "corrupt" Spanish and,
further, as a rejection of the mother tongue. The Chicanos themselves
have been convinced that all they speak is "Tex Mex" or "Spanglish,"
some kind of Spanish that nobody understands. Many speakers speak
some kind of formal standard Spanish but, having had no formal
education through Spanish and thus lacking the criteria for defending
the quality of their speech, they depreciate it. Language policies which
constantly devaluate Chicano local dialects have greatly contributed to
the failure experienced by Chicanos studying Spanish in college and at
the high school level; their failure rate is higher than that of English-
speaking students who are learning the basics of the language.

Future studies dealing with issues related to bilingualism in Chicano
communities will have to address their total sociopolitical and sociolin-

guistic situation. It is not possible to explain the sociolinguistic behavior of the speakers in question by working only within the framework of the standard varieties of the two languages spoken in these communities.

THE TEACHING OF THE SPANISH LANGUAGE TO CHICANO BILINGUALS

Given the sociolinguistic context described above, it is not surprising to find that the Spanish-speaking profession in this country has paid very little attention to the language spoken natively by Chicano bilinguals. For the most part, this profession has concerned itself with the teaching of Spanish as a subject, primarily at the junior high school, high school, and college levels. In keeping with the national preference for elite or academic bilingualism, such instruction has been directed exclusively at monolingual English speakers, who consider the study of a foreign language to be a part of the normal academic curriculum. Within this perspective, it is generally assumed that such monolingual learners will derive a number of important benefits from the study of a foreign language (for example, appreciation of other cultures, understanding of the structure of language in general, the exercise of important intellectual faculties, etc.), if not actually attain communicative competence in the target language.

The Chicano bilingual does not fit comfortably into this established system, and the Spanish-teaching profession—logically, in the light of this general orientation toward its role and purpose—has largely ignored the existence of the large number of native Spanish speakers in the United States. The reasons for this exclusion are, however, complex. On the one hand, members of the profession have been sincere in their confusion concerning how instruction designed to produce basic fluency can in any way profit fluent speakers. On the other hand, it is also clear that other less neutral factors have been of some importance. To begin with, a significant number of Spanish-teaching professionals, particularly those who teach at the junior high school and high school levels, are nonnative speakers of the Spanish language. With some frequency, these persons have taken the required courses for certification but have not achieved the degree of fluency and comfort characteristic of those who have spent a period of time in a Spanish-speaking country or who frequently interact with the members of a Spanish-speaking community. When confronted with native fluent speakers of the language, their response ranges from a fundamental fear of not being able to understand what these natives say, to uneasiness concerning their own fluency, to a compensating disdain for what they take to be an "inferior" form of the Spanish language. Normally, teacher training at the secondary level, and indeed at the college level, does not include training in basic sociolinguistics. Thus, most teachers are unaware of the artificiality of their own classroom register and of that register in which they were trained. Therefore, they often respond to perfectly standard informal speech with suspicion and in many cases label a student's speech defective because the student does not respond in complete sentences.

The disdain for students' home language is not exclusive to nonnative Spanish-speaking teachers of the language, however. Similar prejudices concerning the language of Chicano bilinguals have been expressed by numerous native-speaking professionals from different regions of the Spanish-speaking world. Indeed it was this particular position, the commitment to "undoing the damage that has been done at home," that first resulted in the profession's undertaking of the instruction of Chicano speakers.

Essentially, in its early stages such instruction took place within the foreign language classroom. The approach was one providing remediation by having the student "learn the language from the beginning." In an era deeply influenced by the behaviorist tradition of language learning, it was not considered impossible for a student to "unlearn" one set of habits and to acquire another.

Much has happened within the Spanish-teaching profession within the last several years. Perhaps in line with the interest in minority languages, in ethnicity, and in bilingualism—or perhaps simply as a result of increased enrollment of Chicanos at the university and college levels—Spanish-teaching professionals have begun to examine the entire question of appropriate instruction for native Spanish-speaking students.

Progress includes the fact that at this point it is almost universally accepted that instruction directed at the fluent or almost fluent bilingual cannot take place in the environment of the traditional foreign language classroom with nonspeakers.

In many cases this conclusion was reached after it was seen that the desired expiration of "errors" did not result from "learning the language from the beginning" along with nonspeakers. In such cases, the purpose of the move toward the separation of the two groups was to provide more time and attention to the correction of the many stigmatized features which were considered to be characteristic of *all* Chicano speakers.

In other cases, the desire for separate classes was motivated by the realization that teaching a language as a native language and teaching it as a second or foreign language are two very different processes with little in common with regard to approaches, methods, and techniques.

Essentially, at the moment, professionals concerned with teaching Spanish to Chicano bilinguals have for the most part embraced one of the following philosophies:

1. That the exclusive role of the Spanish language class is to instruct Chicano students in the use of the spoken standard dialect (Barker, 1972; Baker, 1966; De León, 1976).
2. That the role of formal language instruction in Spanish for Chicano students is to provide a comprehensive language development program which focuses on Spanish language literacy as a primary goal and the development of increased oral proficiency, awareness of the norms of the standard dialect, etc. as secondary goals (Sánchez, 1976; Valdés-Fallis, 1976a, 1976b, 1977, 1978).

THE TEACHING OF THE STANDARD DIALECT AS A PRINCIPAL GOAL

Members of the profession concerned primarily with teaching the spoken standard dialect are very similar in orientation to groups within the English-teaching profession who have reacted negatively to the speech of black Americans. They see their primary role as one of remodeling the students' oral language. From this perspective, the ideal end of such Spanish language instruction would be that Chicano students would be able to function undetected among educated Latin Americans.

There is no real agreement on how such a dramatic change will be achieved. One faction, equivalent to those whom Fasold and Shuy (1970) have labeled "eradicators," insists on the abandonment of the language variety students bring with them and requires its substitution with the prestige or standard variety. The other faction, the "biloquialists," claim that the same results can be achieved by providing students with a comparison between varieties and instruction on language appropriateness so that they may be able to choose intelligently the variety they wish to employ.

In general, professionals committed to this type of instruction advocate exposing students to long lists of stigmatized features variously designated *anglicismos, barbarismos, arcaísmos,* etc. (which are thought to be present in the speech of all Chicanos) so that they may remember to replace the "correct" item in their normal speech. Classroom activities include pattern drills, repetition drills, translation, and especially a prescriptively oriented grammatical approach centering on "Chicano errors." As a whole this group of Spanish-teaching professionals seems to be unaware that there is little evidence in the research on second-dialect teaching which suggests that instruction along these lines is effective. Moreover, many of these professionals have not yet understood that their prescriptive approach toward grammar and its concomitant devaluation of the students' language result in negative responses toward the study of Spanish and in very little interest in maintaining it as a resource of some value.

While lip service is given to the question of language diversity, there is no understanding of how it exists in a real-life setting. There is no awareness, for example, of how speech styles alternate in monolingual Spanish-speaking communities and no conception of the fact that both standard and nonstandard varieties are always present in bilingual as well as in monolingual communities. Bilingualism is seen, not as an asset, but as a handicap, and there is little interest in the way two languages function in a bilingual's everyday life. Chicanos are simply considered to be a homogeneous group characterized by the same language "problems," many of them due directly to the influence of English. Little effort is made, therefore, to consider existing studies of Chicano communities. Indeed, it is ironic that members of the profession committed to this first aim, dedicated as they are to changing students' speech, have not developed an approach based on an accurate view of the language of the students with whom they work, an approach which might contribute significantly to the success of now largely unsuccessful efforts.

THE COMPREHENSIVE APPROACH TO THE TEACHING OF SPANISH TO CHICANO BILINGUALS

Unlike the group described above, the members of the Spanish teaching profession who advocate basic literacy as a primary goal have very little in common with the exception of their opposition to the teaching of the standard dialect as a principal aim. They represent a number of views concerning the objectives of instruction for native Spanish-speakers and range in orientation from very strict prescriptivism to the most advanced acceptance of language diversity.

There are those who, disenchanted with the poor effects of instruction which strives to extirpate "errors" by the methods described above, hope to achieve the same ends by concentrating on writing and composition skills. They are optimistic that such an approach will be less objectionable to those who are concerned with students' self-image because comparisons relating to correctness and incorrectness can be made under the guise of teaching the written standard. There are others, on the other hand, who champion this same approach because they believe that in our society the reading and writing of one's language is a basic and fundamental right. They point out that if one does not question the teaching of reading and writing to speakers of English, who in the course of their lifetime may make little use of these abilities, one cannot question the parallel objective for bilingual Chicano speakers in their first language. Still others, however, advocate a teaching commitment which goes beyond instruction in basic literacy and which aims to bring forth the implementation of comprehensive language development programs. Such programs, unlike those designed for the teaching of reading and writing skills, would seek to develop the Spanish proficiency of Chicano bilinguals so that they might approximate the levels of achievement developed in English as a result of their educational experiences in this language. Objectives for instruction, therefore, would include: the development of basic spelling skills, basic reading skills, and basic composition skills; the introduction of traditional grammar; the development and growth of vocabulary; the exposure to a variety of experiences in the spoken language, and the like.

At this time much thought and energy are being devoted to the development of methodologies appropriate to the objectives described above. Considerable work has already been done in the area of teaching orthography, especially with regard to instruction in grapheme/phoneme equivalences, in a situation which exhibits much transfer from English-language orthographical conventions. Recently, increasing attention has been given to the elaboration of materials designed to teach reading effectively. It has become clear that native speakers cannot be expected to begin reading immediately in a language in which their experience has been exclusively oral. It is agreed, therefore, that development of reading skills must be approached in sequential steps which maximize the learner's familiarity with reading in the other language. Significant questions have also begun to be raised concerning the role of grammar as a tool in the teaching of reading and writing as well as its place as a bona fide subject worthy of study for its own sake in a total language development program. Classroom materials are now being written which focus on the structure of the language as an area about which every educated student must know something, rather than as a set of prohibitions and prescriptions. Additionally, attention has focused on the teaching of both oral and written expression. It has been pointed out that in order to provide opportunities for the development of real-language skills, students must be exposed to a variety of language situations in which different styles and levels of speech are used. A classroom context must be provided which, at the very least, encourages the discussion of a number of subjects which have previously been handled by the students in their second language. At the same time, instruction in written expression must make clear that writing goes beyond mere mechanics to the clear expression of ideas.

Significant as these developments are, the total picture which emerges at the moment is one of frustration. Professionals trained in the teaching of a second language are suddenly beginning to perceive that they need to function in areas in which they are not prepared. Most know little about teaching orthography, teaching accentuation, teaching techniques of clarity in writing, and less than nothing about the teaching of reading. They are comfortable with teaching traditional grammar and seriously wonder if it can be taught nonprescriptively. More important, however, they are beginning to become conscious of the importance of language diversity and of its implications for the teaching which they hope to undertake. Increasingly they are becoming conscious of the fact that techniques which are used in the classroom need to be based on information concerning how language *actually* works in a real-life setting.

Questions such as the following have become common:

1. What is a native speaker?
2. Which different kinds of bilinguals have enough proficiency in Spanish to participate in courses for native speakers?
3. What is *enough* proficiency?
4. Does fluency in Spanish correlate with success in attaining reading and writing skills?
5. How does one measure proficiency, fluency, or both?
6. What kinds of placement instruments are appropriate for a bilingual with no reading language skills in Spanish?
7. What are the functions of Spanish in the community?
8. Is language maintenance a legitimate goal, given the language attitudes of the community toward Spanish?
9. What is the attitude of the community toward the value of reading and writing in Spanish?
10. What are the attitudes of the community to various styles or levels of Spanish? To other regional varieties? To their own speech?
11. How can the language situation existing in a community be exploited in order to bring about expansion of total proficiency?
12. What resources in the community—traditions in joke telling, story telling, verbal dueling, and the like—can be incorporated into the curriculum?
13. What is the difference in the effectiveness of instruction using materials that speak to the experience of the working class or

migrant Chicano compared with instruction using materials written for Latin America or Spain, or simply translated from English originals?

THE STUDY OF LANGUAGE DIVERSITY AND THE FUTURE OF LANGUAGE TEACHING

Clearly the answers to the above questions will not be arrived at by Spanish-teaching professionals working alone. Progress will come as there begins to be, or continues to be, collaboration between sociolinguists and language instructors. Major advances will come as ongoing research on Chicano communities is translated into materials and methodologies. Change will come as institutions of higher education incorporate instruction in sociolinguistics into teacher-training programs. Most important, however, significant change will take place if a large enough number of professionals see themselves not as Spanish language teachers or sociolinguists, but rather as language planners and as social engineers. The entire concept of teaching Spanish to minority speakers in this country cannot be seen as a simple or neutral issue. Spanish language instruction for Chicano bilinguals is not equivalent to instruction in a number of other ordinary academic subjects. Rather, instruction in a first language for these speakers involves either continued attack on their self-worth through a devaluation of their home varieties of Spanish, or an opportunity to take pleasure in the development of an existing and valuable resource.

NOTES

1. Spanish-speaking people of Mexican descent living in the United States call themselves Mexicans, Mexican-Americans, Hispanos, Latinos, or Chicanos, depending upon the region in which they have settled, their socioeconomic experiences, their political beliefs, etc. The term "Chicano" was used in the past to designate only lower-class Mexicans, but since the emergence of the Chicano nationalistic movement it has been used as a symbol of the struggle for socioeconomic and linguistic equality, especially with regard to this group's right to maintain and develop their original first language.

2. According to the Census Bureau (1975), the median income for Chicanos in 1975 was $9,546 compared with $13,719 for Anglos, with 79 percent of the Chicanos holding low-wage positions.

3. All studies show that Chicanos are consistently below the other students in *all* academic studies. The 1966 Coleman Report showed that Chicanos fall significantly behind white students in academic achievement. By the twelfth grade, Chicanos are 4.1 years behind the national norm in math achievement, 3.5 in verbal ability, and 3.3 in reading. In Texas, the average Anglo over 25

years old has 12 years of schooling, the average black nearly 9, and the average Chicano 6.7. A study done in 1976 and released by the National Center for Educational Statistics showed that Spanish-speaking students enrolled in grades 5–12 were about twice as likely to be two or more grades below the grade levels expected for their ages (*Forum*, vol. 1, no. 8, October 1978). Similar findings were reported by the Educational Commission of the States in 1977 (National Assessment of Educational Progress Newsletter, Volume X, June 1977).

4. For a more comprehensive and detailed analysis of the treatment of minorities in public schools, as well as a theoretical explanation of the low achievement of Chicanos in public schools, see, among others, Weinberg, 1977, and Cárdenas–Cárdenas, 1973.

5. Chicanos are poorly represented in positions which control or influence educational outcomes. They are considerably underrepresented in the faculties of teacher education programs, on the professional staff of State Departments of Education, and as principals and school board members (USCCR, 1974:73). In spite of the high concentration of Chicanos in the Southwest, the USCCR found that in Southwestern schools they constituted only 10.4 percent of superintendents, 5.4 percent of counselors, 4 percent of teachers, 3.6 percent of librarians, and 7.06 percent of principals (USCCR, 1971:41, 45, 48, 53).

6. The categorization of the Spanish varieties given here is based on a study done in a working-class Chicano neighborhood in Austin, Texas (Elías-Olivares, 1976). It could certainly vary for other bilingual settings.

7. One may argue that the speech varieties shown in the diagram are a continuous range of linguistic variables (Labov, 1966) and not discrete varieties. These varieties are categorical from an ethnographic point of view in that they are named and perceived as distinct by Chicano speakers. However, they could also be treated as linguistic variables; that is, there are also statistically measurable tendencies holding between the varieties. A considerable number of these variables, such as / s / pronunciation, can and should be studied as such. In fact, it is crucial for our understanding of bilingual communities to realize that speakers perceive and conceive of the linguistic situation in discrete, categorical terms even though behaving in variable terms.

8. Research concerning attitudes toward varieties of Spanish is scarce. Teachers in El Paso, Texas, classify all Spanish spoken by Chicanos as "border slang" or "Tex Mex" (Ornstein and Goodman, 1974). In Austin, Texas, older speakers express felings of linguistic insecurity and inferiority regarding the Spanish they use, whereas younger Chicanos look at their ways of speaking as an expression of ethnic pride. Speakers also code-switch in order to demonstrate their bilingualism and their lack of assimilation into the dominant society (Gumperz and Hernández-Chávez, 1972; Elías-Olivares, 1976). In a study done in Edinburg, Texas, it was found that students from Mexico and South America deprecate most varieties of Southwest Spanish. In additon, it was shown that the evaluative dimension and the solidarity dimension do not necessarily run exactly parallel, and that hearers categorize others on the basis of the sound of language varieties heard frequently but not necessarily understood (Amastae and Elías-Olivares, 1978). For a more comprehensive review of the literature, see Ornstein (1978).

REFERENCES

Aguirre, Adalberto. "The Review as Social Commentary." *Language in Society* 6 (1978), 391–433.

Amastae, Jon, and Elías-Olivares, L., "Attitudes Toward Varieties of Spanish." In *The Fourth LACUS Forum 1977*, ed. M. Paradis. Columbia, S.C.: Hornbeam Press, (1978), pp. 286–302.

Andersson, Theodore, and Boyer, M. *Bilingual Schooling in the U.S.* Austin, Tex.: Southwest Educational Development Laboratory, 1970.

Baker, Pauline. *Español para los hispanos.* Skokie, Ill.: National Textbook Company, 1966.

Barker, Marie Eastman. *Español para el bilingue.* Skokie, Ill.: National Textbook Company, 1972.

Cárdinas, Blandina, and Cárdenas, José A., "Chicano—Bright-eyed, Biningual, Brown, and Beautiful." *Today's Education*, NEA Journal, 62:2 (1973), 49–51.

Census Bureau 1976. Persons of Spanish Origin in the U.S. Current Population Reports. Series P-20:302.

Coleman, James, et al. *Equality of Educational Opportunity.* Office of Education, H.E.W. Washington, D.C.: Government Printing Office, 1966.

Cordasco, Francesco, ed. *Toward Equal Educational Opportunity.* New York: AMS Press, 1974.

De León, Fidel. *El español del suroeste y el español standard.* Manchaca, Tex.: Sterling Swift Publishing Company,1976.

Elías-Olivares, Lucía. "Ways of Speaking in a Chicano Speech Community: A Sociolinguistic Approach." Dissertation, University of Texas, 1976.

Ervin-Tripp, Susan. "An Issei Learns English." *Journal of Social Issues*, 23:2, (1967), 78–90.

Fasold, Ralph W., and Shuy, Roger W. *Teaching Standard English in the Inner City.* Washington, D.C.: Center for Applied Linguistics, 1970.

Fishman, Joshua. "Standard Versus Dialect in Bilingual Education: An Old Problem in a New Context." *The Modern Language Journal*, 7 (1977), 315–325.

Gaarder, Bruce. *Bilingual Schooling and the Survival of Spanish in the United States.* Rowley, Mass.: Newbury House, 1978.

Gumperz, John. "Linguistic and Social Interaction in Two Communities." In J. J. Gumperz and D. Hymes (eds.). *The Ethnography of Communication.* Special publication of *American Anthropologist*, 66.6. pt. 2 (1964), 137–153.

————, and Hernández-Chávez, E. "Bilingualism, Bidialectalism and Classroom Interaction." In *Functions of Language in the Classroom*, ed. C. Cazden, V. John, and D. Hymes. New York: Teachers College Press, 1972.

Hernández-Chávez, Eduardo. "Meaningful Bilingual Bicultural Education: A Fairytale." NABE, *The Journal of the National Association for Bilingual Education*, 1., no. 3. (1977), 49–54.

Hymes, Dell. Introduction. "Toward Ethnographies of Communication." In J. Gumperz and D. Hymes (eds.). *The Ethnography of Communication.* Special publication of *American Anthropologist*, 66.6 pt. 2 (1964), 1–34.

————. Preface to *Pidginization and Creolization of Languages*, ed. D. Hymes. London: Cambridge University Press, 1971.

Kjolseth, Rolf. "Bilingual Education Programs in the United States: For Assimilation or Pluralism?" In *Bilingualism in the Southwest*, ed. P. Turner. Tucson: University of Arizona Press, 1973.

Labov, William. *The Social Stratification of English in New York City*. Washington, D.C.: Center for Applied Linguistics, 1966.

Ornstein, Jacob. "Research on Attitudes Toward Chicano (Southwest) Spanish in the United States." Paper presented at the 9th World Congress of Sociology, Uppsala, Sweden, 1978.

Ornstein, J., and Goodman, P. "Bilingualism/Biculturalism Viewed in the Light of Socioeducational Correlates." Paper presented at the 8th World Congress of Sociology, Toronto, 1974.

Peñalosa, Fernando. "Some Issues in Chicano Sociolinguistics." In *Swallow VI: The Bilingual in a Pluralistic Society*, ed. H. H. Key et al. Long Beach, Calif.: California State University, 1978, pp. 150–57.

Sánchez, Rosaura. "Spanish for Native-Speakers at the University: Sugerencias." In *Teaching Spanish to the Spanish Speaking: Theory and Practice*, ed. G. Valdés-Fallis and R. García Moya. San Antonio, Tex.: Trinity University, 1976.

————. "Bilingualism in the Southwest." *In Swallow VI*, ed. H. H. Key et al., 1978, pp. 181–88.

Solé, Yolanda. "Language Attitudes Toward Spanish Among Mexican-American College Students." *Journal of LASSO*, 2.2 (1977), 37–46.

United States Commission on Civil Rights. *Ethnic Isolation of Mexican-Americans in the Public Schools of the Southwest*. Washington, D.C.: Government Printing Office, 1971.

United States Commission on Civil Rights. *Toward Quality Education for Mexican-Americans*. Washington, D.C.: Government Printing Office, 1974.

United States Commission on Civil Rights. *A Better Chance to Learn: Bilingual Bicultural Education*. Washington, D.C.: Government Printing Office, 1975.

Valdés-Fallis, Guadalupe. "Pedagogical Implications of Teaching Spanish to the Spanish Speaking in the United States." In *Teaching Spanish to the Spanish Speaking: Theory and Practice*, ed. G. Valdés-Fallis and R. García Moya. San Antonio, Tex.: Trinity University, 1976a.

————. "Language Development Versus the Teaching of the Standard Language." *Lektos* (December 1976b), pp. 20–32.

————. "Spanish Language Programs for Hispanic Minorities: Current Needs and Priorities." In *Minority Language and Literature*, ed. D. Fisher. New York: Modern Language Association, 1977, pp. 86–98.

————. "A Comprehensive Approach to the Teaching of Spanish to Bilingual Spanish-Speaking Students." *Modern Language Journal*, LXII, no. 3 (1978), 102–10.

Weinberg, Meyer. *A Chance to Learn: A History of Race and Education in the United States*. Cambridge, Mass.: Harvard University Press, 1977.

Conservative Versus Radical Dialects in Spanish: Implications for Language Instruction

JORGE M. GUITART
State University of New York at Buffalo

The labels "conservative" and "radical" in the title of this paper do not refer to the political philosophy of Hispanic speakers but to something perhaps less exciting: their phonetic behavior.

Among radical Spanish dialects I would include my own, Havana Spanish, along with other Caribbean dialects and Mainland Puerto Rican Spanish. Among conservative dialects known to me I would include the varieties spoken in Salamanca (Spain), Lima (Peru), Quito (Ecuador), and La Paz (Bolivia).

One informal way of expressing the difference between a conservative pronunciation and a radical one is to say that a conservative pronunciation is closer to the orthography than a radical one. Many linguistically naive observers would characterize what I call a radical dialect as one whose speakers "pronuncian mal las letras o se las comen" (pronounce their letters incorrectly or "eat" them) and a conservative dialect as one whose speakers "pronuncian bien las letras y no se las comen" (pronounce their letters correctly and do not "eat" them).

Though seemingly confusing letter and sound, these naive observers are actually making some fundamental theoretical assumptions about the relationship between the phonological level and the phonetic level. They know intuitively that a close correspondence exists between the orthographic shape of words and their phonological shape. When they speak of letter eating, for instance, they are assuming that eaters and non-eaters share the same set of letters, or in more sophisticated terms, that both groups of speakers have the same phonological representations.

What the naive observer calls letter eating is what some phonologists call segment deletion, which can be formally expressed as $A \rightarrow \emptyset / B \_\_ C$. Like the naive observer who assumes the letter is there to be eaten, the phonologist assumes the segment is there to be deleted; i.e., there is a sequence / BAC / at the systematic level.

What the naive observer refers to as incorrect pronunciation of letters encompasses a number of phenomena that can be regarded in theoretical terms as involving a difference between phonological representations and phonetic representations, with respect to either the internal feature composition of segments in an utterance or the number and arrangement of the segments in the utterance. Segment-internal changes account for the pronunciation of *cerca* "near" as ce[kk]a in rapid speech in my dialect. That is to say, the articulatory features of phonetic [k] are different from those of phonemic /r/, and the relationship between the two can be expressed by a rule that would have [− back] to the left of the arrow and [+ back] to the right, [+ sonorant] to the left and [− sonorant] to the right, etc. (cf. Guitart, 1976a).

As to the differences regarding the number of segments and/or their arrangement, they can be expressed by rules of epenthesis (addition and insertion of segments) and metathesis (transposition of segments). An instance of the application of a rule of epenthesis in my dialect would have *fuiste* "you went" to the left of the arrow and *fuistes* to the right. An instance of metathesis would have *denle* "give him" to the left of the arrow and *delen* to the right. In the first example I have one more segment at the phonetic level; in the second I have the same segments, but two have traded places.

No Spanish dialect, however conservative, is devoid of assimilatory phenomena, in which segments adopt at least some of the features of the segments they are in contact with. Nasal assimilation is apparently universal and many conservative dialects have voicing assimilation as well (e.g., /s/ is realized as [z] before voiced consonants, as in [mizmo] for *mismo*). And no dialect, however conservative, is devoid of deletion, with certain deletions appearing to be universal; e.g., it seems no one pronounces the j in *reloj*. Some deletions have reached the orthographic code (which was written by conservatives and has been periodically revised by other conservatives); e.g., September used to be written *septiembre* but now it is "officially" *setiembre*. The most conservative speakers delete /s/ before the alveolar trill; e.g., *los rojos* "the reds" is pronounced *lorrojos*. Many conservative speakers delete intervocalic /d/ in past participles in casual speech, e.g., *hablao* for *hablado* "spoken."

But even though every Hispanic dialect shows differences between the phonological and phonetic levels in terms of segmental and sequential changes, the degree of phonetic departure from a hypothetically common phonological base is considerably greater within some dialects than within others.

In the Hispanic world at large, phonetic radicalism is inversely proportional to dialectal prestige. This has a well-known historical explanation. Castilian, the historical standard, was conservative in relation to other dialects of the same diasystem (e.g., Andalusian dialects). Today no variety of contemporary Castilian is regarded as the model of pronunciation by all educated speakers everywhere. But for any country where Spanish is spoken, it is considered that an educated speaker should be able to speak without engaging in deletion.

The correlation between prestige and phonetic conservatism is not absolute, however. A certain amount of deletion is acceptable in colloquial speech; e.g., the deletion of intervocalic /d/ in past-participle suffixes is not stigmatized if it occurs in informal discourse.

Actually it seems that prestige is not the only factor that causes speakers to reduce phonetic radicalism. That is to say, radical speakers have conservative episodes in situations where prestige is not at stake. Evidence is mounting that phonetic radicalism is not always correlated with "casualness" and phonetic conservatism is not always correlated with "formality." Some investigators have discovered that segments tend not to be deleted when they constitute an essential part of the message, no matter what the extralinguistic factors are (see Cedegren, 1973; Terrel, 1976). For instance, when /s/ signals plurality, it will tend not to be realized as ∅ when it is not redundant. In the sentence *vemos unas* "we see some," deletion of plural /s/ will change the message to "we see one." In contrast, /s/ is frequently deleted when it is redundant, as in *dos libros* "two books," where the numeral is sufficient to signal plurality.

Because radicals who would not be considered educated have conservative realizations even in casual speech (see Ma and Herasimchuk, 1971), the phonological shape of some lexical items seems to be the same for all radicals, regardless of educational level. Conversely, in other cases it is obvious that the phonological representation of the same lexical item is different for different groups of radicals. Chilean linguist Andrés Gallardo (personal communication) has found that in the Lake Budi area near Temuco, Chile, the word *red* "net" is pronounced *re* in the singular but *rese* (never *rede*) in the plural. It is obvious that either the phonological representation in the singular is /re/ or it contains another segment that is *not* /d/.

Examples can be multiplied to show that when the phonological representation of the same lexical item differs from one radical group to another, that of educated radicals resembles the orthographic shape of the word and that of uneducated radicals differs from it. The corollary to this is that orthography exerts a decisive influence on the pronunciation of radicals.

Certain instances of hypercorrection seem to provide further evidence of the relationship between orthography and pronunciation. A speaker who says *bacalado* for *bacalao* "codfish" probably does so because he does not know how the word is written; literate radicals never engage in that type of hypercorrection. Actually the hypercorrections of literate radicals can be seen as stemming from an excessive awareness of the orthographic code, as in the pronunciation of *x* as [ks] in preconsonantal position (e.g., [ékstra] for *extra*).

In summary, educated radicals have the same phonological processes as uneducated radicals and essentially the same phonological representations as educated conservatives—with the exception of items involving /θ/ (the interdental fricative) and /ʎ/ (the palatal lateral) which, as is known, are both absent from the great majority of dialects.

Why is it, then, that educated radicals do not stop deleting, weakening, etc., in casual speech? The answer is obviously that it is physiologically easier to produce fewer and weaker sounds, expecially when they are not needed. But then, why is it that certain conservatives *never* delete segments that are highly redundant, even in casual speech? For instance, speakers from Salamanca never delete the final /s/ of *domingos* in the utterance *todos los domingos* "every Sunday," even though both this /s/ and the final /s/ of *todos* are redundant. The answer is that redundancy, though physiologically uneconomical, is perceptually profitable. It is commonly held that the greater the redundancy the greater the assurance of transmission.

In addition, deletion of redundant segments may turn out to be economical only locally, but not so economical when the whole of the grammar is taken into account. For instance, Alvar (1975) observes that in dialects where no distinction is made phonetically between second and third person singular forms (e.g., *vienes* "you come" and *viene* "he/she comes" are both realized as [biéne]) the subject pronoun normally accompanies the verb forms *(tú biene, él biene)* in contexts where it would be omitted in what I call conservative dialects. Alvar reminds us that the loss of final consonants in French made it necessary for the subject pronoun to always accompany conjugated verb forms in that language. Jiménez Sabater (1978), who makes similar observations regarding segment deletion and subject pronoun usage in contemporary Dominican Spanish, offers as an illustration the following contrast:

Dominican Spanish: *Cuando tú acabe, tú me avisa.*
Spanish general norm: *Cuando acabes, me avisas.* "When you finish, let me know."

The use of *tú* is far from redundant here since without the pronouns the sentence can have several meanings (e.g., "when he finishes, he'll let me know," "when you [formal] finish, let me know," "when he finishes, you [formal] let me know," etc.).

It is my personal experience that the phenomenon illustrated by Jiménez Sabater occurs also in Cuban Spanish. It probably occurs in all dialects where the index of deletion of final consonants is very high.

In view of this, it is perhaps best not to propose any direct correlation between phonetic radicalism and economy of transmission, but to say instead that conservatism and radicalism are different solutions to the problems of communicating both clearly and economically.

Returning to the interplay between pronunciation and prestige, I would like to add that a conservative pronunciation does not insure social prestige, since there are uneducated speakers who are phonetically conservative; their deviations from the standard are of a different nature (e.g., lexical and syntactic). For instance, Boyd-Bowman (1960: 71; 105) describes a Mexican dialect in which uneducated speakers are very conservative—as conservative as literate speakers—when it comes to deletion, but they use so-called "double plurals" (e.g., *papases* instead of *papás* "dads"), which is stigmatized.

As to the interplay between spelling and pronunciation, since the same speakers are conservative regardless of their degree of literacy, obviously literacy is not of the essence for phonetic conservatism, and conservatives are so before they are exposed to the orthographic code.

DIALECTS IN CONTACT

When conservatives and radicals come into contact on a regular basis, the result is that radicals tend to be more conservative in their pronunciation but conservatives make no attempt to be more radical. For instance, educated Andalusians living in Castile make successful efforts to suppress weakening and deletion in their contact with Castilian speakers, but Castilian speakers living in Hispanic nations of the Caribbean apparently make no attempt to learn how to delete, weaken, etc.

It is logical to think of social prestige as the factor governing such a difference in phonetic behavior. It seems, however, that fear of sounding uneducated is not the only reason why a radical becomes more careful in the presence of a conservative listener. It is also fear of being misunderstood.

I remember that Cuban radio and television announcers and performers were extremely conservative in their speech as compared even with educated radicals speaking in formal situations of another type (e.g., lecturing in a classroom). Since the intended (domestic) audience was largely radical, there is no reason to believe that such care was exercised to impress a few conservatives. It is logical to assume that the main reason was to insure intelligibility. It is the same reason that brings out the stronger allophones in the speech of not-so-educated radicals when the integrity of a message—not personal prestige—is at stake.

This brings us to the question of mutual intelligibility between conservatives and radicals. It seems that radicals never misunderstand conservatives on the basis of pronunciation. But do conservatives have difficulty understanding radicals who make no concessions?

It seems that conservatives are able to get accustomed to the pronunciation of extreme radicals after a certain period of exposure. According to Peruvian linguist Blas Puente Baldoceda (personal communication), conservative speakers from the Peruvian sierra who have not had any previous exposure to certain very radical speakers from the coastal areas experience trouble understanding them only initially.

I do not recall ever hearing that Peninsular conservatives in Cuba had comprehension problems with the speech of poor, uneducated Cubans. On the contrary: communication seemed to proceed unimpeded, even though these speakers patently made no attempt to pronounce more carefully on behalf of their listeners.

It seems, then, that mutual intelligibility between a conservative dialect and a radical one does not depend exclusively on what radicals do for conservatives.

In theoretical terms, it seems that conservatives are able to reconstruct phonological representations starting from very incomplete and very deviant phonetic samples offered them by radicals. In this task they are surely aided by the large number of things any two Spanish dialects have in common in the area of morphology and syntax.

To my knowledge, dialectal variation involving morphological and syntactic operations is insignificant when compared with phonetic variation. Actually some syntactic peculiarities of radical dialects vis-á-vis standard forms may serve to increase, rather than decrease, intelligibility, as is the case, for instance, of the greater use of personal subject pronouns in the absence of person-number markers in verb forms (cf. the cited data of Alvar and Jiménez Sabater).

DIALECTS IN CONTACT IN INSTRUCTIONAL SITUATIONS

British linguist S. Pit Corder (1971) has advanced the notion that at any point before the acquisition of full competence in a foreign language, a learner speaks a dialect of the target language of which he is the only speaker.

These idiosyncratic dialects, as Corder calls them, approximate more and more a native dialect as learning progresses.

Many of us know from experience that the pronunciation of our better English-speaking students, though not entirely free of interference, is intelligible, especially when the students are able to construct an adequate number of well-formed sentences or sentences which, though not well-formed syntactically, are semantically and pragmatically correct. These students are understood by both conservatives and radicals. Their problem, however, is one of reception. They report their greatest trouble is with natives "who talk too fast and leave a lot of things out" (the radicals). They also have problems with native conservative speakers. Some learners understand only slow, deliberate speech. The reason for this is, of course, lack of exposure.

The idiosyncratic dialects of our learners are unusually conservative. They show almost a one-to-one relationship between phonological and phonetic representations. This is due in great part to the learners' heavy reliance on the printed text—which we do little to discourage. It is also due to lack of training in some basic phonological processes that are common to all dialects, conservative and radical alike. There are three processes of a sequential nature to which the introductory books known to me dedicate only cursory attention: vowel fusion, loss of syllabicity, and resyllabication—the latter at times involving segmental feature changes.

Following is an illustration of the differences in pronunciation between a speaker of an idiosyncratic dialect and a conservative native, both talking at their normal, unemphatic rate of speed. Transcriptions are semiphonetic. For clarity I show syllabic separation:

	Orthography	*Idiosyncratic*	*Native conservative*
1.	Voy a hacer "I'm going to do"	voy-a-a-ser	bo-ya-ser
2.	Ella habla inglés "She speaks English"	e-lla-a-bla-in-glés	e-lla-ƀlain-glés
3.	No le haga el otro "Don't do the other one for him"	no-le-a-ga-el-o-tro	no-lҽa-ǵaҿ-lo-tro

These are some of the operations the learner has failed to execute: in (1), vowel fusion and resyllabication, with the palatal glide turning into a consonant; in (2), vowel fusion and resyllabication, with a vowel becoming a glide (dipthongization); in (3), loss of syllabicity, with syllabic /e/ twice being realized as a medial (nonsyllabic) glide.

It is not hard to see why learners have reception troubles. How could they, for instance, recognize the word *voy* when it is distributed between two syllables and its last segment has become something else? In generative terms, learners do not have the rule that relates surface [y] to an underlying non-obstruent. Learners have few if any rules governing sequential phonetic processes. And they are not being taught those rules; i.e., they are not being exposed consciously and systematically to these phenomena.

At the present time I do not notice any trend toward changing this situation.

If everyone were to agree that we should help our students become less conservative phonetically, the question would then arise as to whether this can be accomplished within a conventional program of instruction, as opposed to directing our students to go abroad and get accustomed to everyday radical speech (which for them is initially that of *any* dialect, however conservative).

We should endeavor to have our students acquire a degree of productive competence similar at the very least to that of conservative natives. We could begin by establishing mastery of sequential allophonic variation as one of the essential goals of instruction. In order to achieve that goal, drilling of sequential phenomena cannot be limited to the few exercises contained in current textbooks but instead must be an important component of every instructional unit. And practice should involve both production and listening comprehension, preferably of meaningful material.

Of course the instructor himself/herself should be able to pronounce like a native conservative, or very close to it.

I would like to go one step further. Why not give our learners some degree of receptive competence in *radical* dialects by exposing them systematically to recordings of radical speakers, or perhaps by encouraging radical instructors to be less conservative in the classroom? We radicals tend to be naturally (or unnaturally) conservative in classroom situations.

Why not offer learners the opportunity of becoming familiar with the communication strategies of radicals? Like native conservatives, they would learn to interpret those strategies without having to adopt them.

Should a student desire to be exposed to radicals *in vivo* he or she does not have to travel abroad. There are many radical speakers in the United States. Mainland Puerto Ricans and Cubans are radical, and apparently so are certain Chicanos (see González Mena de Lococo, 1974).

I believe that English-speaking students who wish to become involved in the education of Hispanic children within bilingual-bicultural educational programs should be given the opportunity through formal training to acquire, at the very least, receptive competence in U.S. Spanish radical dialects.

This brings me to discussing the characteristics of those dialects in the light of the distinctions I have established in the foregoing.

Many U.S. Spanish speakers are radicals without a choice. For many of them, knowledge of Spanish is only oral, and in this they resemble the uneducated radical population in Hispanic countries. Being illiterate in Spanish, they lack that which gives educated radicals essentially the same phonological representations as conservatives: the influence of orthography.

One goal of teaching Spanish to Spanish ethnics should be to give these students the ability to engage in conservative modes of speech. But as I have argued elsewhere (Guitart, 1976b), this goal will not be achieved by teaching these students how to pronounce "correctly" but rather by increasing their level of literacy to that of educated speakers.

I believe that instruction for Spanish ethnics should be directed toward making them text-oriented. I also believe that a careful distinction should be made in instruction between lexical items (words) that have phonological representations different from those of the standard shared by educated speakers, both conservative and radical (e.g., *entodavía,* vs. standard *todayvía* "still"; *cafeses,* vs. *cafés* "coffees"; *celebro* vs. *cerebro* "brain"), and words that seem to have phonological representations identical to those of the standard—for since the speakers also show the standard forms in their speech, e.g., since *lune* and *lunes* alternate for "Monday," the phonological representation must be /lunes/.

No attempt should be made to correct, for example, a Puerto Rican speaker who pronounces *ser* "to be" as [sél] in, say, *ser de noche* "to be evening," because the occurrence of / l / is a purely phonetic phenomenon (an instance of weakening); the same speaker pronounces the word as [ser] in *ser asi* "to be that way," where the environment for weakening is absent. In Guitart, (1976b) I showed that weakening of /r/, which leads to the so-called confusion of *l* and *r*, occurs less in speech influenced by text. By introducing the influence of the printed word as a factor in the competence of our speakers, we are reducing the incidence of this stigmatized phenomenon without demeaning our students with blanket normative statements.

On the other hand, students should be corrected if they use the word *entodavía* in writing. Without condemning the use of *entodavía* in speech, we should point out to them that in written Spanish—which is the mode that all speakers share—the word is *todavía.* I believe that when discussing text-related topics the students will tend to use *todavía.* The choice of continuing to use *entodavía* in other settings will be theirs. But once they acquire the standard form they will have the additional choice of being able to use it when interacting with other educated speakers, whether conservative or radical.

SUMMARY

In the Hispanic world, dialects can be classified as to how much their pronunciation differs from the orthographic code, which in turn reflects the phonological representation of lexical items. Those that depart greatly from it are radical and those that are very close to it are conservative.

Educated radical speakers have phonological representations that are essentially the same as those of educated conservatives. This is so by virtue of the influence of literacy on educated radicals.

Radicals seem to follow a communication strategy that favors phonetic economy, possibly at the expense of syntactic simplicity, while conservatives seem to favor phonetic redundancy, thus apparently not having to complicate other parts of the grammar. On the other hand, phonetic economies on the part of radicals are not indiscriminate and are not effected when communication is at stake.

When conservatives and radicals come into contact, the latter tend to imitate the former but not vice versa. Mutal intelligibility seems assured, no matter how radical an interlocutor is, apparently because of the great morphological and syntactic similarities between any two dialects.

Students learning Spanish as a second language speak idiosyncratic dialects that are highly conservative. This is mainly the outcome of a lack of training in sequential phonetic phenomena. Learners should be exposed systematically to radical realizations so as to impartto them the same degree of receptive competence in radical dialects that native conservatives have. This training is especially relevant if those learners plan to apply their knowledge of Spanish language and culture by serving in bilingual-bicultural education programs in the United States.

U.S. Spanish ethnics who are illiterate in Spanish are in the same situation as uneducated radicals anywhere. Their instruction in Spanish should be directed not at correcting their pronunciation but at making them highly literate, so that they acquire the phonological representations shared by educated speakers.

REFERENCES

Alvar, M. 1975. *Teoría lingüística de las regiones.* Barcelona: Planeta/Universidad.
Boyd-Bowman, P. 1960. *El habla de Guanajuato.* Mexico City: Imprenta Universitaria.

Cedergren, H. 1973. "The interplay of social and linguistic factors in Panama." Cornell University doctoral dissertation.

Corder, S.P. 1971. "Idiosyncratic dialects and error analysis." *IRAL* 9: 147–59.

González Mena de Lococo, V. 1974. "The Salient Differences Between Chicano Spanish and Standard Spanish: Some Pedagogical Considerations." *The Bilingual Review* I, 3: 243–51.

Guitart, J.M. 1976a. *Markedness and a Cuban Dialect of Spanish.* Washington: Georgetown University Press.

———. 1976b. "On the Pronunciation of Puerto Rican Spanish on the Mainland: Theoretical and Pedagogical Considerations." In Valdés-Fallis and García-Moya *infra,* 57-74. Reprinted in Valdés, Lozano, and García-Moya, *infra,* 48–58.

Jiménez Sabater, M.A. 1978. "Estructuras morfosintácticas en el español dominicano: algunas implicaciones sociolingüísticas."In H. López Morales, ed. *Corrientes actuales de la dialectología del Caribe hispánico: Actas de un simposio.* Río Piedras: UPRED.

Ma, R. and E. Herasimchuk. 1971. "The linguistic dimensions of a bilingual neighborhood." In J.A. Fishman, R.L. Cooper, and R. Ma, eds. *Bilingualism in the Barrio.* Bloomington: Indiana University Press.

Terrell, T. 1976. "The Inherent Variability of Word Final /s/ in Cuban and Puerto Rican Spanish." In Valdés-Fallis and García-Moya, *infra,* 41-55.

Valdés-Fallis, G. and R. García-Moya. 1976. *Teaching Spanish to the Spanish Speaking: Theory and Practice.* San Antonio: Trinity University.

Valdés, G., A.G. Lozano, and R. Garcia-Moya. 1981. *Teaching Spanish to the Hispanic Bilingual: Issues, Aims, and Methods.* New York: Teachers College Press.

Structural Linguistics and Bilingual Interference: Problems and Proposals

JOHN M. LIPSKI
Michigan State University

A situation of languages in contact,[1] particularly one characterized by a large amount of bilingual interaction, inevitably leads to the influence of one language upon the other. Such an influence generally occurs in both directions, but, when one of two languages represents a majority and/or prestige language, it is most frequent for this language to exert a more profound influence on the minority language. In such cases, it is usual to speak of linguistic interference, borrowing, and the numerous *-isms* (e.g., Anglicisms, Latinisms, etc.) characterizing studies of bilingual transfer.

Interference between languages, while encompassing every conceivable form of linguistic structure, may be divided into three general categories, via the *substratum, superstratum or adstratum* models of linguistic interference. The first involves lexical interference, that is, borrowing of entire words or phrases. The second case is phonological interference, involving the transfer of sounds or sound patterns from one language to another. Finally, we come to syntactic interference, involving the formation of words and phrases, the transference of patterns of word formation from one language to another, and the shift in meaning of partial or false cognate forms. While all three categories of linguistic interference have been studied, there has by no means been an equal amount of scholarly activity devoted to each. Lexical interference, being perhaps most common, and certainly most easily catalogued, forms the basis for the majority of studies of bilingual interference, studies which run the gamut from mere lists of foreign borrowings to more sophisticated studies seeking to determine the causes for the borrowing of particular words, in terms of the semantic and lexical structures of the languages. Phonological interference, involving transference of sounds and phonemic oppositions, has received due attention, and explanations based on the phonological influence of substrata have traditionally formed part of the stock in trade of historical linguistics. In synchronic analyses, phonological interference is responsible for "foreign accents," which in many instances work their way, after several generations, into the pronunciation of the majority language.[2] Finally, in the realm of syntactic interference, there has been comparatively little investigation, particularly within the framework of modern linguistics. The transference of syntactic patterns has often been felt to be somewhat of a linguistic curiosity, difficult to determine and even more difficult to describe. In 1881, William Dwight Whitney[3] defined a scale of the difficulty with which various linguistic structures are borrowed, with nouns at the end of greatest ease, and sounds at the opposite end. Turning his attention to the borrowing of grammatical patterns, Whitney then noted: "the exemption of 'grammar' from mixture is no isolated fact; the grammatical apparatus merely resists intrusion most successfully, in virtue of its being the least material and the most formal part of language. In a scale of constantly increasing difficulty it occupies the extreme place." More recently, however,[4] it has been admitted that "native speakers . . . seldom make syntactic errors . . . non-native speakers do make syntactic mistakes frequently and stubbornly as they make semantic and morphological mistakes, because they tend to transfer to the foreign language their native syntactical system as well as their morphological habits and semantic values." Linguists have nonetheless tended to avoid questions of grammatical interference, particularly among bilinguals, and have directed their attention instead toward the methodologically less troublesome areas of interference in the lexicon and phonological components, leaving the study of syntactic interference in the hands of often linguistically naive scholars.

The above remarks, while describing the study of bilingual encounters in general, are particularly relevant to the interaction between Spanish and English in the United States and its environs. Given the majority status of English as compared to Spanish, especially in the United States, and given the generally extensive lexical borrowing from English encountered throughout the world's languages, it is reasonable to expect that close contact between Spanish and English would lead to a profound influence of the latter on the former. Studies on the influence of English on Spanish abound,[5] yet the majority cluster around the area of lexical borrowing, with a diminished number treating phenomena of phonological interference. Within the realm of syntactic interference, the most common methodology has been to present as "evidence" a Spanish expression which may or may not be a commonly accepted pattern, together with a similar phrase in English, followed by the claim that the Spanish expression is a calque or loan-translation of the English expression in question. In many cases such claims may be intuitively quite satisfying, especially when gleaned from areas where one is led to expect large quantities of linguistic interference of English on Spanish, but the fact remains that to date, there is no comprehensive linguistic methodology for determining true cases of syntactic interference comparable, for example, to the work which has been done in assessing phonological interference.[6]

To the generality of the preceding comments may be added some specific observations regarding situations of Spanish-English interaction. In particular, the present note will focus on certain claims regarding the influence of English on the Spanish of Puerto Rico, in an attempt to assess the effectiveness of the results hitherto reported. While no comprehensive linguistic methodology will result, due to the embryonic state of research into bilingual interaction, it will be suggested that a greater application of linguistic theory to the study of language contact will yield a clearer picture of the type and extent of interference to be anticipated.

The fact that Puerto Rico is a territory of the United States, thus having English as one of its official languages, leads to inevitable claims of English influence on Puerto Rican Spanish, claims further strengthened by a constant source of linguistic flux attributable to Puerto Ricans in the United States, allegedly removed from extensive contact with the living Spanish language and consequently exposed to a higher degree of unmitigated English influence. Touching on a topic of political and social relevance, claims of English influence in Puerto Rico cannot be divorced from the polemical tirades and impressionistic observations which accompany discussions of foreign interference and independence, and as a result the study of Puerto Rican Spanish has suffered in empirical acceptability, if not in volume.

Studies of Puerto Rican Spanish generally cluster around two poles, those claiming large amounts of linguistic interference from English, and those asserting that, apart from lexical borrowing, Puerto Rican Spanish remains relatively free of foreign influence; relatively few studies strike the middle ground, and thus the reader is left with a feeling of confusion and frustration when attempting to draw his own conclusions. In particular, the studies of Navarro Tomás,[7] Gili y Gaya,[8] and especially that of De Granda[9] have claimed for Puerto Rican Spanish a relatively high degree of English influence, in the syntactic structures as well as in the lexicon. Taking the opposing viewpoint we may cite the studies of Lloréns[10] and Pérez Sala.[11] The work of the latter author is especially significant in that he has devoted an entire monograph to the study of structural syntactic interference of English on

Puerto Rican Spanish; more significantly still, Pérez decries the lack of methodological rigor characterizing earlier studies and calls for a rigid structural linguistic methodology to deal with cases of syntactic interference. In reality, however, it turns out that, after a discussion of structural linguistics in general, Pérez Sala's application of linguistics to the study of syntactic interference is not radically different from that to be found in earlier studies, although undertaken from a much more rational viewpoint. After adopting a set of general categories, such as *noun phrase, verb phrase*, etc., the author compiles a list of Spanish expressions suspected of being "Anglicized," together with the English expressions from which they reputedly came. In order to verify the degree of similarity between the expressions in question, Pérez notes (p. 48, fn. 10) that "basta una ojeada a las tres formas para constatar, con cierta seguridad, que la frase [española] es un calco de la frase [inglesa]." Thus, right from the outset there is no indication of precisely what it means for two phrases in two languages to be sufficiently similar for one to have influenced the other. To assert the similarity after the fact is a totally circular procedure, providing no escape from the impressionism to be found in nearly all works dealing with syntactic interference.

Since Pérez Sala believes that the majority of his examples may be dismissed as false Anglicisms, he proceeds via a process of elimination to provide other explanations for the expressions in question. The general method is to search for another attestation, either in other Spanish dialects, or in earlier periods of the Spanish language. With respect to the first possibility, given the pervasive influence of English in the modern world, a fact amply recognized by Pérez himself, finding an attestation of an expression elsewhere in the Hispanic world is no guarantee that this area has not also been influenced by English. Arguments based on historical parallels are generally much more substantial, for given the highly diversified history of the Spanish language, together with the numerous attested archaic forms, in Puerto Rico and elsewhere, it is not surprising to find that Old Spanish shared many structural patterns with modern English, patterns which may have survived intact in certain regions without having been directly influenced by modern English. However, once these resources have been exhausted, all remaining examples must automatically be relegated to the status of Anglicisms, and thus the appeal to "structural linguistics" seems to have been in vain, since at no point has a true linguistic model been applied.

It is thus seen to be of the utmost importance whether in fact an algorithm can be established which will sort out true cases of foreign interference from spontaneous evolutions within the language, in the absence of additional attestations. In general, it may be affirmed that such a determination is impossible, since, as with any scientific hypothesis, claims of foreign influence can never be totally *proved;* on the other hand, by amassing sufficient counterevidence, the possibility of foreign influence may, in many cases, be reduced to negligible proportions. It is here that a more substantive appeal to structural linguistics may aid in the determination of linguistic interference, for by viewing languages as structured entities instead of bodies of isolated forms, a total view may be obtained.

A natural language is a system in equilibrium, a sort of micro-ecological system, in which both static and dynamic aspects play a role in maintaining the balance. Therefore, despite the polemic accompanying the theory of transformational-generative grammar,[12] there is no incompatibility between linguistic theories stressing static aspects of language and those placing emphasis on the dynamic aspects, as long as there is articulation between the two components. In particular, both the static and dynamic aspects may be relevant to the study of syntactic interference, inasmuch as the process of borrowing is itself *dynamic,* although its results are usually assessed in terms of static after-effects.

In addition to providing a precise description of what constitutes sufficient similarity between two expressions to warrant formation of a calque, a more detailed application of linguistics may also serve in the role of devil's advocate in the determination of linguistic interference, in determining the relation between the underlying system of language and the spoken chain. Ferdinand de Saussure[13] defined the terms *syntagm* and *paradigm* to characterize these notions. Most generally, they relate the set of possible choices available at any given time with the choice that is actually made. The paradigm is the *system,* the set of all possible alternatives for a given element, whether it be sound, word, sentence, or even something more diffuse like narrative unit. The paradigm is highly structured by a number of correlations interrelating the members along various axes. The syntagm, on the other hand, is the *concrete realization* of this underlying system, in which one choice is made for each element in question. As an example, one may consider the total conjugation of a verb as a paradigmatic set, while the occurrence of a particular verbal form in a given sentence belongs to the level of the syntagm. Roman Jakobson[14] has described this relationship by characterizing the paradigm as a relation of *similarity,* where the elements are related by virtue of sharing common traits which would make them appropriate in a given slot; the syntagm generates a relation of contiguity, where the elements are related by virtue of their juxtaposition in the spoken chain.

In the majority of cases, the paradigm or system and the syntagm or concrete realization are opposed to one another, as distinct axes. When these axes overlap, however, striking and unusual results may ensue. Roland Barthes[15] notes, in a description of the syntagm/paradigm dichotomy: "the mode of articulation of the two axes [i.e., syntagmatic and paradigmatic] is sometimes 'perverted,' when, for instance a paradigm is extended into a syntagm. There is then a defiance of the usual distribution *syntagm/system*, and it is probably around this transgression that a great number of creative phenomena are situated."

The interaction of the syntagm and the paradigm has been a particularly fruitful area of investigation in linguistics, particularly in the study of sound change. In general, it is assumed that the paradigm or system exerts pressures of conformity on the syntagm, or spoken chain,[16] although in the field of sound change, the opposite claim has occasionally been made.[17] In the realm of syntactic interference, however, the possible role of the syntagm in shaping the underlying structure of the language has received little attention, outside of a few scattered references in specific studies. For example, speaking of the occasional use of *le vi* instead of the more common *lo vi* in Colombia, Restrepo[18] notes that "an occasional *le vi* was usually an affectation of the peninsular Spanish, or the influence of the written word. However, let us bear in mind the possibility of an expression such as *no le vi la cara* . . . ." The latter observation clearly indicates the possibility for the spoken chain to influence a more fundamental paradigmatic pattern. Similarly, speaking of the frequently occurring *está siendo*, which many have claimed is the result of English influence, Ramos[19] notes "aunque dicho sintagma sea atribuible al inglés (*is being + participio o adjetivo*), podría ser explicado estructuralmente dentro del sistema sintáctico español."[20] In a more comprehensive study, Vallejo[21] attempts to demonstrate that Spanish expressions of the form *por fuerte que sea*, evolved from earlier configurations such as *maguer muy fuerte sea* > *por maguer fuerza tenga* > *por fuerza que tenga* > *por fuerte que sea*, rejecting the Academy's hypothesized evolution from *porque sea fuerte*.

The possibility for the spoken chain to profoundly influence the underlying system or paradigm has, nonetheless, never been systematically explored, especially in regard to cases involving putative bilingual interference. It is here, nonetheless, that structural linguistics can potentially add to the arsenal of facts needed to substantiate or refute claims of foreign influence, by providing yet another alternative to simple cases of calques or borrowings. In addition to arguments involving attestations from earlier historical periods or far-flung dialects, a questionable expression which is structurally similar to one in another language may also be described as the result of a spontaneous internal evolution, stemming from the successive transformation of structures already present in the language, under the influence of dominant syntagmatic patterns. While the determination of such routes of transformation will be, in most cases, purely hypothetical, the amassing of sufficient data, and hopefully precedent evolutions in other areas of the language, may place the overall role of foreign influence in a somewhat narrower perspective. Some concrete cases should serve to demonstrate the potential inherent in such a methodological procedure.

Pérez Sala, and others,[22] note the expression *el pasado presidente* "the past president" instead of what is claimed to be the "correct" Spanish, *el ex presidente*. The former expression is claimed to result from the English version, a claim not unlikely given the occurrence of errors like *pasado año, pasada semana,* etc., frequently encountered among English-speaking students in Spanish classes. To stop here, however, would fail to take into consideration the equally acceptable *el antiguo presidente*, also with preposed adjective, as in English. The adjective *antiguo* belongs to a restricted group of Spanish adjectives which change in meaning, or at least in scope, according to whether they are anteposed or preposed;[23] others include *viejo, pobre, cierto, nuevo,* etc. Compare, for example, *un amigo viejo* "a friend who is old" with *un viejo amigo* "a friend of long standing." While it is quite likely that the English syntactic pattern was instrumental in attracting the adjective *pasado* into the sphere of the variable adjectives like *antiguo*, the presence of *el antiguo presidente*, given the close semantic relationship between *pasado* and *antiguo,* must not be overlooked as having at least contributed to the shift in question.

Another expression branded as an Anglicism is *¿cómo te gustó la película?* instead of simply *¿te gustó la película?;* the former expression presumably comes from English "how did you like the picture?" However, it must be noted that Spanish *gustar* is not syntactically equivalent to English *like*, but rather to *please;*[24] thus, a phrase such as *¿cómo te gustó la película?* would be literally rendered into English as "how did the picture please you?" On the other hand, the English expression asks for a value judgment, given the presence of the interrogative adverb *how;* typical answers would be *a lot, not at all,* etc. The "correct" Spanish *¿te gustó la película?* merely asks for a *yes–no* response, thus providing a totally different type of interrogative structure.[25] Gili y Gaya (*op. cit.*, pp. 137–38) notes, with reference to the expression *¿cómo te gustó la película?* that

> el forastero a quien se dirigen tales preguntas se da cuenta de que en la intención de los hablantes no se proponen decir? ¿De qué manera le gusta P.R.?, ¿De qué manera le gusta mi casa?, y que la respuesta esperada es *sí* o

no, o las expresiones ponderativas *mucho* o *poco*, del mismo caracter afirmativo o negativo. *Cómo* pierde en esas frases su sentido modal. Un hablante hispánico que no se percatara de la intención de su interlocutor, al oír. ¿cómo le gusta la playa de Luquillo? contestaría: *A la luz de la luna*, o *Con poco oléaje.*

While agreeing with Gili y Gaya that *cómo* has lost much of its adverbial force in the expressions in question, we would disagree that *sí* and *no* would be totally acceptable answers to the question, although *mucho, poco*, etc., do fit the situation, as in English. However, again as in English, the semantic erosion of *cómo* does not occur only in this expression, but also with other verbs requiring value judgments. In his encyclopedic Spanish grammar, Ramsey[26] noted that "after *cómo*, *encontrar* 'to find' or *parecer* 'to seem' are preferable to *gustar* in asking an opinion," a statement even implicitly admitting the acceptability of the type-form ¿*cómo te gusta?* although giving preference to other expressions. Given the possibility of variants like ¿*cómo/qué te parece?* as well as ¿*cómo te encuentras?*, all of whose meanings are almost identical to that expressed in ¿*cómo te gusta?*, it is not unlikely that this latter expression has been influenced by structures already present in Spanish. Gili y Gaya, in fact (p. 138, fn. 5), hints at another possible alternative to English influence, noting "Cabría en lo posible que este uso del *cómo* interrogativo fuese una propagación analogica del *cómo* exclamativo en las frases: ¡*Cómo me gusta esta calle!* ¡*Cómo me parece bien esa idea!* y otras parecidas. En este caso, la frase en cuestión vendría de antiguo y no sería anglicada en su origen, si bien el contacto con la expresión inglesa puede haber contribuido a consolidarla y propagarla." The last remark is particularly pertinent, for, in discussing possible cases of foreign interference, it is necessary to differentiate between simple cases of borrowing, and internal evolutions aided by the overwhelming presence of structurally similar expressions in the predominant language.

Also considered to have come from English are expressions like *él sabe cómo hablar inglés* "he knows how to speak English," instead of simply ·*él sabe hablar inglés*, since *saber* + infinitive means "to know how to." This sort of error is frequently heard among English-speaking students of Spanish, and thus claims of English influence are quite plausible. However, it must also be noted that Spanish, in addition to allowing *saber* to be followed by the adverbs *cuándo, dónde*, etc., also permits contrast between *saber* + infinitive and *saber cómo* + infinitive, for example in the pair:

(1) *El no sabe traducir.* "He doesn't know how to translate."
(2) *El no sabe cómo traducir este párrafo.* "He doesn't know how to translate this paragraph."

In sentence (1), general ability is referred to, while in (2), inability on a specific occasion necessitates the use of the adverb *cómo*: he doesn't know how to go about translating a particular paragraph. A literary citation[27] also aids in exemplifying this distinction: "—¡Valérie! ¡Déjame! ¡No sé! ¡No sé hacerlo!—gritó con violencia, tratando de incorporarse—¡No sé cómo hacerlo!" The meanings of *saber* + infinitive "to be able to" [in theory], and *saber cómo* + infinitive "to be able to" [on a specific occasion], are sufficiently close that a certain amount of semantic transference could be anticipated, even in the absence of foreign influence. This situation is parallel to that exhibited by the preterite and imperfect tenses of *poder* + infinitive. Compare:

(3) *Podía abrir la ventana.* "I was able (in theory) to open the window."

(4) *Pude abrir la ventana.* "I was able to open the window (and opened it)."

As the meanings of the preterite and imperfect may merge under certain conditions, so might the difference between *saber* + infinitive and *saber cómo* + infinitive become blurred in the minds of many speakers.

Another example is provided by the expression *hay que darle pensamiento a eso* "it's necessary to give that some thought," instead of preferred *hay que estudiar eso*. Also cited is *darle seguimento a* "to follow up," instead of *tramitar*. In the first case, the structure of the Spanish expression is sufficiently close to that of its English counterpart to make one suspect a calque; in the second example, however, there is no ready syntactic parallel, other than the use of the verb pair *seguir/follow*. In any case, expressions of the form *darle* + noun + *a* are sufficiently common in Spanish in other cases where no English influence is to be suspected. Most common is *darle vueltas a* "to ponder." Encountered in a Nicaraguan novel[28] is *darle pegamento a* "to stick," while the expression *dar nacimiento a* "to give birth to," is found in a novel by a Cuban author not generally given to unintentional use of Anglicisms.[29] Thus it appears quite possible that the Spanish expressions in question are the result of neologisms, following an already established pattern, rather than being ascriable to the influence of English.

As a final example, let us consider the pleonastic usage of the indefinite articles *uno* and *una* in expressions like *la consecuencia es una muy importante* "the consequence is an important one," instead of *la consecuencia es muy importante; el plan parece uno demasiado costoso* "the plan seems a very expensive one," instead of *el plan parece demasiado costoso*, etc. Here the insertion of the unnecessary article in the Spanish expression parallels English usage, thus adding plausibility to claims of structural interference. In English, when the combination of noun and adjective is pronominalized by deletion of the noun, the pronouns *one* or *ones* must be inserted in place of the deleted noun: *I have the blue pens > I have the blue ones; That is an important consequence > that is an important one,* etc. In Spanish, due in part to the greater differentiation provided by gender and number concord in adjectives, pronominalization may be accomplished merely through deletion of the noun: *tengo las plumas azules > tengo las azules; me gusta aquel libro > me gusta aquél,* and so forth. Errors of the form *este uno* for "this one" are frequent in beginning Spanish classes, until students have mastered the process of pronominalization in Spanish.

It is possible, however, to construct acceptable and indeed necessary combinations of indefinite article + adjective in Spanish, paralleling those found in the unacceptable expressions cited above. The requirement is that the article + adjective combination in the predicate must not be co-referential with any noun phrase in the subject, but rather must stand in contrast with it. Compare the following pronominalizations, where unacceptable derivations are marked with an asterisk: *Los problemas son difíciles > *son unos difíciles > son difíciles; el plan es muy costoso > *es uno muy costoso > es muy costoso > buscamos uno menos costoso; el espectáculo no tuvo lugar en un edificio viejo sino en uno nuevo,* etc. In these examples it may be seen that the combination of *uno* + adjective is called for whenever a new, previously unspecified object is being referred to, while *uno* is not permitted in the same frame if the pronominalized adjective is co-referential with an NP in the subject. The crucial question then is whether it would be possible for this requirement of non-co-referentiality to spontaneously disappear, thus permitting transfer of patterns of the type *uno* + adjective to cases involving co-referential noun phrases. At this point, only a speculative answer may be offered, since no data are available which bear directly on the emergence of the questionable Spanish phrases. Clearly, considering only the predicate phrases in both types of expressions could lead to a transfer of the type suggested above, particularly since we do not ordinarily process or produce sentences on a word-by-word basis, but rather in larger, stereotyped chunks which are often retained or modified as integral units.[30] Moreover, there is at least one other case in Spanish where requirements of co-referentiality are being lost, and this concerns the growing use of the disjunctive pronouns *él, ella,* etc., to the exclusion of the reflexive pronouns *sí, consigo,* etc. This process, which Henríquez Ureña[31] dates back to the end of the 19th century, has not reached full generality in Spanish, but certain authors, for example Julio Cortázar, use the pronouns *él, ellos,* etc. consistently in such cases; for example, *lo trajo con él, leía para él,* instead of *lo trajo consigo, leía para sí.* A similar process has taken place in modern French. Thus, the possibility of transfer of patterns involving the combination of indefinite article + adjective to cases involving co-referentiality through spontaneous internal evolution would not be totally unparalleled. More likely, as with most of the previously cited examples, the English expression provided either the initial impetus or reinforcement for a structurally permissible change in Spanish.

In addition to searching for earlier attestations, studying the possibility of internal deformations of already existing patterns cannot definitively disprove claims of foreign linguistic interference. However, a cogent and well-argued linguistic presentation can place claims of structural interference in a different perspective, by giving due consideration to language as a structured entity, capable of complex evolutionary patterns, rather than as a passive mechanism which swallows words and expressions whole merely upon contact with another language. Clearly the rudimentary examples presented in this note make no claims to represent a comprehensive linguistic theory of internal evolution; they were included merely to demonstrate the sort of results that may be anticipated by applying structural models of language to problems of bilingual interaction. Only by giving sufficient consideration to all aspects of the bilingual encounter, linguistic as well as social, can a truly accurate portrayal be realistically approached. The current state of research into bilingualism shows a healthy cooperation of varying disciplines, and it is in the spirit of such interdisciplinary cooperation that the preceding remarks have been offered.

NOTES

1. The literature on linguistic aspects of bilingual is enormous. For a panoramic view, in which the "contact" aspect is emphasized, see Uriel Weinreich, *Languages in Contact* (The Hague: Mouton, 1968 [1st ed. 1953]).

2. For some specific examples of this process, see William Labov, *The Social Stratification of English in New York City* (Washington, D.C.: Center for Applied Linguistics, 1966).

3. William Dwight Whitney, "On Mixture in Language," *Transactions of the American Philological Association* 12 (1881) 5–26.

4. Eric H. Kadler, *Linguistics and Teaching Foreign Languages* (New York: Litton Educational Publishing, Inc. 1970, pp. 86–87).

5. See for example Richard Teschner, "A Critical Annotated Bibliography of Anglicisms in Spanish," *Hispania* 57(1974) 631–78.

6. For instances, as exemplified by André Martinet, *Economie des changements phonétiques* (Bern: Francke, 1955); F. Jungemann, *La teoría del sustrato y los*

dialectos hispano-romances y gascones (Madrid: Gredos, 1956); A. G. Haudricourt and A. G. Juilland, *Essai pour une histoire structurale du phonétisme français* (2nd ed. The Hague: Mouton, 1970).

7. Tomás Navarro Tomás, *El español en Puerto Rico* (3rd ed. Río Piedras: Editorial Universitaria, 1974).

8. Samuel Gili y Gaya, *Nuestra lengua materna* (San Juan: Instituto de Cultura Puertorriquena, 1965).

9. Germán de Granda, *Transculturación e interferencia lingüística en el Puerto Rico contemporaneo (1898–1968)* (Río Piedras: Editorial Edil, 1971).

10. Washington Lloréns, *El habla popular de Puerto Rico* (Río Piedras: Editorial Edil, 1971).

11. Paulino Pérez Sala, *Interferencia lingüística del inglés en el español hablado en Puerto Rico* (Hato Rey: Inter American University Press, 1973).

12. Cf. Noam Chomsky, *Syntactic Structure* (The Hague: Mouton, 1957); Paul Postal, *Constituent Structure* (Bloomington: Indiana University Press, 1964); *Aspects of Phonological Theory* (New York: Harper & Row, 1968).

13. Ferdinand de Saussure, *A Course in General Linguistics*, trans. W. Baskin (New York: Philosophical Library, 1959).

14. See R. Jakobson and M. Halle, *Fundamentals of Language* (The Hague: Mouton, 1956), pp. 48–81; R. Jakobson, *Studies on Child Language and Aphasia* (The Hague: Mouton, 1971), pp. 49–94.

15. Roland Barthes, *Elements of Semiology*, trans. A. Lavers and C. Smith (Boston, Beacon Press, 1970), p. 86.

16. See the references in fn. 6; also, E. Dorfman, "Correlation and Core-relation in Diachronic Romance Phonology," *Word* 24 (1968) 81–98.

17. For one recent study, see K. I. McCalla, "System Attraction and the Syntagm: Modern English Assimilation," *La Linguistique* 9 (1973) 95–104.

18. R. J. Restrepo, "More on 'lo' and 'le'," *Hispania* 52 (1969) 433–34 [p. 433].

19. M. A. Jamos, "El fenómeno de 'estar siendo,' " *Hispania* 55 (1972) 128–31 [p. 129].

20. For further discussion of this same expression, see Gili y Gaya, *op. cit.*, p. 70.

21. J. Vallejo, "Notas sobre la expresión concesiva," *Revista de Filología Española* 9 (1922) 40–51.

22. For example Gili y Gaya, *op. cit.*; Rose Nash, "Spanglish: Language Contact in Puerto Rico," *American Speech* 45 (1970) 223–33.

23. The term "bivalent" has been suggested by William E. Bull, "Spanish Adjective Position and the Theory of Valence Classes," *Hispania* 37 (1954) 32–38.

24. For further discussion of the evolution of *gustar*, see John Lipski, "A Syntactic-semantic Shift in Spanish," *Folia Linguistica* 7 (1974).

25. For a discussion of Spanish interrogative patterns, see R. P. Stockwell, J. D. Bowen and J. W. Martin, *The Grammatical Structures of English and Spanish* (Chicago: University of Chicago Press, (1965), pp. 220–30; Roger L. Hadlich, *A Transformational Grammar of Spanish* (Englewood Cliffs, N.J.: Prentice-Hall, 1971) pp. 115–19.

26. M. Ramsey, *A Textbook of Modern Spanish,* revised by R. Spaulding (New York: Holt, Rinehart & Winston, 1956 [1st ed. 1894]), p. 507.

27. Enrique Lafourcade, *El príncipe y las ovejas* (Santiago de Chile: Editorial Zig Zag, 1961).

28. Lizandro Chávez Alfaro, *Trágame tierra* (Mexico: Editorial Diógenes, 1969).

29. Severo Sarduy, *Gestos* (Barcelona: Seix Barral, 1963).

30. This is a commonly known fact in psycholinguistics. For a novel discussion, in terms of "centos," see Fred Householder, *Linguistic Speculations* (Cambridge: Cambridge University Press, 1971), Chap. 15.

31. P. Henríquez Ureña, "Ello," *Revista de Filología Hispánica* 1 (1939) 209–29 [p. 209]; also, Mercedes Roldán, "Reflexivation in Spanish," in Rose Nash, ed., *Readings in Spanish-English Contrastive Linguistics* (Hato Rey: Inter American University Press, 1973), pp. 197–219 [pp. 202-05].

Spanish in the Inner City: Puerto Rican Speech in New York

WILLIAM G. MILÁN
Yeshiva University

They call it "Spanglish"! To many the term is insulting, since it is often used to refer to a "decadent" dialectal form spoken by a lower-class minority group. Purists despair when they hear it, not so much because of the term itself, or the "mixture" it implies, but because to them it is only a symptom of a greater disease that threatens to destroy the Spanish language. What is most amazing about this whole attitudinal syndrome is that the linguistic phenomenon that causes it, that has prompted so much concern among educators, so much grief among academicians, and so much cross-cultural misunderstanding, has received little attention from the kind of research scholars who would be best equipped to elucidate the problem.

It is ironic that the English spoken by Puerto Ricans in New York City has been the subject of such extensive and valuable research while New York City Puerto Rican Spanish has been neglected.[1] The first significant research project done on mainland Puerto Rican Spanish was Charles W. Kreidler's doctoral dissertation for the University of Michigan in 1958: "A Study of the Influence of English on the Spanish of Puerto Ricans in Jersey City, New Jersey". Kreidler's emphasis was on the acquisition and adaptation of English loan words; his research design, with its forms-oriented questionnaire, was in a sense years ahead of its time. This first attempt to make a systematic analysis of the influence of English on mainland Puerto Rican Spanish continues to be a valuable resource document to this day.

This is a revised version of a paper, "The Influence of Bilingualism on the Evolution of American Urban Spanish: Puerto Rican Speech in New York City, a Case in Point," delivered as part of the Chicano-Riqueño Lecture Series, Indiana University, Bloomington, Indiana, April 1, 1976.

191

Cesáreo Rosa Nieves speaks of the influence of English in New York City Puerto Rican Spanish as the seed that will give rise to a new language some day. His article "El español de Puerto Rico en Nueva York" (1969) consists of a classification of English loan words taken from New York City Puerto Rican speech and, except for a couple of mistaken etymologies, it is rather informative and interesting. It does not represent a major contribution to the field, however.

The turn of the decade saw the New School for Social Research of New York City embark on a new pedagogical extravaganza: the teaching of "Spanglish" as a spoken norm to New York area professionals, supposedly to enable them to communicate with the Puerto Rican population they served. This, of course, became a matter of concern to the Puerto Rican intellectual community in New York City, and to the conventional defenders of the purity of the language who simply could not sit still and accept such humiliation. Carlos Varo took the lead in denouncing the New School's innovative endeavor as being an outright insult to the Puerto Rican community. He presented his case in a "comunicación" to the Second International Congress on the Teaching of the Spanish Language (1971), and the document was subsequently published as a brief monograph entitled *Consideraciones antropológicas y políticas en torno a la enseñanza del "Spanglish" en Nueva York* (1971). It is important to note that Varo's intention was to raise the anthropological and political issues that were implicit in the ill-advised pedagogical practices of the New School. "Spanglish" was not at that time (nor is it today) a standardized linguistic code that could be acquired through formal instruction. His seemingly negative remarks about bilingualism in general should not be interpreted as coming from a contemporary sociolinguistic or psycholinguistic research base, since they are clearly more in the tradition of the Sapir-Whorf theory of language relativity as applied by conservative language philosophers. But he makes a significant contribution by calling our attention to the social dangers inherent in the institutionalization of unconsummated linguistic change. His criticism of the New School and of the political and educational establishments in Puerto Rico serves to expose the serious need for some comprehensive language policy in the case of the Puerto Rican community.

Another voice of protest raised against the New School for Social Research was that of Carlos Hamilton. His "Amenazas contra el español en los Estados Unidos" (1971), though not a significant contribution to the study of New York City's brand of Puerto Rican Spanish, does make a very interesting and most important point: that the teaching and spreading of this particular linguistic variety as if it were a spoken norm may in fact constitute a threat to an equal opportunity education for the Spanish-speaking minorities.

Micho Fernández has written a very short but informative article entitled "El Barrio Diccionario: Spanglish Made Easy" (1972). The article is written for a very broad and diverse audience and it gives a quick overview of the most commonly discussed features of New York City Spanish, some examples, and some facts about the ideological battle between the New School for Social Research and the offended Puerto Rican community. Of a similar journalistic style is Eladio Secades' article "El Spanglish . . . ¡qué horror!" (1972), which appeared in ABC *de las Américas*. It adds very little to the works mentioned above, and it has no pretensions about being a scientifically researched piece of scholarship.

The first attempt to systematically abstract, classify, and discuss the characteristic features of the Puerto Rican Spanish spoken on the mainland is contained within a larger study called; "The Language of Puerto Rico: Three Myths, and Their Realities," co-authored by Adriana L. de Galanes, William G. Milán, and Miguel A. Santiago. The authors have tried to isolate those structural phenomena of New York City Spanish that can be attributed to its contact with English, as well as to describe them and give some examples. I will be discussing some of those "characteristic features" later in this study.

José Luís Monserrate has presented the most novel approach to the subject of continental Puerto Rican Spanish. In his study, "Spanglish, an Attempt Towards a Sociolinguistic Classification," he gives a brief historical account of the events leading up to the establishment of the social context in which New York City Spanish was originally installed and continues to grow, and then proceeds to place it within Stewart's linguistic varieties classification matrix.[2] Using as his criteria some basic sociolinguistic attributes (standardization, historicity, autonomy, and vitality), Monserrate concludes that what is commonly called "Spanglish" is in fact a variety of Spanish, and he places it somewhere between a dialect and a creole.

As we can see, most studies of New York City Spanish can be grouped into three basic categories: those which are primarily descriptive and informative (Kreidler, Fernández, Rosa Nieves, Galanes et al.); those which are primarily argumentative (Varo, Secades, Hamilton); and a third category which must be reserved for Monserrate, who has made the first attempt to look at the phenomenon within a community-based socio-attitudinal framework rather than in terms of its internal structure or political implications.

Perhaps we are ready now to look at this phenomenon that we call "Spanglish" from a different perspective. Rather than studying "Spanglish" as an isolated linguistic phenomenon, we should be taking more into consideration the broader sociolinguistic context in which it originates. And instead of focusing on it as an exclusively contemporary issue, we should be viewing it within the historical continuum of language evolution. In taking this approach, we will soon come to two interesting realizations: that the peculiarities we observe in New York City Spanish are largely due to intragroup bilingualism, and that what we are observing is not a mere accidental change in language *content,* but the structural manifestation of a rather consistent diachronic *process.*

Let us take a look at our first realization. Can these apparently peculiar features of New York City Spanish come about spontaneously, without intragroup bilingualism? Uriel Weinreich's classical definition of "bilingualism" as a situation in which two languages are in contact to the extent that they are used alternatively (1953) sounds a little bit unrealistic in this era of the Sociology of Language, since it implies an alternativeness that would defy the effect that such sociolinguistic constructs as domains, value clusters, social situations, topic, and locale can and do have in code selection. The works of Ferguson (1959), Rubin (1968), and Fishman (Fishman, Cooper, Ma, et al., 1975) have successfully put multilingualism in a societal dimension and have shown that, regardless of the extent of an individual's latent bilingual competence, the ability to speak more than one language is actualized only at a community level and is therefore affected by social constraints.

Along these lines, it is worthwhile to consider Robert Di Pietro's universals in multilingualism (1970). According to the first of Di Pietro's principles, the stability of multilingualism depends on the extent to which the community is capable of keeping the languages in question compartmentalized within different contexts.[3] In other words, the only way to maintain a multilingual situation on a community-wide scale is through diglossia; that way, each language can ideally be kept and safeguarded within its own domains, and "contact" with the other language is minimized. Where such compartmentalization is limited, one of two things is bound to happen: either one language will displace the other, or the two systems will merge, since a community that functions with two alternative codes can do as good a job with just one.[4]

Bearing in mind what could be the result of intensive language contact, Di Pietro's second universal deserves even more careful consideration. It states that since language evolution depends largely on the total context in which such evolution is taking place, the presence of another language within that context will be a major factor in the evolutionary process.[5] The implications of these two principles are rather serious. Whether we agree with Di Pietro or not, we do have to wonder where in the world we can find a case of diglossia (where two different languages are involved) so strict that the two codes would not influence each other. In any situation where two coexisting languages are widely spoken by the same population, mutual influence is inevitable. The degree to which this mutual influence occurs will be determined by diglossic constraints. In the case of a fairly stable diglossia, such as that in Paraguay, where Spanish and Guaraní coexist in a rather well-compartmentalized situation, this cross-linguistic influence is not monumental, but it does exist. Joan Rubin lists several cases of cross-linguistic loan translations and lexical borrowings that occur between Spanish and Guaraní.[6]

In cases where sociolinguistic compartmentalization is less constrained—as in the code-switching situations in the village of Kupwar (Maharashtra, India), where three languages have coexisted for centuries—cross-linguistic influence can be so great that a common converged grammar can develop. Gumperz and Wilson (1971) have studied the structures of the Kupwar varieties of Hindi-Urdu, Marathi, and Kannada and have found that the three languages have influenced each other to the point that they all share the same grammatical rules.[7]

Studies done in the area of continental Puerto Rican bilingualism do not document either one of the above extreme situations.[8] From the research done on the subject, we can conclude that neither an extremely constrained diglossia nor a case of widely spread alternative bilingualism exists in the New York City area Puerto Rican community.

One thing we do know for sure, and that is that there is a great deal of *intragroup* bilingualism in this community. In other words, the speech community in question, contrary to common belief, is not exclusively Spanish speaking. The positive acceptance of this fact would make our study and *understanding* of the peculiarities of New York City Spanish a lot easier. The reasons for this intragroup bilingualism are obvious. The younger Puerto Rican generation is being educated in a school system that still has as its primary objective the achievement by all students of an adequate level of competence in English by the time of graduation. Consequently, the members of the new generation of New York-raised and New York-born Puerto Ricans have received a great deal of exposure to the English language and use it considerably for intragroup communication.[9] Let us not forget also that the political status of Spanish in New York City is that of a migrant language and as such it is often excluded from several important domains (e.g., education and employment).[10] The necessity to interact in those domains daily has forced most New York Puerto Ricans to acquire at least some functional competence in English. It has been my own experience that, even in intragroup conversations in which the subject pertains to these extra-group domains, the English language is frequently used.

Given these two factors, it is impossible to ignore the fact that English is very much a part of Puerto Rican life in New York City and that Spanish is therefore very much exposed to its influence. It is not my intention to discuss whether this is good or bad. My only point is that when we look at New York City Puerto Rican speech we must look at the total picture and thus must take into consideration the existence of that often ignored intragroup bilingualism and the fact that, like it or not, Spanish and English are very much in contact.

I would like to elaborate on the four major "characteristic features" attributed to New York City Spanish as they have been identified in the literature in general and to give particular attention to those discussed by Galanes et al.

1. Semantic reassignment.   This is a very common phenomenon, which consists of a transference of meaning from a word in one language to a word in another language which originally had a different meaning of its own. While semantic reassignments can occur under many different circumstances, ranging from the predictable to the totally arbitrary, at least in New York City Spanish they seem to be limited to pairs of false cognates only. For example, "carpet" in English refers to something used to cover the floors. There is a Spanish word *carpeta* that is commonly used to refer to a small portfolio or loose-leaf binder. In contemporary New York City Puerto Rican speech, the Spanish word *carpeta* has assumed a new meaning: something used to cover floors; thus it has become a true cognate of the corresponding English word. Another example, this one even more interesting, is that of *aplicación*. The word *aplicación* in Spanish and the word "application" in English do share a common meaning; they both correspond to the postverbal nominalization of the verb "to apply" (Spanish: *aplicar*). So in addition to being acoustic correlates, they are also cognates on at least one count. However, the English word "application" also refers to the set of documents that one fills out in order to be considered for employment, membership in an organization, or some other type of benefit; this meaning is not shared by *aplicación* in standard Spanish. Through contact with English, the Spanish word *aplicación* has picked up this new meaning also and has displaced the traditional bona fide standard Spanish term *solicitud*.

I want to stress that this is a common phenomenon and that, while in the case of New York City Puerto Rican Spanish it seems to occur only where there is at least a pair of false cognates, semantic reassignments can and do occur freely even where there is no acoustic similarity between the words involved. We will see some examples of this later.

2. Large-scale word borrowing.   This has been considered the most prominent "characteristic feature" of New York City Spanish. Again, we are dealing with a very common phenomenon. Responding to the pressures of the English language in those domains where it prevails, Spanish has been forced to pick up a great deal of domain-relevant terminology. In addition, an array of words proceeding from multiple semantic fields has penetrated the Spanish language, sometimes out of necessity since there are no adequate words in Spanish to match the borrowed words' meanings, but sometimes for no apparent "justifiable" reason and at the expense of bona fide Spanish words, which are then displaced and eventually lost. In this category we can list *bil* (English: "bill"), which replaces the Spanish words *cuenta* and *factura;* and *jol* (English: "hall"), which replaces the Spanish word *pasillo.*

3. Loan translations.   This is another very common phenomenon. It consists of the adaptation of an expression from the second language into the everyday usage of the native tongue. Essentially, this is accomplished by a literal translation of the expression from one language to the other. Thus the English expression "take advantage of this opportunity" becomes the often heard New York City Spanish construction *tome usted ventaja de esta oportunidad* (Standard Spanish: *aprovéchese usted de esta oportunidad*).

4. Morphosyntactic readjustment.   This fourth "characteristic feature" is the most subtle one, and therefore it is the least noticeable. For example, notice the shift in word order as seen in: *¿Qué usted piensa?* The verb is placed after the pronoun. This is in fact a restructuring of the Spanish word order to fit the English syntax as in "What do you think?" The standard Spanish construction would be: *¿Qué piensa usted?*, with the pronoun following the verb. In addition to adjustments in word order, there have also been some changes in the grammatical role of certain forms. For example, the Spanish present progressive is being used more frequently in place of the present indicative. Thus we hear *estoy teniendo problemas* (English: "I am having problems") instead of the usual *tengo problemas* (English: "I have problems"). While the present progressive construction is not a recent innovation in Spanish, its usage in this context may be linked to language contact.

We now move on to consider our second realization: that the changes we observe in New York City Puerto Rican Spanish are not mere accidental changes in language *content* but are structural manifestations of a rather consistent diachronic *process.* Anybody who has taken the most elementary course on the history of the Spanish language, or who is at least capable of reading Lapesa's *Historia de la lengua española* (1965) with a minimum of understanding, should be able to realize that the so-called "characteristic features" of this brand of New York City

Spanish that some people want to call "Spanglish" are anything but exclusive. All four of the major characteristics discussed above are common everyday linguistic changes that occur naturally in language evolution. Of the four, only the second and third are more likely to occur when two or more languages are in contact. The first and fourth changes can occur spontaneously, as a result of internal currents in language evolution or out of sheer inexplainable arbitrariness. Of course, the presence of another language can make a difference. It can prevent a change, it can precipitate it, or it can shift it. For our historical considerations let us first take those linguistic changes that can occur in a non-language-contact situation and then show how throughout the history of the Spanish language they have been known to come about spontaneously, by themselves, or with the help of a coexisting language. We will be looking, therefore, at semantic reassignments and morpho-syntactic adjustments.

Semantic reassignment is a very common phenomenon in language evolution. Consider, for example, that none of the original roots corresponding to the following "bona fide" Spanish words had the same meaning in Proto-Romanic times that they have today: *juego, casa,* and *pierna.*[11] Instead of "game," "house," and "leg," the corresponding romance roots that yielded these words meant "scorn," "hut," and "ham." The original Latin roots that once bore the meanings presently attributed to these modern forms are now defunct: *ludus* for "game," *domus* for "house," and *crus* for "leg."[12] There is no apparent "justification" for these semantic reassignments, nor is any justification necessary. I have yet to hear any of the conservative defenders of the language complain about these changes or suggest that we resurrect the original forms and restore their meanings.

Semantic reassignments have also occurred in Spanish because of the influence of another language. Take, for example, those reassignments that occurred as a result of the contact between Spanish and Arabic. Notice that these reassignments took place without there even being false cognates. In other words, there was no acoustic resemblance between the two words in question. What apparently brought about the reassignment was the semantic duality of one of the contact words. *Infante,* which originally referred to just "child," took on the meaning of "crown prince," because the Arabic word for child, *walad,* also had that meaning.[13] Note also how a Spanish word like *adelantado* (the one ahead or in front) assumed the Arabic meanings for *almuqaddan,* which, in addition to meaning "the one ahead or in front," also meant "chief," "magistrate," and "authority."[14]

As we can see, semantic reassignments are not major disasters. They have taken place throughout the entire history of the language. They can occur spontaneously, or they can occur under the pressures of a contact language. When they occur through language contact, they occur usually because the two words in question share at least one meaning (*infante–walad*), have some acoustic resemblance (carpet–*carpeta*), or meet both of these criteria (application–*aplicación*).

So far, I myself have been able to document semantic reassignments in New York City Spanish only in cases where the words in question do bear some acoustic resemblance. Some pairs may also share part of their "original" semantic content, but this does not seem to be a prerequisite for the change to take place. If we can accept semantic reassignments as drastic as the internal ones we see in *juego, casa,* and *pierna,* and reassignments that have come about through Arabic influence where there is no acoustic resemblance at all between the words in question, I simply fail to see what is so special about the semantic reassignments occurring in New York Spanish that makes them so offensive.

Like semantic reassignments, morphosyntactic readjustments are part of the everyday process of language evolution. History tells us that grammatical constructions in general and word order in particular are not eternal and sacrosanct. As a matter of fact, most of the grammatical rules prescribed today by the *Academia* did not even exist a few centuries ago.

Literally dozens of Proto-Romance grammatical features have disappeared. There is hardly any trace left in modern Spanish of the once widely used future subjunctive *(que yo fuere)*. The stock of verbs in the ancestral form of Spanish was originally divided into four conjugations. The second and third conjugations merged, thus reducing the number of conjugations to three.[15] And of course, unless we go way back to the proto-embryonic stages of the development of Romance, we can find no trace of declensions or case systems in nouns.[16]

In the course of language evolution, new forms have been created to replace those which were abandoned. For example, the original Latin future tense no longer exists. In its place, a new form has been created consisting of the infinitive stem plus the contracted form of the present indicative of *haber*.[17] Thus, instead of the original Latin *amabo* (I will love), we have *amar he* (modern Spanish: *amaré*).

Some forms have assumed new grammatical roles. For example, both the original Romance pluperfect indicative and the pluperfect subjunctive are now functioning as alternative forms of the Spanish imperfect subjunctive: *cantara, cantase*.[18]

Several grammatical practices have been abandoned or totally displaced. *Ser* is no longer used as an auxiliary to form the past participle of intransitive verbs. We no longer say *son idos*, but *han ido* (they have gone).[19] Notice also how the gender and number agreement between the participle form and the object have been abandoned. We no longer say *"no la avemos usada,"* but *no la hemos usado* (we have not used it).[20]

As far as word order is concerned, let it simply be stated that almost every single word order rule of modern Spanish is an innovation. Syntax as we know it today became necessary only after the loss of the Romance case system. And even when word order became a necessity, it did not start out as a fixed and unchangeable set of rules. In *El Cid*, for example, we have multiple instances in which the object precedes the verb: *el agua nos han vedada* instead of the modern construction *nos han vedado el agua.*[21]

From a structural point of view, I fail to see how these morphosyntactic readjustments that we so agreeably accept today differ from the so-called New York City Spanish constructions that we discussed earlier. Morphosyntactic changes are part of the natural process of language evolution. To what extent some of these changes can be attributed to language contact, we do not know. One thing we do know for sure is that in order for us to have a Spanish language today with something that can be called a grammar of its own, its ancestral Proto-Romance form had to undergo major morphosyntactic changes, next to which the grammatical readjustments found in New York City Puerto Rican speech must be considered minor.

I would like to concentrate now on the two types of changes that are likely to occur most frequently in a language contact situation: word borrowing and loan translations.

Word borrowing is as old as bilingualism itself. When two languages coexist, they will borrow from each other—that is inevitable. The borrowing might be "justified," as in the cases where a foreign word is required to express a foreign concept that does not exist in the original language, or it may simply be gratuitous and arbitrary. I wonder how the defenders of the Spanish language would react if a resolution were presented to the *Academia* to disenfranchise some of the most commonly used "bona fide" Spanish words, such as the following:

A.	B.	C.	D.
camisa	idea	guerra	ropa
cabaña	fantasía	falda	ganso
cerveza	música	dardo	tapa
legua	atleta	albergue	gana

E.	F.	G.	H.
zanahoria	mensaje	piloto	chocolate
azúcar	manjares	atacar	tiza
algodón	viandas	belleza	tocayo
tambor	vinagre	avería	maíz

Every single one of these words is a borrowing from another language. The words in column A are of Celtic origin.[22] Those in column B are of Greek origin.[23] Those in column C are of Germanic origin.[24] Those in column D are of Visigothic origin.[25] Those in column E came from Arabic.[26] Those in column F came from French.[27] Those in column G came from Italian.[28] And those in column H are of Amerindian ancestry.[29]

Whether these words entered the Romance mainstream in Pre-Iberian times, as was probably the case for the first four groups, or whether they became part of an already growing Spanish tongue, as was certainly the case for the latter four groups, all of them have three things in common:

1. They are *not* of Hispanic origin.
2. At the time of their borrowing they were as foreign to the linguistic mainstream that received them as are the English borrowings found in New York City Spanish today.
3. In the course of time, they became generalized, commonly accepted, and finally so well integrated into the Spanish lexical stock that they are no longer considered foreign.

I am troubled by the kind of attitude that would arbitrarily reject a borrowing from contemporary English, when history shows that the Spanish language is full of borrowings from other languages. Whatever the criteria may be for such animosity against English contributions to the Spanish lexicon, it certainly is not justifiable from a diachronic linguistic point of view.

Contrary to common belief, loan translations are not contemporary innovations either. Loan translation is another phenomenon that is most likely to occur in a language contact situation. It is very similar to word borrowing in that once the integration of the translated expression has taken place, hardly anybody will recognize that the expression is foreign. As a matter of fact it may even become part of the "native" folklore. After all, what could be more Hispanic than the prayerful expression *si Dios quiere,* (God willing), or that enthusiastic exclamation *bendita sea la madre que te parió* (blessed be the mother that bore you). Ironically enough, these expressions, which have become part of the very soul of the Hispanic people, are not Hispanic at all. They are both loan translations from Arabic.[30]

My conclusions will be brief and to the point:

1. We need to study the state of the Spanish language in New York City much more seriously than we have done so far. In doing so, we need to pay more attention to the sociolinguistic context in which it is

evolving, a context in which, in addition to intragroup bilingualism, there exist broader extra-group conditions where Spanish is a subordinated language and therefore more exposed to change.

2. The so-called "characteristic features" of New York City Spanish are no more than common changes that naturally occur in language contact situations. If we look at the history of the Romance languages, we see that centuries ago some form of vulgar Latin left the territorial boundaries of Rome, migrated to far-off places, came into contact with other languages, and evolved into what we know today as French, Portugese, Sardinian, Provençal, Rumanian, Spanish, etc. The differences between any two of these languages are good indications of the significance of the different language contact situations that played an important role in their evolution.

3. We simply cannot pretend to stop the course of history. Languages will evolve and change even when in total isolation, let alone when in contact with other languages that can influence them. I disagree with Varo's assertion that when we speak of "Spanglish" we are speaking more of a form of speech full of barbarisms such as we may expect to hear from lower-class uncultured people than of a language in transition or evolution (Varo, 1971, p. 125). If that assertion is true, I have yet to see any convincing proof. As I have shown in this study, the nonstandard elements that we find in New York City Spanish can be easily explained in terms of natural diachronic evolution within a language contact situation. If we go back in time, we see that any language spoken today had a humble origin and was initially regarded as vulgar, barbaric, and low class. It is amusing, and almost prophetic, that only a few centuries ago scholars such as Cicero were making similar remarks about the poor Latin spoken by the Roman citizens of Galia and Hispania. Little did they know that the bastardized dialects they criticized were destined to become the French of Victor Hugo and the Spanish of Cervantes.[31]

4. The hate literature campaign that is being conducted against the Spanish spoken by our New York City Puerto Rican community is creating serious polarization and is doing more harm than good. One cannot attack the way the people speak without attacking the people themselves. The energy of those well-meaning scholars and journalists would be put to better use if they tried to make a positive contribution to the education of those "culturally deprived" people whose language they claim to defend. Let us see these writers do something constructive that, instead of lowering the morale of our New York Puerto Ricans, will serve to increase their self-esteem.

As a final consideration, I would like to propose that both the researchers studying contemporary Puerto Rican speech in New York City and the practitioners striving for an equal educational opportunity for the city's Puerto Rican population make a truly concerted effort to avoid using the term "Spanglish." As a scientific term attempting to designate a particular phenomenon, it is hopeless since it fails to capture the broader context wherein the phenomenon occurs. As a label it is grossly misleading, since it does not even come close to describing either the structure or the nature of its pretended designatum. The inadequacy of the term has been denounced by many outstanding linguists who feel strongly that a more scientifically sound way of referring to this phenomenon must be found. I would think that this brief statement coming from one of them is a fair summary of their concern:

> The term "Spanglish". . . is as misunderstood and misleading as the term "Tex-Mex" in Texas, and particularly gets caught up in misunderstandings of code-switched speech as a hopeless syncretism of the two languages, in which the speakers cannot separate them. Tactically, insisting on New York City, or continental Puerto Rican Spanish as the appropriate terms would be a major contribution to increasing acceptance of it as a legitimate variety.[32]

It is about time that we start referring to this phenomenon as what it really is: a simple, natural, and ordinary series of structural manifestations of the ongoing process of language evolution. And the time is long overdue for us to accept this particular form of speech as a linguistic variety in its own right, with all the traits that it is entitled to on account of its historical, situational, and socio-environmental realities, without vague labels, without any apologies, and without any stigma.

NOTES

1. I highly recommend Richard V. Teschner, Garland D. Bills, and Jerry R. Craddock (1975). Its chapter on Puerto Ricans on the United States mainland' contains the most complete literature search on Puerto Rican mainland bilingualism published to this day, and it serves to illustrate my point that Puerto Rican English has received a lot more attention than Puerto Rican mainland Spanish.

2. As Stewart's classification matrix in Fishman (1972), p. 22.

3. Di Pietro (1970), pp. 18–19.

4. Di Pietro (1970), p. 8. For further information on the subject, consult also Fishman (1968b) and Mackey (1968).

5. Di Pietro (1970), pp. 19–20.

6. Rubin (1968), pp. 118–22.

7. See Fasold (1975), manuscript, Center for Applied Linguistics.

8. Refer to the plethora of studies collected by Fishman, Cooper, and Ma (1975).

9. See Chapter 6 of Fishman, Cooper, and Ma (1975), pp. 117–56, for an informative and enlightening interview with mainland Puerto Rican high school students.

10. This exclusion is imposed by extra-group pressures, but its effect on the sociolinguistic behavior of the members of the Puerto Rican community is so marked that it can be measured. See Lawrence Greenfield and Joshua Fishman, "Situational Measures of Normative Language Views of Person, Places, and Topic Among Puerto Rican Bilinguals" in Fishman, Cooper, and Ma (1975), pp. 233–52.

11. For the purposes of this study the terms "Proto-Romance" and "Romance" will refer to the early ancestral forms of Spanish and other Romance languages. Essentially, we are talking here about the migrating brand of vulgar Latin that was spread throughout the entire Roman Empire by the imperial legions. For further clarification of these terms, see William J. Calvano, "Is Old Spanish a Node on the Stammbaum?" (1975). See also Hall (1950) and Elcock (1960), pp. 18–169, 398–445.

12. Lapesa (1965), p. 59.

13. Lapesa, (1965), p. 109.

14. Lapesa, (1965), pp. 109–10.

15. Menéndez Pidal (1962), p. 284.

16. Elcock (1960), pp. 17–169.

17. Menéndez Pidal (1962), pp. 322–23.

18. Menéndez Pidal, (1962), p. 310.

19. Lapesa (1965), p. 151.

20. Lapesa (1965), p. 152.

21. Lapesa (1965), p. 154.

22. Lapesa (1965), p. 35.

23. Lapesa (1965), p. 44.

24. Lapesa (1965), p. 80.

25. Lapesa (1965), p. 87.

26. Lapesa (1965), pp. 98 ff.

27. Lapesa (1965), pp. 120–21.

28. Lapesa (1965), p. 183.

29. Lapesa (1965), p. 347.

30. Lapesa (1965), p. 110.

31. Canino-Salgado (1975), pp. 23–34.

32. Rudolf C. Troike, 1976, private communication.

REFERENCES

Alatis, James E., ed. *Bilingualism and Language Contact*. GURT 1970. Washington, D.C.: Georgetown University Press, 1970.

Calvano, William J. "Is Old Spanish a Node in the Stammbaum?" In *1974 Colloquium on Spanish and Portuguese Linguistics*, ed. William G. Milán, John Staczek, and Juan C. Zamora. Washington, D.C.: Georgetown University Press, 1975, pp. 12–22.

Canino-Salgado, Marcelino Juan. "El habla de las clases jóvenes en Puerto Rico: proyecciones hacia una lengua futura." In *1974 Colloquium on Spanish and Portuguese Linguistics*, ed. William G. Milán, John J. Staczek, and Juan C. Zamora. Washington, D.C.: Georgetown University Press, 1975, pp. 23–34.

Colhoun, Edward. "Local and Non-Local Frames of Reference in Puerto Rican Dialectology." Doctoral dissertation, Cornell University, Ithaca, N.Y., 1967.

Di Pietro, Robert J. "The Discovery of Universals in Multilingualism." In *Bilingualism and Language Contact*, ed. James E. Alatis. GURT 1970. Washington, D.C.: Georgetown University Press, 1970, pp. 13–24.

Elcock, W.D. *The Romance Languages*. London: Farber and Farber, 1960.

Fasold, Ralph W. "Sociolinguistics: Contributions to Bilingual Education." Paper presented at the Linguistic Society of America Symposium on Bilingualism (sponsored by the National Institute of Education and the Center for Applied Linguistics), San Francisco, December 1975.

Ferguson, Charles A. "Diglossia." *Word*, 15, (1959), 325–40.

Fernández, Micho. "El Barrio Diccionario: Spanglish Made Easy." *New York Magazine*, August 7, 1972, pp. 46–48.

Fishman, Joshua A., ed. *Readings in Sociology of Language*. The Hague: Mouton, 1968a.

———. "Sociolinguistic Perspective on the Study of Bilingualism." *Linguistics*, 39 (1968b), 21–49.

———. *The Sociology of Language*. Rowley, Mass.: Newbury House, 1972.

Fishman, Joshua A.; Cooper, Robert; Ma, Roxana; et al. *Bilingualism in the Barrio*, 2d ed. Language Science Monographs, Vol. 7. Bloomington: Indiana University Press, 1975.

Galanes, Adriana; Milán, William G.; and Santiago, Miguel Ángel. "The Language of Puerto Rico: Three Myths and Their Realities." Paper presented at the Symposium on Puerto Rican Studies (sponsored by the Center for Inter American Studies), Philadelphia, Temple University, 1971.

Gumperz, John, and Wilson, Robert. "Convergence and Creolization: A Case from the Indo-Aryan/Dravidian Border."In *Pidginization and Creolization of Languages*, ed. Dell Hymes. Cambridge: Cambridge University Press, 1971, pp. 151–68.

Hall, Robert A. "The Reconstruction of Proto-Romance." *Language*, 26 (1950), 6–27.

Hamilton, Carlos D. "Amenazas contra el español en Estados Unidos." *Español Actual*, 19 (October 1971), 23–25.

Hymes, Dell. *Pidginization and Creolization of Languages*. Cambridge: Cambridge University Press, 1971.

Kreidler, Charles W. "A Study of the Influence of English on the Spanish of Puerto Ricans in Jersey City, New Jersey." Doctoral dissertation, Ann Arbor, University of Michigan, 1958.

Lapesa, Rafael. *Historia de la lengua española*. 6th ed. New York: Las Américas, 1965.

Mackey, William F. "The Description of Bilingualism." In *Readings in the Sociology of Language,* ed. Joshua A. Fishman. The Hague: Mouton, 1968, pp. 554–84.

Menéndez Pidal, Ramón, *Manual de gramática histórica española.* 11th ed. Madrid: Espasa-Calpe, 1962.

Milán, William G.; Staczek, John J.; and Zamora, Juan C. *1974 Colloquium on Spanish and Portuguese Linguistics.* Washington, D.C.: Georgetown University Press, 1975.

Monserrate, José Luis. "Spanglish; an Attempt Towards a Sociolinguistic Classification." Unpublished manuscript, Amherst, University of Massachusetts, 1975.

Navarro-Tomás, Tomás. *El español en Puerto Rico.* Río Piedras, Editorial Universitaria, 1966.

Rosa Nieves, Cesáreo. "El español de Puerto Rico en Nueva York." *Boletín de la Academia de Artes y Ciencias de Puerto Rico,* 5 (1969), 519–29.

Rubin, Joan. *National Bilingualism in Paraguay.* The Hague: Mouton,. 1968.

Secades, Eladio. "El Spanglish, . . . ¡qué horror!" *A B C de las Américas,* November 11–17, 1972, p. 53.

Teschner, Richard V.; Bills, Garland; and Craddock, Jerry, eds. *Spanish and English of United States Hispanos: A Critical, Annotated, Linguistic Bibliography.* Arlington, Va.: Center for Applied Linguistics, 1975.

Varo, Carlos. *Consideraciones antropológicas y políticas en torno a la enseñanza del "Spanglish" en Nueva York.* Río Piedras, Puerto Rico: Ediciones Librería Internacional, 1971.

Weinreich, Uriel. *Languages in Contact.* New York: Linguistic Circle of NewYork, 1953.

No Case for Convergence:
The Puerto Rican Spanish Verb System in a Language-Contact Situation

ALICIA POUSADA
SHANA POPLACK
City University of New York

INTRODUCTION

In situations of language contact it is often the case that the language of lesser (economic or political) prestige adapts to the patterns of the superordinate language (Bloomfield, 1933; Weinreich, 1953). This kind of convergence may occur at all levels of linguistic structure, although lexical transference has been by far the most widely attested.

The grammatical component of language has traditionally been considered relatively stable and perhaps even impervious to external influence (Meillet, 1921; Sapir, 1921). More recently, however, empirical studies of language use in a wide variety of multilingual communities (e.g., Weinreich, 1953; Gumperz and Wilson, 1971; Clyne, 1972; Klein, 1976; Lavandera, 1981) have demonstrated that grammatical systems in contact can influence each other. In particular, Gumperz and Wilson's seminal study of multilingualism in Kupwar, India (1971) describes a situation in which the grammatical systems of three languages have converged to such an extent that they may be said to have a single syntactic surface structure (p. 256).

The Puerto Rican communities in the United States provide an excellent example of language contact, as many have contained stable bilingual populations since the 1930's. The influence of English on Puerto Rican Spanish has been noted throughout the history of the contact situation (e.g., de Granda, 1968; Klein, 1976; Perez Sala, 1973;

This analysis is part of a research project on Intergenerational Perspectives on Bilingualism supported by the National Institute of Education under NIE-G-78-0091 and the Ford Foundation. The paper has benefited from comments and criticism from Jorge Guitart, Don Hindle, Beatriz Lavandera, and David Sankoff, to whom we are very grateful.

Anisman, 1975; Varo, 1971; Seda Bonilla, 1970). The majority of these observations, however, have been impressionistic and have focused predominantly on the easily discernible process of lexical transference.

GOALS

In this study we examine quantitatively the systems of tense, mood, and aspect in Puerto Rican Spanish spoken in the United States. Verb usage is a sensitive gauge of linguistic influence or change. The verbal system is a tightly knit amalgam of morphology, syntax, and semantics and can signal change at any of these levels. Verbs appear in virtually every sentence, making it feasible to collect a large body of data for analysis. In addition, the number of different forms, though large, is not unmanageable. Finally, there is sufficient overlap of the English and Spanish verb systems to allow meaningful comparisons.

By focusing on these core elements of grammar, traditionally most resistant to change, we hope to shed some empirical light on the general problem of linguistic evolution in multilingual communities: Is the influence of the prestige language as pervasive as has been claimed, or is it largely limited to low-level but highly visible lexical transference?[1] Specifically, we will seek answers to the following questions:

1. Has the system of tense, mood, and aspect used by Puerto Ricans in the United States diverged from Spanish as spoken in Puerto Rico or from standard Castilian Spanish?
2. Are the semantic fields, or ranges of meaning, of verb forms being extended or restricted, and in what direction? Are some forms being extended to cover semantic fields of other forms which have fallen into disuse within the Puerto Rican Spanish system, or is there adaptation to specifically English semantic fields?
3. Who is initiating any divergence from standard varieties? Is the change favored by bilingual or English-dominant speakers of Puerto Rican Spanish? Do these speakers employ some verb forms where they are not used by monolingual speakers of Puerto Rican Spanish?
4. What can we predict about the Puerto Rican Spanish tense/mood system in the speech of future generations?

To answer these questions, this study makes an empirical assessment of the distribution of surface verb forms throughout the entire verbal paradigm, as well as the semantic fields covered by each. We compare the relative frequencies of these forms with data from standard Puerto

Rican Spanish, modern and fifteenth-century peninsular Spanish, and English. Such systematic quantitative analysis should produce valuable evidence with which to corroborate or refute the observations of less extensive, qualitative studies of verb usage in American Spanish which characterize the literature (cited in Floyd, 1978).

Other motivations for a study of verb usage come from educational curricula, methodology, and language proficiency testing. Knowledge of the actual distribution of verb forms in Puerto Rican Spanish would be a helpful tool in the determination of teaching practices and priorities. It is just beginning to be acknowledged (Paulston, 1978) that grammatical structures cannot be taught to native speakers in the same way as they have traditionally been taught to nonnatives: the competence already possessed by the students should be taken into consideration. If certain forms occur rarely or never in Puerto Rican speech, they can be assigned lower priority in the learning load than other more frequent and functional structures.

There are further implications for the testing of language proficiency. Current rating scales are based on indications of successful acquisition of vocabulary items as well as of specific verb forms.[2] However, without data on both the actual frequency of occurrence of given forms and their functional load, any assessment of proficiency based on their acquisition must be arbitrary or, at best, geared toward foreign rather than native linguistic competence. Forms that are members of "regular" grammatical paradigms are not always learned first by the native speaker and, as we will show, some of the most complicated structures are also the most commonly used. Measurements of language proficiency should register these facts.

HYPOTHESIS

Several mechanisms for the grammatical influence of one language upon another have been postulated. De Granda (1968) posits a process of "grammaticalization," or convergence of the Spanish spoken in Puerto Rico to parallel English structures. He claims that the influence of the prestige language (English) forces the subordinate language to select and favor those forms which most closely parallel its own semantic fields or expressive forms while eliminating those which have less correspondence with it (p. 166).

Klein (1976, p. 1) has suggested that such a process might be most likely to occur in areas where the languages in contact have constructions which are parallel morphologically but which only partially overlap in their conditions of use. In a quantitative study of the use of two such constructions in the Puerto Rican Spanish of Spanish-dominant and bilingual speakers in the United States, she found that the bilinguals' system of present reference in Puerto Rican Spanish was converging with English (p. 13).

In explaining the convergence of three grammatical systems in Kupwar to the extent that all speakers now speak "word-for-word translatable codes," Gumperz and Wilson (1971) suggested that it is the need for constant code switching which has led to reduction and adaptation in linguistic structure (p. 271).

In the Puerto Rican speech community under investigation, code switching (along with the monolingual use of Spanish and English) is also an integral part of the communicative repertoire (Pedraza, 1979). Moreover, the code switching behavior of the community has been found (Poplack, 1980, 1981) to obey a syntactic equivalence constraint: codes tend to be switched at points around which the surface structures of the two languages map onto each other. Given this constraint, and the use of code switching as an interactional resource, we might expect to find, as has been suggested by Lavandera (1981) for a bilingual Chicano dialect, that Puerto Rican Spanish verb usage is being reinterpreted on the model of English to provide more potential loci for grammatical code switching.

To examine this possibility, we will first compare the standard Spanish and English verbal systems. For those usages where the two systems already coincide, we cannot expect the influence of one language to cause a change in the other. On the other hand, those areas in which the two systems differ to a greater or lesser extent could conceivably reveal transference from one language to another.

Table 1 shows that of the 26 verb forms under consideration, 10 coincide totally with English usage. None of the six morphological manifestations of the Spanish subjunctive mood corresponds to any English form, as English may be considered to have preserved the subjunctive/indicative distinction only lexically in a closed set of forms involving the first and third person (Quirk and Greenbaum, 1978, pp. 51–52). An additional 10 forms show partially overlapping conditions of usage with English, a situation hypothesized to favor transference from one language to the other. These will be examined in greater detail in the ensuing section.

DISTRIBUTION OF VERB FORMS BY SEMANTIC FIELD

A variety of meanings may be expressed by a single surface verb, and the converse is also true. The various forms in Table 1 may be organized

Table 1

Overlapping Conditions of Usage in Standard Spanish and Standard English Verbal Forms

No Overlap	*Partial Overlap*	*Total Overlap*
PRESENT SUBJUNCTIVE: *bese* 'that I kiss'	SIMPLE PRESENT: *beso* 'I kiss'	PRETERITE PERFECT: *había besado* 'I had kissed'
IMPERFECT SUBJUNCTIVE: *besara* 'that I (would) kiss'	IMPERFECT: *besaba* 'I used to kiss/was kissing'	PRETERITE ANTERIOR: *hube besado* 'I had kissed'
FUTURE SUBJUNCTIVE: *besare* 'that I (will) kiss'	PRETERITE: *besé* 'I kissed/did kiss'	FUTURE PERFECT: *habré besado* 'I will have kissed'
PRESENT PERFECT SUBJUNCTIVE: *haya besado* 'that I have kissed'	PRESENT PERFECT: *he besado* 'I kissed/have kissed'	CONDITIONAL: *besaría* 'I would kiss'
PRETERITE PERFECT SUBJUNCTIVE: *hubiera besado* 'that I had kissed'	PRETERITE AUXILIARY + INFINITIVE: *pude besar, tuve que besar* 'I could/had to kiss'	PRETERITE CONDITIONAL: *habría besado* 'I would have kissed'
FUTURE PERFECT SUBJUNCTIVE: *hubiere besado* 'that I have kissed'	IMPERFECT AUXILIARY + INFINITIVE: *podía besar, tenía que besar* 'I could/had to kiss'	PRETERITE PERIPHRASTIC FUTURE: *voy a besar* 'I am going to kiss'
	PRESENT PROGRESSIVE: *estoy besando* 'I am kissing'	IMPERFECT PERIPHRASTIC: *iba a besar* 'I was going to kiss'
	IMPERFECT PROGRESSIVE: *estaba besando* 'I was kissing'	PRESENT AUXILIARY + INFINITIVE: *puedo besar, tengo que besar* 'I can/have to kiss'
	PRETERITE PROGRESSIVE: *estuve besando* 'I was kissing'	IMPERATIVE: *¡besa!* 'kiss!'
	FUTURE: *besaré* 'I will kiss'	INFINITIVE: *besar* 'to kiss'

into three semantic fields: {PAST}, {PRESENT}, and {FUTURE}. We provide here a summary examination of the surface possibilities for expressing each verbal semantic field in Spanish, as well as a comparison with English possibilities where relevant.

{Present}

Four verbal forms may be used to express the semantic field {PRESENT} in Spanish, as can be seen in (1) below:

1a. *Simple Present:* Yo *soy* de Cayey. 'I'm from Cayey.' (003/016)[3]

1b. *Present Auxiliary + Infinitive:* No *pueden hablar* mucho en inglés conmigo. 'They can't speak much English with me.' (037/383)

1c. *Present Progressive: Estoy economizando* dinero. 'I'm saving money.' (004/029)

1d. *Future:* No sé porqué *será.* 'I don't know why that is.' (052/247)

Simple Present.[4] The Simple Present is most commonly used to describe an imperfective action in the present, a "law" of nature, or a habitual activity, as in (2):

2a. No *saben* de qué eran. 'They don't know what they were from.' (004/021)

2b. Uno *mata* por amor, pero por pena no. 'One kills out of love, but not out of pity.' (052/155)

2c. Yo siempre *voy* por un mes o dos meses. 'I always go for one or two months.' (039/122)

Present Progressive.   The Progressive is generally used to express an activity or condition in progress at the moment of speaking, as in (3):

3. ¡Ave María! *¡Estoy chorreando* yo aquí! 'Oh God! I'm dripping!' (002/001)

Simple Present Vs. Present Progressive.   The conditions of use of the Simple Present and Present Progressive differ from Spanish to English. Although characterization of these differences is complex, they may be generally summed up by the fact that ongoing action, which in English must be conveyed by the Present Progressive, may be expressed in Spanish by either form, as in (4):

4. ¡Mira, el barco *se hunde/se está hundiendo*! 'Look, the boat is sinking!'

Given the low frequency of the Progressive in monolingual Spanish (Zdenek, 1972, p. 499), and the fact that components of the English system of present reference are mutually exclusive while in Spanish they are not, it has been hypothesized (e.g., de Granda, 1968; Klein, 1976) that a large incidence of the Progressive to convey ongoing action in the speech of Puerto Rican bilinguals is due to influence from English.

{Past}

There are many different ways to express an action in the past, depending on the degree of remoteness and the aspectual characteristics of the action. Hadlich (1971) identifies three main aspects for past "tense" verbs: the perfective, the imperfective, and the subsequent.

If an action was perfective and completed in the past, the Preterite or the Preterite Anterior are used, the last being differentiated by the degree of remoteness, as in (5):

5a. Yo *vine* a Caguas como cuando tenía seis años. 'I came to Caguas like when I was six.' (003/071)

5b. Pero no *hubo tenido* intimidades de madre y hija. 'But she hadn't had a close mother–daughter relationship.' (050/130)

If the action was imperfective without any mark of initiation or termination, the Imperfect, Present Perfect, and Preterite Perfect are used, the last two again being differentiated by degree of remoteness in the past, as in (6):

6a. *Imperfect:* ¿*Estaba* feliz? 'Was he happy?' (048/029)

6b. *Present Perfect:* Tienes que pagar los gastos que ellos te *han dado*. 'You have to pay back the money they've given you.' (003/109)

6c. *Preterite Perfect:* No *había tenido* hijos de mi esposo. 'I hadn't had any children by my husband.' (050/114)

Finally, if the action took place in the past and was directed into the future, the Future Perfect and the Preterite Conditional are used. These were not attested in the data. In addition, Past Periphrastic and Progressive forms as well as the Historical Present may be used to convey {PAST}. These are exemplified in (7) below:

7a. *Imperfect Auxiliary + Infinitive:* Mi mamá era pobrecita y *tenía que buscar* sus chavos. 'My mother was poor and had to work hard for her money.' (050/065)

7b. *Preterite Auxiliary + Infinitive: Tuvimos que usar* carbón. 'We had to use coal.' (037/039)

7c. *Historical Present:* Yo entré en la barra y dije "Déme un vaso de agua" ẏ me *mira* Ralph y dijo "¡Qué!" 'I went into the bar and said, "Give me a glass of water" and Ralph looks at me and said, "What!" ' (004/027)

The Simple Present can also be used to express a durative action in the past, as in 7d:

7d. Ella me la *cuida* desde que ella tenía seis meses. "She's taken care of her for me since she was six months old.' (052/250)

Preterite vs. Present Perfect.   In both Spanish and English the Preterite is used to convey perfective as opposed to imperfective aspect. In Spanish the Preterite is used to refer to the beginning, end, or entirety of an event, state, or characteristic occurring prior to the moment of speaking, as in (8a), while the Imperfect is used to refer to the progression or middle of the event (8b). The Imperfect is also used to refer to an event which was in progress when another event took place (8c) and with time expressions, as in (8d). Although the opposition of Preterite and Imperfect is more complicated than has been indicated here (Guitart, 1978), the basic distinction outlined above is sufficient for the present purposes.

8a. Anoche *leí* el libro entero. 'Last night I read the whole book.'
8b. Yo *leía* a menudo ese periódico. 'I often read/used to read that newspaper.'
8c. Yo *estaba* afuera cuando *sonó* el teléfono. 'I was outside when the phone rang.'
8d. *Eran* las tres cuando *sono* el teléfono. 'It was three o'clock when the phone rang.'

English does not distinguish between the Imperfect and the Preterite except by the Past Progressive or the *"used to* + verb" formation. This is an area in which one might expect some degree of convergence toward English on the part of bilingual speakers.

{Future}

Unlike the fields of {PRESENT} and {PAST}, {FUTURE} is not differentiated aspectually, as it is imperfective by its very nature. In Spanish the semantic field {FUTURE} can be expressed by the Future Indicative, the Present Indicative, and the Periphrastic Future, as in (9) below:

9a. Yo *iré* después pa' allá. 'I'll go there later.'
9b. Yo *voy* después pa' allá. 'I('ll) go there later.' (048/079)
9c. Yo *voy a ir* después pa' allá. 'I'm going to go there later.'

All of these verbal forms correspond to English forms.

There are two other sets of forms which may be considered to express futurity: the Subjunctive and the Conditional. Both are characterized by their hypothetical, imperfective, future orientation.

The Subjunctive in Spanish is subject to many complicated rules of usage; however, the basic pattern involves use of this form in subordinate clauses whenever the (surface or underlying) main verb expresses a doubtful, possible, necessary, or desired action.

Theoretically, there is a Subjunctive form to match every indicative form. In reality, only four of the Subjunctive forms are commonly used: the Present, Imperfect, Present Perfect, and Preterite Perfect. The three Future Subjunctives have all but disappeared in modern Spanish usage.

10a. *Present Subjunctive:* Entonces, uno lo tapa para que *coja* olor. 'Then you cover it so that it can take on the aroma.' (050/059)

10b. *Imperfect Subjunctive:* Yo quería que las *conociera.* 'I wanted her to get to know them.' (050/128)

10c. *Present Perfect Subjunctive:* Ningún boricua, menos que no *haya estudiado* suficiente pa' poderlo hablar como se debe. 'No Puerto Rican, unless he has studied enough to be able to speak it the way it should be spoken.' (036/200)

10d. *Preterite Perfect Subjunctive:* Nosotros siempre actuábamos como si *hubiéramos sido* acabados de conocer. 'We always used to act as if we had just met.' (050/362)

There is very little direct overlap with English in conditions for use of the Subjunctive, as English has lexicalized or lost most of the distinctions expressed in Spanish by the Subjunctive. The only areas in which these forms can still be recognized in English surface structure are the third person singular forms of the Present Subjunctive and the Present and Past Subjunctive forms of the verb *to be,* as in (11) below:

11a. It is necessary that he *come* immediately.

11b. If I *were* a rich man . . .

11c. We recommend that he *be fired.*

As Spanish has many obligatory sites for the use of the Subjunctive while English has virtually none, this is a potential locus for transference on the part of bilingual speakers.

The Conditional is used to posit hypothetical events and is often found in the result clause after a Subjunctive form in the if-clause.

12a. No me *gustaría* vivir aquí. 'I wouldn't like to live here.' (003/092)

12b. Si recobrara la salud, *iríamos* a Puerto Rico. 'If he could get back his health, we would go to Puerto Rico.'

As in English, the Conditional can also be used to express politeness:

12c. ¿Te *gustaría* probar las habichuelas? 'Would you like to taste the beans?'

Finally, the Conditional can be used to express conjecture in the past (paralleling the use of the Future for expressing conjecture in the present).

12d. *Serían* las doce cuando vino. 'It was (probably) twelve o'clock when he came.'

METHODOLOGY

Several grammars of Spanish (e.g., Bello, 1970; Alonso, 1964, 1968; Criado de Val, 1966; Stevenson, 1970; Socarras, 1975) were consulted to arrive at the list of 26 possible verb forms in the active voice shown in Table 1. Note that in addition to the tenses and moods traditionally included in prescriptive grammar paradigms, we examined several compound forms and aspectual structures separately: the Present, Imperfect, and Preterite Progressives, and periphrastic formations consisting of auxiliary verbs (with or without prepositions or conjunctions) plus infinitives (e.g., *voy a ir* 'I'm going to go'). These additional forms were included in the analysis because of their function as variants of other Spanish verb forms, because of the fact that like traditional verb forms they may be considered to function as single units, and because of their surface similarity to English forms.

Nonconjugable verbal derivatives such as gerunds (which in Spanish function as adverbs, and in English, as nouns) and past participles (functioning as adjectives) were omitted from this study.

We further distinguished absolute or systemic uses of verb forms from extended or nonsystemic uses (Bull, 1971). *Absolute* uses are those in which the function of the form is defined by its systemic position, i.e., the uses most commonly associated with the verbs. The systemic position may be altered, changing the orientation of the verb form. These alterations are *extensions* of the semantic fields of the surface forms. The meaning of a verb form used in an extended sense is inferred from adverbial expressions, other verbs, or markers of temporal shift which indicate its context in time.

Extensions must be considered separately in order to examine the ways in which tense, mood, and aspect are conveyed in surface structure. Thus, in a sentence like *Mañana voy a Ponce* 'Tomorrow I go to Ponce,' *voy* is considered a manifestation of the present in its surface form and of the future in its extended sense. Apparent divergences from the "standard" as noted in grammar books were checked as potential sites of changing verb usage in order to ascertain whether they occurred in the Spanish of New York City Puerto Ricans, and further, if some verb form usage has been extended either to cover the semantic fields of other Spanish tenses which have fallen into disuse, or to include English semantic fields.

Each occurrence of a verb form (excluding lone gerunds and participles) was coded for speaker, for speech style, and according to whether it was used in an absolute or extended sense. Invariant verb forms such as those occurring in frozen phrases (e.g., *tú sabes* 'you know,' *vamos a poner* 'let's say') and proverbial expressions (e.g., *uno sabe donde nace pero no donde muere* 'you know where you were born, but not where you'll die') were excluded from the analysis.

Percentages of occurrences of each type of form were calculated over all speakers in our primary sample according to language dominance, extended use, speech style, and sex. Intragroup comparisons were made, as well as comparisons with modern Andalusian Spanish, Puerto Rican and historical Castilian standards, and English.

To determine the statistical significance of the results, we compared the log-likelihood of rate estimates for the various groupings separately as compared to that for the combined data. In addition, we examined the distribution of verb forms using rank correlation coefficient measures.

THE SAMPLE

The primary data on which this study is based were collected as part of an interdisciplinary study of language use in El Barrio of East Harlem, New York, one of the oldest continuous Puerto Rican settlements in the United States. This is apparently a stable bilingual community, which includes speakers who are dominant or monolingual in both Spanish and English.

Twelve long-time residents (of at least 10 years) of the community were selected as informants, chosen primarily on the basis of language dominance as determined by self-report, ethnographic observation, and linguistic analysis. Six are Spanish-dominant or monolingual, having migrated to New York at adolescence or later, and six are English-dominant or balanced bilinguals, having arrived in early childhood. The groups are evenly divided by sex, and members range in age from 20 to 57. Only adults were included in this study in order to distinguish dialectal from developmental variation.

Sample members reported more years of schooling than the general Puerto Rican population in New York City (United States Department of Labor 1975, pp. 50–52). Two-thirds have had some high school education, and all but one have completed the seventh grade. Those informants who attended school in both Puerto Rico and New York City (5 out of the 8) reported having received instruction in Spanish and English. The majority of those who claimed to be Spanish-dominant reported Spanish as their habitual language of literacy, while the reverse is true for the English-dominant group.

A questionnaire administered to the informants revealed a near consensus on the attitudes that command of the Spanish language is not necessary to be Puerto Rican, and that Spanish is not well regarded by

American society at large; but that it should nevertheless be kept alive in the Puerto Rican community in New York.

Most respondents (8 out of the 12) claimed to speak "good Spanish," regardless of reported language dominance. Indeed, when asked to rate their Spanish competence on a seven-point scale, the majority rated themselves as "perfect" or "excellent" speakers. "Good Spanish" was described in a variety of ways by these speakers, with good vocabulary and pronunciation being the most frequently recurring characterizations. Only one speaker pointed to grammatical correctness as an identifying feature of good Spanish.

When asked who could be considered to speak Spanish well, only three respondents cited Spaniards. Other responses included "older people," who are mostly Spanish-dominant speakers in this community. Sample members were fairly evenly divided between those who feel that Spanish should be the official language of Puerto Rico and those who would prefer both Spanish and English. All respondents but three plan to return to Puerto Rico to live at some point in the future.

This pattern of responses indicates strong positive feelings towards Spanish language maintenance as well as a clear community awareness of a Puerto Rican Spanish norm distinct from that of Castilian Spanish.

Comparative Data

For purposes of comparison with the Spanish-dominant and bilingual speakers, five other data sets were assembled. Two of these were based on sources of standard Spanish. Standard Puerto Rican Spanish was represented by an interview with José Luís González (González, 1976), a prominent Puerto Rican writer who has evinced concern over the purity of Puerto Rican Spanish. Second, data on early modern Castilian Spanish were provided by a frequency analysis of verb usage in the fifteenth-century picaresque novel *La Celestina* (Criado de Val, 1966).

For purposes of cross-dialectal comparison, we analyzed the speech of a 29-year-old monolingual speaker of peninsular Spanish, who is an upper-middle-class native of Granada, Spain.[5]

Next, two data sets on English speech were collected in order to see whether verb usage in the Spanish data is indicative of language convergence or merely reflects systemic similarities between English and standard Spanish. First, we examined the English verb usage of two additional speakers from East Harlem. These informants considered themselves to be English-dominant bilinguals. They were both born and raised in New York City, and neither has ever lived in Puerto Rico. Both have had a university education and were employed at the time of the sampling in white-collar positions. Then, to correct for any possible influence from Puerto Rican Spanish on the English of these speakers, their verb usage was compared with that of a middle-class, middle-aged non-Puerto Rican New Yorker who is a monolingual speaker of English.

Each informant in the sample was tape-recorded in a variety of speech situations, which included responding formally to a language attitude questionnaire, participating in a semiformal sociolinguistic interview, and using vernacular speech in interacting with peers.

From 29 hours of taped speech, 8,679 Puerto Rican Spanish vernacular verb forms were identified, 6,532 from the Spanish-dominant group and 2,147 from the bilinguals.[6] An additional 270 verb forms representing standard Puerto Rican Spanish were coded from eight consecutive pages chosen at random from the transcribed interview with González. The interview format here provided a certain degree of comparability with the speech of the primary sample, although, because of its written form, this data set can be characterized as far more formal in style. We also included 473 Andalusian Spanish verb forms and 2,258 English forms in the study for purposes of comparison, totaling 11,680 instances of verb usage in all.

RESULTS

A noteworthy result of this study is that there was virtually no divergence from standard usage among the 8,679 Spanish verb forms collected from our primary sample. Uses not attested in prescriptive grammars constituted less than 1 percent of the data.

Of the 26 verb forms listed in Table 2, four were not attested at all: Future Perfect, Future Subjunctive, Future Perfect Subjunctive, and Preterite Conditional. As the first three are highly literary forms, it is not surprising that there were no occurrences. Of the 22 remaining forms, 12 occur infrequently enough to represent 1 percent or less of the data. Table 2 shows that the four inflected forms comprising the subjunctive mood together constitute less than 4 percent of the 8,679 verb forms. Indeed, aside from the two uninflected forms (Infinitive and Imperative), there are only three quantitatively important forms. The largest share of all verbal forms is represented by the Simple Present—it accounts for half of the data. The Preterite accounts for 14 percent, and the Imperfect, 8 percent. All other inflected forms individually represent 3 percent or less of the total of verbal forms.

How does Puerto Rican Spanish express distinctions of tense, mood, and aspect by means of these three favored forms? As mentioned above, each verb use was coded for its surface form as well as its extended

Table 2
Verb Distribution in Vernacular and Standard Puerto Rican Spanish

| | Vernacular PRS | | | | | | Standard PRS | |
| | Spanish Dominants | | Bilinguals | | All Speakers | | | |
Verb Forms	N	%[a]	N	%[a]	N	%[a]	N	%[a]
INDICATIVE								
Present	3,231	49.5	1,078	50.2	4,309	49.6	133	49.3
Preterite	904	13.8	324	15.1	1,228	14.1	25	9.3
Imperfect	543	8.3	148	6.9	691	8.0	15	5.6
Present Perfect	143	2.2	43	2.0	186	2.1	6	1.1
Conditional	49	0.8	14	0.7	63	0.7	10	3.7
Preterite Perfect	22	0.3	5	0.2	27	0.3	2	0.7
Future	12	0.2	3	0.1	15	0.2	5	1.9
Preterite Anterior	0	0.0	1	0.0	1	0.0	0	0.0
Future Perfect	—		—		—		—	
Preterite Conditional	—		—		—		—	
PERIPHRASTIC								
Present Modal + Infinitive	245	3.8	78	3.6	323	3.7	12	4.4
Present Periphrastic Future	158	2.4	43	2.0	201	2.3	4	1.5
Imperfect Modal + Infinitive	23	0.4	16	0.7	39	0.4	0	0.0
Preterite Modal + Infinitive	15	0.2	6	0.3	21	0.2	1	0.4
Imperfect Periphrastic Future	4	0.1	4	0.2	8	0.1	0	0.0
PROGRESSIVE								
Present Progressive	135	2.1	54	2.5	189	2.2	2	0.7
Imperfect Progressive	26	0.4	5	0.2	31	0.4	0	0.0
Preterite Progressive	6	0.1	3	0.1	9	0.1	0	0.0
SUBJUNCTIVE								
Present Subjunctive	257	3.9	51	2.4	308	3.5	7	2.6
Imperfect Subjunctive	71	2.0	10	0.5	81	0.9	2	0.7
Preterite Perfect Subjunctive	4	0.1	2	0.1	6	0.1	0	0.0
Present Perfect Subjunctive	1	0.0	1	0.0	2	0.0	1	0.4
Future Subjunctive	—		—		—		—	
Future Perfect Subjunctive	—		—		—		—	
Imperative	173	2.6	82	3.8	255	2.9	0	0.0
Infinitive	510	7.8	176	8.2	686	7.9	45	16.7
Total	6,532		2,147		8,679		270	

[a]Percentages may not add up to 100 percent because of rounding.

meaning where relevant. Table 3 shows how verb forms are distributed to convey the semantic fields of {PRESENT}, {PAST}, and {FUTURE}. By far the preferred form of expressing present reference is through use of the Simple Present. Preterite and Imperfect forms are generally used to express past reference, with the Present Perfect also representing a sizable though lesser contribution.

Results for the semantic field of {FUTURE}, however, are somewhat less predictable. As can be seen, the single verb form used most frequently to convey futurity is the Present Subjunctive, a form we included in this category because of its imperfective and future-oriented nature. When we examine only those forms used to convey futurity directly, we find that the Present Periphrastic and Simple Present are the preferred ways of expressing this semantic field, with the inflected Future itself accounting for only 2 percent of the remaining data.

This finding explains how speakers of Puerto Rican Spanish express {PRESENT}, {PAST}, and {FUTURE} by means of a basic present ~ past tense distinction: the Present has been extended to cover the semantic field of the Future, which is used only rarely and not necessarily to convey futurity. (Note from Table 3 that one-third of the attested Future forms were used for {PRESENT} reference.)

These findings are in keeping with studies on Spanish in the Southwest reviewed by Floyd (1978). While not directly comparable to ours because they are not quantitative, these studies repeatedly indicate that the Present, Imperfect, and Preterite are the most productive forms, maintaining their usual functions as well as expanding to include those of other verbal forms.

The substitution of the Present as well as the periphrastic construction for the Future has been widely observed in California, Texas, and Colorado, and the use of the Present for the Preterite and the Present Perfect has also been noted, though less generally. The distinctions between the Preterite and Imperfect and between the Preterite and Present Perfect have been maintained in Chicano Spanish, though there have been limited observations of variation between forms. Contrary to the findings reported for the Puerto Rican community below, the use of the Imperfect in either clause of conditional sentences has been frequently noted in Southwest Spanish.

In general, it has been reported that compound forms of both the indicative and subjunctive moods are used infrequently and are occasionally replaced by other forms. Use of the progressives has been widely observed, and they have even been reported to take on functions of the Simple Present and Imperfect. As we will see, this tendency is not exhibited by Puerto Rican Spanish.

Table 3

Distribution of Inflected Verb Forms by Semantic Field in Puerto Rican Spanish of East Harlem Speakers

{PAST}			{PRESENT}			{FUTURE}		
Verb Forms	N	%[a]	Verb Forms	N	%[a]	Verb Forms	N	%[a]
Preterite	1,225	54.1	Simple Present	4,147	88.9	Present Periphrastic Future	201	24.8
Imperfect	689	30.4	Present Modal + Infinitive	323	6.9	Simple Present	131	16.2
Present Perfect	186	8.2	Present Progressive	189	4.1	Future	10	1.2
Imperfect Modal + Infinitive	39	1.7	Future	5	0.1	Past Periphrastic	8	1.0
Imperfect Progressive	31	1.4				Conditional	63	7.8
Simple Present	38	1.4				Present Subjunctive	308	38.1
Preterite Perfect	27	1.2				Imperfect Subjunctive	81	10.1
Preterite Modal + Infinitive	21	0.9				Perfect Subjunctives	7	0.9
Preterite Progressive	9	0.4						
Total[b]	2,265			4,664			809	

Note: The table does not include 255 imperatives and 682 infinitives uttered by these speakers. In addition, it does not include the following 13 forms which were used idiosyncratically:

Simple Present substituted for Present Subjunctive	2
Simple Present substituted for Imperative	1
Infinitive substituted for Simple Present or Present Subjunctive	3
Infinitive substituted for Imperative	1
Preterite substituted for Imperfect	1
Imperfect substituted for Conditional	2
Present Progressive substituted for Simple Present	1
Present Progressive substituted for Past Progressive	1
Present Perfect Subjunctive substituted for Present Perfect	1

[a]Percentages may not add up to 100 percent because of rounding.
[b]N = 7, 738.

Extended Usage

The use of verbs in an extended sense accounts for only 2 percent of our data (n = 179). Eleven types of extended uses occurred, four of which are considered perfectly acceptable by prescriptive Spanish grammars. The occurrence of two others (use of the Present for the Imperative, and the Imperfect for the Conditional) has been noted in descriptions of other Spanish dialects (Floyd, 1978), as well as in standard Spanish grammars. The remaining five types of extended use (eight examples) do not form any particular pattern. These were uttered by both Spanish-dominant and bilingual speakers. Examples of these may be seen in (13) below:

13a. *Simple Present substituted for Subjunctive* (2 examples): Quieren que los nenes no *saben* [sepan]. 'They want the children not to know.' (043/171)

13b. *Subjunctive substituted for Present Perfect* (1 example): ¡No me digas que lo *hayas dejado* [has dejado] puesto! 'Don't tell me you left it on! (004/005)

13c. *Infinitive substituted for Simple Present or Subjunctive* (3 examples): You know, como tú *hablarles* [les hablas/les hables] como si tú—te están hablando contigo—como tú *hablarles*, como tú *corresponderles*. 'You know, the way you speak to them, as if you—they're speaking to you—the way you speak to them, the way you communicate with them.' (037/243)

COMPARATIVE EVIDENCE FROM THE PUERTO RICAN STANDARD

Table 2 reveals strikingly little difference between "standard" verb usage and that of the East Harlem sample. Comparing the log-likelihoods of rate estimates calculated from these figures separately and combined reveals that the most significant differences between the two data sources are in the area of past tense forms (Preterite and Imperfect) which are used more by the East Harlem speakers than in the standard represented by González. This is due to a greater proportion of informal speech in the East Harlem data, which included many narratives of personal experience requiring verb forms in the past.

Of the inflected forms, on the other hand, González uses significantly ($p < .001$) more Conditional and Future than do the other speakers. Use of the Conditional is probably an aspect of academic or learned speaking characterized by hypothetical argument and mitigating suggestions. Finally, although González used more inflected future forms, there was

Table 4

Verb Distribution by Speech Style in Vernacular Puerto Rican Spanish

| | Speech Style | | | | | |
| | Informal | | Questionnaire | | Vernacular | |
Verb Forms	N	%[a]	N	%[a]	N	%[a]
Present	919	36.8	1,766	61.3	1,624	49.3
Preterite	645	25.8	147	5.1	436	13.2
Imperfect	368	14.7	117	4.1	206	6.3
Present Perfect	69	2.8	71	2.5	46	1.4
Conditional	9	0.4	40	1.4	14	0.4
Preterite Perfect	8	0.3	1	0.0	18	0.5
Future	5	0.2	7	0.2	3	0.1
Preterite Anterior	1	0.0	0	0.0	0	0.0
Present Modal + Infinitive	56	2.2	150	5.2	117	3.4
Present Periphrastic Future	52	2.1	45	1.6	104	3.2
Imperfect Modal + Infinitive	15	0.6	8	0.3	16	0.5
Preterite Modal + Infinitive	8	0.3	4	0.1	9	0.3
Imperfect Periphrastic Future	5	0.2	1	0.0	2	0.1
Present Progressive	35	1.4	68	2.4	86	2.6
Imperfect Progressive	9	0.4	7	0.2	15	0.2
Preterite Progressive	4	0.2	2	0.0	3	0.1
Present Subjunctive	53	2.1	122	4.2	133	4.0
Imperfect Subjunctive	28	1.1	17	0.6	36	1.1
Preterite Perfect Subjunctive	0	0.0	0	0.0	6	0.2
Present Perfect Subjunctive	0	0.0	1	0.0	1	0.0
Imperative	24	1.0	40	1.4	191	5.8
Infinitive	186	7.4	269	9.3	231	7.0
Total[b]	2,499		2,883		3,297	

[a]Percentages may not add up to 100 percent because of rounding.
[b]N = 8,679.

no significant rate difference in the use of the Periphrastic Future. As in other languages, such as French and English, the Future in Puerto Rican Spanish is probably largely reserved as a marker of highly formal speech performance. The absence of the Imperative in González's data is due to the interview situation from which they were extracted. Similarly, in the East Harlem data, as seen in Table 4, Imperatives were used least in the informal interview and most frequently in vernacular settings, primarily when addressing children.

CONTRIBUTION OF EXTRALINGUISTIC FACTORS TO VERB USAGE
Sex

Sex of the speaker was not a distinguishing factor in the use of verb forms.

Language Dominance

It had been hypothesized that reported and observed language dominance would play a major role in differentiating patterns of verb usage. Spanish-dominant Puerto Ricans could be considered to be less under the influence of English than are bilinguals.

As can be seen in Table 2, however, there is remarkably little difference between the two groups. Indeed, the most startling aspect of these findings is their great regularity. Log-likelihood tests based on these figures reveal that the only significant area of difference is in the use of the Subjunctive. The bilinguals use somewhat less of these forms than the Spanish-dominant speakers, a tendency which had been hypothesized (e.g., de Granda, 1968) to be due to convergence toward English. Although this possibility cannot be overruled, no conclusive evidence in its favor has yet been presented. Note that the slight increase in use of the Subjunctive by Spanish-dominant speakers is not accompanied by significant rate differences between any other forms. What is more, Table 2' shows that "standard" Puerto Rican Spanish is characterized by Subjunctive usage closer to that of the bilinguals than to that of the Spanish-dominant speakers. These results, then, cannot be considered evidence for any significant degree of convergence of vernacular Puerto Rican Spanish toward English.

CONVERGENCE?

Although the results presented in the preceding sections point to an overwhelming homogeneity of verb usage regardless of language dominance, it would be difficult to substantiate a claim that even the Spanish spoken by Spanish-dominant or monolingual Puerto Ricans has remained uninfluenced by English, considering that Puerto Rico has undergone several periods of official emphasis on English since 1898. Lack of variation might conceivably be explained by the possibility that the Spanish of both groups has been influenced by English.

To account for this possibility, we compared the East Harlem data first with data from fifteenth-century Spanish, then with modern Andalusian Spanish, and finally with English.

Comparative Evidence from the Historical Standard

Figure 1 correlates the rank order of inflected verb-form frequencies of the East Harlem and *La Celestina* data sources. Points lying near the diagonal represent forms of relatively equal importance in each corpus. Strikingly enough, Figure 1 shows that the relative ranking of verb form usage has remained basically unchanged since the fifteenth century. The

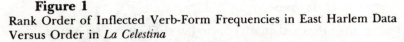

Figure 1
Rank Order of Inflected Verb-Form Frequencies in East Harlem Data
Versus Order in *La Celestina*

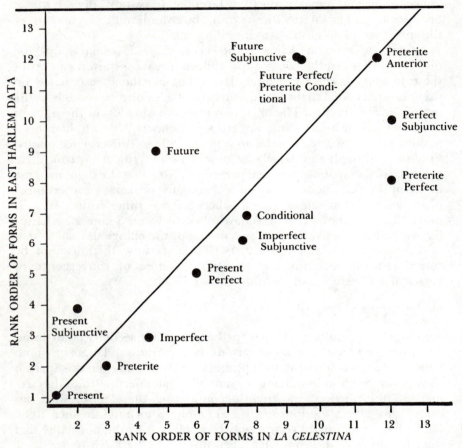

rank correlation of these figures is 0.85 by Spearman's rho measure,
indicating a strong similarity in the distribution of verbal forms. An
apparent exception is the rank order of the Preterite Perfect in the two
data sources. However, as can be seen in Table 5, this form is practically
nonexistent in both the East Harlem data and fifteenth-century Spanish.

A more striking exception involves the inflected Future, precisely the
form we have seen to be practically displaced by the Simple Present in
modern-day vernacular Puerto Rican Spanish.

Table 5

Verb Distribution in Vernacular Puerto Rican Spanish and
Fifteenth-Century Spanish

Verb Forms	Vernacular Puerto Rican Spanish		La Celestina	
	N	%^{a}	N	%^{a}
Present	4,309	62.3	18.0	53.7
Preterite	1,228	17.8	3.5	10.4
Present Perfect	186	2.7	1.5	4.5
Imperfect	691	10.0	2.0	6.0
Preterite Perfect	27	0.4	0.1	0.3
Preterite Anterior	1	0.0	0.0	0.3
Future	15	0.2	2.0	6.0
Conditional	63	0.9	0.6	1.8
Future Perfect/Preterite Conditional	0	0.0	0.5	1.5
Present Subjunctive	308	4.5	4.0	11.9
Imperfect Subjunctive	81	1.2	0.6	1.8
Future Subjunctive	0	0.0	0.5	1.5
All Perfect Subjunctive	8	0.1	0.1	0.3
Total	6,917		33.4	

Note: The data in this table include only forms comparable to those studied by Criado de Val. The totals for the *La Celestina* data were converted from relative frequencies over all grammatical categories. Raw frequencies were not available.

^{a}Percentages may not add up to 100 percent because of rounding.

Comparative Evidence from Modern Andalusian Spanish

Table 6 compares verb distribution in vernacular Puerto Rican and Andalusian Spanish.

Figure 2 shows that the rank orders of verb-form frequencies in the East Harlem and Andalusian data sets are again very highly correlated, at 0.79 by Spearman's rho coefficient. One major difference is in use of the Imperative, a form not attested at all in Andalusian Spanish, because of the semiformal nature of the interview situation from which the data were extracted. Other apparent exceptions in Figure 2, such as those involving the compound Preterite forms and the Imperfect Periphrastic Future, are due to sparse data (Table 6).

Comparative Evidence from English

When we compare the vernacular Puerto Rican Spanish verbs with English (Table 7), on the other hand, we find that their distribution is significantly different for every verb form but one, the Present Progres-

Table 6
Verb Distribution in Vernacular Puerto Rican Spanish and Modern
Andalusian Spanish

Verb Forms	Vernacular Puerto Rican Spanish		Modern Andalusian Spanish	
	N	%[a]	N	%[a]
INDICATIVE				
Present	4,309	49.6	248	52.4
Preterite	1,228	14.1	24	5.1
Imperfect	691	8.0	54	11.4
Present Perfect	186	2.1	7	1.5
Conditional	63	0.7	9	1.9
Preterite Perfect	27	0.3	0	0
Future	15	0.2	6	1.3
Preterite Anterior	1	0.0	0	0
Future Perfect	—		1	.2
Preterite Conditional	—		0	0
PERIPHRASTIC				
Present Modal + Infinitive	323	3.7	22	4.7
Present Periphrastic Future	201	2.3	5	1.1
Imperfect Modal + Infinitive	39	0.4	9	1.9
Preterite Modal + Infinitive	21	0.2	0	0
Imperfect Periphrastic Future	8	0.1	0	0
PROGRESSIVE				
Present Progressive	189	2.2	2	.4
Imperfect Progressive	31	0.4	3	.6
Preterite Progressive	9	0.1	0	0
SUBJUNCTIVE				
Present Subjunctive	308	3.5	19	4.0
Imperfect Subjunctive	81	0.9	7	1.5
Preterite Perfect Subjunctive	6	0.1	1	.2
Present Perfect Subjunctive	2	0.0	1	.2
Future Subjunctive	—		0	0
Future Perfect Subjunctive	—		0	0
Imperative	255	2.9	0	0
Infinitive	686	7.9	55	11.6
Total[b]	8,679		473	

[a]Percentages may not add up to 100 percent because of rounding.
[b]N = 9,152.

Figure 2
Rank Order of Verb-Form Frequencies in East Harlem Versus
Andalusian Data

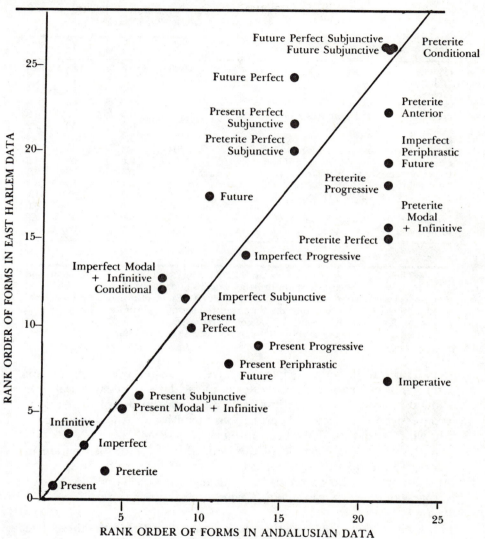

Table 7

Verb Distribution in Vernacular Puerto Rican Spanish and in English

Verb Forms	Vernacular Puerto Rican Spanish		English	
	N	%[a]	N	%[a]
Present	4,309	49.6	888	39.3
Preterite/Imperfect	1,919	22.1	714	31.6
Present Perfect	186	2.1	29	1.3
Conditional	63	0.7	86	3.8
Preterite Perfect/Preterite Anterior	28	0.3	20	0.9
Future	15	0.2	50	2.2
Present Modal + Infinitive	323	3.7	122	5.4
Present Periphrastic Future	201	2.3	11	0.5
Imperfect/Preterite Modal + Infinitive	60	0.6	99	4.3
Imperfect Periphrastic Future	8	0.1	2	0.1
Present Progressive	189	2.2	53	2.3
Imperfect/Preterite Progressives	40	0.5	28	1.2
Subjunctive	397	4.6	1	0.0
Imperative	255	2.9	46	2.0
Infinitive	686	7.9	109	4.8
Total[b]	8,679		2,258	

Note: These 2,258 English forms consist of 1,144 from the Puerto Rican informants and 1,114 from the non-Puerto Rican informants. Log-likelihood tests of significance showed that while verb distribution in the English of Puerto Rican informants differed from standard English on some points, the former differed from Puerto Rican Spanish on all points. All English verbs were therefore considered together.
[a]Percentages may not add up to 100 percent because of rounding.
[b]N = 10,937.

sive, a form frequently cited as indicative of transference from English. This is not evidence for convergence, particularly since statistical tests show that there is no significant rate difference in use of the Present Progressive in vernacular Puerto Rican Spanish and Andalusian Spanish, which could not have been influenced by English.

Moreover, the correlation of the rank order of verb distribution in Puerto Rican Spanish and English is only 0.53 (Figure 3). In fact, the Andalusian data show even greater similarity to English than do those of vernacular Puerto Rican Spanish, with a Spearman's rho coefficient of 0.57.

It is more likely that even this much similarity between the three data sets reflects either universals in tense distribution or sheer coincidence rather than the results of any historical relationship between English and the other two dialects.

Figure 3
Rank Order of Verb-Form Frequencies in East Harlem Versus English Data

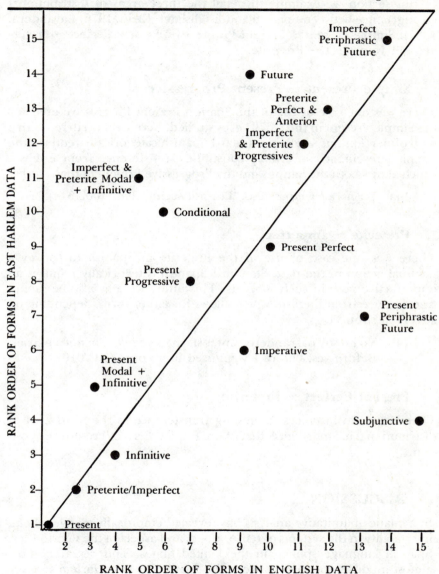

AREAS OF DISTRIBUTIONAL INCONGRUENCE

In this section we examine in detail the three areas of distributional incongruence between Spanish and English (cf. Klein, 1976; Lavandera, 1981): Simple Present ~ Present Progressive, Present Perfect ~ Preterite, and Imperfect ~ Preterite.

Simple Present ~ Present Progressive

There was one case of use of the Spanish Present Progressive used for the Simple Present in the 8,679 verbs studied. Because it occurred with a verb of perception, which in standard Spanish categorically requires the Simple Present, it conceivably constitutes transference from English, which allows both the Simple and the Progressive Present in these verbs.

14a. Yo no *estoy viendo* eso. 'I'm not seeing that.' (002/314)

Preterite ~ Imperfect

There was one case of use of the Preterite in Spanish to convey a habitual action in the past. Standard Spanish categorically requires an imperfective verb in such contexts. This utterance may also be due to transference from English, which allows for either form, depending on adverbial support.

14b. Yo no soy parrandero. Antes sí, antes yo *salí*. 'I'm not a partier. Before yes, before I went/used to go out.' (003/010)

Present Perfect ~ Preterite

There were no instances suggesting transference in the third area of distributional incongruence, that of the Present Perfect/Preterite opposition.

DISCUSSION

Systematic quantitative analysis has revealed empirically an overwhelming stability in the systems of tense, mood, and aspect in the Puerto Rican Spanish language spoken in the United States. This research shows almost no differentiation between the Spanish of East Harlem speakers and the Puerto Rican Spanish standard, represented by the speech of a prominent Puerto Rican author. Moreover, there was great similarity between vernacular Puerto Rican and Andalusian Spanish, a dialect which has not been in extended contact with English. The differences which do emerge may be attributed to the nature of the speech situations from which the data were extracted.

We have also presented evidence that the relative importance of the various verb forms has remained basically unchanged in Spanish since the fifteenth century. The area of greatest divergence is in use of the inflected Future, a form which has practically been replaced by the Periphrastic Future in contemporary vernacular Puerto Rican Spanish, and which now appears to be reserved for use in formal speech styles. This finding is not surprising in view of the long history of vacillation between inflected and periphrastic Future forms, beginning with Classical Latin. Displacement of the Future by periphrastic forms is widespread in all of Latin America (Lapesa, 1968, p. 359) as well as in other Romance languages and English.

This study also shows little or no divergence between bilingual and Spanish-dominant speakers in the distribution of Spanish verb forms. Influence of English does not appear to have affected these core areas of the Spanish language. A minor trend toward what has been construed as convergence with English (de Granda, 1968) was evidenced in the data by a lesser incidence of the Subjunctive on the part of the bilingual group. However, this difference was not accompanied by significant rate differences in use of other forms, and thus it was difficult to attribute it with any degree of certainty to influence from English. Indeed, we have shown that distribution of verb forms in vernacular Puerto Rican Spanish differs significantly from English patterns on all points but one (the Present Progressive). Increase in use of the Present Progressive has also been attributed (Klein, 1976; de Granda, 1968) to convergence. However, no conclusive evidence of actual *increase* can be drawn from this or other studies.

Extended use of verb forms in general was shown to correspond to accepted standard usage, with the exceptions representing less than 1 percent of the data. Only two examples of what might be considered extensions in the direction of English were attested. Because of the current lack of any general tendency in extended use, we would not expect the emergence in the near future of a norm in Puerto Rican Spanish verb usage different from the standard.

In sum, the only factor which may be said to differentiate verb usage in any significant way is the speech style in which the form was uttered. Different speech situations were shown to favor different proportions of verbal forms, providing yet another example of the inherent stylistic variation which characterizes natural languages.

This research indicates that the verbal paradigm has remained stable in a situation of language contact, despite hypotheses that this should accelerate linguistic change (Lavandera, 1981).

Such conclusions were not drawn in qualitative studies of verb usage in other varieties of United States Spanish. However, these studies have concentrated on supposed deviations from the standard, without quantitative study of this standard itself (Bills, 1975, p. vii).

This study shows that when apparent deviations are placed within the context of the entire system, they are seen to constitute only a minuscule proportion of the total verbal output. This leads us to suggest that emphasis on deviations in multilingual situations on the part of researchers, educators, and intellectuals is merely stereotyping due to the phenomenon of categorical perception (Labov, 1966), whereby deviation from a norm may be seen as far more prominent than its negligible frequency would warrant.

What explanation could reasonably account for the lack of convergence? On the one hand, the time scale in this contact situation is considerably less than that involved in Gumperz and Wilson's study. On the other hand, enough time (several generations) has elapsed to permit at least some movement, so that the resistance of convergence must be attributed to other factors. It is probable that the circulatory pattern (Campos and Bonilla, 1976) which characterizes Puerto Rican migration to and from the United States has a stabilizing effect on the Spanish language. Because of this there are always some monolingual speakers of Spanish in the Puerto Rican community. The increasing presence of other Hispanics in New York City adds to this effect. Finally, the social implications of linguistic assimilation for the community should not be underestimated. Desire for Spanish language maintenance is unanimous among community members (Attinasi, 1978). The language attitudes reported above reveal the value attached not only to the Spanish language, but to a specifically Puerto Rican variety.

Community members themselves are aware of Puerto Rican Spanish as a distinct variety which is correctly perceived as characterized by low-level but highly visible differences from the Castilian standard. Their criteria for "good Spanish" are pronunciation and vocabulary, not grammatical correctness. This assessment accurately reflects the area in which vernacular Puerto Rican Spanish usage diverges most from that of other dialects.

Because this variety is close to, if not identical with, the standard insofar as verb usage is concerned, it would be ill-advised to try to impose another norm upon speakers of vernacular Puerto Rican Spanish.

These facts should be considered in the planning of bilingual curricula and in the preparation of language tests for native speakers of Spanish. Knowledge of the actual distribution and use of verb forms in the community should aid teachers in determining learning priorities.

Examiners could also reevaluate their methods of rating language competence based on grammatical knowledge and usage. For example, in many tests administered at present, mastery of the Subjunctive is considered an indication of maximal proficiency in Spanish, while mastery of a regularly inflected form like the Future represents a lower level of proficiency. According to the findings of this study, this practice does not properly measure native abilities. Before constructing tests of native language proficiency, examiners should obtain reliable statistics on the actual distribution of linguistic features in the particular dialect of the speaker being tested. Without this information, any results will be due to inherent biases toward a specious "standard" which reflects the speech of neither the teachers nor their students.

NOTES

1. The term "prestige" is used here in its technical sense only.
2. An example of such a test is the Foreign Service Institute exam used to test Peace Corps and other government applicants. It has also been used in screening bilingual teachers in several areas.
3. Numbers in parentheses refer to speaker and example. Examples not followed by these codes were created for expository purposes but reflect the recorded speech.
4. This includes the present modal plus infinitive.
5. These data, which consist of informal speech elicited by a sociolinguistic interview, were collected by Poplack in 1976.
6. The disparity between the totals reflects the fact that the bilinguals produced less Spanish and more English than did the Spanish-dominant speakers.

REFERENCES

Alonso, Martín. *Evolución sintáctica del español.* Madrid: Aguilar, 1964.
————. *Gramatica del español contemporáneo.* Madrid: Ediciones Guadarama, 1968.
Anisman, Paul Harry. "Some Phonological Correlates of Code-Switching in the English of Puerto Rican Teenagers in New York City." Unpublished doctoral dissertation, University of Rochester, 1975.
Attinasi, John. "Results of a Language Attitude Questionnaire Administered Orally to an Ethnographically Chosen Sample of 91 Residents of a Block in East Harlem, New York, 1977–1978." Manuscript, 1978.
Bello, Andrés. *Gramática de la lengua castellana.* Ed. R. Cuervo. Argentina: Sopena, 1970.
Bills, Garland D. "Linguistic Research on United States Hispanics: State of the Art." In *Spanish and English of United States Hispanics: A Critical, Annotated Linguistic Bibliography,* ed. R. Teschner, G. Bills, and J. Craddock. Arlington, Va.: CAL, 1975, pp. v-xxii.

Blansitt, Edward L., Jr. "Progressive Aspect." *Working Papers on Language Universals,* 18 (1975), 1–34. Stanford University.

Bloomfield, Leonard. *Language.* New York: Holt, Rinehart & Winston, 1933.

Bull, William E. *Time, Tense, and the Verb: A Study in Theoretical and Applied Linguistics with Particular Attention to Spanish.* Berkeley, Los Angeles, and London: UCLA Press, 1971.

Campos, Ricardo, and Bonilla, Frank. "Industrialization and Migration: Some Effects on the Puerto Rican Working Class." *Latin American Perspectives,* 3, issue 3 (1976), 66–108.

Clyne, Michael. *Perspectives on Language Contact.* Melbourne: The Hawthorne Press, 1972.

Criado de Val, Manuel. *Gramática española y comentario de textos.* Madrid: SEATA, 1966.

de Granda, Germán. *Transculturación e interferencia lingüística en el Puerto Rico contemporáneo (1898–1968).* Bogotá: Instituto Caro y Cuervo, 1968.

Floyd, Mary Beth. "Verb Usage in Southwest Spanish: A Review." *The Bilingual Review,* 5: 1 & 2 (1978), 76–90.

Gili Gaya, Samuel. *Curso superior de sintaxis española.* 11th ed. Barcelona: Biblograf, 1973.

González, José Luís *Una conversación con José Luís González.* ed. A. Díaz Quiñones. Río Piedras, Puerto Rico: Ediciones Huracán, 1976. pp. 38–45.

Guitart, Jorge M. "Aspects of Spanish Aspect: A New Look at the Preterite/ Imperfect Distinction." In *Contemporary Studies in Romance Linguistics,* ed. M. Suñer. Washington, D.C.: Georgetown University Press, 1978.

Gumperz, John J., and Wilson, Robert. "Convergence and Creolization: A Case from the Indo-Aryan/Dravidian Border in India." In *Language in Social Groups: Essays by John J. Gumperz,* ed. A. Dil. Stanford, Ca.: Stanford University Press, 1971.

Hadlich, Roger L. *A Transformational Grammar of Spanish.* Englewood Cliffs, N.J.: Prentice-Hall, 1971.

Holt, Miriam P., and Dueber, Julianne. *1001 Pitfalls in Spanish.* Woodbury, N.Y.: Barrons, 1973.

Klein, Flora. "A Quantitative Study of Syntactic and Pragmatic Indicators of Change in the Spanish of Bilinguals in the United States." Paper read at N-WAVE V, Georgetown University, 1976.

Labov, William. *The Social Stratification of English in New York City.* Washington, D.C.: Center for Applied Linguistics, 1966.

Lapesa, Rafael. *Historia de la lengua española.* 10th ed. Madrid: Escelicer, S.A., 1968.

Lavandera, Beatriz. "*Lo quebramos,* but only in Performance," In *Latino Language and Communicative Behavior,* ed. R. Durán. Norwood, N.J.: Ablex Publishing Corp., 1981.

Meillet, Antoine. *Linguistique historique et linguistique générale.* Paris: La société linguistique de Paris, 1921.

Paulston, Christina Bratt. "Teaching English to Speakers of Other Languages: The State of the Art." *In Bilingual Education,* ed. H. LaFontaine, B. Persky, and L. Golubchick. Wayne, N.J.: Avery Publishing Corp., 1978.

Pedraza, Pedro. "Ethnographic Observations of Language Use in El Barrio." Manuscript, 1979.

Pérez Sala Paulino. *Interferencia lingüística del inglés en el español hablado en Puerto Rico.* Hato Rey, Puerto Rico: Inter American University Press, 1973.

Poplack, Shana. "Social and Syntactic Functions of Code-Switching." In *Latino Language and Communicative Behavior,* ed. R. Durán. Norwood, N.J.: Ablex Publishing Corp., 1981.

————. "Sometimes I'll Start a Sentence in Spanish Y TERMINO EN ESPAÑOL': Toward a Typology of Code-Switching." *Linguistics,* 18:7/8 (1980).

Quirk, Randolph, and Greenbaum, Sidney. *A Concise Grammar of Contemporary English.* New York: Harcourt, Brace, Jovanovich, Inc., 1978.

Sapir, Edward. *Language.* New York: Harcourt, Brace, Inc., 1921.

Seda Bonilla, Edwin. *Réquiem por una cultura: Ensayos sobre la socialización del puertorriqueño en su cultura y en ámbito del poder neo-colonial.* Río Piedras, Puerto Rico: Editorial Edil, 1970.

Socarras, Cayetano J. *Gramática de la lengua española.* New York: Las Américas Publishing Company, 1975.

Stevenson, C.H. *The Spanish Language Today.* London: Hutchinson University Library, 1970.

United States Department of Labor. *A Socioeconomic Profile of Puerto Rican New Yorkers.* New York: Bureau of Labor Statistics, 1975.

Varo, Dr. Carlos. *Consideraciones antropológicas y políticas en torno a la enseñanza del "Spanglish" en Nueva York.* Río Piedras, Puerto Rico: Ediciones Huracán, 1971.

Weinreich, Uriel. *Languages in Contact.* New York: Linguistic Circle of New York, 1953.

Zdenek, Joseph W. "Another Look at the Progressive." *Hispania,* 55:3 (1972), 498–99.

IV | Attitudes Toward Spanish and Bilingual Education

Research on Attitudes of Bilingual Chicanos Toward Southwest Spanish: Progress and Problems

JACOB ORNSTEIN
The University of Texas at El Paso

BACKGROUND AND DEVELOPMENT

The fact that relatively little work has been done on attitudes toward U.S. varieties of Spanish reflects the marginal status which they have until recently occupied in the scholarly work, particularly because of their supposed nonstandard nature through contact with English.[1] Of these varieties, including Boricua (Puerto Rican), Cuban, "Luiseño" (Louisiana and elsewhere), Judeo-Spanish (Ladino), only the first two, together with Mexican-American (Chicano) Spanish, claim any considerable number of active speakers. No exact figures exist but U.S. Spanish varieties are probably spoken by over 15 million, with Chicanos representing from 6 to 9 million. For the most part, Mexican-Americans, like Amerindians, constitute "territorial minorities," to employ a term introduced by De la Garza, Kruszewski, and Arciniega (1973). It would be unjust to omit the mention of another Southwest variety, that of New Mexican Spanish (northern New Mexico and southern Colorado), a vestigial remnant of the sixteenth-century *conquistadores*, hence Peninsular in its base although merging increasingly with General Southwest Spanish (hence: SwS).

With the possible exception of Cuban and Ladino Spanish, these varieties have also been neglected because of their association with the "cultures of poverty." As noted, their marginality of.status is owed in part to the tendency of linguists to concern themselves with formal

---

Revision of paper prepared for 9th World Congress of Sociology, 1978. Uppsala Sweden, in the framework of RC 25, Section 6, "Bilingualism and Bidialectalism in the U.S.: Sociolinguistic and Sociopolitical Realities."

241

"standard" languages or with "regional" rather than "social dialects," which these varieties mostly represent.

The rather negative picture painted above has been radically altered in the wake of ethnic and civil rights movements and the growth of the bilingual education movement. The latter, in particular, has created an unprecedented demand for more knowledge and insights into the often nonstandard social dialects, which sociolinguists have established as legitimate objects of inquiry. The overwhelming majority of the youngsters enrolled in the 800-odd bilingual programs of the 50 states are largely speakers of dialects or varieties diverging considerably from formal standard languages, and what is more, most of them are from ethnically Hispanic homes. Thus from a position of obscurity, the "home" varieties must now be reckoned with as teachers and administrators are forced to make decisions regarding these varieties' relationship in the classroom to "standard" Spanish (or other language) and English.

While much in this paper is applicable to all U.S. Spanish varieties, its main thrust is toward SwS. Up to the present only two full-scale books have been published on the subject (Hernández, Beltramo, and Cohen, 1975; Bowen and Ornstein, 1976).

The cold, hard fact is that despite the reality that speakers of Spanish constitute America's largest foreign language ethnic group, research on the varieties represented is still insufficiently developed, and much of it consists of master's theses and doctoral dissertations or articles in regional publications of limited circulation. The same holds true for attitudinal research on these varieties, such research usually being performed within some sort of sociolinguistic framework, with psychologists prominently represented. The pioneering work in language attitudes performed by such Canadian scholars as Lambert. Tucker, Anisfield, and others involving French and English are well known and need no labored repetition here. Certainly the ingenious "matched guise" technique and the Osgood-Suci "semantic differential" scale, have had wide appeal and have been replicated frequently (the Osgood-Suci approach is, of course, not Canadian, but associated with the University of Illinois in the United States). Beyond this, sociolinguistic research on the speech of black Americans (with some 20 million, our largest minority) has included brilliant work by a number of scholars, including Labov, Shuy, Wolfram, Fasold, Orlando Taylor, Kochman, DeStefano, and others. Related investigations on Spanish are only recently coming to the fore.

At this point, we will briefly touch upon some of the studies performed on attitudes toward Spanish varieties, mostly during the past decade, limiting ourselves for the most part to SwS. It ought to be noted that, by and large, the lion's share of related research has focused on reactions to the accented English of Spanish-English bilinguals. Ryan, a psychologist, and Carranza, a sociologist, appear to have carried out the most work in this area with at least a half-dozen articles prepared on their findings, which have tended to focus on differences in the reactions of judges to samples of accented and "standard" speech in different domains of living. (Cf., for example; Carranza and Ryan, 1975; Ryan and Carranza, 1975; Ryan, Carranza, and Moffie, 1977.) In general, it was hypothesized that accented speakers were rated higher in informal domains, whereas unaccented ones were rated higher in formal domains. Galván, Pierce, and Underwood (1975, 1976) have elicited reactions of future teachers to the Mexican-American accent and found that these tend to be traditionally negative, despite the fact that the majority if not all of the subjects had taken basic linguistic courses in which subjective value judgments about language varieties are vigorously attacked. In addition, incidental references in our literature and in education journals regarding the stigmatizing nature of Mexican-American and other "nonstandard" accents also occur. "Remedial" English courses at numerous colleges have as their aim, not only the improvement of grammatical mastery, but often also the "elimination" of phonological "deviations" from a supposed homogeneous standard.

One may well reflect that although our nation justifiably prides itself on tolerance of religious, racial, and ethnic diversity, a "foreign accent," even of persons born here, is still regarded by many as a sign of inferiority and still functions at times as a tacit reason for denial of positions to otherwise qualified applicants.

Investigations of attitudes toward varieties of Spanish are even less numerous than studies of accented speech, obviously because problems related to English as the dominant language in school and elsewhere are bound to attract attention. Nevertheless, as the home vernacular of millions of Americans, Spanish deserves far more attitudinal research than it has thus far received or is presently receiving. MacIntosh and Ornstein (1974), who distributed a written questionnaire to a limited sample, found that a high percentage both of Anglo and Mexican-American teachers of Spanish in the El Paso area public schools considered the local variety "border slang." Elías-Olivares (1976a) arrived at a similar finding in studies made in the lower Río Grande Valley of Texas, in the area of Edinburg and McAllen, which like El Paso, is adjacent to the U.S.-Mexico International border. By contrast, in another study (1976b) she observed a frequent sense of language inferiority regarding Spanish among older informants, while younger subjects often manifested ethnic pride in the regional variety, making extensive use of code switching as a symbol of their bilingualism and nonassimilation into the dominant Anglo culture. Gumperz and Hernández-Chávez (1972), in research with Bay Area Chicanos, came to similar conclusions about code switching as an identity marker, but Valdés-Fallis (1975) believes that this has been overrated as a triggering cause, according to her investigations in the Las Cruces, New Mexico, area.

Other scholars who have concerned themselves with attitudinal factors include Hannum and Amastae and Elías-Olivares. Hannum (1978), employing as subjects Spanish-speaking students from Spain, Latin America, New Mexico, and elsewhere in the U.S. Southwest, had them listen to samples of speech from different parts of the Spanish-speaking world. While informants from countries where Spanish is the national language tended to rate varieties of SwS low, New Mexican and other U.S. students did the opposite, obviously manifesting a growing ethnic pride in them, significant to a positive self-image.[2]

Thus it can be seen from the foregoing that much of the research alluded to focuses on attitudes toward one more or less "standard" language versus another; however, MacIntosh and Ornstein, Hannum, and Amastae and Elías-Olivares concentrate more on reactions to varieties of the same language. Hence it appears important in this branch of our field to differentiate the various patterns and goals represented, rather than lumping them into one potpourri.

A rather extensive study was carried out in the Lower Río Grande Valley of Texas by Amastae and Elías-Olivares (1976) and involved the Pan American University's Language and Linguistics Research Center. That study concerned itself with "infra" rather than "interlanguage" attitudes (a technical term submitted to colleagues apparently for the first time in their paper). Instead of utilizing the same passage rendered in various varieties, as predecessors had done, this team, reacting to criticisms of that practice, varied the content. A different taped passage was presented to subjects in the following varieties: formal standard Spanish, popular Spanish (fairly homogeneous throughout the Spanish-speaking world), *español mixtureado* (SwS with a considerable amount of integrated and nonintegrated English loans, mostly lexical), code-switching variety (with alternating stretches of Spanish and English), and Caló (normally termed Pachuco Caló or argot).

Four primary populations served as Ss in the Pan American University investigation: bilinguals and monolinguals who were enrolled there and had completed a linguistics course; students who had not taken a linguistics course; students from Mexico and other Latin American countries; and Mexicans residing in the border zone. Altogether the sample consisted of 125 Ss randomly selected, and stratified by age, education, birthplace, and ethnicity. As is frequently the practice, the Osgood-Suci differential scale was employed, as was an open-ended interview on topics which induced Ss to express themselves freely and with as much conviction as possible. Each respondent was handed a booklet containing a biographical background sheet to be filled out, and rating sheets. The latter sheets contained fourteen semantic differential scales consisting of bipolar adjectives which were found by previous investigators to be significant in reflecting the dimensions of affective meaning; these scales included evaluation, potency, activity, and solidarity. Solidarity stressing was represented by such polarized pairs as nice/mean, beautiful/ugly. Good/bad, careful/sloppy were examples of pairs designated as evaluative in an overall sense, and potency-activity scales were represented by such examples as sharp/dull, fast/slow. Each scale contained six spaces between each polar adjective. The experiment booklets were in English or Spanish, applied according to origin and ethnicity. Ss were told that the study aimed only at testing reactions to intonation patterns and that they were to concern themselves only with these rather than lexical, syntactic, or other aspects of the passages. Each passage was then played twice, with the respondents marking the rating sheets.

While a complete discussion of results is impossible here, a few findings may be reported. The researchers' hypothesis that Mexican nationals and other Spanish-Americans tend to deprecate most varieties of SwS was clearly confirmed. The second hypothesis, that Mexican-Americans tend to deprecate their own language variety was partially confirmed, partially disconfirmed. The third hypothesis, that other significant factors were influential, was generally supported. Other dynamics of linguistic attitudes of this particular speech community manifested themselves, and the solidarity dimension turned out to be an important overall factor in language attitudes, while the evaluative dimension was shown not necessarily to run parallel with the solidarity one. In addition, speakers categorized users of other varieties on a sort of sound "configuration" or "gestalt" (the author's own expressions) even if they did not necessarily grasp their entire denotative and, of course, connotative import. Persons involved in bilingualism should be interested in this statement by Amastae and Elías-Olivares:

> The fact that there are not only several varieties of Spanish in the community but also a well-developed complex of attitudes toward these varieties should be considered in the designing of educational programs.

No attempt is being made in this paper to report all of even the scant attitudinal literature relating to Spanish and English of Mexican-Americans. Those wishing a more complete review are heartily urged to consult Teschner, Bills, and Craddock's *Spanish and English of United States Hispanos; A Critical, Annotated, Linguistic Bibliography* (1975). One more research study, nevertheless, will be briefly noted, carried out by Yolanda Solé (1977). In general, her research design is based on the attitudinal work and notions in the now classic *Bilingualism in the Barrio* (Fishman et al., 1971) study and a more recent writing by Cooper and Fishman, "The Study of Language Attitudes" (1974). In the Solé study, 164 Mexican-American students at the University of Texas, Austin, served as Ss, reflecting a wide distributional range of background and behavior patterns. Important variables involved were: language proficiency, currently and developmentally; language usage habits; socioeconomic status; provenance and generation of residence in the United States. Occupational status of fathers ranged from manual laborers to professionals, with the mean status a low one. Metropolitan and nonmetropolitan areas were both represented. The majority of subjects had been born and spent their childhood years in areas of predominantly Chicano concentrations, although half were of foreign-stock parentage and half were born in the United States.

The methodology involved the use of mailed questionnaires containing the data on all variables: demographic, linguistic, and attitudinal. Thus the researcher depended on self-report of language proficiency and of distributional usage of Spanish (and English) by domains, as well as language attitude and loyalty. Following Fishman (and Cooper) with their Puerto Rican Ss in the *Bilingualism in the Barrio* study, Solé included a "commitment" question, asking what if any measures they had undertaken during the past two years to strengthen their knowledge of Spanish. She found in the analysis (which employed analysis of variance and other rigorous techniques) that professed language loyalty was generally high throughout this heterogeneous sample. The consensus was that Spanish was an important referent or symbol for the continuation of intergroup community life (84.5 percent); an almost equal percentage thought that Spanish usage should be encouraged and that socialization in Spanish was more important than effecting an attitudinal change among the dominant Anglo community. Over half of the respondents (63.4 percent) attributed greater expressiveness to Spanish than English for certain topics. Nevertheless, when it came to queries on which language they themselves employed in most situational domains, it turned out that Spanish was employed mostly in interaction with the older generation. Linguistically, there was no doubt that the sample was English-dominant, even in affective domains where emotions were concerned.

Solé found that older and less well-to-do Mexican-Americans equated English with status improvement and associated bilingual education programs with disadvantaged minorities, but more affluent and self-assured Chicanos, at least as an ideal, favored the nurturing of bilingualism/biculturalism. She provides food for thought when she concludes:

> The validation of cultural pluralism among those who favor it is rooted, however, in the past rather than the present. Support is sought from those very attributes that are least relevant to daily existential patterns and are embedded in home and hearth. (p. 46)

Courageously she challenges one of the cherished assumptions of bilingual educationists regarding ethnicity:

> If in fact the ethnic individual finds himself more at ease with the high and more distant ethnic-related culture than his own variant, then it would seem that the inclusion of contrastive existential patterns between the majority and the minority child in the cultural component of bilingual programs and in teacher training programs might achieve less for the minority child's sense of security than the teaching of the high culture. (pp. 45–46)

AN INVESTIGATION IN A SOUTHWEST U.S. BORDER AREA

In the preceding section, some idea was afforded of the types of surveys performed thus far on attitudinal aspects of SwS and, *en passant*, other U.S. Spanish varieties. At this juncture, we concern ourselves with a sociolinguistic survey carried out a few years ago, utilizing students enrolled at the University of Texas at El Paso as informants. The study has been reported in professional literature both here and abroad (see References), but the attitudinal factors, comprising only a portion of the study, have been reported *in extenso* by the writer only in a paper titled "La investigación de actitudes hacia el español chicano (Méjico-americano) del suroeste de Estados Unidos," which was delivered at Caracas, January 9–13, 1978, at the 8th Congress of ALFAL and which will be included in the *Proceedings*. One of our main concerns in the attitudinal portion of the questionnaire employed in the investigation was to elicit from both Anglo and Hispano Ss their perceptions of what type(s) of Spanish are utilized in the U.S. Southwest, as well as their subjective reactions to these. While, indeed, the sampling was biased in the direction of Ss already involved in higher education, hence an elite group, it nevertheless has an advantage in that if misconceptions and prejudices manifested themselves substantially in a group like this, one could extrapolate existence of a much higher degree of negative attitudes in non-college individuals, particularly at the "grass roots." Unfortunately, we did not include a question on whether respondents had studied introductory (or advanced) linguistics, but would estimate that less than 7 to 10 percent had done so.

Let us briefly describe the survey. A *Sociolinguistic Background Questionnaire* was first devised by Brooks, Brooks, Goodman, and Ornstein (1972), representing an educational administration specialist, an educational psychologist, a sociologist specializing in the "cultures of poverty," and the author, as linguist. The questionnaire included 106 items of a demographic nature, mostly multiple choice, followed by questions on distributive usage of English and Spanish in a number of domains and situations, self-report of fluency in the two languages, attitudes toward the two languages and toward Anglo and Mexican-American cultures, as well as a group of items aimed at measuring vocational and life aspirations. We endeavored to secure a 5 percent stratified sample of our entire full-time undergraduate population (randomly selected), as to ethnicity, sex, age, specialization, and year of college. This resulted in a total of 301 Ss, almost evenly distributed between Chicanos and Anglos. In addition, a subsample, similarly stratified, was taken of the total bilinguals, amounting to 30 Ss, representing about 10 percent of the overall sample and 20 percent of the total bilinguals. The latter group agreed to our battery of linguistic elicitation, consisting of an open-ended interview (20 minutes to an hour) in the two languages respectively, and the writing of three compositions on identical themes in Spanish and English. They were free to choose from three sets of topics in Spanish and English, arranged in ascending order of semantic and grammatical complexity; the topics could also, if the peer interviewers so desired, serve as the basis for the interviews. As was to be expected, the writing skill (poorly represented in American sociolinguistic experimentation) proved more difficult in Spanish than in English since most of their formal schooling had been in the latter language.

In soliciting students' evaluations of varieties of SwS in the questionnaire, we assumed no linguistic technical background and presented four choices; for these, no claims of excellence are made, and improvement of the set is possible. At any rate, Table 1 reports the evaluations given by both the Anglo and Mexican-American groups, with six Ss failing to respond to this item.

As may be observed, the students believed that all four varieties are available in the Southwest. A mere 5 percent of the Chicanos considered that "Formal, educated" Spanish is employed, while no Anglos thought so, so that only 2 percent of the overall sample chose this designation. The most frequent response was unhappily "Border slang" (41 percent), comprising 51 percent of Anglo and 31 percent of Chicano respondents. The second most frequent choice, far more realistic, was "Informal, everyday," chosen by 37 percent of the entire sample, representing 32 percent of Anglos and 40 percent of Mexican-Americans. The remaining Ss chose "Southwest dialect," and again this was favored by more

Table 1
Students' Evaluations of Types of Spanish Used in the Area

Type	Anglo		Mexican-American		Total	
	N	%	N	%	N	%
Formal, educated	0	0	7	5	7	2
Informal, everyday	46	32	62	40	108	37
Southwest dialect	24	17	36	24	60	20
Border slang	72	51	48	31	120	41
Total	142	100	153	100	295	100

Note: Kolmogorov-Smirnov one-tailed test, X^2 = 11.01 p. 001.

Chicano than Anglo students, 24 percent versus 17 percent. It is regrettable that "Informal, everyday" and "Southwest dialect" somewhat criss-cross each other semantically, but in all probability no set of choices would be without underlying ambiguities. A statistically significant difference between the two groups existed at the 0.001 level.

In accordance with our hypothesis that SwS varieties would be given rather unfavorable ratings, both groups indeed reacted in that wise. We were, however, surprised that a higher percentage of favorable or neutral evaluations (i.e., "Informal, everyday" and "Southwest dialect") were not forthcoming from Mexican-American respondents, although their ratings were significantly higher than the Anglo ones. However, the research described in the literature regarding attitudes toward Mexican-American Spanish and English present a generally unfavorable consensus for both. Nevertheless, very recent experiments, some informally reported and not yet widely available, perceive and upward trend in attitudes toward the two varieties, to a large extent as a function of more tolerant views toward "ethnic variation" promoted by civil rights drives, the Chicano movement, and equal opportunity legislation.

However, almost more important than the above finding, which is common in the literature, is strong evidence that both Chicanos and Anglos reveal widespread confusion about Southwest varieties in general—again hypothesized by us initially. Obviously the failure of schools to include basic linguistic facts somewhere in the curriculum is fundamentally at fault here. At any rate, some of the confusion is reflected in Table 2. Here, the Ss were asked to select the one variety which they best control. For obvious reasons we are reporting only the reactions of the bilingual sample, and some contradictions vis-à-vis Table 1 will readily become apparent.

Table 2

Bilingual Students' Self-Report on Variety Best Controlled by Them

Variety	Number	Percentage
Formal, educated	49	32
Informal, everyday	87	57
Southwest dialect	14	9
Border slang	3	2
Cannot handle	1	1
Total	154	

While the choice of either "Informal, everyday" or "Southwest dialect" is soundly realistic, the remaining selections are at odds with informants' perceptions of the types of varieties employed in this region. The most striking of these was that 49, or 32 percent, claimed control of "Formal, educated" Spanish, although only 7, or 5 percent, had thus character-ized the regional variety. Moreover, while 48 Mexican-Americans or 31 percent had termed it "Border slang," a mere step from the more pejorative "Tex-Mex, " only 3, or 2 percent, cared to claim an obviously low-status variety. The fact that language is a very vital and sensitive component (or extension) of one's self-esteem is a commonplace. Never-theless, limitations of space prevent our discussing the frequently unfavorable semantic connotation of "dialect," and of "slang" (if taken as an individual's entire language system, although it is acceptable for showing solidarity with special groups or colorful current informal discourse). Pachuco Caló was omitted as a choice since hardly anyone considers it among normal varieties of most speakers of SwS.

Thus it appears that not all linguistic prejudices are attributable to what might be termed "domestic xenophobia." The problem of depre-cating or holding in low esteem all but "standard" varieties of school type is obviously one that linguists by themselves cannot solve merely by providing excellent descriptions, but rather by effecting changes in traditional attitudes within the societal mainstream as well as among ethnic minorities themselves. As a parting shot let us mention briefly two other findings. One is that language and cultural loyalty had no significant correlation with performance in either Spanish or English. As noted, the bilingual subsample wrote essays in both languages, and three independent judges assigned them ratings in the separate language skills and gave an overall rating based on the compositions and tape-recorded interviews. In addition, it was found that although the subsample Ss rated their Spanish capabilities realistically enough, they tended to rate their English knowledge rather low. (Elaboration on these points is available in writings cited in References, particularly those by Goodman, Renner, Brooks, and Ornstein.)

SOME IMPLICATIONS

The writer has dared here to say little or nothing about outstanding work and writings on the subject, such as the collection by Shuy and Fasold (1973) and the prolific and insightful works by Giles and collaborators (1977); in these works a number of new directions in attitudinal research are suggested. Likewise work by Williams and colleagues (1970) is highly useful and suggestive. Peñalosa (1978) disputes many of the assumptions in current research on Chicano language attitudes, arguing for work in a "conflict" model framework.

Perhaps no aspect of sociolinguistics involves so many converging disciplines as that of language attitude study, yet one observes that primarily linguists and psychologists are involved, particularly the latter, with only a sprinkling of sociologists—those who are concerned with society in both micro- and macro-contexts. Anthropologists and other practitioners are here and there represented, but sparsely, although some specialists in "speech," such as Williams, have pointed out paths which few colleagues in his own field appear to have followed.

It is an understatement to say that work in attitudes toward the Spanish and English of U.S. Hispanos is poorly developed, as this paper has underlined repeatedly. Yet the crying need is not for more copious writings and an indefinite amount of research replications of pioneers in attitudinal studies, but new directions in which the word "interdisciplinary" is not merely a hollow term, scarcely reflected in the investigations.

As in previous talks and writings, I would like to urge the formation of regional consortia, much like those carrying out work on regional dialect geography, with interdisciplinary groups studying attitudes toward urban, semi-urban, and rural language varieties. The Spanish and English of the Southwest, for example, would lend themselves to this type of approach, which would be preferable to the disparate efforts now observable, often duplicating one another. That the data gained would be useful both to theorists and applied linguists and social scientists (e.g., those working with minority groups) is a foregone conclusion.

NOTES

1. Acknowledgment of research support is made to The University of Texas' Research Institute, Hogg Foundation for Mental Health, Austin, Texas, Spencer

Foundation, Chicago, Cross-Cultural Southwest Ethnic Study Center.

2. Cf. also: Janet B. Sawyer, "Social Aspects of Bilingualism in San Antonio, Texas," *American Dialect Society*, 1965, pp. 7–16.

REFERENCES

Amastae, Jon, and Elías-Olivares, Lucía. "Attitudes Toward Varieties of Spanish." Language and Linguistic Research Center. Pan American University, Edinburg, Tex., 1976. Typescript.

Bowen, J. Donald, and Ornstein, Jacob, eds. *Studies in Southwest Spanish* Rowley, Mass.: Newbury House, 1976.

Brooks, Bonnie S., Brooks, Gary; Goodman, Paul W.; and Ornstein, Jacob. *Sociolinguistic Background Questionnaire: A Measurement Instrument for the Study of Bilingualism.* Rev. ed. El Paso: University of Texas, Cross-Cultural Southwest Ethnic Study Center, 1972.

Carranza, Miguel A., and Ryan, Ellen Bouchard. "Evaluative Reactions of Bilingual Anglo and Mexican American Adolescents Toward Speakers of English and Spanish." *International Journal of the Sociology of Language*, no. 6 (1975), 83–104.

Cooper, Robert L., and Fishman, Joshua. "The Study of Language Attitudes." *International Journal of the Sociology of Language*, (1974), 9–23.

De la Garza, R.; Kruszewski, Z. A.; and Arciniega, T., eds. *Chicanos and Native Americans: Territorial Minorities.* Englewood Cliffs, N.J.: Prentice-Hall, 1973.

Elías-Olivares, L. "Ways of Speaking in a Chicano Community: A Sociolinguistic Approach." Dissertation, University of Texas, Austin, 1976a.

————. "Un cuestionario sociolingüístico: Problemas en la interpretación de datos." Presented at SWALLOW V. San Antonio, Texas, April 22, 1976b.

Fishman, Joshua A., et al. *Bilingualism in the Barrio.* Bloomington: Indiana University Press, 1971.

Galván, J. J.; Pierce, J.A.; and Underwood, G. "Relationships Between Teacher Attitudes and Differences in the English of Bilinguals." Presented at SWALLOW IV, San Diego, California, April 11, 1975a. Also in *Journal of Lasso*, 1976.

————. "The Effects of Teachers' Social and Educational Characteristics on Their Attitudes Toward Mexican-American English." *Journal of the Linguistic Association of Southwest* (LASSO), 1976, p. 1.

Giles, H., ed. *Language, Ethnicity and Intergroup Relations.* New York: Academic Press, 1977.

Giles, Howard, and St. Clair, Robert, eds. *Language and Social Psychology.* Baltimore, Md.: University Park Press, 1979.

Goodman, Paul W., and Brooks, Bonnie S. "A Comparison of Anglo and Mexican-American Students Attending the Same University." *Kansas Journal of Sociology*, 10 (Fall), 181–203.

Goodman, Paul W., and Renner, Kathryn S. "Social Factors and Language in the Southwest." In *Problems in Applied Educational Sociolinguistics*, ed. Glenn Gilbert and J. Ornstein. The Hague and Berlin: Mouton and De Gruyter, 1978, pp. 55–62.

Gumperz, J. J., and Hernández-Chávez, E. "Bilingualism, Bidialectalism and Classroom Interaction." In *Functions of Language in the Classroom*, ed. C. Cazden, V. John, and D. Hymes, New York: Teachers College Press, 1972, pp. 74–110.

Hannum, Thomasina. "Attitudes Toward Spanish: A Field Report." Presented at Symposium on Bilingualism and Bilingual Education. University of Texas, El Paso, June, 1978.

Hernández-Chávez, Eduardo; Beltramo, Anthony F.; Cohen, Andrew D., eds. *El Lenguaje de los Chicanos*. Arlington, Va.: Center for Applied Linguistics, 1975.

MacIntosh, Roderick, and Ornstein, J. "A Brief Sampling of West Texas Teacher Attitudes Toward Southwest Spanish and English Language Varieties." *Hispania*, 57:4 (1974), 920–26.

Ornstein, Jacob. "Relational Bilingualism. A New Approach to Linguistic-Cultural Diversity." *Ethnicity*, 5 (1978a) 148–66.

––––––. "La investigación de actitudes hacia el español México-Americano (Chicano) del suroeste de EE. UU." *Proceedings of 8th International Congress of ALFAL*, Caracas, Venezuela, January 9–13, 1978b.

Peñalosa, Fernando. "Sociolinguistics and the Chicano Community." In *Proceedings of the 6th Southwest Area Language and Linguistics Workshop: The Bilingual in a Pluralistic Society*, ed. Harold H. Key, G. G. McCullough, and J. B. Sawyer. Long Beach: California State University, pp. 150–57. Revision of paper presented at 6th Annual Southwest Area Language and Linguistics (LASSO) Workshop.

Ryan, E. B., and Carranza, M. A. "Evaluative Reactions of Adolescents Toward Speakers of Standard English and Mexican-American Accented English." *Journal of Personality and Social Psychology*, 31:5 (1975), 855–63.

––––––. "Ingroup and Outgroup Reactions to Mexican-American Language Variation." In *Language, Ethnicity and Intergroup Relations*, ed. H. Giles. New York: Academic Press, 1977.

Ryan, Ellen Bouchard; Carranza, Miguel A.; and Moffie, Robert W. "Reaction Toward Varying Degrees of Accentedness in the Speech of Spanish-English Bilinguals." *Language and Speech*, 20 (1977), 267–73.

Shuy, Roger, and Fasold, Ralph, eds. *Language Attitudes: Current Trends and Prospects*. Washington, D.C.: Georgetown University Press, 1973.

Solé, Yolanda. "Language Attitudes Toward Spanish Among Mexican-American College Students." *Journal of Linguistic Association of Southwest*, 2:2 (1977), 37–46.

Teschner, Richard V.; Bills, G. B.; and Craddock, J. R. *Spanish and English of U.S. Hispanos: A Critical, Annotated Linguistic Bibliography*. Arlington, Va.: Center for Applied Linguistics, 1975.

Valdes-Fallis, Guadalupe. "Code-Switching and Language Dominance: Some Initial Findings." Presented at Border Linguistic Circle, New Mexico State University, Las Cruces, February 22, 1975.

Williams, Frederick, ed. *Language and Poverty*. Chicago: Markham, 1970.

Language Loyalty
and Language Attitudes
Among Cuban-Americans

CARLOS A. SOLÉ
University of Texas at Austin

Although the study of attitudes has long been the object of research among behavioral scientists and a great deal of literature is available on theoretical as well as methodological formulations, sociolinguists have only recently incorporated attitudinal variables in their own investigations. The relevance of language attitudes is obvious to sociolinguistic endeavors. Attitudinal variables may influence language maintenance and language shift processes, differential evaluations of speech varieties, language choice and differential code allocations among bilingual populations, language policies and language planning endeavors, as well as interdialectal intelligibility or the lack thereof. While sociolinguists agree on the importance of language attitudes, they do not share a common understanding of what language attitudes are and how they differ from other attitudinal variables.[1]

This lack of consensus arises partly from the fact that sociolinguists and attitude theorists have worked in relative isolation from one another. Some sociolinguists define language attitude in terms of its referent, "Elicitable shoulds on who speaks what, when and how."[2] This definition, which covers attitudes toward a language, language use, and language variants, fails, however, to include attitudes toward language

The data gathering for this study was made possible through a summer grant awarded by the Institute of Latin American Studies of the University of Texas at Austin in 1975; the statistical analyses were funded by the University Research Institute of the same university. I am most indebted to Dr. Herminia Cantero, Coordinator of Bilingual Education, Dade County Public School System, for her invaluable assistance in distributing the questionnaire. I am also grateful to the schools' principals, teachers, and staff for their cooperation; but above all, my thanks go to all those students who by answering the questionnaire made this study possible.

254

planning efforts, language maintenance, and language shift processes, as well as other areas which are an integral part of the sociology of language. Thus it is too restrictive. Other researchers suggest a more comprehensive scope whereby language attitudes would encompass all the attitudinal variables that may influence language behavior and behavior toward language. This latter conceptualization, on the other hand, is not sufficiently restrictive as it fails to differentiate between language attitudes *per se* and other attitudinal variables at large.

Joshua A. Fishman defines language attitudes in terms of their referent, including language, language behavior, and referents of which language or language behavior is a marker or symbol.[3] Thus, attitudes toward Spanish, toward features of Spanish such as speech varieties, toward the use of Spanish for specific purposes, or toward Spanish as an ethnic group marker would all be considered language attitudes. On the other hand, attitudes toward Mexican-Americans, Puerto Ricans, or Cubans would not be language attitudes *per se* although they might be reflected by attitudes toward the mother tongue of these populations. In exploring and discussing language attitudes among Cuban-Americans, Fishman's definition is accepted.

The presence of Spanish in the United States has been a palpable one in the life of this country for centuries. Today it is not only the largest foreign language group but also the country's fastest growing minority. Although the Spanish-speaking communities are united by two powerful sources—their language and their Catholic religion—this population is by no means homogeneous. The three main subgroups—Mexican-Americans, Puerto Ricans, and Cubans—differ greatly in their sociodemographic profile and migratory characteristics. Differences of race and class divide these and other Hispanic groups: the Caribbean blacks, the "mestizos," the Castilian Spanish, the aristocratic Spaniards of the American Southwest.[4]

At present, the Spanish-speaking minorities, particularly the Mexican-Americans and the Puerto Ricans, are in the process of actively claiming their rights in an English-speaking society. They are aware that access to the institutions that will enable them to strengthen themselves socially is possible only through English. Monolingual and even bilingual groups admit the need for English, the official language. They are also aware that while Spanish serves the purpose of keeping and strengthening the ethnic consciousness of the group, as a unique instrument of communication, Spanish is of little pragmatic value since it limits, and in many cases even hinders, social mobility in an alien world.

Associated primarily with a minority concept, Spanish is not viewed as a prestigious language within the mainstream. In spite of the fact that

the United States has been for several decades an important center of
Hispanic studies, the cultural and literary prestige of Spanish is acknowledged only within a very small sector of the mainstream society.
Whether these attitudes prevail among the Spanish-speaking communities or whether they differ or are correlated with language shift or
behavioral commitment to Spanish maintenance is open to question and
remains the object of important sociolinguistic research.

There are few studies dealing systematically with language attitudes
toward Spanish among Hispanic populations in the United States. Two
of these studies, which appeared in the mid-Sixties, deal with sample
populations of Mexican-Americans in San Antonio and Los Angeles.[5]
Among these subpopulations the desire for language retentiveness
seems to be positively correlated with social status. It was mentioned far
more often among the well-to-do than the dispossessed. In San Antonio,
however, mother tongue continuity when considered desirable was not
justified upon ethnic grounds (i.e., the preservation of the group as a
distinct entity), but rather upon the basis of humanistic and cultural
values. Contrastively, respondents from Los Angeles, where Mexican
origin is less of a liability because of the greater opportunity for upward
social mobility, claimed preference to Spanish maintenance by a
far larger margin (51%).

A more recent study conducted among college students in Austin,
Texas, reinforces these findings.[6] Among this younger and more
socially mobile population, attitudinal language loyalty was found to be
high. In fact, the majority view the Spanish language as a positive
referent and feel that its usage should be encouraged because it
represents an important component of community life.

A comprehensive study on the Puerto Rican situation in New York
City, based on two socially different samples—the neighborhood
population and the so-called "intellectuals" (i.e., leaders, artists, writers)—shows a general positive attitude toward Spanish, particularly
among the intellectuals.[7]

Through the press and other sources, we have learned that some
Hispanic groups have been exercising considerable pressure on the
in-group as well as the dominant society to recognize the importance of
Spanish as a symbol of ethnic identity worth protecting and maintaining.
Yet, in spite of these claims by some, attitudes toward Spanish and
language consciousness among Mexican-Americans and Puerto Ricans
are not consistently associated with ethnic pride and behavioral commitment. For many, particularly the less socially mobile population, Spanish-language usage is associated with stress regardless of the fact that it
may be an important component of group identity or community life.

There are no data on language attitudes among the Cuban-American subpopulation, whose sociocultural and demographic profile contrasts with that of Mexican-Americans, Puerto Ricans, and other recent immigrant groups. Due to political events, Cuban immigrants were warmly welcomed in the United States as a people who had refused to accept an ideology incompatible with that of their new homeland. Most Cuban immigrants were upper- or middle-class city dwellers whose pre-immigrational background showed a high level of professional, technical, and occupational achievement. As a result, Cubans have managed to consolidate their socioeconomic position in the United States without much difficulty.[8]

Given their high socioeconomic status and their immigrational recency, one would expect the Cuban subgroup to show a distinct pattern of language loyalty and to hold attitudes different from those held by Puerto Ricans or Mexican-Americans. The present study is an attempt to explore the attitudinal orientation toward Spanish among a young generation of Cuban-Americans, to determine what linguistic and demographic variables are correlated with differential language attitudes, and to ascertain to what extent, if any, attitudinal commitment to Spanish correlates with behavioral commitment to Spanish language maintenance.

The data for this study were gathered in Miami, Florida, during the fall of 1975. They covered language usage patterns and language attitudes among a young generation of Cuban-Americans. Only the latter aspect will be discussed here in detail. The participants were high school students, ranging from 14 to 18 years and representing the first generation of Cubans raised and educated in the United States from elementary school on. To ensure a heterogeneous sample, students from both public and private schools located in different sections of the city were selected. From a total distribution of 350 questionnaires, 268 usable responses were collected, and they constitute the basis of this study.

The questionnaire had three main sections. In the first section, demographic data were elicited: age, sex, place of birth, years of residence in the United States, professional goals of the participants, educational and occupational status of the parents. Section two of the questionnaire dealt with language proficiency and language choice (Spanish or English) within a wide range of different contexts of social interaction and in relation to different age groups. Information was elicited concerning the participants' language proficiency and language dominance in all four skills (understanding, speaking, reading, writing), both developmentally and currently. The last section of the questionnaire was intended to elicit the respondent's attitudinal posture through a series of open-ended questions covering a wide range of topics such as: the importance of knowing Spanish; opinions concerning the ongoing language shift perceived among the younger generation; the expressiveness of Spanish compared to English in relation to different topics or domains; the rationales for encouraging or discouraging Spanish maintenance; the disadvantages of using Spanish; the disadvantages of not knowing English; the measures necessary to ensure Spanish maintenance; attitudes toward bilingualism and bilingual education.

The sociodemographic profile of the sample population attests that we are dealing here with an urbanized, socially and economically well-established ethnic group. The vast majority of the respondents were born in Cuba, 62% in Havana and 15% in other Cuban cities, while 12% were U.S. born. From those born in Cuba, 48% arrived in the United States between the ages of 1 and 3 years, 27% between the ages of 5 and 8, and 22% between 10 and 13 years of age. Sex distribution was roughly even, 49% were males and 51% females. The respondents showed a high level of personal and professional ambition: 37% hoped to obtain an M.A. degree; 44% hoped to attain a doctorate degree either in medicine, law, or humanities. The high educational aspirations held by the respondents correspond to actual trends among Cuban-American youth. Statistics show that in 1976, 72% of the high school graduates of Hispanic origin in Dade County pursued their education at the college level. This is not surprising if one examines the high educational and occupational level of the respondents' parents: 80% of the fathers had completed their education in Cuba and today 20% are professionals, 5% business owners or managers, 37% white-collar workers and 22% skilled laborers. In 61% of the cases, the father's occupation in the United States coincided with the one held in Cuba.

The educational and occupational level of the respondents' mothers was also high: 24% had finished high-school, 16% had had some college education, while 11% had earned a university degree. In 92% of the cases, the mothers were educated in Cuba. At present, 51% of the mothers are employed: 2% are professionals, 30% white-collar workers, and the rest skilled laborers.

Language attitudes toward Spanish among the young generation of Cuban-Americans are highly favorable. Nonetheless, language attitudes do not correlate with a strong behavioral commitment toward exclusive Spanish language usage. The linguistic ideal of the young generation of Cuban-Americans seems to be directed more toward bilingual usage rather than the exclusive choice of Spanish within those domains under private control.

The overwhelming majority of the respondents viewed Spanish as a positive referent: 96% felt that Spanish is indeed necessary because it represents an important component of their cultural heritage; 75% felt that Spanish should be encouraged, and 72% did not see any disadvantage in using the language. On the other hand, only 55% regretted the ongoing language shift they claim to perceive among their peers while 13% did not express any concern over it.

The results of this study concerning language usage patterns show that language choice among young Cuban-Americans does not respond to a diglossic system in which each language has different code allocations according to different contexts of social interaction.[9] Language choice seems to respond primarily to the linguistic competence of the speakers, which in turn is governed by generational differences, years of residence in the United States, and age at the time of arrival. It is interesting to note that a trend toward language shift is suspected and suggested by the respondents themselves: 78% of them felt that the younger generation is using less Spanish than the older generations. On the other hand, although 71% of the respondents know and use as much Spanish today as they did five years ago, only 30% preferred Spanish over English; 25% preferred English over Spanish; and 42% preferred to use both languages, depending on the topic or the interlocutors. Linguistic proficiency in English determined language preference for 24% of the respondents; for 46%, language preference was determined by the linguistic appropriateness of each of the two languages according to topic or domain, while (only) 21% of the respondents based their preference for Spanish on affective or expressive grounds.

The rationale advanced against generational language shift covered different areas: loss of ethnic pride and identity (32%); the fear that Spanish may disappear (16%), the fact that bilingualism is enriching (25%). For 25% of the respondents language shift is either unimportant or even desirable because English is the official language and an indispensable tool. Thus, the less Spanish used, the faster the individual will master English.

Only 46% of the respondents attributed greater expressiveness to Spanish than to English, while 49% were undecided on this matter. When questioned as to the appropriateness or expressiveness of Spanish/English in specific speech situations, the respondents were overwhelmingly unable to decide. Only three categories showed any appreciable ratings insofar as Spanish is concerned: cultural matters (14%), affective matters (16%), and social interactions (12%). Insofar as differential linguistic expressiveness is concerned in such domains as religious matters, technical or academic pursuits, occupational pursuits, sports activities, music, literature, and politics, the respondents were unable to choose. The lack of responses in this area can be explained by several factors. First, the entire sample population claimed to have acquired English. There was not a single respondent who claimed to be a Spanish monolingual. Second, the frequency of English usage claimed either exceeded or equaled that of Spanish in all spheres, except those which involve communication with the older generations. Since language choice seems to be primarily determined by the linguistic proficiency of the interlocutors (and therefore by generational differences), rather than by a diglossic norm for both Spanish and English, it should not be surprising that difficulties arise in conceptualizing domain separations when in actual speech situations few if any obtain. On the other hand, one should not overlook the fact that bilingual high school students between the ages of 14 and 18 who have been educated in the mainstream culture and language since early childhood would be less likely to conceptualize and verbalize this type of linguistic behavior than older but less culturally assimilated respondents. As previously mentioned, only 21% of the respondents justified their preference for Spanish on affective and sentimental grounds. The greater expressiveness of Spanish claimed by some is attributed to the fact that Spanish is their mother tongue (the first language learned and heard) and home language. Preference of Spanish is thus the result not of a cognitive awareness about the structural and lexico-semantic expressiveness of the language itself but of habitual use.

For the rest of the population studied, language choice was influenced by fluency of the speaker and/or interlocutor rather than by linguistic expressiveness of either language. A substantial number of the participants tended to view bilingualism as an ideal linguistic situation, although the respondents were not able to describe the conditions in which a stable and coordinated bilingualism could obtain. A vast percentage (81%) claimed not to experience any social or inner discomfort when using Spanish. However, half of the sample population could not give any reasons behind their secure or insecure feelings in relation to Spanish usage. Among those who could verbalize their feelings, 30% of those who experience tension when using Spanish, indicated the presence of English monolinguals was the main reason. Only 8% specifically referred to American prejudice as a possible deterrent of Spanish-language usage.

On a closely related question, 72% of the respondents indicated they saw no disadvantage in using Spanish while at the same time 91% felt that English is indeed indispensable. It is interesting to point out that among those who considered Spanish usage undesirable, 17% felt that it is disadvantageous only for the Spanish monolingual, while only 10% attributed the disadvantage to prejudice on the part of the dominant group.

The enriching values of bilingualism were one of several arguments offered by the respondents when attempting to justify Spanish usage, the need for encouraging Spanish, the need to know English, the need to know Spanish, and the meaning of Spanish itself. While the percentages allocated to this argument are not very large, (24%, 17%, 21%, 31% and 14%, respectively), the value of bilingualism and the pride of being bilingual were a consistently recurrent response in answer to more than one question. Considering that in each case the response was one of several other possible choices, one cannot ignore the fact that bilingualism as an ideal plays an important role among the respondents. Consistent with this claim, 92% of the respondents advocated sustained bilingual education, while only a very small minority, 8%, viewed it as a bridge to English.

The highly positive and problem-free attitude toward a dual linguistic loyalty among Cuban-American high school students can be explained by a number of factors. First and probably most important is the nature of the Cuban immigration. Being a highly skilled and well-educated group, Cubans not only very quickly achieved a high employment and income level which assured their economic independence within a different linguistic and cultural milieu, but gradually and increasingly became an important force in the economic expansion of Greater Miami. The Cuban immigration not only had the political sympathy of the dominant society but, since it brought skills and know-how, it also had the moral and economic support of those in power.

Second, only one-fifth of the sample population arrived in the United States between the ages of 10 and 13 years. The large majority arrived in this country during critical ages for language acquisition (48% between 1 and 3 years; 27% between 5 and 8) or were U.S. born (12%). Thus, they acquired English at a very early stage in their lives and consequently were enabled to function optimally within the educational system. In fact, the Hispanic community, which comprises one-third of Dade County's pupil population, scores well above other Dade County students in both mathematics and English achievement tests and, as already mentioned, in 1976, 72% of high school graduates entered a college or university.[10]

Third, the innovative philosophy of the early bilingual education programs in Dade County contributed to the positive reinforcement of Spanish.[11] Thanks to the foresight of educators, community leaders, and administrators, and to the financial support of government agencies and private foundations, the basic philosophy of the early bilingual education experiments called for cultural maintenance without ethnic segregation. Cubans and Americans would become familiar with the culture of the other while each would maintain his or her own home language, cultural values, and identity.

Finally, the rising status of ethnicity in the United States since the last Sixties has created a favorable climate which enhances the values of biculturalism and bilingualism.

As a result of all of these factors, Spanish was not negatively reinforced in Dade County nor did it become a politicized issue. Cuban children were never chastised nor ridiculed for using Spanish, as has been the case with Mexican-American children. Therefore, no defensive reaction was necessary on the part of the Cuban population. The linguistic policy of Dade County itself has been one of *laissez-faire*, tolerance and even recognition that Spanish plays an important role in the economic expansion of the area. All of this has facilitated the acculturation process of the young and their rapid assimilation of a new linguistic code that ensures their success within the mainstream society without conflicting with the preservation of their mother tongue. It is, then, only natural that for the young Cuban-American, bilingualism should be viewed as problem-free and an asset in itself.

The highly positive evaluation of Spanish among young Cuban-Americans is based on three grounds:

1. Ideological;
2. Instrumental/pragmatic;
3. Sentimental/affective.

Ideological support for Spanish does not come primarily from a strong feeling of ethnicity *strictu sensu*, nor does it come from the awareness of the primacy of the Spanish speaking in Florida, nor from a strong conscience of the cultural and literary achievements of the Hispanic world. The younger generation of Cubans are quite conscious of the circumstances that brought their families into exile. They seem to be quite aware of the impact that this experience has had among their older relatives, particularly when familial and friendship ties still remain in Cuba. The young seem to have a strong feeling of respect and admiration for the traditions and institutions known and loved by their elders. Spanish more than a symbol of Hispanic tradition is a symbol of Cubaness, of the "free and ideal" Cuba. The mother tongue is thought of as a cultural bond that unites all Cubans in exile, a symbol of pride and identity that needs to be preserved. Cubans share a common ethnic heritage with most other Hispanic groups and, because they were part of the Empire until the end of last century, there is in them a stronger feeling of attachment and admiration for Spain than in other Spanish-American countries. However, the trauma and sad experiences of exile are something they do not share with any other Spanish-speaking country. The Spanish language is undoubtedly a symbol of group solidarity but a solidarity based more on nationalistic identifications than on purely ethnic and cultural values.

Within the second category Spanish is valued for practical and instrumental reasons. Spanish is viewed as necessary because it serves the purpose of interpersonal communication, particularly between the younger and older generations in Miami and other cities in the United States. It is also important for communicating with friends and relatives exiled throughout many Spanish-speaking countries. Young Cubans seem to be very aware of the steady transit of Spanish-speaking tourists and business people through the Miami area and of the fact that communication with this group is achieved through Spanish. This was another reason for validating Spanish. Equally important are the usefulness and advantage of knowing Spanish in occupational pursuits. Considering the important role played by the Hispanic community in the economic development and expansion of Dade County, this is not surprising. Apart from pragmatic considerations, the respondents as a whole feel that knowing more than one language is an enriching and fulfilling experience and a source of personal pride and accomplishment.

On sentimental and affective grounds, Spanish is cherished not so much in itself or for its pragmatic values but rather because it is evocative of childhood memories and reminiscent of intimate, familial or close bonds, particularly in relation to the older generations. Spanish represents the language of their parents and relatives, whom they love, admire, and respect.

Attitudinal orientation toward Spanish language maintenance is highly favorable, as may be expected—75% of the respondents strongly feel that Spanish should be encouraged and preserved. They also strongly favor the use of Spanish in the socialization process at home as well as at school: 92% advocate language maintenance as the basic philosophy for bilingual education programs and 80% feel that parents should play an important role in language maintenance through the socialization process. In addition, 82% of the respondents feel that contact with other Cubans is essential if Spanish is to be preserved. Yet the results of language usage patterns show that there is not enough behavioral

implementation and commitment beyond the home context. There is no
indication that any of the respondents have taken any specific, deliberate
measures to maintain or improve their proficiency in Spanish.

Although the Spanish media in Miami are potentially important
sources for language retentiveness (there are three TV stations, one with
full programming and two with half-time programming in Spanish; five
radio stations with full-time Spanish language broadcasting), only 20%
of the respondents take advantage of them and then only as a supplementary source to the English media. On the other hand, for 61% of
the sample population, the English press is their only source of information, although there are about twenty Spanish magazines and newspapers—one of them, *El Diario de las Américas,* having a daily distribution of
65,000 copies.

Continued bilingual education is favored by nearly all Cuban-
Americans. Funding for these types of projects, however, is becoming
more difficult to obtain. For as long as Cuban-Americans are not an
academic problem and as English becomes increasingly their dominant
language, it is unlikely that Spanish language maintenance can succeed
on the basis of present bilingual-schooling practices unless it is heavily
funded on a continuous basis. Mother tongue retentiveness cannot be
guaranteed by a positive attitudinal orientation unless overt maintenance efforts and behavioral implementation exist.

There are no overt negative attitudes toward Spanish. Nevertheless,
roughly one-fifth of the respondents showed some kind of negative
response when confronted with certain questions. For instance, 22% felt
that lesser use of Spanish among the young was a positive trend; 21%
remained indifferent to the question of socialization in Spanish; 19% felt
that parents should not play any role in this socialization process one way
or another; 19% felt uncomfortable when using Spanish, and 27%
admitted that there were disadvantages in using the mother tongue.

Apart from purely pragmatic considerations, there is little reason to
assume that negative responses are attributable to overt pressures
stemming from the mainstream society. By and large, Cubans feel quite
at home in Miami. Although they perceive the instrumental needs of
English, they do not feel pressured to abandon their mother tongue. As
a whole, Cubans feel quite secure about their particular speech variety
when communicating with native speakers of other nationalities. Only
an insignificant percentage (6%) prefer not to use Spanish for fear of
making mistakes. Cubans in Miami have succeeded educationally, socially, and economically. As a result, they are respected by the dominant
group. Therefore, they are not hesitant nor do they feel uncomfortable
being and behaving as Cuban-Americans. If any negative attitude

toward Spanish is perceived among the young, it is less likely to come from stress or negative reinforcement than from the rapid assimilation and acculturation process that is taking place among them. This assumption is corroborated not only by replies from this study but by outside sources as well.[12] To an open-ended question regarding the disadvantages of not knowing English, 35% of the respondents answered that "in America one must be an American."

Most immigrant groups tend to have a positive attitudinal orientation toward their own mother tongue, although the reasons underlying language loyalty may vary according to time, place, and circumstances. Cuban-Americans at large seem to have a more consistent and unambivalent attitude toward Spanish than other Hispanic groups; this attitude has been partly facilitated by recent events within the dominant society. The civil rights movements, the bilingual education act, the revival of the ethnic conscience, and the Chicano movement have all brought a heretofore unseen reevaluation and vitalization of Spanish in this country. Thus, Spanish has become a source of ethnic identity for Hispanics, a symbol of the ideals and aspirations of the group in their crusade for claiming their share in the English-speaking society. Yet for many Spanish-speaking communities, their language has also been associated with economic deprivation, with retardation in gaining access into the mainstream, and with social prejudice, and as such it is viewed as having little pragmatic value. For Cuban-Americans, however, Spanish has consistently been associated with their cultural heritage, culture not in the anthropological sense but in the sense of national identity. Spanish represents for Cuban-Americans a symbol of group solidarity and group identity based on national pride for what they have accomplished as Cubans who were forced to leave their homeland. "Suddenly we lost everything and were confronted with potential poverty and hunger. Fear spurred us to work our tails off and to regain what we once had," says Frank Soler, editor of the Spanish-language edition of the *Miami Herald*. And Cuban writer José Sánchez Boudy insists: "We have been the most successful immigrants this country has received since it was founded." This sense of group identity is translated into a kind of nationalistic linguistic pride: "History will write Miami's future in Spanish and English," claims Carlos Arboleya, a prominent banker and community leader in Miami.[13]

For Cuban-Americans the Spanish language has not been associated with school failure, it has not hindered their socioeconomic success, nor has it been associated with major social stress or prejudice. Because of the high demographic concentration of the group (about 430,000 Cubans have settled in Dade County, roughly one-third of its total population), because of their high socioeconomic status, and because of their impact on the economic and cultural growth of Miami (they generate an estimated $1.8 billion in annual income, have created 100,000 jobs, and have given the city a distinct flavor), Spanish has come to acquire almost as much instrumental value as English. Bilingualism and biculturalism seem to be the order of the day.[14] In fact, bilingual educators and community leaders warn that if English-speaking high school graduates expect to obtain jobs in the area, they will need Spanish as much as Cubans or other Hispanics need English. This possibility is already the cause of friction with other non-Spanish speaking minorities in the area.

The negative response to Spanish perceived among a small sector of the young Cuban-American population and the lack of a stronger behavioral implementation among those sustaining a high attitudinal orientation are the result of incipient language shift and acculturation. These processes are generally more accelerated among the better educated and more socially mobile groups than among the uneducated and less mobile.

There were few variables, demographic or linguistic, which were correlated with differential language attitudes. This may be due largely to the restricted range of variance on all attitudinal questions since most of the respondents showed a positive orientation toward the Spanish language and its maintenance. Nonetheless, the respondent's birthplace, the time of arrival in the United States, the ethnic composition of the respondent's neighborhood, the parents' educational and occupational status, and the way in which the respondent perceived the Spanish language itself had a differential impact on the attitudinal and behavioral orientation toward the mother tongue.

Spanish language maintenance was more likely to be favored by those who arrived in the United States during their early childhood than those who arrived in their early teens and might therefore be less secure with their status. The need for Spanish language maintenance and the importance of the Spanish language itself was more likely to be stressed by those who live in ethnic neighborhoods, and who therefore need to use Spanish more often, than by those who live in predominantly English-speaking areas. The importance of the Spanish language for Cubans was also more often perceived and acknowledged by those respondents who have an ideologized stance toward the language, who view Spanish as a symbol of their own culture or an ethnic marker, than by those respondents for whom Spanish is primarily expressive of affective ties and/or instrumental values. On the other hand, Spanish language preference, as opposed to bilingual usage—which is favored by the majority—occurred most often among the foreign born and/or most recent arrivals as well as among those respondents whose parents have low educational and occupational status. Those respondents who arrived in the United States before their teens and whose parents have higher socioeconomic status tended to favor both Spanish and English. Behavioral commitment to Spanish, as manifested by preference for this language, would thus seem to be determined largely by linguistic proficiency rather than by attitudinal factors *per se.*

Although a good degree of ideological mobilization has existed among Cuban exiles, creating strong feelings of allegiance to their cultural and linguistic heritage which in turn has helped to offset the loss of their home country, there is also a growing feeling that the United States is indeed home. If language loyalty and language maintenance succeed in Dade County, they will probably respond more to instrumental needs than to deliberate maintenance efforts or ideological elaborations. They will respond to the continuous influx of Spanish-speaking groups into and through the area and the growing importance of the port of Miami as a trade center with Latin America. International trade with Latin America today accounts for $4 billion in state revenues; it has created some 167,000 jobs, and it has attracted about 80 firms in Coral Gables alone, some very powerful ones such as Exxon, General Electric, and Dupont having established their Latin American headquarters in the area. On the other hand, as Cubans become increasingly more interested in political involvement and government participation (they are now taking U.S. citizenship at the rate of 1,000 per month, and about 100,000 of the 351,000 eligible Spanish speaking voters are actually registered), it might be possible to sustain language loyalty by political implementation. Such gain, however, would be offset by generational distance. The intensity of attachment to Spanish would decrease with generational distance if and when Spanish ceases to be the home language of second- and third-generation Cuban-Americans and English becomes their mother tongue.

NOTES

1. R.L. Cooper and J.A. Fishman, "The Study of Language Attitudes," *International Journal of the Sociology of Language,* 3, (1974), 9–23. R. Shuy and R.W. Fasold, eds., *Language Attitudes: Current Trends and Prospects* (Washington, D.C.: Georgetown University Press, 1973).

2. Charles A. Ferguson, "Soundings: Some Topics in the Study of Language Attitudes in Multilingual Areas," Paper presented to the Tri-University Meeting on Language Attitudes, Yeshiva University, January, 1972.

3. Cooper and Fishman, "The Study of Language Attitudes," p. 10.

4. Carlos A. Solé, "El español en los Estados Unidos: Perspectiva sociolingüística," *Thesaurus*, (BICC), 30, (1976), 318–37. "Hispanic Americans: Soon The Biggest Minority," *Time*, 112, no. 16 (October 16, 1978), 48–61.

5. J.B. Sawyer, "Social Aspects of Bilingualism in San Antonio, Texas," *American Dialect Society* (1965), pp. 7–16. R.G. Hayden, "Some Community Dynamics of Language Maintenance," in *Language Loyalty in the United States*, ed. J.A. Fishman (The Hague: Mouton and Co., 1966), pp. 191–205.

6. Yolanda Solé, "Language Attitudes towards Spanish among Mexican-American College Students," *The Journal of the Linguistic Association of the Southwest*, II, no. 2 (1977), 37–46.

7. J.A. Fishman and H. Casiano, *Bilingualism in the Barrio*, Indiana University Publications, Language Science Monographs, No. 7 (The Hague: Mouton and Co., 1971).

8. Carlos J. Arboleya, "La colonia cubana: pasado, presente y futuro," *Diario de las Américas*, Miami, September 3, 1975. *The Latin Community of Dade County: A Socio-Economic and Demographic Study*, conducted by Human Communications, Miami, 1975.

9. Carlos A. Solé, "Selección idiomática entre la nueva generación de cubano-americanos," *The Bilingual Review/La Revista Bilingüe*, VI no. 1 (1979).

10. "Hispanic Americans," *Time*, p. 52.

11. W.F. Mackey and Beebe Von Nieda, *Bilingual Schools for a Bicultural Community. Miami's Adaptation to the Cuban Refugees* (Rowley, Mass., Newbury House, 1977).

12. Carol Finemann, "Attitude Toward Assimilation: Its Relationship to Dogmatism and Frigidity in the Cuban Refugee" (M.S. thesis, University of Miami, 1966). Eleanor Meyer Rogg, *The Assimilation of Cuban Exiles: The Role of Community and Class* (New York: Aberdeen Press, 1974). J. Szapocznik, M.A. Scopetta, W. Kurtines, and M. Aranalde, "Acculturation: Theory, Measurement and Clinical Implications " (Unpublished report on study conducted under NIDA Grant No. SH 81 DA 01699-02, Department of Psychiatry, University of Miami), Miami, Fla., 1976).

13. "Hispanic Americans," *Time*, pp. 51–52.

14. On April 16, 1973, the County Commissioners unanimously approved a resolution declaring Dade County a Bilingual and Bicultural County, and an office for Bilingual/Bicultural Affairs was also created. The complete text of the resolution may be found in *Guide for Spanish Translations of Official Dade County Documents*, prepared by Amaury Cruz, Dade County, Fla., 1975.

Language Attitudes and the Achievement of Bilingual Pupils in English Language Arts

ARNULFO G. RAMÍREZ
State University of New York at Albany

EDGARDO ACRE-TORRES
ROBERT L. POLITZER
Stanford University

INTRODUCTION

It is widely assumed that teachers' attitudes toward pupils influence teachers' expectations and result in a self-fulfilling prophecy concerning the pupils' achievements (e.g., see Rosenthal & Jacobson, 1968). Seligman, Tucker, and Lambert (1972) have demonstrated that speech style, or dialect, among other pupil characteristics, has a strong impact on teacher expectations and attitudes. The forms that attitudes and expectations based on speech style can take have also been scrutinized by various scholars, chiefly Fredrick Williams (1973), whose findings show that teacher attitudes toward pupils' habits of speech can be broken down into two clusters that form judgmental dimensions. One cluster, made up of such adjective pairs as "standard American—marked ethnic style," "white-like—nonwhite-like," "low social status—high social status," and "disadvantaged—advantaged," was labeled by Williams "ethnicity and nonstandardness." The other cluster was made up of such adjective pairs as "unsure—confident," "active—passive," "reticent— eager," "hesitant—enthusiastic," and "like talking—dislike talking," which Williams interpreted as indexing an overall evaluation of a child's

This article is a slightly revised version of Research Memorandum No. 146 published by the Stanford Center for Research and Development in Teaching. The research reported in this article was supported by funds from the National Institute of Education (Contract No. NIE-C-74-0049). The opinions expressed in this publication do not necessarily reflect the position, policy or endorsement of the National Institute of Education.

269

"confidence—eagerness." It is, of course, the latter factor that is often responsible for the prophecy of failure, which then establishes in the teacher's mind this casual link: nonstandard speech → lack of eagerness → low achievement.

The assumption that teachers' attitudes toward language are crucial for educational outcomes has been stated succinctly in a recent book on American sociolinguistics:

> Our experience in working with teachers has indicated that the most crucial contribution that the study of social dialects can make to education is in the area of teacher attitudes. A teacher who has been freed from the opinion that nonstandard dialect is simply distorted English will be a better teacher even without new materials and techniques specifically designed to deal with language variation. (Wolfram & Fasold, 1974, pp. 178–179)

The language attitudes of pupils have been investigated by, among others, two of the authors of this memorandum, who found that in a bilingual program pupils rated Spanish higher than hispanized English and standard English, evidently as the result of their exposure to bilingual instruction (Politzer & Ramírez, 1973a).

A hypothesis linking pupils' language attitudes to achievement has rarely been advanced, but one can easily be made since the pupil's view of his own language is assumed to be strongly linked to his self-concept. The hypothesis that low self-concept is directly related to low achievement is, of course, a dominant one in the vast and rapidly multiplying literature that is attempting to explain the low educational achievement of some ethnic groups.

The main purposes of this study are, therefore, the following:

1. To measure the attitudes of teachers and pupils toward specific speech varieties that might occur in a bilingual (English/Spanish) school environment.
2. To determine whether introducing teachers to the concept of bilingual balance and the nature of sociolinguistic speech variation would have any impact on their language attitudes.
3. To determine whether there is any evidence that specific language attitudes held by either teachers or bilingual pupils have a demonstrable link to pupil achievement in reading and English.

METHOD

Subjects

Eighteen teachers and 279 pupils took part in the study. The subjects were fourth- and fifth-grade pupils and teachers in the Franklin-McKinley School District, San Jose, California, a low-income district.

The majority of the pupils in the district come from homes in which the wage earners are unskilled workers. Schools within the district have a great deal of autonomy, although some uniformity in programs exists among schools funded through Title I programs. Classroom organization is predominantly the traditional classroom type. The teacher/pupil ratio in instructional programs is 1 to 28 for the whole district but 1 to 20 in programs operating under Title I. As will be pointed out below, one group of teachers and pupils taking part in this study took part in a Title I program, the other did not. Spanish-surnamed pupils constitute 47 percent of the total school district enrollment. The pupils in our sample were all Spanish-speaking, although the predominant speech variety among them was code-switching (i.e., an alternate use of English and Spanish in which the change from one language to the other can occur in the midst of a discourse or even within a sentence). With two possible exceptions the teachers were not bilingual, and no bilingual programs were in effect in any of the classrooms of the participating teachers. (The teachers of Group II were, however, simultaneously participating in an E.S.E.A. Title I program on teaching students from lower-income areas.)

Procedures

The teachers were divided into two groups: one group took part in a workshop on language variation; the other did not. The second group was included in order to enlarge the sample for the investigation of the relations between teacher attitudes and pupil gains in reading (see below), and between teacher attitudes and pupils' grades in reading and English. Teacher Group I took an attitude test both before and after the two-session workshop; Group II took it only once.

The pupils of the teachers in Group I took the same attitude test as the teachers and, in addition, took a bilingual test of oral language proficiency. They took the attitude measure after the teacher workshop in the spring of 1975, and the language tests were administered by members of the research staff at the same time. The other pupil achievement measures—reading gains and grades in reading and English—were obtained for some pupils of both groups. Grades were from the end of the academic year 1974–75; relative gains in reading were computed from test scores from the end of the 1973–74 and 1974–75 academic years.

The composition of the two groups in the sample was as follows:

	Group I	Group II
Teachers	9	9
Pupils	82	197

Attitude Variables

SCRDT Bilingual Attitude Measure.   The language attitudes of both teachers and pupils were measured by a matched guise test of the type first developed and frequently used by Wallace Lambert and his research group (Lambert, Frankel, & Tucker, 1966); similar tests, for pupils only, were used earlier within the context of Spanish/English bilingualism by Politzer and Ramírez (1972a, b). The test used in this experiment was the SCRDT Bilingual Attitude Measure (Program on Teaching and Linguistic Pluralism, SCRDT). It consists of seven different guises spoken by four adult speakers (two men and two women). The test measures the subjects' reactions to the tape-recorded voices of the same speakers using different dialects (speech varieties). The subjects' reactions to the guises are used as indications of their attitudes. The seven guises are (see Appendix A, pages 286–88):

    I. Standard English.

    II. English with hispanized (Spanish accented) phonology and morphology.

    III. English with hispanized phonology, morphology, and syntax.

    IV. Code-switching between English and Spanish (an alternate use of English and Spanish in which the change from one language to the other can occur in the midst of a discourse or even within a sentence).

    V. Spanish which deviates from standard in syntax as well as in phonology and morphology.

    VI. Spanish which deviates from standard in morphology and phonology.

    VII. Standard Spanish.

A general description of the linguistic variables distinguishing the guises will appear in the teacher's manual being prepared for the SCRDT Bilingual Attitude Measures and goes beyond the scope of this study.

Partly because of time constraints, partly because the teachers who participated in this study had little or no knowledge of Spanish, guises V and VI were not used in this study. The teachers were asked to react to guises I–IV and VII.

The subjects were asked to listen to each speech sample and react to its *appropriateness for school,* its *correctness,* and the *likelihood of achievement in school* by the speaker, and to rate each speech sample on a scale of 1 to 4 in each of these three categories. Every subject heard all four speakers' voices for each guise, and the individual subject's scores on each guise for appropriateness, correctness, or achievement had a potential range of 4 (a score of 1 for each speaker) to 16. The higher the score, the more favorable the subject's attitude.

In addition to scores on the attitude dimensions of each guise, *difference scores* were used to measure subjects' differential reactions to different guises presented by the same speaker. For example, a subject reacting to Guise I (standard English) with a likelihood-of-achievement score of 15 and to Guise IV (code-switching) with a score of only 10, has a I–IV difference score of 5 for likelihood of achievement. Thus the magnitude of the difference score on each attitudinal dimension can be interpreted as measuring the degree to which one guise is valued over another.

Treatment Variable

Workshop. One of the goals of the study was to determine whether exposure to some facts concerning language variation would bring about a change in teacher attitudes, especially attitudes toward code-switching, which was the predominant language variety of the pupils in this study. We chose to use for the purpose the teacher's manual for the SCRDT Spanish/English Balance tests (Program on Teaching and Linguistic Pluralism, SCRDT). The exposure to the manual and the workshop in which the manual and the test were explained can thus be considered a treatment variable.

Two workshops were conducted, each lasting two and a half hours. During the first workshop, the description, administration procedures, and uses of the Spanish/English Balance Tests were explained to the teachers. Each teacher received the complete test battery and forms for recording the pupils' responses. Examples of pupils' responses in English on the Grammar Production Test (one of those in the battery) were discussed. Linguistic analysis of responses such as "These childs eat" and "Today the boys not know the answer" was used to introduce the teachers to bilingualism, standard and nonstandard varieties of English and Spanish, and language attitudes. Each teacher was also given a copy of the teacher's manual and asked to administer two of the Spanish/English Balance Tests to at least five pupils (test key is shown in Appendix B, page 288).

During the second workshop, two weeks later, teachers were helped to make up bilingual profiles for each pupil and for the class. (The test materials include profile sheets, and the teacher's manual explains their use.) These profiles graphically illustrated the concept of relative proficiency in English and Spanish for the individual pupil as well as for the class. Questions related to language variation were further explored.

Achievement Variables

Relative Reading Gain Scores.   Since one of the purposes of the study was to determine the influence of teachers' attitudes on student achievement, we wished to measure the relative gains in reading made by each pupil under the guidance of a particular teacher during the school year. The measure was the difference (either positive or negative) between the pupil's 1975 score on the reading section of the California Test of Basic Skills (CTBS) and his predicted reading score based on the line of regression of 1975 scores over 1974 scores. Although the subjects used in this study were at two different grade levels, they were given the same forms of the CTBS test. In interpreting relative gain scores we must keep in mind that they indicate positive or negative distances from a line of regression. In other words, the average relative gain score is by definition zero; a positive score indicates a gain greater than average and a negative score a gain smaller than average. Negative relative gain does not necessarily indicate either a loss or an absence of gain. (The R value of the regression of 1975 over 1974 scores was 0.75.)

Grades in Reading and English.   Grades given by teachers for achievement in reading and English were also used as dependent variables for the obvious reason that they could reflect teachers' attitudes as well as pupil achievement. Final grades for the 1974–75 school year were used.

SCRDT Spanish/English Balance Tests.   Two of these tests were used as a third objective measure of the language development of the pupils in the sample. The tests were a Grammar Production Test and a Grammar Multiple-Choice Test.* Both had 32 English items and 32 corresponding Spanish items. For the production tasks, pupils were asked to produce an utterance on the model of a key sentence. On the multiple-choice test, they selected one of the three possible alternatives to complete an unfinished sentence.

Scores on the Spanish Production, Spanish Multiple-Choice, and English Production tests had no significant relationship to achievement in reading and English or to pupil and teacher attitudes. Although these scores were not analyzed further, they are included in the various tables as useful information for the reader.

---

*Test reliability in this administration was as follows:

English Production	Cronbachα = .84
English Multiple-Choice	Cronbachα = .71
Spanish Production	Cronbachα = .96
Spanish Multiple-Choice	Cronbachα = .90

RESULTS

Teacher Attitudes

The mean scores assigned by the teachers to different guises for the attitudinal dimensions of correctness, appropriateness for school, and likelihood to achieve in school are presented in Tables 1A, 1B, and 1C. Correctness is defined here as the degree of conformity to the speech variety generally accepted by teachers in a school environment. Significant differences between mean evaluations of different guises are indicated in the tables by double-line brackets (p < .01) or single-line brackets (p < .05) between the two means. These differences indicate the strength of the subjects' preference for one guise over another.

The evaluation along the *correctness* dimension (Table 1A) for Group I teachers shows that on both the pretest and the posttest, Guise I (standard English) is definitely rated higher than the nonstandard guises (II, III) and code-switching (IV). The only difference between the pre- and post-results is the introduction of some new significant differences in the evaluation of the nonstandard guises relative to code-switching.

Table 1A

Teachers' Mean Scores, Standard Deviations, and Standard Errors for Guises I–IV on the Correctness Dimension

Group and Variable	Mean Score[a]	Standard Deviation	Standard Error
Group I, Pretest (N = 9)			
Guise I	14.56	1.74	0.58
Guise II	8.22	1.79	0.60
Guise III	7.89	2.15	0.72
Guise IV	7.33	2.69	0.90
Group I, Posttest (N = 9)			
Guise I	14.22	1.64	0.55
Guise II	8.78	1.64	0.55
Guise III	8.22	1.79	0.60
Guise IV	6.33	2.60	0.87
Group II (N = 9)			
Guise I	14.33	1.66	0.55
Guise II	8.89	1.17	0.39
Guise III	7.67	0.87	0.29
Guise IV	8.44	2.74	0.92

▓ = The difference between the connected means is significant at the p = 0.05 level.
░ = The difference between the connected means is significant at the p = 0.01 level.
[a]Maximum possible mean score = 16.

Table 1B

Teachers' Mean Scores, Standard Deviations, and Standard Errors for Guises I–IV on the Appropriateness-for-School Dimension

Group and Variable	Mean Score[a]	Standard Deviation	Standard Error
Group I, Pretest (N = 9)			
Guise I	14.73	1.48	0.49
Guise II	8.78	1.79	0.60
Guise III	7.56	1.67	0.56
Guise IV	6.78	2.28	0.76
Group I, Posttest (N = 9)			
Guise I	14.33	1.66	0.55
Guise II	8.67	1.41	0.47
Guise III	8.33	1.50	0.60
Guise IV	6.44	2.79	0.93
Group II (N = 9)			
Guise I	14.56	1.42	0.48
Guise II	8.78	2.33	0.78
Guise III	7.44	2.51	0.84
Guise IV	7.44	2.56	0.85

[a]Maximum possible mean score = 16.

Table 1C

Teachers' Mean Scores, Standard Deviations, and Standard Errors for Guises I–IV on the Likelihood-of-Achievement Dimension

Group and Variable	Mean Score[a]	Standard Deviation	Standard Error
Group I, Pretest (N = 9)			
Guise I	13.11	1.27	0.42
Guise II	10.22	1.56	0.52
Guise III	10.11	2.03	0.68
Guise IV	9.22	2.68	0.89
Group I, Posttest (N = 9)			
Guise I	13.22	1.39	0.47
Guise II	10.67	1.32	0.44
Guise III	9.89	1.62	0.54
Guise IV	8.89	1.97	0.66
Group II (N = 9)			
Guise I	13.22	1.86	0.62
Guise II	11.11	1.05	0.35
Guise III	9.56	1.81	0.60
Guise IV	11.89	1.36	0.46

[a]Maximum possible mean score = 16.

The attitude toward code-switching seems to have deteriorated slightly after the workshop treatment; the posttest evaluation of Guise IV is significantly lower than that of guises II and III. Group II teachers (those not involved in the workshop) did not judge the guises very differently from the workshop group. They scored standard English highest by a wide margin, as expected, on the correctness dimension.

The *appropriateness judgments* (Table 1B) correspond by and large to the correctness evaluations. Standard English is preferred to guises II, III, and IV on both the pretest and the posttest and by both groups. Differences between the pretest and posttest and between the two groups of teachers are relatively minor. The teachers in Group II did not rate code-switching quite as low as the workshop group, just as in the case of the correctness dimension.

Evaluation on the *likelihood-of-achievement* dimension (Table 1C) shows that Group I teachers rated Guise I as more likely to be associated with achievement in school than all others on both the pretest and the posttest. The only difference introduced by the posttest is a deterioration of the attitudes toward code-switching, which on the posttest is rated significantly lower than accented English. The Group II teachers, however, show a quite different pattern of ratings. Standard English is still rated higher than the hispanized English guises, but the rating given to the code-switching guise is exceptionally high. It is evaluated higher than Guise III, and the difference between the evaluation of code-switching (Guise IV) and standard English (Guise I) is *not* significant. What caused this significant difference between the teacher groups in attitudes toward code-switching? We cannot offer a certain explanation, but only a suggestion. The teachers of Group II took part in a special Title I Program, offered within the school district, which concentrated on increasing the academic achievement of students from lower income areas; the activities of this program may have either brought about a change in attitudes or attracted teachers with specific attitudinal characteristics.

Pupil Attitudes

The attitudes of the pupils of Group I teachers only were analyzed. The mean pupil ratings of the different guises (i.e., the ratings of each teacher's class), and significant differences between them on each dimension are shown in Tables 2A, 2B, and 2C. (Again, a double-line bracket is used to indicate significance at the .01 level, and a single-line bracket to indicate significance at the .05 level.)

Unlike the teachers, the pupils evaluated Guise VII, standard Spanish. They evaluated standard Spanish differently from standard English *only*

Table 2A

Pupils' Mean Scores, Standard Deviations, and Standard Errors on the
Correctness Dimension (N = 74)

Variable	Mean Score[a]	Standard Deviation	Standard Error
Guise I	13.24	1.90	0.22
Guise II	7.42	2.05	0.24
Guise III	7.36	1.83	0.21
Guise IV	9.32	2.80	0.33
Guise VII	13.51	2.13	0.25

▨ = Difference significant at p < 0.01 level.
[a]Maximum possible mean score = 16.

Table 2B

Pupils' Mean Scores, Standard Deviations, and Standard Errors on the
Appropriateness-for-School Dimension (N = 74)

Variable	Mean Score[a]	Standard Deviation	Standard Error
Guise I	13.38	1.78	0.21
Guise II	7.03	2.16	0.25
Guise III	7.32	2.02	0.24
Guise IV	8.46	2.82	0.33
Guise VII	11.85	3.29	0.38

[a]Maximum possible mean score = 16.

Table 2C

Pupils' Mean Scores, Standard Deviations, and Standard Errors on the
Likelihood-of-Achievement Dimension (N = 74)

Variable	Mean Score[a]	Standard Deviation	Standard Error
Guise I	13.54	1.70	0.20
Guise II	7.81	2.30	0.27
Guise III	8.10	2.06	0.24
Guise IV	9.55	2.62	0.31
Guise VII	13.26	2.63	0.31

[a]Maximum possible mean score = 16.

on the appropriateness dimension and not with regard to correctness or likelihood to succeed in school. The only interpretation of this finding is that the pupils think the speaker of standard Spanish is likely to succeed in school conducted in Spanish, but unfortunately this attitude has no application to the monolingual English school the children attended.

In the evaluation of the *correctness* of the guises (Table 2A) the pupils seem to have been able to make the "correct" and justifiable judgment that the most hispanized version of English (Guise III) is the least "correct" guise. (By contrast, their teachers, on the posttest, rated code-switching as the least "correct" guise.)

On *appropriateness* (Table 2B), the two versions of hispanized English (guises II and III) were again rated lowest. Code-switching (rated lowest by the teachers) was again ranked higher than hispanized English by the pupils.

With regard to the judgments concerning *likelihood of achievement* (Table 2C), the same pattern is repeated: the hispanized English guises are rated lowest. Pupils agree with the Group II teachers in ranking code-switching higher than hispanized English and disagree with the Group I teachers who put the code-switching pupil either in the same category as the hispanized English speaker (pretest) or at an even lower level (posttest).

Since code-switching is characteristic of the language of the pupils in this study, judgments about the achievement potential of the code-switchers are of particular interest. Both pupils and teachers agree that code-switchers are not as likely to succeed in school as the speakers of standard English, though in the case of Group II teachers the difference is not significant.

Teacher Attitudes and Pupil Achievement

In order to investigate a possible relation between teacher attitude and pupil achievement, three difference scores on the likelihood-of-achievement attitude dimension were found for each teacher: the evaluation of Guise I minus, separately, the evaluations of guises II, III, and IV. The rationale behind this procedure is that the magnitude of the difference score can be assumed to be proportional to the teacher's negative attitude toward guise II, III, or IV relative to standard English. Or, put another way, the difference score is a measure of the degree of preference for standard English. Tables 3A, 3B, and 3C show each teacher's difference score, his group affiliation (pretest scores are used for Group I teachers), the relative gain score in reading for his class, and mean pupil grades in reading and English (grades were measured on a 4-point scale from A = 4 to F = 1). (continued on page 283)

Table 3A

Teacher Difference Scores I–II on the Likelihood-of-Achievement Dimension and Class Achievement Measures (N = 18)

Teacher Difference Score I–II	Teacher Number	Teacher Group	Relative Gain Scores in Reading[a] Pupil N	x̄	SD	Grade in Reading Pupil N	x̄	SD	Grade in English Pupil N	x̄	SD
0	2	I	5	-.34	0.58	15	2.67	0.49	15	2.80	0.68
0	6	I	2	-.38	0.03	7	2.29	0.76	7	2.86	0.69
0	11	II	7	.01	0.53	17	2.65	0.79	17	2.53	0.80
0	15	II	19	.23	0.69	23	3.00	0.30	23	3.09	0.29
0	18	II	0	0	0	20	3.25	0.72	19	3.37	0.68
1	5	I	3	-.80	0.34	6	3.00	0.63	6	2.50	1.05
1	14	II	9	-.01	0.38	16	2.63	0.62	16	2.75	0.68
1	16	II	16	-.06	0.67	19	2.90	0.46	19	3.00	0.33
2	7	II	2	-.61	0.34	5	2.20	0.45	5	2.20	0.84
2	12	II	11	.67	0.66	16	3.19	0.40	16	3.06	0.25
3	3	II	11	-.33	0.43	15	2.47	0.83	15	2.53	0.83
4	1	I	5	-.27	0.43	11	2.64	0.67	11	2.73	0.91
4	8	I	2	-.16	0.52	11	2.46	0.52	11	1.97	0.54
4	10	II	1	-.48	0	8	2.25	0.46	8	2.13	0.64
5	17	II	20	.06	0.77	21	2.86	0.57	21	2.86	0.48
6	4	I	4	-.33	0.41	7	2.57	0.79	7	2.14	0.90
6	9	I	4	.09	1.16	4	3.00	0.82	4	3.00	1.41
6	13	II	10	-.12	0.53	17	2.65	0.70	17	2.88	0.86

[a]Actual reading achievement score minus predicted score.

Table 3B

Teacher Difference Scores I–III on the Likelihood-of-Achievement Dimension and Class Achievement Measures (N = 18)

Teacher Difference Score I–III	Teacher Number	Group	Relative Gain Scores in Reading[a]			Grade in Reading			Grade in English		
			Pupil N	x̄	SD	Pupil N	x̄	SD	Pupil N	x̄	SD
0	2	I	5	-.34	0.58	15	2.67	0.49	15	2.80	0.68
0	6	I	2	-.38	0.03	7	2.29	0.76	7	2.86	0.70
0	7	I	2	-.61	0.34	5	2.20	0.45	5	2.20	0.84
0	14	II	9	-.01	0.38	16	2.63	0.62	16	2.75	0.68
0	15	II	19	.30	0.69	23	3.00	0.30	23	3.09	0.29
1	11	II	7	.01	0.53	17	2.65	0.79	17	2.53	0.80
2	5	I	3	-.80	0.34	6	3.00	0.63	6	2.50	1.05
2	8	I	2	-.16	0.52	11	2.46	0.52	11	1.91	0.54
2	18	II	0	0	0	20	3.25	0.72	19	3.37	0.68
3	16	II	16	-.06	0.67	19	2.90	0.46	19	3.00	0.33
4	12	II	11	.67	0.66	16	3.19	0.40	16	3.06	0.25
5	3	I	11	-.33	0.43	15	2.47	0.83	15	2.53	0.83
5	4	I	4	-.33	0.41	7	2.57	0.79	7	2.14	0.90
6	1	I	5	-.27	0.43	11	2.64	0.67	11	2.73	0.91
7	9	I	4	.09	1.16	4	3.00	0.82	4	3.00	1.41
7	17	II	20	.06	0.77	21	2.86	0.57	21	2.86	0.48
8	13	II	10	-.12	0.53	17	2.65	0.70	17	2.88	0.86

[a]Actual reading achievement score minus predicted score.

Table 3C
Teacher Difference Scores I–IV on hte Likelihood-of-Ahcievement Dimension and Class Achievement Measures (N = 18)

Teacher Difference Score I–III	Teacher Number	Group	Relative Gain Scores in Reading[a]			Grade in Reading			Grade in English		
			Pupil N	x̄	SD	Pupil N	x̄	SD	Pupil N	x̄	SD
0	2	I	5	-.34	0.58	15	2.67	0.49	15	2.80	0.68
0	6	I	2	-.38	0.03	7	2.29	0.76	7	2.86	0.69
0	11	II	7	.01	0.53	17	2.65	0.79	17	2.53	0.80
0	12	II	11	.67	0.56	16	3.19	0.40	16	3.06	0.25
0	14	II	9	-.01	0.38	16	2.63	0.62	16	2.75	0.68
0	15	II	19	.30	0.69	23	3.00	0.30	23	3.09	0.29
0	16	II	16	-.06	0.67	19	2.90	0.46	19	3.00	0.33
2	5	I	3	-.80	0.34	6	3.00	0.63	6	2.50	1.05
2	7	I	2	-.61	0.34	5	2.20	0.45	5	2.20	0.84
2	13	II	10	-.11	0.53	17	2.65	0.70	17	2.88	0.86
2	18	II	0	0	0	20	3.25	0.72	19	3.37	0.68
4	1	I	5	-.27	0.43	11	2.64	0.67	11	2.73	0.91
4	3	I	11	-.33	0.43	15	2.47	0.83	15	2.53	0.83
5	8	II	2	-.16	0.52	11	2.46	0.52	11	1.91	0.54
5	17	II	20	.06	0.77	21	2.86	0.57	21	2.86	0.48
7	9	I	4	.09	1.16	4	3.00	0.82	4	3.00	1.41
7	10	II	1	-.48	0	8	2.25	0.46	8	2.13	0.64
11	4	I	4	-.32	0.41	7	2.57	0.79	7	2.14	0.90

[a]Actual reading achievement score minus predicted score.

Table 4

Correlations Between Mean Teacher Difference Scores on Likelihood of Achievement and Class Achievement Measure

Source of Teacher Difference Scores[a]	Relative Gain Score in Reading (N = 17 teachers)	Grade in Reading (N = 18 teachers)	Grade in English (N = 18 teachers)
I–II	.01	-.16	-.33
I–III	.08	.03	-.05
I–IV	-.24	-.21	-.50[b]

[a]Pretest scores were used for Group I teachers.
[b]p < .05

Table 4 presents relationships between these scores, i.e., between teacher attitude and pupil achievement. A Pygmalion effect would, of course, be suggested by a negative correlation between a teacher's difference score and the mean achievement of his pupils (i.e., the greater the teacher's preference for Guise I, the lower the pupils' achievement). A significant negative correlation between achievement measures and difference scores I–IV would especially be indicative of a Pygmalion effect, since code-switching (Guise IV) is the characteristic speech behavior of the pupils. All the correlations between the three pupil achievement measures and difference score I–IV are indeed negative, but only one of them (I–IV and grade in English; $r = .50$) reaches the .05 level of significance. This single result, however, gives a rather clear indication that the teachers' negative attitudes toward code switching (and corresponding stongly positive attitudes toward standard English) generate low assessments of their pupils' language and performance and lead to low grades in English.

Pupil Attitudes and Achievement

To examine the relation of pupil attitudes to pupil achievement, we did a correlation analysis of pupil difference scores on the likelihood-of-achievement attitude dimension and pupil achievement measures (see Table 5). The difference scores comparing Guise I (standard English) and guises II, III, and IV (all "nonstandard" varieties) all have a significant positive relation to the pupils' performance on the Grammar Multiple-Choice Test in English. This relation is not surprising, since to some extent the evaluation of the nonstandard guises and the multiple-choice test involve overlapping or similar tasks, that is, the recognition of

Table 5

Correlations of Pupil Difference Scores on the Likelihood-of-Achievement
Dimension with Pupil Achievement Measures

Source of Pupil Difference Scores	Relative Gains in Reading (N = 35)	Grade in Reading (N = 73)	Grade in English (N = 73)	Spanish Multiple Choice (N = 67)	English Multiple Choice (N = 68)	Spanish Production (N = 17)	English Production (N = 23)
I–II	.13	-.05	.09	.03	.24	.33	-.04
I–III	.20	.26ᵃ	.14	.04	.25ᵇ	.23	.09
I–IV	.38ᵃ	.12	.17	.13	.22ᵇ	.02	.17
I–VII	.05	-.04	-.16	-.11	-.12	.00	.11

ᵃ p < .01
ᵇ p < .05

standard as opposed to nonstandard English speech. The positive
correlation between the grade in reading and the pupil difference score
I–III can be explained in much the same way: both the reading grade
and the evaluation of different guises are likely to involve an ability to
distinguish between standard and nonstandard speech varieties. Somewhat surprisingly, all the achievement measures are positively related to
the degree to which pupils downgrade code switching compared to
standard English (I–IV), though only two correlations are significant.
These findings suggest that pupils' grades and actual reading achievement may have some relation to the congruence of pupils' attitudes with
teachers' attitudes.

CONCLUSIONS

The important results of this investigation may be summarized as
follows:

1. Teachers and pupils have well-defined and largely similar attitudes toward specific speech varieties found in a Spanish/English
   bilingual environment. Teachers and pupils agree in rating
   standard English higher than nonstandard speech varieties on
   correctness, appropriateness, and likelihood of achievement in
   school; and most teachers agree with pupils in rating standard
   English significantly higher than code switching. After the
   workshop, the participants (Group I teachers) tended to rate
   code switching even lower than heavily hispanized English
   (Guise III). However, another group of teachers involved in a
   year-long special program did not share this judgment, and
   ranked code switching higher than hispanized English on likeli-

hood of achievement and even went so far as not to rank the achievement potential of code-switchers significantly lower than that of speakers of standard English.

2. The workshop conducted for Group I teachers apparently did not bring about changes in attitude in the desired direction. Indeed, attitudinal change may have taken place in the opposite direction. Although the workshop presentation stressed, among other sociolinguistic facts, the naturalness of code switching as a legitimate and expressive form of communication among bilinguals, post-workshop attitude measures seem to indicate a further deterioration of teacher attitudes toward code switching, compared to other nonstandard speech varieties. The results suggest that relatively short-in-service workshops may be an unsuitable vehicle for bringing about predictable attitudinal change on the part of teachers.

3. Bilingual pupils' language attitudes have some relation to their achievement in reading and English. Their ranking the achievement potential of speakers of standard English higher than that of speakers of nonstandard varieties, including code switching, has a positive relation to their achievement.

4. There is some evidence that teachers' attitudes regarding the likelihood of success of code-switching bilingual pupils are directly related to pupils' grades as well as to their relative reading gains as shown by an objective test.

The next step in research may not be further documentation of the self-fulfilling prophecy, but a detailed study of specific teaching behaviors as well as specific characteristics of pupils that mediate between the teacher's attitude and the achievement of the pupils (cf. Alpert, 1975; Dusek, 1975). Only investigating the dynamics and importance of teacher-pupil interactions in the classroom and their effects on pupils' learning will tell us how to plan the kind of intervention that will result in maximum benefit to the pupil.

REFERENCES

Alpert, J.L. "Teacher Behavior and Pupil Performance: Reconsideration of the Mediation of the Pygmalion Effect." *The Journal of Educational Research,* 69 (1975), 53–57.

Dusek, J.B. "Do Teachers Bias Children's Learning?" *Review of Educational Research,* 45 (Fall 1975), 661–684.

Lambert, W.E., Frankel, H., and Tucker, G. R. "Judging Personality from Speech: A French-Canadian Example." *Journal of Communication,* 16 (1966), 305–321.

Politzer, R.L., and Ramírez, A. G. *Judging Personality from Speech: A Pilot Study of the Effects of Bilingual Education on Attitudes toward Ethnic Groups* (R&D Memorandum No. 106). Stanford, Ca.: Stanford Center for Research and Development in Teaching, 1973a. (ERIC No. ED 076 278)

Politzer, R. L. L., and Ramírez, A. G. *Judging Personality from Speech: A Pilot Study of the Attitudes toward Ethnic Groups of Students in Monolingual Schools* (R&D Memorandum No. 107). Stanford, Ca.: Stanford Center for Research and Development in Teaching, 1973b. (ERIC No. ED 078 992)

Program on Teaching and Linguistic Pluralism, Stanford Center for Research and Development in Teaching. "SCRDT Bilingual Attitude Measure." Stanford, Ca.: Stanford Center for Research and Development in Teaching, in preparation.

Program on Teaching and Linguistic Pluralism, Stanford Center for Research and Development in Teaching. "SCRDT Spanish/English Balance Tests." Stanford, Ca.: Stanford Center for Research and Development in Teaching, in preparation.

Rosenthal, R., and Jacobson, L. *Pygmalion in the Classroom.* New York: Holt, Rinehart and Winston, 1968.

Seligman, G. P., Tucker, G. R., and Lambert, W. E. "The Effects of Speech Style and Other Attributes on Teachers' Attitudes toward Pupils." *Language and Society,* 1 (1972), 131–142.

Williams, F. "Some Research Notes on Dialect Attitudes and Stereotypes." In R. W. Shuy and R. W. Easold, eds., *Language Attitudes: Current Trends and Prospects.* Washington, D.C.: Georgetown University Press, 1973. Pp. 113–128.

Wolfram, W., and Fasold, R. W. *The Study of Social Dialects in American English.* Englewood Cliffs, N.J.: Prentice-Hall, 1974.

APPENDIX A

Paragraph I

STANDARD ENGLISH (GUISE I)

Ann is thirteen years old. She likes to play with her brother Richard who is eight years old. Ann's mother brought her a red shawl for her birthday. When Ann was going to put on her shawl, she couldn't find it because Richard had hidden it under some boxes. Ann was very angry, but her mother told her not to be upset because her brother was only playing a game.

STANDARD ENGLISH WITH PHONOLOGICAL AND MORPHOLOGICAL DEVIATIONS (GUISE II)

Ann is thirteen[4] years old. She[1] likes to play with her brother Richard who is[2] eight years old. Ann's mother bring[6] her a red shawl[1] for her birthday. When Ann was going to put[3] on her shawl,[1] she[1] couldn't find it[2] because Richard had hidden it[2] under some boxes. Ann is[2,6] very angry, but her mother told her not to be upset because her brother was only playing a game.

STANDARD ENGLISH WITH PHONOLOGICAL, MORPHOLOGICAL, AND SYNTACTICAL DEVIATIONS (GUISE III)

Ann__[7]thirteen[4] year[5] old. She[1] likes to play with her brother Richard who is[2] eight year[5] old. Ann's mother bring[6] her a red shawl[1] for her birthday. When Ann was going to put[3] on his[8] shawl,[1] she[1] no[10] could find it[2] because__[9] had hidden it[2] under some box__[5]. Ann is[2,6] very angry, but her mother told her to be no[10] upset because her brother was only playing a game.

ENGLISH/SPANISH CODE SWITCHING (GUISE IV)

Ana tiene thirteen years. She likes to play con su hermano Richard que tiene eight years. Ana's mother le trajo un red shawl para su birthday. When Ana se fue a poner su shawl, she couldn't find it porque Richard lo había escondido under some boxes. Ana was very angry, pero su madre le dijo not to be upset porque su hermano was only playing a game.

STANDARD SPANISH WITH PHONOLOGICAL, MORPHOLOGICAL, AND SYNTACTICAL DEVIATIONS (GUISE V)

Ana tene[18] trece años. A e' a[12] le gusta jugar con su hermano Ricardo, quien tene[18] ocho[11] años. L'[15] [14]amá de Ana le trujo[17] a e' a[12] un rojo[19] rebozo para su cumpleaños. Cuando Ana jue[13] a ponerse su[20] rebozo, no lo pudo encontrar porque Ricardo lo había escondido debajo de una__[16] cajas. Ana estaba furiosa, pero su '[14] amá le dijo que no se '[14] nojara porque su hermano sólo estaba jugando.

STANDARD SPANISH WITH PHONOLOGICAL AND MORPHOLOGICAL DEVIATIONS (GUISE VI)

Ana tene[18] trece años. A e' a[12] le gusta jugar con su hermano Ricardo, quien tene[18] ocho[11] años. L'[15] [14] amá de Ana le trujo[17] a e' a[12] un rebozo rojo para su cumpleaños. Cuando Ana jue[13] a ponerse el rebozo, no lo pudo encontrar porque Ricardo lo había escondido debajo de unas cajas. Ana estaba furiosa, pero su '[14] amá le dijo que no se enojara porque su hermano sólo estaba jugando.

STANDARD SPANISH (GUISE VII)

Ana tiene trece años. A ella le gusta jugar con su hermano Ricardo, quien tiene ocho años. La mamá de Ana le trajo a ella un rebozo rojo para su cumpleaños. Cuando Ana fue a ponerse el rebozo, no lo pudo encontrar porque Ricardo lo había escondido debajo de unas cajas. Ana estaba furiosa pero su mamá le dijo que no se enojara porque su hermano sólo estaba jugando.

APPENDIX B

Key to Phonological, Morphological, and Syntactical Variations

ENGLISH

Phonological Variations

    (1) /"sh"/ - /"ch"/ confusion.

    (2) /I/ - /i/ confusion.

    (3) /u/ - /U/ confusion.

    (4) /θ/ → /t/.

Morphological Variations

    (5) Misuse of pluralization rules.

    (6) Incorrect simple past tense.

Syntactical Variations

    (7) Omission of a form of the auxiliary "be."

    (8) Confusion in use of the possessive pronoun.

    (9) Misuse or omission of third-person pronoun.

    (10) Incorrect negation.

SPANISH

Phonological Variations

    (11) /"ch"/ - /"sh"/ confusion.

    (12) The weakening of the intervocalic [y].

    (13) /f/ → /X/.

    (14) Aphaeresis (loss of initial sound or syllable).

    (15) Elision.

Morphological Variations

    (16) Gender or number disagreement.

    (17) Archaism.

    (18) Regularization of irregular verbs.

Syntactical Variations

    (19) Adjective-noun word disorder.

    (20) Possessive redundance.

Mexican-American Perceptions of Parent and Teacher Roles in Child Development

ELENA PARRA
University of Arizona

RONALD W. HENDERSON
University of California at Santa Cruz

The origins of interest in bilingual/bicultural programs for Americans of Spanish surname and language background are difficult to trace through the tangled web of educational, political, and social issues which gave rise to this movement (Padilla, Warner-Grough, Amaro-Plotkin, and Amodeo, 1975). Clearly, the movement is part of a larger expression of dissatisfaction with traditional American values, particularly those relating to the narrow technical, economic and bureaucratic goals of American society, and those associated with the "melting pot" philosophy which fashioned institutions to assimilate Americans of differing cultural traditions into a homogeneous population. From Colonial times onward a unified educational system has been advocated on the premise that such a system would result in a more uniform citizenry. Benjamin Rush, a Colonial leader, member of the Continental Congress and a signer of the Declaration of Independence, advocated such an educational undertaking, believing that a homogeneous population could be more easily governed than one consisting of culturally diverse groups (Henderson and Bergan, 1976).

The melting pot philosophy is gradually giving way to a view that sees richness in cultural diversity. This outlook advocates that we consciously and systematically attempt to preserve valued aspects of the native cultures of diverse groups of Americans. This shift in values has provided a favorable climate for the development of educational programs designed to foster cultural pluralism, but to date the literature of cultural pluralism is almost exclusively comprised of statements of opinion and philosophy, with little empirical data either to validate existing bicultural programs or to provide the basis for more effective program development and implementation. As a result, many educators are uncertain about precisely what populations their multi-cultural programs are targeted at, how to communicate their program objectives to the community, the range of cultural similarities and differences within the targeted population, or what differences may be considered cultural and which are attributable to social class.

In brief, information relating to the nature of the Spanish-speaking populations of the United States is spotty, and contradictory assertions and misconceptions concerning their educational problems are rampant. As Padilla and his associates (1975) stated in the introduction to their recent review of research on this topic, "All of the information gathered in the preparation of this state-of-the-art paper has given us insight into what is known but *mostly not known*, about the SS/S [Spanish-speaking/Spanish surnamed] preschool child, his family, community and BL/BC [Bilingual/Bicultural] education" (p. 2, emphasis added).

If bilingual/bicultural programs are to be successful, policy must be guided by knowledge of present relationships between the schools and the family patterns of target populations. Padilla and his colleagues feel that if the child is to succeed in school, it is essential that parental and teacher expectations mesh with each other. Their arguments support the need for research designed to examine these relationships. Citing Getzels (1974), Padilla et al. (1975) state that

> in the absence of formal empirical evidence there is some indication that parents and teachers have different, and possibly incompatible, role expectations which conflict and interfere with the academic success of children. (p. 18)

The purpose of the present investigation was to obtain descriptive data on Mexican-American* perceptions of socialization roles of teachers and parents. Although there is evidence that a substantial degree of cultural heterogeneity exists even within the Mexican-American population of a single large community (Henderson and Merritt, 1968), few investigations have explored differences within a Chicano population. Therefore, similarities and differences between two socioeconomic levels were also examined in the present investigation. The study was designed as a pilot effort to generate hypotheses for future investigations of continuities and discontinuities in socialization role perceptions of Mexican-American families and their schools. The specific areas selected for study were child management practices,

---

*Throughout this paper the terms Mexican-American and Chicano are used interchangeably because of individual differences in preference for terms of self-reference within the population involved in this study.

sex-role perceptions relating to children, age-related behavioral expectations, capabilities and qualities valued in children, learning outcomes valued, and educational and occupational expectations for the child.

METHOD

Subjects. A total of 95 Chicano parents from two socioeconomic levels served as subjects for this study. Twenty-five parents receiving welfare payments and/or public housing benefits constituted the lower socioeconomic level group. The 70 subjects who were classified as middleclass were enrolled in courses at a community college and were self-supporting in skilled or "higher" occupations. The lower-class subjects were drawn entirely from a government housing project and from night school GED and arts and craft classes. All members of these groups who could be contacted were asked to participate in the study. Only two of the lower socioeconomic status families contacted refused to be interviewed. All of the middle-class parents attended introductory psychology classes taught by a community college instructor who agreed to announce the project to her classes. Only four potential subjects enrolled in these classes declined to participate in the interview.

Instrument. An interview schedule was developed to elicit information on child management practices, sex-role perceptions, age-related behavioral expectations for children, qualities valued in children, learning outcomes valued and responsibility (school or family) for these outcomes, and educational and occupational expectations held by parents for their children. These were all areas of inquiry for which experience or existing literature suggested that social status differences might exist, or for which expectations of the ethnic subculture might be inconsistent with expectations of professional educators.

The interview schedule consisted of 22 focused items calling for constructed responses on the part of the interviewees. Examples of items for each of the subject areas addressed are as follows:

> Child management practices: "Suppose you want your child to do something he/she doesn't want to do (like washing dishes or cleaning the yard). How would you get him/her to do it?"
>
> Sex-role perceptions: "Name some things that are OK for boys to do but not for girls."
>
> Age-related behavioral expectations: "If a child 3 years old or younger begins to cry, how would you react? What if the child is older than 3 years old?"
>
> Qualities valued in children: "Can you think of any specific thing your child has done in the past few days that you have shown approval of?"

Learning outcomes valued and focus of responsibility: "What are some of the things that you think are most important for a child to learn in school? At home?"

Educational and occupational expectations: "What types of work would you like to see your child do when he/she grows up?"

Procedure. The interview was administered in each subject's preferred language by a Spanish surnamed female graduate student. Following the subject's response to each question, the interviewer prompted further responses by saying "Anything else?" When the respondent had nothing further to say about that item, the interviewer proceeded to the next question. The interview schedule required an average of about 30 minutes to administer, exclusive of the time required in establishing rapport and post-interview discussions.

Data were analyzed by classifying responses to each set of questions for analysis by the z test for proportional differences in populations (Glass and Stanley, 1970). If a subject suggested more than one approach to child management, for example, each response was classified and entered into the relevant analysis.

RESULTS

Language Preference. The first comparison does not bear directly upon the primary questions addressed in this study, but from a descriptive point of view it is interesting to note that while participants were afforded the opportunity to have the interview conducted in their language of choice, 83% of the interviews with middle-class parents were conducted in English, while 80% of the interviews with lower-status parents were conducted in Spanish. A related point of interest not reflected in these percentages was that middle-class parents shifted from one language to the other more frequently than lower-class subjects, regardless of which language they chose for the interview.

Child Management. In response to items about child management, participants suggested a number of different means of controlling and directing the behavior of their children. Responses were categorized as explanation (inductive procedures), positive reinforcement, negative reinforcement, verbal punishment (scolding) and corporal punishment. Sixty-eight percent of the parents interviewed suggested the use of explanation as a means of managing child behavior. The frequency of mention of inductive procedures did not differ by socioeconomic status of subjects. Moreover, approximately half of each group also suggested practices that could be classified as negative reinforcement (i.e., removal of a reinforcer as a means of increasing a desired behavior).

There was a significant difference between the two groups in reports of verbal punishment ($z = 1.96$, $p < .01$). The middle-class parents reported significantly less use of verbal punishment (7.5 percent) than the lower-status parents (47.6 percent).

While the majority of parents in both groups reported the use of positive reinforcement procedures, there was a significant difference ($z = 2.44$, $p < .05$) between the groups in the ratio of positive reinforcement to punishment when verbal and physical punishment were combined. In the middle-class group, 77.2 percent of the parents reported the use of positive reinforcement while only 22.8 percent suggested punishment. In the lower socioeconomic group, 55.3 percent suggested positive reinforcement compared to 44.7 percent who mentioned punishment.

Fewer parents reported the use of physical punishment as a control procedure than for any other category. Lower-status parents (33.3 percent) suggested such procedures relatively more frequently than middle-status parents (19.8 percent), but the difference was not significant.

Sex-Role Perceptions.   Lower- and middle-class subjects did not differ in their expectations and/or demands for boys and girls. However, a majority (56.5 percent of the middle-class and 75 percent of the lower-class parents) reported holding different expectations for boys than for girls. There was, nevertheless, a clear consciousness on the part of many parents that sex-role distinctions were fading.

Age-Related Differentiation in Expectations.   Eighty-nine percent of the middle-class parents and 95 percent of the lower-class parents reported that they would respond differently to children's behaviors, depending upon the child's age. The difference between the two groups was not significant.

Activities and Qualities Valued.   One way of looking at the kinds of qualities people value in their children is to examine the kinds of activities in which they encourage their children to participate. This examination rests upon the assumption that parents believe that participation in specified activities helps their children to develop the skills or qualities stressed in those activities. None of the comparisons in this area revealed any significant differences between the two groups of parents. Fifty-six percent of the middle-class parents and 52 percent of the lower-class parents reported that they placed a high value on activities having a recreational content. Forty-three percent of the lower-class parents reported placing highest value on activities having educational content, in contrast to 36 percent of the middle-class parents who reported this emphasis. Comparisons based on the qualities approved or disapproved of in their children's friends were not possible, because most responses were too general, merely indicating that the friends should have "acceptable behavior patterns."

Learning Outcomes and Focus of Responsibility.   Responses relating to this set of variables were categorized on the basis of the kinds of expectations that parents held for socialization activities of the home and the school. Of the middle-class parents, 78.7 percent reported that they viewed the school's principal responsibility as one of teaching academic skills. Almost 73 percent of the lower-status parents reported the same expectation. This is not to say that these parents overlooked the school's responsibility for promoting social and emotional development. Sixty percent of the lower-class and 70.4 percent of the middle-class parents expressed dissatisfaction with the job the schools were doing. Of these parents, half of the lower-class and 65.8 percent of the middle-class parents recognized social and emotional development as an important part of the school's responsibility, which they felt was not being adequately met. The remainder of the dissatisfied parents focused their complaints on the teaching of academic skills.

When responses were categorized to reflect whether parents perceived the socialization responsibilities of the home and school as the same or different, there was a significant difference ($z = 2.9$, $p < .01$) between the two social classes. Lower-class parents were more prone than middle-class parents to see the responsibilities of the home and the school as congruent, in the sense of sharing the burden for fostering some common aspect of the child's development. However, agreement that the home and school were both responsible for the child's socioemotional development accounted for nearly all of the apparent congruence in role perceptions. Of the total number of subjects, only two parents indicated that both the home and the school were responsible for fostering intellectual development or academic achievement, and both of these were from the middle-class sample. All of the others saw this responsibility as solely the province of the schools. Quite clearly, most of the parents, 98 percent, perceived the main socialization task of the home as the fostering of socioemotional development.

Aspirations and Expectations.   This category of perceptions was examined by comparing the educational and occupational expectations and aspirations that parents held for their children. None of the comparisons performed yielded significant differences between the groups, but descriptively the results were rather interesting. A majority (69 percent for the lower class and 61 percent for the middle class) of the parents reported that they had aspirations for their children to enter professional occupations. Thirty-one percent of the lower-class and 18 percent of the middle-class parents reported that they would be satisfied if their children went into any sort of honest occupation. Other reported aspirations accounted for 21 percent of the responses.

Questions distinguishing between the kinds of work a parent would like to see his/her child doing in adulthood and the sorts of work the parents thought the child might actually be doing in adulthood revealed an interesting pattern. Analysis of the data revealed discrepancies between the aspirations and the actual expectations of 52 percent of the lower-class parents and 55 percent of the middle-class sample.

Most parents (74 percent of the lower-class sample and 83 percent of the middle-class sample) reported that they had aspirations for their children to attend college. Of those who held college aspirations for their children, only 43.6 percent of the middle-class and 66.6 percent of lower-class parents had expectations that their children would actually complete college. When asked about their specific plans or preparations to fulfill their expectations for their children, most of the parents (54 percent of the lower class and 49 percent of the middle class) reported that they planned for their children to be academically prepared for college. Only 38 percent of the lower-class and 49 percent of the middle-class parents reported any financial preparation for the higher education of their children.

DISCUSSION

The results of this study must be viewed as tentative because the samples cannot be assumed to accurately represent middle- and lower-class Mexican-Americans in general. Nevertheless, the findings have implications that warrant the consideration of educators and suggest areas requiring further study by researchers.

Relatively few differences were identified between the views of middle and lower-class Mexican-Americans. This may result in part from the fact that the middle-class subjects seemed to be largely from families whose middle-class status had been attained only within the present generation. Nevertheless, the fact that there was a large and significant difference in the language of preference of the two groups, as defined in this study, suggests that the samples did indeed represent different populations of Mexican-Americans.

The major group differences in opinions regarding child management were identified. Lower-class parents suggested the use of verbal punishment, or scolding, as a means of influencing children's behavior with significantly higher frequency than did middle-class parents. When all forms of punishment were compared with practices employing principles of positive reinforcement, the data indicated that lower-class parents leaned toward the use of punishment to a significantly greater degree than did middle-class parents.

The results also suggest that most parents in both groups have an extensive range of child management procedures in their repertories, including explanation, positive reinforcement, and punishment. The nature of the questionnaire did not make it possible to direct comparisons of preference hierarchies for these control procedures, but the findings do suggest that new studies of the actual child management practices employed by Mexican-American parents are needed, and that socioeconomic differences should be examined in these investigations. Much of the present literature on the child-rearing practices of Mexican-Americans is based upon self-report data from a single socioeconomic strata (Henderson and Merritt, 1968) or observations of the teaching procedures employed by mothers as they present their children with a problem-solving task (Steward and Steward, 1973, 1974). For example, data reported by Steward and Steward suggest that Chicano mothers employ large amounts of negative feedback in teaching interactions with their children, relative to the practices employed by Anglo and Chinese-American mothers. Social class differences were not examined in these studies. Since mothers in both socioeconomic groups in the present investigation appeared to understand the use of a wide range of alternative methods of child management, it would be appropriate to determine the influence of situational variables on the kinds of management practices used. If Chicano mothers do not see themselves as teachers of intellectual skills as Steward and Steward (1973) suggest, then behaviors displayed in the parent-child interaction situations employed in observational studies may not be representative of strategies employed in managing their children's behavior in other domains and settings. Both observational and self-report studies should be undertaken to determine the range of variation in child management practices of Chicano families and the influences of situational determinants of parent-child interaction.

No social class differences were found in parental perceptions of sex-roles for children, with a majority of the parents from both groups reporting that they held different expectations for boys and girls. Many respondents indicated their awareness of changes within the large society toward less differentiation in sex-roles. As one mother put it, "Where is the cut-off line in society now? With E.R.A. almost in the Constitution, there's hardly anything that will be thought good for boys and not for girls." Another parent stated the case very directly by saying that "Nowadays, what's good for the boys is good for the girls."

The vast majority of both groups of parents reported that the age of a child has a determining influence on how a parent should respond. The information available from the present study is too limited to identify the specific areas of behavior for which this may be true, but it does indicate that the parents differentiate their responses on the basis of the age of the child.

The data on the kind of qualities that parents value in their children suggest a fair balance of interest in both groups between social and recreational skills on the one hand and academic ability on the other. These results are most interesting when considered in the context of information concerning the kinds of learning outcomes parents valued and their opinions about whether the home or the school was primarily responsible for the development of those capabilities. A large majority of both groups believed that the school's primary responsibility was to teach academic skills. In contrast, they saw the fostering of the social and emotional development of their children as the primary responsibility of the home, and they did not perceive the parental role as one of deliberately promoting the intellectual development and academic achievement of their children. On this dimension there were no differences between the two socioeconomic levels, and the results tend to confirm the contention (Steward and Steward, 1973) that Chicano mothers do not perceive themselves as teachers. On the other hand, there was no apparent support for the contention that Mexican-American parents were not concerned with academic skills.

While parents believed that the school's principal responsibility was to teach academic skills, they also expressed the belief that the schools should provide an atmosphere to promote the social and emotional development of children, and there was a considerable amount of dissatisfaction with the school's accomplishments along both of these dimensions.

The most striking fact about parental expectations and aspirations for the education and future employment of their children was the discrepancy between the expectations and aspirations of the samples. Regardless of socioeconomic status, a very large proportion of the parents interviewed did not expect their children to achieve goals as high as the aspirations held for them. There was a non-significant trend for lower-class parents to express a greater discrepancy between aspirations and expectations than the middle-class sample. If such a trend were confirmed, it might reflect differential access to or acknowledgement of social realities.

There was evidence in the responses of some parents that part of their dissatisfaction with schools stemmed from the belief that the methods employed by teachers failed to take the children's cultural background into consideration. When asked if there were some things the schools should be doing better, one parent made the case that schools should provide ". . . better methods of teaching minority children instead of teaching their middle-class methods to minority children. They should provide better materials, support for recreation, and minority teachers who have been exposed to the Barrios." Such comments were relatively few in number and no one spontaneously mentioned bicultural/bilingual programs as either a reason for satisfaction or dissatisfaction.

Although the evidence is indirect, respondents did not seem to have been greatly influenced by the public appeal of some Chicano leaders for more bilingual/bicultural programs. On the other hand, the public rhetoric on cultural pluralism and multicultural education leads some school officials to believe that the goals advocated by Chicano parents who do press for educational reform are quite different from those traditionally held by educators. This view is buttressed by statements in the psychological literature suggesting that Chicano parents are not interested in the academic accomplishments of their children (Steward and Steward, 1973; Durrett, O'Bryant, and Pennebaker, 1975). Obviously, some goals of multicultural education differ from those of traditional programs, but the data from the present study suggest that Chicano parents are very much concerned with the academic progress and socioemotional development of their children—the same central goals professed by educators. With better provisions for communication between the school and the home, it should be possible to build cooperatively toward these shared goals, and some successful procedures for increasing continuity have been demonstrated in the literature (Swanson and Henderson, 1976).

While a core set of aims of parents and educators do seem to mesh, the present data suggest an important area in which parental and school expectations instrumental to these aims are discrepant with each other. Parents in these samples did not perceive their role as teachers of intellectual capabilities, at least for the sorts of abilities generally considered to be important in academic achievement. If contemporary psychological and educational literature has influenced the thinking of educators at all, we would expect them to believe that basic intellectual abilities and academic motivation are developed in substantial degree in the home environment before children attend school and that the home is the primary source of continuity in supporting academic growth. Clearly, discontinuities in parental and educator perceptions of home and school roles in the socialization process is a critical area requiring the cooperative attention of community groups, school administrators and researchers. There should be reason for some optimism that differences in perception are not irreconcilable because research has shown that family activities that bear positive relationships with academic growth are not in conflict with valued Mexican-American customs (Henderson and Merritt, 1968; Henderson, 1972).

In conclusion, we would propose that arguments about cultural deficiencies versus cultural differences have served the useful purpose of alerting educators to the assertion that different cultural backgrounds teach different intellectual capabilities to the children who are socialized in them. While it would be quite overly optimistic to assume that the cultural difference point of view has been widely accepted among educators, it seems unlikely that further arguments along those lines would produce many additional converts. A more direct course of action is now needed, in which common goals are identified, the effects of discontinuities in perceptions of socialization roles examined objectively, and programmatic experimentation employed to find solutions to this problem.

REFERENCES

Durrett, M.E., O'Bryant, S., and Pennebaker, J.W. Child-rearing reports of white, black, and Mexican-American families. *Developmental Psychology*, 1975, *11*, 871.

Getzels, J.W. Socialization and education: A note on discontinuities. *Teachers College Record*, 1974, *76*, 218–225.

Glass, G.V., and Stanley, J.C. *Statistical Methods in Education and Psychology*. Englewood Cliffs, N.J.: Prentice-Hall, 1970.

Henderson, R.W. Environmental predictors of academic performance of disadvantaged Mexican-American children. *Journal of Consulting and Clinical Psychology*, 1972, *38*, 297.

Henderson, R.W. and Bergan, J.R. *The Cultural Context of Childhood*. Columbus, Ohio: Charles E. Merrill, 1976.

Henderson, R.W. and Merritt, C.B. Environmental backgrounds of Mexican-American children with different potentials for school success. *Journal of Social Psychology*, 1968, *75*, 101–106.

Padilla, A.M., Warner-Grough, J., Amaro-Plotkin, H. and Amodeo, L.B. Preschool bilingual/bicultural education for Spanish-speaking/surnamed children: A research review and strategy paper. Spanish-Speaking Mental Health Research Center, University of California, Los Angeles, December, 1975.

Steward, M., and Steward, D. Effect of social distance on teaching strategies of Anglo-American and Mexican-American mothers. *Developmental Psychology*, 1974, *10*, 797–807.

―――. The observation of Anglo, Mexican, and Chinese-American mothers teaching their young sons. *Child Development*, 1973, *44*, 329–337.

Swanson, R.A. and Henderson, R.W. Achieving home-school continuity in the socialization of an academic motive. *Journal of Experimental Education*, 1976, *44*, 38–44.

V | Research on Bilingual Instruction and Assessment

Reversing the Roles of Chicano and Anglo Children in a Bilingual Classroom: On the Communicative Competence of the Helper

CAROLE EDELSKY
SARAH HUDELSON
Arizona State University

BACKGROUND

Despite exciting findings on processes (Ervin-Tripp, 1974; Dulay and Burt, 1974), reevaluation of stages (Hakuta and Cancino, 1977), and social and discourse strategies (Fillmore, 1976a, 1976b; Hatch, 1978; Peck, 1978) involved in second language acquisition, attention to the political nature of the second language learning situation has been largely absent in the research literature. The subjects in most studies either have been native speakers of minority languages learning English, a majority language, as a second language, or have been linguists' children, also learning a majority or unmarked language as a second language during their parents' field work or sabbaticals.

As Fishman (1976) explains, a marked language is one which requires some deliberate activity in its behalf before it is used as a language of a particular institution or domain (for example, the designation of Language X as a language of instruction, as opposed to a subject, in a school). An unmarked language, on the other hand, is one which would be used anyway as the language of that institution or within that domain without the need for consciously devising a language policy to make that happen. It is the language the general community takes for granted will "naturally" be the language of that institution, domain, or set of interactions.

Our general impression was that with the exception of Schumann's (1976) propositions concerning good and bad language-learning situations and Fishman's (1976) report on survey data relating language markedness, bilingual programs, and school achievement, few studies explicitly acknowledged possible effects of a language hierarchy. The longitudinal work on process and strategies used by young children has especially ignored the issue. This leads us to question whether the conclusions based on a seemingly skewed population might more properly be considered conclusions concerning acquiring an unmarked second language rather than acquiring a second language in general.

We reasoned that if we chose a bilingual classroom where the teacher planned for and desired mutual second language learning for both ethnic groups, and if we chose a few Anglo students learning Spanish as a second language and followed them for one school year, we might begin to balance our picture of second language acquisition.

At this point, we must admit to our naiveté. We had not yet become familiar with the ethnomethodological literature on the actual allocation and function of two languages in the daily life of bilingual classrooms, nor did we truly understand the power of "unmarkedness" to override teachers' plans and intentions. Had we been more sophisticated, we would have chosen a different situation, one where the teacher at least received school- or district-wide support for her desire for mutuality. Nevertheless, unaware, we posed general questions concerning strategies the Anglo children might use, the nature and function of their moment-to-moment interactions in the second language, the speech acts encompassing these interactions—general questions for which we thought reversing the usual power hierarchy of the target and native languages might reveal some different answers.

Method

Our setting was a bilingual first grade in a greater Phoenix, Arizona, school with a transitional bilingual program. The teacher and the aide were both bilingual Chicanos. The teacher wanted the second language learning to be a mutual enterprise, although that was not one of the goals of the school district. Use of Spanish for all the children was planned for the opening of the day, for social studies, and for some end-of-the-day singing games and activities.

Of the 23 children in the class, 16 were designated as Spanish dominant, and 7 as English dominant. Of the 7 English speakers, one was black, three were Native American, and three were white. We selected the three who were white to make sure we were looking at "nonunderdogs" in as many senses as we could. Unfortunately, one of our choices, Tiffany, was not really without prior experience with Spanish, a fact we discovered two months after beginning the study. Some of her maternal relatives were Spanish-speaking Mexican-Americans. Spanish was thus used around her at home when relatives would visit and to her in what she described as rather deliberate Spanish-teaching efforts by her mother. The latter may have been merely songs and routines; still, despite the teacher's categorization of her language profile, her Anglo surname, and her native English proficiency, Tiffany was not a total newcomer to Spanish as were the other two, Robbie and Jenny.

We paired each of the three Anglos with a same-sex Spanish-speaking peer and took each pair to a special room every two weeks from October through March for half-hour language/play sessions. (Because of some absences, we used four different Spanish-speaking helpers rather than three.) One of us posed as a monolingual Spanish speaker in order to justify our demand that the sessions be conducted in Spanish. It was this researcher who conducted the sessions. The other was present in the background, making a running commentary on context into a tape recorder. Another tape recorder, a Pioneer Model KD-11, sat on the play table. One child wore the Realistic Condenser microphone clipped to his/her clothing.

At the beginning of each session, we presented the Anglos with pictures and phrases to test their comprehension of the plural morpheme, gender, and a few lexical items. We followed that by using the same pictures and phrases as a repetition task. The phrases were:

Es un/a muchacho/a grande/chiquito/a
Es una pelota verde/roja
Es un perro grande/chiquito
Las muchachas están corriendo
El muchacho está caminando

When the "work" was over, we gave them their choice of things to play with—Play-Doh, magic slates, puppets, books in Spanish, etc. The "monolingual" Spanish researcher would then play also. Beginning with the third session, we left the room for about ten minutes, leaving the tape recorder on. The room had a one-way mirror so we could see what transpired in our absence in addition to hearing the tape.

Additionally, we each observed in the classroom and on the playground a total of five times for 1½ to 2½ hours each time. During those observations, we followed our three Anglo Ss around in order to quickly write down who was addressing them in Spanish, for what functions, under what circumstances, and how the Anglo Ss responded.

Answers to Our General Questions

The key answer to our questions was that we were to have no answer, that we had made a grave error in our assumptions. Our observational records show that outside of our research sessions, no one addressed Spanish to our Anglo Ss. As documented by Shulz (1975), Bruck and Shulz (1977), Genishi (1976), and Legarretta (1975), English was allocated the bulk of the classroom time. Spanish was used in large-group settings at which the Anglo Ss were present, and was used between Chicanos in one-to-one interaction. Except for our research sessions, it was not used by anyone on a one-to-one basis with any of the Anglo children. If, as Hatch (1978) suggests, language learning occurs in the process of learning to carry on a conversation (as opposed to the process of hearing one person address a large group), our Ss not only lacked the language input but the entire learning context. It is no wonder then that our major finding regarding second language acquisition was that, for our two monolingual Anglo Ss, no Spanish was acquired with the exception of one routine—rote counting, two color words, and a possible understanding in our test setting of the word *chiquito*. Our third subject, Tiffany, demonstrated different Spanish language behaviors in March than she did in October. Since she demonstrated understanding of at least parts of rather complex utterances back in October, however, it is difficult to be certain whether it was language learning that had occurred or simply an increased comfort and familiarity over time that permitted her to more fully perform her bilingual competence.

We want to emphasize this rather simple finding. These children participated in SSL sessions, were exposed to Spanish as part of a group, and were certainly surrounded by it often as Chicano interacted with Chicano in their presence. However, the group and bystander role allowed them to tune out, as they often did when we observed, and it virtually eliminated the possibility that the second language input data would have any tailored-for-the-individual quality.

Fillmore (1976b) notes anecdotally the lack of second language acquisition among Anglos in bilingual classrooms. Genishi (1976), Hudelson (1978), McClure (1977), and Shulz (1975) present data on code choice on the part of bilingual Chicano children to other bilinguals and to monolinguals which show that in informal contexts, English is used with people who are more comfortable with English. Unfortunately, we documented the same language acquisition phenomenon and the code choices related to it. We believe, however, that the absence of sustained or *any* one-to-one interaction in Spanish with Anglos was not merely a matter of a code choice norm of "address the listener in his/her preferred language." Rather, it went beyond that rule to a sociopolitical context which produces the phenomenon of markedness. That is, in this classroom and school, where the unmarked language is English, Spanish/English bilinguals sometimes used English on a one-to-one basis with non-English speakers, expecting some understanding and eventual learning. They did not, however, use Spanish, the marked language, on a one-to-one basis with non-Spanish speakers, except in stereotyped ways when Spanish was the content of the lesson. It appears that one more aspect of the marked/unmarked distinction is that the aforementioned code choice rule is not applied equally to all listeners. In a school where language learning, not just language-comfortable interaction, is an acknowledged goal, if the speaker or code-chooser is bilingual and the listener is *less* comfortable with a target language which is *un*marked, there is still some likelihood that the code choice will sometimes result in use of the *non*preferred or *un*marked target language. If, on the other hand, the listener's preferred language is already the unmarked language and the target language in that classroom, there is minimal likelihood that a code choice will result in the use of the nonpreferred, marked language.

We did find individual differences in the three Anglos' approaches to Spanish in the language/play sessions, and also in aspects of the communicative competence of the four Chicano partners. It is to the Chicanitos that we now turn.

Others have reported Chicano children's abilities to switch codes depending on listener attributes (Genishi, 1976; Hudelson, 1978; Lance, 1972; McClure, 1977; Shulz, 1975). In addition to displaying their agility in this area, these children also revealed their tacit notions of what counts as a translation, of how one helps another with a language task, and of style shifting.

FEATURES OF THE CHICANO PARTNERS' COMMUNICATIVE COMPETENCE

Their General Style

Pedra, who acted as partner to both Tiffany and Jenny, was the youngest of the four Chicano children, (5:10 that fall) and the only one who was not originally a monolingual Spanish speaker. She was a willing participant, spontaneously volunteering information and initiating topics. Veronica M., a U.S. resident for two years and the other partner Tiffany had, was seven and the oldest of the four. From the time we met her in November until our last session in March, she was considerably less vocal than the others while we were present. She responded with what was minimally necessary to answer a question, and initiated a topic only once. On 20 different occasions her responses to our questions or directives consisted of silence. When we were out of the room, however, she was a much more willing and animated conversational partner. Juan, Robbie's partner, had arrived from Mexico the preceding year. He would wait to initiate topics until another task or topic was complete and would then provide the monolingual researcher with many unprompted details. Neither he nor Veronica M. ever tried to compete with the Anglo child for the adult's attention during the comprehension/repetition work sessions. Jenny's other partner, Veronica Q., also a two-year U.S. resident, provided quite a contrast. Her efforts to totally maintain the position of prime verbal interactor were varied, clever, and ultimately exasperating. She would initiate new topics with a focus on herself in the midst of test/work with the Anglo child:

(1) S (Spanish "monolingual" researcher): Okay, Jenny, *ahora quiero que digas "es un muchacho grande." Veronica te ayudará.*
Veronica Q (to S): *Tengo una hermanita.*

Veronica Q. would translate everything, including head nods, to the Spanish-speaking adult, drop intriguing self-focused remarks into an ongoing stream of talk to change its direction, etc.

(2) Jenny: *uno, dos, tres . . . cuarenta* (sigh).
S: *Muy bien. ¡Qué bien! Sí, sabes.*
VQ: *Ay, me ponen como crema.*
S: *¿Cómo crema? ¿Dónde tienes crema?*

She tried to obstruct our interaction with Jenny:

(3) Jenny (to S): They (some new clothes) came from a church. I got new socks too.
VQ (to S): *Unuhn. No es verdad. Son puras mentiras.*

She would rhythmically repeat the same syllable while Jenny tried to repeat our test phrase, sang directly into the microphone when Jenny was "working," and so on. When we were gone, however, the competition stopped, and she and Jenny made plans together and discussed their respective activities.

The Meaning of the Task

After several sessions, all the children, regardless of native language, knew that the order of events in the sessions was: a few amenities, "work" with cards, then play with toys with the monolingual researcher. Their notion of the point of the "work," however, was interesting. Since the Chicanos were placed in the role of broker or translator between the supposedly monolingual adult and the Anglo peer, it was *their* perspective on "the point of the game" that became immediately apparent. Once, the direction the Chicano relayed to the Anglo coincided exactly with our intention.

(4) S: *Dilo tú, Jenny.*
    VQ (to J): Say *"una pelota verde."*

One time, Pedra partly understood the task, translating the phrase to her own wording (*es una muchacha chiquita* became *una chiquita chavalita*), then issuing her own directive for an exact repetition (*Say what I say. "Una"*). On one occasion Juan managed to string all but one of the elements of our intention across several turns in an extended interaction (indicating that verbal production was to be the activity and that repetition of what the researcher offered was desired, but not verbalizing that exact repetition meant repeating in Spanish).

(5) S: *Mhm. Y diga "es un muchacho chiquito."*
    Robbie (points to picture)
    S: *Mmm. Ayúdale.*
    Juan: Say it, Robbie.
    R: What?
    J: The thing he is saying to you, reading to you.
    S: *Ayúdale.*
    J: Talk. Talk about that.
    R: What?
    J: Say that. He tell you to say that. You say it. He want to say it.

After five months, Juan once mentioned his suspicion that production of Spanish was the point of the task. When we asked him to help, he asked *¿En español o en inglés?* However, at all other times, in over 100 other instances, the perspective the Chicanos seemed to have of the point of the work with the cards was that the Anglos' task was not to comprehend the Spanish sentence by pointing to the correct picture, nor to repeat the Spanish phrase that described a picture; rather, they thought the Anglos' work was to demonstrate understanding of the concepts shown on the cards (big and little, red and green, one and two). When the Anglo did not respond to our direction and we told the Chicano partner to help, thinking he/she would give the direction (point vs. say) either in English or Spanish and repeat the phrase in Spanish (for example, we were expecting, "Point to the picture that shows '*el muchacho grande*' "), each of the four Chicanos instead said things like *the big one* in English. They kept trying to relate the task to concept meaning, acting as though they thought that if the Anglo was having trouble responding, it was because he/she did not understand the idea of big/little, etc. Therefore, if they could communicate the idea represented on the cards, the Anglo would be able to respond to our request. So each of them said to their Anglo partner things like *the red ball* or *that a big one*, expecting ensuing successful emission of anything meaning "red-hued sphere," i.e., *red ball* or *es una pelota roja*. After Jenny didn't respond to Pedra's prompt in Spanish:

> (6) S: *Ahora tú, Jenny, "es un muchacho chiquito."* (to Pedra) *Digale.*
> Pedra: *Es un muchacho chiquito.*
> S: *Y ahora tú, Jenny.*
> J (no response)
> P: He's a little boy.
> S: *Si, pero quiero que Jenny diga la frase en español. Le puedes ayudar.*
> P: It's a little boy.
> S: *Uhm, si, pero en español.*
> P: *Chiquito chavalito.*
> S: *Uhm, chiquito chavalito. Dígale a Jenny que repita la frase "es un muchacho chiquito."*
> P: She said to—it's a little boy.
> S: *Digalo. Es.* (to Pedra) *Tú dilo. Es.*
> P: She said say it.
> J: *Es.*
> S: *Muy bien. Un muchacho chiquito.*
> J (to Pedra): Ask her if we can play with those.

and then

> (7) S: *Ahora, Robbie, digalo. Es un muchacho grande.*
> Juan: Say it.
> S: *Digalo. Es.*
> Juan: Uh, Robbie, she's asking "a big boy."
> S: *Es.*
> Other Researcher: Try it.
> Juan: Big boy. C'mon Robbie. C'mon Robbie.

Veronica Q. even tried a word-for-word relating of Spanish to English, "That's like 'a ball red,' " as though proof of its meaningfulness plus a display of contrastive word order would encourage Jenny, silent until then, to respond. If the Anglo still was silent after the cue of meaning, then the Chicano acted as though the problem was a generalized language production, one requiring tutoring/prompting in English.

The Anglos shared that perspective. Evidence for the joint viewpoint was displayed both negatively and positively; i.e., no Anglo said anything like, "But I still can't say it in Spanish," and positively but stranger still, the native English-speaking Anglo would accommodatingly repeat the translated and segmented phrase sometimes offered as "help" by their partners, as though they too thought they needed word-for-word cues for their English. For example:

(8) S: *Es una muchacha grande.*
    Pedra: It's.
    Jenny: It's.
    P: A.
    J: A.
    P: Tall.
    J: Tall.
    P: Boy.
    J: Boy.
    P: Tall boy.
    J: Tall boy.

and also

(9) S: *Di, Jenny. Es un perro chiquito.*
    Jenny: *Es.*
    S: Mmm.
    J: *Un.*
    S: Mmm.
    Pedra: *Chi* . . .
    J: *Chi* . . .
    P: *Chiquito perrito.*
    J: Huh?
    P: I said *"un chiquito perrito."*
    J: Say it one at a time cause I can't hear you.
    P: I said "a little dog."
    J: Little dog.
    P: Purple dog (the brown color was actually purplish).
    S: *En español.*
    P: It's a little dog purple.
    J: It's a little dog purple.
    P: *Un chiquito perrito* purple.

Number (9) shows not only that the two girls seemed to share a definition of the task, but also that they recognized and acquiesced to its artificiality. Pedra's noun-adjective word order in Spanish was often influenced by English, but neither she nor Jenny ever used such contorted sequences in their spontaneous interactions.

Veronica M. and her partner Tiffany would use the cards and label them in English.

(10) Tiffany: Big, big. Little, little.
     Veronica M: Big one, little one.

Essentially then, the comprehension/repetition task was not understood by the children in the same way we had intended. Moreover, its opaqueness, the sociolinguistically bizarre aspect of the whole situation, and children's willingness to go along with and try to make sense of artificial language situations in school must have contributed to the Anglo's acceptance of the role of being tutored in their native language.

How to Help

When the Anglos' task (from our perspective) was merely to match a picture with a phrase, and when the Chicanos were told to help, they interpreted "helping" as translating the phrase into English or as themselves pointing to the right picture. None relayed the directive (point/show her) verbally.

Occasionally, after an incorrect first move by the Anglo (pointing to two rather than one boy in the array of two boys and two girls), the Chicano-as-helper would highlight the problem in English (*one, one, one*).

On the repetition task, the adult had to give permission to each Chicano to begin to help; Juan and VM needed some prodding before they would enter the activity. All, however, conceived of helping with the repetition task as providing English meaning at times and also as making the language easier by slowing it down and breaking it up. Veronica M. broke the phrases into single words. Veronica Q. and Pedra used a combination of phrases, words, and syllables, some of them unconventional.

(11) S: *Ayúdale.*
     Veronica Q: *Es.*
     Jenny: *Es.*
     VQ: *Un.*
     J: *Un.*
     VQ: *Na.*

J: *Na.*
VQ: *Mu.*
J: *Mu.*
VQ: *Chacha.*
J: *Chacha.*
VQ: *Chi.*
J: *Chi.*
VQ: *Quita.*
J: *Quita.*

Pedra would divide at *es/una/pe/lota/verde.* She would also provide a type of "forward buildup."

(12) Pedra: *Es.*
Jenny: *Es.*
P: *Una.*
J: *Una.*
P: *Chi.*
J: *Chi.*
P: *Chiquita.*
J: *Chiquita.*
P: *Chiquita chavalita.*
J: Huh?

The deliberate segmentation into syllables seemed to reveal a notion of: (1) two kinds of words—those that could not be segmented (single-syllable words, color words, *grande*), and those that could (some multi-syllabled words); and (2) where and how often the segmentation could occur (once, between the first and second syllables).

Breaking the phrase apart seemed to be related more to the style of the helper than to the Spanish competence of the Anglo. Both Robbie and Jenny were English monolinguals, yet Juan would break Robbie's test sentences into words and phrases while Pedra and Veronica Q. used smaller segments. Pedra even segmented the original phrase into words for Tiffany, although Tiffany previously had been able to repeat the entire test phrase.

The Chicanos' Roles

Our conflicting demands.   Handling our two-part directives and helping were only some of the aspects of the roles of the Chicano children. Our conflicting expectations certainly must have complicated their construction of a role for themselves. We expected the children to translate directives and questions into English for their Anglo partners and so did the Anglos ("What did she say" and "Tell her that . . ." from the Anglos run throughout the transcripts). The Chicanitos' facility with the broker position was epitomized by Veronica Q. In (13) she translates at first on request and then on her own initiative.

> (13) S (to V): *Digale a Jenny en inglés que le vas a ayudar a platicar en español.*
> Jenny (to V): Tell her if we can play with that.
> Veronica Q (to J): I'm going to help to talk Spanish with me, OK?
> J: You are gonna help me (s)peak in (S)panish with you?
> V: Yeah.
> J: But tell her if we can play with the clay.
> S: *¿Qué quiere hacer Jenny?*
> J: And to make that. The dolls.
> V (to S): *Qué jugamos.*
> S: *¿Con los monitos o la plastilina?*
> V: *Con los monitos y la plastilina.*
> S: *Las dos cosas,* OK. *En un ratito. ¿Puedes hablar unos dos minutos? ¿Si? Vamos a hacer esta cosa y luego vamos a jugar.*
> V (to J): We're gonna do this thing and then we're gonna play with that.

However, in addition to expecting and indeed demanding that they act the Spanish-to-English intermediary for the Anglo child, we also asked the children to try to talk in Spanish only. To compound the problem, yet staying in tune with the established language hierarchy, we sometimes made this and other procedural statements in English.

The Roles. Despite our conflicting demands and our setting-up of the Chicano as broker, each child resolved the role question in an individual way, and each child's Anglo partner contributed, roles being reciprocal constructions. Veronica Q. played the constant go-between, translating every signal Jenny emitted, jumping in to help as soon as the monolingual adult set out the task, indeed deciding what Jenny's answers should be rather than always strictly "going-between."

> (14) S (to Jenny): *¿Vas hacer una tortilla como la mia?*
> VQ (to Jenny): Say yes.
> Jenny: Yes.

Much of this was related to her efforts to stay in the limelight. A strategy to that effect was to establish herself in the role of colleague of the adult, commenting on Jenny's performance to the adult (*aprendió eso, dice* "*grachito*" —as opposed to "*chiquito*"), praising Jenny, sighing and rolling her eyes to the adult as Jenny dawdled, giving the adult an account for how Jenny came to give a correct response, and joining in as a tester by continuing some of the *qué color es este/cuántos son* questions the adult asked while playing. In addition, she corrected our lexical choices in the test phrases, preferring *niño* to *muchacho*, providing an authority for the substitution (*mi mami me dice que les dice "niños"*).

In contrast, because of Tiffany's ability to understand some Spanish, Veronica M. did not have to be a Spanish-to-English broker. She even increased her use of Spanish with Tiffany as the months went on (from single words to entire directives), demonstrating her awareness of Tiffany's receptive abilities in Spanish. Because of her own problem with English and her reticence when the adults were present, she acted the English-to-Spanish intermediary only with some prodding. She assumed the role of Tiffany's singing/acting impresario and coach when we left the room, also criticizing the accuracy of Tiffany's Spanish lyrics and her occasional Spanish phrases. Tiffany, for her part in Veronica M.'s role, did not look to her for Spanish-to-English translations, but did occasionally tell her something in English to tell the adult in Spanish. As frequently, Tiffany would use the other adult as her bridge.

Pedra willingly took on the broker role but sometimes had problems knowing when she was using which language. She took credit for her Anglo partner's successes, and Jenny at least looked to her for translations and explanations. Like Veronica Q. and Juan, Pedra also saw herself as having the right to change our test phrases and comment on the change.

Juan on the other hand, initially refused the role of broker because of the "impossible" language situation among the threesome at the beginning of the year.

> (15) S: *Pregúntale. ¿Cuántos años tiene?*
> Juan (silence)
> S: *Pregúntale.*
> J: *Pero él no entiende en español.*
> S: *Si, pero quiero que le preguntes a él en inglés.*
> J: *Yo no sabo en inglés.*

He eventually played the translator, though he did not voluntarily do this during the testing task, nor did Robbie ask Juan to translate for him though he looked to Juan to provide him with answers to the comprehension task. Juan would occasionally answer for Robbie, as Veronica Q. answered for Jenny. Once, early in our study, he appeared to be operating on a co-equal status with the adult by: praising Robbie's

Spanish counting and, instead of showing off his own skill in that area, by: expressing surprise because Robbie *nunca conta* (never counts); and by commenting on Robbie's performance (*dice "arroz" en vez de "adios,"* laughing at Robbie's *muchacha* instead of the test word *muchacho*). Juan's initial resistance to the role of intermediary surfaced again at midyear. After January, he stopped helping Robbie with the comprehension/repetition work.

> (16) S: *Ahora, Robbie, enséñame "las muchachas están corriendo."*
> R (no response)
> S: (to Juan) *¿Le quieres ayudar?*
> J (shakes head no and does not help)

He implied in (17) that when talk was not directed to us, we did not have to have it translated.

> (17) S: *Es un paquete.*
> Robbie (to Juan): That was funny.
> S (to Juan): *¿Qué dijiste?*
> Juan: *Me dijo a mi.*

While resisting the translating job, he also must have been quite cognizant of the difference between recoding someone else's talk and encoding his own when he took part in the exchange shown in (18).

> (18) S: *¿Cómo se llama tu hermano, Robbie?*
> Robbie: What?
> Juan: I don't want to say it.
> R: What?
> S: *Digale.*
> J: What you said Robbie.
> R: *What* did you say?
> J: I didn't. I didn't say nothing.

Translating

It must be noted that translating between two languages requires considerable proficiency in those languages. Pedra was the only one who met that requirement in October.

> (19) S: *Ahora ¿qué vas a hacer, Tiffany? ¿Una tortilla?*
> Tiffany (to VM): Tell her that it's a swimming pool.
> S (to VM): *¿Qué va a hacer?*
> VM: *Una mesita.*
> (20) S: *Y qué dijo la Sra. López?*
> Tiffany: Mrs. Lopez don't say nothing.

      S: *Que ¿qué?*

      VM: *Que ella no dijo nada a la Sra. Lopez.*

(21) S (to Robbie): *Se llama Tony. ¿Tienes una hermana también?*

      Juan: Uh, uh, uh you get a friend, a girl?

      Robbie: A girlfriend?

(22) Jenny (to S): You know what? My brother gots one of those.

      Veronica Q: *Que su, que su . . .*

      J: My BIG brother.

      VQ: *Que su hurmana tiene unos do esos.*

(23) S: *Dile que vamos a jugar en un ratito.*

      VQ (to Jenny): We gonna play in a little—in a little mmm mmm.

Veronica Q. sometimes tried to hold the slot she knew she was not able to fill with a legitimate English word as in (23). Juan verbalized his difficulties with making translations into English. In October, he simply claimed he did not know the language (15). By March, the English abilities of the three had increased greatly. At this point, Juan accounted for his translation problems by blaming Robbie (*me habla muy despacito*).

In addition to the initially minimal proficiency with English, all these children, being very young, obviously would not have been adult-like in their first language competence either. Therefore, sometimes their translation difficulties may have also stemmed from not understanding Spanish in the way it was intended.

(24) Pedra (to Tiffany): Do the "n."

      Other Researcher: *En español, Pedra.*

      Pedra: *Haz la "n."* Try it. Right there.

      S (to P): *Dígale en español que haga la "n."*

      P: *Haga la "n."*

Hearing *decir* as a directive to repeat exactly is a common confusion among young Spanish speakers (Edelsky and Muiña, 1977). When she encoded her own meaning and then translated it in (24), Pedra made correct translations. However, when she participated in a bizarre speech act (if the researchers wanted Tiffany to hear that particular meaning in Spanish, they could have told her themselves, rather than asking Pedra to do it), she heard the Spanish incorrectly. Perhaps, then, other translation errors stemmed partly from the Chicanos' child-competence in Spanish (interacting with a most peculiar context for the use of Spanish) rather than entirely from their second language problems with English.

In addition to dual language proficiency, deliberate translating also requires a conscious awareness that there are two codes and that each one has boundaries. The children all demonstrated some knowledge in regard to multiplicity of codes. They would vary their choice of codes, without being asked, depending on their addressee. They would make some speech changes when directed to translate (from recoding in the other language to expanding the utterance but maintaining the original language).

Sometimes a false start let us know that as translators, these children knew that idioms could not be changed word for word from one language to another.

> (25) S: *Y ella ¿cómo se llama?*
> P: Jenny.
> S (to Jenny): *¿Quieres hablar, Jenny? ¿Cómo te llamas?*
> J (to Pedra): What did she say?
> Pedra: How do—what's your name?

Their knowledge of translation purposes and procedures also had some contradictory aspects; they knew: (1) that translating was needed in order to include a noncomprehending participant; (2) that the original encoder had an intention and meaning to convey and that the purpose of translating was to convey meaning to the other; and yet, (3) that the monolingual recipient sometimes needed a translation only of the last part of an exchange rather than its full intent.

The first bit of knowledge was evidenced by their spontaneous, unprompted translations for the benefit of either the monolingual adult or the Anglo child.

The second aspect, that the purpose was to convey the original speaker's meaning, was shown when they would make extended efforts to paraphrase if they did not know an English word.

> (26) S: *¡Qué bien! Dice aqui, Robbie. ¿Robbie qué? ¿Que es tu apellido?*
> *¿Robbie qué? Como Juan Fuentes. ¿Robbie qué?*
> Juan: Robbie what?
> Robbie: What?
> J: Robbie. And your next name?
> S: *¿Qué es tu apellido, Robbie?*
> J: What your next name? Your name, Robbie. How about your name? How about your 'nother name? 'Nother name?

This aspect was also demonstrated when they added to the original statement in the translation, maintaining and predicting expansions of the speaker's intent.

> (27) S (to Robbie): *¿Con qué quieres jugar? Vamos a jugar.*
> Juan: Robbie, what you wanna play, **the clay or what?**

and then

>   (28) S: *Digale en inglés que vamos a platicar y que vamos a jugar.*
>   VQ (to J): We gonna talk and we gonna play, **OK?**

The third aspect, that the other person needs only the last segment translated, contradicting the first, that he or she needs a translation because of lack of competence with one of the languages, was revealed in the following truncated translations.

>   (29) S: *¿Jenny entiende que le vas a ayudar? ¿Si, si entiende?*
>   VQ: You understand?

and also

>   (30) S (to Pedra): *Pero quiero que diga en español. ¿Puede hablar español? Pregúntale. Pregúntale.*
>   P (to Tiffany): Can you?

The English-to-Spanish translations often showed the same quality of missing information, but they contained more than just the ending. We believe that in these cases the omitted message was due to the translators' inability to completely understand the English they heard; thus they were constrained to recode only what they could make sense of.

Translating had functions beyond recoding a message. McClure (1977) found that children appeared to use immediate translations for emphasis. Besides emphasis, children used them for clarifying and contextualizing Spanish through English. (From Juan: "Lookit, lookit, *mira*, lookit"; from Veronica Q: "What do you want, Jenny. *¿Qué quieres tú, Jenny?*"; from Juan: "*¿Qué es?* What is it? *¿Qué es, Robbie?*") Veronica Q. used this device to gain attention:

>   (31) S: *Ahora Jenny enséñame la pelota verde.*
>   VQ: *Se llama* "green."
>   S (to VQ): *Le dijiste.*
>   VQ: "Green" *se llama. En español se dice, se dice "verde."*

Juan, knowing he could not be challenged by Robbie, "translated" in order to "put one over" on his partner.

>   (32) Juan: I gonna play with you.
>   Robbie: No.
>   J: Yes you are.
>   S: *¿No le puedes decir en español? ¿Van a pelearse?*
>   J: *A él.*
>   R: Give me it. Give me it.
>   S: *Peléanse en español.*
>   J: She say I could play with you.

When the Chicanos were not acting as our intermediaries, when they were encoding their own intents and meanings, they were still sometimes translators, making sure that their own English to the other child was understood by the Spanish-speaking adult, or, when we were out of the room, occasionally repeating an idea in the other language as if for emphasis, as we have mentioned.

We have said that part of an ability to translate readily is an awareness that there are two codes or two sets of variants involved. We believe there was such an awareness at some level: code switching is evidence for fine tacit knowledge of this type.

> (33) Juan (to S): *Luego, Caperucita Rosa ven—lleva este a su abuelita.*
> (to Robbie): Turn it (the page).
> (to S): *Su mamá dijo que lleve esta a su abuelita.*

Once, Juan asked the monolingual adult, in Spanish, if she wanted to know what Robbie had written on a heart while we were gone and then reported the written message to her in English, the language in which it had been written. We are uncertain, however, about the children's consciously held ideas of the boundaries between the two codes. There seemed to be a lag between tacit and full awareness. Robbie and Juan had this exchange in our absence.

> (34) Robbie: Feel this, Juan.
> J: Ooh.
> R: Cold, huh.
> J: Yeah, *está blandita ¿verdad? ¿Verdad que está blandita? Cuchi Cu.*
> R: What is that Juan? What does that spell?
> J: I'm talking Spanish.
> R: What does it spell?
> J: It spell—it say "*cuchi cuchi cu,* for you, for you," that's what.

Pedra, bilingual from infancy, had problems in translating the test phrase and in keeping the translations separate in (9). She would often offer the monolingual Spanish adult an expanded English version as her translation of English. Her translations into Spanish would include English words with English phonology within the Spanish utterance, even though she would later reveal knowledge of the Spanish equivalent. Some of Pedra's English-to-Spanish translation mixing and her repetitions may have been examples of slow, overt rather than quick, covert planning which she needed to do in order to eventually produce a complete shift into Spanish.

(35) Pedra (to S): *El* brother *de la Andrea queria hacer* beatup *a ella y nos hizo* chase *a mi y a ella y a Irma.*
S: *¿Se pelea Verónica? ¿Con quién?*
P: *Dice, dice, que* don't—*no juegas con la Verónica otra.*
S: *¿Con quien se pelea? ¿Con Jenny?*
P: *No, no. Se pelea con con*—she fights with me.
S: *¿Qué¿*
P: *Pelea conmigo.*

and also

(36) S: *¿Qué hicieron—qué bonita estrella.*
P: We both share the cl—(the clay) the white.
S: *¿Qué dijiste?*
P: We are both sharing the—*lo blanco. Estamos haciendo* share *lo blanco.*

Pedra did not display this mixing in English. Since the occasion never arose when we overtly asked her to "say it in English," we do not know if her Spanish-to-English translations-on-command required overt planning. She did seem to shift more easily (more quickly and more completely) from Spanish to English. Pedra, then, may have been demonstrating a tacit awareness of the politics of the language context into which she was born; i.e.: (1) her experienced-backed disbelief that there might be a Spanish-speaking adult in a school who does not also know some English, although there would be English-speaking adults who did not know Spanish, and (2) her greater comfort with English in the school setting (and possibly in other settings as well, due perhaps to a greater proficiency in English).

Style Shifting

When interacting as non-go-betweens, especially in our absence, the Chicanos shifted styles. When they talked for puppets or dolls, they used raised pitch, usually using only one word, if any, of Spanish (*ola, mira,* followed immediately by its English equivalent). Juan, when his English was apparently still minimal, talked "black" paralinguistically for a brown-colored plastic doll, using intonation contours with highest pitch levels, exaggeratedly drawing out the vowels, and saying "tha's good" rather than his own "that good." The two Veronicas each went into second language drilling routines, calling the "student's" name, using artificial stress, and expecting a string of answers.

(37) VM: Tiffany, Tiffany, what *can* ↑ you do ↓ ?
　　　T: I can walk.
　　　VM: What *can* you do? I can—
　　　T: I could run, I could walk, I could type, I could—
　　　VM: I can, I can ride the—
　　　T: I can ride the bike.
　　　VM: Tiffany, what *can* you do?
　　　T: *Verónica, cállate la boca.*

There were also a few instances where the Chicano children adopted our style of talking to the Anglos in Spanish, using an attentional comment (*mira la flor*), followed by a compliment (*qué bonita*), followed by a language eliciting question (*¿cómo hiciste?*). Almost always, when they used Spanish in our absence, the Chicanos were momentarily taking on our roles of materials provider (*¿Qué quires tú, Jenny?*); of tester (*¿Qué es?*); of organization prompter (*¿Qué vas a hacer tú, Robbie?*). Such statements were mostly followed by immediate translations into English or by provision of nonverbal meaning clues (pointing, holding up an object) for the Spanish utterance. Because of the Chicanos' contextualizations, then, the Anglos sometimes responded appropriately.

(38) VQ (holding can): *¿Quieres ésta? ¿Quieres éste, Jenny?* Go. Here.
　　　Jenny: I don't want that.

Most often, though, the Anglos responded to these researcher-role utterances in Spanish by either ignoring them or by blatantly putting a stop to them ("none of your beeswax").

Language Use in the Absence of Adults

A display of metalinguistic awareness, play with taboo language behavior, and a hugely expanded range of language functions characterized the segments after we left the room.

Juan gave us an inkling of either what constitutes a word for him or of how he evades censure for using a taboo word.

(39) Juan: I'm gonna tell if you say a bad word or something.
　　　Robbie: I didn't say a bad word.
　　　J: You said—it start with a "f." (Whispered) Fuck.
　　　R: You said it. You said the whole thing. I just said—where'd she put my [unintelligible] there.
　　　J: And I just say "fff" (pause) "uck." I didn't say the bad word. I just say (whistles) (pause) "uck."

Evidently, whispering does not count as saying; breaking up the speech stream with pauses changes its status as a word. Juan's metalinguistic legalisms extended to his distinction between writing and some other kind of message-producing marking on a page.

(40) Juan (to S):—*Lo puso* "I love Tiffany. Robbie"
   S (to Robbie): *¿Tiffany es tu novia?*
   R (to J): You wrote it.
   J: I didn't wrote it. I only went like that.
   R: You wrote it.
   J: I didn't wrote it, man. I went like that.

Veronica M. accepted Tiffany's Spanish-pronounced nonsense as a word for two sessions until she finally asked, *¿Qué quiere decir 'muriosa'?* Her question was never answered, but *muriosa* remained part of that dyad's singing play while we were gone.

As with roles, which require some co-participant construction, the contrasting attributes of adult-present and adult-absent talk cannot be attributed solely to one child in each dyad. Still, we would like to mention the range of functions of language displayed by both Chicano and Anglo while we were gone, as opposed to the very narrow repertoire in our presence. It must be noted that we were not seen as ogres by the children. Rather, when we went to their classroom to take them to the special room, they showed pleasure and excitement and the other children in the class begged to go too. Still, they were inhibited with us. Aside from the talk we initiated by placing them in the broker role, their child-child talk was almost nonexistent in our presence. The range of functions they employed was correspondingly limited. As soon as we left them alone, however, they bloomed linguistically. They used talk for threatening, planning, insulting, conspiring, informing, directing, fantasying, word play. Almost all the talk was in English despite the limited English proficiency of three of the Chicanos, especially early in the school year. Veronica M. was somewhat of an exception. Acknowledging Tiffany's ability to comprehend some Spanish, Veronica M.'s use of Spanish with Tiffany increased over the six months, although it never approached the amount of English that was used. Like us though, bowing to the power of the unmarked language, when Veronica M. wanted Tiffany to use Spanish, she told her so in English. From the beginning, Pedra used only English to the Anglos unless we were present and insisted on Spanish. Even then, she obeyed us in letter but not spirit, translating only the utterance immediately preceding *pero dígale en español* and then returning to English. Regardless of its source (language dominance or political dominance), Pedra was clearly more comfortable using English, the language of the school, in that institution. Unlike Pedra, as mentioned earlier, Veronica Q. did use Spanish in small phrases or single words when we were out of the room. Like Pedra, though, she immediately retreated to English when Jenny would ignore her, laugh, or even simply respond in English. Juan's last Spanish word to Robbie was uttered in January.

And so we come full circle. In addition to the varied picture we have described, this too was part of the competence of the Chicano— knowing, despite overt and contradictory instructions, which one was the unmarked language. The Anglos helped to teach them that by generally not responding at all to the offerings in Spanish. Learning which was the unmarked language entailed learning which second language it was that learners were expected to acquire. There being no expectations for Spanish language acquisition on the part of either group of children, the Chicanos never played out their potential as teachers of Spanish.

REFERENCES

Bruck, Margaret, and Shulz, Jeffrey. "An Ethnographic Analysis of the Language Use Patterns of Bilingually Schooled Children." *Working Papers on Bilingualism,* 11 (1977), 60–91.

Dulay, Heidi, and Burt, Marina. "Errors and Strategies in Child Second Language Acquisition." *TESOL Quarterly,* 8, no. 2 (1974), 129–36.

Edelsky, Carole, and Muiña, Virginia. "Native Spanish Language Acquisition: The Effect of Age, Schooling and Context on Responses to *Dile* and *Pregúntale.*" *Journal of Child Language,* 4, no. 3 (1977), 453–76.

Ervinn-Tripp, Susan. "Is Second Language Acquisition like the First?" *TESOL Quarterly* 8, no. 2 (1974), 111–28.

Fillmore, Lily Wong. "Individual Differences in Second Language Acquisition." Paper presented to Asilomar Conference on Individual Differences in Language Ability and Language Behavior, Monterrey, Cal., November 9–11, 1976a.

———. "The Second Time Around: Cognitive and Social Strategies in Second Language Acquisition." Unpublished Ph.D. dissertation, Stanford University, 1976b.

Fishman, Joshua. *Bilingual Education: An International Sociological Perspective.* Rowley, Mass.: Newbury House, 1976.

Genishi, Celia. "Rules for Code-Switching in Young Spanish-English Speakers." Unpublished Ph.D. dissertation, University of California, Berkeley, 1976.

Hakuta, Kenji, and Cancino, Herlinda. "Trends in Second-Language-Acquisition Research." *Harvard Educational Review,* 47, no. 3 (1977), 294–316.

Hatch, Evelyn. "Discourse Analysis and Second Language Acquisition." *Second Language Acquisition,* ed. Evelyn Hatch. Rowley, Mass.: Newbury House, 1978.

Hudelson, Sarah. "Videotape Analysis: Beto at the Sugar Table." Arizona State University, 1978. Unpublished manuscript.

Lance, Donald M. "The Codes of the Spanish-English Bilingual." *The Language Education of Minority Children,* ed. Bernard Spolsky, Rowley, Mass.: Newbury House, 1972.

Legarretta, Dorothy. "An Analysis of Teacher Talk and Pupil Talk in Bilingual Classrooms." University of California, Berkeley, 1975. Mimeograph.

McClure, Erica. "Aspects of Code Switching in the Discourse of Bilingual Mexican-American Children." *Technical Report No. 44,* University of Illinois–Urbana: Center for the Study of Reading, 1977.

Peck, Sabrina. "Child-Child Discourse in Second Language Acquisition." *Second Language Acquisition,* ed. Evelyn Hatch. Rowley, Mass.: Newbury House, 1978.

Schumann, John. "Second Language Acquisition: The Pidginization Hypothesis." *Language Learning,* 26, no. 2 (1976), 391–408.

Shulz, Jeffrey. "Language Use in Bilingual Classrooms." Harvard Graduate School of Education, 1975. Unpublished manuscript.

Cloze Procedure with Spanish, English, and Bilingual Adults

ADELA ARTOLA STEWART
University of Arizona
ANN MARIE BERNAZZA HAASE
New York State Education Department

The past decade has evidenced the emergence of an ever-increasing number of bilingual education programs. Federal funds have become available to schools where there is a large population of children whose home language is other than English. Teachers, parents, administrators, taxpayers, and federal agencies are asking, "How can dual language reading competency be assessed?" "How can we measure transfer of reading skills from one language to another?" "How effective is bilingual instruction in terms of reading?"

Currently, there are being marketed a wide array of formal and informal measures for assessing language skills, particularly for the early grades (Cohen, 1976). On the other hand, reading tests which are constructed in two languages specifically to measure parallel skills are almost nonexistent. The need for dual-language reading assessment instruments in bilingual programs is obvious and urgent.

The cloze procedure has been proven to be an effective tool for studying language variables related to reading in English (Weaver and Bickley, 1967; Bloomfield and Miller, 1966; Louthan, 1965; Taylor, 1956). In English, it has been shown to measure readability (Bormuth, 1969, 1968, 1966, 1963) and specific comprehension of reading materials (Ransom, 1968; Bormuth, 1969, 1963; Blumfield, 1962; Taylor, 1957, 1956).

The readability and validity of the cloze procedure were examined by McLeod (1976) in French, German, Czech, and Polish. He constructed parallel cloze tests in these four languages and English, and presented them to children between the ages of eight and fourteen. His results showed high reliabilities and validities for the different linguistic forms of the test within each language. However, no significant differences across languages were found.

Another cross-lingual study was conducted by Grudin, Courtney, Langen, Pherrson, Robinson, and Sakamato (1978). English-, Japanese-, and Swedish-speaking children in grades four and five participated by responding to three prose passages, each in their own languages. An every-fifth-word deletion pattern and the conventional number-right method of scoring were used. Those authors concluded that there was a variation between languages because Japanese children obtained higher scores than English- or Swedish-speaking children.

Even though cloze procedure studies have been conducted across lingual areas, a search of the literature revealed no study examining the use of cloze procedure as an assessment instrument in Spanish. The only studies that approach assessment in Spanish are Spaulding (1956, 1951) and Patterson (1972), each of whom provided a readability formula for determining the relative level of difficulty of Spanish written material for school-age children.

The purpose of this study was to ascertain if the cloze procedure was a reliable measure across both the Spanish and the English languages. If this occurred, an analysis of the language groups by scoring procedures would be conducted. The interaction between type of scoring of the cloze passages and type of language then could be investigated. This would provide pertinent information for further research into the potential for assessment of reading comprehension by bilingual speakers.

PROCEDURE

Sample

Eighty-eight adults aged 20 to 60 years old participated as volunteers in this study. Included in this sample were 32 monolingual Spanish-speaking adults from the state of Jalisco in Mexico, 28 monolingual English-speaking Americans, and 28 bilingual adults who speak Spanish and English. The monolingual Spanish sample consisted of 17 males and 5 females, and the bilingual sample contained 18 females and 10 males. The monolingual English sample consisted of 8 males and 20 females. All subjects were comparable in terms of formal education, having a minimum of two years of college.

INSTRUMENTATION

The article "Liberación a la Limeña" was selected from the magazine *Americas,* published in English, Spanish, and Portuguese by the General Secretariat of the Organization of American States. Only the English and Spanish versions were used. This was not a word-by-word translation that adhered to the syntactic structure peculiar to each language concerned. All content information appeared to be the same in all three passages, and the paragraph divisions were maintained exactly. The article appears to be written in English and Spanish by the same person. These versions were then mutilated as follows: the first and last sentences were left intact, and from the remaining passage every fifth word was deleted, except when the word was a proper noun, an adjective, or a numerical symbol. The blank spaces were all kept equal at ten spaces of underlined type. The selection was taken to a logical end, which in both cases was at the end of a paragraph. Because the deletion-of-every-fifth-word rule was adhered to, the deletions between the English and Spanish versions were not the same.

The English selection was 369 words long and had 58 deletions while the Spanish passage was 399 words long and had 62 deletions. There were 12 sentences in the English passage and 13 in the Spanish.

Instructions

The following instructions were given verbally prior to distributing the passages: "Please read through the entire passage first, then try to fill in the blanks with the word you believe the author would have written. Please use only one word per blank. There is no time limit."

Scoring

Both passages were scored in two ways: (1) exact replacement, and (2) exact replacement plus synonym. Criteria for acceptability of a synonym was that the alternate word had to be of the same syntactic class and that it appears in a dictionary (De La Canal, 1977; De Robles, 1963; Devlin, 1961; Barcia, 1948) or thesaurus (Lewis, 1972) as a synonym for the original word. In the Spanish version, the auxiliary of the pluperfect subjunctive was accepted as exact replacement in its two forms which exist in free variation in all dialects.

RESULTS AND DISCUSSION

For assessing the reliability of the cloze tests, Cronbach's alpha were calculated within each language group with both scoring procedures.

Table 1

Test Reliabilities by Language Group

| Language | Alpha | | (Scoring) |
	Exact	Exact/Syn	
English	.806	.820	.99
Bilingual	.644	.643	.97
Spanish	.802	.855	.96

This resulted in six coefficients which ranged from .64 to .86, which were all significant to the .01 level. To assess the equivalence of scoring procedures, three correlation coefficients were computed. All coefficients presented in Table 1 are significant at the .01 level.

As the paragraphs were found reliable for all three language groups, an analysis of the language groups by scoring procedures was performed. A two-way analysis of variance was conducted using percent correct as the dependent variable, and language group membership (Spanish, bilingual, and English) and type of scoring (exact or exact plus synonym) as independent variables. Type of scoring was treated as a repeated measure. The results indicated that group membership was not significant. Type of scoring ($F = 151.82$, $df = 1$, 85; $p < .01$) and the interaction between group membership and type of scoring ($F = 15.85$, $df = 2$, 85; $p < .01$) were found significant (see Table 2 and Figure 1). Tukey post-hoc test was employed to interpret the interaction. The following differences were found to be significant: (a) type of scoring for Spanish, (b) Spanish versus bilingual on exact synonym, (c) Spanish versus English and exact plus synonym. No significant differences were found among language groups on exact scoring.

Table 2

Percentage Correct by Language Groups and Type of Scoring

| Language | Type of Scoring | |
	Exact	Exact Plus Synonym
English	47.50	50.92
Bilingual	49.92	51.32
Spanish	49.09	54.28

Figure 1
Percentage of Correct Responses by Language Group on Exact and Exact
Plus Synonym Replacement Scoring Procedures

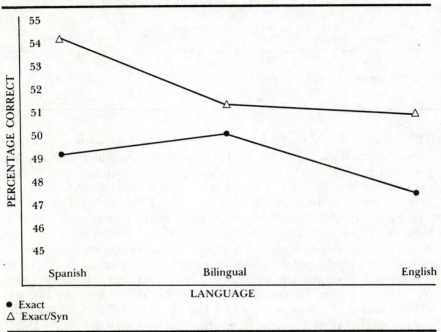

● Exact
△ Exact/Syn

This result may be due to redundancy factors in Spanish or to language group differences. However, the data do suggest that exact replacement scoring procedures could be used to assess readability and comprehension of the reading materials for bilingual adult readers.

Although further research is needed to develop tests which are constructed in English and Spanish to assess parallel skills, these results are heartening. They indicate that it is possible to use existing testing procedures formulated in English in the assessment and diagnosis of the Spanish and bilingual reader. Perhaps the assessment of dual language competency is not as far away as some believe.

Another interesting facet of these results is that they add to the growing body of knowledge of the scoring of cloze procedure. Taylor (1956), Ruddell (1964), and Gallant (1965) have found that the method of exact replacement was most useful and efficient. These data corroborate the findings of these studies across three language groups.

REFERENCES

Barcia, Roque. *Sinónimos castillanos.* Buenos Aires: Editorial Sopena Argentina, 1948.

Bloomfield, J.P., and Miller, H.R. "Improving Reading Through Teaching Grammatical Constraints," *Elementary English,* 43 (1966), 752-55.

Blumfield, John. "Cloze Tests as a Measure of Readability and Comprehension Ability." Unpublished doctoral dissertation, Indiana University, 1962.

Bormuth, John. "Cloze as a Measure of Readability." *Proceedings of the International Reading Association,* 8 (1963), 131–34.

———. "Readability: A New Approach." *Reading Research Quarterly,* 1 (Spring 1966), 79–135.

———. "The Cloze Readability Procedure." *Elementary English,* 45 (April 1968), 429–36.

———. "Factor Validity of Cloze Tests as Measures of Reading Comprehension Ability." *Reading Research Quarterly,* 4 (Spring 1969), 358–65.

Cohen, A. D. "Assessing the English-Speaking Skills of Bilingual Children." Paper presented at the Council for Exceptional Children's Annual Convention, 1976.

De la Canal, Julio. *Diccionario de sinónimos e ideas afines.* Mexico D.F.: Compañía Editorial Continental, 1977.

De Robles, Federico Carlos Sainz. *Diccionario español de sinónimos y antónimos.* Madrid: Aguilar, S. A. de Ediciones, 1963.

Devlin, Joseph. *A Dictionary of Synonyms and Antonyms.* New York: Popular Library Inc., 1961.

Gallant, Ruth. "Use of Cloze Tests as a Measure of Readability in the Primary Grades." *Proceedings of the International Reading Association,* 10 (1965), 286–87.

Grudin, H.; Courtney, L.; Langen, J.; Pherrson, R.; Robinson, H.; and Sakamato, T. "Cloze Procedure and Comprehension: An Exploratory Study Across Three Languages." In *Cross Cultural Perspectives on Reading and Reading Research,* ed. D. Feitelson. Newark, Del.: International Reading Association, 1978.

Holmgren, V. C. "Liberación a la Limeña." *Américas,* 29, 6 (1977), 12.

Lewis, Norman. *The New Roget's Thesaurus.* New York: Berkley Publishing Corp., 1972.

Louthan, V. "Some Systematic Grammatical Deletions and Their Effects on Reading Comprehension." *English Journal,* 54 (1965), 295–99.

McLeod, J. "Uncertainty Reduction in Different Languages through Reading Comprehension." *Journal of Psycholinguistic Research,* 4, 4 (1976), 343–55.

Patterson, Frank. *Como escribir para ser entendido.* El Paso, Tex.: Casa Bautista del Publicaciones, 1972.

Ransom, Peggy E. "Determining Reading Levels of Elementary School Children by Cloze Testing." *Proceedings of the International Reading Association,* 12, part 1 (1968), 477–82.

Ruddell, Robert. "A Study of the Cloze Comprehension Technique in Relation to Structurally Controlled Reading Material." *Proceedings of the International Reading Association,* 9 (1964), 198–302.

Spaulding, Seth. "Two Formulas for Estimating the Reading Difficulty of Spanish." *Educational Research Bulletin,* 30 (May 15, 1951), 117–24.

———. "A Spanish Readability Formula." *Modern Language Journal,* 40 (December 1956), 433–41.

Taylor, Wilson "Recent Developments in the Use of the 'Cloze Procedure.' " *Journalism Quarterly,* 33 (1956), 42.

———. "Cloze Readability Scores as Indices of Individual Differences in Comprehension and Aptitude." *Journal of Applied Psychology,* 41 (February 1957), 19–26.

Weaver, W. W., and Bickley, A. C. "Structural-Lexical Predictability of Materials which Predictor Has Previously Produced or Read." *Proceedings of the 75th Annual Convention of the American Psychological Association,* 1967, pp. 289–90.

Bilingual Schooling and Spanish Language Maintenance: An Experimental Analysis

ANDREW D. COHEN
The Hebrew University of Jerusalem

Studies which trace the progress of children schooled bilingually have appeared abroad and are beginning to appear in the United States (see Cohen, 1972; Cohen, 1975; Engle, 1975; Bowen, 1977). In evaluational studies, mention is made of tests that the students took and of their charted progress. Occasionally, mention is also made of the language used by the children at school and in the home, but rarely has there been any systematic study of the effect of bilingual schooling on the child's language use over time. Neither has there been any systematic study of how the child's language use in school (in and out of class) relates to his language use out of school and to the language use patterns within the child's family.

Kjolseth (1972) asserts that a real innovation in researching bilingual education programs would be to investigate the language use patterns, as opposed to simply assessing changes in the individual's language skills and language attitudes. Two other advocates of research in bilingual education, Ornstein and Gaarder, also emphasize the importance of investigating language use. Ornstein (1971) includes "distributive roles of Spanish vs. English in Southwest communication networks" in his "sociolinguistic research kit," and Gaarder (1971) refers to "specialized (language) use by domain and interlocutor" as one of the socio-cultural factors affecting the maintenance or shift of Spanish in the U.S.

The only study I have seen so far which considers a bilingual education program from a sociolinguistic perspective (e.g., use of language by societal domain)[1] was conducted in a small community in

A revised version of a paper presented at the California Teachers of English to Speakers of Other Languages Conference, San Francisco, California, April 26–28, 1974.

Special thanks go to Robert L. Cooper, Theodore Andersson, and J. Donald Bowen for their assistance in revising this paper. However, I take full responsibility for the ideas expressed herein.

333

Albuquerque, New Mexico, by Mallory (1971). She looked at whether a bilingual program affected "a sociolinguistic performance change" in six selected first graders in the program as compared with older children in their families. The sociolinguistic performance of the children was also compared with that of their parents. Unfortunately, the author was unable to conclude very much about the effects of bilingual schooling on language maintenance because the children demonstrated only minimal familiarity with Spanish and the study was not conducted over time (i.e., longitudinally).

What will be considered in this paper is the effect of several years of bilingual schooling on language maintenance. A number of articles have appeared concerning what language Mexican Americans are reading and how well (e.g., Guerra, 1965), but little research addressing itself to the question of their language use. This paper will concern itself with the following basic questions about language use:

1. Does a bilingual program promote greater use of Spanish among its Mexican American participants than is found among comparable children schooled conventionally (i.e., in English only)?
2. Does a bilingual program influence participants who use Spanish more than English at the outset to continue doing so over time?
3. What effect might the child's participation in a bilingual program have on family language use patterns?

If bilingual schooling has an interventionist effect, then perhaps the children in the program might be observed to use as much Spanish several years after entering such a program as they did at the outset. On the other hand, comparable children in a conventional program might be expected to be using Spanish less after a similar period of time. The conventionally schooled group would not only be receiving all or most of its instruction in English, but would also be learning implicitly (and perhaps even explicitly) that English is the dominant, official, and prestigious language in the majority society, and that they should lose the vestiges of Spanish as a natural part of the assimilation process.

Furthermore, a Mexican American child's participation in a bilingual program might stimulate his family (particularly older siblings) to continue using Spanish, whereas a comparable child schooled exclusively in English might promote the increased use of English among family members.

The Redwood City School District began a bilingual schooling program in the fall of 1969, under the auspices of the ESEA Bilingual Education Program, Title VII. The Redwood City project was initiated with one Pilot first grade class of 20 Mexican Americans and 10 Anglos at the Garfield Elementary School. The following year, another first grade and kindergarten were added. In the fall of 1970, a two-year longitudinal study was begun with these three classes of bilingually schooled students and their families, along with comparison students and their families from a neighboring school, as the population under study.

Since one of the aims of the Redwood City Bilingual Education Project was to maintain the minority group's language and culture, a component of the research design called for extensive study of language use patterns over time (see Cohen, 1975). The intent was to be able to make some statements about the project's effect upon language maintenance.

METHOD OF DATA ACQUISITION

Subjects: The student group consisted of the 14 bilingually schooled and 16 conventionally schooled Mexican American children who were kindergartners at the outset of the study (the fall of 1970) and first graders at the termination of the study (the spring of 1972). Given that the program was initiated with a first grade, rather than with a kindergarten, and that a first grade and a kindergarten were added the following year, only the kindergarten group had the benefit of bilingual schooling from the outset of their school career. The other two groups had one year of English-only instruction first. For this reason, only the group starting in kindergarten will be considered in this paper. (All three groups are reported on in Cohen, 1972, and Cohen, 1975).

The parental group consisted of the 30 sets of parents of the bilingually and conventionally schooled children. These families had, for the most part, immigrated from Mexico within the previous 11 years and had lived in Redwood City for an average of 7 years. Generally, only the men had some oral skills in English and neither the men nor the women reported appreciable reading and writing skills in English (Cohen, 1972). Thus, these parents represented Spanish-dominant households, in contrast to the population Mallory (1971) studied in New Mexico.

Procedure: All the students were individually administered a Pupil's Language Use Inventory (based on Fishman, Cooper, Ma et al., 1971) at school, on a pretest-posttest basis (in October 1970, and again in April 1972). Each child was asked the language he used and the language used by others to address him when he was with various members of his family at home, with classmates at school, with peers in the neighborhood, and at church with his companions.[2] Responses were coded as "Spanish," "English," and "both."

As part of a Home Interview Questionnaire, the parents were asked about the student's language use patterns by domain (based on Fishman,

Cooper, Ma et al., 1971). The parents were asked what language the student used at home to speak with adults, to speak with children, to read books or magazines, and to write letters, and what language he used to talk with peers in the neighborhood. Both the student and parent interview data were collected by bilingual Mexican American college students.

A Language Use Observation Instrument (based primarily on Cooper and Carpenter, 1976) was used to obtain a direct measure of the language use of the Mexican American children in four different contexts at school: two within the classroom setting (math and social studies/science) and two outside of the classroom setting (lunchroom and playground).[3] The two classroom settings were intended as more formal, and lunchroom and playground were intended as more informal. The observers watched 7 students randomly selected from each group for one minute (after the children started talking) in each of the four settings on three different days.[4] The observer noted the language that the child used (Spanish or English); to whom the child addressed his remarks (to a Mexican American or Anglo adult—teacher, aide, volunteer helper, etc., or to a Mexican American or Anglo student); the grouping arrangement that the child was in (whole class, small group, or individual); and the language that the adult was using at the time (if an adult was present). The observation instrument was administered in February/March of the second year of the study (1972), by bilingual Mexican American college students.

METHOD OF DATA ANALYSIS

The seven items relating to the student's own language use on the Pupil's Language Use Inventory were combined into an index of "student language use/student report" (Spanish = 2, both = 1, English = 0). The six items relating to the language use of other family members were combined into an index of "family language use/student report." The five parent response items concerning student's language use patterns were combined into an index of "student language use/parent report." Although some descriptive power is lost in using indices, indices facilitate statistical analysis and may increase the explanatory power of the findings.

Mean Bilingual and Comparison group scores for the three indices were submitted to an analysis of covariance. This procedure takes into account initial differences between an experimental and a comparison group by using the pretest score as a covariate to adjust group means in posttesting. Data from the Language Use Observation Instrument were expressed as percent of observation time in which the student used

Spanish or English in class (based on 100%) and out of class (also based on 100%). One-way analysis of variance was run comparing mean percentages for the Bilingual and Comparison groups (see Cohen, 1972; Cohen, 1975, for a complete discussion of the statistical procedures).

FINDINGS

1. *Mexican American students in the bilingual program were found to be using Spanish more after several years than comparable children schooled conventionally.* The Bilingual students did report themselves to be using significantly more Spanish than the Comparison group (F = 12.13, df = 1/27, p < .01) (Table 1). This student self-report was corroborated by the parent report, which also indicated that the Bilingual group used Spanish to a significantly greater extent than the Comparison group (F = 6.27, df = 1/27, p < .05) (Table 1). On the Language Use Observation Instrument, the Bilingual group was observed to use significantly more Spanish with adults in class (F = 7.87, df = 1/12, p < .05) and with other Mexican-American students out of class (F = 20.01, df = 1/12, p < .01). On the other hand, the Comparison group was observed to use English more with other Mexican American students out of class (F = 15.48, df = 1/12, p < .01) (Tables 2 and 3).

Table 1
Report of Language Use Patterns

Indices	Group	Pretest Mean	Posttest Mean	Posttest mean Adjusted for Pretest	df	F
Student Language Use/ Student Report (14-point scale)	Bilingual	11.0	10.3	10.0	1/27	12.13[a]
	Comparison	10.1	7.4	7.6		
Student Language Use/ Parent Report (10-point scale)	Bilingual	6.1	5.9	5.8	1/27	6.27[b]
	Comparison	5.7	3.3	3.3		
Family Language Use/ Student Report (12-point scale)	Bilingual	8.6	7.9	7.7	1/27	2.14
	Comparison	6.9	6.6	6.7		

[a] p <.01.
[b] p <.05.

Table 2
Language Use Observation in Class (Math and Social Studies/Science)

Language and Addressee	Group	Average % of Observation Time (based on 100% for each group)	df	F
Spanish to Mex. Am. Student	Bilingual	34	1/12	1.11
	Comparison	25		
English to Mex. Am. Student	Bilingual	17	1/12	2.67
	Comparison	30		
English to Anglo Student	Bilingual	12	1/12	1.63
	Comparison	6		
Spanish to Adult	Bilingual	13	1/12	7.87[a]
	Comparison	0		
English to Adult	Bilingual	24	1/12	2.30
	Comparison	39		

[a] $p < .05$.

Table 3
Language Use Observation Out of Class (Lunchroom and Playground)

Language and Addressee	Group	Average % of Observation Time (based on 100% for each group)	df	F
Spanish to Mex.-Am. Student	Bilingual	63	1/12	20.01[a]
	Comparison	13		
English to Mex.-Am. Student	Bilingual	22	1/12	15.48[a]
	Comparison	64		
English to Anglo Student	Bilingual	15	1/12	1.52
	Comparison	23		

[a] $p < .01$.

Of the total in-class observation time, Bilingual students spent 47% speaking Spanish: 34% to other Mexican-American student and 13% to adults. (The use of Spanish to Anglo students is not included in the analysis because the incidence was so slight.) The remaining 43% of the time they were observed speaking English: 24% to adults, 17% to other

Mexican-American students, and 12% to Anglo students. The Comparison group spent only 25% of the time speaking Spanish in class, always to other Mexican-American students, never to adults. Seventy-five percent of their time was spent speaking English: 39% to adults, 30% to other Mexican-American students, and 6% to Anglo students (Table 2).

Of the total *out-of-class* observation time, Bilingual students spent most of their time (63% speaking *Spanish* to Mexican-Americans (with 22% of their time spent speaking English to other Mexican-American students and 15% speaking English to Anglo students). Comparison students, however, spent most of their time (64%) speaking *English* to other Mexican-American students (with only 13% of their time spent speaking Spanish to other Mexican-American students and 23% speaking English to Anglo students) (Table 3).

2. *The Mexican-American students in the bilingual program continued to use Spanish more than English over time, while Comparison students schooled only in English shifted to greater use of English.* Whereas the Comparison group reported that they used Spanish half the time and English half the time after two years of English-only schooling (adjusted posttest mean = 7.6, where 14 = Spanish only, 0 = English only), the Bilingual group still reported using Spanish more than English (adjusted posttest mean = 10.0). At the outset of the study, both groups reported themselves using Spanish considerably more than English (Bilingual pretest mean = 11.0; Comparison pretest mean = 10.1). According to parental report, the Comparison students used considerably more English than Spanish at the end of first grade (adjusted posttest mean = 3.3, where 10 = Spanish only, 0 = English only), while the Bilingual students were reported to still be using slightly more Spanish than English (adjusted posttest mean = 5.8) (Table 1).

3. *Family language use patterns were not noticeably associated with their child's participation or non-participation in the bilingual program.* The differences over time in language use patterns in the home between the Bilingual and Comparison groups did not reach a level of statistical significance, and generally showed little change—just slightly more use of English overall. At the outset, the Bilingual students reported more use of Spanish than English (pretest mean = 8.6, where 10 = Spanish only, 0 = English only), and two years later they still indicated somewhat more use of Spanish (adjusted posttest mean = 7.7). The Comparison students also reported more use of Spanish than English at the outset (6.9 on a 10-point scale) and two years later (adjusted posttest mean = 6.7) (Table 1).

The five items in this index included the language used by the father, the mother, the older siblings, and the younger siblings to address the student at home, and the language used by the parents in conversing with each other. Thus, three of the five items reflected parental language use. Such behavior would perhaps be least affected by the student's language use, particularly in a community such as Redwood City, where the adults used Spanish almost exclusively at home. This could help explain why there was no great change in language used by family members.

DISCUSSION AND CONCLUSION

Student report, parent report, and direct observation all contributed to the conclusion that the students going from kindergarten to first grade in the bilingual education program were using more Spanish over time than Comparison students. It would, of course, be expected that only the Bilingual students would use Spanish to adults in class since the conventional classrooms did not have Spanish-speaking teachers or teacher aides. But that would not necessarily prohibit the Comparison students from using Spanish out of class. These findings suggest, however, that the general effect of English language use in the classroom, and particularly the attitudes that are generated in the classroom as to the "appropriate" or "acceptable" language, may have a carry-over effect upon language use in the lunchroom, on the playground, as well as in the surrounding community and at home. And this "transition" to English may go on even while Spanish language use by others at home remains considerable and relatively constant.

It should also be noted that since this Bilingual group was the third to be involved in the program, some of the Hawthorne effects of a new, special program should have worn off.

It appears that the Redwood City Bilingual Education Project did contribute to the maintenance of the Spanish language by encouraging the use of Spanish among the students involved. The fact that the students were given formal schooling in Spanish and used Spanish as a vehicle for learning subject matter appeared to have acted as an incentive for them to continue to use Spanish regularly in a variety of social interactions.

These language use results are most promising for the prospects of bilingual education. If, in fact, a bilingual program is intended to encourage bilingual youngsters to use their language of heritage, then these results show that this *is* going on. Student report, parental report, and direct observation all provide evidence to that effect.

An irony of bilingual schooling is that program staffs are now encouraging minority children to behave in a way that had been shunned for 50 years or more in most U.S. schools: to use their native language at school. In a sense, the new pattern is one of reverse socialization. In the past, school children had been subjected to the English-only rule whereby they were punished, even suspended or expelled, for using a language other than English in school (see Espinosa, 1917; Bernal, 1969; Carter, 1970; Ortega, 1970; Cannon, 1971), while now they are being encouraged to use that language at school.

To my knowledge, no other study of a bilingual project in the U.S. has systematically contrasted the language use patterns of students in the project with those of comparison students. Thus, it is not possible to relate these findings to those of other projects. Hopefully, other such studies will appear in the future. The language use studies on Spanish speakers that are available pertain to patterns in Texas and New Mexico (see Mahoney, 1967; Thompson, 1971; Timmins, 1971), and generally conclude that Spanish language use is on its way out, except in certain rural areas. However, these results do not deal with California. Neither do they pertain to students enrolled in bilingual programs.

It should also be remembered that the Bilingual students were for the most part from families that had immigrated to the United States from Mexico within the previous ten years. Thus, the children were first- and second-generation Spanish speakers. For this reason, one might have expected Spanish to be used considerably, both among the Bilingual and the Comparison children. Instead, Spanish language use appeared to be on the decrease among the Comparison students. The significant differences in the language use patterns of these two groups seem to be attributable to the interventionist effects of the bilingual program.

NOTES

1. Fishman (1971) defines a domain as a cluster of social situations which are typically constrained by a common set of behavioral rules. The domains which are relevant for a given bilingual community may vary, but they often include family, neighborhood, religion, education, and the occupational sphere. Note that a domain is more than a context or a place. A domain also comprises the roles of interlocutors within the particular setting and the topics that these interlocutors are likely to discuss. For instance, within the educational domain, the teacher and the pupil (two interlocutors in a socially prescribed role relationship) may be talking in the classroom (setting) about a math problem (topic).

2. The domains of family, neighborhood, education, and religion were chosen in replication of a study by Edelman, Cooper and Fishman (1971), and based on a year of participant observation and focused interviews and discus-

sions with representative informants of a Puerto Rican barrio in Jersey City. The intent was to see if the domains that differentiated language use patterns for one group of children of Latin American background also applied to another group, from a Mexican-American barrio in California. The results of research in Redwood City tend to validate these domains as useful delimiters of Mexican-American sociolinguistic patterns as well (see Cohen, 1975).

3. Fishman (1969) points out that self-report as a means for determining language use is in need of empirical validation. Self-report data, particularly from young children, may suffer from the Hawthorne effect. The children know they are in a program in which a premium is put on say, Spanish. Consequently, they may *say* they speak it more than they actually do. The Language Use Observation Instrument was introduced into the Redwood City study to provide the necessary empirical validation of language use.

4. One-minute periods were chosen in replication of other studies (see Cohen, 1972, p. 271). Longer observation periods may not add much descriptive data. Rotation of observers might have helped improve the reliability of the measure, and could be considered for future research.

REFERENCES

Bernal, Joe J. 1969. "I am Mexican-American." *Florida Foreign Language Reporter* 7.1:32, 154.

Bowen, J. Donald. 1977. "Linguistic Perspectives in Bilingual Education." In B. Spolsky and R. L. Cooper, eds., *Current Trends in Bilingual Education*. The Hague: Mouton & Co.

Cannon, Garland. 1971. "Bilingual Problems and Developments in the United States." *Publications of the Modern Language Association*, pp. 452–458.

Carter, Thomas P. 1970. *Mexican Americans in School: A History of Educational Neglect*. New York: College Entrance Examination Board.

Cohen, Andrew D. 1972. "Innovative Education for La Raza: A Sociolinguistic Assessment of a Bilingual Education Program in California." Unpublished Doctoral Dissertation, Stanford University.

———. 1975. *A Sociolinguistic Approach to Bilingual Education: Experiments in the American Southwest*. Rowley, Massachusetts: Newbury House.

Cooper, Robert L., and Susan Carpenter. 1976. "Language in the Market." In M. L. Bender, J. D. Bowen, R. L. Cooper, and C. A. Ferguson, et al., *Language in Ethiopia*. Nairobi: Oxford University Press, pp. 244–255.

Edelman, Martin, R. L. Cooper, and J. A. Fishman. 1971. "Young Puerto Rican Schoolchildren." In J. A. Fishman, R. L. Cooper, R. Ma, et al., *Bilingualism in the Barrio*. Indiana University Publications. Language Science Monographs no. 7. The Hague, Netherlands: Mouton & Co., pp. 298–304.

Engle, Patricia L. 1975. "Language Medium in Early School Years for Minority Language Groups." *Review of Educational Research* 65:283–325.

Espinosa, Aurelio M. 1917. "Speech Mixture in New Mexico: the Influence of the English Language on New Mexican Spanish." In H. H. Stephens and H. E. Bolton, eds., *The Pacific Ocean in History*. New York: MacMillan Co, pp.

408–428. Also in E. Hernández-Chávez, A. D. Cohen, and T. Beltramo, *El Lenguaje de los Chicanos: Regional and Social Characteristics of Language Use of Mexican Americans.* Washington, D.C.: Center for Applied Linguistics, 1975, pp. 99–114.

Fishman, Joshua A. 1969. "Some Things Learned: Some Things Yet to Learn." *Modern Language Journal.* 53:255–258.

———. 1971. *Sociolinguistics: A Brief Introduction.* Rowley, Massachusetts: Newbury House.

Fishman, Joshua A., R.L. Cooper, R. Ma, et al. 1971. *Bilingualism in the Barrio.* Indiana University Publications, Language Science Monograph no. 7. The Hague, Netherlands: Mouton & Co.

Gaarder, A. Bruce. 1977. "Language Maintenance or Language Shift." In W.F. Mackey and T. Andersson, eds., *Bilingualism in Early Childhood.* Rowley, Massachusetts: Newbury House, pp. 409–434.

Guerra, Manuel H. 1965. "Why Juanito Doesn't Read." *CTA Journal,* October 1965, pp. 17–19.

Kjolseth, Rolf. 1972. "Bilingual Education Programs in the United States: For Assimilation or Pluralism?" In B. Spolsky, ed., *Language Education of Minority Children.* Rowley, Massachusetts: Newbury House. Pp. 94–121.

Mahoney, Mary K. 1967. "Spanish and English Language Usage by Rural and Urban Spanish-American Families in Two South Texas Counties." Unpublished M.S. Thesis, Texas A&M University.

Mallory, Gloria E. 1971. "Sociolinguistic Considerations for Bilingual Education in an Albuquerque Community Undergoing Language Shift." Unpublished Doctoral Dissertation, The University of New Mexico.

Ornstein, Jacob. 1971. *Sociolinguistics and the Study of Spanish and English Language Varieties and Their Use in the U. S. Southwest, With a Proposed Plan of Research.* Available from SWCEL, 117 Richmond Drive, N.E. Albuquerque, New Mexico 87106.

Ortega, Phillip D. 1970. "Montezuma's Children." *The Center Magazine.* Center for the study of Democratic Institutions, Box 4068, Santa Barbara, California. 3.6:23–31.

Thompson, Roger M. 1971. "Language Loyalty in Austin, Texas: A Study of a Bilingual Neighborhood." Unpublished Doctoral Dissertation, The University of Texas at Austin.

Timmins, Kathleen M. 1971. "An Investigation of the Relative Bilingualism of Spanish Surnamed Children in an Elementary School in Albuquerque." Unpublished Doctoral Dissertation, The University of New Mexico.

Individualizing Instruction in the Bilingual Classroom

RICHARD A. FIGUEROA
University of California, Davis

In his *Lau* vs. *Nichols* opinion (1974), Justice Douglas noted that "there is no equality of treatment merely by providing students with the same facilities, textbooks, teachers, and curriculum; for students who do not understand English are effectively foreclosed from any meaningful education" (p. 3). Initially hailed as a landmark decision for bilingual education, the Supreme Court did not, in fact, endorse bilingual education as the most appropriate educational model for children from language backgrounds other than English (though with regard to Spanish-background children such a case can be readily made from a considerable body of empirical evidence). *Lau* "asks only that the Board of Education be directed to apply its expertise to the problem and rectify the situation" (p. 2). Likewise, the decision is not based on the "equal protection clause" in the Constitution. Rather, it rests on Section 601 of the Civil Rights Act of 1964 and the H.E.W. regulations related to that section, which delineate and outlaw the inherent discrimination and diminished educational opportunity involved in not providing for the language differences of some students. Yet, for all that it is not, the decision does set a unique precedent. In *Brown* vs. *Board of Education* (1954), the basic thrust was towards treating all children similarly in the provision of physical and human resources and in equal access to wherever these resources were provided. *Lau* sets forth the principle of *differential* treatment where this is a necessary first step to a "meaningful opportunity to participate in the educational program" (p. 5). In this context, *Lau* affirms the individualization of instruction where language differences require it.

For those engaged in the struggle for the education of Mexican-American children throughout the Southwest, there is little doubt that bilingual education is the most appropriate educational model for precisely such individualization. The history and practice of English-language instruction for Mexican-American children, be it in the form of an ESL model or in the form of punitive rules that forbade (and

344

forbid) the use of Spanish in the schools (United States Commission on Civil Rights, Report No. 3, 1972), can be held directly and indirectly responsible for: (1) the low percentages of Mexican-American students who finish school (U.S.C.C.R. Report No. 4, 1972), (2) the isolation of Mexican-American students and staff in schools throughout the Southwest (U.S.C.C.R. Report No. 1, 1971), (3) the suppression of Mexican-American culture in the schools (U.S.S.C.R. Report No. 3, 1972), (4) the low degree of Mexican-American students' extra-curricular participation (U.S.C.C.R. Report No. 3, 1972) and curricular participation (U.S.C.C.R. Report No. 5, 1973), and (5) the vulnerability of Mexican-American children to the misuse of psychological tests and to being labeled mentally retarded in the schools (Mercer, 1971; *Diana* vs. *State Board of Education,* 1970).

Bilingual education, as the most appropriate educational model for Mexican-American children, promises to correct these inequities by providing a reasonable and fair means for Mexican-American children to acquire: competency in English, educational achievement, respect and sensitivity on the part of educators for their culture, and a predictive validity component in mental test results that will require, if not force, integrating language factors into test scores, interpretation, and research. Defined in these terms, however, the "appropriateness" of bilingual education for Mexican American students can be erroneously interpreted by wholly designating it as a remedial or compensatory function. Such a mistaken view can easily obscure the more important individual benefits accruing to bilinguality, particularly for Mexican-American children. For them, bilingual education can deal much better with their individuality by enhancing their unique aptitudes (Kagan & Madsen, 1971; Ramírez & Castañeda, 1974) and their unique intelligence (Jensen, 1973). It also promises to educate children who because of their bilinguality, may, as in other countries where bilingual education is routinely provided, show greater cognitive enhancement (Friedman & Ianco-Worral, 1972), more creativity (Carringer, 1972), and more tolerance towards other cultures (Lambert & Tucker, 1973). Most of these "benefits" evolve not simply because of the development of dual mental and language systems (Kolers, 1968), but also because of the cultural-anthropological ambiance associated with and incorporated into truly bilingual instruction.

California has instituted a credential in Spanish-bilingual/cross-cultural specialization. Programs for the training of these specialists require that Spanish be dealt with not as an isolated skill but as an integral component of Mexican-American culture, values, and traditions. The first four training programs approved in California early in the fall of 1974 reflected this orientation by requiring courses dealing principally with Mexican-American culture: e.g., Culture and Civilization of Mexico and Mexican-Americans, Mexican-American Culture, Sociology of the Barrio, and Research Methods in the Chicano Community. However, as an extension of the *Lau* orientation to individualize instruction, and as sources for actualizing all the possible beneficial effects to be derived from a truly bilingual/multicultural education, these programs may be too narrow.

The Spanish-speaking population in the United States, and especially in the Southwest, is not homogeneous. Individualizing Spanish-bilingual education requires an understanding and knowledge of Mexican-American children (be they urban or rural migrant children) *and* of immigrant Latino and Mexicano children. At present the latter are both invisible and unknown. Training specialists to teach in bilingual/single-culture (Mexican-American) classrooms fails to meet their cultural needs, their value orientations, their historical/familial traditions, and their total existential situation.

With their Mexican-American brothers and sisters, these children share ancestry and even genetic ties. They suffer the same educational inequities and the same sociopolitical inequalities in this country. But they are unique, and if Spanish-bilingual/multicultural education is to address itself to individual needs, it must account for them and it must therefore expand the present meaning of multiculturality. But who exactly are they?

Census data (U.S. Bureau of the Census, 1972) indicates that approximately 16% of the Spanish surnamed population in the Southwest is not "Mexican." It is assumed that this group is composed predominantly of Latino immigrants from Central and South America. Also, even though the Census did not differentiate between "Mexican" and "Mexican-American," the distinction is critical. Both Mexicano and Latino immigrants share in the unique experience of adapting to a different culture. For the purpose of this study, the two groups are undifferentiated. In effect, then, the 16% not categorized as "Mexican" in the Census is an underestimate of the Spanish surnamed population with a cultural heritage other than Mexican-American in the southwestern United States. Taking into account the Census error with respect to this group, the non-Mexican-American Spanish surnamed population in the Southwest may total well over one million persons.

Yet, their invisibility is singularly unique. In California, for example, a survey of non-English-speaking and limited English-speaking students is taken annually to determine the need for bilingual education (California State Legislature, 1972). In 1973, 47,508 students were identified as non-English-speaking and 140,651 as limited English-speaking students from Spanish-speaking homes. It would be interesting to determine the homogeneity of this group and, by extension, the type of cultural emphasis that would necessarily have to be integrated within their bilingual/multicultural education. This author predicts that the immigrant group would be represented in such a survey well above the Census estimate of 16%. What should a bilingual teacher, therefore, need to know about such a population?

Research on these children is sparse. There is, however, some information on the effects of migration, the variable most likely to permeate, color, and perhaps determine their lives.

Mexicano and Latino immigrants, like their Mexican-American relatives, share a binding sense of family love and loyalty. The process of migrating to a new country often engenders a serious if not traumatic sense of separation. Ample psychiatric evidence attests to the strains placed on individuals and families that migrate (Fabrega, 1969; Dworkin, 1971; Sommers, 1964), particularly when the migration entails separation from loved ones. However, even when this form of separation does not occur, as in the case of many Latino and Mexicano immigrants due to the legal prerequisite of having a sponsor who is capable and willing to support the immigrant and who is usually a relative, a different sense of "separation" inevitably taps the adaptive capacity of individuals and families. The changes in behavioral, social, and language customs, even when foreseen, always carry with them varying degress of anxiety. Coping with a new environment where the stimulus-response cues are different often produces a sense of disorientation. Shopping, procuring employment, or exploring the urban environment can become potential sources for constricted, if not regressive, behavioral options. These, in turn, often lead to feelings of lowered self-esteem, accentuated when the "host" culture already perceives one's culture as somehow not quite as good, or second class, or even "foreign" (Derbyshire, 1969). If the migration has been to a Mexican-American or Latino community or barrio, the effects of the change may be buffered insofar as the community provides cultural and linguistic support. Sensitive, experienced bilingual teachers, eminently aware of the psychological dictum that a child reflects the emotional tone in the family (Robinson, 1972), can readily appreciate and understand the possible consequences of this entire family process on an immigrant child.

This author's clinical experience readily verifies the effect of this form of stress within immigrant Latino-Mexicano families and its reflection in the children. Clients in a community mental health agency, in describing their difficulties, would recount how much they had wanted to come to the United States in order to improve their condition economically or in order to attain greater freedom, and after arrival (once the reality of their linguistic, behavioral, or employment difficulties became glaringly real) how often they longed to return. Their experience was not lost on the children. They would invariably show withdrawing, fearful, and aggressive behaviors which, according to their parents, were not typical or developmentally continuous with previous patterns. Their visibility in school increased. Referral for psychological services followed and more often than not for reasons such as "extreme shyness," "withdrawal," "will not talk."

In order to explore the effects of migration, particularly in children, data was systematically collected during the 1972–1973 and 1973–1974 school years on most of the Spanish-speaking, immigrant population registering their children in a large Northern California school district. Table 1 presents a breakdown of the countries from which the children and their families migrated. These percentages are not generalizable throughout the Southwest, but they do offer a glimpse at the possible international variety that any given Spanish-bilingual teacher may encounter.

Table 1
Distribution by Nationality of the Spanish-Speaking Immigrant Group That Registered Their Children in a Northern California School District in 1972–1973 and 1973–1974

| | 1972–1973 | | 1973–1974 | |
Country	N	%	N	%
Nicaragua[a]	148	50%	38	14%
El Salvador	65	22%	75	29%
Mexico	55	19%	97	38%
Puerto Rico	8	3%	2	1%
Cuba	3	1%	8	3%
Colombia	3	1%	1	1%
Peru	3	1%	3	1%
Ecuador	3	1%	2	1%
Guatemala	2	1%	16	6%
Costa Rica	2	1%	—	—
Honduras	2	1%	3	1%
Argentina	1	1%	—	—
Bolivia	1	1%	7	3%
Chile	1	1%	3	1%

[a]The large number of Nicaraguan children can be attributed to the relaxation of immigration laws after the disastrous earthquake in 1972.

Additional data, collected only during the 1973–1974 school year, revealed that for approximately 102 families (82% of the total sample) the process of changing cultures was a first-time occurrence. Likewise, over the two-year period, approximately 15% of the children returned to their countries, while 5% moved within the United States. At the time of registering for school (1973–1974), most families (61%) with whom the children were living had been in the country less than a year. Critically important, in the sense of requiring teacher and school sensitivity, was the fact that 58% of the children were not living with the same family that they lived with in their native country, and that most of these children (88%) had only recently arrived. In these situations the probability of school problems, both behavioral and cognitive, is quite high. As an educational concern, this merits teacher awareness at the very least.

School referrals for a substantial number of these children increased as the 1973–1974 year progressed. Typically, many children found it difficult to adjust to several aspects of the Anglo school, even when the school was in the predominantly Spanish-speaking area. Teacher behavior and appearance were described by the children, and often echoed by the parents, as strange, lacking authority, with no direction, unable to control pupils, and sloppy ("bastante chuco"). "Hippy" was a particularly derogatory description often used to refer to even the milder types of beards, beads, and boots.

Ramírez and Castañeda's (1974) model for a field sensitive curriculum would greatly aid in the education of these students since it provides for the sort of consistent structure that is more congruent with their teacher and classroom expectations. This is a curious sort of Pygmalion Effect and one that might really be related to these students' achievement. Sensitivity to dress or at least to the reaction of the children to the more informal teacher dress styles in this country is a subject more than worthy of bilingual teacher-training programs.

An unusual number of children who were referred for psychological services by their teachers within the first three months evidenced "poor retention," "troubles with remembering," and "perceptual problems." Psychological tests failed to verify any form of disability. Time alone, in most cases, was a sufficient remedy. Cultural stress created by the recent migration and/or a "new" family probably accounted for the referred "problems." Teacher patience and understanding would do much to help the children adjust without any need for the sort of psychological intervention that, in the case of Mexican-American children, has often led to gross misplacements in special education classes.

Prolonged exposure to the "dominant culture" did not always bring adequate adaptation. In many family counseling situations arising out of school-related problems, it was noted by this author that there was a critical element of differential rates of acculturation between the parent(s) and the child that often caused interpersonal and adjustment problems. The student was inadvertently and imperceptibly being socialized in school in a manner quite different from that at home. The parent, out of deference to a "perhaps-that's-how-it's-done-here" attitude, often acquiesced to unacceptable behaviors only to react violently when too many cultural norms about child-behavior had been violated. Many parents failed to realize that some of the socialization is not how it's done here, but rather peculiar to low socioeconomic culture, if not to anti-social, delinquent culture. Teachers can greatly aid parents in either redefining or reaffirming behavioral norms and standards. For the Mexicano and Latino population this form of "community involvement" on the part of the bilingual teacher may not only lessen cultural disorientation but also enhance cultural identity and family stability.

A precaution should be stated. When dealing with the Mexicano/Latino child, the bilingual teacher should not stereotypically expect to find an anxiety-ridden, cognitively restricted pupil who is incapable of effective academic development. The observations and data presented here serve principally as sources for understanding and sensitivity, not for a blanket classification.

The final set of data collected in the school district on Mexicano/Latino children revolved around their low educational achievement (Friedman, 1972). This set of data, more than any other, dramatically highlights the possible consequences of "homogenizing" the Spanish surnamed population throughout the Southwest and of developing a multicultural emphasis that is blind with respect to some one million persons and with respect to the educational histories of their children.

Table 2 presents the different ages when children begin schooling in Latin American countries.

The variation is sufficient to warrant at least inquiry into each child's educational history. Failure to do so, particularly in the high school years, may lead to disastrous misplacements of many children. Table 3 documents what can happen when the instruction of these children is neither individualized nor planned.

Students get placed in grades that are not sequentially related to their educational background, though their placement may be naively considered "appropriate" in terms of chronological age. Considering that they will have added demand placed on them relative to the acquisition of English competency, it is not surprising to find their academic attainment far less than adequate. The results of such misplacement are particularly devastating in high school. In at least one high school studied, an examination of three counselor lists within the ESL program

Table 2
Age When Schooling Begins in Latin American Countries

Country	Preprimary	Primary
Argentina	3	6
Bolivia	4	6
Brazil	4	7
Colombia	5	7
Costa Rica	4	6
Chile	4	7
Ecuador	3	6
El Salvador	4	7
Guatemala	3	7
Honduras	4	6½
Mexico	3	6
Nicaragua	5	7
Panama	5	7
Paraguay	5	7
Peru	4	6
Uruguay	3	6
Venezuela	4	7

Source: Organización de los Estados Americanos, 1973.

Table 3
Grade Misplacement of Latino/Mexicano Students Entering a Northern California School District (1972–1973, 1973–1974) Resulting from the Use of Chronological Age Rather Than Educational Age In Determining Educational Programs

	Elementary		Secondary [a]	
	1972/73	*1973/74*	*1972/73*	*1973/74*
Sample size	184	171	162	148
Number misplaced [b]	40	47	67	81
Percentage misplaced	21%	27%	41%	54%
Range of years of misplacement	1–4	1–5	1–6	1–7
Average number of years of misplacement	1.5	1.57	2	2.41

[a]Including junior and senior high school.
[b]Kindergarten included as a grade.

showed that the Latino/Mexicano students who reached 18 years of age by either the end of their 1973–1974 academic year, or who would be 18 by the beginning of their 1974–1975 year, averaged 92.5 completed units (range: 5 to 189.5). Two hundred units are needed to graduate. Their post-high school career options would seem exceedingly limited. Teachers, particularly bilingual teachers, should not be party to such an insidious form of chronological-age tracking.

Realizing that "disadvantaged" status might be used to justify either a diluted curriculum or depressed levels of educational achievement, Mercer (1972) conducted a comparative study of sociocultural characteristics known to correlate with academic achievement on the approximately 140 families registering their children into the school district for the 1973–1974 school year. Mercer derived these sociocultural characteristics specifically for use with a Mexican-American population. Five dimensions that statistically accounted for a substantial portion of the variance in IQ measures within a Mexican-American sample define a given Mexican-American family's "modal"/"non-modal" status. The more "modal," or "Anglicized" as Mercer prefers to designate it, the greater the probability of academic success as predicted from IQ. In the study Mercer found that Mexican-American children who were "modal" and therefore had a greater probability of success in school were more likely to:

a. Come from less crowded homes (fewer than 1.4 per room).
b. Have mothers who expected them to get some college education.
c. Have fathers who grew up in cities and who had completed at least the ninth grade.
d. Come from home-owning families.
e. Come from homes in which English is spoken most of the time.
(Mercer, 1972, p. 47)

The Mexicano/Latino children:

a. Come from homes where the persons-per-room index is 1.45 (statistically not different from 1.4).
b. Have mothers who expect them:
to go to college: 56%
to go to university: 7%
to go to school as long as possible: 28%
to go to high school: 7%
c. Have fathers who were born in large cities (82% of the fathers) and completed an average of 8.96 years of school (statistically not different from 9).
d. Live in predominantly rented housing (80%).
e. Come from homes in which Spanish is spoken most of the time (86%).

To the degree that Mercer's predictive model is appropriate and to the degree that the responses taken from the immigrant sample were accurate and reliably applicable, the Mexicano/Latino sample fares well on three out of the five sociocultural characteristics. This proportion is effectively reduced to three out of four if the child receives bilingual instruction, since the predictive validity associated with the last sociocultural characteristic (English spoken in the home) is, in fact, nullified. These results serve to deflate any self-fulfilling expectation of low academic achievement for these children due to social "non-modal" status. They also indict the educational system for the children's low levels of measured academic achievement (Mercer, 1973).

For a bilingual teacher, Mercer's model can serve as a vantage point from which she or he, through some very indirect data, can get a sense of a child's environment and from it move to either enhance or improve the child's academic standing. The present results from this model also serve to set a favorable expectation based on sociological variables relative to academic achievement *provided* that programs are individualized bilingually, academically, and emotionally.

Spanish-bilingual teachers and Spanish-bilingual/cross-cultural specialist training programs should carry out the *Lau* mandate to individualize instruction and should actualize the educational promises of bilingualism in accordance with the needs of the Spanish-surnamed population throughout the Southwest and, indeed, the entire United States. This means recognizing that a substantial number of students are not Mexican-American but rather Latino or Mexicano. Central to understanding and meeting the needs of these children is the process of migration and adaptation faced by them and by their families. Concomitantly, curricular and cultural programs require individualization based on *their* needs and *their* educational background. The mandate for Spanish-bilingual teachers with regard to these students is unique.

This mandate can be operationalized by expanding the cultural component in the bilingual teacher-training programs to include the various possible ethnic differences of Spanish-surnamed youngsters, especially in the Southwestern United States. Individualizing instruction within this mandate entails an emphasis on assessment calling for the development of empathy and awareness skills relative to the possible temporary affective stress involved in cross-cultural migration. Knowledge of the educational systems throughout the Americas is essential. Use of parent and student expectations about teacher roles, appearance, and behavioral management should also be in the "community involvement" component of the training programs. Planning in terms of educational needs requires the use of each individual's educational "age," or educational history, as well as sociological background. It is this form of multicultral emphasis that really leads to individualized instruction in bilingual classes.

REFERENCES

Brown v. *Board of Education*, 347 U.S. 483 (1954).

California State Legislature. *The Bilingual Education Act of 1972*, Section 5761.3, 1972.

Carringer, D. C. "The Relationship of Bilingualism to the Creative Thinking Abilities of Mexican Youth." Unpublished Doctoral Dissertation, University of Georgia, 1972.

Derbyshire, R. L. "Adaptation of Adolescent Mexican-Americans to United States Society." In E. B. Brody (ed.), *Behavior in New Environments: Adaptation of Migrant Populations*. Beverly Hills: Sage, 1969, pp. 117–144.

Diana v. *State Board of Education*, C.A., C-7037, N.D. California (Feb. 1970).

Dworkin, A. G. "National Origin and Ghetto Experience as Variables in Mexican-American Stereotypy." In N. Wagner and M. Haug (eds.), *Chicanos; Social and Psychological Perspectives*. St. Louis: Mosby, 1971, pp. 80–84.

Fabrega, H. "Social Psychiatric Aspects of Acculturation and Migration: A General Statement." *Comprehensive Psychiatry*, 10 (4), July, 1969.

Friedman, M. "Spanish-Bilingual Students and Standardized Tests." Unpublished Masters Thesis, California State University, Hayward, 1972.

Friedman, M., and Ianco-Worral, A. D. "Bilingualism and Cognitive Development." *Child Development*, 34 (4), December, 1972.

Jensen, A. R. "Level I and Level II Abilities in Three Ethnic Groups." *American Educational Research Journal*, 10 (4), Fall, 1973.

Kagan, S., and Madsen, M. C. "Cooperation and Competition of Mexican, Mexican American, and Anglo American Children of Two Ages Under Four Instructional Sets." *Developmental Psychology*, 5 (1), 1971.

Kolers, P. A. "Bilingualism and Information Processing." *Scientific American*, March 1968.

Lambert, W., and Tucker, R. "The Benefits of Bilingualism." *Psychology Today*, September, 1973, pp. 89ff.

Lau v. *Nichols*, U.S. 72-6520 (1974).

Mercer, J. R. "Institutionalized Anglo-centrism: Labeling Mental Retardates in the Public Schools." In P. Orleans and W. R. Ellis (eds.) *Race, Change, and Urban Society*. Urban Affairs Annual Review, Sage, 1971.

———. "IQ: The Lethal Label." *Psychology Today*, September 1972.

———. *P.R.I.M.E. Evaluation of Integration Following Desegregation: Student Output Variables-Summary Profile*. San Francisco Unified School District, 1973.

Organización de los Estados Americanos, *América en cifras, 1972*. Washington, D.C.: Secretaria General de la Organización de los Estados Americanos, 1973.

Ramírez III, M., and Castañeda, A. *Cultural Democracy, Bi-cognitive Development and Education*. San Francisco: Academic Press, 1974.

Robinson, J. F. "Psychiatric Examination of the Child." In Freedman and Kaplan (eds.), *The Child, His Psychological and Cultural Development: Vol. I*. New York: Atheneum, 1972.

Sommers, V. "The Impact of Dual Cultural Membership." *Psychiatry*, 27 (November 1964).

United States Bureau of the Census, U.S. Department of Commerce. *Selected Characteristics of Persons and Families of Mexican, Puerto Rican, and Other Spanish Origin: March 1972*. Washington, D.C.: U.S. Government Printing Office, 1972.

United States Commission on Civil Rights. *Mexican American Education Study, Report 1: Ethnic Isolation of Mexican Americans in the Public Schools of the Southwest*. Washington, D.C.: U.S. Government Printing Office, April, 1971.

United States Commission on Civil Rights. *Mexican American Education Study, Report 2: The Unfinished Education, Outcomes for Minorities in the Five Southwestern States*. Washington, D.C.: U.S. Government Printing Office, October 1971.

United States Commission on Civil Rights. *Mexican American Education Study, Report 3: The Excluded Student, Educational Practices Affecting Mexican Americans in the Southwest*. Washington, D.C.: U.S. Government Printing Office, May 1972.

United States Commission on Civil Rights. *Mexican American Education Study, Report 4: Mexican American Education in Texas: A Function of Wealth*. Washington, D.C.: U.S. Government Printing Office, August 1972.

United States Commission on Civil Rights. *Mexican American Education Study, Report 5: Teachers and Students: Differences in Teacher Interaction with Mexican American and Anglo Students*. Washington, D.C.: U.S. Government Printing Office, March 1973.

Reading in Spanish as a Mode of Language Maintenance in the United States

CHESTER CHRISTIAN
Texas A & M University

In the early 1960's the Language Resources Project gave considerable attention to minority language publications as an aspect of language maintenance in the United States (Fishman, Hayden, and Warshauer, 1976, pp. 51–74), but although this pioneering study has stimulated interest in and research on Spanish language maintenance for more than fourteen years, the written language has been virtually ignored except as a manifestation of the nonstandard elements in the spoken language. It is rare to see even a suggestion such as that of Guadalupe Valdés-Fallis:

> Hispanic minorities, in particular Chicanos and Puerto Ricans, have much to gain from reading Spanish language masterpieces in their original form. Within this literature can be found not only the traditional ideas, aspirations, and beliefs of the Hispanic world but also the stylistic excellence and genius of its people. (1977, p. 86)

This lack of attention to the role, both as reality and as possibility, of written Spanish in the preservation not only of all forms of the language, but also of the cultural values they represent, may be due as much to professional bias as to the presumably modest proportion of native speakers who read and write Spanish.

More than a century ago, Wilhelm von Humboldt expressed an attitude toward written language which seems to have become an article of faith in contemporary linguistics, subscribed to enthusiastically by amateur as well as professional linguists:

> Properly conceived of, language is something persistent and in every instant transitory. Even its maintenance by writing is only an incomplete, mummified preservation, necessary if one is again to render perceptible the living speech concerned. (1971, p. 27)

This attitude is presently embedded in the doctrine firmly established since Bloomfield (1933) that spoken language is *real* and written language is *artificial;* spoken language is *alive* and written language is *dead.* It is an integral part of introductory textbooks on linguistics; in such a text, for example, Ornstein and Gage discuss the importance of being able to speak and then continue:

> By contrast, reading and writing—marks on paper that stand for speech sounds—are much less important. In fact, half the people on earth, even in this modern and advanced day, are illiterate or unable to read and write. Many of the world's languages, probably a large majority, have no writing system at all. . . . People who cannot read or write may still get along quite well in our society, and even become successful. (1969, p. 8)

Another source of bias against the study of literacy in Spanish as a mode of language maintenance is the assumption that the "natural" domain of Spanish in the United States is the home and neighborhood, and that of English the school and government. This "social allocation of functions to different languages or varieties," described by Fishman (1972, p. 102) as "diglossia," is seen as essential to the maintenance of a minority language in any society. It is sometimes taken to imply the inappropriateness of the duplication in Spanish of the school functions of reading and writing.

Jacobson (1975, pp. 123–38) has discussed the implications for Spanish/English bilingual programs of the duplication and/or compartmentalization of language functions in terms of the analysis of diglossia by Fishman, and has offered a "conciliatory solution," the "nonredundant full bilingual maintenance program," which involves code switching in oral Spanish and English in the classroom, and the development of some degree of literacy in Spanish; he indicates that the degree of literacy might be determined by socioeconomic factors, with those of the upper levels attaining a higher degree of biliteracy than those of the lower, since in the latter case the "child does obviously not need to develop the skill of fully performing in two mutually exclusive settings." Again, the natural domain for that child seems to be assumed to be the home and neighborhood.

A third reason for implicit scholarly opposition to education in written Spanish is closely related to the aforementioned: the written word is perceived as implied criticism of the spoken dialects in the United States, as disparagement of the culture of those using these dialects, and even as an attempt of those for whom Spanish is a second language to maintain their authority with respect to its use. Books which prescribe usage for native speakers, such as those of Baker (1966) and Barker (1972)—the latter a native speaker—represent for many this type of power struggle.

It is common to insist that children be given to read only works written in the dialect they speak, that the only literature worth studying for them is that embryonic body of works produced by members of their own group, and that culture heroes from Spain and Spanish America are inappropriate subjects of study for them.

Scholarship thus reinforces entrenched political and pedagogical opposition to the use of written materials in Spanish with children in the United States who speak the language. However, it is possible that use of such materials as are standard in Spanish-dominant countries facilitates not only the maintenance of Hispanic language and culture, but higher standards of academic achievement for the child. This is due to the contrasts between the English and Spanish writing systems and between the type of materials used for reading in other countries, such as Mexico, in part as a result of differences in the writing systems.

While it is not possible here to offer a contrastive analysis of the English and Spanish writing systems, the scale of difference is indicated by the fact that in the Spanish system there is one and only one way to pronounce the letter *a,* and there is one and only one way to represent the sound. In English there are six sounds associated with the same letter, and forty-three ways to represent them in writing. In Spanish, there is one rule for silent consonants (the *h* is always silent), and in English there are twenty, including "rules" such as "the *d* is silent in *some* words, such as *handsome, Wednesday.*" In summary, there are approximately twice as many sounds in English as in Spanish, and approximately six times as many ways of representing them in writing. Also, in Spanish the rules are completely reliable, while in English their applicability seems at times almost random.

These linguistic criteria have provided a rationale which has been used at times as a justification for initial teaching of reading in Spanish for those who speak the language. Gaarder (1967, p. 53), explaining the results of a Columbia University study in Puerto Rico, concluded:

> What they were actually saying is that because Spanish has a much better writing system than English (i.e., the writing system matches the sound system) speakers of Spanish can master reading and writing very quickly and can begin to acquire information from the printed page more easily and at an earlier age.

This ease of acquiring information from the printed page has been documented many times in my experience with more than a thousand Mexican-American students in high school and college who have read masterpieces of Spanish literature in my classes, and with what I believe to be a significantly higher level of competence than their Anglo peers were able to read English. It has also been demonstrated by the high proportion of Spanish-Americans I have known with little or no education who read literary classics for entertainment; these include, for example, a Mexican maid with a total of six weeks of schooling who in eight years of working in my home read almost everything that I studied or taught, as well as a highly literate secretary from Nogales, Arizona, whose only formal training in Spanish was having been taught to read the newspaper by her father when she was in first grade.

There are some data to indicate that this experience is not misleading; a survey of Mexican-American sophomores in four South Texas counties indicated that 88 percent could read Spanish, although only 56 percent of the males and 62 percent of the females had had a course in the language (Patella and Kuvlesky, 1975). Other surveys had indicated that one-third to more than one-half of high school students in South Texas, El Paso, and Colorado read newspapers and/or magazines in Spanish (Kuvlesky, 1973). This type of reading seems particularly significant, since it would almost always be of the student's own volition.

Spanish provides an almost "ideal" writing system, as that term was used by a group of specialists on the use of vernacular languages in education in reporting to UNESCO in 1951 (Fishman, 1968, p. 704). In an ideal system, each sound of the language is represented by one and only one letter, and no letter represents more than one sound. The Venezuelan scholar and poet Andrés Bello in 1836 recommended "perfecting" Spanish in this sense by the introduction of eight rules of orthography, but in spite of influential personal and governmental support, tradition prevailed (as it usually does in matters of language), so that the written *h* has no sound, the sound /s/ may be represented by an *s*, a *c*, or a *z* in American Spanish, and there are a few other minor inconsistencies.

These are insignificant, however, in comparison with the complexities of the writing system of English. In discussing a paper on alphabets (Fishman, 1968, pp. 750–51), Fishman cites the researcher, Don Stuart, who mentions his daughter's experience with three languages—Japanese, Dutch, and English—stating that at the age of six and a half she had been reading "Japanese literature in *hiragana*" for more than a year, was beginning to read Dutch, "which has a semiphonemic spelling," but that "it goes without saying that she has made least progress of all in English with its completely unsystematic orthography." In the case of another child (Christian, 1977) even the slight irregularities of the Spanish system, such as the identical pronunciation of the *b* and the *v*, were protested at the age of two years.

Case studies of the development of reading skills in Spanish beginning at the age of two and before have been made by Kay E. Past (1975), Alvin W. Past (1976), and C. Christian (1977, 1978). Mariana Past learned to speak and read both English and Spanish at the same time; Aurelio and Raquel Christian learned Spanish first, not receiving specific instruction in English reading until they were in school. Reading in Spanish provided an excellent foundation for English reading, with both in first grade scoring at the 99th percentile in "reading readiness" in terms of norms for monolingual English-speaking children.

While the environments of these children are much more oriented toward academic learning than those of most children whose home language is Spanish, little time (15–20 minutes daily) was spent in teaching them reading. And records of 394 "brain-injured" children (Doman and Melcher, 1978, pp. 209–22) given reading lessons showed that almost all could learn before the age of five.

Funds are available for "preschool programs preparatory and supplementary to bilingual education programs," but Andersson and Boyer (1978, p. 166) point out that little or no attention has been given to this provision because of the assumption that children are the responsibility of parents during the preschool period and that the latter usually have little knowledge of possibilities or processes associated with early reading. Nevertheless, in principle, preschool literacy in Spanish seems nearly an ideal solution to the social and psychological, as well as the educational, problems of the child who speaks Spanish at home.

Some of the psychological and social problems which result from initial literacy in a language not spoken by the child's parents may include damage to the self-concept resulting from the presumed rejection by the "generalized other," represented principally by the school, of "significant others" represented by parents and friends (Christian, 1976, pp. 18–23). Preschool literacy in Spanish, or even exposure to printed materials in the language, can serve to identify the child's home environment with the reading process so that upon entering school it is not alien to the self.

Not only is the reading process usually alien to the child who speaks Spanish, but so is the content of reading he or she is given in the school. A pattern of culture as well as of language is implicit in whatever material is used for the teaching of reading, and materials in English represent some of the facets of the dominant culture most contradictory to traditional Hispanic values. A comparison of the following two poems representing relationships between parents and children, one from a reader in the United States and one from a Mexican reader, both for children in first grade just past the preprimer stage, indicates the type of cultural as well as linguistic contrasts typical of readers in English and readers in Spanish in general. They reflect differences in the characteristics of the two languages, in the nature of the reading process, in the concept of the child's maturity level, and in the nature of the society and culture.

From *Something to Tell,* Grade 1, Level 6, second poem (O'Donnell, 1972a, p. 80):

Play Catch with Me

Daddy is home,
And we can play ball.
This is the game
That I like best of all.

Play catch with me, Daddy,
Here comes the ball,
Why, Daddy! Oh, Daddy!
You let that ball f . . .

From *Mi libro de primer año,* segunda parte, first poem (Domínguez Aguirre and León González, 1960, pp. 90–91):

Amor filial

Yo adoro a mi madre querida,
yo adoro a mi padre también
ninguno me quiere en la vida
como ellos me saben querer.

Si duermo, ellos velan mi sueño;
si lloro, están tristes los dos;
si río, su rostro es risueño;
mi risa es para ellos el sol.

Me enseñan los dos, con inmensa
ternura, a ser bueno y feliz.
Mi padre, por mí lucha y piensa;
mi madre ora siempre por mí.

Yo adoro a mi madre querida
yo adoro a mi padre también;
ninguno me quiere en la vida
como ellos me saben querer.

—Amado Nervo

Filial Love

I adore my beloved mother,
I adore my father as well,
Nobody in this life loves me
as they know how to love me.

If I sleep, they watch over me;
if I cry, both of them are sad;
if I laugh, their faces are smiling;
my laughter is sunshine for them.

Both of them teach me, with immense
tenderness, to be happy and good.
My father struggles and thinks for me;
my mother always prays for me.

I adore my beloved mother,
I adore my father as well,
Nobody in this life loves me
as they know how to love me.

—Translation by C. Christian

In the English reader there are five other examples of rhymed trivia; in the reader from Mexico there are thirteen other examples of poems from the pens of outstanding writers from half a dozen countries. The contrast in second-grade readers is even greater, especially in the vocabulary and conceptual level of the prose selections. The same series in English presents a group of unrealistic and unimaginative stories stressing the kind of experience that many adults (especially teachers) suppose that children experience: "I Want to Be Best," "Front-Page News," "Keep Your Fingers Crossed," and "Oh, No! It Couldn't Be!" for example. The Spanish reader covers a broad range of themes representing home life, social awareness, country life, daily routine, a tour of Mexico City, organs of the body, social life, patriotism, nature, and miscellaneous classics and historical sketches.

As an example of contrast in content, the English reader, in dealing with the newspaper, represents the "news" of a dog who follows a postman on his route; the Spanish reader tells of the news of a flood, as a result of which the father goes to check on relatives and returns with a rural Indian boy who has been orphaned by the disaster and is adopted by the family. Apparently children who read Spanish are expected to do so not only on a higher verbal but also a higher conceptual level than those who read English.

Even where readers in Spanish follow the trend of U.S. pedagogy, there are still quantitative differences which are noteworthy. For example, Bettelheim has discussed vocabulary limitations, observing that in the United States "all four preprimers in one widely distributed series of readers contain only 78 extremely simple words, which are endlessly repeated. The basic primer of the series adds but another 104 words" (1978, p. 56). There is a beginning set of readers from Spain which follows this pattern, except that there are 79 different words in the one preprimer, and 404 words in the basic primer. And the language does lean slightly toward the vacuousness of the U.S. readers.

Bettelheim criticizes U.S. readers as representing life in terms of "being cute and having fun," and as failing to depict the contributions of children "to family life and to the society at large" (p. 58). Almost all readers in Spanish do what he suggests readers in English should do—and they do so in part by utilizing masterpieces of literature geographically and historically distant from the world of the child, and in a dialect often quite distinct from the local one. This is thought to contribute to education, not detract from it. To a great extent education consists of the acquisition of language varieties, but U.S. texts typically utilize about 2 to 5 percent of the vocabulary already known by the child, making reading a spiritless and mindless chore.

The foregoing is offered as evidence that Hispanic minorities indeed "have much to gain from reading Spanish language masterpieces in their original form" and that this gain need not be postponed beyond first grade. It is possible, in fact, to initiate it early in the life of the pre-school child. The possibility has been suggested by the Director of the Office of Bilingual Education, Dr. Josué González, who, in an interview soon after he was named to the position, was reported as favoring "teaching reading at a very early pre-school age in the home language—perhaps in a collaborative arrangement in the home" (Ebel, 1978, p. 1). He also stated that even though he interprets the intent of the law* to be in support of "transitional" bilingual programs, where instruction in Spanish is eliminated as soon as possible, he favors reading instruction in Spanish, through "maintenance" bilingual education offered by local initiative. His reasoning is that without this instruction children could lose their native-language literacy skills as a result of continuing in school.

Institutional support for reading in Spanish can be expected to continue at a minimal level, however, just as institutional support for the use of Spanish in instruction has been minimal even in bilingual programs. But just as Spanish continues to be used by millions of U.S. citizens without institutional support, a significant proportion of these millions will continue to learn to read even the masterpieces of Hispanic literature with minimal institutional support.

In summary, the oral language bias in linguistics, the assumption that home versus official domain is appropriate for Spanish, and the ideal of dialectical democracy have combined to reinforce the popular political and pedagogical philosophy that there is no reason to encourage reading in Spanish on the part of those citizens who speak the language.

---

* *Lau* v. *Nichols*, 1974 and the 1975 "*Lau* Remedies."

Research almost invariably stresses the endless permutations of oral language production and focuses on the nonstandard elements in that production to the point of giving the impression to the scholar as well as the general public that United States Spanish is a "different language" from what is written in Spanish, except perhaps for "Chicano literature," and that the latter, like all written language, is but a pale shadow of the spoken language. Few investigators seem to realize that a significant proportion of those who speak Spanish in the United States also can and do read it, that the nonstandard aspects of the language comprise only a small proportion of all the utterances made in Spanish in the United States in any one day, and that most of these are similar to utterances produced in Spain and Spanish-American countries. One even finds much of what is listed as the nonstandard Spanish of South Texas or Detroit or Los Angeles written in such classic works of literature as the Argentinian gaucho epic "Martín Fierro." Rosaura Sánchez (1972) has catalogued many of these characteristics.

It may be true that "no society can be motivated to maintain two languages if they are really functionally redundant" (Fishman, quoted in Jacobson, 1975, p. 125), but differences in the functions of Spanish and English as written languages may be both more subtle and more significant than generally supposed. One of the Spanish functions, for example, is to express an intensity of emotion which is rarely expressed in English without embarrassment or even shame. Taking another example from first-grade readers (O'Donnell, 1972a, p. 110, and Domínguez Aguirre and León González, 1960, p. 108), consider the representation of friendship:

David and I

I like to play ball with David.
We like to climb a *tree*.
This morning I said to my mother,
"May he stay and eat with me?"

"We are out of ice cream," said Mother.
But I said just in fun,
"All he wants is a hamburger,
A hamburger on a b . . ."

Dos rosas*

Cultivo una rosa blanca
en junio como en enero

---

*I grow a white rose / in June as in January / for the sincere friend / who gives me his open hand. /   And for the cruel one who tears out / the heart with which I live / I grow neither thistle nor nettle / I grow a white rose. (Translation by C. Christian)

> para el amigo sincero
> que me da su mano franca.
>
> Y para el cruel que me arranca
> el corazón con que vivo,
> cardo ni ortiga cultivo,
> cultivo una rosa blanca.

—José Martí

This type of contrast is represented in the prose of the two books as well as in the poetry. Admittedly, the "function" of both the poems in this context is to teach reading; however, the function of the *reading* is to contribute to the formation of attitudes, values, and character appropriate to the corresponding culture. The children whose home language is Spanish are pressured, by reading the English poem, to change their culture as well as their language.

The lack of representation of local dialectical peculiarities in Spanish reading textbooks seems not to be a problem in any country or area where Spanish reading is taught, since materials from all countries are found in almost all textbooks. There is, of course, a tendency for there to be a greater proportion of materials from the country where the book is used, but almost every aspect of the dialect used is international or "standard" Spanish, although in every country there are the same kinds of *spoken* variations as exist in the United States. Critics of the use of the standard tend to concentrate on a few lexical items which vary by region, as, for example, the use of the word *dado* in the Mexican reader to refer to a child's building block whereas the Anglicism *bloque* would probably be used in the United States.

Emphasis on the nonstandard aspects of U.S. Spanish dialects has been such that many native speakers do not know when they are speaking standard Spanish; one university teacher asked a group of Mexican-American students to make a list of "Chicano" words and was given a list of 42 words, 38 of which were in use in other countries and 30 of which were standard literate Spanish everywhere. Literacy provides awareness of language generally understood, outside every local group. A person who assumes that his or her language variety is understood only locally is unlikely to attempt to develop the ability to use the language in other situations or places.

Many of the dialectical variations of Spanish found in the United States are found also in masterpieces of Hispanic literature in such works as the Argentine *Martín Fierro:* "*y ansina* me *vide* pronto *obligao* a andar *juyendo*" and the Spanish (Castilian) *La malquerida:* "si *hubiea querío* recordarse, no *hubiea* usted *sabío* decir lo que había *hablao*." Through study of literature, students learn in what social levels, under what circumstances, and in what regions language such as this is found. On the other hand, since standard Spanish tends toward the pronunciation of every written letter, and the representation of every element of sound in writing, they learn standard pronunciation through reading, i.e., *aire* instead of *aigre*. However, when they *write* before they are very familiar with reading, they follow this rule and write the sounds as they make them—and language teachers attack them body and soul.

Once reading abilities are developed, a language may be developed as well as maintained with little or no continuing contact with others who speak it, and the spoken language can be expanded to new levels of usefulness where there are groups of people who use it. Neither tendency is favored by the propagation of the idea—too often associated with scholarly research—that there is an abyss between dialects of Spanish spoken in the United States and the standard written form of the language. This notion may result in large part from the forms of professional bias described.

REFERENCES

Andersson, Theodore; Past, Alvin W.; and Past, Kay E. "Early Childhood: The Best Time to Become Bilingual and Biliterate." *Childhood Education*, 54 (1978), 155–61.

Andersson, Theodore, and Boyer, Mildred. *Bilingual Schooling in the United States*. 2d ed. Austin, Tex.: National Educational Laboratory Publishers, 1978.

Baker, Pauline. *Español para los hispanos*. Skokie, Ill.: National Textbook Company, 1966.

Barker, Marie Eastman. *Español para el bilingüe*. Skokie, Ill., National Textbook Company, 1972.

Bettelheim, Bruno. "Learning to Read." *Harpers* (April 1978), pp. 56–58.

Bloomfield, L. *Language*. New York: Holt, 1933.

Christian, Chester C., Jr. "Social and Psychological Implications of Bilingual Literacy." In *The Bilingual Child: Research and Analysis of Existing Educational Themes*, ed. António Simões, Jr. New York: Academic Press, 1976.

———. "Early Reading in Spanish," Unpublished manuscript, 1978.

———. "Minority Language Skills Before Age Three." In *Bilingualism in Early Childhood*, ed. William F. Mackey and Theodore Andersson. Rowley, Mass.: Newbury House, 1977.

Doman, Glenn, and Melcher, Daniel. "How Brain-Injured Children Learn to Read." In *Bilingual Schooling in the United States*, 2d. ed., ed. Theodore Andersson and Mildred Boyer. Austin, Tex.: National Educational Laboratory Publishers, 1978.

Domínguez Aguirre, C., and León González, E. *Mi libro de primer año*. México, D.F.: Secretaría de Educación Pública, 1960, pp. 90–91, 108.

Ebel, Carolyn, interviewer. "Josué González Named OBE Director," NABE News, II, no. 1 (November 1978), 1.

Fishman, Joshua A. *Readings in the Sociology of Language.* The Hague: Mouton, 1968.

———. *The Sociology of Language.* Rowley, Mass.: Newbury House, 1972.

Fishman, Joshua A.; Hayden, Robert G.; and Warshauer, Mary E. "The Non-English and the Ethnic Group Press, 1910–1960." In *Language Loyalty in the United States,* ed. Joshua A. Fishman. The Hague: Mouton, 1976, pp. 51–74.

Gaarder, A. Bruce. "Statement of A. Bruce Gaarder, Chief, Modern Foreign Language Section, U. S. Office of Education." *Hearings Before the Special Subcommittee on Bilingual Education of the Committee on Labor and Public Welfare, Part I.* Washington, D.C.: U.S. Government Printing Office, 1967.

Galicia Ciprés, Paula. *Mi libro de segundo año.* México, D.F.: Secretaría de Educación Pública, 1960.

Humboldt, Wilhelm von. *Linguistic Variability and Intellectual Development.* Coral Gables: Miami Linguistic Series, 1971.

Jacobson, Rodolfo. "The Dilemma of Bilingual Education Models: Duplication or Compartmentalization." In *New Directions in Second Language Learning, Teaching, and Bilingual Education,* ed. M. Burt and H. Dulay. Washington, D.C.: TESOL, 1975.

Kuvlesky, W. P. "Use of Spanish and Aspirations for Social Mobility Among Chicanos: A Synthesis and Evaluation of Texas and Colorado Findings." College Station, Tex.: Author, 1973.

O'Donnell, Mabel, *Something to Tell.* New York: Harper & Row, 1972a, pp. 80, 110.

———. *Sunshine and Shadows.* New York: Harper & Row, 1972b.

Ornstein, Jacob, and Gage, W. "Language and Myths About Language." In *Language: An Introductory Reader,* ed. J.B. Hogins and R. E. Yarber. New York: Harper and Row, 1969.

Past, Alvin W. *Preschool Reading in Two Languages as a Factor in Bilingualism.* Ph.D. dissertation, University of Texas at Austin, 1976.

Past, Kay E. *Reading in Two Languages from Age Two: A Case Study.* M.A. thesis, University of Texas at Austin, 1975.

Patella, V. M., and Kuvlesky, W. P. "Bilingual Patterns of Nonmetropolitan Mexican-American Youth: Variations by Social Context, Language Use, and Historical Change." College Station, Tex.: Unpublished manuscript, 1975.

Sánchez, Rosaura. "Nuestra circunstancia lingüística," *El Grito,* 6, 1 (Fall 1972), 45–74.

Valdés-Fallis, Guadalupe. "Spanish Language Programs for Hispanic Minorities: Current Needs and Priorities." In *Minority Language and Literature,* ed. Dexter Fisher. New York: Modern Language Association, 1977.

The Instruction of Hispanic American Students: Exploring Their Educational Cognitive Styles

RICHARD E. BAECHER
Fordham University

Authorities in minority groups and bilingual education have documented the low levels of educational development attained by Hispanic American students. (Carter, 1970; Coleman, 1966; Fitzpatrick, 1971; Liem, 1972; Moore, 1970; Steinberg, 1974). Various reasons are stated for these low achievement levels: (1) language and cultural experiences, (2) socioeconomic status, (3) school experiences, and (4) inadequate testing (Andersson and Boyer, 1970; Cannon, 1971; Cordasco and Bucchioni, 1968; Montenegro, 1972; Plakos, 1971; Robinett, 1971).

Another reason is the litle attention given to the cultural diversity and learning styles of bilingual students by the educational establishment. Proponents of this psychological approach advocate rigorous research to determine variations and individual differences in learning styles in pupils from different ethnolinguistic groups (Cornejo, 1974; Leichter, 1973; Smithers, 1974; Ramirez and Castañeda, 1974). According to Taba (1966, p. 231), "knowledge of the cognitive styles is needed to provide optimum opportunities for learning."

However, theories pertaining to "learning styles," "cognitive styles," "socialization styles," and "educative styles," to mention a few, represent a confusing variety of conceptual outlooks to the educational practitioner. Rarely has there been any systematic investigation from an educational framework as to how bilingual pupils come to know the world in which they live and how they relate to it through the use of various symbols.

This paper considers the unique and multiple ways in which Hispanic American students seek meaning in English and Spanish, respectively. What is investigated are the "educational cognitive styles" of these pupils. Little research has been devoted to diagnosing and recording in a systematic manner the cognitive functioning of these pupils that use their cultural and lingual resources. The following basic questions served as research hypotheses of the study:

1. What differences exist among Chicano and Puerto Rican students in listening comprehension, or, "theoretical auditory linguistic" ability, when English and Spanish are employed, respectively?
2. What differences exist among these two groups in reading achievement, or more accurately, "theoretical visual linguistic" ability, in English and Spanish?
3. How do the "collective" cognitive styles of Chicano and Puerto Rican subjects differ with respect to (a) symbolic meaning, (b) cultural influences, and (c) reasoning patterns?

In the past, researchers and educators have neglected to determine specific levels of educational development in listening and reading among Hispanic American pupils, especially in their own native Spanish. Today, much emphasis is placed upon use of the child's language as a medium of instruction in bilingual programs. It follows, then, that information pertaining to an individual's educational development expressed in terms of composite grade levels involving his measured ability in vocabulary, language usage, reading and listening comprehension in Spanish and English has become essential for effective and successful bilingual instruction.

Since an individual's lingual abilities as manifested in listening and reading tasks do not occur in a vacuum but within a context accompanied by other forms of communication and social factors, an analysis of other elements in that individual's "cognitive style" is required. Such an assessment, based upon subcultural and cognitive textures, can provide important data to make comparisons between an individual's unique strengths and those that characterize the group of which he may be a member. With this information, educational practitioners can initiate individualized group instruction for bilingual/bicultural students.

A brief description of the educational science of cognitive style, as defined by Hill (1968; 1970; 1972; 1981), will clarify the author's educational framework. The approach within the Educational Sciences attempts to describe a broad pattern of consistent cognitive behavior using symbolic language to represent preferences for different types of symbols, preferred cultural roles, and preferred reasoning patterns. Cognitive style, then, is a relative concept that attempts to dynamically describe an individual's predominant mode of behavior in coming to know. Specifically, cognitive style is identified in an individual's disposition to: (1) use certain types of symbolic forms versus others, e.g., English and Spanish symbols, (2) derive meaning of symbols from the cultural role the individual finds most satisfying, and (3) use one reasoning pattern in preference to others in reaching conclusions from assorted data. (See Berry, Sutton, McBeth, 1975; and Appendix A, "Explaining the Educational Cognitive Style Map," at the end of this paper, for more information.) A graphic representation of the elements included within the three sets, i.e., Symbols, Cultural Determinants, and Modalities of Inference, is called a "map." This map provides a picture of the way in which the individual derives meaning from his environment based upon his symbolic orientations, personal experiences, and methods of reasoning. (See Appendix B, "Illustrated Cognitive Style Map-Profiles," for a list of variables investigated in the present study.)

METHOD OF DATA ACQUISITION

Subjects.   The student group consisted of 20 Puerto Ricans and 13 Chicanos who were in the fourth and fifth grades (Spring 1973) of a bilingual program in Pontiac, Michigan. Both grades were treated as a single unit in the program and were designated as "team 002." The Puerto Rican subjects had a mean age of 11 years and had resided in Pontiac an average of 2.5 years. The Chicano students averaged 9 years in age and had lived in Pontiac an average of 3.5 years.

The samples employed in the study can be described as "purposive," i.e., they were selected on the basis of what the researcher considered from his past experience to be a typical, or representative, sample. (Hill and Kerber, 1967, p. 43). The samples were representative insofar as the subjects were: (1) of Chicano and Puerto Rican background, (2) enrolled in the Pontiac bilingual program for the 1972–73 school year, (3) currently in the fourth and fifth grades, (4) bilingual to a certain degree in English and Spanish, and (5) approximately 80% of the total number of Hispanic American students in these grades. It was reasoned that this purposive, small sample would allow intensive analysis of their educational cognitive styles.

Procedures.   Initially, all the students belonging to team 002 were individually administered an interview schedule (based on Spolsky, Murphy, et al., 1972), by the bilingual personnel of the program in December, 1972. Its purpose was to ascertain each student's use of English and Spanish at home. Only those subjects who communicated in both languages at home were selected for further cognitive style mapping. Each pupil was asked the language he used with certain individuals, e.g., members of the family, teachers, friends, and his attitude toward speaking Spanish. Responses were coded as "Spanish dominant," "English dominant," and "Spanish-English."

As part of the process to adapt the standardized basic skills tests (Fishman, 1964), all pupils were administered a research-constructed "student interest questionnaire," thereby yielding information concerning the subject's interest in reading books, magazines, playing games and watching television. These data were collected by the bilingual staff, appropriately categorized, and served in the adaptation of the instruments.

Next, oral and written forms of selected subtests of the Iowa Tests of Basic Skills (Levels 9, 10, 11) were given in English and Spanish to all the subjects on a volunteer basis. (Out of a total of 6 tests administered to 33 students, 7 subjects decided not to take the Spanish vocabulary and grammar tests.) The vocabulary, language usage and reading subtests were modified, adapted, and administered by the bilingual staff under the direction of the author. Each subtest and its most appropriate level (9, 10, 11) was individually determined for each subject. For instance, one student may have received a level 10 listening test, level 11 vocabulary, and a level 9 grammar test, depending upon his teacher's judgment. The vocabulary subtest included Chicano, Puerto Rican, and basic Spanish items, e.g., "ranchero," "guagua." The Spanish grammar subtest followed Catford's model on translation (1965) and his suggestion on "level shifts," i.e., word level to phrase level translation shifts. These efforts—using bilingual examiners, lexical items from the subject's home language, and the appropriate level—were interpreted as enhancing the content validity of the instruments, thereby yielding efficient scores for the respective elements of cognitive style.

The listening comprehension subtest, adapted from parts of the reading test, was administered in the following manner: (1) a Mexican American taped the Chicano version; (2) a Puerto Rican teacher intern taped the version for the Puerto Rican pupils, and (3) the author recorded the English version. With not more than 4 students at any one testing session, pupils were instructed to listen to a series of passages and to respond to questions that were written.

All the subtests including listening were scored in percentiles according to the *Teacher's Guide* for administration and interpretation of the Iowa tests. These data were then used to determine the levels of educational development for the cognitive style elements of: "theoretical auditory linguistic" (listening to spoken symbols), and "theoretical visual linguistic" (obtaining meaning from printed symbols).

In the final stage of the study, a self-report inventory, translated and modified from the Oakland Community College Cognitive Style test battery, was administered to each subject in either Spanish or English.

Each student responded to questions that probed selected cognitive style elements, i.e., "qualitative code empathetic," "qualitative code ethic," cultural determinants, and modalities of inference. (See Appendix A for a listing of the elements in the study). All the diagnostic testing, or cognitive style mapping, was completed in the first three months of 1973.

Responses for the Iowa Tests of Basic Skills and the Cognitive Style Inventory-Selected Elements were recorded according to these principles:

I. If the bilingual student manifests an element in the 50-99th percentile range, i.e., in the top half of the population exhibiting such an element, then assign a *major* orientation in the element to that pupil.

II. If the element is placed in the 26-49th percentile range of the population, assign a *minor* orientation in the element.

III. If the element lies in the 0-25th percentile range of the distribution, i.e., in the lowest quarter of the distribution, then assign a *negligible* orientation in the element, meaning that the respective element does not appear on the student's map. (Radike, 1973, p. 18)

Data derived from these instruments were recorded for all 33 subjects and by means of the process of "empirical mapping," i.e., classifying the cognitive style elements on a "makes sense" or "doesn't make sense" basis, cognitive style maps were formulated. The original study includes all the maps with test scores (Baecher, 1973).

METHOD OF DATA ANALYSIS

The Kolmogorov-Smirnov statistical test model was applied to find out whether the two samples were drawn from the same population. This two-sample test is concerned with the degree of agreement between the two cumulative distributions of the relative frequencies observed in the respective samples (Siegel, 1956, p. 127). Since the samples were small in size and the level of data was ordinal in nature, the Kolmogorov-Smirnov test was the most appropriate and sensitive. The significance level for each null hypothesis (16 in all) was set at .05.

The second analytical technique applied to the data was called "comparative analysis" (Good and Scates, 1954, p. 260). It supplemented those descriptions and interpretations of data that were uncovered from the Kolmogorov-Smirnov test. In the original study (Baecher, 1973, p. 100), this technique is illustrated by showing how the elements in the cognitive style of an individual are compared with the elements comprising the "collective" cognitive style map of the group of which the student is a member.

The validity and reliability of the instruments were reported and explained in terms of content validity and domain sampling theory. It was concluded that the instruments were of high content validity because of the procedures followed by the bilingual personnel in the administration and modification of the instruments. The reliability coefficients for the listening and reading tests were .86 and .84 respectively. For the "empirical mapping" technique, the Kuder-Richardson Formula 20 yielded a .675 reliability coefficient. More information pertaining to these characteristics of instrumentality construction is contained in the original study.

RESULTS

1. Chicano students in the bilingual program were found to have higher listening comprehension achievement than Puerto Rican students. The listening in English and Spanish, respectively (Max De for T $(AL)_e$ = .466, p<.05; Max De for T $(AL)_s$ = .466, p<.05) (Table 1). There were proportionately more "majors" in listening ability in both languages among the Chicano students than among the Puerto Rican subjects (Table 1).

The average level of educational development, i.e., composite grade level for the Puerto Rican subjects in listening (English) was fourth grade level below the 50th percentile, and for the Chicano students, the fifth

Table 1

Major and Minor Chicano and Puerto Rican Subjects in "Theoretical" Symbolic Orientations

Element	Chicano	Puerto Rican	Max D_o	Max D_c
Theoretical auditory linguistic—English T $(AL)_e$	9/13	4/20	.492	.466[a]
Minor theoretical auditory linguistic—English T' $(AL)_e$	13/13	20/20		
Theoretical auditory linguistic—Spanish T $(AL)_s$	10/13	6/20	.469	.466[a]
Minor theoretical auditory linguistic—Spanish T' $(AL)_s$	13/13	20/20		
Theoretical visual linguistic—English T $(VL)_e$	0/13	0/20	0	0
Minor theoretical visual linguistic—English T' $(VL)_e$	13/13	20/20		
Theoretical visual linguistic—Spanish T $(VL)_s$	2/13	10/20	.346	.466
Minor theoretical visual linguistic—Spanish T' $(VL)_s$	13/13	20/20		

[a]Significant at the .05 level, consulting Table 17 in Conover (1971, p. 401) for the Kolmogorov-Smirnov two-sample test.

Note: Max D_o refers to maximum difference observed; Max D_c refers to maximum critical value of the distance. Subscripts *e* and *s* refer to the English and Spanish forms of the instruments, respectively.

grade level above the 50th percentile. Listening comprehension (Spanish) for the Puerto Rican subjects was third grade level above the 50th percentile, and for the Chicanos, it was fourth grade level above the 50th percentile (Figure 1).

2. No significant differences were found in reading achievement between the two groups when grade equivalent scores were used. Inspection of the "collective" cognitive style maps for both groups indicates that the Chicano sample was reading approximately one grade level above the Puerto Rican sample in English (Table 2).

Moreover, significant differences did not occur in general ability to acquire meaning from printed materials, i.e., "theoretical visual linguistic" ability, T(VL). The average level of educational development for Puerto Rican subjects in this element was second grade level below the 50th percentile (English and Spanish). For the Chicano subjects, the average level was third grade below the 50th percentile (English and Spanish) (Table 2).

3. The Chicano sample did not differ significantly from the Puerto Rican sample in these elements: "qualitative code empathetic," "qualitative code ethic," cultural determinants, and modalities of inference. However, inspection of the "collective" cognitive style maps of each

Figure 1
Level of Educational Development

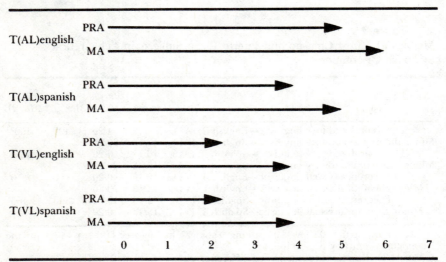

Note: Average Levels of Educational Development in T(AL) and T(VL) for Puerto Rican American (PRA) and Mexican American (MA) subjects.

Table 2

Collective Cognitive Style Map of Mexican American Students in the Fourth and Fifth Grades

Present Grade: *4–5*   Mean Age: *9.3*   Ethnic Origin: *MA*   Mean Months in Pontiac: *41*

I. Symbolic Orientations   II. Cultural Determinants   III. Modalities of Inference

$$
g = \left\{
\begin{array}{cc}
\overset{5}{\text{T(AL)e}} & \overset{3}{\text{T'(VL)e}} \\
\\
\overset{4}{\text{T(AL)s}} & \overset{3}{\text{T'(VL)s}} \\
\text{Q'(CEM)} & \\
\text{Q'(CET)} &
\end{array}
\right\}
\times
\left\{
\begin{array}{c}
\text{I} \\
\\
\text{F'}
\end{array}
\right\}
\times
\left\{
\begin{array}{c}
\text{M} \\
\\
\text{D'}
\end{array}
\right\}
$$

Collective Cognitive Style Map of Puerto Rican American Students in the Fourth and Fifth Grades

Present Grade: *4–5*   Mean Age: *11.06*   Ethnic Origin: *PRA*   Mean Months in Pontiac: *30.7*

I. Symbolic Orientations   II. Cultural Determinants   III. Modalities of Inference

$$
g = \left\{
\begin{array}{cc}
\overset{4}{\text{T'(AL)e}} & \overset{2}{\text{T'(VL)e}} \\
\\
\overset{3}{\text{T(AL)s}} & \overset{2}{\text{T'(VL)s}} \\
\text{Q'(CEM)} & \\
\text{Q'(CET)} &
\end{array}
\right\}
\times
\left\{
\begin{array}{c}
\text{I} \\
\\
\text{F'}
\end{array}
\right\}
\times
\left\{
\begin{array}{c}
\text{M} \\
\\
\text{R'} \\
\text{D'}
\end{array}
\right\}
$$

group (Table 2) indicates that the majority of the subjects were assigned *minor* orientations in "qualitative code empathetic," and "qualitative code ethic," i.e., in the 26–49th percentile range.

Additionally, both groups exhibited a strong "individuality" (I) element among cultural influences, tempered by a minor "family" influence (F'). With respect to modalities of inference, both samples indicated a preferred "magnitude" orientation (M), i.e., a preference to think in terms of categories and classifications, and the Puerto Rican subjects manifested an additional element, "relationships" (R'), in their cognitive style, meaning the tendency to reason in terms of relationships in making decisions (Table 2).

DISCUSSION

This study has demonstrated that the educational science of cognitive style, as defined by Hill (1981), can be used in a fruitful way with Hispanic American students. It was shown that the educational cognitive styles of Chicano and Puerto Rican samples can be identified in a coherent and systematic fashion. This represents a definite advantage among the variety of educational theories that are being proposed for the study of bilingual students.

Through such instruments as modified standardized tests, listening tests, and self-report assessment inventories, specific levels of educational development were derived for each subject. Provided the lingual and cultural backgrounds of the subjects are seriously taken into account in any diagnostic procedures, such attempts are successful and accurate, thereby providing teachers with realistic estimates of the current strengths of their pupils. Furthermore, through the technique of "empirical mapping," i.e., classifying and judging the presence or absence of cognitive style elements, teachers can be directly involved in discovering ways to observe, listen to, and elicit cognitive style elements. The involvement and participation of the bilingual and monolingual staff in the study confirms the feasibility of this technique.

While significant differences were found between both groups in listening ability (English and Spanish), their "collective" cognitive style maps indicated a definite preference for activities involving listening rather than reading for information. One immediate implication of this finding is greater use of this ability in all educational tasks. In addition, this study was the first serious effort to diagnose Hispanic American pupils in their native language in the bilingual program, and the results showed the importance of this procedure, especially for bilingual programs that seek to maintain the student's native tongue.

Another feature of the study is the recognition given to the cultural influences and reasoning patterns exhibited by these students. In other words, the "bicultural" origins and context of these pupils were ascertained in a dynamic way along with their lingual abilities through educational cognitive style. The qualitative knowledge of these subjects, the influence of one's family, friends and individuality, and their preferred reasoning patterns, were integrated and combined within the entire study. This information is essential for prescribing successful education tasks (Baecher, 1975; 1976; 1981; Radike, 1973).

In conclusion, bilingual/bicultural education can benefit from the common language and conceptual framework of educational cognitive style analysis. It offers the teacher an effective diagnostic-prescriptive strategy oriented to individual differences with special focus upon lingual, bicognitive, and cultural factors. Moreover, it offers the researcher a viable and practical theory to conduct systematic educational research and to generate significant hypotheses for future investigation.

REFERENCES

Andersson, Theodore and Boyer, Mildred, 1970. *Bilingual Schooling in the U.S.* Washington, D.C.: U.S. Government Printing Office.

Baecher, Richard E., 1973. "An exploratory study to determine levels of educational development, reading levels, and the cognitive styles of Mexican American and Puerto Rican American students in Michigan." Unpublished doctoral dissertation, University of Michigan, Ann Arbor, Michigan.

———, 1975. "Focusing on the Strengths of Bilingual Students," in L. Golubchick and B. Persky (eds.), *Innovations in education.* Dubuque, Iowa: Kendall-Hunt Publ. Co.

———, 1976. "Bilingual children and educational cognitive style analysis," in A. Simoes (ed.), *The bilingual child: research and analysis of existing themes.* New York: Academic Press.

———, 1981. "Matching the educational cognitive styles of bilingual students and modes of understanding required by bilingual education," in Raymond V. Padilla (ed,), *Bilingual education technology.* Ethnoperspectives in Bilingual Education, Vol. III. Ypsilanti: Department of Foreign Languages, Eastern Michigan University.

Berry, J. J.; Sutton, T.J.: McBeth, L.S., 1975. *Bibliography of the educational sciences with commentary.* Bloomfield Hills, Michigan: The American Educational Sciences Association (2480 Opdyke Road).

Cannon, Garland, 1971. "Bilingual Problems and Development in the United States," *Publications of the Modern Language Association,* 86:452–458.

Carter, Thomas., 1970. *Mexican Americans in school: A history of educational neglect.* New Jersey: College Entrance Examination Board.

Catford, J. C., 1965. *A linguistic theory of translation: An essay in applied linguistics.* London: Oxford University Press.

Coleman, James S., and Associates, 1966. *Equality of educational opportunity.* Washington, D.C.: U.S. Government Printing Office.

Conover, W. J., 1971. *Practical nonparametric statistics.* New York: John Wiley and Sons, Inc.

Cordasco, Francesco, and Bucchioni, Eugene, eds., 1968. *Puerto Rican children in mainland schools: A source book for teachers.* Metuchen, N.J.: The Scarecrow Press, Inc.

Cornejo, Ricardo, 1974. *A synthesis of theories and research on the effects of teaching in first and second languages: Implications for bilingual education.* Austin, Texas: National Educational Laboratory Publishers, Inc.

Fishman, Joshua A., Chairman, 1964. "Guidelines for testing minority group children." *Journal of Social Issues* 20:129–145.

Fitzpatrick, Joseph P., 1971. *Puerto Rican Americans: The meaning of migration to the mainland.* Englewood Cliffs, New Jersey: Prentice-Hall, Inc.

Good, Carter V., and Scates, Douglas E., 1954. *Methods of research: Educational, psychological, sociological.* New York: Appleton-Century-Crofts, Inc.

Hill, Joseph E., 1968. "The educational sciences." Bloomfield Hills, Michigan: Oakland Community College.

———, 1970. "Cognitive style as an educational science." Bloomfield Hills, Michigan: Oakland Community College.

———, 1972. "An outline of the educational sciences." Bloomfield Hills, Michigan: Oakland Community College.

———, 1981. *The educational sciences.* Privately published. Available from Hill Educational Sciences Foundation, P.O. Box 5053, West Bloomfield, MI 48033.

Hill, Joseph E., and Kerber, August, 1967. *Models, methods and analytical procedures in education research.* Detroit: Wayne State University Press.

Leichter, Hope J., 1973. "The concept of educative style." *Teachers College Record,* 75:239–250.

Liem, G. Ramsay, et al., 1972. *A report card for the New York City schools.* Paper commissioned by ASPIRA, Inc.

Montenegro, Raquel, 1972. "Bilingual education: A bandaid for educational neglect," *in Claremont Reading Conference: 36th Yearbook,* edited by Malcolm, D. Douglas. California: Claremont Graduate School.

Moore, Joan W., 1970. *Mexican Americans.* Englewood Cliffs, N.J.: Prentice-Hall, Inc.

Plakos, John, 1971. *Report of survey findings: Assessment of needs of bilingual education programs.* Calmont, Fort Worth, Texas: National Consortia for Bilingual Education.

Radike, Floyd (ed.), 1973. *Handbook for teacher improvement utilizing the educational sciences.* Bloomfield Hills, Michigan: American Educational Sciences Association.

Ramirez, Manuel, and Castaneda, Alfredo, 1974. *Cultural democracy, bicognitive development, and education.* New York: Academic Press.

Robinett, Ralph, 1971. "Teaching of bilingual children," *in The Encyclopedia of Education.* Vol. I. New York: The Macmillan Co. and the Free Press, Crowell-Collier Educational Corp.

Siegel, Sidney, 1956. *Nonparametric statistics for the behavioral sciences.* New York: McGraw-Hill Book Co.

Smithers, James E. P., 1974. "An investigation into the effect of culture and acculturation on the formation of cognitive style." Unpublished dissertation, Wayne State University. Detroit.

Spolsky, Bernard; Murphy, Penny; Holm, Wayne; Ferrel, Allan, 1972. "Three functional tests of oral proficiency." *TESOL Quarterly* 6:221–235.

Steinberg, Lois, 1974. *Report on bilingual education: A study of programs for pupils with English language difficulty in New York City public schools.* New York: Department of Public Affairs, Community Service Society of New York.

Taba, Hilda, 1966. "Cultural deprivation as a factor in school learning" in Judy F. Rosenblith and Wesley Allensmith (eds.), *Causes of Behavior*. Boston: Allyn and Bacon, 2nd edition.

APPENDIX A:
Explaining the Educational Cognitive Style Map

Numerous different elements are included in one's educational cognitive style map. Each element is recorded as a major, a minor, or a negligible score.

A *Major* score means that your score is above average in the element under consideration (50th percentile or above). It is shown as a capital letter, T(VL).

A *Minor* score means that your score is below average in the element (50th percentile) but above the bottom quarter (25th percentile). It is shown as a capital letter with a prime ('), T'(VL).

A *Negligible* score means that your score is below the 25th percentile, indicating a below-minimum preference for using the element in your cognitive style. The element does not appear on the map.

I. Symbols and Their Meanings

*T(AL): Theoretical Auditory Linguistic—Ability to acquire meaning through spoken words, talking, listening.

T(AQ): Theoretical Auditory Quantitative—Acquiring meaning in terms of quantities (numbers, measurements) you hear.

*T(VL): Theoretical Visual Linguistic—Obtaining meaning from words you see and graphic symbols.

T(VQ): Theoretical Visual Quantitative—Ability to find meaning in terms of written quantities, i.e., numerical symbols and measurements that you see.

Q(A): Qualitative Auditory—Ability to perceive meaning through sense of hearing sounds other than words, e.g., tones, pitch, dialects, etc.

Q(O): Qualitative Olfactory—Perceiving meaning through the sense of smell, e.g., odors, aromas.

Q(S): Qualitative Savory—Deriving meaning through taste.

Q(T): Qualitative Tactile—Ability to gain meaning by the sense of touch, e.g., textures, etc.

Q(V): Qualitative Visual—Perceiving meaning through seeing things other than T(VL), e.g., pictures, scenes, etc.

Q(P): Qualitative Proprioceptive—Ability to integrate a number of symbolic mediations into a performance of a complex task, e.g., typewriting, playing a musical instrument; or an immediate awareness of a possible set of inter-relationships between symbolic mediations, i.e., dealing with "signs."

---

*Denotes the variables that were selected and probed for the study.

*Q(CEM): Qualitative Code Empathetic—Sensitivity to another's feelings, ability to put oneself in another person's position.

Q(CES): Qualitative Code Esthetic—Ability to appreciate beauty of an object or an idea, e.g., in music, art, nature; well-turned phrase.

*Q(CET): Qualitative Code Ethic—Dedication to a specific value system, a group of moral principles, obligations and/or duties.

Q(CH): Qualitative Code Histrionic—Ability to deliberately stage behavior to produce some particular effect on other persons, e.g., good actor.

Q(CK): Qualitative Code Kinesic—Communicating by non-linguistic functions such as facial expressions and body movements, e.g., smiles and gestures.

Q(CKH): Qualitative Code Kinesthetics—Motor skills, muscular coordination with correct form, e.g., sports or tasks where skillful use of hands is involved.

Q(CP): Qualitative Code Proxemics—Ability to behave with appropriate physical and social distance as defined by the other person.

Q(CS): Qualitative Code Synnoetics—Personal knowledge of oneself objectively in qualitative and theoretical forms in relation to one's environment, e.g., setting realistic goals.

Q(CT): Qualitative Code Transactional—Ability to communicate with others in a way that significantly influences their goals, e.g., salesmanship.

Q(CTM): Qualitative Code Temporal—Ability to respond according to time expectations imposed on an activity by members in the role-set associated with that activity, e.g., timed tests, language drills, etc.

II. Cultural Determinants

*A: Associates—Interpreting symbolic information predominantly as one's associates or peers do.

*F: Family—Interpreting symbolic data predominantly in ways which have been learned from one's family.

*I: Individual—Interpreting symbolic information predominantly from one's own perspective independently arrived at.

III. Modalities of Inference

*M: Magnitude—Inductive reasoning process that utilizes norms, rules, and definitions to draw conclusions; a form of "categorical thinking."

*D: Difference—Inductive reasoning pattern that uses one-to-one contrasts or comparisons of selected characteristics or measurements in reaching a decision.

---

*Denotes the variables that were selected and probed for the study.

*R: Relationship—Inductive reasoning process that synthesizes a multitude of relationships between two or more characteristics or measurements.

*L: Appraisal—Reasoning process that employs all three of the above approaches giving equal weight to each.

®: Circle K—Deductive reasoning or logical proof that yields a necessary conclusion derived from given information.

APPENDIX B:

Illustrated Cognitive Style Map-Profiles

Bilingual Student Number One

Present Grade: 4th   Sex: M   Ethnic Origin: 5.0 Reading Grade (Eng)
Age: 9 yrs. 10 mos. Mexican American   2.7 Reading Grade (Sp)

$$g = \left\{ \begin{array}{cc} 5 & 4 \\ T(AL)e & T'(VL)e \\ 4 & 3 \\ T(AL)s & T'(VL)s \\ Q(CET)e & \end{array} \right\} \times \left\{ Ie \right\} \times \left\{ \begin{array}{c} Me \\ D'e \end{array} \right\}$$

In narrative form, the "map" would read as follows:

$$\left\{ \begin{array}{l} \text{Processes information} \\ \text{better through listen-} \\ \text{ing than through read-} \\ \text{ing printed materials,} \\ \text{in both English and} \\ \text{Spanish.} \\ \text{Can dedicate himself to} \\ \text{a set of values and} \\ \text{rules; works diligently} \\ \text{at educational assign-} \\ \text{ments; requires little or} \\ \text{no supervision.} \end{array} \right\} \times \left\{ \begin{array}{l} \text{Is an individualist and} \\ \text{prefers to make up his} \\ \text{own mind; likes to} \\ \text{work alone and define} \\ \text{things in his own} \\ \text{words.} \end{array} \right\} \times \left\{ \begin{array}{l} \text{Categorizes and classi-} \\ \text{fies things and events} \\ \text{according to obvious} \\ \text{features; likes to follow} \\ \text{specific directions.} \\ \text{Compares and con-} \\ \text{trasts on a one-to-one} \\ \text{basis; perceives many} \\ \text{differences.} \end{array} \right\}$$

Note: e refers to the English form of the instrument; s refers to the Spanish form of the instrument.

Source: Adapted from Baecher, 1973, p. 158.

---

*Denotes the variables that were selected and probed for the study.

Bilingual Student Number Two

Present Grade: 4th   Sex: M   Ethnic Origin: 5.1 Reading Grade (Eng)
                      Age: 9 yrs. 11 mos. Puerto Rican   3.1 Reading Grade (Sp)

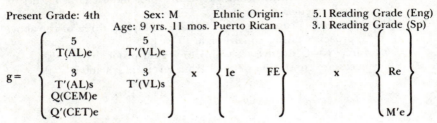

$$g = \begin{Bmatrix} 5 \\ T(AL)e \\ 3 \\ T'(AL)s \\ Q(CEM)e \\ Q'(CET)e \end{Bmatrix} \begin{matrix} 5 \\ T'(VL)e \\ 3 \\ T'(VL)s \end{matrix} \times \begin{Bmatrix} Ie \quad FE \end{Bmatrix} \times \begin{Bmatrix} Re \\ \\ M'e \end{Bmatrix}$$

In narrative form, it would look like this:

Processes oral and written information in English equally well, and is above grade level . . . Shows listening and reading abilities one grade level below in Spanish . . . Identifies with the feelings of others; shows concern for others; helps his peers with their work. Completes tasks assigned.	Acts independently; makes his own decisions. Will take directions from authority figure; relates home and family experiences often.	Sees relationships among things, events and qualities; likes examples in doing educational tasks; sees similarities . . . Makes statements of fact; classifies objects.

Note to both profiles: e refers to the English form of the instrument; s refers to the Spanish form of the instrument.

Source of both profiles: Adapted from Baecher, 1973, pp. 173, 190.

Bilingual Student Number Three

Present Grade: 5th	Sex: M	Ethnic Origin	2.5 Reading Grade (Eng)
	Age 14 yrs. 6 mos.	Puerto Rican	2.7 Reading Grade (Sp)

$$g = \left\{ \begin{matrix} \overset{2}{T'(AL)e} & \overset{2}{T'(VL)e} \\ \overset{2}{T(AL)s} & \overset{2}{T'(VL)s} \\ Q(CEM)s & \\ Q'(CET)s & \end{matrix} \right\} \times \left\{ \begin{matrix} As \\ \\ F's \end{matrix} \right\} \times \left\{ \begin{matrix} Ds \\ \\ M's \end{matrix} \right\}$$

In narrative form, it would look like this:

$\left\{ \begin{matrix} \text{Acquires meaning from symbols in oral and visual form about the same in English and Spanish, but at the second grade level.} \\ \text{Empathizes with others.} \\ \text{Capable of dedicating himself to a set of rules and principles.} \end{matrix} \right\}$ x $\left\{ \begin{matrix} \text{Strongly influenced by his peers; likes to work in groups; seeks and follows the suggestions of others.} \\ \text{Sometimes prefers to have teachers explain and not classmates.} \end{matrix} \right\}$ x $\left\{ \begin{matrix} \text{Contrasts objects and events on a one-to-one basis; quick in identifying differences in shape, color, size; divides.} \\ \text{Appeals to rules and standards in making decisions.} \end{matrix} \right\}$

VI | How Young Children Become Bilingual

Language Acquisition
in the Bilingual Child

AMADO M. PADILLA
ELLEN LIEBMAN
University of California, Los Angeles

The study of language acquisition in children has become increasingly important in recent years. From the normative studies of the 1930s (McCarthy, 1954), we have age-related milestones for the language development of children. From the more recent psycholinguistic research based on transformational grammar (Brown and Bellugi, 1964; Chomsky, 1957, 1965; Menyuk, 1969) we know further that a child's language is not acquired through a simple associational learning process but rather with the grasp of a complex set of rules underlying the structure of language.

The psycholinguistic research is beginning to demonstrate that there are definite relationships between linguistic and cognitive universals (Slobin, 1971). That is, when describing child language, researchers suggest that there are relationships between psychological and linguistic processes that occur from the inception of an idea to its actual phonological manifestation and from the time the child begins to utter his first word until he becomes an adult user of the language. The best indication of these universals is that children all over the world learn language according to a set of underlying principles that appear to be the same. There appears to be a series of processes that all children progress through in acquiring language.

The first stage in language acquisition is that of one-word speech. This stage occurs somewhere between 8 and 17 months. One-word speech is described as holophrastic or "rich in meaning" (McNeill, 1966). That is, a single word may mean a complex set of ideas. Speech at this stage is also predicative in that the child generally lacks verbs. However, he

This report is an expanded version of a paper presented at the annual meetings of the Western Psychological Association, San Francisco, 1974.

The research reported in this study was funded by a grant from the University of California at Santa Barbara Senate Research Committee.

seems to be saying something about the world. For instance, if the child says "milk," he may mean "I want milk," or "there is a glass of milk sitting on the table," or "give me a glass of milk." Along with this, at the one-word stage, it is important to note that any description of a child's language at this point must be based upon how the observer interprets the situation and the utterances. The child at this stage cannot use his speech to elaborate or to get his meaning across at all times. Thus as Bloom (1970) has pointed out, it is important to include the context of the utterance in an attempt to make the meaning of that utterance clearer.

Brown (1973) described child language in terms of five stages through which a child progresses. He uses a range of the Mean Length of Utterance which increases with age to characterize each stage. Thus instead of dividing each stage up in terms of the number of words per stage, Mean Length of Utterance (MLU) is more indicative of development than are number of words per utterance per stage.

Stage I of Brown's description is characterized by the use of semantic roles. Speech at this stage is analyzed in terms of meaning and inferences of the observer. It has been called "telegraphic speech" because the child communicates using only content words (nouns and verbs) much like a telegram (e.g., ball go, play that, give me).

The retention of content words and omission of functor words (adjectives, adverbs, prepositions, articles) is also found in imitation tasks of very young children (Ervin, 1964). Word order is maintained along with stressed words. It also appears that even when children progress past this stage of development, they revert back to it during imitation tasks. This suggests that language acquisition is a continuous process. Before progressing to a new stage, the child must have control of earlier structures. Brown (1973) calls this phenomenon the process of cumulative complexity.

Stage II involves the modulation of meaning. At this stage, the child begins to use functor words. Meaning now becomes more elaborated (i.e., "eat Ellen coffee," "man do that"). At Stage III, the child begins to use different modalities. The child now appears to be using simple forms of negative, question, and imperative sentences (e.g., no go, no play; where my dog? what that? give me that, play with that). Stage IV involves the use of different types of embedding and it is at this point that the child's speech begins to resemble an adult's. Finally, Stage V is characterized by coordination and conjunction of simple sentences with the use of "and," "but," "or," etc.

Brown (1973) analyzes the language development process of children acquiring different languages. He describes the acquisition of different languages within the framework of his five stages of cumulative complexity of language acquisition. Clearly Brown's analysis points out that all children acquire language at different rates even though they all progress through the same invariant stages.

Child Bilingualism

In spite of the growing interest in developmental psycholinguistics, most researchers have concentrated their efforts on the acquisition of one language. There is a noticeable lack of literature on bilingual language acquisition. Slobin (1971) has suggested that in studying bilingual children, psycholinguistics may be provided with answers to some of the complexities of the formal rules of languages. This may, in turn, yield information regarding the rule making abilities of all speakers.

Prior to the advent of structural linguistics, Leopold (1939, 1947, 1949a, b) recorded, over a four year period, detailed language samples of his German and English-speaking daughter. As such, it was mainly a diary-type study. In this classic study, the language samples included discussions of the contexts of many utterances, development of vocabulary and parts of speech, and the problems which the child seemed to encounter as she learned two languages simultaneously. The study lacks linguistic analysis of the language samples.

Burling (1959) observed his Garo-and English-speaking son over a two year period. This study describes the child's phonological development in two languages by comparing the child's development of English and Garo sounds. Another study is that of Imedadze (as reported by Slobin, 1971), who studied her Russian-Georgian-speaking daughter's language development over a period of several years.

The most in-depth study of child bilingualism to date suggests that the simultaneous acquisition of two languages does not differ significantly from the acquisition of a single language (Swain, 1972). Swain suggests that a child, whether in a bilingual or in a monolingual environment, uses a single set of rules in the learning of a language in his particular "linguistic milieu." That is to say, that as any child learns to speak, there is an initial stage of code mixing found to be universal in linguistic acquisition.

This argument is based on the author's definition of a code as

> any linguistic system used for interpersonal communication . . . languages, dialects, and varieties of dialects are thus all examples of codes . . . in the case of the "bilingual" individual it is argued that the codes used and the switches made are simply more obvious to the listener than in the case of a monolingual individual. To the user of the code, whether the code is a language, a dialect, or a variety of a dialect, it is not at all clear that the bilingual/monolingual distintion is a meaningful one. (p. 4)

Thus, in order to determine how Swain suggests an initial period where one set of rules is used, it is important to look at her definition of a code.

Swain further suggests that following this initial period of code mixing, the rules of each code begin to differentiate. At this stage the child starts using a different set of rules for each of his languages. Consequently, Swain suggests that bilingual language development is 4 to 5 months behind monolingual language development because the bilingual child has more to acquire and differentiate than the monolingual child. This suggestion is based upon Swain's study of wh- and yes/no questions in bilingual (French and English) children. However, when reviewing the development of language in children, it is important to recognize that even for monolingual speakers there are different rates of development. Swain seems to suggest that there is one and only one age at which a child will acquire and produce a form.

Though the study to be described below concerns itself only with bilingual (Spanish and English) children, the methods employed in the description of monolingual language acquisition have been used to gather a corpus of language for analysis. Since the study involves the development of more than one language, an overview of the theories and research on adult bilingualism is provided as a background from which to understand the simultaneous acquisition of the two languages in children.

Theories and Research on Bilingualism

In an attempt to define or describe what is meant by the term "bilingualism," psychologists have devised several distinctions between different types of bilingual speaker-listeners. Several attempts have tended to place bilingual speaker-listeners on a continuum of proficiency in order to determine the speaker-listeners' dominance, or lack thereof, in one or the other of his languages (e.g., Lambert, Havelka, and Gardner, 1959). Rating scales based upon frequency of usage in different environments, use of reaction time tasks in recall for both languages, and tests of the speaker-listener's ability to translate passages have also been used to determine the degree of bilingualism or the degree of bilingual proficiency of the speaker-listener (MacNamara, 1967).

Another method of defining bilingualism is based upon the encoding and decoding skills of the speaker-listener (MacNamara, 1967). MacNamara argues that when we use a language, there are many different levels at which we function. For instance, a user of a language is basically able to encode (i.e., production skills) a language by speaking or writing or both. Within any of these four skills (listening, speaking, reading, writing) the speaker-listener processes language at the phonological level, the lexical level, the syntactic level, and the semantic level. For the bilingual speaker-listener, two languages are involved and the complexity of language usage is doubled. Thus, the bilingual: (a) uses encoding and decoding skills in his two languages; and (b) as a result may or may not be proficient when processing each of the different levels in two languages.

The first attempt to determine the psychological processes of a bilingual speaker-listener is that of the compound-coordinate distinction developed originally by Weinreich (1953) and later elaborated upon by Ervin and Osgood (1954). This distinction refers to the semantic aspects of language in an attempt to distinguish different bilingual speaker-listener patterns in psychological processing. An example of a compound bilingual is one who has acquired his languages in a home where two languages are spoken interchangeably by the same people in the same situations (Ervin-Tripp, 1973, p. 16). Consequently, this speaker-listener attributes identical meanings to corresponding words and expressions in his two languages. Hence, the meaning of alternate linguistic signs (i.e., one in English—horse, and one in Spanish—*caballo*) is coded with the same meaning within the nervous system.

The coordinate bilingual differs in that this speaker-listener has learned his two languages in different situational contexts (e.g., one language at home, another at school, or first the mother language and then a second language). The important consideration here is that the linguistic signs in one language (i.e., horse) have different representations in the nervous system for the same set of signs in the other language (i.e., *caballo*). Thus, although the compound/coordinate distinction is a semantic one, it is based on where and how the bilingual speaker-listener learned his languages.

In an attempt to characterize how a bilingual speaker-listener uses his two languages, Kolers (1968) has suggested that the bilingual speaker-listener processes and stores in memory lexical items from each of his two languages in one of two ways: (1) in one storage bin where the lexical items from both languages are kept, or (2) in two separate storage bins—one bin for the first language and another bin for the second language. The process of storing and retrieving lexical items from separate storage bins has been called linguistic independence. As Kolers further suggests, with regard to the bilingual speaker-listener, a combination of both the separate and shared processing systems is probably the best description of how a bilingual speaker-listener stores and retrieves lexical items from memory.

Another approach used in describing bilingualism suggests that certain social factors play an important role in bilingualism. Hymes (1967) and Fishman (1967) have pointed out that the components of speaking and listening will be chosen depending upon the interaction of language within the social environment. Language choice or use is often affected by social pressures. People behave within a community according to the rules and the actions of other members of the community. Thus children acquire not only language(s) in a social setting, but they also acquire attitudes and values regarding the use of language(s). It would appear possible, then, to attempt to define bilingualism and its use upon the basis of the community mores in which the languages were acquired. Gumperz (1967) has suggested that a child will acquire language(s) that are most suited to the community, its values, its actions, and its social pressures. Thus in a bilingual community, the most appropriate language system to learn is the bilingual one. Thus any attempt to define bilingualism is a complex task, whether the attempt is based on psychological, linguistic, or sociological grounds. Any meaningful attempt at such a definition or description would ultimately have to include information about the bilingual speaker-listener from each of these points of view.

Some Linguistic Considerations of Spanish and English

The Spanish and the English languages are both subject-verb-object languages—that is, on a structural basis they are word order languages. Thus in determining the meaning of a sentence, the appropriate ordering of the words is important. Besides being a word order language, Spanish is also a more highly inflected language than English (Stockwell, Bowen, and Martin, 1965). Certain parts of speech are unambiguously marked with endings that determine their relationship to other words in the sentence. Therefore, while word order is essential to preserve meaning in Spanish, these endings are also essential to the preservation of meaning.

At the basic level of phrase structure grammar both Spanish and English can be rewritten as S→ NP + VP. The NP can be rewritten as NP→ (determiner) + (adjective) N in English, and in Spanish, optionally as NP→ (determiner) + N (adjective). The difference is in the placement of the adjectives; before the N in English and usually following the N in Spanish. The VP can be rewritten as VP→ V + (NP) in both languages.

Other differences occur beyond these simple levels. In English, there is only one sense of the verb "to be," but in Spanish there are two senses represented by *"ser"* (to be, to exist, to happen, to be characteristic of, to be permanent) and *"estar"* (to locate, to hurry, to be less permanent). Although there are four basic rules which can be used in both languages (i.e., addition, deletion, permutation, and substitution), we find that the actual manifestation of the transformational rules for each of these languages is somewhat different.

At the lexical level, both languages seem to have the same distinctive features (i.e., + -human, + -animate, + -count, + -solid, etc.). Thus, in mediating and putting lexical items together into a meaningful sequence, the same basic principles are operating. However, the actual manifestations of the lexical items at the phonological level are different. For instance, while English has vowels that change shape in production, the Spanish vowels are steady-state and are not usually altered during production (Hadlich, 1971).

Language Acquisition in the Bilingual Child

The above overview of bilingualism demonstrates the complexity involved in the use of two (or more) languages by adult bilinguals. There is also an obvious scarcity of literature on child bilingualism. The purpose of this research is to begin an analysis of a corpus of language from three children who are simultaneously acquiring two languages (Spanish and English). It is expected that the analysis of this corpus will begin to provide a more complete insight into the processes involved in bilingualism. The data will be compared with that of Brown (1973) and González (1970), who have studied English and Spanish monolingual language acquisition, respectively. It is felt that this comparative analysis will begin to provide the theoretical framework necessary for better understanding of both monolingualism and bilingualism.

METHOD

Subjects

Three Ss were observed over a period ranging from three to six months. Two of the children were still under observation at the time of this writing. Several considerations were used in selecting subjects. The most obvious factor was that the child's language input consist of an environment where both Spanish and English were used with consistency. Along with this, there was a conscious attempt by the parents to establish a plan or a strategy for rearing their children as bilingual speaker-listeners. Secondly, in order to eliminate possible confounding language influences of other siblings the children selected were first born, only children. Finally, it was hoped that all three children would be fairly verbal, though this was not an essential criterion, since one of the children was too young at the onset of the study to determine this.

Two boys and a girl were selected for the study. Their ages at the onset of the study were two years, two months (2.2); two years, one month (2.1); and one year, five months (1.5). The fathers of two of the children were graduate students at the University of California, Santa Barbara, while the parents of the third child were high school graduates.

A brief description of each subject is as follows:

JOAQUIN

Birthdate: November 7, 1970   Birthplace: Santa Barbara, California

Joaquin was the oldest of the three children. He was 2.2 years at the onset of the study. He was observed over a 5 month period in his home and at his babysitter's home. His parents were bilingual (Spanish and English) speakers and both were native Californians. Joaquin spent his days with his mother and a monolingual, Spanish-speaking babysitter. Joaquin spoke predominantly English, particularly in the experimenter's presence. However, when the mother was instructed to input only Spanish one hour prior to the session, more Spanish was observed.

BOBBY

Birthdate: January 25, 1972   Birthplace: Santa Barbara, California

Bobby was the second boy observed. He was 2.1 at the onset of the study and is still under observation at the time of this writing. Bobby's father was trilingual (Spanish, English and Italian). However, he only spoke two languages at home—Spanish and English. He was a native Californian. Bobby's mother was bilingual (Spanish and English) and was from Mexico. She had been in the Santa Barbara area for 13 years and had learned English since coming to the United States. Bobby spent two days a week in a bilingual (Spanish and English) day care center with other bilingual children.

MICHELLE

Birthdate: April 4, 1972   Birthplace: Los Angeles, California

Michelle, the only girl observed, was 17 months at the onset of the study. Though still under observation, she was 23 months at the time of this writing. Michelle's parents were bilingual (Spanish and English) speakers. While her father was a native Californian, her mother was born and reared in Mexico and learned English in private schools in Mexico. Michelle has been cared for by a series of babysitters. The first was monolingual, English-speaking, while the last two were monolingual, Spanish-speaking. Also Michelle went to Mexico City for a three week period during observation. While there, she was exposed to only Spanish. While she heard English from her parents and from television, she was predominantly Spanish-speaking.

Methods

Each subject(s) was visited on an average of once a week in as many of the child's environments as possible (i.e., home, school, babysitter, etc.) The experimenter (E) tried to remain a mere observer for most of the sessions, but often had to stimulate speech with the child or with the parent. Both Spanish and English were used in the sessions in an attempt to keep them as close to the child's speaking environment as possible.

Each session averaged one hour. All speech was tape recorded except for Michelle's first four sessions and Bobby's first session. In addition to tape recording each session, E also kept a written record of the child's speech and the context in which it occurred.

Materials

A portable Sony cassette tape recorder was used for all of the sessions. Trac—60 minute cassette tapes were used for recording. As each child had his own toys, they were used if necessary to engage the child in conversation. When necessary, E used the child's storybooks to stimulate spontaneous speech. Following each session the tape was transcribed and the context was added to the language samples.

RESULTS

Since the data presented here were obtained in a naturalistic fashion, it is necessary to elaborate upon some of the data. This method of reporting will make the data clear. The language samples were analyzed so that they could be compared to language acquisition studies of monolingual English-speaking children (Brown, 1973) and monolingual Spanish-speaking children (González, 1970).

In order to assess the child's rate of language acquisition the total Mean Length of the Utterance (MLU-T) was calculated for each child based on Brown's rules for calculating MLU (Brown, 1973, p. 54). MLU was used as one index of language acquisition since it increases with age and with the increase of complexity of grammatical structures. Besides the MLU-T, the MLU for Spanish utterances (MLU-S), the MLU for English utterances (MLU-E), and the MLU for mixed Spanish and English utterances (MLU-M) were calculated.

In order to calculate the MLU-S and the MLU-M, it was necessary to add several steps to Brown's rules:

(1) Count as separate morphemes all singular and plural inflectional endings on the verb if the subject/noun was missing, as well as the verb itself. Justification is that each Spanish verb must take an inflectional ending to denote person and number.

(2) Count as separate morphemes all inflectional endings on adjectives. Justification is that adjectives in Spanish agree in gender and number with the noun they modify.

(3) Count those morphemes pronounced with a Spanish accent as Spanish, and all those morphemes pronounced with an English accent as English (/tʃ o-ko-la-té/vs./tʃ ok-lət/;/tʃ I-li/vs./tʃ i-le/).

(4) Count an utterance as mixed if it contains at least one phonological representation from each language (*está* raining, *dame* that).

Table 1 presents the computed values of MLU-T, MLU-E, MLU-S, and MLU-M for each of the three children.

Inspection of Table 1 shows the rate of language development of the three bilingual children and the similarities and individual differences at specific age levels. In order to adequately use the MLU in the study of simultaneous language acquisition, it is important to account for the components of the bilingual's speech. When viewing the MLU-E and the MLU-S, we see an orderly increase in the language development for the three children. In the case of Michelle, however, we see that her language production is greater in Spanish than in English. The MLU-M, although seemingly indexed by a larger value than the other three MLUs, should be interpreted with caution. The reason for this is that out of a mean of approximately 100 utterances per session the children typically only produced two-to-three mixed utterances. The MLU-T, which is the composite of all morphemes, shows a growth rate similar to the increases found in the MLU-E and MLU-S.

MICHELLE

As expected at 17 months, Michelle was at the one-word stage in her development of language. At this stage, Michelle had a limited vocabul-

Table 1
Computed Mean Length of Utterance for the Three Children

Chronological Age	MLU-T	MLU-E	MLU-S	MLU-M
Joaquin				
26 months	1.61	1.80	1.42	2.00
27 months	2.01	1.69	1.65	3.16
28.5 months	3.16	2.01	1.70	2.10
29.5 months	4.47	2.44	2.21	3.20
30.5 months	5.19	4.80	2.42	1.60
Bobby				
25 months	2.52	1.90	1.91	3.00
25.5 months	2.16	2.23	1.76	3.25
26 months	2.25	2.40	2.00	3.00
26.5 months	2.20	2.25	2.25	2.85
27 months	2.31	2.35	2.25	3.10
28 months	3.01	2.55	2.50	3.00
28.5 months	3.25	3.10	2.65	3.00
Michelle				
17 months	—	—	—	—
18 months	1.35 1.25		1.16	1.00
18.5 months	1.56	1.14	1.42	3.00
19.5 months	1.60	1.50	1.66	2.50
20.5 months	1.63	1.14	1.90	
20.5 months	1.20	—	1.20	—
21 months	1.60	—	1.60	—
21.5 months	1.77	—	1.77	—
22 months	1.57	—	1.57	—
23 months	1.93	1.00	1.93	—
23.5 months	1.96	—	1.96	2.00
24 months	2.01	—	2.01	—
24.5 months	2.07	1.00	2.07	—
25 months	2.00	—	2.00	—

ary and often communicated by means of gestures. For instance, she was asked by *E* where her dog was. She responded by pointing to her dog. However, at 18 months, though still at the one-word stage, she would name objects, use simple one-word imperatives (i.e., *dame, ten*), or ask questions by adding a rising intonation at the end of the word (i.e., *¿qué?*). Although Michelle was not verbalizing a great deal at this stage, she displayed instances of one-word speech in both of her languages (i.e., mine, *tenga, pan,* puppy). Because Michelle's speech development was at the one-word stage, language mixing was apparent.

It is worth noting that Michelle possessed both forms of the Spanish imperative of the verb *tener* (to have), that is *ten* and *tenga*. González (1970) in his study of monolingual Spanish-speaking children at 2 years observed the imperative form, *ten*. The importance of this is that both forms of the imperative of the verb *tener* are correct. However, *ten* is only used in the expression *ten cuidado* (be careful), while *tenga* is the more commonly found imperative form.

Imitation in both languages is also seen particularly on words stressed in the adult model or on the last word of what had just been said to her. Two such examples can be seen below:

> *E:* Have some milk.   *M:* milk
> *E: Está lloviendo*   *M: vendo*

Language comprehension was much more developed than was production at this stage. Michelle was able to carry out simple commands and answer questions directed toward her. It is interesting to note that she would usually, though not always, respond in the language of the utterance directed to her. For example, *E* asked her "Who fixed your hair?" Her response was "Mommy." Immediately following this response, her father asked her ¿Qué quieres? (What do you want?). Her response was "*Mamá* cookie.". The first word of her response, closest to the question which was in Spanish, was answered in Spanish. It should also be pointed out that Michelle used the appropriate lexical term for "mother" in the language directed toward her.

At this stage, her responses seemed "loaded." Although they were mostly one-word utterances, they seemed to convey a complex set of ideas. For instance, at one point in the third session, Michelle went to a kitchen drawer, opened it, turned to *E* and said *Mamá*. Though she could have meant a variety of ideas, none were clear to the observer. In this case the context should have been the only clue to the child's meaning. However, in this particular case, context did not add to the meaning of Michelle's utterance.

Until around 19 months, the development of both Spanish and English seemed to be progressing at the same rate. This observation is based on the comparisons of Michelle's one-word sentences in both languages as well as on the computed MLU for Spanish and English (i.e., MLU-S 1.66 and MLU-E 1.50).

At 20 months, Michelle's Spanish began to be somewhat more frequent and more complex than her English. This is particularly evident in the fact that her MLU-S was now 1.90 while her MLU-E decreased, due to the less frequent use of English, to 1.14. Another indication of this was that quantitatively there were more verbs present in Spanish than in English. The presence of more verb forms was indicative of increasing complexity in Michelle's speech at this stage. Previously, Michelle's speech was very action-oriented and represented by many predicative notions (i.e., the child is making a comment about his world; however, the verb form is absent) in both of her languages. Now what is observed in the language samples is the decrease in the use of predicative notions in Spanish. We also see the first appearance of the plural "s" in Spanish and not yet in English. The first appearance of a negative was the placement of the word "no" in front of a sentence. This also occurred only in Spanish.

At around 21 months, Michelle began to consistently use two-word utterances. As with Brown's (1973) children, Michelle's utterances mostly looked like N + N, M + N, V + N. These utterances were telegraphic in that the content words were used as a means of communication while the smaller words or functors were not yet evident. The modifiers (M) at this stage were very simple and had not yet begun to differentiate into adjectives, articles, etc. Table 2 presents some examples of Michelle's speech at this stage.

As is evident in this small sample, the major portion of Michelle's speech is in Spanish, and where English appears, it is within a mixed utterance. Again, much the same as with the one-word stage, two words could have a variety of meanings (i.e., "mommy Molly" could mean "Mommy, here is doll, Molly" or "mommy's name is Molly" or "Mommy, where is Molly"). Again, we must depend on the context to give us clues to such an utterance. However, even with the more elaborated language that Michelle was using, the context was not always a clue to the semantic notion behind the utterances.

Use of the negative sentence and the wh- or *qu-* question and the yes/no or *sí/no* question still consisted of "no" + sentence and the sentence plus a rising intonation, or wh- or *qu-* with a rising intonation

Table 2
Samples of Michelle's Two-Word Speech at 21 Months

Utterance	Structure	Context
arriba munjeca	M + N	*¿Dónde está la munjeca negrita?*
mommy Molly	N + M	Gives it to her mother
baila mommy	V + N	Asks her mother to dance
por papá	M + N	Gives toy to father
hello *papá*	M + N	Goes to her father
es chonge	V + N	Points to herself
that *papel*	M + N	Points to a piece of paper

plus the sentence (i.e., *no fea, no torné; ¿está?, ¿qué* that?). These various modalities were only observable in Spanish or in mixed utterances as is seen above. González (1970) provided instances from his recorded language samples of similar constructions for children at age two.

Because of the noticeable lack of English found in Michelle's language samples, a discrimination task was presented to her at 22 months to determine her receptive knowledge of English. *E* placed three objects in front of Michelle (i.e., a book, some keys, and a toy dog). *E* asked Michelle the following questions:

(1) Where is (are) the *perro?*
                                  libro
                                  claves
(2) Where is (are) the dog?
                                  book
                                  keys
(3) *¿Dónde está(n) el (los)* dog?
                                  book
                                  keys
(4) *¿Dónde está(n) el (los) perro?*
                                  libro
                                  claves

Michelle responded to questions one and four by correctly pointing to the objects. Where the object was named in Spanish, at least for these objects, Michelle responded appropriately. However, she made non-task related responses to questions two and three. If the object was named in English, there was an inappropriate response. The language of the carrier phrase did not appear to aid or to hinder her response. Instead, naming of the object in Spanish by the *E* seemed to aid Michelle in responding appropriately to the task.

At this same age there is the first appearance of the plural inflection in Spanish. Some examples are Michelle's use of *niños* (babies) and *claves* (keys). However, the inflectional plural form only appeared marginally. Other inflections such as the Spanish participle -*(i)endo* or *ando* occurred only in imitative responses.

Michelle's use of modifiers appeared to begin differentiating at 23 months. There were now two classes of modifiers: the article modifiers (i.e., *un, una, la, lo*) and a general group of modifiers which included possessives (e.g., *mío, tuyo*) and descriptive adjectives (e.g., *fea, otro*). The use of the masculine definite and indefinite article often occurred with a feminine gender noun. This suggested that Michelle had not yet fully mastered the modifier agreement rules between nouns and articles in Spanish.

Between 24 and 25 months, Michelle's speech production in Spanish indicated the development of several new forms of sentence complexity. The first included the use of descriptive adjectives on a much wider basis (e.g., *globos azules*). Along with this is the occurrence of the indefinite article before the noun and the descriptive adjective after the noun. This can be seen in *una globos azules*. What is interesting about this example is that although the modifier placements are correct, the modifier agreement rule between *una globos* is incorrect according to the adult model, which requires the use of the masculine plural indefinite article *unos*.

Another indication of increasing sentence complexity was the correct use of the reflexive pronoun.

> *Mira, niña se pica.*
> *A que se carga.*
> *Mamita, se me va mi coche.*

The age of the occurrence of the reflexive pronoun in Michelle's speech corresponded to González (1970), who also noted the occurrence of this form within the range of two to two and-a-half years. González pointed out that this form is one of the most difficult to acquire for an adult learning Spanish as a second language. Like González's three informants, Michelle did not appear to have any difficulty using this form.

BOBBY

Bobby at 25 months was at Brown's (1973) second stage of development. Though Bobby still used simple, one -and two-word utterances, longer utterances with finer and more complex meaning had begun to appear. One word, usually a noun, was used in a variety of utterances. Various types of functor words were occurring around this word. These functor words were occurring in both languages and in mixed utterances. Table 3 provides some examples from Brown's Adam, and our Bobby and Joaquin.

Table 3

Examples of Functor Words for Two Bilingual Children and for Brown's (1973) Adam

Adam[a]	Bobby	Joaquin
Adam write ball	man do that	man watching
hit ball	that a boat man	*eso hombre aquí*
Adam hit ball	a man *tu casa*	man watching horsie
where the ball go		*es* a baby horsie

[a]Taken from Brown, 1973.

The large class of modifiers had split into articles, adjectives, adverbs, and prepositions. At this point in Bobby's development, meaning was not dependent specifically on context. These functor words served to elaborate and clarify the meaning of Bobby's utterances.

In the mixed (Spanish and English) utterances that occurred above, Bobby mixed his two languages appropriately. When functor words were used, they appeared in the proper relation to the noun they modified. "A man *tu casa*" appeared, not *"a man *casa tu*." As this differentiation occurred in the modifier class of words, Bobby appeared to be expanding his vocabulary as well as the structural length of the utterances in both languages. Evidence for this was seen where Bobby developed comparable forms in both languages. If a form developed in one language, that form also occurred in the other language. For instance, for the English words "this" and "that" now occurring at this stage, the Spanish *esta* and *eso* were also noted in Bobby's speech.

At this stage, Bobby began to use the subject noun where it had been absent before. This demonstrated that he was developing more complex forms of language. For example, "man do that" or "daddy *está*" appeared in Bobby's language samples. The subject noun was present instead of implied as was common at an earlier stage of development. Evidently, this phenomenon was occurring in English and in mixed utterances, but not in Spanish alone.

This is not to say at this level that Bobby's use of Spanish was not as complex as his use of English. For instance, Bobby used forms of the Spanish equivalents of the English verb "to be." These forms of *ser* and *estar* occurred in Bobby's language samples.

González (1970) informants between 2 years and 2.6 years demonstrated the use of *ser* and *estar* also. These children only used these verbs occasionally. However, appropriate use was noted when the verbs were used. Bobby's language samples showed only limited use of the possible constructions of *ser* and *estar* and González noted the same phenomena. As with Bobby, the main function of *estar* (to denote location) appeared; and the use of *ser* as a copula or linking verb appeared infrequently. However, they were used appropriately when they did occur. For instance, when Bobby said "daddy *esta*" he pointed in a westerly direction to where his father was working, thus denoting location. This is one of the main functions of the verb *estar*. In another phrase, he said *es un cama* meaning "this is a bed." He was referring to a permanent quality or characteristic or name of the object being referred to. This is one of

---

*An asterisk preceding an utterance means that this is not a grammatical sentence.

the main functions of the verb *ser* to be used when naming an object, person, or thing.

At 26 months, the progressive inflectional endings "-ing," and *-e(a)ndo* were occurring in Bobby's speech (i.e., *llorando, comiendo,* "crying" and "eating"). At this stage in both English and Spanish, the auxiliary form of the verb "to be" that occurs before a progressive verb form was absent.

Bobby used full sentence negation in English beginning at 27 months (e.g., "daddy no home," "I no see it"). Other forms of negative particles began appearing at this same time in English (i.e., can't, nothing). However, use of the negative in Spanish was limited to the negative plus noun in non-sentence forms (e.g., *no agua*). Further, the use of more complex negatives was not yet apparent in Bobby's Spanish language samples. This might have been due to the influence of the experimenter's use of English.

At 27 months, Bobby began using the conjunction "and" in English (i.e., "mommy and me," "and the boat"). This form had not yet begun to show in Bobby's Spanish.

Full sentence question forms in both English and Spanish were first used by Bobby at 27 months. Some examples were

> What you do?
> *¿Qué es?*
> *¿Qué es eso?*

While Bobby used the wh (*qu*)-question in both languages, the yes/no; *sí/no*-question had not yet occurred in the language samples. González (1970) also noted a prevalence of the *qu*-type question in Spanish with the limited occurrence of the *sí/no* question in his informants.

It would be difficult to determine which language had developed to a more complex level based on the evidence just presented. However, if we look at the MLU-E and the MLU-S for Bobby as well as the quantity of output of the English language, quantitatively, English was predominant. It is important to note that this effect may have been due primarily to the English-speaking influence of *E*.

JOAQUIN

When first observed at 26 months, Joaquin's language development appeared to be at Brown's second stage. That is, simple one- and two-word utterances were still evident. However, Joaquin was also using longer utterances with a wider variety of meaning. Much like Bobby, Joaquin would use one word in many different utterances. Around this word, generally a content word, we find functor words. This phenomenon occurred in English, in Spanish, and in mixed utterances. (See examples in Table 3).

Joaquin's utterances as shown in Table 3 indicate that when functor words appeared, they appeared appropriately. This is particularly evident in the mixed utterance "*es* a baby horsie." The article appeared before the noun phrase and after the verb phrase instead of *"a *es* baby horsie" or *"*es* baby a horsie." Along with this development, the same lexical items began to appear in both languages. For instance, for the English words "a" and "here," the Spanish equivalents *una* and *aquí* began to appear within the same language sample.

At 27 months, subject nouns began appearing. Joaquin used the noun and the pronoun as subjects, (i.e., frog ride, I go). The plural inflection also began to appear in English and in Spanish. A yes/no question appeared in the form of a sentence plus a rising intonation ("remember mule?"). This question form does not appear in Spanish nor does it appear again in English. The present progressive inflection (-ing) had also begun to appear, but only in English.

One month later, Joaquin's language samples indicated the use of negative contraction forms. Previously, Joaquin had used only the negative particle "no" plus a sentence. At 28 months, he began to use "can't" plus a sentence, while at the same time he began using the complex double negative. An example would be Joaquin's frequent use of "no touch him no more." It should be noted that the negative contraction form does not exist in Spanish. Interestingly, the negative contraction form never appeared in Joaquin's mixed language utterances.

Around the age of 29 months, Joaquin's language samples showed evidence of the use of different sentence modalities (i.e., question, negative, complex imperatives) in both languages. Wh-questions, *qu*-questions, and yes/no questions appeared. The Spanish equivalent of the yes/no question, the *sí/no* question, was not observed in the language samples. Some examples of these question forms are found in Table 4.

In the above examples some of the complexities of these forms are evident in the presence of and the correct use of "do" insertion for the yes/no question along with subject-verb inversion. For the wh-question form in both Spanish and English, there was evidence of permutation of the wh-form to the front of the sentence along with subject-verb inversion.

While Joaquin's MLU-S had begun to level off at 29 months, his MLU-E continued to increase (See Table 1). English appeared to be more predominant possibly due to *E's* more predominate use of English.

Table 4

Question Forms Found in Joaquin's Speech at 29 Months

Wh-/qu-Questions	Yes/No Questions
¿Qué es eso?	do you like this?
¿Quién es?	this fits?
¿Cuándo cena?	
What is that?	

However, Joaquin spoke more Spanish during a session when his mother was instructed to speak only Spanish to him for at least one hour prior to the session. This is an important observation because it demonstrates the significance of language input and its relationship to the language production of bilingual children. Support for this can be seen in the language samples of all three children since they would answer a question, imitate, or command in the language which was spoken to them.

An imitation task was devised by reviewing Joaquin's earlier language samples from which E selected utterances which were made grammatically correct according to an adult model and/or elaborated or lengthened. The purpose of this task was to determine whether Joaquin had more knowledge of his language than was evident in the spontaneous language samples. E started the task with one-word utterances and proceeded to four- and five-word utterances of increasing complexity. The first session of the imitation task was conducted in English while the second session was conducted in Spanish. The same sample utterances were used in both languages. Although direct translation from English to Spanish was not always possible due to idioms and structural differences, the meaning of each word or phrase was held constant. Examples from both sessions can be found in Table 5.

In both languages, Joaquin maintained word order. If words were deleted from the stimulus phrase, the meaning was preserved. It also appeared that Joaquin modified the stimulus phrase to fit into his existing repertoire of language or into the context of the phrase. For example, when asked to imitate "don't touch" he said, "no touch." Although Joaquin used "don't" plus a verb earlier in his language samples, he would change this form to "no" plus a verb (i.e., no like you no more). If the stimulus phrase was a question form, but read without a rising intonation, Joaquin would answer the "question" instead of imitating the phrase. For example, to the stimulus phrase "say 'do you like' " he said, "Yeah, I like that."

Table 5

Examples from Joaquin's English and Spanish Imitation Task

Stimulus Phrase	Imitation
English	
/say/ I don't touch	no touch
/say/ don't touch me anymore	no touch me no more
/say/ I am writing it	I writing it
/say/ this goes	this goes this way
Spanish	
/diga/ pontélo	pontélo
/diga/ lo pones aquí	pones aquí
/diga/ los estoy escribiendo	escribiendo
/diga/ en la bolsa	airplane bolsa

Analysis of the complexity of imitated phrases in both languages contradicted the earlier suggestion that Joaquin's English was more complex than his Spanish. However, without any apparent understanding or knowledge of the sentence structure, Joaquin imitated some phrases that were purposely made longer and more complex by the *E* than any found in his prior language samples (i.e., "I will help you."). Thus, while the imitation task provided some interesting data, it failed to provide information that was not already apparent in his earlier language samples.

Finally, in analyzing the lexical, syntactic, and phonological structures we find that each child appeared to be using two distinct sets of rules for language production. For example, at the lexical level, at the same time that "this" occurred in English, *eso* appeared in Spanish. There were some exceptions to this; for instance, Joaquin always said *boca* but not "mouth." The mixed utterance language samples also indicated that there were no additional lexical items or reduplication of items first in one language and then in the other. For instance, *"chanclas por by here"* did not occur, but "*chanclas por* here" did.

At the syntactical level, the appropriate use of both languages even in mixed utterances was evident; that is, correct word order was preserved. For example, there were no occurrences of *"raining está"* or *"a es baby"* but there was evidence for such utterances as "*está* raining" and "*es* a baby." There was also an absence of the redundance of words in the mixed utterances as well as the absence of unnecessary words which might tend to confuse the meaning. That is, *"*dámelo* that" or *"*es un* a baby pony" did not appear, whereas "*dame* that" and "*es un* baby pony" did occur.

The clearest evidence for separate systems was at the phonological level. Even in mixed utterances where evidence for some assimilation of sounds, particularly in young language learners, might have appeared, none was found. English morphemes were pronounced with an English accent and Spanish morphemes were pronounced with a Spanish accent. Within a word boundary there was no switching from one language to the other. Examples of this in narrow transcription are [está renin] and [wʰ∧t ar dedos].

DISCUSSION

The present study was concerned with the simultaneous acquisition of Spanish and English in three children. The methodology employed was similar to that of Brown (1973). At various points throughout, comparisons were made between the bilingual children of this study and Brown's monolingual English-speaking children and González's (1970) monolingual Spanish-speaking children. It was hoped that these comparisons would shed some light on the rate of language acquisition for the children of this study who, because of their bilingual environment, were learning two languages simultaneously.

In this study, instead of being primarily concerned with linguistic competence, i.e., the abstract knowledge of the languages' underlying performance, we were directly concerned with our subjects' linguistic performance, i.e., the actual forms produced in speech. Analyses of the language, samples of our bilingual children indicated that these subjects, in spite of the linguistic "load" forced onto them due to their bilingual environments, were acquiring their two languages at a rate comparable to that of monolingual-speaking children. There was no evidence in the language samples that might suggest an overall reduced or slower rate of language growth for the bilingual children of this study. This finding contradicts a reported slower rate of language acquisition in bilingual children shown in the data of Swain (1972). In her study, Swain analyzed the development of question forms in young French/English bilinguals and observed that the development of yes/no questions was delayed in her subjects. However, these data should be interpreted with caution since the delay in acquisition was confined only to the yes/no question form. As Swain herself notes, several interpretations may be offered for the delay; it may be that the bilingual child "has already learned several ways to ask questions, and so has concentrated his efforts on learning other aspects of the codes. Perhaps the delay, when seen in terms of the bilingual's complete linguistic systems, is not really a delay at all. Perhaps at any particular level of development he has a greater number of linguistic structures available to him than does a monolingual child" (Swain, 1972, p. 243).

In commenting on studies of child bilingualism, Slobin (1971) has suggested that "Studies of bilingual children yield valuable suggestions as to what sorts of formal devices may be simpler to acquire than others" (p. 181). By this comment, Slobin is proposing the notion that if a child develops a similar grammatical form in both languages, the linguistic complexity of that particular form is the same in both languages; or, if a child developed one grammatical structure in one language before the comparable structure in the second language, the language in which the earlier form appeared could possibly be less complex than the language in which the later developing form appeared. To support his argument, Slobin refers to the observation of Imedadze, who noted the simultaneous appearance of the genitive and instrumental forms in her Russian-Georgian bilingual daughter. This observation led Imedadze to conclude that these forms "express the very same semantic relationships in analogous fashion [in Russian and Georgian]" (Slobin, p. 181).

Though there may be some validity to Slobin's reasoning, our work with bilingual children suggests that before such a conclusion can be drawn it is important to make certain that the bilingual child has received an equal input in both languages and that there be no stated or observed preference or dominance of one language over the other. In our work, we have consistently found that bilingual children acquiring two languages simultaneously demonstrate a preference in their language output for one language over the other. This appears to be true even though there are reports from parents that the child is proficient in both languages and/or that no language preference is expressed by the parents in speaking to the child.[1] Accordingly, it would be in error to suggest that grammatical structures appear in one language earlier than they appear in the second language because the languages differ in linguistic complexity. These differences may only reflect the subtle realities of the child's bilingual environment as well as individual variations in language development.

A related issue is that of attempting to determine the extent of bilingualism in a child speaker. Some authors have suggested that there are adult bilinguals who are "balanced" bilinguals (Ervin-Tripp, 1964) because these speaker-listeners encode and decode with equal proficiency at each of the four linguistic levels specified by MacNamara (1967), i.e., the phonological, lexical, syntactic, and semantic levels. As discussed above, the results of this study indicate that it is impossible to speak of "balanced" bilingualism among our subjects. This is true in spite of the appearance that at initial contact with our subjects, the children were receiving an equal input in both of their languages and that the parents were "committed" to rearing their children bilingually. The importance of this observation leads us to suggest that future researchers of child bilingualism should exercise caution in drawing conclusions about differences in linguistic structures between two languages, as suggested by Slobin, unless some very precise technique is employed to determine the actual extent of bilingualism in the young child.

In her discussion of child bilingualism, Swain hypothesizes that initially, bilingual children do not differentiate their languages into two linguistic systems. She suggests that the mixed utterance forms so often observed in her bilingual subjects confirm this position. Swain says that it is only later, when children output utterances in a single language, that the child differentiates the two languages into separate systems. The data reported here contradict the hypothesis advanced by Swain. The subjects of this study demonstrated the use of one set of rules for each language which was most evident particularly at the phonological level as discussed in an earlier section of this paper. This can also be seen at the lexical and syntactic levels. If there is a stage when young bilingual speakers cannot (or do not) differentiate between two linguistic systems, then the transition from non-differentiation to differentiation occurs quite early for the children reported in this study. Moreover, it should be noted that the use of mixed utterances, as proof of lack of differentiation between linguistic systems, may not be a useful index with Spanish/English bilingual children in the Southwestern and Western sectors of the United States. This is most likely the case because these Spanish/English bilingual children may be far more accustomed to hearing mixed utterance forms from their adult language models than is true of the children studied by Swain in Quebec, Canada.

The findings reported here, along with the data obtained by Swain, suggest that a fuller description of the child's mixed utterances should be undertaken. It may be that the children reported here did not differentiate between their two languages at the phrase structure level. This may be true because at the phrase structure level the linguistic framework of Spanish and English is very similar. At the transformational level—that is, where structural changes begin to appear—the child begins to differentiate his grammatical rules into two separate systems—one system for each language. This is most clearly evident in the mixed utterance form. For example, we find our subjects saying the following:

Joaquin	*Bobby*	*Michelle*
es a baby horsie	*una* baby	*¿Qué* that?
es un baby pony	*es* a baby	*dame* that

The striking thing about these mixed utterances is that when the child performs a transformational change, he does so appropriately for each language. He does not include extra lexical items that are unnecessary. That is, if a child uses an article in Spanish, he does not add the same item from English; the child does not say *"*es un* a baby pony" since the use of the article in English would be redundant.

NOTE

1. A much larger study presently being conducted in the Santa Barbara–Goleta, California, area adds confirmatory evidence to this observation.

REFERENCES

Bloom, L. *Language Development: Form and Function in Emerging Grammars.* Cambridge, Mass.: M.I.T. Press, 1970.

Brown, R. *A First Language: The Early Stages.* Cambridge, Mass.: Harvard University Press, 1973.

Brown, R., and Bellugi, U. Three processes in the acquisition of syntax. *Harvard Educational Review,* 1964, 34: 133–151.

Brown, R., Bellugi, U., and Cazden, C. The child's grammar from I to III. In John P. Hill (ed.), *Minnesota Symposia on Child Psychology,* Vol. II. Minneapolis: University of Minnesota Press, 1969. Pp. 28–73.

Burling, R. Language development of a Garo and English-speaking child. *Word,* 1959, 15, 45–68.

Chomsky, N. *Syntactic Structures.* The Hague: Mouton, 1957.

————. *Aspects of the Theory of Syntax.* Cambridge, Mass.: M.I.T. Press, 1965.

Ervin-Tripp, S. M. Imitation and structural change in children's language. In Eric H. Lenneberg (ed.), *New Directions in the Study of Language.* Cambridge, Mass.: M.I.T. Press, 1964. Pp. 163–189.

Ervin-Tripp, S. M. *Language Acquisition and Communicative Choice.* Stanford, California: Stanford University Press, 1973.

Ervin, S. M., and Osgood, C. Language learning and bilingualism. *Journal of Abnormal and Social Psychology,* 1954, 49, 139–146.

Fishman, J. Bilingualism with and without diglossia; diglossia with and without bilingualism. *Journal of Social Issues,* 1967, 23, 29–38.

González, G. "The Acquisition of Spanish Grammar by Native Spanish Speakers." Unpublished Doctoral Dissertation, University of Texas at Austin, 1970.

Gumperz, J. J. On the linguistic markers of bilingual communication. *Journal of Social Issues,* 1967, *23,* 48–57.

Hadlich, R. L. *A Transformational Grammar of Spanish.* Englewood Cliffs, N.J.: Prentice Hall, Inc., 1971.

Hymes, D. Models of the interaction of language and social setting. *Journal of Social Issues,* 1967, 23, 29–38.

Kolers, P. A. Bilingualism and information processing. *Scientific American,* 1968, 218(3), 78–86.

Lambert, W. E., Havelka, J., and Gardner, R. C. Linguistic manifestations of bilingualism. *American Journal of Psychology,* 1959, 72, 77–82.

Leopold, W. *Speech Development of a Bilingual Child: A Linguist's Record.*
Volume 1: *Vocabulary Growth in the First Two Years,* 1939.
Volume 2: *Sound Learning in the First Two Years,* 1947.
Volume 3: *Grammars and General Problems in the First Two Years,* 1949 (a).
Volume 4: *Diary from Age Two,* 1949 (b).
Evanston, Ill.: Northwestern University Press.

MacNamara, J. The bilingual's linguistic performance—a psychological overview. *Journal of Social Issues,* 1967, 23, 58–77.

McCarthy, D. "Language development in children." In L. Carmichael (ed.), *Manual of Child Psychology.* New York: Wiley, 1954.

McNeill, D. Developmental psycholinguistics. In Frank Smith and George Miller, (eds.), *The Genesis of Language: A Psycholinguistic Approach.* Cambridge, Mass.: M.I.T. Press, 1966. Pp. 15–84.

Menyuk, P. *Sentences Children Use.* Cambridge, Mass.: M.I.T. Press, 1969.

Slobin, D. I. Cognitive prerequisites for the development of grammar. In E. D. Dingwell, (ed.), *A Survey of Linguistic Science.* College Park, Maryland: University of Maryland Linguistics Program, 1971. Pp. 298–400.

Stockwell, R. P., Bowen, J. D., and Martin, J. W. *The Grammatical Structures of English and Spanish.* Chicago: The University of Chicago Press, 1965.

Swain, M. K. "Bilingualism as a First Language." Unpublished Doctoral Dissertation. University of California, Irvine, 1972.

Weinreich, E. *Languages in Contact: Findings and Problems.* New York: Linguistic Circle of New York, 1953.

Development of Interrogative, Negative, and Possessive Forms in the Speech of Young Spanish/English Bilinguals

AMADO M. PADILLA
KATHRYN J. LINDHOLM
University of California, Los Angeles

The study of language acquisition in monolingual children has increased in recent years (e.g., Bloom, 1970; Bowerman, 1973; Brown, 1973; McNeill, 1970; Menyuk, 1969). These studies have all contributed to our knowledge of the processes involved in language learning. An equally important and possibly more complicated aspect of language acquisition is bilingualism, especially the learning of two languages simultaneously by children. With the exception of a few studies (e.g., Burling, 1959; Leopold, 1939, 1947, 1949a, b; Padilla and Liebman, 1975; and Swain, 1972), little is known about child bilingualism.

In an earlier study of three bilingual children (Padilla and Liebman, 1975), we showed that the rate of acquiring two languages was approximately the same as in monolingual children. Further, we suggested that our bilingual children appeared able to keep the grammatical rules of the two languages they were learning separated from a very early age. In this study, we intend to examine the development of speech of bilingual children in greater detail. We will focus on the development of interrogative, negative, and possessive forms in both Spanish and English of young bilingual speakers.

To provide a frame of reference, the adult transformational rules involving interrogative, negative, and possessive grammatical structures

This report is an expanded version of a paper presented at the annual meetings of the Western Psychological Association, Sacramento, 1975.

The research reported in this study was supported by Research Grant GY11534 from the National Science Foundation and by Grant MH24845 from the National Institute of Mental Health to the Spanish Speaking Mental Health Research and Development Program at UCLA.

in Spanish and English will first be discussed. These transformation rules will then be applied to the speech of our bilingual children. Using this approach, we hope to be able to answer such questions as: Do children learning two languages develop parallel grammatical structures in the two languages at the same time? Or, are some grammatical structures of one language easier to learn and therefore acquired first, and then, later, learned in the second language? What kinds of grammatical interference problems are encountered by children learning two languages? Questions such as these have rarely been posed by investigators of child bilingualism although a good deal of speculation exists concerning the deleterious effects of child bilingualism (e.g., Axelrod, 1974; McCarthy, 1946; Riley, 1972).

METHOD

Subjects

Nineteen bilingual children were selected for observation. The children included: three two-year-olds, with a range from 2.0 to 2.10; four three-year-olds, ranging from 3.1 to 3.9; six four-year-olds, with a range from 4.3 to 4.11; three five-year-olds, ranging from 5.1 to 5.9; and three six-year-olds, who ranged from 6.1 to 6.4. The children were chosen in accordance with the following criteria: (1) that the amount of Spanish and English that the child heard and used be about equal; (2) that the parents be of Mexican descent; and (3) that the children be verbal enough to communicate in both languages with strangers. Of the 19 children, 11 were males and 8 were females. Within each age group, there was at least one male and one female child.

Although socio-economic status was not specifically controlled for, all of the children were from working-class families. Eighteen of the fathers and all but four of the mothers of the children were born in Mexico. All of the children, however, were born in the U.S. The parents of 12 children indicated that the children had spoken both Spanish and English from the time their language production began. The parents of the remaining 7 children indicated that their children had first produced Spanish utterances and then, at some later point, produced English utterances.

Equipment and Recording

Sony cassette tape recorders, TC-110, with Scotch C60 minute and C90 minute tapes, were used to collect the language samples. Experimenters also recorded utterances and context by hand on legal-sized tablets. Toys (e.g., airplanes, boats, doctor and nurse kits, telephones, blocks, drawing materials, picture books, etc.) were used to encourage spontaneous speech.

To collect a representative language sample from each child in Spanish and in English, a minimum of 400 utterances was collected in each language. When one language was used more frequently by a child, it was necessary to record more than the minimal requirement of utterances in the more frequently occurring language in order to obtain the minimum of 400 utterances in the language which occurred less frequently.

To standardize the procedure of counting the utterances across children, an utterance was operationally defined as: (1) a complete thought process; (2) a grammatical phrase; (3) an incomplete phrase due to the child's shift in attention, e.g., "the boy was . . ." (child stops talking and becomes interested in something else); (4) a one-word utterance (e.g., dog or *perro*); and (5) a repetition of an utterance, elicited by huh?, *¿cómo?* (how?), or *¿qué?* (what?) on the part of another individual, which differs from the initially produced utterance.

Procedure

Four pairs of female experimenters collected the language samples. Each pair consisted of one Spanish-English bilingual and one English monolingual who, in most cases, had some knowledge of Spanish. The bilingual experimenter spoke only Spanish and the monolingual experimenter spoke only English during all interactions with the child. Three of the pairs of experimenters collected language samples from five children each, while the fourth group of experimenters gathered language samples from four children. An entire language sample for each child was collected by the sample pair of experimenters.

The language sample for each child was based primarily on interaction between the experimenters and the child. However, since the sample was obtained in the child's home, other people (e.g., mother or siblings) frequently interacted with the child during a session.

To insure consistency in the collection of language samples, several procedural guidelines were established for all groups of experimenters prior to the start of the study. These guides were: (1) do not prompt; (2) try not to ask questions that require a "yes" or "no" answer; (3) try to avoid questions which require only a naming or labeling response; and (4) if the child does not speak clearly, ask for a repetition.

The language samples of each child were always transcribed by the same pair of experimenters who had obtained the language sample.

Notes taken during the taping session were used to facilitate transcription. An attempt was made to transcribe every utterance made by the child. However, some utterances occurred that could not be understood even after having been listened to at least three times. The utterances were then considered unintelligible and were noted as such in the sequence of the child's utterances.

RESULTS AND DISCUSSION

In terms of the three grammatical structures to be analyzed, the interrogatives will be discussed first, followed by the negatives and lastly by the possessives. A developmental stage framework will be presented for each of the grammatical structures to be analyzed. The acquisition of each grammatical structure will be discussed in each language separately. Then the developmental stage framework will be used to compare and contrast the acquisition of the same grammatical structure in both Spanish and English. A brief introduction to the adult rules for each structure will precede each section to ensure a clearer conception of the child's development of each grammatical structure as it approaches the adult model.

Interrogatives

The Spanish and English adult interrogative structures are comparable in terms of the transformational rules applicable to both languages. A short discussion of the transformational rules of each language will be followed by a comparison of the rules for each.

The two basic forms of the English interrogative are the yes/no questions and the interrogative word or wh-questions. Klima and Bellugi-Klima (1966), who have analyzed the interrogatives in monolingual English speakers, state that in the adult model, either the whole sentence may be questioned (a yes/no question) or one or more parts may be questioned (a wh-word question). However, these two forms are similar in that they adhere to a common interrogative rule:

$$S \rightarrow Q^{wh}\text{——}NP\text{——}aux\text{——}VP$$

Both question forms involve transformations to prepose the wh-word and invert the noun phrase with the verb. Yes/no questions, though, include the additional transformational rule of inverting the intonation pattern from falling to rising.

The transformations of the yes/no question involve: (1) preposing the interrogative, which is not a lexical realization (Klima & Bellugi-Klima,

1966), but is nevertheless a transformational realization; (2) inserting the "do" verb (if the auxiliary verb is only specifying tense); (3) inverting the noun phrase and the verb; and (4) transforming the intonation pattern from falling to rising. For example, in the declarative sentence:

John eats apples at home   ↓ *

the transformations mentioned above would change the declarative to:

(1) (wh) John eats apples at home   ↓
(2) (wh) John does eat apples at home   ↓
(3) (wh) Does John eat apples at home   ↓
(4) (wh) Does John eat apples at home   ↑

A less common type of yes/no question, the "echo" question, merely inverts the intonation pattern in a declarative sentence without application of transformational rules 2 and 3.

The wh-questions interrogate only part of the sentence, and therefore the wh-word refers to the particle of the sentence which requires information. The transformations for the wh-questions are: (1) wh-preposing; (2) "do" insertion, which only occurs if an auxiliary verb is absent or simply specifies tense; and (3) noun phrase-verb inversion. The transformations would change the declarative sentence;

John eats apples at home

according to the particle requiring information (e.g., subject, object, or location), as follows:

   I. *Who* eats apples at home?   (subject)
  II. John eats *what* at home?   (object)
      a. John does eat what at home?
      1. What John does eat at home?
      2. What does John eat at home?
 III. John eats apples *where?*   (location)
      a. John does eat apples where?
      1. Where John does eat apples?
      2. Where does John eat apples?

Spanish has the corresponding two classes of questions: the *sí/no* and k/d-questions (Stockwell, Bowen, & Martin, 1965). The *sí/no* and k/d-question types correspond to the English yes/no and wh-question types. *Sí/no* questions are of two types: (1) where transformations include (a)

---

* ↓ will refer to a falling intonation pattern while a ↑ will refer to a rising intonation pattern.

preposing the k/d-words, (b) inverting the entire verb phrase and the noun phrase, and (c) inverting the intonation pattern; and (2) where only the intonation pattern is inverted from falling to rising. The transformation of the declarative sentence:

Juan come manzanas en casa ↓ (Juan eats apples at home)

would produce the following results:

(a) (k/d) *Juan come manzanas en casa* ↓
(b) (k/d) *Come manzanas en casa Juan* ↓
(c) (k/d) *Come manzanas en casa Juan* ↑

The second type of *sí/no* question would result in:

(2) (k/d) *Juan come manzanas en casa* ↑

The k/d-questions are more complex than the *sí/no* questions because some k/d-words must agree in number with the particle in question [e.g., *cuál-es* (which), *quién-es* (who), *cuánto-s* (how much/many)]. Also, one k/d-word must agree in gender with the noun requiring information *(cuánto-a).* Another complexity involved in the k/d-questions concerns the use of prepositions, such that preposing the k/d-word requires also preposing the preposition [e.g., *por qué* (why), *adónde* (where), *por dónde* (whereabouts), *para qué* (why), *de cuál* (of which), *de quién* (whose), *para qué* (what for), etc.]. The transformations required for the k/d-type questions are: (1) preposing the k/d-word; (2) inverting the verb phrase with the noun phrase; (3) inserting the preposition at the beginning of the sentence; (4) number agreement; and (5) gender agreement. For the declarative sentence:

Juan come manzanas en casa

the transformations would form a k/d-question as follows:

I. *¿Quien come manzanas en casa?* (subject) (Who eats apples at home?)

II. *¿Juan come qué en casa?* (object)
   1. *¿Qué Juan come en casa?* (What does Juan eat at home?)
   2. *¿Qué come Juan en casa?*

The declarative:

Las muchachas van a casa (The girls are going home)

needs number and gender agreement and prepositional-preposing k/d-words:

I. *¿Cuánto-a(s) muchachas van a casa?* (quantifier) (How many girls
are going home?)

    4. *¿Cuánto-as muchachas van a casa?* (number agreement)

    5. *¿Cuánto-as muchachas van a casa?* (gender agreement)

II. 1. *¿Dónde las muchachas van?*   (location)   (Where are the
girls going?)

    2. *¿Dónde van las muchachas?*

    3. *¿A dónde van las muchachas?*

In comparing the structures of Spanish and English interrogatives, we can see that both languages employ equivalent transformations of interrogative preposing and inversion of verb and noun phrase. Additionally, the *sí/no* and yes/no question forms both involve the transformation of inverting the intonation pattern. However, k/d - *sí/no* questions differ from wh - yes/no questions because in Spanish the auxiliary verb ("do") is not inserted. Another difference is that the entire verb phrase is inverted with the noun phrase in Spanish whereas only the auxiliary verb (or "do") is inverted with the noun phrase in English (Stockwell et al., 1965):

The boys can go home   → Can the boys go home?

Los muchachos pueden ir a casa→ *¿Pueden ir los muchachos a casa?*

Also, in English one does not insert a presentential preposition as part of the wh-word nor does the structure require gender and/or number agreement.

A final comparison can be made with a less common type of question termed the tag question. Tag questions seek only to affirm what has previously been stated in the sentence. The words used in these types of questions are equivalent in Spanish and English:

eh	huh
a ver	see
verdad	okay; right

In summary, similarities exist in the structures of English and Spanish interrogatives. The transformational differences which occur between the two languages cannot be used to infer that the acquisition of the interrogative is easier in one language than in the other.

We will now proceed to a developmental analysis of interrogatives, first looking at English interrogative acquisition and then at Spanish interrogative acquisition, and finally comparing the structures of the two languages.

Klima and Bellugi-Klima (1966) have suggested that the acquisition of the English interrogative structure is divisible into three stages. By the end of the first stage, the child has already acquired the two transformations of wh-word preposing in both the yes/no and the wh-questions and rising intonation in yes/no questions. During stage two, the child develops some superficial structures of the interrogative (e.g., pronouns, articles, modifiers, and some inflections), but does not add any new transformations to his two existing rules. By stage three, the child is employing all the transformational rules necessary so that his interrogative structure approximates the adult pattern.

The bilingual children whose language development is reported here followed the three stages that Klima and Bellugi-Klima have outlined. In stage one, the five bilinguals who were 2.0 to 3.2 years of age had acquired the two transformations of interrogative preposing and rising intonation. Most of the wh-questions were of the form:

What - NP - (do)[1]
Where - NP - (go)

Some examples of the children's utterances are:

What that?
What you do?
Where he go?
Where it go?
Where gun?

Wh- preposing is obviously acquired by this first stage. The noun phrase follows the wh-word, with some sentences containing a verb. Many times the children would produce the wh-words "where" and "what" with the contraction for "is" attached:

What's that?
What's this go?
Where's the pennies?

However, there is no evidence of the contraction being a formal rule. Rather it seems that the "what's" and "where's" are lexical entries. Another word appeared in the samples of two children. These children produced the wh-word "who."

Who that?
Who is that?
Who's in there?

The verb "is" appeared in many of the "who" questions, as in the second example above.

The yes/no questions followed the rule written below, with the two transformational rules of preposing the interrogative (written as $Q^{yes/no}$) and inversion of the intonation pattern.

$$S \rightarrow Q^{yes/no} \text{ - Nucleus}$$

$$\text{Nucleus} \rightarrow \text{NP - (VP) - (NP)}$$

The following examples indicate a nucleus which is marked by a rising intonation:

Cows   ↑
Right here   ↑
Want it   ↑
Wanta see   ↑

These representative examples from stage one indicate that both transformations are evident. The rising intonation is perhaps more obvious than is the transformation of preposing. However, we can argue that the children seem to be preposing the interrogative word for two reasons. First, the children are forming questions, and second, preposing of the interrogative word structurally marks a question.

The stage one children have acquired two transformational rules: (1) preposing of the wh-word for both yes/no and wh-questions, and (2) rising intonation for the yes/no questions.

Four of the bilingual children who were in stage two were between 3.5 and 4.3 years old. Also, one child who was 6.4 years old produced utterances which structurally followed the rules of stage two. This one child had learned English at a later time than any of the other children and was more advanced in some respects, but will still be discussed in stage two. New transformational rules were not added during this period, but superficial structures (e.g., pronouns, modifiers, etc.) were expanded. For the wh-questions, the structure was:

$$S \rightarrow \left\{ \begin{array}{l} Q^{what} \\ Q^{where} \\ Q^{why} \end{array} \right\} \text{ - Nucleus}$$
$$\text{Nucleus} \rightarrow \text{NP - V - (NP)}$$

Some examples include:

Where I put it?
Where you get this, huh Kathy?
What you got?
Why you not put this up?
Why he like that?

The transformation of preposing is still the only transformation, but the questions are expanded from stage one with noun phrases and verbs. "Why," which has been added as a new wh-question word, is a more complex wh-word because it is more abstract. As in stage one, "who" appears as a wh-word but does not follow the structure of most questions, since a verb always follows:

Who are they?
Who are these fall in the water there?

The yes/no questions of the second period are similarly marked as:

$$S \rightarrow Q^{yes/no} - Nucleus$$

$$Nucleus \rightarrow NP - V - (NP)$$

with examples clearly supporting this rule:

She's a girl or boy ↑
Wanta use telephone ↑
Here this is top ↑
They go right there ↑

The rising intonation is, again, found in these examples. Both the wh- and the yes/no questions of this stage, as compared to the first stage, are longer, due to the addition of noun phrases and verbs in the questions.

The age range of the nine bilingual children who produced interrogative utterances which could be classified at stage three was 4.3 to 6.2 years of age. Children at this final stage added two new interrogative transformational rules. The two new transformations for both yes/no and wh-questions were: (1) insertion of auxiliary verbs, and (2) inversion of noun phrase and auxiliary verb.

Wh-questions now include three transformational rules, so that the stage three children's utterances approximate the adult model. The wh-structures were of the form:

$$S \rightarrow Q^{wh} - aux - NP - VP$$

Representative examples include:

Where should I put this?
Where does he go?
Why don't you play with this?
Now, which one's heavy and which one's light?
Whose is this?
What are you planning to do?
How could you do something like that?

New wh-words such as "which," "whose," and "how" have been acquired in addition to the new transformational rules. Children during this final stage show not only preposing of the wh-word, but they also insert auxiliary verbs into their questions and invert the auxiliary verb with the noun phrase. Klima and Bellugi-Klima's (1966) monolingual children did not evidence the inversion of auxiliary verb and noun phrase. Evidently, the final step of inversion of the noun phrase with the verb would have been the next stage for the children reported in the Klima and Bellugi-Klima study.

The yes/no questions, similarly, contained not only wh- preposing and intonation inversion, but also auxiliary verb insertion and noun phrase-auxiliary verb inversion, as evidenced in the examples below:

> Can I do it first, Kathy?
> Do you know what I'm gonna make?
> Didn't I talk of that?
> Could I hear it all?
> Shall we put it like this?

In sum, the three stages advanced from the two transformations of preposing and intonation inversion in the first stage to an expanding on the question forms by means of the addition of a verb in stage two. The children then progressed to stage three, with preposing of the wh-word, insertion of an auxiliary verb, insertion of the noun phrase and auxiliary verb, and inversion of the intonation pattern. This final stage in the development of the interrogative in our bilingual children resembles the English speaking adult-model form.

In the acquisition of Spanish interrogatives, only two developmental stages are found. In the first stage; we find three transformational rules: (1) preposing of the k/d-word; (2) inverting the noun phrase with the verb phrase; and (3) inverting the intonation pattern. The second-stage child adds three more transformational rules to his repertoire: (1) number agreement; (2) gender agreement of the k/d-word with the particles of the sentence the k/d-word is replacing; and (3) preposing the prepositions belonging to the k/d-word questions.

Six children, between the ages of 2.0 and 3.5 years, were found to be in stage one. The form of their k/d-questions was:

$$S \rightarrow Q^{k/d} - VP - (NP)$$

They utilized two transformational rules: (1) k/d- preposing, and (2) noun phrase-verb phrase inversion. A wide variety of k/d-question words are noted in this stage, as seen in the following examples:

¿Dónde está el otro?	(Where is the other one?)
¿Qué pasó acá?	(What happened over here?)
¿Quién es?	(Who is it?)
¿Cuál?	(Which?)
¿Por qué se cayeron?	(Why did they fall?)

Four of the children used the k/d-word *por qué* (why) even though *por qué* structurally belongs in the second stage because of its prepositional *(por)* preposing. A possible explanation for the occurrence of *por qué* is that it is a common k/d-word and is, in fact, more common than the remaining k/d-words that are used with prepositions.

Two transformational rules were applied in composing the *sí/no* questions. These rules were: (1) preposing of the interrogative word, and (2) inverting the intonation pattern from falling to rising. The two types of *sí/no* questions (discussed above) are already differentiated at this first stage. The reason for this differentiation is shown by the elaboration of the sentence's structure. That is, the intonation-only type questions are full declaratives with rising intonations, whereas the regular type of *sí/no* question, at this point, consists mostly of a fragment of a sentence (e.g., a noun phrase or a verb phrase, but no full structures with both noun and verb phrase). In the following examples, only the last one is of the intonation only type:

Esta ↑	(This?)
Aquí ↑	(Here?)
Otra vez ↑	(Again?)
Este pescado ↑	(This fish?)
Esta es tuya ↑	(This is yours?)

We can see that the children of stage one have acquired three transformational rules: (1) preposing of the interrogative word in both *sí/no* and k/d-questions, (2) inverting the noun phrase with the verb phrase in the k/d-questions, and (3) inverting the intonation pattern in *sí/no* questions. The k/d-question forms appear to be more elaborate structurally, and the large vocabulary of k/d-words which the children possess is also apparent. Both forms of the *sí/no* questions appear to be differentiated in this first period of development.

Our analysis of Spanish interrogative development indicates that the second and final stage is marked by three additional transformational rules for the k/d-questions and one more transformational rule for the *sí/no* questions. The three new transformational rules in the k/d-questions are: (1) preposing the preposition belonging to the k/d-word,

(2) number agreement, and (3) gender agreement. The structure of the k/d-question is:

$$S \rightarrow (prep) - k/d - VP - (NP)$$

Language samples indicated that the bilingual children had attained stage two in their development of the interrogative form by age 3 years, 8 months.

Some examples include:

¿Adónde vamos?	(Where are we going?)
Hey, ¿con qué puedo hacer algo?	(Hey, what can I make something with?)
Esto, ¿para qué es?	(This, what's it for?)
¿A cuánto está?	(How much is it?)
¿De quién es?	(Whose is it?)
¿Cuántos tienes?	(How many do you have?)
¿Cuáles?	(Which ones?)
¿Cuál hombre?	(Which man?)

Both types of *sí/no* questions are, again, apparent in stage two. The intonation-only type is similar to that seen in stage one, as evidenced below:

Ese es tu carro ↑	(That is your car?)
Esa es una casa ↑	(That is a house?)
Este es tu libro ↑	(This is your book?)

However, the *sí/no* questions are now full forms, because they are more elaborate and because of the addition of the new transformational rule of noun phrase-verb phrase inversion. Some examples include:

Ya no hay más cosas ↑	(Aren't there any more things?)
Quieres que me ayudes ↑	(Do you want to help me?)
Se puede quitar este ↑	(Can this be taken off?)
Mañana, vas a venir ↑	(Tomorrow, are you coming?)

To summarize, we see that from stage one to stage two a complexity in sentence structure and transformational rules develops, with stage one k/d-questions characterized by k/d-word preposing and noun phrase-verb phrase inversion. Stage two expands the form with the addition of number and gender agreement as well as prepositional preposing in k/d-questions. With the *sí/no* questions, stage two acquires a more elaborate structure and noun phrase-verb phrase inversion. The two types of *sí/no* questions are already differentiated by stage one.

Table 1

Summary of the Developmental Stages of the wh- and k/d-Interrogative in English and Spanish

Stage	English	Spanish
1.	A. Structure What-NP-(do) Where-NP-(go) B. Transformations 1. wh- preposing	A. Structure $S \rightarrow Q^{k/d}$-VP-(NP) B. Transformations 1. k/d- preposing 2. Inversion of noun and verb phrases
2.	A. Structure $$S \rightarrow \left\{ \begin{array}{l} Q^{what} \\ Q^{where} \\ Q^{whv} \end{array} \right\} \text{-Nucleus}$$ Nucleus$\rightarrow$NP-V-(NP) B. Transformations (No new transformations)	A. Structure $S \rightarrow$(prep)-k/d-VP-(NP) B. New Transformations 1. Number agreement in k/d-word 2. Gender agreement in k/d-word 3. Preposing prep. belonging to k/d-word
3.	A. Structure $S \rightarrow Q^{wh}$-aux-NP-VP B. New Transformations 1. Insertion of auxiliary verbs 2. Inversion of noun phrase and auxiliary verb	

Tables 1 and 2 depict the developmental stages of the interrogative forms in the two languages.

In contrasting the acquisition of interrogatives in English and in Spanish, the stage analysis reveals a more rapid initial development of the interrogative in Spanish than in English. Why this occurs may be due to the semantic variability of verb phrases in the two languages. In Spanish, the verb phrase reflects not only the verb but, in most cases, also the noun. On the other hand, in English the noun must be specified, since the noun is not a part of the verb. The language samples clearly indicate this difference in specification of noun and verb. When the bilingual children speak English, they are noun-oriented, as evidenced by the literature citing telegraphic speech (Brown, 1973). They change to being verb-oriented when they speak Spanish, as evidenced by the following examples:

Table 2

Summary of the Developmental Stages of the Yes/No and *Sí/No*
Interrogative in Spanish and English

Stage	English	Spanish

1.	A. Structure
	  $S \rightarrow Q^{yes/no}$-Nucleus
	  Nucleus $\rightarrow$ NP-(VP)-(NP)
	B. Transformations
	  1. Interrogative preposing
	  2. Intonation inversion
		A. Structure
		  $S \rightarrow Q^{sí/no}$-Nucleus
		  Nucleus $\rightarrow$ (VP)-NP
		B. Transformations
		  1. Interrogative preposing
		  2. Intonation inversion

2.	A. Structure
	  $S \rightarrow Q^{yes/no}$-Nucleus
	  Nucleus $\rightarrow$ NP-V-(NP)
	B. Transformations
	  (No new transformations)
		A. Structure
		  $S \rightarrow Q^{sí/no}$-VP-(NP)
		B. New Transformations
		  1. Noun-verb phrase inversion

3.	A. Structure
	  $S \rightarrow Q^{yes/no}$-aux-NP-VP
	B. New Transformations
	  1. Insertion of auxiliary
	    verb
	  2. Inversion of auxiliary
	    verb and noun	

¿Dónde está?	(Where are you?) (Where is he/she/it?)
¿Qué tiene?	(What do you have?) (What does he/she/it have?)
¿Qué va aquí?	(What goes here?)

Now compare the above with the following English examples:

What these?
Where the soldiers?
That the cowboys?

In both languages the children presuppose that the listener has knowledge of what is being referred to, that is, the noun or the verb. A possible
explanation for this noun/verb orientation may be how verb phrases are
structured in Spanish and English. In the Spanish adult model, the noun
is included in most verb phrases and need not be specified. However, in
English the verb phrase is more complicated, due to obligatory inser-
tions of the noun and the auxiliary verbs, such as in "Where should I put
this" or "How could you do something like that?" Thus, the contrast in
the variability of developmental stages may reflect the differences
between the verb phrases of both languages.

When we compare acquisition of the interrogative form using a stage analysis, we see in both languages the preposing of the question word and inversion of the intonation pattern in the first stage. Also, in Spanish the children are inverting the noun and verb phrases. The second stage of English is an elaboration period where no new transformations are added, but where structural expansion occurs. In the final stages of both languages, new transformational rules are added so that the interrogative structure reaches the adult model. In Spanish, the children add the transformations of preposing the prepositions belonging to the k/d-word and number and gender agreement. The new transformational rules which the children add in English are auxiliary verb insertion and auxiliary verb and noun phrase inversion. In sum, we can conclude that children acquiring Spanish and English simultaneously show a similar progression from initial use of the interrogative to the acquisition of the adult model form.

Negatives

The negation rules for both languages, Spanish and English, will now be discussed briefly, in order to compare and contrast the negative forms.

For the English adult negative structure, the form may be written as:

$$S \rightarrow NP \text{ - aux - } VP$$

$$aux \rightarrow T \text{ - } V^{aux} \text{ - neg*}$$

The auxiliary verb accepts the negative particle in the form of a contracted "not" (n't), or by "not" following the auxiliary verb. The two transformations inherent in this structure are: (1) "Negative Transportation" and (2) "Do Support" (McNeill, 1970). Negative Transportation (Neg Trans) involves moving the negative element from the beginning of the sentence to a position behind the auxiliary verb. Neg Trans also changes indeterminants (some, somebody, somewhere, etc.), if they are following a negative, to indefinites (any, anybody, anywhere, etc.). Negative words such as the pronouns "nobody" and "nothing," and the adverbs "nowhere" and "never" are inserted in their proper positions as dictated by the parts of speech they represent and also by the rule Neg Trans. If no auxiliary verb is present in the sentence, the insertion of "do" is obtained by the rule "Do Support." Therefore, the declarative sentence:

He wants something

---

*T signifies tense marking of the verb.

could be transformed to a negative in the following ways:

(1) He want (neg) something (neg)
(2) He doesn't want something (neg)
(3) He doesn't want anything

In the Spanish negative system, negation is always inserted before the verb phrase by Neg Trans. However, it takes two forms: (1) "no" is inserted preverbally when there is no proverbal element that can take a negative form (i.e., *algo, alguien*); or (2) "Neg Spread," which occurs when there is a preverbal element capable of taking the negative form. The preverbal element is inserted before the entire verb phrase and then dictates that a negative be attached throughout the verb phrase wherever it can be accepted (Stockwell et al., 1965). The negative elements include *nadie, nada, nunca, ningún,* etc. Thus, the declarative sentence:

Él quiere algo

would be transformed in the following ways:

(1) *Él no quiere algo* (Neg Trans)
(2) *Él no quiere nada* (Neg Spread)

In comparing the negative structures in Spanish and English, we can see that both languages employ the transformational rule Neg Trans, inserting the negative element preverbally. However, a Spanish speaker inserts the negative element before the entire verb phrase while an English speaker inserts the negative particle between the auxiliary verb and the main verb. Also, the Neg Trans rule results in double negative structures for Spanish speakers, but does not form double negatives in English. Another contrast occurs with the use of the rule "Do Support." English speakers need a rule to insert the auxiliary verb "do" if no other auxiliary verbs are present. In Spanish, on the other hand, one need not insert the auxiliary verb. A comparable process transpires in the two languages with the changing of indeterminants to negative elements, from the Neg Trans rule.

In summary, we can see that both Spanish and English employ the Neg Trans rules, although the end result is different in the two languages. In English, an additional rule is needed for auxiliary verb insertion. Also, both languages utilize Neg Trans to negate their indeterminants.

We will now proceed to the developmental stages of negation, first in English and then in Spanish.

Klima and Bellugi-Klima (1966) have proposed that there are three stages of development in English negation. These stages are: (1) "no" inserted presententially; (2) a negative particle inserted between a noun phrase and a verb phrase, by Neg Trans; and (3) negation inserted between the auxiliary verb and the main verb, by the Neg Trans rule and possibly also by "Do Support."

Only our youngest bilingual subject, who was 2.0 years old, produced utterances that were still in the first period. The rule for this initial stage was:

$$S \rightarrow no - (nucleus)$$

Some examples of negative utterances consisted of:

> Kitty no
> No

These utterances obviously fit into the negation rule of "no" plus an optional nucleus.

The ages of the bilingual children whose utterances fit into the second period were between 2.6 and 3.8 years. This second stage showed the development of Neg Trans in moving the negative element from the beginning of the sentence to between the noun phrase and the verb phrase. The negative elements consisted of "no," "not," "can't," and "don't" as well as "nobody" and "nothing." The structure at this stage can be notated as:

$$S \rightarrow NP - neg - VP$$

$$Neg \rightarrow \begin{Bmatrix} no \\ not \\ V^{neg} \end{Bmatrix}$$

$$V^{neg} \rightarrow \begin{Bmatrix} can't \\ don't \end{Bmatrix}$$

Some examples of this stage are:

> And they no more
> He can't see me
> Don't want to
> No go in here
> No give it
> He's no talking like that
> Nobody
> Nothing

"No" attached preverbally was still the most common form of negation. The two negative words "nobody" and "nothing," both of which are pronouns, occurred only in isolation. The contracted auxiliary verbs "can't" and "don't" were found at this stage but there was no evidence of separation into "cannot" and "do not," leading us to the contention that "can't" and "don't" are negative lexical items. Klima and Bellugi-Klima (1966) also observed similar lexical items in the language samples of their monolingual children.

The distinction between stage two and stage three occurs with reference to the auxiliary verbs. In stage three, auxiliary verbs are either contracted with the negative element "not" or merely followed by the word "not," by the application of the Neg Trans rule. Use of the rule "Do Support" is also evidenced. The form for the third period is:

$$S \rightarrow NP - aux - VP$$
$$aux \rightarrow T - V^{aux} - neg$$

$$V^{aux} \rightarrow \left\{ \begin{array}{l} do \\ can \\ be \\ will \\ could \end{array} \right\}$$

Our bilingual children at this third stage of development were 4.3 to 6.2 years of age. Examples of their negative utterances are:

My mother doesn't let me
Her mother won't let her
There wasn't a gorilla
He isn't
The other one couldn't
I cannot
I can't even see that

These examples substantiate the rule that the negative particle is inserted between the auxiliary verb and the main verb. Some children had problems, at times, understanding which verb takes the tense marking—the auxiliary verb or the main verb:[2]

You don't have to told me that
And we didn't went on that boat
It didn't came out
I didn't saw that

There are also negative elements such as the pronouns "nothing" and "nobody" as well as the adverbs "never" and "nowhere" transformed into the sentences:

> He's saying just nothing
> There was nothing else
> Nowheres
> Nobody see me
> I never saw a green cow

Negating of a time element was also observed; these negations were correctly formed and used in appropriate circumstances. For example:

> Not now
> Not today
> Not yet

The largest undeveloped category which appeared was the formation of double negatives, which are inappropriate in English. McNeill (1970) explains the occurrence of double negatives in monolingual English-speaking children as an overgeneralization from the affirmative structures. Since the result of an affirmative structure is positive, the child overgeneralizes that the result of a negative structure will also be positive, so he inserts two negatives and transforms the sentence into a double negative. The reasoning is explained structurally as:[3]

> I want$^+$ some
> I want$^+$ none$^-$ or I don't$^-$ want any$^+$
> I don't$^-$ want none$^-$

Language samples from the bilingual children studied here support McNeill's explanation of how children form double negatives. Some examples are:

> But it's *don't* have *none* of those
> Then you *won't* have *nothing* of my cake
> I'm *not* gonna make *nothing*
> No, snakes *don't* have *none*
> And *don't never* get my garage
> He *don't* look like *nothing*

There were also examples of children learning the correct usage of indefinites:

> There was nothing *else*
> You don't have *any*
> I can't read this one *anymore*
> *Some* aren't fighting

Even the more complex usage of placing indeterminants in a negative sentence and using them in the proper position is evidenced in the last example.

Accordingly, we see in the three stages a progression from "no" plus a nucleus to the use of Neg Trans in moving "no" or "not," "can't" or "don't" to their position before the verb phrase. Then we observe the more complex auxiliary verb contraction of "not" before the main verb, the beginning of the use of indefinites as opposed to double negatives, and the use of the "Do Support" rule.

The Spanish adult model of negation was also completed in three developmental stages. The first period consists of "no" in isolation. In the second stage, "no" is inserted before a verb phrase, employing Neg Trans, and in addition the negative word *nada* is used. Stage three advances to the use of a greater variety of negative words. These negative elements are inserted into the sentence and extended into the verb phrase wherever possible by use of Neg Spread, forming double negatives.

Only one bilingual child, who was 2.0 years of age, was still at the first stage of negative development. Her utterances consisted of *no* used in isolation.

Our second-stage bilingual children ranged from 2.6 to 3.2 years. The structure of their utterances can be expressed as:

$$S \rightarrow (NP) - no - VP$$

This rule is apparent in the following stage two utterances:

No que éste	(None of that)
No traes	(Don't bring)
No me puches porque te pego	(Don't push me because I'll hit you)
Él no vive	(He doesn't live)
Yo no puedo hacer	(I can't make)
Tú no quiere a comer	(You don't want to eat)
No me gusta	(I don't like it)

The transformation employed in this second stage was that of Neg Trans. In utilizing Neg Trans, *no* was inserted before each verb phrase, and then a noun phrase followed if one was present. Also, the negative word *nada* was evidenced in the language samples of several children. However, it was always observed in isolation.

Stage three utterances expanded the second period utterances through the substitution of negative particles for corresponding sentential particles using the Neg Trans rule. The following structures correspond to the utterances:

$$(1) \ S \rightarrow N^{(neg)} - VP - N^{(neg)}$$

$$N^{neg} \rightarrow \left\{ \begin{array}{c} nada \\ nadie \end{array} \right\}$$

$$(2) \ S \rightarrow VP^{neg} - VP - (NP)$$

$$VP^{neg} \rightarrow \left\{ \begin{array}{c} nunca \\ ningún \end{array} \right\}$$

Some examples of this rule used in utterances are:

Nadie juega conmigo	(No one plays with me)
Yo no falto nada	(I'm not missing any)
Dije nada	(I didn't say anything)
Nunca va con eso porque vamos a jugar	(Never go with that because we are going to play)
Yo no, nunca he ido	(Not me, I never have gone)
Nada más tengo una	(I only have one)

These negative elements are inserted before the verb phrase and in many cases are further negated in the verb phrase by Neg Spread, as evidenced by the following utterances:

No hay nadie allí	(There's no one over there)
No se llama nada	(It's not called anything)
Esto no hace nada	(This doesn't do anything)
Porque casi no tenemos nada de comida	(Because we hardly [or barely] have anything to eat)

The rule for the Neg Spread utterances is:

$$S \rightarrow (NP) - no - VP - (N^{neg})$$

$$N^{neg} \rightarrow \left\{ \begin{array}{c} nada \\ nadie \end{array} \right\}$$

Another development is in the inherently negative element *tampoco*. *Yo tampoco* (me neither) was observed in several instances, thus beginning the realization of negation in words other than the negative particles.

In sum, the first stage of negation in Spanish is limited to *no* and the second stage to *no* plus the verb phrase. This structure is expanded in the third stage to include more complex negative structures with noun phrases and double negatives. The substitution of negative words for their affirmative complements is also observed in the language samples.

Table 3 presents the developmental stages of the negative form in both Spanish and English.

Table 3
Summary of the Developmental Stages of Negation in English and Spanish

Stage	English	Spanish
1.	A. Structure $S \rightarrow$ no - (nucleus) B. Transformation (none)	A. Structure $S \rightarrow$ *no* B. Transformations (none)
2.	A. Structure $S \rightarrow$ NP - neg - VP $Neg \rightarrow \begin{Bmatrix} no \\ not \\ V^{neg.} \end{Bmatrix}$ $V^{neg} \rightarrow \begin{Bmatrix} can't \\ don't \end{Bmatrix}$ B. Transformations 1. Neg Transport	A. Structure $S \rightarrow$ (NP) - *no* - VP B. Transformations 1. Neg Transport
3.	A. Structures 1. $S \rightarrow$ (N) $^{(neg)}$ - VP - (N) $^{(neg)}$ $N^{neg} \rightarrow \begin{Bmatrix} nobody \\ nothing \\ no\ one \\ none \end{Bmatrix}$ 2. $S \rightarrow VP^{neg}$ - VP - (NP) $VP^{neg} \rightarrow \begin{Bmatrix} (never) \\ (nowhere) \end{Bmatrix}$ 3. $S \rightarrow$ NP - aux - VP aux $\rightarrow$ T - V^{aux} - neg $V^{aux} \rightarrow \begin{Bmatrix} do \\ can \\ be \\ will \\ could \end{Bmatrix}$ B. New Transformations 1. Do Support	A. Structures 1. $S \rightarrow$ (N) $^{(neg)}$ VP - (N) $^{(neg)}$ $N^{neg} \rightarrow \begin{Bmatrix} nada \\ nadie \\ ninguno \end{Bmatrix}$ 2. $S \rightarrow VP^{neg}$ - VP - (NP) $VP^{neg} \rightarrow \begin{Bmatrix} nunca \\ ningún \end{Bmatrix}$ 3. $S \rightarrow$ (NP) - *no* - VP - (N^{neg}) $N^{neg} \rightarrow \begin{Bmatrix} nada \\ nadie \\ ninguno \end{Bmatrix}$ B. New Transformations 1. Neg Spread

In comparing English and Spanish, we can see that negation in both languages requires three developmental periods. The first negation stage in both languages is comparable, since we see in both English and Spanish the use of "no" in isolation or preceding a nucleus. Also, the second negation stage in English is very similar to the second Spanish stage in the formation of the structures: NP - neg - VP and (NP) - *no* - VP. However, English seems more complex because of the use of contractions (e.g., "can't and "don't"). The negative words of English, "nothing" and "nobody," are semantically equivalent to the first Spanish negative elements learned, *nada* and *nadie*. Proceeding into the final stage of each language, we see that negation in English appears more complex than in Spanish. In negating a sentence English speakers must insert the auxiliary verb "do" if no other auxiliary verb is present. Then the negative element must be inserted between the auxiliary verb and the main verb; or, alternatively, the negative element can be contracted with the auxiliary verb. When speaking Spanish, the speaker only has to learn to negate the entire verb phrase, which as shown above results in double negation. The double negative is formed by the application of the Neg Spread transformational rule. In English, the speaker must learn to confine the negation to only that sentential particle which requires negation. The formation of double negatives in English appears prior to the structuring of the fully formed negative adult model (McNeill, 1970). It is this progression from double negatives to the specification of the sentential particle requiring negation that leads us to suggest that the formation of negatives is more complex in English than in Spanish.

A similarity between Spanish and English exists regarding the substitution of negative elements for their corresponding affirmative structures (e.g., indefinites). That is, both languages have replacement of:

Spanish	English
nadie for *alguien*	nobody for anybody
nada for *algo*	none, nothing for any
ningún for *algún*	nowhere for anywhere

To conclude, we have shown that when Spanish-English bilingual children are learning negative forms, their first structures are not necessarily distinguishable in terms of which language's "no" they are using—that is, the English "no" or the Spanish *no*. However, as the children proceed to learn the complexities of each language's negation rules, it readily becomes apparent which rules they are using for negation.

Possessives

The possessive structures of English and Spanish can be compared and contrasted in a number of ways: (1) the position of the possessive element in sentences; (2) the use of possessive pronouns; (3) the breakdown of pronouns into gender and number agreement; (4) the inflectional affix /'s/, and "of " or *de;* and (5) the transformational rules used to derive these forms. As with the negatives and interrogatives, adult structures will be discussed and compared to ensure a clearer understanding of the acquisition of possessive structures in English and Spanish.

First, it is important to point out that transformational grammarians have argued that possession is derived from simple sentences with the verb "have" (Lyons, 1967). This theory focuses on the premise that the deep structure of possessives is similar to the deep structure of relative clauses. We will begin the discussion of both languages with a consideration of the transformational rules for forming possessives. This will be based on the argument that "have" or *tener* sentences are possessive in structure and therefore derive the alternate possessive forms /'s/, "of," and *de*.

Possession in English occurs in two ways: (1) by noun inflection of /'s/ (i.e., man's) and (2) by the use of possessive pronouns. The pronouns are either feminine (her), masculine (his), or neuter (its, your, their). Inherent in the possessive structure is a number reference, so that singularity and plurality are determined by selecting from person-number forms to identify the possession (my book versus my books; our book versus our books). Possession can occur in two environments: before nouns (with pronouns or /'s/) or elsewhere, such as after the verb "be" and after nouns. In the latter, in nominal functions, the possessive must be part of a prepositional phrase (i.e., the house of the man). An inherent possessive form is found in the question word "whose," a wh-question word which always indicates possession.

The transformational rules for deriving possessive structures can be notated in the following way:

(1) NP_1 - have - $NP_2 \rightarrow NP_1$ - /'s/ - NP_2*

(2) NP_1 - /'s/ - $NP_2 \rightarrow NP_2$ - of - NP_1

"Have" forms derive the /'s/ forms, which in turn derive the "of" forms. In forming possessive pronouns, the following transformational rules apply:

(3) NP_1 - have - $NP_2 \rightarrow NP_1{}^{ProN}$ - NP_2

(4) ProN $\rightarrow$ Number agreement (singular, plural)

(5) ProN $\rightarrow$ Gender agreement (masculine, feminine, neuter)

From the following declarative sentence:

The man has a house

the possessive will be formed as follows:

---

* NP_1 refers to the Possessor and NP_2 refers to the Possessed.

(1) The man's house

or (2) The house of the man

or (3), (4), and (5) ProN-singular, masculine → His house

A total of five transformational rules apply for possessive structures, with the pronouns responsible for the existence of three of the rules.

Spanish possessives are also of two classes: pronouns and possessive noun phrases utilizing the word *de*. The first class, the pronouns, are adjectival and therefore show gender and number agreement (Stockwell et al., 1965). Two kinds of number agreement are needed: reference to the possessor, and reference to the possessed. That is, the correct first or second person form must be used as well as a singular or plural inflection depending on whether the possessed item is singular or plural. The gender agreement is made to the possessed item (i.e., when the possessed object is masculine, the gender will be masculine). Before nouns, the possessive pronouns *mío, tuyo,* and *suyo* are shortened to *mi, tu* and *su*. The possessive pronouns occur in three positions: (1) after nouns, where they function as adjectives; (2) after the verb *ser* (to be), where they again function adjectivally; and (3) before a noun, where they function as determiners. When the nominal case is used, the pronouns require determiners. The second form of possession requires the use of *de* in noun phrases. It is also used to distinguish the third person forms of *suyo,* since *suyo* is used in both the singular and plural third person forms (Stockwell et al., 1965). The question form *de quién* is inherently possessive since it always requires a possessive form as a response.

The transformational rules in Spanish can be notated as:

(1) (NP_1) - *tener* - NP_2 → NP_2 - *de* - NP_1

(2) (NP_1) - *tener* - NP_2 → ProN - NP_2

(3) ProN - NP_2 → (NP_2) - *ser* - ProN

(4) ProN → Gender (masculine, feminine)

(5) ProN → Number (singular, plural) to possessor

(6) ProN → Number (singular, plural) to possessed

Using the six transformational rules, the sentence:

El hombre tiene dos carros   (The man has two cars)

would be derived for the possessive form as follows:

(1) . . . *dos carros del hombre*   (Two cars of the man = The man's two cars)

(2), (4), (5), (6) *Sus dos carros*   (His two cars)

(3), (4), (5), (6) *Los dos carros son suyos*   (The two cars are his)

In comparing the structures of the English and Spanish possessives, we can observe that both languages have two major possessive structures: pronouns, and the /'s/, "of," and *de* forms. Possessive pronouns in both languages have gender and number agreement, but only one form of number agreement corresponds in the two languages: that of agreement to the possessor—that is, the correct singular or plural first, second or third person form. Each language has possessives occurring in positions before nouns, after nouns, and after the corresponding verb *ser* or "to be." Also, the structures /'s and *de* are similar to the extent that the prepositional "of " form of the inflectional /'s/ is a transformational derivative, and is semantically equivalent to the Spanish *de* form. For example, *La casa del hombre* is equivalent to "the house of the man," which is equivalent transformationally to "the man's house." The verbs "have" and *tener* are related as possessive constructs and in transformationally deriving the alternative possessive forms: the pronouns, and the *de*, /'s/, and "of " forms. Another similarity is noted in the two corresponding possessive question forms *de quién* and "whose."

In contrast, we find that the English gender agreement is to the possessor while the Spanish gender agreement is to the possessed. English has three gender classes (feminine, masculine, and neuter) while Spanish has only two (feminine and masculine). Also, in Spanish there is an additional number agreement with the possessed object. Another difference is that the Spanish possessives are adjectives while the English possessives are simply pronouns.

We will now see how bilingual children acquire these possessive forms. Development of English possessives is divided into two periods. The first period shows development of three transformations with use of possessive pronouns containing gender and number agreement. The acquisition of the two additional transformations—inflectional /'s/ and "of " for the prepositional phrase form—occurs in the second stage. Also developing in the second stage is the "whose" question.

In stage one we note the following utterances:

Mine
The train mine
I gonna kill my face
Your hand on it
Oh, where his *mano* (hand)?
What's your name?
It's her fire
Our playground

The bilingual children at this first stage were 2.0 to 4.3 years old. Their English language samples reveal a number of possessive pronouns, all of which agree in number and gender. By this first stage, children are already using three of the five transformational rules.

An interesting occurrence was the word "mines," which two children generalized when the possessed noun was plural. Menyuk (1964) also noted this occurrence of the carry-over of the plural object that was being possessed into the word "mine," making it "mines."

Stage two is comprised of children who range in age from 4.3 to 6.4 years old. Their structures are marked by the two additional transformational rules: forming the prepositional phrase possessives with "of" and using the inflected suffix /'s/ possessives. Some examples of stage two utterances are:

Those are mines
It's not theirs
Because their mother went to get some apples
It's a monkey's tail
It's not yours, it's Jay's remember?
The hair of the prince
The leg of the grandma
Here comes a friend of them

From these examples, we can see that the children are acquiring the two transformational rules stated above. Also found at this stage is the possessive construct "whose."

Whose is bigger, his or his?
Whose is this?

This question word, as well as the inherently possessive word "belong," shows that the child is beginning to understand possession in its more abstract form:

This belong to me
They belong to me
Who does this belong to?

Thus by the second stage, the children are employing more complex forms of possession. In short, they are elaborating on the already developed pronouns of the first stage and adding more pronouns.

Two stages comprise the development of the Spanish possessive system. The first period consists of the transformational rules for deriving pronouns with correct number and gender agreement and for formation of the shortened form of the pronouns. The verb *tener* is also well developed in the first period. Stage two encompasses the addition of the *de* form as well as the *de quién* question form.

The utterances in stage one are from children who ranged in age from 2.0 to 3.8 years. They show understanding of both the shortened and the regular forms of the possessive pronouns:

Es mío	(It's mine)
Son tuyas	(They are yours)
Éste es tuyo	(This is yours)
Esos míos	(Those mine)
¿Dónde está mi sombrero?	(Where is my hat?)
A su mamá	(To his mother)
Estos son mis amigos	(These are my friends)
¿Es tuyo el tren?	(Is the train yours?)

Also apparent are both number and gender agreement.

In stage two the children were 4.3 to 6.4 years of age. Their structures included the addition of the forms *de* and *de quién*. The following examples are typical:

¿Dónde están las patas de la abuelita?	(Where are the grandmother's feet?
Son de mi mamá	(They are my mother's)
Una es de mi hermana	(One is my sister's)
Son del pato	(They are the duck's)
La mano de Plu	(Plu's hand)
A la oficina del doctor	(To the doctor's office)
¿De quién es?	(Whose is it?)

Thus, to the well developed pronouns acquired in stage one, the children add the possessive forms *de* and *de quién*.

The developmental stages for the possessive form in both Spanish and English are shown in Table 4.

In comparing the possessive development of the children in English and Spanish, we can see that in both languages the pronouns are developed first and occur with both number and gender agreement. The structures *de* and /'s/ as well as the prepositional phrase form with "of" are acquired next, and the "whose" and *de quién* question words follow. In both English and Spanish the first stage is marked by the focus on the application of transformational rules to form the possessive pronouns.

In sum, the developmental stage analysis indicates that the possessive structures appear to be acquired at the same rate in both languages. In

Table 4

Summary of the Developmental Stages of the Possessive Form in English and Spanish

Stage	English	Spanish

1.	A. Structure
	 1. Pronouns
		A. Structure
		 1. Pronouns
		  a. Shortened
		  b. Lengthened

	B. Transformations
	 1. Gender agreement
	 2. Number agreement
		B. Transformations
		 1. Gender agreement
		 2. Number agreement
		  a. To possessor
		  b. To possessed

	3. Have → Pronoun Trans.	3. *Tener* → Pronoun Trans.
2.	A. Structure 1. /'s/ form 2. Prep. form ("of ") 3. "Whose"	A. Structure 1. *De* form 2. *De quién* form
	B. New Transformations 1. Have → /'s/ form 2. 's/ → "of" form	B. New Transformations 1. Tener → *de* form

drawing this conclusion, it is interesting to point out two complexities in acquiring the possessive form that bilingual children must overcome. First, there is the fact that in Spanish there are two forms of the possessive pronouns—shortened (*mi, tu, su*) and lengthened (*mio, tuyo, suyo*)—that the child bilingual speaker must acquire. Second, we note that the two English possessive forms—"of " and /'s/—are equivalent to the single form *de* in Spanish. These differences, however, do not appear to create problems for bilingual children learning to form the possessive in Spanish and English.

SUMMARY AND CONCLUSIONS

Play sessions with 19 Spanish-English bilingual children provided a corpus of spontaneous speech for an investigation of children's ability to use the interrogative, negative, and possessive forms in both languages. The purpose of this study was to compare and contrast the development of these grammatical structures in bilingual child speakers. In order to make such an analysis meaningful, we first discussed the adult patterns of each of these grammatical structures in Spanish and English. Then we employed a stage analysis as a framework around which to demonstrate how the child comes to approximate the adult structure in his/her use of the interrogative, negative, and possessive forms in both Spanish and English.

In comparing the developmental stages for each of the three grammatical structures in English and Spanish, it was found that children attained the adult model for interrogatives at different times (i.e., two stages in Spanish versus three stages in English). This developmental difference was not observed in the acquisition of either the possessive or the negative forms.

The acquisition of English interrogatives appeared to be initially slower than the development of Spanish interrogatives. It was hypothesized that the difference was due to a contrast in emphasis on verb phrases. That is, in Spanish the speaker often need not specify a noun with his/her verb. However, in English, both the noun and the verb must be specified. Further, there is an obligatory rule in English which requires the insertion of an auxiliary verb in the interrogative sentence. A similar rule does not exist in Spanish. Tables 1 and 2 summarize both wh - k/d and yes/no - *sí/no* question structures and the transformational rules deriving these interrogative forms. We can see that interrogative preposing is the first transformational rule acquired in Spanish and English for both question forms (wh - k/d and yes/no - *sí/no*). The other apparent transformational rule that is similar in both languages at the first stage is intonation inversion in the yes/no - *sí/no* questions. The next transformational rules in both languages involve the inversion of the verb (phrase) with the noun (phrase). In Spanish, this inversion is acquired by the first stage for the k/d-questions and by the second stage for the *sí/no* questions. In English, on the other hand, inversion does not occur until stage three, after the auxiliary verb is inserted. New question words are added in the second stage of both languages. In Spanish, at this second stage the children acquire transformational rules to derive correct number/gender agreement as well as preposing of the prepositions belonging to the k/d-word.

Negation in English was found to be comparable to the stages of development in Spanish negation. In stage one (see Table 3), we see the similar Spanish and English structures "no" uttered either in isolation or preceding a nucleus. The form of the second stage in both languages necessitates employment of the transformational rule Negative Transport to derive the structures of an optional noun phrase followed by some sort of negation and a verb phrase. The negative elements used, at this point, are "can't," "don't," and "not" in English, and *no* in Spanish. To arrive at the final stage in each language, the transformations of Negative Spread (in Spanish) and Do Support (in English) are added. From these rules, auxiliary verb insertion followed by some kind of negation occurs in English, while double negatives are evidenced in Spanish. It appears that the English negative structure is more complex at this point due to the insertion of the negative element between the auxiliary verb and the main verb. Further, the negation many times results in contractions. At the final stage in Spanish the children develop double negatives. Double negatives appear to be easily formed, since children speaking English progress through double negatives before mastering the English form, where only one negative element exists. In the third stage, negation in both languages is refined through the addition of another structure, which involves replacement of a negative element for an affirmative element. The resulting forms in Spanish and English are analogous (refer to Table 3, stage 3, structures 1 and 2).

The developmental stages of the possessive structures, like those of the negative forms, proceed similarly in English and Spanish from stage one to stage two. The first evident structure is the formation of possessive pronouns. In Spanish, the children learn both the shortened and lengthened forms, while in English there exists only one form to be learned. The transformations for the pronouns in both languages involve the derivation of the pronouns from the verbs "have" and *tener,* as well as gender and number agreement. In advancing to the second and final stage, the children develop the similar forms *de* and /'s/ from the "have" and *tener* verbs. Additionally, in English the children acquire the "of" form from the /'s/ structure. Another form emerging at this final stage is the question words *de quién* and "whose."

We will now turn to addressing several of the questions posed at the beginning of this paper. First, we asked whether grammatical structures were more easily learned first in one language and then later transferred to the second language. Analysis of the developmental stages suggests that there is no transfer, since the grammatical structure that varies (interrogative) requires different transformational rules to derive the correct form. Since different rules are required, speakers cannot develop one grammatical structure—for example, in English—and then apply the same rules to derive a similar grammatical structure in the other language. Another question posed was whether there was any interference from one language to another which could have deleterious effects on how bilingual children acquire either of their two languages. The answer to this question is that little, if any, interference was apparent in the language samples obtained from the 19 children. Further, although this study was not designed to compare the rate of language acquisition in monolingual and bilingual children, our analysis of the data do lead us to suggest that bilingual children do not develop language at a slower rate than monolingual children. These results fail to support Swain (1972), who has indicated that the acquisition of the interrogative form was delayed in the speech development of French/English bilingual children. The data reported here, on the other hand, support the earlier findings of Padilla and Liebman (1975), which showed that in developing grammatical structures, bilingual children do not appear to lag behind monolingual children. In sum, we may conclude that bilingual children can separate the grammatical rules for each language and that there is not the interference between languages so frequently discussed in the literature on bilingualism. Finally, in confirming the earlier findings of Padilla and Leibman, we would here argue that the deleterious effects of child bilingualism suggested by recent literature (e.g., Axelrod, 1974; Riley, 1972) are unconvincing.

Finally, we recommend that when language acquisition is to be studied in bilingual children a stage analysis be employed. Such an approach allows for a more refined contrastive analysis of the similarities and differences between equivalent grammatical structures in the two languages. The value of this approach is that a more organized and interpretative analysis of the language development of bilingual children can be presented. From this, more empirically based and linguistically sound conclusions can be reached about the relative merits and/or problems of child bilingualism.

NOTES

1. Adapted from Klima and Bellugi-Klima (1966).
2. This confusion in verb tense marking was also observed by Klima and Bellugi-Klima (1966).
3. From McNeill (1970).

REFERENCES

Axelrod, J. Some pronunciation and linguistic problems of Spanish-speaking children in American classrooms. *Elementary English*, 1974, *51*, 203–206.

Bloom, L. *Language Development: Form and Function in Emerging Grammars.* Cambridge, Mass.: M.I.T. Press, 1970.

Bowerman, M. *Early Syntactic Development: A Cross-linguistic Study with Special Reference to Finnish.* Cambridge, England: Cambridge University Press, 1973.

Brown, R. *A First Language: The Early Stages.* Cambridge, Mass.: Harvard University Press, 1973.

Burling, R. Language development of a Garo and English-speaking child. *Word*, 1959, *15*, 45–68.

Klima, E. S., & Bellugi-Klima, U. Syntactic regularities in the speech of children. In J. Lyons and R. J. Wales, eds., *Psycholinguistics Papers*. Edinburgh, England: Edinburgh University Press, 1966.

Leopold, W. *Speech Development of a Bilingual Child: A Linguist's Record*. Vol. 1: *Vocabulary Growth in the First Two Years*, 1939. Vol. 2: *Sound Learning in the First Two Years*, 1947. Vol. 3: *Grammars and General Problems in the First Two Years*, 1949a. Vol. 4: *Diary from Age Two*, 1949b. Evanston, Ill.: Northwestern University Press.

Lyons, J. A note on possessive, existential and locative sentences. Foundations of Language, 1967, *3*, 390–396.

McCarthy, D. Language development in children. In L. Carmichael, ed., *Manual of Child Psychology*. New York: Wiley, 1946.

McNeill, D. *The Acquisition of Language: The Study of Developmental Psycholinguistics*. New York: Harper & Row, 1970.

Menyuk, P. Alternation of rules in children's grammar. *Journal of Verbal Learning and Verbal Behavior*, 1964, *3*, 480–488.

———. *Sentences Children Use*. Cambridge, Mass.: M.I.T. Press, 1969.

Padilla, A. M., & Liebman, E. Language acquisition in the bilingual child. *The Bilingual Review/La Revista Bilingüe*. 1975, *2*, 34–55.

Riley, G. D. Language problems of culturally disadvantaged children. In M. V. Jones, ed., *Language Development: The Key to Learning*. Springfield, Ill.: Charles C. Thomas, 1972, 78–105.

Stockwell, R. P., Bowen, J. D., & Martin, J. W. *The Grammatical Structures of English and Spanish*. Chicago: University of Chicago Press, 1965.

Swain, M. K. "Bilingualism as a First Language." Unpublished Doctoral Dissertation. University of California, Irvine, 1972.

Order and Pace
in the Syntactic Development
of Bilingual Children

BARBARA J. MERINO
University of California, Davis

Although the simultaneous acquisition of two languages in young children has long been the object of investigation by scholars from many disciplines (see Leopold, 1948, for a review of earliest efforts), until recent years the language development of older bilingual children has been largely neglected.

Recently, the most substantial and detailed studies of language development in a bilingual context have focused on monolingual children's acquisition of a second language in the school environment (Chun and Politzer, 1975; Dulay and Burt, 1974; Fathman, 1976). But as succeeding generations of bilinguals enroll their children in school, we can expect a growing number of children to arrive in school already bilingual. To date, aside from a limited number of case studies of preschool children (most notably Leopold, 1949; Padilla and Liebman, 1975) and even fewer cross-sectional studies (Kessler, 1971; Martínez-Bernal, 1972; Keller, 1976), very little can be said about the bilingual child's capabilities and limitations in two languages.

To what degree can we expect that the development of a bilingual child's two languages will be comparable in order and pace? Order and pace in the development of bilinguals have been studied principally in comparison to monolinguals (Swain, 1972; Padilla and Liebman, 1975). Swain, for example, compared her subjects' results with those described earlier by Bellugi (1967) in English and those outlined by Gregoire (1947) in French. Though studies such as these are of value, the difficulty with such comparisons is that they are made across very

This article has been excerpted and adapted from the author's dissertation, "Language Acquisition in Bilingual Children: Aspects of Syntactic Development in English and Spanish by Chicano Children in Grades K–4." The author wishes to acknowledge the thoughtful guidance and assistance of Dr. Charles Ferguson, Dr. Eduardo Hernández-Chávez, and Dr. Robert Politzer, members of the dissertation reading committee.

446

different populations, on data collected under very different circumstances, with small samples.

Limiting the comparison to the development of semantically similar structures across the bilingual's two languages can prove to be a very productive avenue for research. As Slobin (1973) has pointed out, if a given semantic relationship, expressed in structure X in language *a* and in structure Y in language *b*, appears at the same time in both languages of a bilingual child, we can suppose that formal devices (X and Y) in the two languages are similar in complexity. Many definitions of linguistic complexity have been posited (depth hypothesis, number of transformations, etc.). Since the issue is yet to be resolved, it seemed wise to follow Brown's (1973) empirically based definition: a structure that involves A + 1 is more complex than one that involves A or 1 alone. For example, Imedaze (1960), in describing the language development of her Russian-Georgian bilingual daughter, reports the simultaneous emergence of the genitive and the instrumental cases in both languages. She concludes that these forms express the same semantic relationships in analogous fashion. By extension, if structure X from language *a* appears later than structure Y from language *b* in a bilingual child with equal exposure to both languages, difference in formal complexity may be implied. The study of Mikes and Vlahovic (1966) with Serbo-Croatian/Hungarian bilingual children provides empirical evidence for this assertion. Locative relations which are formally simple in Hungarian appeared sooner than in Serbo-Croatian, where they are formally more complex, requiring a locative preposition before the noun as well as a case inflection attached to the end of the noun.

The order and pace of acquisition of semantically similar structures have also been studied in larger cross-sectional samples of bilinguals. Kessler (1971), in her investigation of Italian-English bilinguals, found what she termed a "remarkable parallelism" in the sequencing of syntactic structures in English and Italian (p. 55). Padilla and Lindholm (1976) reported that adverb and adjective structures were acquired simultaneously at approximately the same ages in Spanish and English; however, in the acquisition of the interrogative word structures, the inversion rule was employed about one and one-half years sooner in Spanish than in English. To explain the age difference, they suggest that the children concentrated on auxiliary verb insertion of English and did not employ the rule for inversion until the rule for insertion had been learned. However, not all differences in the acquisition of semantically similar structures can be explained by complexity, as Keller (1976) has suggested in his study on the acquisition of passives in Spanish and English. Frequency may explain why some structures which are semantically similar may be produced in one language but not the other.

As commendable as many of these efforts are, the study of bilingual language acquisition is only in its initial stages and has a long way to go. Most of the work has been done in very young bilinguals. In an effort to gain a better understanding of the language development of bilingual children of *school age,* a cross-sectional study of language acquisition in bilingual children was undertaken.

The main purposes of this study were: (a) to describe significant developmental trends in the acquisition of specific structures of Spanish and English in bilingual Chicano children in kindergarten through fourth grade, (b) to compare the control of these structures across tasks (Comprehension and Production) and languages (Spanish and English), and (c) to outline the order of difficulty of the structures by task and language.

Subjects for this study included all the children at a school in the San Francisco Bay area who were balanced bilinguals; that is, they could speak and understand English and Spanish with equal or near-equal proficiency when they entered school at the age of 5 years. There were nine children in kindergarten, four in the first grade, nine in the second grade, ten in the third grade, and nine in the fourth grade.

SELECTION OF STUDENTS

Since the study focused on the language development of bilingual children over time, the following steps were taken to ensure that the children under study had been balanced bilinguals at the time of their enrollment in school. (Balanced bilingualism was used as a criterion for selection because it was important to exclude children who were in the process of acquiring English as a second language.)

1. All Spanish surnamed children in grades kindergarten through fourth at the school were interviewed to establish whether they were able to speak English and Spanish upon school entry.
2. The kindergarten and first grade teachers who had been teaching at the school for the past five years were interviewed. The teachers were asked to select, from all the children in kindergarten through fourth grade, those children who could speak and understand Spanish and English with equal or near-equal facility at school entry.
3. Fluency scores (Word Listing by Domain, Cohen, 1976) from previous years—1972, 1973, 1974—when the subjects were in

the first and second grades, were available for approximately one-half of the sample (22). A t test (for dependent means) was conducted on these scores and no significant differences were found between their performances in English and Spanish, indicating that at first and second grade levels the children's English and Spanish were developing at a comparable pace (Merino, 1976).

4. To verify further the validity of the teachers' and children's evaluation of the language abilities of the subjects upon school entrance, the parents were sent a questionnaire. (Parent Questionnaire on Children's Retrospective Abilities, Merino, 1976). To operationally define the range of abilities of the children in both languages, the parents were asked if their children could perform in English and Spanish several tasks judged to be within the ability of 5-year-old children. These tasks ranged from greetings and commands to simple conversations, and finally to the ability to speak and understand both languages with equal ease.

Most of the parents (92 percent) stated that their children could conduct a conversation typical of a child of that age in both Spanish and English and could describe an object he or she had seen as well as an experience that had happened to the child. This, coupled with the reports of the children and their teachers, indicated that at school entrance, most—if not all—of the children were, indeed, bilingual.

DEVELOPMENT OF THE TEST

An instrument, the Bilingual Language Acquisition Scale (BLAS) (Merino, 1976), was developed to measure proficiency in comprehension and production. The instrument included items for each of the following seven categories: number, gender, past tense, word order, Spanish subjunctive/English equivalents, relatives, and conditionals. These categories were selected on the basis of a review of the literature on first and second language acquisition in English and Spanish (see Merino, 1976). The criteria for preliminary consideration were: (a) semantic equivalence between Spanish and English—items such as you/*tú, usted*, which convey the additional feature of formality in Spanish, were avoided, (b) range of difficulty—a concerted effort was made to include some structures that are generally acquired early, and some that appear late, (c) amenability of forms to elicitation by pictorial stimuli. Each category included from two to four subcategories of items. For instance, the category "past tense" contained three subcategories: regular preterite, irregular preterite, and imperfect.

Item Construction. In total, twelve items were written for each type, three for each subscale: English comprehension, English production, Spanish comprehension, Spanish production. A careful selection process was used to determine which items would appear in the final version of the test. Items were first submitted for evaluation to adult bilinguals from the community. They were then piloted on a sample of 20 children. On the basis of statistical analyses, a final selection was made—20 items for each subscale—comprehension and production/ Spanish and English.

To ensure that all vocabulary difficulties had been eliminated, once the items had been selected and all necessary adjustments made, the drawings were shown to two monolingual English-speaking children and two monolingual Spanish-speaking children, ages 6 and 9 years. These children were asked to identify all relevant items in the drawings. Neither set of children encountered any difficulty with the vocabulary.

TESTING PROCEDURES

In the comprehension tasks the subject selected (by pointing) one of the two pictures which matched the sentence that he or she heard. In the production tasks, each child was shown two pictures involving some grammatical contrasts, and heard a sentence describing each picture. As the experimenter pointed to one picture, the child was asked to produce the appropriate stimulus, which he or she had heard previously.

Final Test: Statistical Analyses

Reliability. In evaluating each of the four subscales—English comprehension, English production, Spanish comprehension, and Spanish production by item—the following analyses were made: (a) The Point-biserial correlation coefficient was computed for each of the items with its subscale and total language score for both pilot and final. (b) To estimate the internal consistency of each of the subscales, Cronbach's Alpha coefficient was computed (see Table 1). The internal consistency of the production scales was high (in the range of .80 to .90+) at the pilot, and only slightly lower at the final, with a shortened version of the test. Cronbach's Alpha, in the comprehension subscales dropped from highs of .80 and .70 at the pilot to a lower but still respectable .55 and .42 at the final.

Test-Retest Reliability. To determine the reliability of the BLAS, the

Table 1
Intraclass Correlations of Pilot-Final Administration (Cronbach's Alpha)

	Alpha	Mean	SD	Standard Error
Spanish comprehension				
Pilot	.80	25.4	5.1	2.3
Final	.55	15.9	2.4	1.6
Spanish production				
Pilot	.88	20.2	6.7	2.3
Final	.82	13.7	3.7	1.6
English comprehension				
Pilot	.71	23.3	4.1	2.2
Final	.42	16.9	1.9	1.5
English production				
Pilot	.93	24.9	8.5	2.3
Final	.86	15.0	4.1	1.5
English scale				
Pilot	.93	48.2	12.2	3.2
Final	.84	31.8	5.5	2.2
Spanish scale				
Pilot	.91	45.6	10.8	3.3
Final	.80	29.6	5.2	2.3
Comprehension scale				
Pilot	—	—	—	—
Final	.64	32.7	3.6	2.2
Production scale				
Pilot	—	—	—	—
Final	.89	28.7	7.0	2.3

Note: Number items: 40 = Pilot; 20 = Final.

20 children who were tested at the pilot were administered the final version of the test (one-half of the items in the pilot) approximately a month later. Test-retest reliability coefficients were never lower than .70 for English comprehension and were as high as .94 for the Spanish scales:

Spanish Comprehension	Spanish Production	English Comprehension	English Production
.74	.86	.70	.82

Spanish	English	Comprehension	Production
.94	.88	.76	.89

Test Validation

Concurrent.   Fishman and Cooper (1969) and Lambert, Havelka, and
Crosby (1958) have shown that one of the best predictors of bilingualism, the one with the highest correlations with other indirect measures,
was a fluency measure in which the subject was asked to give continuous
free association to either selected stimulus words (Lambert et al., $r =$
.82) or domains (Fishman and Cooper, $r =$ .75). Since the Word Listing
by Domain instrument had been used with many of these same subjects
in the past and their scores were available, it was adopted once again.
Highest correlations were obtained between the production scales and
fluency in both English and Spanish (all significant at the .01 level, as
shown in Table 2). Correlations of fluency scores with the comprehension scales, although lower than production, were nonetheless significant at the .05 level in Spanish, at the .01 level in English.

Adult.   To ensure that the difficulties encountered by the children
were real ones and not artifacts of the test, the BLAS was administered
to a small sample (4) of adult bilinguals. All responded correctly to all of
the items.

METHOD OF ANALYSIS

Between Subjects.   The effects of two independent variables—grade
and sex—on performance in the comprehension and production subscales were measured through analysis of variance. Analysis of variance
was also used to determine the effect of grade as a source of variance on

Table 2
Bilingual Language Acquisition Scale Subscales Correlated with Fluency

	FLSP	SCTOT	SPTOT	ECTOT	EPTOT	SPAN	ENG
FLENG	.57	.19	.26	.36	.50	.27	.51
p	.001	.12	.05	.01	.001	.043	.001
FLSP		.32	.42	.27	.30	.45	.33
p		.022	.003	.046	.028	.002	.020

Note 1: N = 41.
Note 2:
FLENG = Fluency English.   SPAN = Spanish: Comprehension and
FLSP = Fluency Spanish.   Production Subscales.
SCTOT = Spanish Comprehension Subscale.   ENG = English: Comprehension and
SPTOT = Spanish Production Subscale.   Production Subscales.
ECTOT = English Comprehension Subscale.

performance in each of the seven categories—number, gender, past tense, word order, Spanish subjunctive/English equivalent, relatives, and conditionals. The interaction between grade and sex was measured through two-way analysis of variance.

Within Subjects.   Within-subject comparisons were made ($2 \times 2 \times 7$ factorial design) by task (comprehension, production), language (English, Spanish), and category. Two-way ANOVA for repeated measures was used to determine the effect of grade and language within each category.

Rank Order.   The rank order (Spearman's Correlation Coefficient) of all the types of items was correlated across tasks, grades, and languages.

Control Variables.   To ensure that differences among grades were not being influenced by accidents of the administration of the test (times tested, order of test), personal history (such as place of birth or order of language acquisition), or language-use patterns (retrospective as well as current), ANOVAS were conducted on these types of variables.

RESULTS AND DISCUSSION

General Effect of Grade and Sex.   The interaction of grade and sex did not affect performance to a significant degree. Most development occurred between kindergarten and the upper grades in the English comprehension and production subscales. In Spanish production, significant differences appeared between kindergarten and the upper grades, to grade 3. In grade 4, performance dropped sharply, with children performing almost at the kindergarten level. There were no significant differences by grade in Spanish comprehension, as shown in Tables 3 and 4.

Effect of Grade by Category.   In Spanish production (see Table 5) significant differences among grades occurred in the more complex categories (conditionals and subjunctives). In English production (see Table 6) there were significant differences by grade in all categories except number. Very few significant differences were apparent in the comprehension scales (relatives in English, past tense in Spanish). In English, with most categories development was chronological. Generally, the older children performed better than the younger. The notable exception was the smaller sample (4) in the first grade which included two gifted children (a boy and a girl) and two average-ability girls. These children performed with a very high degree of accuracy. In Spanish, however, by grade 4, children were performing with significantly lower accuracy than the younger children, particularly in the more complex structures (subjunctive and conditional). In these categories, as in the

Table 3
Bilingual Language Acquisition Scale: Production Subscales by Grade

Grade	Mean	SD	Percentage Correct	Significant Pairwise Differences	Duncan's Range Statistic	p
			Spanish			
Kinder-garten	11.1	2.4	56%	Kg.-1	13.3	< .05
Fourth	12.8	4.1	65%	Kg.-3	12.9	< .03
Second	14.1	2.4	71%			
Third	15.3	4.4	77%			
First	16.8	2.5	84%			
			English			
Kinder-garten	10.33	4.9	52%	Kg.-1	16.3	< .01
Second	14.89	2.8	75%	Kg.-2	13.7	< .01
Third	16.20	3.3	81%	Kg.-3	18.1	< .01
Fourth	17.22	2.9	86%	Kg.-4	20.7	< .01
First	17.25	1.0	86%			

Note: N = 41.

Table 4
Bilingual Language Acquisition Scale: Comprehension Subscales by Grade

Grade	Mean	SD	Percentage Correct	Significant Pairwise Differences	Duncan's Range Statistics	p
			English			
Kinder-garten	15.22	2.2	76%	Kg.-4	5.5	< .01
Second	16.89	1.8	85%	Kg.-1	6.0	< .05
Third	17.20	1.6	86%	Kg.-3	6.1	< .05
Fourth	17.66	1.7	88%			
First	17.75	1.0	89%			
			Spanish			
Kinder-garten	14.66	.9	73%			
Third	15.50	2.3	75%			
Fourth	15.90	.4	80%			
Second	16.77	2.1	84%			
First	17.25	1.0	86%			

Note: N = 41.

scales as a whole, results suggest that the older children were undergoing language loss.

Effect of Grade and Language. The fundamental question here is whether language contributed, in a significant degree, to performance in any of the categories. As mentioned earlier, Slobin (1973) has suggested that bilinguals offer a unique opportunity to study the effect of language complexity on language acquisition. Balanced bilinguals can, in essence, function as their own controls. If a child is exposed to two languages more or less equally and is able to use a grammatical marker that conveys a particular semantic notion in one language but not in the other, it may be assumed that the grammatical marker is more complex in one language than in the other. The "caveat" here is that this conclusion is valid only as long as we can assume equal exposure to and equal abilities in both languages, as established by other measures of language proficiency.

The effects of grade and language were significant in the Spanish subjunctive and its English equivalents in the production subscales and in the past tense and conditional categories in the comprehension

Table 5

Bilingual Language Acquisition Scale: Analyses of Variance by Grade, Spanish Categories

Category	df	MS (Grade)	MS Error	F	p
		Comprehension Subscale			
Number	4,36	.00	.00	—	—
Gender	4,36	.03	.05	.63	n.s.
Tense	4,36	1.01	.33	3.03	.03
Word order	4,36	.20	.59	.35	n.s.
Subjunctive	4,36	1.77	.78	2.27	n.s.
Relatives	4,36	.50	.39	1.28*	n.s.
Conditionals	4,36	1.32	.90	1.46	n.s.
		Production Subscale			
Number	4,36	.06	.09	.62	n.s.
Gender	4,36	.16	.18	.88	n.s.
Tense	4,36	.48	.40	1.21	n.s.
Word order	4,36	.71	.58	1.24	n.s.
Subjunctive	4,36	3.77	1.05	3.57	01
Relatives	4,36	.84	.67	1.26	n.s.
Conditionals	4,36	4.28	1.13	3.77	.01

Table 6

Bilingual Language Acquisition Scale: Analyses of Variance by Grade,
English Categories

Category	df	MS (Grade)	MS Error	F	p
		Comprehension Subscale			
Number	4,36	.03	.03	.88	n.s.
Gender	4,36	.08	.07	1.24	n.s.
Past tense	4,36	.18	.31	.56	n.s.
Word order	4,36	.61	.43	1.42	n.s.
English equiv.– Span. subjunct.	4,36	.72	.34	2.15	n.s.
Relatives	4,36	1.10	.39	2.86	.037
Conditionals	4,36	.66	.85	.78	n.s.
		Production Subscale			
Number	4,36	.36	.15	2.36	n.s.
Gender	4,36	.35	.12	2.96	.032
Past tense	4,36	1.50	.56	2.69	.046
Word order	4,36	1.68	.64	2.63	.050
English equiv.– Span. subjunct.	4,36	2.93	.48	6.11	.001
Relatives	4,36	1.85	.53	3.48	.017
Conditionals	4,36	5.51	1.70	3.25	.022

subscales. The effect of language alone was a significant source of
variance in the following categories: word order and conditionals in the
production scales, and Spanish subjunctives and their English equivalents in the comprehension scales (see Tables 7 and 8). This indicates
that although Spanish word order and conditionals in production and
Spanish subjunctives and conditionals in comprehension were significantly more difficult for the whole sample, when each grade was
considered, differences by language were not great enough to be
significant. To identify in which language the categories were easier, the
t test for dependent means was used. In every instance categories were
easier in English.

Since the parent questionnaires, as well as the teachers' and students'
reports, indicated that all grades had roughly similar language skills in
both languages at school entry the following assumption could be made:
either (a) the Spanish constructions are more complex than their English
equivalents, or (b) language development in Spanish in some of the

grades has not kept up with English. To evaluate this second position, it was necessary to check the current abilities of the children in English and Spanish, through an independent measure.

The children's fluency scores (Word Listing by Domain) showed no significant differences across languages, except at the fourth grade. In terms of word fluency, then, it can be said that most of these children were balanced (see Table 9). The balance scores (obtained through the Fishman formula) gave additional clues about what might have been going on. Results showed that there were three subjects in the fourth grade who were English dominant. It seems, then, that differences across language in the fourth grade could be attributed to current language abilities and/or the complexities of the Spanish structures. However, for all other grades, differences are more likely due to the complexities of the language itself.

Table 7

Bilingual Language Acquisition Scale: Production Subscales Within Subject Comparisons, Effect of Grade and Language

Variable	df	Source	MS	MS Error	F	p
Number	4,36	Grade	.13	.11	1.14	n.s.
	1,36	Language	.31	.14	2.19	n.s.
	4,36	Gr. & lang.	.30	.14	2.14	n.s.
Gender	4,36	Grade	.28	.14	1.59	n.s.
	1,36	Language	.05	.16	.30	n.s.
	4,36	Gr. & lang.	.29	.16	1.79	n.s.
Past tense	4,36	Grade	1.64	.59	2.78	.04
	1,36	Language	.01	.37	.03	n.s.
	4,36	Gr. & lang.	.34	.37	.93	n.s.
Word order	4,36	Grade	2.25	.87	2.58	.05
	1,36	Language	1.48	.35	4.27	.04
	4,36	Gr. & lang.	.15	.35	.42	n.s.
Span. subjunct.–English equiv.	4,36	Grade	4.70	1.00	4.67	.004
	1,36	Language	3.95	.53	7.47	.009
	4,36	Gr. & lang.	2.00	.53	3.78	.01
Relatives	4,36	Grade	2.44	.95	2.55	.05
	1,36	Language	.05	.25	.20	n.s.
	4,36	Gr. & lang.	.26	.25	1.03	n.s.
Conditionals	4,36	Grade	7.64	1.79	4.27	.006
	1,36	Language	6.45	1.04	6.20	.016
	4,36	Gr. & lang.	2.15	1.04	2.07	n.s.

Table 8
Bilingual Language Acquisition Scale: Comprehension Subscales Within Subject Comparisons, Effect of Grade and Language

Variable	df	Source	MS	MS Error	F	p
Number	4,36	Grade	.01	.01	.88	n.s.
	1,36	Language	.01	.01	.99	n.s.
	4,36	Gr. & lang.	.01	.01	.88	n.s.
Gender	4,36	Grade	.10	.05	2.11	n.s.
	1,36	Language	.01	.07	.18	n.s.
	4,36	Gr. & lang.	.01	.07	.16	n.s.
Past tense	4,36	Grade	.32	.40	.81	n.s.
	1,36	Language	.01	.25	.05	n.s.
	4,36	Gr. & lang.	.87	.25	3.48	.01
Word order	4,36	Grade	.53	.65	.82	n.s.
	1,36	Language	.44	.37	1.18	n.s.
	4,36	Gr. & lang.	.28	.37	.75	n.s.
Span. subjunct.–English equiv.	4,36	Grade	2.11	.68	3.11	.03
	1,36	Language	5.90	.43	13.67	.001
	4,36	Gr. & lang.	.37	.43	.86	n.s.
Relatives	4,36	Grade	1.30	.34	3.80	.01
	1,36	Language	.05	.44	.11	n.s.
	4,36	Gr. & lang.	.31	.44	.70	n.s.
Conditionals	4,36	Grade	.43	1.20	.37	n.s.
	1,36	Language	3.12	1.54	5.43	.02
	4,36	Gr. & lang.	1.54	1.54	2.69	.05

Table 9
Current Language Abilities: Fluency and Balance Scores by Grade

	Kindergarten (n = 9)		Grade 1 (n = 4)		Grade 2 (n = 9)		Grade 3 (n = 10)		Grade 4 (n = 9)		Total (N = 41)	
	Mean	SD	Mean	SD	Mean	SD	Mean	SD	Mean	SD	Mean	SD
Fluency in Spanish	25.6	8.6	27.8	9.1	35.8	6.5	33.8	7.5	36.0	2.8	32.3	8.7
Fluency in English	28.7	9.2	31.5	3.4	42.2	7.8	37.4	7.6	50.6	3.7	38.9	11.5
Balance score	.45	6.2	.40	8.2	.44	9.8	.46	14.3	.36	2.7	.42	10.1

Because the performance on the subjunctive category in production seems to demonstrate most clearly the role of language complexity on these bilingual children's performance, I will limit myself to discussion of this category only.

In the Spanish subjunctive/English equivalents category, there were significant differences between English and Spanish, not only in the whole sample, but within the following grades: kindergarten, second, and fourth, always with the Spanish items more difficult than their English equivalents. The Spanish subjunctive items included the optative, purposive, and dubitative (*tal vez*) constructions (Lozano, 1972). The optative and the purposive use embeddings in English, the dubitative form does not.

Why would the subjunctive delay acquisition of such structures as the purposive? The obvious answer is that the subjunctive is in some sense more complex than the present. But why should a change from one verb ending to another—e.g., *lee* to *lea*, or *lava* to *lave*—cause so much difficulty? Some of this difficulty can be explained in terms of universal operating principles that children adopt in acquiring language. Slobin (1973) suggests that the use of grammatical markers should make semantic sense (Operating Principle G). By extension, he stipulates that semantically consistent grammatical rules are acquired early and without significant error. Although attempts have been made to organize the subjunctive mood in such a way that it does make semantic sense (Lozano, 1972), these have not been in every way successful, nor have they met with total agreement.

In the development of productive and receptive control of the structures in both languages, the principal outcomes are (a) language loss occurred among older children, usually fourth graders, but sometimes third or even second graders; (b) loss usually first affects those skills and categories that are generally acquired last (production, for example) and the more complicated structures (conditionals and subjunctives, for instance); (c) development in Spanish does occur but is generally limited to the lower grades—note significant differences in the subjunctive between kindergarten–second, and kindergarten–third grades in Spanish productions; (d) in some categories (word order in Spanish production), though loss has not reached significant levels, trends seem to indicate that accuracy is reduced; (e) comparisons of performance in English with performance in Spanish reveal that in those instances where loss is not occurring in Spanish, no development is taking place (relatives, Spanish production, and Spanish comprehension, in most categories). Generally, those psycholinguists who have talked about language loss (Ervin-Tripp, personal communication,

1974) believe that loss will begin with more complex skills and structures first. The findings of this study give empirical support to this belief.

How consistent was the order of difficulty of the items across languages?

Production. Rank order correlations across languages in the production scales were very high in the lower grades through second grade (.73 to .83) and were significant at the .001 level; but they were lower in the third and fourth grades (.47 and .44) though still significant (see Table 10). The discrepancy in performance across languages is less often comparable for the third and fourth grades than it is for other grades. One possible interpretation for this finding is that as subjects began to lose their proficiency in Spanish, their performance became more erratic.

Comprehension. Rank order correlations across languages were lower in the comprehension scales, though still significant. Correlations in

Table 10

Bilingual Language Acquisition Scale: Rank Order Correlation of Items (Spearman's RHO) Across Languages by Grade

Comprehension	Rho	*p*
English comprehension, kindergarten Spanish comprehension, kindergarten	.49	.01
English comprehension, 1st grade Spanish comprehension, 1st grade	.51	.01
English comprehension, 2nd grade Spanish comprehension, 2nd grade	.53	.01
English comprehension, 3rd grade Spanish comprehension, 3rd grade	.75	.001
English comprehension, 4th grade Spanish comprehension, 4th grade	.44	.02
Production	Rho	*p*
English production, kindergarten Spanish production, kindergarten	.73	.001
English production, 1st grade Spanish production, 1st grade	.83	.001
English production, 2nd grade Spanish production, 2nd grade	.80	.001
English production, 3rd grade Spanish production, 3rd grade	.47	.02
English production, 4th grade Spanish production, 4th grade	.44	.03

Note: N = 20 Items.

these scales were usually in the .40 to .50 range, with the exception of third grade, which reached .75 (see Table 10). It is difficult to evaluate this finding because the reliability of the comprehension scales was not as high as the production scales and the results for these scales may have been more easily influenced by chance factors.

Effect of Control Variables. Of those variables that were likely to affect performance on the test and that were taken into consideration in this study, only visits to Mexico had any significance. Children who had not been to Mexico scored significantly lower in the Spanish production, English comprehension, and English production subscales than children who had.

Since children who had been to Mexico constituted most of the sample, reducing the number of children who had *not* to a very small number, it would be foolhardy to assume that children who have never been to Mexico are automatically at a disadvantage. It is likely, though, that families who have never taken their children to Mexico probably have fewer contacts with Spanish, which would explain lower scores in Spanish production. But children who had not been to Mexico also scored lower in the English tasks. In a previous study (Kimball, 1968) birthplace of the family in Mexico has been found to contribute to achievement. It is possible that greater exposure to Mexico (a place where Mexicans would not be treated as a lower status minority), where they would be made aware of their heritage in a positive way, might affect self-concept and thus would, in turn, influence overall achievement.

CONCLUSIONS AND IMPLICATIONS

As many sociolinguists have documented (Kloss, 1966; Fishman, 1966), the forces against maintenance of minority languages, especially in this country, are formidable. Sudies of bilingual children in the United States have documented parallel development of both languages, with very young children (Padilla and Liebman, 1975; Padilla and Lindholm, 1976) and with young school-age children, first and second graders (Kessler, 1971). With older children, however, recent investigations have demonstrated continuing development in English but static development in Spanish (McKay, 1974). It may be that the Kessler study failed to record loss because it did not include older children in whom loss is most likely to occur. The McKay study analyzed free speech samples only. It may be that in free speech children undergoing loss simply avoid using structures in which they are no longer competent (Schacter, 1974). Yet, when children are called upon to deal with specific structures as they were in this study, an upsurge of errors will occur among the older children.

The bilingual children in this study are in a situation which, by and large, should encourage maintenance of their two languages. They live in a community which is Spanish speaking to a high degree (40 percent). They attend a school in which Spanish speakers are well represented (45 percent). Most of these children participate in a bilingual program which has been commended (Cohen, 1976) for its efforts to encourage achievement of the bilingual child in both languages. However, despite all of these factors, the pressures of the dominant society are taking their toll; Spanish is not developing at a pace comparable to English and is in many instances losing ground.

The schools, of course, cannot hope to single-handedly counteract the pressures of the society as a whole. They can, however, be agents for change. Those educators who accept the premise that the goal of bilingual education is to ensure the parallel development of both of the child's languages must be made aware that this goal is not being fulfilled. Obviously bilingual programs must do much more than they are doing at the present time. Concrete steps must be taken to ensure that real development in Spanish continues beyond the lower grades. Children must be exposed to a greater variety of activities and materials in Spanish. Spanish must be not only the language of the family, but in a real sense the language of the school as well.

REFERENCES

Bellugi, U. "The Acquisition of Negation." Unpublished Doctoral Dissertation, Harvard University, 1967.

Brown, R. *A First Language*. Cambridge, Mass.: Harvard University Press, 1973.

Chun, J., and Politzer, R. *A Study of Language Acquisition in Two Bilingual Schools*. Stanford Manuscript, School of Education. Stanford, Cal.: Stanford University, 1975.

Cohen, A. "Innovative Education for la Raza: A Sociolinguistic Assessment of a Bilingual Education Program in California." Unpublished Doctoral Dissertation, Stanford University, 1972. Later published as *A Sociolinguistic Approach to Bilingual Education*. Rowley, Mass.: Newbury House, 1976.

Cronbach, L. J. *Essentials of Psychological Testing*. New York: Harper & Row Publishers, 1970.

Dulay, H. C., and Burt, M. K. "Natural Sequences in Child Second Language Acquisition." *Language Learning*, 24 (1974), 37–53.

Ervin-Tripp, S. *Personal Communication*. Berkeley, Cal.: 1974.

Fathman, A. "Variables Affecting the Successful Learning of English as a Second Language." *TESOL Quarterly*, 10 (1976), 433–41.

Fishman, J. A. *Language Loyalty in the United States*. The Hague: Mouton, 1966.

Fishman, J. A. and Cooper, R. L. "Alternative Measures of Bilingualism." *Journal of Verbal Learning and Verbal Behavior*, 8 (1969), 276–82.

Gregoire, A. *L'apprentissage du language: Les deux premières années*. Vol. 1. Paris: Droz, 1947.

Imedadze, N. "K Psikhologicheskoy prirode rannego dvuyazychiya." *Voprosy Psikhologii*, 6, no. 1 (1960), 60–68.

Keller, G. "Acquisition of the English and Spanish Passive Voices Among Bilingual Children." In *Bilingualism in the Bicentennial and Beyond*, ed. G. Keller, R. Teschner, and S. Viera. New York: Bilingual Press, City University of New York, 1976.

Kessler, C. *The Acquisition of Syntax in Bilingual Children*. Washington, D.C.: Georgetown University Press, 1971.

Kimball, W. L. "Parent and Family Influences on Academic Achievement Among Mexican-American Students." Unpublished Doctoral Dissertation, University of California, Los Angeles, 1968.

Kloss, H. "Types of Multilingual Communities: A Discussion of Ten Variables." *Sociological Inquiry*, 36 (1966), 135–45.

Lambert, W.; Havelka, J.; and Crosby, C. "The Influence of Language-Acquisition Contexts on Bilingualism." *Journal of Abnormal Social Psychology*, 56 (1958), 239–44.

Leopold, W. "The Study of Child Language and Infant Bilingualism." *Word*, 4 (1948), 1–17.

———. *Speech Development of a Bilingual Child: A Linguist's Record*. Vol. 3. Evanston, Ill.: Northwestern University Press, 1949.

Lozano, Anthony. "Subjunctives, Transformations and Features in Spanish." *Hispania*, 5, no. 1 (1972), 76–90.

Martínez-Bernal, J. A. "Children's Acquisition of Spanish and English Morphological Systems and Noun Phrases." Unpublished Doctoral Dissertation, Georgetown University, 1972.

McKay, M. "Spoken Spanish of Mexican-American Children: A Monolingual and Bilingual School Program." Unpublished Doctoral Dissertation, Stanford University, 1974.

Merino, B. "Language Acquisition in Bilingual Children: Aspects of Syntactic Development in English and Spanish by Chicano Children in Grades K–4." Unpublished Doctoral Dissertation, Stanford University, 1976.

Mikes, M., and Vlahovic, P. "Razvoy gramtickih kategorija u decjem govoru." *Prilozi proucavanju jezika*, II, Nove Sad, Yugoslavia, 1966.

Padilla, A. M., and Liebman, E. "Language Acquisition in the Bilingual Child." *The Bilingual Review*, 1, no. 2 (1975), 34–35.

Padilla, A. M., and Lindholm, K. "Acquisition of Bilingualism: An Analysis of the Linguistic Structures of Spanish/English Speaking Children." In *Bilingualism in the Bicentennial and Beyond*, ed. G. Keller, R. Teschner, and S. Viera. New York: Bilingual Press, City University of New York, 1976.

Sánchez, R. "Nuestra circunstancia lingüística." *El Grito,* 6, no. 1 (1972), 45–74.

Schacter, J. "An Error in Error Analysis." *Language Learning,* 24, (1974), 205–14.

Slobin, D. "Cognitive Prerequisites for the Development of Grammar." In *Studies of Child Language Development,* ed. C. Ferguson and D. Slobin. New York: Holt, Rinehart and Winston, 1973.

Swain, C. "Bilingualism as a First Language." Unpublished Doctoral Dissertation, University of California, 1972.

Emerging Styles in Child Speech: Case Study of a Bilingual Child

ALVINO E. FANTINI
School for International Training
Brattleboro, Vermont

The number of linguists concerned with the structure of child language has increased to an amazing degree in recent years. Yet few works to date have focused on sociolinguistic aspects of the acquisition process. And although sociolinguists have made significant contributions to our knowledge and understanding of language use, they, like linguists before them, have concerned themselves primarily with the adult speaker. The present paper, therefore, aims at describing one aspect of developmental sociolinguistics, namely, the emerging linguistic styles and language use observed in child speech.

THE CASE STUDY: BACKGROUND

This study is based on ongoing research which has focused on an examination of language development through longitudinal study of one bilingual child—the author's son—over the past nine years. Initial efforts, as with most other works, concentrated on the linguistic progress of the child; however, the child's use of his two languages early became the central interest of the study. It became apparent that the child was both linguist and ethnographer, learning not only the language or languages of his environment but also how to use them in accordance with changing social contexts. Consequently, as much contextual data were recorded as possible in addition to linguistic notations in an

This study was updated and revised with the aid of a Summer Seminar Stipend from the National Endowment for the Humanities. Appreciation is also expressed to Dr. Bernard Spolsky, Director of the Seminar at the University of New Mexico, Albuquerque, and to the other participants who provided helpful suggestions and comments. This paper was first presented at the Seventh Annual International Bilingual/Bicultural Education Conference in San Juan, Puerto Rico, April 24–28, 1978.

attempt to examine the relationship of speech acquisition and the social milieu.

From the time of the child's birth, data were systematically collected in a speech diary, based on observation, recordings, and occasional video tapes. The limitations inherent in the study of a single child are immediately apparent given that social circumstances are naturally unique for each individual. However, the study of even one individual can shed light on both bilingual behavior and the interrelatedness of speech acquisition and social context.

The subject of this study—Mario—was born in Vermont in 1968 of an Italian-American father and a Bolivian mother. Spanish was the language of the home and the language used with the child from his birth. Contact with English was limited at first to that provided by visitors, television and radio, and the environment outside the home. His first prolonged and intensive contact with English during his pre-school years occurred between ages 2;2 and 2;4 when he attended a nursery with English-speaking children. Consequently, English was a somewhat tardy development which manifested itself as a productive skill beginning about 2;8. Periods of English alternated intermittently with periods of almost exclusive contact with Spanish during occasionally but lengthy trips to Bolivia and Mexico. Exposure to both languages to age five was uneven, with probably more exposure to Spanish than to English. After age five, however, when Mario began kindergarten, exposure to both languages was more nearly equal. His formal education was conducted entirely in English.

At the time he entered school, Mario might be described as a coordinate bilingual, having acquired each of his languages from separate speakers and under quite separate circumstances. This was reflected as well in his use of each language, each of which he clearly reserved for the appropriate situation with an amazingly low degree of interference. Various test results substantiated Mario's control of Spanish and English on about the same level as the average monolingual child of comparable age. In addition, he also had a passive knowledge of Italian.

LINGUISTIC MODIFICATIONS AND EXTERNAL CUES

All speakers alter their language in various ways in relation to the particular social circumstances at the moment of the speech act. How these non-linguistic factors (or external social cues) affect linguistic elements is of central interest to sociolinguists. The bilingual speaker presents an especially interesting case for study in this respect. Not only does he modify his language stylistically like the monolingual speaker, but he also has another option—that of switching from one language to another, wholly or in part. Such linguistic modifications are not arbitrary or erratic behavior, but rather under the control of the speaker consciously or otherwise, and are normally related to specific social factors.

As linguistic modifications are considered, one area deserves special mention: namely, when do modifications constitute a shift in a particular way of speaking as opposed to a complete change in language (style-shifting as opposed to code-switching)? Both terms are imprecisely defined in the literature. For example, Gleason (1971) uses "code" to mean a particular style of speech used within a particular social circumstance. Ervin-Tripp (1973), on the other hand, points out that "registers, styles, marking, and so forth" are terms which have not yet been fully developed and defined. What these terms do share in common is that they all allude to modifications of linguistic elements producing variations in speech. In this paper, "code" is used as synonymous with "language," whereas "style" refers more specifically to a particular cluster of linguistic features characteristically used in relation to a particular social circumstance with a common purpose.

As most researchers of bilingualism are aware, it is often difficult to specify when modifications in speech entail a style versus a partial to complete language shift. The same problem underlies Haugen's definition of linguistic interference, although not specifically addressed. Haugen (1965, p. 39) described interference (or "diffusion" as he preferred to call it) as that influence "in which a single item is plucked out of one language and used in the context of another." The question, however, is whether "item" might refer to a single phoneme, a word, or to a given segment of speech which might then be viewed as full code-switching.

Can it not be viewed that style, which entails the modifications of sets of linguistic signals, forms part of a continuum, such that if sufficient linguistic modifications are made, eventually they result in a complete change of code? What remains unclear, then, is when a code is so modified by the speaker that it becomes, in fact, another language.

To be able to switch codes to this extent requires not only the inputs from at least two language systems but also an awareness of the basic social conditions calling for the use of one code or the other. Mario began active use of Spanish at 1;4. At the onset of his second tongue at 2;6, he was immediately faced with the task of sorting appropriate linguistic sets for each situation. To communicate, he had to make an appropriate linguistic choice—with the right persons, at the right time and place. Although this seems an inordinate task for such a young child, mixing of Spanish and English, limited as they were, occurred for only a brief period of time. During the next two months a sorting of lexical items was apparent. Sorting was assisted by both linguistic considerations (such as the phonological shape of words) and social considerations (such as the persons and contexts with which words were associated). Nonetheless, sorting was rapid, so that complete and appropriate code-switching was the norm only three months after the introduction of English words into Mario's speech.

In Mario's case, the first social variable that influenced language choice was the interlocutor. Given the child's limited environment, the right language was determined almost entirely in accordance with the person speaking with the child. However, as his language developed, and also as his world enlarged, other social factors influenced language choice. The next major factor was the setting of the speech event. Initially there were two clear-cut divisions—the home and the world outside the home. The original, simplistic framework affecting choice was revised, and subsequent revisions were continually made by the child as additional social variables affected his life.

Mario began to differentiate and categorize people based on their physical appearance. This assisted him in anticipating the proper code to use with others, particularly with those unknown to him. Characteristics of place were another determinant of language choice: for example, whether the event occurred in a predominantly English-speaking milieu (such as Vermont) or in a Spanish-speaking milieu (such as Mexico or Bolivia). Because there was a high degree of consistency in the patterns of language behavior that were displayed in a given situation, it is possible to construct a framework reflecting the interrelationship between the social variables and language choice. The accuracy of this framework is confirmed by the fact that Mario normally reacted in some way when the language used in a given situation was other than what he expected as "normal" for the circumstances. The following anecdote illustrates the child's linguistic expectations:

> At age 4;9, a friend whom Mario had originally met in Mexico and in Spanish visited the home. The visitor, although Greek, "looked" Latin. The mother's conversation with him was conducted in English rather than Spanish. As Mario entered the room he was surprised by what he witnessed and eventually interrupted with a puzzled question to his mother *sottovoce:*

> Mario →Mamá: ¿Por qué hablas así, mamá? No hables así . . . blaka, bla. Así como yo estoy hablando ahola (ahora).

The framework governing language choice, however, holds true only when the child is engaged in unmarked dialog. When the child attempted to produce special effects upon his listeners (e.g., to amuse, surprise, or shock), or when the act assumed some special form (e.g., role playing, singing, play language, or quoting something or someone), then the language selected was often the opposite of the normal choice. Hence, form and function of the speech act also became factors affecting language choice.

In summary, code-switching began about 2;6. By 2;8 it was fairly well established and well executed, and from that point on the child made appropriate language choices—he switched codes consciously, rapidly, and naturally. He behaved like a normal five-year-old—in either of the two languages—with the appropriate people and in the right time and place.

LINGUISTIC STYLES AND LANGUAGE USE

In a sense, we have already referred to two of the styles present in Mario's speech, Spanish and English. Most researchers, however, treat full code-switching separately from style variations within the same language. Whether bilingual behavior is considered a code shift or a style variation, it is perhaps the most dramatic evidence that the child is indeed capable of controlling varying sets of linguistic features at a very young age. If he can control two full codes, there should be no doubt that he can control other styles as well. Yet, Gleason's is one of the few other works which has even considered styles in children's language, focusing primarily on children between four and eight. Gleason (1971, p. 7) starts out by affirming: "By and large we were not primarily looking for evidence of code switching or stylistic variation in the children under four." Although children under four were included in the research, she makes it clear that "These children were included in the sample because we wanted to get examples of the adults and older children talking to them for evidence of babytalk style." Almost as an aside, she makes the observation that "even the tiniest children make some distinctions." This, in fact, is what Mario did, beginning in infancy.

COMMUNICATIVE BEHAVIOR
DURING THE EARLY YEARS

It may be possible to view the infant as possessing two expressive modes: crying or silence. Through his cries, the infant conveyed his various needs—hunger, distress, pain, fear. Ostwald and Peltzman (1972) investigated differentiated cries in infants and made similar observations.

Tape recordings likewise show that not all of Mario's crying was alike. In fact, his mother was able to discern different styles of crying, and often she was able to tell by the pitch and intensity of his cry which of his needs was being expressed. For example, a sharp, piercing cry immediately aroused his mother to say something like: "Ay caray, algo pasa . . . yo sé cuando él está llorando así. Debe tener un gancho abierto." Within a few months, and certainly by 0;4, Mario not only cried and screamed, but he also used body motions along with his sounds, waving his arms and legs, and moving his head from side to side. When content, he sometimes cooed, sighed, or gurgled. Hence, several distinct vocalizations had emerged, each serving a different purpose.

The following months saw the appearance of many more sounds; however, by 0;9 the infant favored certain sounds which he repeated more often than others. These were predominantly consonant plus vowel formations. This pre-speech phase concluded when he eventually gained increasing control over the sounds he made so that he could produce specific combinations at will. The appearance of words between 1;4 and 1;10 marked a new stage in the child's progress. Mario emitted two types of vocalizations; some had meaning and others did not. Those with meaning served to communicate with other people; the others (whether they were for self-expression or practice) served no communicative function.

By the end of his second year, Mario had a sizeable lexicon consisting primarily of nouns with which he labeled his surroundings. However, a few other words also extant had a purely social function. Two favored expressions were "ciao-ciao" (used in the Italian sense so that it served either to greet or to take leave of someone) and "bye-bye." The child usually waved his hand when saying good-bye. However, it was noticed that Mario often fell silent precisely at the moment when he was told to say good-bye, especially with people he did not know well. After the individuals left, he began waving and saying /táw-táw/ (ciao-ciao) several times. This possibly suggests the beginning of another style, one related to the degree of familiarity between the child and the interlocutor. The style shift was vocalization versus non-vocalization; sound and motion as opposed to complete silence.

During this period of limited speech, Mario expressed himself a great deal by pointing, screaming, crying, and jumping up and down. Motions and gestures were more important to the communicative act than language. The early diary, in fact, is replete with contextual comments, but few vocalizations. His utterances alone were insufficient to permit us to understand what transpired. However, as language developed, he used language more and more to communicate; besides, there was increasing social pressure for him to do so. After learning sufficient vocabulary, pointing was then met with responses like: "¡Pues, a ver. Dí lo que quieres; no señales!" The two-, three-, or four-year-old was expected to abandon typical pre-speech behavior and to use language to communicate. Nevertheless, as long as it was tolerated, the child had two options—linguistic or non-linguistic communication; he used gestures or he used words.

Some of these gestures of course were permitted to continue, but as para-linguistic expressions—expressions which accompanied rather than replaced oral language. At only one point did Mario tend to revert to non-linguistic means. This occurred at about 3;5, when he was immersed in situations where he did not have adequate command of English. At such times he often compensated by acting out with motions and onomatopoetic sounds whatever it was that he wanted to convey.

Another interesting development occurred by 2;7. Mario delighted in creating nonsense sounds which seemed to have several functions: at times they were merely sound play; sometimes they were expressive vocalizations; and sometimes he used them when he was bored, uninterested, or otherwise did not wish to reply to his interlocutor:

```
Age 2;7  /Silal, luxála, kapála, tistópi, bakók/
         /tapála, anís, kopála, tokála, kopíl/
         /kakíli, pis:ín, kokála/
         /kopála, pinzála, pinsmála, balamkúm/
Age 2;8  /papál, papál, papópu, popópo, popípi/
Age 3;2  /tobíya, stopáka, sisíya, stubíta, búbi/
```

Although used in a different way and for a different purpose, this style was akin to the language/silence distinction cited earlier. Mario used nonsense sounds for approximately one year, after which they disappeared gradually from his speech. What is surprising is that even though days, and sometimes months, went by before the next use of nonsense sounds, they always preserved a familiar form and rhythm despite their spontaneity. Furthermore, in spite of their originality, these sounds followed the phonological rules of Spanish in almost every detail.

The selective use of whining also took place during this same period. Whining seemed to be a special form of expression used primarily with his caretakers but not with other adults. It involved a sing-song intonation accompanied by higher than normal pitch. It is interesting to note that Gleason (1971, p. 7) made a similar observation. Mario was observed at times playing happily in the nursery until he caught sight of his parents. Immediately he began to whine no matter what he wanted. The nursery attendant reported, however, that he never whined at other times. Similar observations were made when Mario stayed with other persons—an aunt, grandparent, babysitter. Whining began only after the parents returned, and it was reserved exclusively for them. Consequently, this may be considered a style variation related to specific interlocutors (in this case, the child's caretakers).

Socializing pressures, however, did not permit this style to endure. Beyond 3;0, increasing intolerance was demonstrated so that examples of whining were rare as the child grew older. Whining was noted, for example, once at 5;9 when the child was awakened from a nap in kindergarten when his parents visited. But when the child whined at 8;11, he was met with a stern: "¡Habla bien!" and thereby made to repeat his statem'ent in an acceptable manner.

PEER TALK

Although Mario had played with children in Bolivia and Mexico, English was most closely associated with peer talk. This was probably due to his intensive contact with English-speaking children at the nursery. The language he used with peers was characterized in distinctive ways, setting it apart from the speech styles used with adults. Peer talk, for example, contained a high incidence of direct commands, many expressive interjections, frequent onomatopoetic sounds, an almost complete absence of courtesy terms and diminutives, imitated utterances, and an occasional interspersing of songs, recitations, and the like. This was certainly not at all like the verbal behavior he displayed with other people.

Since peer talk was predominantly English, Mario's first speech patterns were often in the form of unmitigated commands in English learned from other children: "Move! Gimme! No!" (meaning: "Don't do that!"), and "My!" (meaning "Give me!" and said while snatching an object from another child). At home, the language of his role playing and play with imaginary friends was filled with the same:

Age 3;4 Get auta here!
     Shut up!
     Don't do dat! No do dat no more!
     My, my! Not yours!
     I want this seat! Mus (move)!
     Close it! Come on!
Age 3;5 No touch dat . . . is bwoken.
Age 3;6 I punch you right da nose!

Entire dialogs with imagined friends were typically filled with rather aggressive statements. The style, of course, reflected the type of interaction going on between children—often filled with conflict, power plays, attention seeking, possessive behavior, and sometimes egocentric displays of indifference—reflected in many of Piaget's investigations (1971). This was not the interplay the child had with the adult, and the difference was reflected in language.

Courtesy terms were conspicuously absent from data recorded during peer involvement. Conversely, there was a fairly frequent use of the not-so-courteous "Stupid!" and "Shalup!" (Shut up!). Yet Mario was aware of the potency of this expression and its challenging nature. This became apparent one evening while watching television. Mario misunderstood the sports announcer who said: "The Philadelphia team *shut out* the other," to which he exclaimed with astonishment, "Grampop, he say 'shut up'!!!" Apparently, courtesy terms serve little function among children, whose social interaction is forthright, candid, and sometimes aggressive. Yet it was obvious Mario knew these terms for he occasionally used them with adults (with some prompting). Furthermore, he sometimes demonstrated his awareness of courtesy expressions during role plays. Pretending to be a playmate, Corey, he sneezed and immediately said to himself: /ga sɛs yu, kówi/ (God bless you, Corey).

Peer talk also contained many expressive interjections such as "yuk, hey, bla, gosh, ouch," and the like. Mario copied these and other expressions from his peers often without the least modification of their statements. This repetition was usually done in an echo-like fashion, apparently serving no other purpose. Piaget (1971, pp. 69-72) provides various interpretations of this phenomenon.

Throughout his development, Mario rarely used diminutives with his peers, possibly owing to the fact that diminutives in English are generally not as widespread as in Spanish. The few diminutives used were in words such as "doggie," and also in some names such as Bobby and Ronnie. However, these were fairly frozen expressions and they cannot be considered the same as spontaneously created forms. Peer language style contained no notes of endearment. And although Mario had many friends whom he obviously admired (as evidenced by his predilection to assume their role when playing), he did not address his friends affectionately. Yet Mario did use many affectionate expressions with adults who were intimately related to him.

Mario favored onomatopoetic sounds, whether playing with others or alone. The diary contains numerous examples of sounds made during play, some of which were so amazingly faithful that they were impossible to transcribe. He imitated animals, tractors, airplanes, rockets, car brakes, monsters, motors, explosions, sirens, hammers banging, and so forth.

Talk with peers was also distinct from other styles in that it contained frequent outbursts of songs, recitations, quotes from commercials, snatches of nursery rhymes, etc. Mario's repertoire included lines from "Cululucucu, Paloma," (Cucurrucucu, Paloma); The Cat in the Hat; Doggie, Doggie, Where's Your Bone?; the A-B-C's; Old MacDonald; Los Pollitos Dicen Pío, Pío, Pío; Intsy, Teentsy Spider; Someone in the Kitchen with Dinah; Poca Fortuna; Mary Had a Little Lamb; Señor Don Gato sobre el tejado; plus many of his own improvised tunes often created around a word overheard while playing.

Peer-talk style evolved rapidly beyond the age of 5;0 when the child began kindergarten. School provided increased contact with other children, and also a norm for interaction within the classroom context. Mario's peer style nonetheless continued to be almost exclusively associated with English, with the exception of language addressed to his younger sister, and its most outstanding characteristic was the use of a specific code.

BABY TALK: A STYLE FOR YOUNGER CHILDREN

Mario's parents had used baby talk with him as an infant, but beyond infancy they employed this style rarely and only to express endearment. His mother's baby talk was characterized by extreme variations in intonation, a higher than normal frequency of voice, the extensive use of diminutives (morphologically derived from both Spanish and Italian), the frequent use of certain frozen expressions, and occasional phone substitutions. For example, at 5:0:

Mother →Mario: Mi chiqu*itico* tan bonito, amoro*sito*.

However, earlier as an infant:

Mother →Mario: ¿Qué paŝó mi nenito, mi guagüita (*little baby*) tan quir*iru*?

In the first example, the speech primarily involved affectionate expressions intensified by the addition of the diminutive *-ito* and the double intensifier *-itico* (*-ito* plus *-ico*). In the second, however, there were also various phone substitutions such as /s →ŝ/, /e →i/, /d →r/, and /o →u/. Apparently, all vowels were leveled to form one of those of the basic triangle /a/i/u/ (which, incidentally, is a common form of interference in Spanish heard among the native Quechua-speakers of Bolivia).

After the birth of his younger sister, Mario began to employ a baby-talk style himself when addressing the younger child. Although in principle he emulated the style described above, he did not copy all of the same features but added many of his own. He adopted the expressive voice pattern and the higher voice frequency, but he often improvised his own diminutives. He did not employ phone substitutions of either vowels or consonants, but sometimes inverted whole syllables instead:

> Age 4;6   Hola, hermanita . . . tu frentita, Carlitita, Carlinina.
> Carla, Carla, Carla, . . . oy, su baguicita (barriguita), tengo a (sic) taparla.
>
> Age 5;7   My darling, my darling!
> La mosicola, mosiquilla, moquilla, mocosilla.
>
> Age 5;8   Ay Carlina, Carlitita, Carlinina . . . qué monita, qué monita.

These utterances all shared the typical voice qualities associated with baby talk, plus the extensive use of diminutives (*-ita*, *-illa*, and *-ina/inina*, the latter being Italian forms). "My darling" was possibly learned from television or some other source as an endearment. In the statement made at 5;7, there was also play with the word "mocosa" (used with little children sometimes as endearment; or, depending on the tone of voice, it might also convey hostility or contempt).

None of the examples of Mario's baby talk were at all like his own real baby talk of an earlier age. As a matter of fact, he did not recall anything of his earlier speech. Gleason (1971: 13) also observed that baby talk is learned, not something one retains from earlier years. Once when role-playing a baby, he said only "agú, agú," but nothing else. He sometimes asked his parents out of curiosity how he had said certain words when he was a baby, and he always found it amusing to listen to tapes of his earlier speech. At 8;11 he discovered diary notes of his earlier speech and he read with fascination, with an occasional outburst of laughter: "¿Así hablaba cuando era 'baby'? ¡Qué chistoso!" But he obviously did not directly recall any of his earlier speech. This suggests that the style he adopted beginning at 4;6 for speaking to his younger sister was a new development, a style for a specific instance.

Baby talk was also a transient style, appropriate only for a limited period of time. By 6;3 Mario considered himself too old to be addressed with any features reminiscent of baby talk, even to the point of lexical choices:

> Papá →Mario: Mario, no hagas así. Te vas a hacer *chichiu*.
> Mario →Papá: No se dice "chichiu," se dice "lastimar."
> Papá →Mario: Ah . . . ok.

Whereas at the same age, Mario prompted his mother to use Bolivian baby expressions with his sister:

Mamá →Carlina:	Carlina, belleza.
Carlina →Mamá:	¿Yo soy bonita, mami?
Mamá →Carlina:	Sí, amor.
Mario →Mamá:	(interjecting) Díle *"musi, musi,"* mamá

Yet scarcely two years later (8;4), Mario considered baby talk inappropriate not only for himself, but also for his sister, now 4;1:

Mamá →Carlina:	Es mi guagüita.
Carlina:	(Pretending to be a baby) Las guagüitas dicen "gu-gu."
Mario:	(Protesting) ¡No es guagüita! ¡Ya tiene cuatro años!

From these and similar examples, we can surmise that Mario viewed four to six as the transitional period from babyhood to childhood, requiring a corresponding change in the way individuals of this age be addressed.

A STYLE FOR INTIMACY

In contrast to the spontaneous development of a baby-talk style when the need arose, affectionate language was evidenced throughout the speech diary. Mario used an affectionate style with his parents and sister and also with certain relatives and close friends. It was marked by the wide use of diminutives, occasionally improvised terminations, and occasional terms of endearment. Samples are abundant:

Age 3;1	Papá, papini.
Age 3;2	Papapito, mamapita.
Age 3;3	Diosito.
	Señolito (sēnorito).
Age 3;6	Fantinito . . . un momentito.
	Mamapita, papito, papisini.
Age 4-6	Carlitita, Carlinina.

The samples of endings in Mario's speech were probably more diverse than those found in the speech of other young Spanish speakers due to the varied inputs provided by his caretakers, derived from the morphological systems of several languages.

Another sign of intimacy reflected in Mario's speech usage was the peculiar tendency to revert to Spanish even when the normal choice would have been English, given the language of his interlocutors. For example, with two persons in particular, both well-liked by the child and intimately associated with him, Mario used English appropriately but with an inclination—almost an expressed desire—to switch intermittently to Spanish. The first was a close family friend who was especially gentle and showed considerable interest in Mario. The other was an elementary school teacher who liked small children and who had also shown interest and affection. Mario knew their language was English, yet he slipped back and forth into Spanish. He did this with no others.

Since Spanish was the language of his home and a language associated with those of intimacy, it conveyed a degree of unity and affection not yet attributed to English. Mario's frequent interjections in Spanish seemed an attempt to convey this to his two special friends. This is plausible since there were no persistent attempts to interject English when speaking with Spanish-speaking interlocutors also intimately related to the child.

Mario became increasingly sensitive to linguistic features which conveyed intimacy. He demonstrated this not only by his own use of such features but also by comments which revealed his detection of intimacy and affection in the speech of others. For example, at 5;8 he was recalling experiences he had on a recent visit to Bolivia:

Mario → Parents: La Teresita de la abuelita Alina me decía "cara sucia."

Mama´→ Mario: No . . . "k'ara" cochino. "K'ara" es aymara para decir "niño de la calle."

Mario: No, "cara sucia" me decía . . . pero sólo de cariño.

Two months later (age 6;0), while waiting for a neighbor who had promised to buy him a toy for his birthday, he reflected:

Mario → Parents: Anne me va a comprar dos juguetes.

Papá: ¿Cómo sabes?

Mario: Porque me dice "sweetie pie."

One of the most pervasive markers in adult Spanish—the pronoun *tú* with its corresponding verb forms—was as yet an unreliable indicator of intimacy. Mario, as with many children even up to age 9;0 and beyond, had not yet been required to employ the contrasting form *usted* and it was only rarely noted in his speech diary. This distinction—a most interesting linguistic and social development—will be discussed more fully below.

A STYLE FOR ADULTS

When speaking with adults, Mario used a form of speech which was stylistically distinct from that used with peers and with children younger than himself. Because of the fixed relationship between the researcher and the child, this was the most abundantly recorded style. Since it is closest to adult usage, it is easier to describe by the absence of features attributed to other styles plus the inclusion of endearment forms (as appropriate for specific adults), courtesy and etiquette terms, and titles of respect. Here we shall also consider the pronoun/verb markings of Spanish which connote social intimacy or distance. Since endearment expressions have already been discussed, we shall limit our examination to courtesy terms, titles, and other linguistic social markers related to the adult style.

The first courtesy expressions were recorded at 2;2: /áŝ:yas/ (*gracias*). However, early use of "thank you" was usually limited to purely imitative action prompted by adults; in fact, prompting was necessary for its occurrence for several years. For the child the term probably served a superfluous function in that it was uttered *after* an action was already completed. *De nada* fell into this same category. On the other hand, *por favor* was a *request* for action and, as such, was a requirement, for without it, Mario's parents often failed to respond. Consequently, *por favor* occurred much earlier in spontaneous use, and much more regularly from 2;7 on (appearing first as /palaló/ and later as /pasalól/). Other expressions spontaneously used were:

Age 2;7	/bái bái/	Bye Bye.
Age 2;8	/peyíso/	Permiso.
Age 2;9	/sae lúts/	¡Salud!
	/salút, ĉin ĉin/	¡Salud! ¡Cin-cin! (an Italian toast).
Age 3;7	/gyáŝyas/	Gracias (spontaneous use).

Leave-taking expressions (bye bye) were usually fun and they were often accompanied by waving. Besides, departures of friends or relatives were usually a lengthy process and the ritual of leave-taking was an exaggerated moment. Much attention was given to the child's participation in this act. *Permiso* and *por favor* also had functional importance since approval was often withheld until these phrases were uttered. In some cases it was almost guaranteed that a request would be granted if the child added the ending *-ito*, as in *por favorcito* at age 3;8. The addition of the diminutive indicated a special plea meriting special consideration. By 6;0 Mario was well aware of the power of these terms, when properly used, toward the attainment of his goals, as, for example, when he asked to borrow his father's flashlight, an item usually denied to him. Whispering into his father's ear, he begged: "¿Puedo usar tu linterna . . . solo por favor?"

Salud and *cin-cin* were fun in that they accompanied the act of consuming some beverage and were often said while raising glasses in a toast. Other social amenities appeared, such as *buen provecho* and *con permiso* at 3;7, usually uttered so rapidly that Mario could not possibly have understood the component words of each expression. Nonetheless, these were ritualistic formulas which obtained permission to leave the table, serving in this way a particular function. However, the spontaneous—yet still sporadic—use of *gracias* made its tardy debut at 3;7, long after many other phrases were already in common use. By approximately 5;0, courtesy expressions had become a rather fixed aspect of the child's speech used with adults, including *gracias*. At 5;9, his parents were impressed (and pleased) to note that Mario spontaneously thanked his teacher for a cookie she handed him at an open-house at the school. Mario was also fairly consistent about extending his hand when introduced and kissing all adults present upon retiring. Only recently was any hesitancy noted about kissing certain adult males, but mainly in response to the consternation of those persons at being kissed by a nine-year-old boy. Certainly this type of behavior is rare for the United States, although far more common to Bolivia.

Even though Mario sometimes failed to use courtesy expressions himself at various stages, it was obvious from comments he made when others failed to use them that he knew social amenities formed part of adult speech. For example:

Age 3;6   His mother punished him erroneously for something he had not done. When it became clear that he was not to blame, he said to her (incorporating her own typically Venezuelan expression "epa"):
Epa, mamá, ahora dí: 'penón' (perdón).

Age 3;7   Requesting a cookie from his aunt, she fails to respond. Mario quickly directs her attention to the proper form of his request by saying:
/Gimi a máy kúki . . . ay tɛl yu plis/
(Give me a "my" cookie . . . I tell you "please").

Age 5;7   A boy comes to the door selling magazine subscriptions. Mario's mother refuses by saying "no, thank you," yet she obviously received nothing. Mario questions this peculiar use:
¿Por qué dijiste "no, gracias"?

Age 8;11 Mario sneezes several times. Everyone else is occupied
and his sneezing goes unnoticed until he announces:
Yo estornudé cuatro veces y no me dijiste "salud."

The use of titles often reflects position and social distance. Sometimes
titles are used to precede a name; in other cases, they substitute for the
name in direct address. From the child's point of view, titles as used in
the first case were probably superfluous and optional. In the second
case, titles were needed when he wished to call someone's attention by
substituting the title for the name. In Spanish, more so than in English, it
is permissible to use titles such as *señor, señora*, etc., without the surname.
This is not so for English since one does not normally address anyone as
"Mr." or "Mrs." without also adding the last name.

Señora was the first title that Mario used spontaneously at 3;0. *Señor*
plus *tío/tía* (used for respect rather than relationship) appeared by 3;7.
Other forms of direct address were used unerringly when they were
learned upon initial contact as part of a person's name, as with the
nursery attendant, Mario's school teacher, the medical doctor, etc. In
spite of these developments, Mario preferred to call people's attention
by simply yelling "hey," often omitting both titles and names, even up to
his fifth year. "Hey" was acquired from his peers and it served a very
functional purpose.

In indirect address, too, Spanish requires the referent *señor, señora*,
etc. rather than *hombre, mujer*, etc. This is akin to referring to a third
party in English as "that gentleman" rather than "that man." However,
titles of indirect address appeared to be bothersome and unnecessary for
the child, even if considered appropriate by adults. Despite constant
reminders, the following behavior was typical:

At 8;2 Mario was sitting in his father's office when the phone rang.
His father entered just as the child was hanging up. When asked
who had called, Mario responded:

Mario → Papá: Ese hombre. (Referring to someone they had seen
a while earlier.)
Papá → Mario: ¡Señor, Mario, señor!

One of the important social markers of adult Spanish speech—as in most
Romance tongues—is the distinction connoted by the choice between the
pronouns *tú/usted* (you) and their corresponding verb endings. Brown
and Gilman (1970, pp. 252-75) termed these "the pronouns of power
and solidarity." To employ this distinction, however, requires mastery of
a considerable amount of morphological detail, but more importantly,
an awareness of varying types of social relationships. In Mario's dialect,
the norm was to use *tú* with his parents (in contrast with other areas

where *usted* is employed with parents) and consequently *tú* was the first form to appear in his speech.

The form *tú* was implicit in some of the earliest frozen expressions used by the child at 2;2: *dáme, toma,* and *te quiero.* It was also implicit in many of the verb forms used at 2;7: *ven aquí, papá; alélala (arréglala); ayaya (agarra); ves; salúlala (salúdala),* and *viste.* However, its first spontaneous use did not occur until 3;0, when it showed up both in the pronominal form as well as in the sometimes accurate verb inflection: *¿Tú no va? (¿Tú no vas?); ¿Qué haces?; ¿Qué comes?; ¿Ya cabáte? (?Ya acabatse?).*

By 3;0 Mario had almost completely mastered both the pronoun *tú* and its relevant verb forms for declarative statements, although he still erred in positive and negative commands because of their aberrant patterning:

Age 3;0　¡Tú no cant*as*!
　　　　　(Intended as the negative command: ¡No cant*es*!)
　　　　　¿No se va tú?
Age 3;1　¿No te vas?
　　　　　Tú sacate. (Tú sacaste.)
　　　　　¿Qué haces ahola (ahora)?
Age 4;1　Tú *es* mi papá. (Tú *eres* mi papá.)

The alternate form *usted* was implicit for the first time at 3;0, when Mario addressed a maid in Mexico with the phrase: "¿Señora, qué hace? ¿Se va?" Since this utterance was made on the same day when he had told his father "¡Tú no cantas!," it was possible that he fully intended the distinction signified by the addition of *-s* to the verb used with his father. Later the same month, he used the pronoun *usted* for the first and only time until fully a year later: "Usted veye (duerme) aquí." However, this time it was said to an intimate person, and therefore its use was incorrect. Nonetheless, these were at least signs that Mario had begun to notice the form, having used it himself once or twice, even though incorrectly. The distinction apparently served no purpose and *usted* was momentarily disregarded.

Yet even by nine Mario did not employ the *tú/usted* distinction; *tú* was the sole form used with few exceptions. The occasional exception was his alternation with the typically Bolivian form *vos,* which requires the same verb forms as *tú* (unlike the Argentine practice). Because this form was frequently used by the child's Bolivian nursemaid, it was used almost exclusively with her and often in direct imitation of her model, as for example at age 7;9:

Mario's nursemaid had lost her ring and asked the child to help her pray so that her ring would be found.

| Nursemaid →Mario: | Vos puedes ayudar. Reza a San Antonio. |
| Mario →Nursemaid: | Vos reza porque a mí no me escucha. No me entiende. |

Aside from *tú* and *vos* there was a hint that Mario may have temporarily grasped part of the rather complex social rule underlying the contrastive pronouns. At 5;5, while role-playing in La Paz with his parents and grandparents, he assumed the role of teacher and assigned the others to be pupils. He adopted a rigid posture, crossed his arms and with a serious face, directed the class. The task he assigned was to translate utterances he gave into English. When his playful students laughed, he called them back to order and, reprimanding his grandmother (now in the role of a little girl), he said:

Mario → Grandmother:	¡Niná, ven acá! ¡Siéntese!
Grandmother:	(Smiles and laughs.)
Mario → Grandmother:	¡Cállese usted, niña!

Although he was linguistically inconsistent in the first phrase, in which *tú* was implicit in the choice of the verb *ven*, he did use correct forms of *usted* in the two subsequent verbs said in the command form. His spontaneous use of *usted* was correct both in form and in application in this imaginary social situation, suggesting that Mario had some awareness of the pronominal distinction which he had not previously displayed. In spite of what he may or may not have perceived at this age, Mario continued to use *tú* with all interlocutors, without regard for age, role, or social distance. Yet adults showed complete acceptance of this form of address from the child, whereas the same would not be true of another adult making an incorrect choice.

In spite of the example just cited, *usted* simply did not reoccur. Its lack of utility for the child may have caused its dismissal from his performance, and possibly from his competence as well. Several incidents between his eighth and ninth year suggest that he had neither linguistic mastery nor a recognized social need:

Age 8;0 A teacher friend was visiting. Because he was interested in Mario's language development, he asked the child to address him with *usted*. Mario was obviously confused by his request:

Mario →Visitor:	¿Cómo estás?
Papá →Mario:	(Intervenes)
	No, dí lo mismo con "usted."
Mario:	¿Cómo?

Age 8;7   Mario began religious instruction in Bolivia, given privately by an elderly priest. Mario used *tú* with the priest even after he was corrected several times by his parents. During all ensuing sessions, *tú* continued to be his only spontaneous form of address for the priest.

Age 8;11   An attempt was made to assess Mario's linguistic control of verb forms corresponding to *usted*. He was therefore asked to change a series of statements from *tú* to *usted*. The child proved to be correct only with the fairly common greeting: "¿Cómo está usted?" In all other cases he merely adopted *usted* but retained the verb ending for *tú*, as in the examples: "Usted fuiste," and "¡Usted haz eso!"

The child's lack of familiarity with this form was rather surprising. Obviously Mario's experiences up to now had not required this social/linguistic expression. The question which arises is when do adults expect this formal expression from children, and correspondingly, when do children employ the contrastive social marker in speech? Observations of other children in diverse situations and questioning of Spanish-speakers indicated great variance in both, related to one's social class, type of education, country and regional differences, and so forth. A child of a lower class family, for example, might well begin to use *usted* early by copying the behavior of his parents in a society where they must address many people formally although they themselves are addressed by *tú* in return (reflecting inferior-superior relationships within their society). On the other hand, children of upper class families use *tú* in many more situations, reflecting also their status in society. As another example, a child attending a rural public school might use *tú* more commonly throughout the elementary levels than a child educated in a religious private school. A child raised in most areas of Venezuela might use *tú* in more situations than would be tolerable in most of Bolivia. With such variance, one might best judge Mario's usage by the reactions of Bolivian speakers in a relationship with him. On this basis, then, his pervasive use of *tú* produced no social awkwardness. Several Bolivian Spanish-speakers of the same social class confirmed that they considered eleven or twelve a transitional period. Puberty seemed to be the critical time for acknowledging social relationships and encoding such information through linguistic markers.

Besides the appropriate uses of *tú/usted*, marked use of either often conveys other meanings. For example, not to use *usted* with adults when it is clearly appropriate is a transgression of social norms, possibly interpreted as an insult, a belittlement of one's social role or position, or simply rudeness. Similarly, parents who address a child as *tú* sometimes switch abruptly to *usted* to produce calculated effects. For example, when Mario's father was irritated or angered by the child's behavior, he made statements like: "¡Y *usted va* a marchar a la cama ahora mismo . . . y no me *llame* más!" This change of linguistic form conveyed much more than the purely literal message of its words. The use of *usted* where *tú* would normally have been employed served to underscore the severity of the message and the anger of the speaker. Mario's speech in his role as school teacher conveyed similar effects. This and other examples demonstrate his sensitivity to this particular usage of *usted*. At 7;1, when his mother got angry with him and addressed him in this manner, he took offense and said:

Mario →Mamá: ¡No me llames "usted" . . . eres mi gente!

Two months later (7;3), when his father entered the kitchen upon return from work and greeted Mario formally, the child reacted in the same way:

Papá →Mario: ¡Hola! ¿Cómo esta usted?
Mario →Papá: ¡No me llames "usted"!
Papá →Mario: ¿Por qué?
Mario →Papá: Eres mi gente.

Although Mario did not yet acknowledge many dimensions of status normally reflected through the *tú/usted* distinction, he did show an awareness of status in other ways. At age 5;6 he demonstrated cognizance of his role and relationship with the chauffeur and servants in La Paz. This was not detected from his use of *tú* with them (appropriate anyway in this case) but rather from other behavior—verbal and otherwise. Commands and manner towards the servants were direct and blunt, lacking courtesy terms: "Ven . . . tráeme la mamadera . . . deja eso . . ." Naturally he had observed others using similar abrupt and direct commands with servants, often devoid of courtesy modifiers. When his father told him to thank Basilio, or to say please to Irma, he answered: "No tengo a (sic) decirlo . . . es mi gente." Although this statement might make many an English speaker shudder, it nonetheless neatly explains his behavior, entirely appropriate within the Bolivian context.

The evidence presented of Mario's development and use of the *tú/usted* distinction—or lack of it—touches upon a rather intriguing question: whether linguistic development or social need is more essential for its eventual appearance. Certainly there were signs that he had begun to pick up the form *usted* and its corresponding verb forms at an early age, but for some reason he failed to incorporate these features as a permanent aspect of speech. Furthermore, by five or six he had acquired practically all of the morphological requirements for the third person singular, which corresponds in detail to *usted* as well. The only linguistic requirement lacking, then, was to relate *usted* to these third person endings already in use. This would seem to be a relatively minor linguistic feat; hence, social need seems to be the critical factor. One might wonder whether Mario's limited experience in a Spanish-speaking society (and therefore limited interactions with speakers of diverse social backgrounds) might account for the lack of a sociolinguistic rule for usage. However, comparisons with other Bolivian children of similar social background and age rules this out since Mario appears to comply with their norm. Besides, we know that he was sensitive to other sociolinguistic dimensions. He knew, for example, that persons belonging to the same family unit do not address each other as *usted* except as marked behavior. He knew also quite a lot about the rules of interaction appropriate for use with those in a socially ascribed inferior position. Hence, his lack of a formal form and its use seem to be linked to his particular social role and his current age. When his failure to employ *usted* begins to cause his parents discomfort (evidenced, for example, for the first time in Mario's sessions with the priest), their reactions will eventually provide the socializing force needed to cause Mario to attend to a feature which up to now has not affected him in his role as a child.

One other development deserves comment in our examination of the child's acquisition of a style acceptable with adults. Slowly he is learning to reformulate his requests through the incorporation of linguistic mollifiers. One of the most notable examples in the diary was the appearance of *quisiera,* which gradually took the place of *quiero.* This would be equivalent in English to ".I would/should like" instead of simply "I want." This was a fairly recent development, beginning in his eighth year. Initial attempts to have the child soften his requests sometimes met with humorous responses; for example, at 8;2:

> Mario was looking through a listing of children's books which he had brought home from school, when he spotted a particular book he wanted.
>
> Mario →Nursemaid: Marina, sabes que quiero ese libro . . . ése.
> Nursemaid →Mario: Mario, no se dice "quiero" . . . se dice "quisiera."
> Mario →Nursemaid: No, pero vo *estoy seguro* que quiero . . . no "quisiera."

Obviously the child understood the linguistic difference between the forms *quiero* and *quisiera;* what puzzled him was this peculiar directive to mollify a request which he was so sure about. However, later on he began to rephrase his statements (especially when met with glaring eyes as a response) and increasingly used *quisiera* spontaneously as a more acceptable form for communicating his wants—no matter how certain he was of what he wanted, nor the intensity of his desire. This social tactic, accomplished through linguistic means, was a significant development toward participation in the adult world.

VARIATIONS FOR OTHER NEEDS

Besides the styles discussed thus far, still other speech variations were used for other special needs: namely, modifications for certain formal public settings, a narrative style, telephone talk, taboo forms, regional dialectical adjustments, and linguistic accommodation for speaking with bilingual speakers of limited proficiency in one of the languages involved. These also deserve comment.

One interesting variety involved voice control, without involving other linguistic modifications aside from certain lexical items. Within certain fixed settings, it was necessary to speak more softly than in others. In church, in a doctor's waiting room, in a public theater or restaurant, Mario was often reminded to speak quietly, sometimes in a whisper. In addition, he was sometimes reprimanded for using certain words. For example, once when his mother spoke to him quietly in a doctor's office, he replied each time with an even louder *¿Qué?* In church he persisted in using the same tone he had used on the street, attracting the attention of everyone around. Furthermore, the content of his remarks was sometimes inappropriate to the setting: "Mira, Diosito está en calzones," observing that Jesus was not fully clothed on the cross; or, "Esos señores parecen indios," likening the dress of the bishop and other priests to Indians in full attire. In other public places, Mario yelled out his toilet needs with complete abandon—"¡¡Pis!! ¡¡Caca!!" Apparently it was difficult to discern the special characteristics of those situations which required a softer voice, for between 2;0 and 5;0 Mario still had not displayed voice control. Voice modulation was a slow development, as well as the knowledge underlying restrictions and constraints on the content of the child's speech. Socialization through school probably hastened this development beyond 5;0.

Among the variations recorded, there was evidence that Mario had adopted a special form for narrations. The style used for storytelling was clearly distinct from that used in dialog and conversation. Narrative style involved the predominant use of declarative statements, a fairly similar intonational pattern maintained with each utterance, and the beginning of most statements with the Spanish conjunction *y*. In addition, the entire narrative was set off with the conventional opening phrase common to Spanish, "Había una vez," and it concluded with "Colorín, colorado, el cuento ha terminado." Immediately upon conclusion there was a marked shift back to normal conversation style. For example, at age 3;3:

Child's Utterance	*Standard Language*
Aquí stava un nene chitito,	Aquí estaba un nene chiquito,
Y decía "bye-bye."	Y decía "bye-bye."
El nenito tene un bastón.	El nenito tiene un bastón.
Y este nenito stava un nenito aquí con su papá.	Y este nenito estaba un nenito aquí con su papá.
Y este nenito stava con bastón largo!	Y este nenito estaba con bastón largo!
Y este nenito stava y jalava el pelo	Y este nenito estaba y jalaba el pelo

Although his linguistic talents had improved considerably by age 5;5, his narrative remained substantially unchanged:

> Este es un "Cuernote" (pointing to a demon with big horns which he has drawn). Es mucho, mucho malo; pero él sólo mata Dr. Mártins y Drácula. Y no come niños y niñas.
>
> Y abajo de él, hay un dragón bueno que es el ayudante del Cuernote. Y el dragón tira fuego por la nariz y por la boca. Y también sale humo de la nariz. Y también cuando el dragón encuentra niños y niñas se los lleva cargando donde Cuernote.
>
> Y también cuando Cuernote le (sic) habla a los niños y las niñas, le pregunta si le ha mordido el Dr. Mártins . . . etc., etc.

On the telephone, Mario invariably used the proper introductory and closing remarks. In the sense that speaking on the telephone requires certain linguistic modifications, it may be viewed as a limited style for a specific circumstance.

Above we have given a few examples of how the socialization process relegated a small core of utterances into a taboo category. The parents' prohibitions against certain words gave them a special aura they did not previously have. Mario used these special words when he became angry or wished to anger others. Although hardly a speech style, the use of this body of phrases was directly related to context. It was a specific social context that gave these words their special power and not the simple act of saying the sounds. As Mario realized what types of words were condemned (principally those related to the sexual organs and bodily functions), he became more imaginative, saying not only things he had learned from direct experience, but also creating his own combinations of potentially powerful phrases:

¡Fastidioso tú, con potito!
¡Pis y caca en tú cara!

Although his taboo repertoire increased rapidly after entering school, so also did his sensitivity about the use of these terms. In fact, he developed such a conservative attitude about the use of certain words that he was reluctant to pronounce them under any circumstances. For example, at 8;4 the following incident was recorded:

Mario had just finished reading a comic book and he was impressed by the number of words uttered by his heroes which he considered unspeakable.

Mario →Papá: En mi libro hay muchas palabras malas.
Papá →Mario: ¿Ah sí?
Mario →Papá: ¿Puedo decir?
Papá →Mario: A ver . . . ¿cuáles?
Mario →Papá: Yo no las digo. Sólo las miro y las pienso.

Mario is obviously reluctant to say the words for his father. When encouraged, he spells them out.

Mario →Papá: D-a-m-m-i-t . . . y . . . h-e-l-l . . .

Remembering another word he had heard elsewhere, he adds:

Mario →Papá: Y también . . . G-o-d-d-a-m-m-i-t.

Mario was also aware that the Spanish he heard did not always sound the same; some people spoke in different ways. In fact, when he heard Mexicans, Bolivians, Venezuelans, Uruguayans, Spaniards, and others speak, he often showed some visible reaction. In some cases, he hesitated while trying to discern whether they simply spoke a different "style" or whether they were speaking a different language. This occurred, for example, when he spoke with Portuguese speaking individuals whose speech sounded strange but was similar enough to comprehend. After dealing with persons who spoke other dialects for any period of time, Mario sometimes began to emulate their intonation and expressions. For example, after a summer in Mexico his tone clearly reflected the speech patterns of his caretaker there; he also used typically Mexican expressions such as "popote, qué padre," and "ándale, ándale." When told not to say this, he retorted: "Pero Andrés (the maid's brother) dijía (decía) 'ándale, ándale.' "

At 5;6, after only two days of play with two Brazilian children he met on a train to Cuzco, his intonation began to reflect theirs, and he already began to say such things as:

> Mario: Esta pistola no funciona . . . está *quebrada*. (To include the dental, rather than fricative /d/ required in Spanish.)

Later:

> Mario: Vamos a *brincar* arriba. *(brincar*, Portuguese for *jugar)*

He was obviously aware of their differing style, and commented on it:

Hearing one of the children reply *não,* he asked:

> Mario: ¿Por qué dice asi . . . "não"?

Or when his friend Alexandro said to his mother:

> Alexandro: Limpa a nariz dêle! (Wipe his nose!)

Mario, surprised by the construction, laughed and remarked:

> Mario →Papá: El dice "limpia la nariz *del.*" (Apparently focusing on the peculiar contraction and pronunciation and unconsciously changing the verb and noun to Spanish forms.)

In addition, Mario commented on the Castilian pronunciation of a Spanish woman who came to dinner. In Venezuela, he made several remarks concerning the speech of children with whom he played. He was sharply attuned to the accents of other persons, both in Spanish and English, and readily detected the dominant or native language of Spanish-English bilinguals. These examples and many others illustrate the child's awareness and sensitivity to speech features different from his own.

As a younger child, his ability to detect the dominant language of others guided Mario in the selection of which of his two languages to use. Often, when he determined that his interlocutor was not sufficiently proficient in Spanish, he changed automatically to English even if the other speaker tried to maintain the conversation in Spanish. However, by 7;0, Mario had learned to accept the attempts of others to speak to him in Spanish even if they lacked sufficient fluency and native pronunciation. In a sense, his linguistic accommodation to such persons constituted the beginnings of another style of speech, one reserved for those who were not native speakers. If his interlocutors switched or mixed codes, he did likewise even though he normally maintained a rigid separation of his languages. It was also noted that he often spoke more slowly, sometimes more loudly, and made conscious attempts to enunciate as clearly as possible. These were salient aspects of his style for those whose Spanish was limited.

CONCLUSION

To summarize, we have noted the relationship between language use and linguistic form through examination of data taken from one child's speech. As an infant, Mario used differentiated vocalizations to express varying physical needs. As he became an increasingly social being, his developing speech was continually shaped by social patterns, and he correspondingly modified his linguistic expression in response to varying social needs. Whether the child addressed younger children, peers, or adults; whether his interlocutors were well known, casual associates, or socially distant; whether they were socially superior, inferior, or equal; or whether they were in a formal or informal setting—all were factors affecting the child's use of language. His communicative competence included not only an ability to produce grammatical constructs but also to modify these in distinct ways related to each situation. Inappropriate forms of expression were less and less tolerated by adults as the child matured. Negative feedback was provided in various ways when the child did not comply with social expectations. In each case, proper or aberrant verbal behavior was determined by the social factors present at the moment of speech, with each set of circumstances affecting the child's language output in specific ways.

Although linguists generally agree that children acquire much of their native language by age five, the literature does not comment on the ability of children to differentiate and produce diverse styles. Yet differentiated communicative behavior probably begins in infancy. And although the younger child does not yet control many of the elements of his language, he nonetheless displays speech variations even with limited language. The bilingual child, in particular, presents convincing evidence of this by his very ability to shift entire codes. Other examples from the data confirm that the child also modifies speech signals in other distinctive ways in accordance with contextual variables.

Speech styles, then, are characteristic not only of adults but of children too. Occasional clues as to the child's perception of social norms and concomitant styles even when not used in his own speech were witnessed in role-play situations, in his reaction to others when they transgressed social rules, as well as in his own comments. Hence, it cannot be assumed that the child did not possess those abilities he did not display actively. Given the proper circumstances, he demonstrated sensitivity even to several styles not related to his present status. Obviously, certain styles are relevant to a speaker only at different stages of development and are therefore temporal in nature. Such styles come and go inasmuch as they are contingent upon the differing roles and relationships the child establishes within his developing world. For example, code differentiation was an immediate necessity and was well handled by the middle of the second year; various styles within each language were also clearly discernible before the third. Yet other styles were already discarded before the child was seven: a communicative style dependent primarily on non-linguistic expression (by about 3;6); whining (last witnessed about the fifth year); and baby talk (no longer acceptable by the sixth year in accordance with the child's own judgments). Furthermore, Mario had learned not only to use unmarked language; he employed marked language as well by adopting a given style out of context to create some special effect. Indeed, he became quite adept at invoking styles not normally appropriate for a given situation for a special purpose. In such cases he conveyed much more than the literal message of the grammatical statement.

Two other aspects of stylistic development deserve comment: the relation of style to status and social class, and the relevance of a diversified "society of speakers" to varied speech behavior. Despite the limitations of a single case study, there is some indication that the individual's ability to control styles, as well as the number of styles he acquires, may be less related to social class in any fixed manner than it is to the need for a child—any child—to behave in the various ways demanded of him. For example, Mario used only one form of address by age 9;0, in contrast with demands placed upon servant children younger than himself to employ multiple forms. Secondly, interaction within a diversified group of speakers also seems essential in order for a wide range of speech styles to develop. Speakers of differing ages, sex, role, relationship, social class, and so forth, provide variables which foster the development and maintenance of a great range of styles. Conversely, the child who has had limited social interaction is constrained by the reduction of social variables. The bilingual child reared apart from a society of speakers of one of the two languages he is acquiring indeed has less opportunity to experience diversified speech behavior. Although linguistic development is stimulated and sustained by the child's family, stylistic development may be truncated for want of a more diversified experience. Bilingual-bicultural education programs, however, may now provide a new source that may help each language to develop with a richness of styles.

Finally, language form and function are intimately related as a dynamic of language use throughout the acquisitional process. As the child advances into a continually expanding world from his base in the family nucleus, so also does his language evolve and change in content and style to meet his new social needs. What began in infancy is a process which continues throughout life—from childhood on into adulthood.

APPENDIX

Styles and Usage Noted in Mario's Speech Data

Age	Emerging Styles	Characteristics and Use
Infancy	Differentiated crying	To express basic physical needs
0;4	Crying or other vocalizations (accompanied by physical motion/silence)	To express physical needs; contentment; self-expression
1;4— 1;10	Emergence of speech vs. non-speech sounds	Communication vs. self-expression or linguistic practice
	Speech (with social terms) vs. silence	Related to interlocutor (known/unknown)
	Oral language vs. physical gestures (pointing)	Socially accepted communication or disapproved (depending on age)
2;0	Developing style with adults (marks the emergence of a vast amount of language input)	Characterized by courtesy and etiquette terms, titles, grasp of some aspects of *tú/usted*. Used with adults for communication; expresses social norms; marks the setting, role, and relationship of participants
	Beginning of voice control	Related to settings: formal/informal
	Taboo phrases	Related to interlocutor and setting
2;6	Spanish/English code distinction	Related to interlocutor and setting
2;7	Speech vs. nonsense sounds	Speech for communication; nonsense sounds used as self-expression; also reflects boredom, non-compliance
	Normal speech vs. whining	Whining used with parents only
3;1	Affectionate language	Marked by diminutives, selected terms, improvised terminations; used only with intimates
3;3	Narrative style	Formalized beginning and ending; fixed utterances commonly begin with a conjunction
3;4	Peer language fully developed (begun about 2;2)	Marked by direct commands, expressive interjections, onomatopoetic sounds, no endearment, lack of courtesy terms or titles, few diminutives, frequent eruptions of song or recitations; used with others of same age

Appendix *(continued)*

Age	Emerging Styles	Characteristics and Use
3;6	Cessation of communicative style using only non-linguistic means (begun about 1;4)	
4;6	Baby-talk style	Higher voice frequency, varying intonation, diminutives, some phone or syllable substitutions, selected expressions; used with younger children
5;6	Style used with servants	Direct commands, lack of courtesy terms; related to social class
5;6	Increased sensitivity to regional accents, dialects	
5;9	Cessation of whining style (begun about 2;7)	
6;3	Cessation of baby-talk style addressed to the child (upon his request)	
7;0	Linguistic accommodation with non-native speakers	Marked by slower pace, increased volume, deliberate enunciation. Related to interlocutors with foreign accents and/or insufficient fluency

REFERENCES

Bates, Elizabeth. *Language and Context: The Acquisition of Pragmatics.* New York: Academic Press, 1976.

Bernstein, B. "Some Sociological Determinants of Perception. An Inquiry into Sub-Cultural Differences." In Fishman, J. (ed.), *Readings in the Sociology of Language.* The Hague: Mouton, 1970.

Brown, R., & A. Gilman. "The Pronouns of Power and Solidarity." In Fishman, J. (ed.), *Readings in the Sociology of Language.* The Hague: Mouton, 1970.

Ervin-Tripp, S. *Language Acquisition and Communicative Choice.* Stanford, Ca.: Stanford University Press, 1973.

Fasold, Ralph W., & Roger W. Shuy (eds.). *Analyzing Variation in Language.* Washington, D.C.: Georgetown University Press, 1975.

Giles, H., & P. F. Powesland (eds.). *Speech Style and Social Evaluation.* London: Academic Press, 1975.

Gleason, J. B. "Code Switching in Children's Language." Unpublished paper presented at the Linguistic Institute, Buffalo, New York, 1971.

Goodman, Mary Ellen. *The Culture of Childhood.* New York: Teachers College Press, 1970.

Haugen, E. *Bilingualism in the Americas.* University, Ala.: University of Alabama Press, 1965.

Hymes, D. *Foundations in Sociolinguistics.* Philadelphia: University of Pennsylvania Press, 1974.

Jakobson, R. *Child Language: Aphasia and Phonological Universals.* The Hague: Mouton, 1968.

Joos, Martin, *The Five Clocks.* New York: Harcourt, Brace & World, Inc., 1961.
———— "The Isolation of Styles." In Fishman, J. (ed.), *Readings in the Sociology of Language.* The Hague: Mouton, 1970.

Kelly, L. G. (ed.). *Description and Measurement of Bilingualism.* Toronto: University of Toronto Press, 1969.

Labov, William. *Sociolinguistic Patterns.* Philadelphia: University of Pennsylvania Press, 1972.

Mackey, William F. & Theodore Andersson (eds.). *Bilingualism in Early Childhood.* Rowley, Mass.: Newbury House Publishers, 1977.

Ostwald, P. F., & P. Peltzman. "The Cry of the Human Infant." *Scientific American,* March 1972, pp. 84–90.

Piaget, J. *The Language and Thought of the Child.* Cleveland: World Publishing Co., 1971.

Slobin, D. I. "Cognitive Prerequisites for the Development of Grammar." In Ferguson, C. A., & Slobin, D. I. (eds.), *Studies of Child Language Development.* New York: Holt, Rinehart & Winston, 1973.

Index

495